Aesthetic Subjects

Aesthetic Subjects

Pamela R. Matthews and David McWhirter, Editors

MINNESOTA

University of Minnesota Press
Minneapolis
London

Chapter 1 was originally published as part of *Filozofski vestnik* 20, no. 2 (Ljubljana, 1999): 63–85; copyright 1999 Filozofski institut ZRC SAZU. Chapter 5 is derived from *Caravaggio's Secrets* by Leo Bersani and Ulysse Dutoit (Cambridge: M.I.T. Press, 1998); copyright 1998 M.I.T. Press; reprinted by permission of M.I.T. Press. Chapter 13 is reprinted from Audrey Jaffe, *Scenes of Sympathy: Identity and Representation in Victorian Fiction* (Ithaca, N.Y.: Cornell University Press, 2000); copyright 2000 by Cornell University; used by permission of the publisher, Cornell University Press. Chapter 15 originally appeared as "Reflections on the Eames House" in Donald Albrecht, ed., *The Work of Charles and Ray Eames: A Legacy of Invention* (New York: Harry N. Abrams, 1997), 126–49; copyright Lucia Eames/Eames Office, www.eamesoffice.com; used by permission. An earlier version of chapter 16 was published as "Red Kant, or the Persistence of the 'Third Critique' in Adorno and Jameson," *Critical Inquiry* 26 (summer 2000): 682–724; copyright 2000 University of Chicago. Chapter 17 originally appeared in *Modernism/Modernity* 6, no. 2 (April 1999): 1–28; copyright The Johns Hopkins University Press; reprinted by permission of The Johns Hopkins University Press.

Published by the University of Minnesota Press
111 Third Avenue South, Suite 290
Minneapolis, MN 55401-2520
http://www.upress.umn.edu

Library of Congress Cataloging-in-Publication Data

Aesthetic subjects / Pamela R. Matthews and David McWhirter, editors.
p. cm.
Based on a conference held in spring 1998 at Texas A&M University.
Includes bibliographical references and index.
ISBN 0-8166-3992-2 — ISBN 0-8166-3993-0
1. Aesthetics—Congresses. I. Matthews, Pamela R. II. McWhirter, David.
BH19 .A465 2003
111'.85—dc21 2002154943

Printed in the United States of America on acid-free paper

12 11 10 09 08 07 06 05 04 03 10 9 8 7 6 5 4 3 2 1

For the viola section
Matthew Berthold, Gabriel McWhirter, Joshua McWhirter

Contents

Acknowledgments xi

Introduction: Exile's Return? Aesthetics Now xiii
Pamela R. Matthews and David McWhirter

PART I
Locating Aesthetic Experience: Sites, Situations, Discourses

ONE
Drifting into Dangerous Waters:
The Separation of Aesthetic Experience from the Work of Art 3
Martin Jay

TWO
Armed Assault 28
Alphonso Lingis

THREE
Reinventing the Wall: Looking into Zaha Hadid 44
Kay Bea Jones

FOUR
Pleasures Incarnate: Aesthetic Sentiment in the
Nineteenth-Century Work of Art 70
Judith Stoddart

FIVE
Caravaggio's Secrets 99
Leo Bersani and Ulysse Dutoit

PART II
Aesthetics in Social Contexts: Economies and Ethics

SIX
The Moral Content of Nabokov's *Lolita* 125
Susan Bordo

SEVEN
The Aesthetics of Jewishness: Shelley Winters 153
Joseph Litvak

EIGHT
Theorizing Popular Practice in Eighteenth-Century Aesthetics:
Lord Kames and Alexander Gerard 171
Maureen Harkin

NINE
The Labor Theory of Beauty: Aesthetic Subjects, Blind Justice 190
Douglas Mao

TEN
Sinthom-osexuality 230
Lee Edelman

PART III
Aesthetic Subjects: Bodies, Minds, Identities

ELEVEN
The Combinatorial Aesthetics of Neurobiology 251
Barbara Maria Stafford

TWELVE
Cloth Wounds: Queer Aesthetics of Debasement 268
Kathryn Bond Stockton

THIRTEEN
Embodying Culture: Dorian's Wish 295
Audrey Jaffe

FOURTEEN
Bad Taste, the Root Evil: I. A. Richards and the
Postnational Subject 313
Howard Horwitz

PART IV
Rethinking Aesthetics: Secrets and Magic, the Gift and the Child

FIFTEEN
The Gift: Reflections on the Eames House 347
Beatriz Colomina

SIXTEEN
What Is Construction, What's the Aesthetic, What Was Adorno Doing? 366
Robert Kaufman

SEVENTEEN
The Secret Life of Things:
Virginia Woolf and the Matter of Modernism 397
Bill Brown

EIGHTEEN
Arresting Images 431
Kathleen Stewart

NINETEEN
The Adult's Imagination of the Child's Imagination 449
Michael Taussig

Contributors 469

Index 475

Acknowledgments

This volume grew out of the conference "Aesthetic Subjects: Pleasures, Ideologies, and Ethics," sponsored by the Interdisciplinary Group for Humanities Studies at Texas A&M University in the spring of 1998. We wish to thank Jeffrey N. Cox, then director of the Interdisciplinary Group; James Rosenheim, director of the Interdisciplinary Group's successor, the Melbern G. Glasscock Center for Humanities Research; and conference director Mary Ann O'Farrell. We are grateful to the many individuals at Texas A&M who contributed to the success of the conference, which was supported by the Office of the Associate Provost for Graduate Studies; the College of Liberal Arts; the departments of English, history, modern and classical languages, philosophy, and speech communications; and the Women's Studies Program. We also thank all the presenters, whether or not their work is represented in this collection, who helped make this such a productive occasion for intellectual exchange.

Research awards from the Department of English, the College of Liberal Arts, and the Center for Humanities Research furthered our work by affording us the time and funding to bring this project to completion. The enthusiasm and informed commitment of University of Minnesota Press editor Richard Morrison to this book are much appreciated. Several individuals at Texas A&M helped with the manuscript preparation: Patricia Brooke, Ede Hilton-Lowe, Sara Anna Horton, Steve Marsden, Joseph Sims, and Larry Van Meter.

It has been our unusual good fortune that our work as coeditors has strengthened an already long-standing friendship. That friendship also includes those closest to us. Special thanks go to Dennis Berthold for his insights and suggestions at various stages of the project and, as always, for his support in the form of intellectual companionship, flowers, vegetables, and swimming pools; and to Mary Ann O'Farrell, not only for organizing a stimulating conference and contributing in countless ways to this volume, but also for beach adventures, Spanish dinners, being friends with the kids, and (ultimately) productive distractions.

Finally, thanks to Matthew, Gabe, and Josh for all the hugs, laughter, conversation, music, and good-humored patience.

P. R. M. and D. M.
College Station, Texas

INTRODUCTION

Exile's Return? Aesthetics Now

Pamela R. Matthews and David McWhirter

According to a 1998 *Chronicle of Higher Education* headline, "Beauty is Back." Yet the article itself, which mentions several recent books and a spate of conferences (including the one from which this project originates) as evidence of "renewed attention to aesthetic criteria in criticism," suggests that the (mostly literary) scholars it cites are far from certain about the feasibility—or even the desirability—of a return to what one interviewee describes as the "forbidden subject" of aesthetics. After thirty years of ideological critique, cultural conservatives, to be sure, are volubly eager for the forbidden subject's return from exile—an exile they view as the result of the aesthetic's unfair stigmatization at the hands of political correctnesses of various stripes. Most of the scholars quoted in the *Chronicle* article, however, sound a far more tentative note: one expresses genuine puzzlement about "whether we can recuperate the aesthetic"; another muses vaguely that "something else must be done," even if we're "not sure what."[1]

Our title, *Aesthetic Subjects,* is meant to signal what we see as productive tensions—the undecidability or fundamentally enigmatic relationships between subject(ivity) and object(ivity), autonomy and repression, art and ideology—in aesthetics. Subjects are simultaneously topics and human beings; aesthetics encompasses the "things" of aesthetic encounters, the philosophical traditions that speculate on the encounters, the act of "aestheticizing" by subjects who are also constrained by the economies of taste in which they participate. Approaching aesthetics from a wide range of disciplinary perspectives (history, philosophy, art history and architectural theory, literary studies, and cultural anthropology), the nineteen essays gathered in this volume undoubtedly reflect—and even welcome—the field's current theoretical instability. Indeed, what is perhaps most singular—and, these essays suggest, potentially most productive—about recent calls for a return to aesthetics is their emergence precisely at a moment when, to paraphrase Adorno, it is increasingly evident that nothing concerning aesthetics is self-evident anymore. As Geoffrey Harpham observes, "We seem to be approaching a maximum of theoretical confusion" that may also, paradoxically, suggest an approach to "the most definite and precise definition of the aesthetic that has yet been ventured—precisely *as* 'theoretical confusion.'" It may be, in other words, that our current confusion is a measure of our progress toward finally recognizing and clarifying fundamental ambivalences and undecidabilities inherent in a discourse—and no discourse, Harpham insists, is "more fundamental to modernity than the aesthetic"—that "gathers into itself and focuses norms and notions crucial to the self-description of an enlightened," modern culture.[2]

Concerned to recover the value of aesthetic experience for artistic, cultural, and social analysis, this volume's contributors also begin from a shared recognition that ideological readings of the aesthetic *have* provided insights difficult—we would say impossible—to ignore. By insisting that aesthetics be historicized and by exploring more rigorously its social functions, contextualized analyses have shown us much about the conditions that shape the experience of aesthetic encounters. Critics such as Terry Eagleton, for example, have analyzed the history of aesthetic discourse productively in order to question the universalizing tendencies of prevailing standards of aesthetic judgment. The so-called canon wars over "classic" literary status have highlighted the tendency of aesthetic criticism to universalize beauty in ways that dismiss the aesthetic criteria and experiences of others: women, non-Western peoples, minority racial and ethnic populations. The study of cultural institutions—museums, markets, and universities, to name just a few—has increased awareness of the interplay between seemingly detached aesthetic judgments (in culturally privileged discourses of high art, for example) and economic forces. Most globally, the insights of theorists like Pierre Bourdieu and John Guillory have helped us to understand that those judgments are never innocent or impersonal, that taste—recognized as a carrier of prestige or cultural capital—cannot be evaluated properly in isolation from its entanglements with power.[3]

But this unmasking of the aesthetic as a discourse—and perhaps an especially powerful one—contributing to the hegemony of bourgeois society and the regulation of modern subjectivities has too often served to elide the specific ways in which aesthetic experience functions as a social and cultural practice in particular historical and material circumstances. The stress on ideology—aesthetic experience, it turns out, isn't a view from nowhere—has proven less helpful in providing a viable language for explaining aesthetic pleasure and for understanding what happens at the moment when a specifically situated subject experiences beauty. Part of the problem, we believe, is that contemporary critiques have left intact—even as they have denounced—the terms the conservative defenders of the aesthetic have used to define it: as a privileged, autonomous, and apolitical locus of putatively absolute, universal, or even transcendent values. If the political arguments against beauty are, as Elaine Scarry remarks, "incoherent," it may be because those arguments have tended simply to invert an overdetermined distinction between politics and aesthetics while preserving the aesthetic in its "own" terms as the depoliticized zone of meaning and experience its beleaguered champions advertise it to be.[4] Positioning the "aesthetic" and the "political" as the discursive antitheses of current critical thought, both parties have conflated aesthetics with a particular, increasingly untenable, concept of aesthetic value.[5] This impasse, as John Guillory notes, has produced "a certain inarticulateness of the aesthetic," an uneasy sense that the language we have inherited is inadequate to the task of describing our actual experiences of aesthetic pleasure and a widely shared intuition that the cultural and ideological critique of aesthetic value nonetheless "always has a remainder, which is nothing other than aesthetic experience."[6]

Reflecting their diverse disciplinary investments in the category of aesthetics, the contributors to this volume work in multiple and complementary ways to explore the specificity, variety, and ubiquity of aesthetic experience even as they resist the temptation to "recuperate," "reclaim," or "resurrect" aesthetic discourse as a discourse of purity.[7] *Aesthetic Subjects* might best be described as an effort to resituate aesthetic pleasure in the mixed, *impure* conditions characteristic of every social practice and experience, however privileged or marginalized. What happens to the aesthetic, these essays ask, if we consider it apart from, or at least in tension with, its dominant discursive formulation—a formulation that, by enjoining a reductive choice *between* "politics" and "aesthetics," and by restricting the field of aesthetic inquiry to a narrow range of high-culture artifacts, has increasingly left the entire subject suspended between uncritical, celebratory calls for its "resurrection" and wholesale rejections of its validity as a category of cultural analysis? What might be gained through a renewed effort to distinguish aesthetics from (or at least to reconsider its entanglements with) the quite startling array of overdetermined concepts to which this experiential realm has been so insistently linked: truth, knowledge, form, the sacred, morality, eros, even art itself?

Any useful (as opposed to merely nostalgic) effort to recover aesthetics—an effort that would, for example, respond to rather than simply dismiss the challenge implied by the title of Tony Bennett's 1990 essay "Really Useless 'Knowledge': A Political Critique of Aesthetics"[8]—requires, we would argue, a willingness to articulate and explore what Wolfgang Welsch calls an "aesthetics beyond aesthetics." We need, that is, to expand the traditional understanding of aesthetics as an *artistics,* an explication of the concept of art with particular attention to beauty, to include "the whole range of *aisthesis* in everyday life, science, politics, art, ethics, and so on."[9] The essays in this volume thus address aesthetic experience from multiple and interdisciplinary perspectives in order to suggest alternative vocabularies and different contexts—or old perspectives and contexts freshly approached—for understanding the subject, and subjects and objects, of aesthetic discourse. For some contributors this means a readiness to explore the pleasures contingent on encounters with objects and sites not traditionally invested with aesthetic value: the screen performances of Shelley Winters, for example, as well as the paintings of Caravaggio; ordinary objects and social practices as well as the productions of high culture; advertising, fashion, and the human body in addition to the canonical literary texts of Dickens or Nabokov. For others it demands a sustained attentiveness to the particular identities—as shaped by factors ranging from class, nationality, and ethnicity to gender, sexuality, and even biology—so often concealed behind the supposedly universal subject of aesthetics.

As several of the essays included here suggest, moreover, the current impasse in discussions of aesthetics is the result not only of contemporary culture wars, but also of contradictions embedded in aesthetic discourse from its inception. The resurgence of interest in Adorno, for example, may be in part attributable to his sometimes tortured refusal of the choice between politics and aesthetics. As a Marxist critic working both within and against the grain of classical aesthetics, Adorno anticipates our current confusion about the place of aesthetics—our desire, on the one hand, to recover the specificity of a variant of experience that might be called aesthetic; our suspicion, on the other hand, of the aesthetic's claims to autonomy and disinterestedness—even as he insists that the confusion is as old as modernity itself.

Although cultural conservatives often seem resistant to the idea that aesthetics even *has* a history (or at least one that might matter to them), the rise of a sustained discourse of philosophical aesthetics in the eighteenth century is in fact coincident with still-resonant shifts in modes of artistic production and consumption. Aesthetic discourse emerged at about the same time that objects previously entangled in religious, political, or other functional contexts began to be valued solely as works of art, available *for* consumption. What Benjamin terms the loss of the art object's aura is, in other words, a product of the same historical conditions that stimulated philosophical, psychological, and scientific efforts to account for aesthetic experience largely, but not exclusively, in terms of disinterested contemplation. As Eagleton has reminded us, aesthetics, often understood today as "a flight from corporeal existence," originates not as a theory of art, but as "an idiom of the body" and an analysis of the mechanisms of sensual perception.[10] Similarly, one of the key strands in contemporary critiques of the aesthetic—the perception that claims about the value of the art object have worked to conceal the aesthetic's function of formulating a regulatory model of "universal" subjectivity—can be understood not only as a challenge to Kant's famously problematic claim that "the judgment of taste" involves "a title to subjective universality," but also as an echo of his less-noticed admission that the enigmatic subjectivity of aesthetic experience can be articulated only through a discourse that attributes beauty to the object.[11] Indeed, aesthetics as a field involves a more or less founding confusion between "particular kinds of objects and the [subjective] attitude[s] appropriate to judging them."[12]

Our contributors' strategies for pluralizing aesthetics as a concept—exploring aesthetic experiences beyond the confines of "art" and in the contexts of variant identities; recovering the multiplicity and contradictoriness too often elided within the history of philosophical aesthetics itself—are also a way of acknowledging that aesthetics has, since its beginnings, increasingly pushed its way into the core of knowledge and truth in disciplines that at first glance would seem to have little to do with any philosophy of art. As Harpham, Eagleton, and others have begun to demonstrate, the aesthetic, for all its putative associations with the timeless and the universal, is in fact the surest and most particular sign of the onset of modernity, for it constitutes a domain in which one confronts what political philosopher Luc Ferry calls "the key problem" of the modern secular universe in general: "how to ground objectivity on subjectivity, transcendence on immanence." The birth of aesthetics is inseparable from the withdrawal of the divine, and since Kant, Ferry argues, "the history of aesthetics is the place par excellence where the subjectivization of the world occurs." Thus "*Homo Aestheticus*" becomes the central actor in "the political problem of democratic individualism"; our "Democratic Age" is inseparable from "The Invention of Taste."[13] Welsch, in his suggestively titled *Undoing Aesthetics,* similarly argues that

> modern thought, since Kant, has subscribed to the insight that the nature of the underlying condition we call reality is aesthetic. Reality has proven itself again and again to be constituted not "realistically" but "aesthetically." Where this insight has penetrated—and by now it is just about everywhere—aesthetics has lost its character as a special discipline relating solely to art and become a broader and more general medium for the understanding of reality.[14]

One scholar quoted in the *Chronicle* article mentioned above remarks that "the public doesn't much understand—and isn't much interested in supporting—a humanities that doesn't address the aesthetic."[15] But the irony of our current cultural situation is that, in the standoff between those who *would* address the aesthetic by uncritically "resurrecting" a reductive and increasingly unsatisfactory conceptual model and those who in their determination to unmask its mystifications sometimes seem bent on dismissing the subject of aesthetics altogether, neither party has done justice to this pervasive yet enigmatic realm of human experience. The mantra of autonomy, disinterestedness, sublimity, and aesthetic purity is no longer adequate to describe our art, let alone the more palpably mixed pleasures of our everyday encounters with beauty. But aesthetic experience, as Michael Taussig insists in his essay for this volume, is also "far more mischievous and complicated and real" than contemporary ideological critiques of the subject allow. *Aesthetic Subjects* is a collective effort to move beyond this impasse by generating the vocabularies and concepts for a new address, one committed to rediscovering not only the specificity of aesthetic experience, but also its profound and various sociality.

"In that which is called philosophy of art, usually one thing is missing: either Philosophy or Art." Schlegel's remark, intended by Adorno as the epigraph for his *Aesthetic Theory,* suggests how our commitment to resituating aesthetics involves a willingness to disturb the term's comfortable reference to a well-defined strand of traditional philosophical discourse.[16] The essays collected in Part I, "Locating Aesthetic Experience: Sites, Situations, Discourses," offer multidisciplinary perspectives on the "places" one might look for understanding aesthetic experience.

Those places are sometimes the symbolic spaces of intellectual inquiry inviting us to look again at the relationship between aesthetic experience and the work of art. Martin Jay, for example, in "Drifting into Dangerous Waters," cautions against separating aesthetic experience from the work of art. Jay calls for a revised account of aesthetics that respects the distinction between artwork and lifeworld and recognizes subjects and objects as irreducible to—but not isolated from—one another. Enacting the very confusion of art and life that worries Jay, Alphonso Lingis in "Armed Assault" finds the space formed at the intersection of unlikely aesthetic subjects (two prisoners and lovers, middle-aged junkies, one a transvestite, both HIV-positive, one already sick with AIDS) and the aesthetically aware scholarly account that foregrounds those subjects a productive site for exploring aesthetic experience. In the process, he radically redefines prevailing concepts of beauty and sublimity. The space Kay Bea Jones considers in "Reinventing the Wall" is the more literally apprehended material space of several structures designed (and, less often, built) by architect Zaha Hadid. Hadid's conceptually porous walls serve as metaphor for an architecture that questions notions of demarcated space by merging inside with outside, building with site, urban setting with the world beyond it—even abstract design with built object. Jones finds in Hadid's liberated spaces (as well as in her implicit challenges to a masculine architectural status quo) an example of a "well-ordered," yet flexible and indeterminate, postmodern world.

In Judith Stoddart's "Pleasures Incarnate," the space for productive inquiry into aesthetics is not contemporary architectural space but the ideological space of eighteenth- and nineteenth-century institutions: museums, exhibitions, the bodies of viewers, and the sentimental as a conceptual tool. Working to recover a chapter of art history judged aesthetically wanting by the standards of a privileged modernism, Stoddart reminds us of Pierre Bourdieu's dictum that there is no "natural" response to art, only particular cultural competencies shaped by powerful but contingent institutions. In "Caravaggio's Secrets," Leo Bersani and Ulysse Dutoit suggest, moreover, that categories such as aesthetic value remain unstable because aesthetic experience is the name we give to a fundamentally enigmatic desire. Bersani and Dutoit read through and beyond the erotic solicitations of Caravaggio's paintings, arguing that the aesthetic is not the royal road to the "secret" of the unconscious, or to a concealed interiority. Rather, and more radically, it opens on a disseminated and "unmappable extensibility of being" that may be incompatible with both sexuality and life itself.

Does the aesthetic necessarily promote, create, or partake of justice? Finding the experience of aesthetics in what once might have been seen as all the wrong places, the authors of the five essays in Part II, "Aesthetics in Social Contexts: Economies and Ethics," explore the ways in which the aesthetic is bound up with ethical and political questions, especially the ethics of representation. In considering such questions, and by attending to individuals and groups of people usually left out of discussions of aesthetics, these authors understand that there's no such thing as "just aesthetics": what once could be regarded as pure aesthetic experience cannot be recovered so easily after the insights of ideological critiques have demonstrated the complex play of power relations in that experience. At the same time, representation is an ethical problematic: depending as it does upon the absence of the represented, representation always distorts its own attempt at representativeness. That is, in speaking for those marginalized by and in the history of taste, the contributors to Part II know that in the effort to represent, justice may be undercut as much as served. The origins of aesthetics in the body, these essays suggest, has become a more complicated issue than one of sensation versus conception; bodies are difficult to represent justly.

For Susan Bordo in "The Moral Content of Nabokov's *Lolita,*" textual and visual representations of Lolita by Nabokov (1955), Kubrick (1962), and Lyne (1998) help us read cultural shifts in attitudes toward the bodies of "girl-children." Arguing that what looks to be individual can be cultural (although not, importantly, universal), Bordo unmasks the larger theoretical issue Nabokov in particular helps her make: divorcing aesthetic pleasure from ethical consciousness is dangerous to actual people. Locating aesthetic and ethical considerations not in the body of Bordo's girl but rather in that of a mature woman, Joseph Litvak in "The Aesthetics of Jewishness" argues that the figure of actress Shelley Winters exemplifies a counteraesthetic of Jewish performance. As an actor in and against the aesthetic codes defining beauty, sexiness, and ridiculousness, Winters—by modeling "a Jewish mannerism of bad manners, a formalism of bad form—not just aesthetic vulgarity, but an aesthetics *of* vulgarity"—helps Litvak theorize ethnic identification and disidentification, and challenge reigning definitions of aesthetic pleasure.

Shifting the social context to eighteenth-century Europe, Maureen Harkin in "Theorizing Popular Practice in Eighteenth-Century Aesthetics" returns to the scene of the crime: the origins of aesthetics as a separate category of inquiry. Focusing on the now relatively unknown aesthetic theories of Lord Kames and Alexander Gerard, Harkin argues that the presence of disempowered or socially marginal figures (variously incarnated as foreigners, the young, the uneducated, and, especially, women and the lower classes) offers deviations from the standard of taste by introducing the disturbance of social diversity into a discourse otherwise invested in managing difference in an emerging bourgeois culture. Human beauty is messier than the beauty of art or nature, Douglas Mao observes in "The Labor Theory of Beauty," in part because the incommensurability between "comeliness" and moral goodness questions the traditional assumption of an unproblematic link between ethics and aesthetics. Reminding us that aesthetics began, in Kant and others, as a discourse of the body, Mao discerns in today's beauty industry—plastic surgery, cosmetics, and gym culture, for example—the signs of an effort to reconnect the rewards of beauty with labor.

In "*Sinthom*-osexuality," Lee Edelman turns to queer theory and practice to situate ethical choices within economies of aesthetics and sexual desire. Through Dickens's *A Christmas Carol* and George Eliot's *Silas Marner* in particular, Edelman reads gay sexuality as the Lacanian *sinthome* (the "irreducible" symptom of *jouissance*). The displaced figure for the antithesis of aesthetic idealization, the homosexual, Edelman argues, has an ethical imperative to resist the lure of aesthetic sublimation and to embody its very opposite, thus opening a space of internal resistance to heterosexual culture's destructive fetishization of "futurity" in the figure of the child. Here, as in the other essays in Part II, what once might have seemed a given—a natural conjunction between the beautiful and the good—has become a much more vexed question of the complex relationship between ethics and aesthetics.

The four essays gathered in Part III, "Aesthetic Subjects: Bodies, Minds, Identities," explore the varied implications of aesthetics for understanding the nature, formation, and instantiation of selves and identities. Does aesthetic experience reveal—or perhaps produce—the subject in ways not duplicated by other modes of experience? And if aesthetics does offer privileged or unique access to the subject, what kind of subject are we talking about? A Kantian subject, at once individual and universal? A Freudian subject of unconscious desires? A Foucauldian self-regulating subject, simultaneously autonomous and subject to repressive law? A decentered postmodern subject with no illusions about individual agency? If, as many have argued, aesthetics from Kant onward has always been concerned fundamentally with the relation between the perceptive or receptive subject and the object—what Eagleton calls the "drama of subject and object" whose "couplings and splittings, matchings and misalliances, have so consistently dominated the modern philosophical stage"[17]—in what ways and to what extent does the aesthetic encounter still work to constitute a self, however we might define it?

Barbara Maria Stafford's subject is constituted through, and explanatory of, what she calls "The Combinatorial Aesthetics of Neurobiology." If understanding itself occurs when disparate things are compelled to converge, the imaging arts have much to contribute to the study of human consciousness in fields as disparate as analytic philosophy, cognitive science, computer programming, and neurobiology. The "sophisticated workings" of analogy, according to Stafford, offer no less than a visual rhetoric for constructing and understanding selfhood.

In "Cloth Wounds," Kathryn Bond Stockton focuses on a "queer aesthetics of debasement"—what she calls the "divine humiliation" of a devotion to cloth and clothing—as a means of exploring the constitution of queer identities. Constellating Freud and Bataille with texts by Radclyffe Hall, Leslie Feinberg, and Jean Genet, Stockton traces a trope of "sartorial sacrifice" in which clothing emerges as the fabric that fosters group fantasy and sets the group apart in an aestheticized sociality. For Audrey Jaffe reading *The Picture of Dorian Gray* in "Embodying Culture," Wilde's late-nineteenth-century fantasy of the beautiful, desirable individual-become-group representative (in this case, representative of an emergent homosexual identity) reveals and predicts the aesthetic foundations of modern symbolic politics of identity. Identity politics, viewed by cultural conservatives as the antithesis of aesthetic appreciation, paradoxically is grounded in a paradigmatic aesthetic difference, the difference between beauty and ugliness.

In "Bad Taste, the Root Evil," Howard Horwitz explores the aesthetic underpinnings of the "postnational subject" theorized by postcolonial critics such as Homi Bhabha. Horwitz views Bhabha's hybrid subject as repeating, ironically, the "ontological idealism" of I. A. Richards's aesthetic formalism and questions our continuing preoccupation with the idealized aesthetic subject: whether we understand it as unified (Richards) or multiple (Bhabha), the subject so conceived is, Horwitz argues, irrelevant and counterproductive to our understanding of the relationship between aesthetic and political or social experience.

Perhaps in part because the traditional (and still-pervasive) language of aesthetics seems inadequate or distorting or even obstructionist for exploring aesthetics now, the contributors to Part IV, "Rethinking Aesthetics: Secrets and Magic, the Gift and the Child," approach the aesthetic through a surprising array of metaphors: secrets, magic, the gift, and the imagined imagination of the child. Not coincidentally, they also apprehend aesthetic experience not in its traditional associations with "high" art or sublime encounters, but in its ordinary and everyday manifestations, apart from (yet aware of) Marxist-inspired notions of commodity and exchange.

In "The Gift," for example, Beatriz Colomina understands the architectural work of Charles and Ray Eames as grounded in an aesthetics of celebration, play, and gift giving. Displacing the single eye (and I) of the historical avant-garde with multiple eyes, the Eameses shifted modern design practices, including but not limited to architecture, away from a Miesian focus on the exterior and toward an emphasis on the interior as a space for intersubjective encounters with the objects and people of everyday existence. In "What Is Construction, What's the Aesthetic, What Was Adorno Doing?" Robert Kaufman uses Jameson's reading of Adorno's reading of Kant to argue that Adorno understood what many theorists now overlook: that the aesthetic, typically formulated as being opposed to the material, the historical, and the social, does not prevent critique but enables it. Rethinking the assumptions behind ideological critiques of the aesthetic, Kaufman finds in Adorno the potential for "mak[ing] the aesthetic's case from within a Marxian vocabulary and syntax."

In an essay focused on Virginia Woolf's short story "Solid Objects," Bill Brown explores "The Secret Life of Things," which, like the artifacts in the Eames house, matter outside the usual subject/object dyad or systems of consumption and/or exchange. Reading Woolf in the context of World War II scarcity and economic depression, Brown argues that the story resists through aesthetic display the utilitarian trajectory of government mandates: aesthetically apprehended objects cannot be merely "reassembled" as they had been before the war. The actors in "Arresting Images," Kathleen Stewart's performative narrative of an addicted, stigmatized underclass in search of redemption and public recognition, act out the ways in which aesthetic destruction and defacement become, in class terms, attempts to imagine the secrets of an unimagined existence. Challenging abstract notions of the aesthetic, Stewart theorizes a concrete aesthetics and explores the dreams and necessities that promote its daily reenactments.

In the volume's concluding essay, Michael Taussig undertakes an ethnography of what he calls "The Adult's Imagination of the Child's Imagination." Exploring cultural sites ranging from contemporary media, state propaganda, and secret societies to "The Emperor's New Clothes" and the phenomenon of Santa Claus, Taussig argues that the child's imagination constitutes a "vast cultural resource" for adult fantasy. In the child who "still loves secrets, as gifts to be unwrapped, as secrets to be spent," adults recognize the public secrecy that grounds social intercourse: the "knowing unknowing" where aesthetics and ethics meet.

In his recent meditation on the status of aesthetics in contemporary theory and culture, Giorgio Agamben reminds us that "the entrance of art into the aesthetic dimension . . . is not as innocent and natural a phenomenon as we usually take for granted." And it may be that nothing is more urgent—if we really want to engage the problem of art in our time: to recover the value of beauty for and in our individual and collective lives, and to reclaim (as Scarry wants us to) beauty's fundamental importance for education—than "a *destruction* of aethetics that would, by clearing away what is usually taken for granted, allow us to bring into question the very meaning of aesthetics as the science of the work of art," and so liberate art from what Welsch describes as "the golden cage of autonomy" in which it has been "ghettoiz[ed]" by traditional aesthetic discourse.[18]

But might not such a "destruction," Agamben goes on to worry, risk "the loss of any possible horizon for the understanding of the work of art?"[19] There is, moreover, another risk involved in the reconfiguration of aesthetics we are advocating, one Martin Jay addresses in his essay here when he cautions against separating aesthetics from the work of art. While he is concerned, like many of this volume's contributors, with extending aesthetic appreciation to cultural artifacts hitherto dismissed by prevalent, deceptively "universal" standards of beauty, Jay also worries that if all objects, whether or not they were ever intended as works of art, can be redeemed in aesthetic terms, we run the risk of promiscuously aestheticizing or "reenchanting" the entire world—a danger recognized by Benjamin in his warning against the fascist aestheticization of politics.[20] Thus, Jay insists, aesthetic experience cannot be freed entirely from a consideration of which objects and events may justifiably evoke it, or else it courts the charge that it produces an ethically problematic "theodicy of beauty." "Or rather," he continues, "it cannot avoid that rebuke if we remain within the terms set by the eighteenth century's version of that experience."

Jay's qualification is crucial, for it articulates the space of this volume's intervention, its contributors' shared recognition of the need for a reconceptualized aesthetics adequate to our own historical situation. As Arthur Danto has argued in a recent book on contemporary art, "Art has gone through a revolutionary moment, one that invalidated forever the easy transit from aesthetics to art criticism."[21] Indeed, as Philip Fisher remarks, "we have for two hundred years built up a more and more intricate theory for a type of art that we do not actually have and would not care for if we did have it."[22] Perhaps, then, Jay is right: if our aesthetics—too often, as Fisher notes, a strategy for "hold[ing] on to covert religious feelings under an aesthetic disguise"[23]—no longer describes even our art, we had best be wary of its claims to reenchant the everyday. Viewed in this light, our current skepticism—a situation, Scarry laments, in which "the vocabulary of beauty has been banished or driven underground in the humanities"[24]—may seem a necessary, if potentially costly, retrenchment.

But aesthetics need not be conflated with a transcendent sublime or a "theodicy of beauty"; there are in fact quite urgent reasons for resisting the lure of that conflation. As Leo Bersani argues in *The Culture of Redemption,* assuming that "the repetition of experience in art repairs inherently damaged or valueless experience," or even "redeems" the "presumed raw material of experience," results in the devaluation of both historical experience and art itself:

> The redemptive aesthetic asks us to consider art as a correction of life, but *the corrective virtue of works of art depends on a misreading of art as philosophy.* Art . . . cannot have the unity, the identity, the stability of truth; it does not belong to the world of perfectly intelligible ideas. A redemptive aesthetic based on the negation of life . . . must also negate art.[25]

Resisting the desire to recover or resurrect a redemptive purity that never was, we, along with the contributors to this volume, seek instead to rethink the connection between art and aesthetics by revising aesthetics as a discipline in light of the changes that have revolutionized critical practice in the past thirty years. Through interdisciplinary dialogue and exchange, this volume works to affirm what might be called an immanent aesthetics: a language for articulating aesthetic experience and value that echoes rather than denies art's own rich sociality and productive capacity for critique. Only by refusing nostalgia for the aesthetic's inviolability, and by acknowledging the aesthetic's entanglements in systems of power, repression, and exclusion, can we begin to recover beauty's still-surprising capacity, not to save, but to provoke us to rethink and change our lives, to lead us to "a more capacious regard for the world," and to bring with it, "in contrast to the withering track of cause and effect, the desire to live, a sense of the abundance, the plentitude of life."[26]

Notes

1. Scott Heller, "Wearying of Cultural Studies, Some Scholars Rediscover Beauty," *Chronicle of Higher Education,* 4 December 1998, A15, A16. Among the recent books mentioned in the article are James Soderholm ed., *Beauty and the Critic: Aesthetics in an Age of Cultural Studies* (Tuscaloosa: University of Alabama Press, 1997); and

George Levine, ed., *Aesthetics and Ideology* (New Brunswick, N.J.: Rutgers University Press, 1994).

2. Geoffrey Galt Harpham, "Aesthetics and the Fundamentals of Modernity," in *Aesthetics and Ideology*, ed. Levine, 135, 124. The current confusion and instability surrounding aesthetics are reflected in the titles of several recent studies, beginning with Hal Foster, ed., *The Anti-Aesthetic: Essays on Postmodern Culture* (Seattle: Bay, 1983). See also Michael P. Clark, ed., *Revenge of the Aesthetic: The Place of Literature in Theory Today* (Berkeley: University of California Press, 2000); Stuart Sim, *Beyond Aesthetics: Confrontations with Poststructuralism and Postmodernism* (Toronto: University of Toronto Press, 1992); Wolfgang Welsch, *Undoing Aesthetics*, trans. Andrew Inkpen (London: Sage, 1997).

3. See Terry Eagleton, *The Ideology of the Aesthetic* (Oxford: Basil Blackwell, 1990); Pierre Bourdieu, *Distinction: A Social Critique of the Judgement of Taste*, trans. Richard Nice (Cambridge: Harvard University Press, 1984); John Guillory, *Cultural Capital: The Problem of Literary Canon Formation* (Chicago: University of Chicago Press, 1993).

4. Elaine Scarry, *On Beauty and Being Just* (Princeton, N.J.: Princeton University Press, 1999), 57. Scarry goes on to argue that "it may even be the case that far from damaging our capacity to attend to problems of injustice, [beauty] instead intensifies the pressure we feel to repair existing injuries" (57); see esp. pt. 2, "On Beauty and Being Fair" (57–124).

5. In arguing for "rethinking the category of the aesthetic," Isobel Armstrong similarly notes that "the traditional definition [of aesthetics] has not shifted much, whether it is reflected as radical or conservative, undermined or confirmed. Neither radical critique nor conservative confidence works with the possibility that social and cultural change . . . might have changed or might change the category itself. Both in its deconstruction and consecration the model of the aesthetic remains virtually unchanged" ("Introduction: A Case for Rethinking the Category of the Aesthetic," in *The Radical Aesthetic* [Oxford: Blackwell, 2000], 5).

6. Guillory, *Cultural Capital*, 271, 335, 327.

7. "Recuperate" is both Anne Mellor's term (quoted in Heller, "Wearying of Cultural Studies," A16) and Christopher Beach's ("Recuperating the Aesthetic: Contemporary Approaches and the Case of Adorno," in *Beauty and the Critic*, ed. Soderholm, 94–112); "resurrect" comes from Soderholm's introduction to *Beauty and the Critic* (6); "reclaim" is George Levine's term in his introduction to *Aesthetics and Ideology* (1).

8. Tony Bennett, "Really Useless 'Knowledge': A Political Critique of Aesthetics," in *Outside Literature* (London: Routledge, 1990), 133–66.

9. Welsch, *Undoing Aesthetics*, 78, ix.

10. Eagleton, *The Ideology of the Aesthetic*, 171. See also James Kirwan's claim that "the association of art and beauty seems, in retrospect, . . . to have been simply an interlude"—the product of a particular age. Provocatively, Kirwan asserts that "beauty, far from being preserved by a certain attitude toward art (or even a certain kind of art), only began to decline through becoming too closely associated with art" (*Beauty* [Manchester: Manchester University Press, 1999], 94).

11. Immanuel Kant, *Critique of Judgement*, trans. J. H. Bernard (New York: Hafner, 1951), 46.

12. Harpham, "Aesthetics and the Fundamentals of Modernity," 124.

13. Luc Ferry, *Homo "Aestheticus": The Invention of Taste in the Democratic Age*, trans. Robert de Loaiza (Chicago: University of Chicago Press, 1993), 25, 19.

14. Welsch, *Undoing Aesthetics*, ix.

15. Giles Gunn, quoted in Heller, "Wearying of Cultural Studies," A16; see also Elaine Scarry's advocacy of "beauty [as] a starting place for education" (*On Beauty*, 31 and passim).

16. Friedrich Schlegel, quoted in Martin Jay, *Adorno* (Cambridge: Harvard University Press, 1984), 111, 180 n (Jay's translation).

17. Eagleton, *Ideology of the Aesthetic*, 70.

18. Giorgio Agamben, *The Man without Content*, trans. Georgia Albert (Stanford, Calif.: Stanford University Press, 1999), 6; Welsch, *Undoing Aesthetics*, 98.

19. Agamben, *The Man without Content*, 6.

20. Walter Benjamin, "The Work of Art in the Age of Mechanical Reproduction," in *Illuminations*, trans. Harry Zohn (New York: Harcourt Brace, 1968), 217–51. In contrast to Jay, Welsch suggests that various historical changes—the aestheticization of material reality in the wake of new material technologies, of social reality as a result of its mediation through mass media, and of subjective reality following the dissolution of moral standards by "self-styling"—have made an expansion of aesthetics beyond its traditional focus on the work of art not only inevitable but necessary to ground effective diagnosis and critique of "the globalization and fundamentalization of the aesthetic" in modernity (*Undoing Aesthetics*, 7, 82).

21. Arthur Danto, *After the End of Art: Contemporary Art and the Pale of History* (Princeton, N.J.: Princeton University Press, 1997), 93.

22. Philip Fisher, *Wonder, the Rainbow, and the Aesthetics of Rare Experiences* (Cambridge: Harvard University Press, 1998), 3.

23. Ibid., 2.

24. Scarry, *On Beauty*, 52.

25. Leo Bersani, *The Culture of Redemption* (Cambridge: Harvard University Press, 1990), 1–2.

26. Scarry, *On Beauty*, 48; Kirwan, *Beauty*, 124.

Part I

Locating Aesthetic Experience: Sites, Situations, Discourses

CHAPTER ONE

Drifting into Dangerous Waters

The Separation of Aesthetic Experience from the Work of Art

Martin Jay

Modernization, runs a familiar story, is typified by the increasing differentiation of value spheres, each with its own immanent logic and relative autonomy. Initially expressed in philosophical terms by Kant, whose three critiques neatly divide the mental world into cognitive, ethical, and aesthetic realms, the process was given sociological grounding in the writings of Max Weber, who explored the institutional underpinnings of the differentiation based on specialization of function and the creation of separate cultures of expertise. In his more recent defense of the project of modernity, Jürgen Habermas has soberly appraised the benefits and costs of the splits among the spheres, as well as between them and an allegedly prior lifeworld of unreflective practices out of which the spheres emerged. In the tradition broadly circumscribed by these three names, the differentiation of value spheres is by and large acknowledged as a progressive or at least irreversible process, which has allowed the clarification of theoretical issues and the increased efficiency that often accompanies a division of labor. Although what Habermas has called the troubling "colonization" of one realm by another may be problematic, the solution has been the restoration of a balance rather than an overcoming of the distinctions themselves.

Against such a reading, a formidable array of critics has bemoaned the loss of the allegedly integrated world that preceded the split into distinct and incommensurable value spheres. Mobilizing the now familiar rhetoric of dissociation of sensibility, alienation, or diremption, these critics yearn to dedifferentiate, or at least render more permeable, the boundaries separating the spheres. They have sought ways to restore a condition of reconciliation or harmony that they believe once existed or at least posit it as a normative goal for a future in which the putative wounds of modern life would be healed. What has become transcendent and abstract they hope to restore to immanent concreteness, and perhaps in so doing reenchant a world from which meaning seems to have fled or retreated into isolated enclaves. Even those critics normally placed in the postmodernist camp, who dismiss such a quest as little more than nostalgia for an imaginary prelapsarian bliss that never obtained and never will, are no less hostile to the alleged autonomy and self-sufficiency of the three value spheres, whose boundaries and limits they eagerly transgress, or rather claim are always already self-transgressed.

In what follows, I do not want to add another round to this now familiar debate, which has taken many different forms and at times has spilled out over the walls of the academy to inspire fervent movements of cultural, religious, and political renewal. Instead, I want to concentrate on one corner of it, in which a differentiation within a differentiation has taken place. That is, I want to examine the consequences within the aesthetic sphere of the distinction between works or objects of art and what has come to be called *aesthetic experience.* I will have to ask your indulgence for not attempting a serious analysis of what might count as an object or work of art, itself a distinction that cannot be entirely ignored. I simply don't have the space here to rehearse the debates generated by Nelson Goodman's pathbreaking *Languages of Art,* with its opposition of "autographic" and "allographic" works, the former understood as singular, material objects, such as paintings, with claims to authenticity based on their production history, and the latter as ideal objects, such as musical compositions or works of literature, with the ability to generate an infinity of valid instantiations.[1] Nor am I able to consider here the further refinement between immanent and transcendent works recently introduced by Gérard Genette, the former implying identity between the work and its material instantiation (or, if allographic, instantiations) and the latter suggesting the ways in which works can exceed those instantiations and produce plural aesthetic effects.[2] I will simply take as given the heuristic usefulness of the distinction between art object, however it may be defined, and the experience it generates. In so doing, I hope to provide some insight into the dangers involved when the differentiations of modernity become too firmly reified or, conversely, when the desire to overcome them results in a problematic confusion or conflation of categories, leading to that drift into dangerous waters suggested by this chapter's title.

Although an awareness of the specificity of a variant of experience that might be called aesthetic has been discerned as far back as Pythagoras, it was perhaps not until the nineteenth century that the center of gravity in aesthetic discourse decisively shifted from the idea of beauty assumed to reside in objects in the world to the experiences of the humans who responded to them. The shift was evidenced by, inter alia, the ascendency of psychological accounts of that experience in the scientific work of Gustav Fechner and others in the 1860s and the general cult of experience in the so-called philosophies of life later in the century, in which intensity of experience (in the sense of vital *Erlebnis,* rather than cognitive or dialectical *Erfahrung*) was the highest value.[3] The ground, however, was already laid in the eighteenth century with the development of a distinct branch of philosophical discourse focusing on "art," a generic category under which all of the separate Muses were subsumed.[4] That discourse, it is often noted, emerged at a time when objects that had previously been revered as sacred and played a role in religious worship or were appreciated as emblems of social or political power were redescribed and newly legitimated as works possessing purely artistic value. As Hegel was among the first to point out somewhere in his *Lectures on Aesthetics,* the cadavers of dead cults could be revived through redescription as living works of art. No longer expected to imitate an ideal world, illustrate mythic stories, or re-create historical events, they could be justified in self-referential terms privileging form over content or function. The recontextualization of such objects in the heterotopic, atemporal space of the public museum—the classical example being the transformation of the palace of the Louvre during the French Revolution into a repository of the nation's cultural patrimony—accompanied and abetted the new discourse, which also emerged in the wake of an accelerated market for objects of beauty by private collectors outside of the aristocracy or the church. Concomitant with the change was the new distinction between fine artist and merely skilled artisan, neatly symbolized by the decision to exclude engravers from the newly created Royal Academy of the Arts in London in 1768.

These aspects of the story have been widely remarked. What is perhaps less frequently realized is that at virtually the same moment that freshly redefined artworks were being freed from their entanglement in religious, political, or utilitarian contexts, allowed to circulate in a new network of value, at once cultural and economic, and housed in secular temples of culture open to the people, they were paradoxically losing their integrity as self-sufficient entities in the world, definable in intrinsic terms as objective exemplars of universal beauty.[5] In the vocabulary made familiar by Walter Benjamin, this loss meant the progressive dissipation of the cultic aura that surrounded such entities, an aura predicated on the presence of a unique object that was distant and distinct from the beholder. Although it is undeniable that some of the numinous atmosphere clinging to sacred objects was transferred to certain fetishized works of elite art, whose cultural capital was accordingly high, the philosophical legitimation of that transfer tacitly abandoned the claim that such objects possessed an aesthetic version of the religious notion of "real presence," an incarnation of ultimate value that was prior to the beholder's response to it. In a context of increased openness to cultural difference, which mirrored the uneven but widening toleration of religious pluralism and appreciation of geographic diversity, absolute and universal hierarchies of beauty were harder to maintain. The classical standards of a Boileau, confidently grounded in an objectivist belief in the order of nature, were challenged by the "sentimentalism" of a Dubos, who focused instead on the feelings of those who responded to specific works.[6] Increasingly, in fact, eighteenth-century aesthetic theory shifted attention to the experience of that beholder or the community of beholders. As David Hume famously put it in his essay "Of the Standard of Taste," "Beauty is no quality in the things themselves: It exists merely in the mind which contemplates them; and each mind perceives a different beauty."[7]

The Greek *aiesthesis*, the origin of the Latin word *aesthetica* used by Alexander Baumgarten as the title for his two-volume work of 1750 and 1758, implied gratifying corporeal perception, the subjective sensual response to objects rather than objects themselves. One of its antithetical terms was *noesis*, which signified pure conceptual thought separated from the senses. Another was *poiesis*, the active making of objects, artistic or otherwise. Some of that activism may have been retained in the ancillary notion of taste, with its connotation of tactile intervention in the world,[8] which implied experience as experimentation. But even here the emphasis was on the emotional, even irrational, reception of art epitomized by the "je ne sais quoi" attitude of ineffability that became emblematic of the retreat from conceptualization and production. As John Dewey was later to note with chagrin, the very concept of the "aesthetic," when set apart from the overlapping but not equivalent term *artistic,* tends to render experience as "appreciative, perceiving and enjoying," rather than productive or creative.[9] Although the discourse concerning aesthetic judgment that culminated in Kant's third *Critique* went beyond the passive and conventionalist subjectivism of taste represented by Hume and sought more universal criteria, it too focused on the response rather than the object per se. Kant did, to be sure, provide an account of the genius who created without criteria—a productive correlate of the beholder, who, as we will see, judges without them as well—but the main emphasis of his aesthetics was on reception.[10]

This is not the place to trace the complex ways in which such Enlightenment theorists as Baumgarten, Shaftesbury, Hutcheson, Hume, Kames, Moritz, Dubos, and Kant developed the concept of aesthetic experience, or to untangle the web of meanings surrounding the crucial term *taste,* but a few central points need to be made.[11] First, whether the ground of aesthetic experience was assumed to be an innate capacity, an unmediated, non-rule-bound sense of what was beautiful comparable to an inbred moral sentiment (as it was for the neo-Platonist Shaftesbury), or understood instead to derive from purely empirical encounters with the world (as the more skeptical Hume believed), it was irreducible to a mere recording of what was intrinsically there in objects deemed artistic or beautiful. The same conclusion was shared by those who saw the source of the aesthetic sense in personal psychology, communal, intersubjective consensus, or the more philosophically grounded "reflective judgment" that Kant had posited as a way to get beyond the apparent antinomy of taste, at once personal and universal. In all of these cases, the stress was on the one or ones who did the experiencing rather than on the intrinsic qualities of the object that was experienced. "The beautiful," as Kant would argue, appeared only as the predicate of a judgment, not as a quality of an object. In some ways reminiscent of the epistemological limits on knowing objects in themselves—whether couched in the empiricist vocabulary of lacking access to primary as opposed to secondary qualities or the transcendental idealist vocabulary of unknowable noumena—the object as such was less important than its aesthetic appreciation or enjoyment. Here too a kind of "Copernican revolution," to cite the famous metaphor identified with Kant's first *Critique*,[12] took place in which ontological or axiological questions were subordinated to those concerning the epistemological or, in this case, aesthetic subject. Objects were admired not for what they were in themselves, but for what they could do to us. The telos of this Copernican reversal was an increasing indifference to the object as such, perhaps even extending to its very existence.

Before that conclusion was reached, and this is the second point worth emphasizing, the sensual pleasure produced by the object in aesthetic experience had to be distinguished from that enjoyed in other relations between self and world. As early as Johannes Scotus Erigena's ninth-century "De divisione naturae," the spectatorial, noninstrumental nature of the aesthetic attitude had attracted attention.[13] Although one might also covet the same objects for what a later age would call their commodity or exchange value, they were appreciated qua objects of art only from a more lofty point of view. Rejecting the egocentric anthropology of a Hobbes, Shaftesbury stressed the fallacy of reducing everything to the question of private interest or need. Instead, and this was related to his belief that aesthetic experience was intertwined with civic virtue and moral sentiment, "disinterested" benevolence was its crucial characteristic.[14]

It was, of course, in Kant's aesthetic theory that the concept of disinterestedness was fully articulated. In the *Critique of Judgment*, Kant claimed that our ability to experience pleasure takes three forms. The first, which he called the "agreeable" or "the pleasant" *(das Angenehme)*, is caused directly by sensual stimulation. It involves a purely private and subjective response of attraction and aversion, without any meaningful cognitive or intersubjective dimension. Here the individual body, with all its appetites and antipathies, is the arbiter, not a cultural or universal norm. Personal gratification or lack thereof is all that matters. The second variety connects pleasure to the question of the "good." That is, we can derive "delight in the good" *(das Wohlgefallen am Guten)* through working for and achieving a beneficent goal, which is set by ideas and principles external to sensual gratification. In this case there is always a functional or utilitarian dimension to our pleasure, which is not an end in itself. The real end is the good that is realized, not the pleasure we have in realizing it, although that pleasure may be a subsidiary part of our motivation as well.

The third form of pleasure *(das Wohlgefallen am Schönen),* Kant argued, is what we can properly call aesthetic. As in the case of the "agreeable," the senses play a role and the body is involved, but with a crucial difference. Whereas in the former the object that produces the pleasure must actually exist—we cannot find a meal pleasant unless there is real food on the table—in the latter, it may not. Or, more precisely, our perception of the aesthetic object and its intrinsic properties or qualities need not coincide, as they must with an agreeable meal (food may look appetizing, but it must taste good to bring us genuine pleasure). Because of this distinction, we have no direct interest in the object, only in its representation or semblance. To be still more precise, because the media of representations can themselves be understood as objects (a gold statue is, after all, made of a substance whose value we find difficult to forget), what is important is a certain kind of experience of the object. Our pleasure in beauty, in short, is disinterested because we are indifferent to the actual object, which is not itself an object of direct sensual desire. We are no longer immersed in being—*inter-esse,* as the etymology of the word *interest* suggests—but rather somehow outside it. We enjoy an aesthetic meal, as it were, without having to taste and swallow the food, as in the case of certain variants of nouvelle cuisine in which visual more than gustatory pleasure, let alone actual nutrition, seems the main purpose of what is on the plate. It is the same disinterestedness that permits the transformation of the lust-arousing naked human form into the idealized, marmoreal nude and allows us to distinguish between pornography and high art (both of which may be representations of real objects, but are differentiated according to our interest or disinterest in their referents as objects of desire).

Aesthetic experience is, however, also akin to the second form of pleasure in its going beyond preconceptual sensual gratification or remaining on the level of what Kant dismissively called the mere "egoism of taste." Aesthetic experience mobilizes cognitive powers, as synthesizing transformations of pure sensation that evolve into truth or at least value claims, which are then assumed to have universal validity. But it does so without subsuming specific cases under discursive rules, a priori categories, or general principles, as is the case with the determinant judgments of the understanding. The latter seem to come from above, as if through the coercive dictates of a ruler. In contrast, aesthetic judgments, singular rather than categorical, are allowed a kind of nonhierarchical, free play in which each of us can make universal claims of beauty on the basis of analogical and paradigmatic rather than subsumptive or deductive reasoning. We move from particular to particular rather than from universal to particular, as was the case with the synthetic a priori judgments of cognition discussed in the first *Critique*. The concepts involved are thus "indeterminate" because they cannot be expressed in schematic form, as can the cognitive concepts of the understanding. They appeal to a virtual *sensus communis*, an intersubjective community that is to be made, not simply found, as innatist neo-Platonists such as Shaftesbury had thought possible. A crucial aspect of disinterestedness for Kant—although not, as we shall see, for the devotees of *l'art pour l'art*—was precisely this assumption that aesthetic judgments evoke enjoyment and appreciation that are not just one's own, but can be shared by all. To the extent that judgment was an inherent dimension of aesthetic experience, and not something added to it after the initial response of the senses, disinterestedness had this crucial communicative implication, which was lacking in expressions of idiosyncratic taste.

What also distinguishes aesthetic experience, Kant argued, from the delight in the good, where practical outcomes are sought, is the intrinsic nature of the purposes involved, which are akin to the immanent telos of play rather than work, whose end is a transformation of the world. Kant's celebrated definition of art as "purposiveness without purpose" was designed precisely to set it apart from those activities in which extrinsic purposes dominate and real objects are there to be produced, consumed, possessed, or exchanged.

Whether or not the distinction between determinant and reflective judgments really solves the riddle of the antinomy of taste, at once subjective and objective, or provides a useful model for intersubjective consensus rather than merely an ideological simulacrum of one, are not questions I want to address now. Nor do I want to rehearse the debate over whether aesthetic judgment and experience are based on a purely psychological concept of the beholding self or a more logically generated one, comparable in some ways to the transcendental, synthesizing self that Kant introduced in the first *Critique* to provide a foundation for epistemology. I am equally reluctant to take sides in the argument over the extent to which Kant's position can be reduced to nothing but a defense of an aesthetic attitude or mental state, which has exercised such commentators as Jerome Stolnitz, George Dickie, and Mary McCloskey.[15]

What I want to do instead is focus on the implications of disinterestedness for the art object, which must be distinguished from objects in general, and the larger question of the differentiation of value spheres in modernity. Although aesthetic judgments are normally made by means of a rhetoric of objectivity—"The Mona Lisa *is* a beautiful painting," not "*I think* it is a beautiful painting"—Kant stresses that it is the subject who is really the source of the judgment. Objectivity, as one of Kant's recent interpreters, Eva Schaper, has pointed out, is merely an "as-if" concept in his understanding of aesthetics.[16] That is, such judgments act as if they were directed at objects, but those objects are never analyzable for Kant entirely in intrinsic terms, and they become important solely for what they produce in their beholder. Or as another student of the *Critique of Judgment,* John Zammito, puts it: "While Kant stresses the degree to which the subject is affected *(afficiert)* in the experience, nevertheless it is striking how not merely the object but even the representation of the object shifts far into the background. Its form serves as the occasion, becomes at most a catalyst, for a complex subjective response."[17]

It is often argued, as we have seen, that the nature of that response is inherently contemplative, passive, and spectatorial, distancing the self from the world and our appetite to possess or consume it. Although this primarily visual characterization may seem an odd way to describe ways in which some art can seize us and invade our interiority—an experience we undergo perhaps most obviously in aural terms, when we listen to music—even here the subject may not always be actively and productively engaged in intervening in the world. Attentive listening, as James Johnson has recently shown, was an acquired skill in the eighteenth century, based on the suppression of the kinesthetic body and the concentration of faculties on only one sensory input.[18] The experience of passive listening was carefully segregated from that of dancing or communal singing as the ear was educated to have contemplative aesthetic experiences. The public concert hall worked like the museum to deracinate works that had their origins in the church or aristocratic chamber, turning them into what nineteenth-century aestheticians such as Eduard Hanslick would call "absolute music." In literature as well, the habit of looking for actual personal references in concocted narratives had to be lost and what Catherine Gallagher has called "nobody's story," the realization of acknowledged fictionality, put in its place before the novel could come into its own.[19]

There is, in short, no practical or possessive intention realized in the act of listening, reading, or beholding qua aesthetic experience. We may, to be sure, also want to own the object for its value in the marketplace or because of our passion to collect, but this is not the same as a purely aesthetic response. The possibility of that experience may be situated in an institutional context or cultural field, as philosophers such as George Dickie and sociologists such as Pierre Bourdieu have argued,[20] but the experience itself cannot be reduced to a mere reflex of that enabling context, for it entails precisely the distance from extrinsic functionality that such reductionism wishes to impose on it from without. It is for this reason that Habermas can claim that "the problem of grounding modernity out of itself first comes into consciousness in the realm of aesthetic criticism."[21]

This is not, to be sure, to argue that the boundaries of aesthetic experience themselves are entirely impermeable. Recent scholarship has stressed how the third *Critique* itself struggled to find a way to bridge the gap between cognitive and moral judgments and their aesthetic counterpart.[22] The larger project of the third *Critique* was, after all, to explore the ways in which nature could be understood teleologically rather than mechanistically, thus going beyond the rigid limitations on knowledge set by the first *Critique*. The purposiveness in art could thus be found in nature as well, which suggested a possible reunification of the varieties of reason. "Beauty," Kant also went on to claim, could be understood as "the symbol of morality,"[23] because of its emphasis on purposiveness without extrinsic purposes, which was parallel to the moral ideal of treating every person as an end itself implied by the categorical imperative. Although the link between art and ethics could not be established discursively, drawing on rational arguments, it could be suggested symbolically and analogically. In both cases, the self-reflective subject had to achieve a certain distance to allow judgment to occur. Even more decisively, that dimension of aesthetic experience Kant followed Longinus in calling "the sublime" provided a link with the noumenal origins of practical reason, because it got us in touch with supersensible realities that could not be grasped by synthetic a priori judgments, helping produce a feeling of respect for the moral law that was also beyond cognitive understanding. Here the objective correlate to our feelings is even more remote than it is in the case of the beautiful, as the paradoxical attempt to represent the unrepresentable is the essence of the sublime, which registers both the grandeur and the futility of the quest.

How successful Kant's *Critique of Judgment* actually was in reintegrating what his earlier work had seemed so powerfully to split asunder is, of course, a matter of some dispute; the entire subsequent history of German idealism suggests that at least his immediate successors thought it was a failure. Beginning as early as Schiller's *Letters on Aesthetic Education,* they sought to reunite art with the other spheres in the hope of reenchanting life, a project that continued well into the twentieth century with not much success to show for it. It has often been remarked that when Kant's ideas were vulgarized in the nineteenth century, as they were by certain French philosophers like Victor Cousin, they could easily be taken to countenance the opposite conclusion, the extreme aesthetic separatism that became the mark of the *l'art pour l'art* movement.[24] With Schopenhauer's 1818 *World as Will and Representation,* aesthetic experience was reduced to the attitude of nonpractical contemplation, a way to fend off, at least temporarily, the meaninglessness of the world.[25] Perhaps one of the reasons for this outcome was the difficulty of reconciling the disinterestedness of aesthetic experience—now understood without the public, communicative moment Kant had attributed to it[26]—with the interested qualities of both its cognitive and moral counterparts. In the case of the former, it was impossible to suspend for very long our interested involvement with the world, which gratified or frustrated our corporeal needs and desires. In the case of the latter, real objects or at least other human beings were necessary to test our will to act morally and be involved in the world of practical consequences. As Paul Crowther has noted, "For Kant the burden of emphasis in moral existence falls on obstacles and responsibilities in relation to the expression of freedom. In aesthetic experience it does not. . . . Hence, whilst the pure aesthetic judgment might figure in a moral image of the world, it could just as easily, if not more so, incline us to a life of self-indulgent or indolent contemplation, wherein the demands of moral duty were the least of our preoccupations."[27] There was, in other words, a certain tension between the aristocratic leisurely premises of aesthetic disinterestedness—the ability to see a beautiful landscape where peasants toiling in the fields could see only recalcitrant soil—and the moral imperative to treat everyone as an end in him- or herself.

But whether or not Kant or anyone else achieved a successful reintegration of the three spheres, the tacit uncoupling of aesthetic experience from the art object within the sphere of the aesthetic allowed a problematic slippage between spheres that is the real subject of this essay. Schematically put, there were two implications that could be drawn from the withdrawal of emphasis on beauty in the object itself in favor of subjective or intersubjective response. One, to which I have already alluded, was the progressive obliteration of the object, which paralleled the disappearance of the thing-in-itself in post-Kantian epistemology. Not only was the real-world referent of the artwork bracketed in the service of pure fictionality, so too the materiality of the representation itself was often suppressed and forgotten. The second and seemingly opposite implication was the indiscriminate elevation of all objects to potential works of art, depending on the attitudes of their beholders. In either case, the specificity of the work of art as such was undermined. Let me take each tendency in turn. Technologies of simulacral mechanical reproduction such as photography and the cinema may have abetted the first outcome, leading to what has been called the "immaterialization of reality,"[28] but it was already foreshadowed, I want to argue, in the privileging of disinterestedness in aesthetic theory. An object that was prohibited from soliciting any desire or interest, an object that could never be possessed or consumed, was an object that would ultimately squander its power to engage the very corporeal response that *aisthesis* had sought to explore. Further erosion followed from the leveling of the distinction between works of art and their critical reception, a tendency that culminated in deconstruction's pantextualist breaching of the boundary between ergon and parergon (work and frame). By 1981, the literary critic Murray Krieger could loudly lament in a work called *Arts on the Level* the "obliteration of the realm of art, its objects, its museums . . . everything immersed within the indivisible flood of experience."[29]

In the visual arts, the same alarm bell was sounded a few years earlier by Michael Fried in his celebrated and controversial essay "Art and Objecthood."[30] According to Fried, the specificity of pictures as such was being undermined by a new literalness, which foregrounded the anti-illusionist, material support of the flat canvas, and a style of beholding he called "theatrical." By the latter, he meant an indifference to the specific media of the separate arts and a willingness to privilege the experience of the beholder over time rather than the art object itself. The often-cited example he provided of the new sensibility was an account given by the artist Tony Smith of a car ride he had taken on the New Jersey Turnpike, in which he realized that traditional art was dead. In Fried's gloss, the result was that "the experience alone is what matters."[31] Fried's fierce resistance to this trend was not very successful, as he would be the first to admit. If postmodernism has meant anything, it has meant a further erosion of the integrity of the work of art.

When the minimalist art that Fried bemoaned was joined by an even less pictorial conceptual art, the radical potential of leveling was still more powerfully realized. Artists like Joseph Kossuth or Michael Asher abandoned the materiality of the work entirely in favor of a textual surrogate (with only a residue of the acknowledgment that inscribed texts can themselves be treated as material objects). Marcel Duchamp's readymades, in which random objects from everyday life rather than ones designed by artistic intention and fashioned by artistic talent were imbued with artistic value by the fiat of the artist, were a way station on the path to this end. Duchamp's famous visual indifference, his disdain for mere "retinal" pleasure, meant that not only the art object was being obliterated, but so too was the sensual dimension of aesthetic experience, which became a more cerebral, theoretically driven game, like the chess he began playing seriously in the 1920s as an alternative to producing—or rather designating—even readymade works of art. Here, ironically, the end of aesthetics turned out to be a kind of anesthesia in which not only the object stimulating the senses had vanished, but so too had the senses it was supposed to affect. Hegel's notorious claim that philosophy would and should replace art seemed fulfilled by this outcome.

Duchamp's elevation of urinals, snow shovels, and bottle racks into objects worthy of being included in the sacred space of the museum was, however, more than a parodic gesture mocking the pretensions of art objects to possess inherent qualities of beauty, more than a denial of the pleasure of the gaze, more than a victory of the concept over the image. From a different angle, it exemplified the second main implication that could be and was drawn from the privileging of aesthetic experience over art objects, which involved the drifting I have invoked in my title. That is, rather than debunking art by bringing it down to the level of ordinary life, using, as Duchamp provocatively recommended, the Mona Lisa as an ironing board, it could seek to elevate life by bringing it up to the putative level of art. In other words, it could promote the promiscuous reenchantment of the entire world, the "transfiguration of the commonplace,"[32] as if any object or event, however mean, were a legitimate occasion for aesthetic experience. As Jauss has noted, "Aesthetic experience does not seem to develop 'organically,' on a field of its own, but to progressively expand and maintain its area of meaning at the expense of bordering experiences of reality, and this by usurpations and compensations, the crossing of boundaries, the offer of competing solutions."[33] The result was a leveling up rather than down, a conflation of representation with reference, a kind of imperialism of aesthetic sublimation in which every object could be redeemed in aesthetic terms.

Duchamp himself, to be sure, would have scoffed at so lofty a program, but by lowering the threshold of what could be construed as an object of aesthetic appreciation and enjoyment (or at least their conceptual counterpart), he was drawing on, if in some ways also reversing the valence of, a venerable tradition that began as early as the Romantics and continues to our day. It could emerge only when the long-standing disdain for nature as a realm of fallen and debased matter in comparison with elevated spirit was reversed, a transformation that was anticipated by certain heterodox philosophies such as Spinoza's pantheism in the seventeenth century. It was also evident, if in slightly displaced form in social or cultural terms, in that increasing incorporation of formerly "low" subject matter into allegedly "high" art, the democratization of content evident in the genre paintings of early modern Dutch art, the bourgeois domestic tragedies of the Enlightenment, and most of all the rise of the novel. It was apparent as well in the Romantic incorporation of the fragment, the sketch, and the incomplete or ruined torso into the canon of genuine art. It came into its own with what M. H. Abrams has followed Carlyle's *Sartor Resartus* in calling "natural supernaturalism,"[34] the infusing of the natural world with all of the numinous meaning that had hitherto been reserved for transcendent spirit. Now the everyday, the commonplace, could be understood as glowing with immanent significance, or at least potentially possessing it through poetic transfiguration, which sought to fill the vacuum left by the withdrawal of religious sacralization.[35]

In a recent work titled *Into the Light of Things,* George Leonard has traced what he calls the "art of the commonplace" from Wordsworth through Carlyle and Ruskin to John Cage, whose celebrated composition

"4′33″" imbued even seemingly unmusical silence or, more precisely, the ambient noise left when no notes were sounded, with aesthetic value.[36] In visual terms, Leonard detects a similar transition already taking place between the time of Sir Joshua Reynolds and John Constable. Although he notes that Wordsworth more likely got his antihierarchical ideas about aesthetic experience from the English critic Archibald Alison's *Essays on the Nature and Principles of Taste* of 1790 than directly from Kant, whose German he could not read, the end result was similar. Alison also argued against elite art objects and in favor of the subjective reaction we can have to anything, however trivial or mundane. Even the sublime, which had been reserved for awesome and unfathomable experiences in the eighteenth century, could now be applied to the commonplace, just as long as the aesthetic sensibility of the beholder was capable of appreciating it in this manner.

There was, to be sure, an important distinction between natural supernaturalism and the Kantian notion of aesthetic experience, which Leonard does not remark. Whereas the former implied a pantheistic project of reenchanting the world, somehow imbuing it with a secularized religious meaning, Kant had explicitly decried such attempts in his own day. In the famous "pantheism controversy," which divided German intellectuals in the decade after F. H. Jacobi's 1785 attack on Lessing's supposed embrace of Spinozist atheism, he was a fervent critic of the rationalist immanentism implied in the Greek slogan *hen kai pan* (the one is the all) revived by Lessing.[37] Kant vigorously resisted what he saw as the determinist implications of that position, which undermined the possibility of human freedom and made practical reason's exercise of will meaningless. He thus never went as far as the natural supernaturalists in reinvesting the world with any kind of aesthetic cum religious "real presence,"[38] preserving instead a more orthodox believer's faith in a transcendent God.

But what Kant's stress on the disinterestedness of aesthetic experience did allow, even if unintentionally, was the possibility of having such experiences in the face of objects or events or actions that had not been intended as works of art or deliberately created to provide aesthetic pleasure. In fact, Kant himself distinctly preferred natural to artifical beauty, the real thing to man-made representations. For this reason, he could be construed as an unwitting precursor of natural supernaturalism. Insofar as this implication was a necessary accompaniment of the redefinition of previously sacred or ornamental objects as purely artistic ones, it produced a valuable disarticulation of the inherent logic of the aesthetic sphere from its cognitive and moral counterparts. The same might be said of the later reevaluation of ritual or utilitarian objects from so-called primitive cultures as objects of formal beauty, which took place during the modernist era. Here too the extension of aesthetic appreciation to cultural artifacts that had hitherto been dismissed as mere examples of less advanced peoples can be accounted an advance in cosmopolitan understanding (however problematic such decontextualization may seem to defenders of the integrity of individual cultures).

But when carried to an indiscriminate extreme, such an extension could lead to a promiscuous aestheticization of the entire world, reducing it to a mere occasion for disinterested subjective pleasure. All objects or events, whether or not they were ever intended as works of art, could be redeemed in aesthetic terms, if they produced experiences that somehow measured up to whatever the common sense of the time called aesthetic. As Jauss notes, "The aesthetic experience of role distance can be intensified and become aestheticism when it is taken up in a real-life situation where the conventions of morality or tact demand a wholly serious involvement. When, for example, a work such as the Isenheim altar is perceived and interpreted solely as a carrier of aesthetic qualities and abstraction is made from everything that makes the representation of the martyrdom shocking, cruel, and thereby exemplary, it is not only a devout sensibility that will be offended. Such an attitude is also inappropriate to the understanding the object itself demands."[39]

Perhaps the most troubling implications of this indifference to the qualities of the object were evident in what Walter Benjamin famously called the "aestheticization of politics." This is not the place to launch a full-fledged rehearsal of its divergent implications, a task I have attempted elsewhere,[40] but several points should be made. Benjamin's critique was directed explicitly at what he saw as fascist aestheticized politics, in which human suffering could become an occasion for aesthetic delectation. Most clearly evident in the celebration of war as a spectacle in the work of Futurists such as Marinetti, it also appeared in his own day in the threnodies to apocalyptic violence in Ernst Jünger's technological sublime. Perhaps the most frequently cited expression of this attitude was the remark made by the symbolist poet Laurent Tailhade in reaction to a deadly anarchist bomb thrown into the French Chamber of Deputies in the 1890s: "N'importe les victimes, si le geste est beau." Here contemplative disinterestedness was given an especially sinister twist because the object to be "enjoyed" was the destruction of human life. The rigid distinction between aesthetic and ethical values, which derived much of its impetus from a reductive misreading of Kant's third *Critique,* combined with the uncoupling of aesthetic experience from works of art to countenance what in other spheres would be quickly understood as problematic. That is, in the realm of cognition, epistemological judgments about objects that do not exist are normally called hallucinations or fantasies, and are separated from those that can claim some warrant in the world external to the self. If ethical judgments are applied to behavior or events that have not occurred or that did not involve the exercise of human will, we worry about our inappropriately moralizing what should be understood in different terms. The same caution, it would seem, should apply with regard to aesthetic experience when it seeks its detached pleasure anywhere it can find it. However much we may applaud the democratic expansion of the realm of art objects beyond the limits of their elite predecessors, however much we may recognize the value of learning to salvage objects that have lost their initial functional purpose in aesthetic terms, it may be wise to acknowledge limits to how far the aesthetic reenchantment of the world can go. The natural supernaturalist project, like all pantheist affirmations of immanence, comes up against the radical evil that exists in the world that it tries to valorize. Although violence can be aesthetically transfigured and represented in works of art—how else could we read with admiration *The Iliad* or stand comfortably before Picasso's *Guernica?*[41]—when the frame is broken, representation is confused with reference, and unmediated reality becomes fair game for aestheticization, the effect is very different. Aesthetic experience, in short, cannot be entirely freed from a consideration of which objects and events may justifiably evoke it, or else it courts the charge that it produces a theodicy of beauty, which is no less problematic than its ethical counterpart.

Or rather, it cannot avoid that rebuke if we remain within the terms set by the eighteenth century's version of that experience. But what if another notion of aesthetic experience could be defended that would avoid the privileging of subject over object and thus avoid the dangers of drifting? In fact, John Dewey presented one such alternative in his well-known *Art as Experience,* which has recently been revived in the work of Richard Shusterman, in particular his *Pragmatist Aesthetics* of 1992.[42] Dewey's ire was directed at all aspects of what he took to be the Kantian version of aesthetic experience, which he denounced as the fruit of excessive Enlightenment rationalism, with its compartmentalizing mania for categorical distinctions. Against the isolation of aesthetic experience from other variants, he argued for their ultimate integration in an ongoing, participatory interaction between humans and their environment. Against the passive and contemplative notion of aesthetic experience, he argued for an active, practical, and productive alternative that would overcome the gap between artistic creativity and aesthetic reception. Against the tacit elevation of the visual arts through the spectatorial bias of traditional aesthetic theory, he stressed the need to involve the entire sensorium. Against the privileging of disinterestedness and psychological detachment as foundations of the aesthetic attitude, he argued that desire and interest were as integral a part of our sensual encounters with art as with the rest of the world.

But most important for our purposes, against the evisceration of the object in the name of subjective or intersubjective response, Dewey rallied to the defense of the artwork not entirely for itself as an exemplar of a Platonic notion of beauty, but as an integral dimension of aesthetic experience, rightly understood. The extreme separation of organism from world, he argued, "lies behind the idea that esthetic quality does not belong to objects as objects but is projected onto them by mind. It is the source of the definition of beauty as 'objectified pleasure' instead of as pleasure in the object, so much *in* it that the object and pleasure are one and undivided in the experience."[43] "There can be no esthetic experience," he argued, "apart from an *object,* and . . . for an object to be the content of esthetic appreciation it must satisfy those *objective* conditions without which cumulation, conservation, reenforcement, transition into something more complete, are impossible."[44] Whereas a preliminary distinction between self and world may be justified in certain other areas of endeavor, such as natural science, "the uniquely distinguishing feature of esthetic experience is exactly the fact that no such distinction of self and object exists in it, since it is esthetic to the degree in which organism and environment cooperate to institute an experience in which the two are so fully integrated that each disappears."[45]

Such a disappearance does not, however, betoken the same thing that is implied by the loss of the referential object in eighteenth-century aesthetic theory or the religious cum aesthetic reenchantment of the world in the natural supernatural tradition. Although Dewey hoped for the ultimate reconciliation of life and art, he also recognized that it had not yet happened. Therefore, the artwork as object set apart from subject represented a covert protest against the unfulfilled potential for integrated experience in the modern world. The possibility for genuine experience in that world, he paralleled Benjamin and Adorno in lamenting, was severely limited: "Zeal for doing, lust for action, leaves many a person, especially in this hurried and impatient human environment in which we live, with experience of an almost incredible paucity, all on the surface. No one experience has a chance to complete itself because something else is entered upon so speedily. What is called experience becomes so dispersed and miscellaneous as hardly to deserve the name."[46] The work of art, as Dewey described it, provided a promise of the order, completeness, and integration of experience that was missing in everyday life and that was wrongly projected onto the world in its present state.

This argument, which was similar in certain respects to those made by members of the Frankfurt school, must, however, be set against the relatively optimistic expectations of the pragmatist tradition, in which fulfilled experience is now a possibility, despite obstacles that may prevail in the external world. Dewey may perhaps have been a bit too quick to dissolve the distinction between esoteric fine art, the art of museums and concert halls, and life lived aesthetically. As Shusterman has conceded, for Dewey aesthetic experience "could be achieved in virtually any domain of action, since all experience, to be coherent and meaningful, required the germ of aesthetic unity and development. By rethinking art in terms of aesthetic experience, Dewey hoped we could radically enlarge and democratize the domain of art, integrating it more fully into the real world which would be greatly improved by the pursuit of such manifold arts of living."[47] As a result, despite its laudable intention to redress the balance lost by Kantian aesthetics, the pragmatist attempt to fashion a new notion of experience, including both subject and object in an equiprimordial interaction, may too easily produce the same outcome as that of the natural supernaturalist tradition: the indiscriminate leveling of the distinction between artwork and lifeworld through the projection of the qualities of the former onto the latter.[48]

To avoid such an outcome, a certain respect for the continued distinction between the two may be required, at least as long as the reintegration remains more a desideratum than a real possibility. Such a distinction would involve acknowledging that works of art, although inevitably intended to produce aesthetic experience in their beholders, somehow exceed that outcome. Honoring this difference does not mean fetishizing the elite object or ascetically denigrating any pleasure in the present, as some defenders of aesthetic experience fear.[49] It entails instead a recognition of the fruitful constellation that keeps subjects and objects irreducible to each other, even as they cannot be understood in isolation. As formed material objects—a characterization more self-evidently true for certain kinds of art than others, but arguably the case for all—artworks resist reduction to nothing but the form-giving or form-appreciating qualities of the creative or receptive subject. In this sense, they preserve the otherness of the nonhuman world that should not be made into a mere occasion for aesthetic delectation as exemplars of natural beauty.

As specifically *art* objects, they resist leveling—either up or down—with other objects in our environment.[50] The necessarily illusory quality of works of art—what German aesthetics designates by the word *Schein* (at once semblance and appearance)—sets them categorically apart from the objects that we encounter cognitively or morally. The pleasure they provide, if indeed in all cases they can be said to produce pleasure, is not of the same order as that provided by other objects that satisfy our desires and interests.[51] The celebrated claim made by Stendhal and repeated by Nietzsche and Marcuse that art is *une promesse de bonheur* must be understood not only as a rebuke to the coldness of the tradition of disinterested detachment, but also as a recognition that such happiness is not necessarily achievable in the present.

Moreover, as George Steiner has noted, "the objects of scientific speculation and investigation, however uncertain their reality-status outside the relevant hypothesis and observation, are, nevertheless, *given.* They are prior and determinant in ways which differ fundamentally from the 'coming-into-thereness' of the aesthetic. . . . Only in the aesthetic is there the absolute freedom 'not to have come into being.' Paradoxically, it is that possibility of absence which gives autonomous force to the presence of the work."[52] However much we may admire a sunset for its beauty or be awed by the sublime chaos of a battle, the experience we have of works created by human intentionality can never forget their unique status in this regard. Even if such works can no longer be understood as perfectly formed, organic wholes, an assumption that was laid to rest with modernism (and the demise of which was foreshadowed by the Romantic cult of the fragment), they nonetheless still possess some residue, perhaps solely in negative terms, of the utopian implications of that impulse.[53] Not until the world is itself made by humans who can fashion their environment to realize such an outcome—a telos that may well be unattainable, and may even be itself a deeply problematic goal—can we forget the victims and praise the beautiful gesture that led to their demise. For the present, it is wiser to hold on to the irreducible constellation of objects and the experiences they engender that prevent us from collapsing one variant of experience into another. However porous the boundaries may be, however great the yearning for a fully integrated form of life, the differentiations of modernity—not only among value spheres, but within them as well—may have a validity that we sacrifice at our peril.

Notes

1. Nelson Goodman, *Languages of Art: An Approach to a Theory of Symbols* (Indianapolis: Indiana University Press, 1968).

2. Gérard Genette, *The Work of Art: Immanence and Transcendence,* trans. G. M. Goshgarian (Ithaca, N.Y.: Cornell University Press, 1997).

3. See the discussion in Wladyslaw Tatarkiewicz, "Aesthetic Experience: The Early History of the Concept," *Dialectics and Humanism* (autumn 1973); and Wladyslaw Tatarkiewicz, "Aesthetic Experience: The Last Stages in the History of a Concept," *Dialectics and Humanism* 1, no. 1 (1974). Richard Shusterman argues the importance of the "philosophy of life" in "The End of Aesthetic Experience," *Journal of Aesthetics and Art Criticism* 55 (1997): 29.

4. For a recent discussion of the problematic implications of that generic subsumption, see Jean-Luc Nancy, *The Muses,* trans. Peggy Kamuf (Stanford, Calif.: Stanford University Press, 1996).

5. It might be argued, to be sure, that such a condition of objective self-sufficiency, like other modes of lost plenitude, was an ex post facto projection backward of a yearning for wholeness rather than one that once really existed. But insofar as newly described art objects, at least those with religious origins, retained traces of their ritual aura, it seems likely that they possessed a power that was not yet entirely attributable to their beholders' response to them.

6. For a still-useful account of the transition, see Ernst Cassirer, *The Philosophy of the Enlightenment,* trans. Fritz C. A. Koelln and James P. Pettegrove (Boston: Beacon, 1955), chap. 7.

7. David Hume, "Of the Standard of Taste," in *Essays: Moral, Political, and Literary,* ed. Eugene F. Miller (Indianapolis: Liberty Fund, 1987), 230. Later in the essay, Hume retreats from the anarchic implications of this statement and asserts the likelihood that "the principles of taste [are] nearly, if not entirely the same in all

men" (241), but adds that few are educated to realize what they are. Here, in a nutshell, we have the perennial problem of reconciling Hume's skeptical side with his naturalist one. For a good short account of his thoughts on aesthetics, see Peter Jones, "Hume's Literary and Aesthetic Theory," in *The Cambridge Companion to Hume,* ed. David Fate Norton (Cambridge: Cambridge University Press, 1992). Jones underscores the importance of social context and conventions in Hume's account of judgment. For a defense of Hume's position against Kant's, see George Dickie, *The Century of Taste: The Philosophical Odyssey of Taste in the Eighteenth Century* (Oxford: Oxford University Press, 1996).

8. For a discussion of the origins of taste in these terms, see Howard Caygill, *Art of Judgement* (Oxford: Blackwell, 1989), chap. 2.

9. John Dewey, *Art as Experience* (New York: Capricorn, 1934), 47.

10. It is true that what Kant called "productive imagination" plays a role in aesthetic appreciation, as it does in normal cognition, albeit under the guidance of the understanding. But what was produced was a mental synthesis, not an active intervention in the world. For a discussion of its importance, see Michael R. Neville, "Kant's Characterization of Aesthetic Experience," *Journal of Aesthetics and Art Criticism* 33 (winter 1974): 197.

11. For useful accounts, see Dabney Townsend, "From Shaftesbury to Kant: The Development of the Concept of Aesthetic Experience," *Journal of the History of Ideas* 48 (April–June 1987): 287–305; Hans Robert Jauss, *Aesthetic Experience and Literary Hermeneutics,* trans. Michael Shaw (Minneapolis: University of Minnesota Press, 1982). For a more general history, foregrounding the questionable political implications of aesthetic discourse, see Terry Eagleton, *The Ideology of the Aesthetic* (Oxford: Blackwell, 1990).

12. Whether or not the metaphor, which in this precise form did not appear in Kant, adequately describes the innovations of the *Critique of Pure Reason* need not concern us here. For a skeptical account of its applicability, see Robert Hahn, *Kant's Newtonian Revolution in Philosophy* (Carbondale: Southern Illinois University Press, 1988).

13. See the discussion in Tatarkiewicz, "Aesthetic Experience: The Early History," 23. Jauss points to other examples of medieval anticipations of aesthetic experience, which produce anxiety because they are linked with idle curiosity about the world rather than immersion in the word of God (see *Aesthetic Experience,* 4).

14. For a history of the concept, see Jerome Stolnitz, "On the Origins of 'Aesthetic Disinterestedness,'" *Journal of Aesthetics and Art Criticism* 20 (winter 1961): 131–43.

15. See, for example, Jerome Stolnitz, *Aesthetics and the Philosophy of Art Criticism* (Boston: Houghton Mifflin, 1960); George Dickie, *Art and the Aesthetic* (Ithaca, N.Y.: Cornell University Press, 1974); Mary A. McCloskey, *Kant's Aesthetic* (Albany: State University of New York Press, 1987). There were many other issues in the long-running debate between Stolnitz and Dickie. For a useful overview, see Peter J. McCormick, *Modernity, Aesthetics, and the Bounds of Art* (Ithaca, N.Y.: Cornell University Press, 1990), 147–57.

16. Eva Schaper, *Studies in Kant's Aesthetics* (Edinburgh: Edinburgh University Press, 1979), chap. 6. The concept of "as-if" is, of course, taken from Hans Vaihinger, but Schaper wants to restrict it to aesthetic judgments, not to the cognitive ones discussed in Kant's first *Critique.*

17. John H. Zammito, *The Genesis of Kant's "Critique of Judgment"* (Chicago: University of Chicago Press, 1992), 113.

18. James H. Johnson, *Listening in Paris: A Cultural History* (Berkeley: University of California Press, 1995).

19. Catherine Gallagher, *Nobody's Story: The Vanishing Acts of Woman Writers in the Marketplace, 1670–1820* (Berkeley: University of California Press, 1994).

20. See George Dickie, *Aesthetics* (Indianapolis: Pegasus, 1971); Pierre Bourdieu, *The Field of Cultural Production: Essays on Art and Literature*, ed. Randal Johnson (New York: Columbia University Press, 1993). For a critique of Dickie, see Richard Shusterman, *Pragmatist Aesthetics: Living Beauty, Rethinking Art* (Cambridge, Mass.: Blackwell, 1990), 38–41. For a critique of Bourdieu, see Paul Crowther, "Sociological Imperialism and the Field of Cultural Production: The Case of Bourdieu," *Theory, Culture & Society* 11, no. 1 (1994): 155–69.

21. Jürgen Habermas, *The Philosophical Discourse of Modernity*, trans. Frederick Lawrence (Cambridge: MIT Press, 1987), 10.

22. See in particular Zammito, *Genesis*, in which he discusses what he calls the "cognitive and ethical turn" in the third *Critique*.

23. This was the title of section 59 of the third *Critique*.

24. See John Wilcox, "The Beginnings of *l'Art pour l'Art*," *Journal of Aesthetics and Art Criticism* 11 (June 1953); Gene H. Bell-Villada, *Art for Art's Sake and Literary Life: How Politics and Markets Helped Shape the Ideology and Culture of Aestheticism, 1790–1990* (Lincoln: University of Nebraska Press, 1996).

25. For an account of the debates concerning the reduction of experience to attitude initiated by Schopenhauer, see Bohdan Dziemidok, "Controversy about Aesthetic Attitude: Does Aesthetic Attitude Condition Aesthetic Experience?" in *Possibility of Aesthetic Experience*, ed. Michael H. Mitias (Amsterdam: Dordrecht, 1986).

26. According to Jauss, "As the new ideal of aesthetic pleasure, self-enjoying subjectivity abandoned the *sensus communis* as the expression of a sociable sympathy at the same moment the aesthetics of genius finally replaced the aesthetics of rhetoric" (*Aesthetic Experience*, 26).

27. Paul Crowther, "The Significance of Kant's Pure Aesthetic Judgment," *British Journal of Aesthetics* 36 (April 1996): 118.

28. Paul Crowther, *Critical Aesthetics and Postmodernism* (Oxford: Clarendon, 1993), 18. See also Arthur Danto, *The State of the Art* (Englewood Cliffs, N.J.: Prentice Hall, 1987).

29. Murray Krieger, *Arts on the Level: The Fall of the Elite Object* (Knoxville: University of Tennessee Press, 1981), 56.

30. Originally published in 1967, "Art and Objecthood" is included with other essays of that period and a long introduction answering subsequent criticism in Michael Fried, *Art and Objecthood: Essays and Review* (Chicago: University of Chicago Press, 1998).

31. Ibid., 158.

32. Arthur Danto, *The Transfiguration of the Commonplace: A Philosophy of Art* (Cambridge: Harvard University Press, 1981).

33. Jauss, *Aesthetic Experience*, 111–12.

34. M. H. Abrams, *Natural Supernaturalism: Tradition and Revolution in Romantic Literature* (New York: Norton, 1971).

35. This impulse was later to be rechanneled into the quasi-political project of the avant-garde to imbue life with the energies of art, a project whose problematic implications Peter Bürger has foregrounded in *Theory of the Avant-Garde,* trans. Michael Shaw (Minneapolis: University of Minnesota Press, 1984).

36. George J. Leonard, *Into the Light of Things: The Art of the Commonplace from Wordsworth to John Cage* (Chicago: University of Chicago Press, 1994).

37. For a good account of Kant's role in the debate, see Zammito, *Genesis,* chaps. 11–12.

38. The urge to do this is still alive, as evidenced by George Steiner's recent book *Real Presences* (Chicago: University of Chicago Press, 1989), in which, to be sure, he tries to see art from the point of view of the creator rather than the beholder or critic and, in so doing, stress its links with freedom.

39. Jauss, *Aesthetic Experience,* 6.

40. Martin Jay, "'The Aesthetic Ideology' as Ideology: Or What Does It Mean to Aestheticize Politics?" in *Force Fields: Between Intellectual History and Cultural Critique* (New York: Routledge, 1993).

41. Kant himself makes this point when he notes that at least in one respect man-made art is superior to natural beauty: "Beautiful art shows its superiority in this, that it describes as beautiful things which may be in nature ugly or displeasing. The Furies, diseases, the devastations of war, etc., may (even regarded as calamitous) be described as very beautiful, as they are represented in a picture." Immanuel Kant, *Critique of Judgment,* trans. J. H. Bernard (New York: Hafner, 1951), sec. 48, p. 155.

42. Dewey, *Art as Experience;* Shusterman, *Pragmatist Aesthetics.* See also Richard Shusterman, *Practicing Philosophy: Pragmatism and the Philosophical Life* (New York: Routledge, 1997); Shusterman, "The End of Aesthetic Experience"; Alexander Nehamas, "Richard Shusterman on Pleasure and Aesthetic Experience," *Journal of Aesthetics and Art Criticism* 56 (winter 1998): 49–50; and Richard Shusterman, "Interpretation, Pleasure, and Value in Aesthetic Experience," *Journal of Aesthetics and Art Criticism* 56 (winter 1998): 51–52.

43. Dewey, *Art as Experience,* 248. It is passages like this that allow Shusterman to argue that ultimately Dewey privileges "dynamic aesthetic experience over the fixed material object which our conventional thinking identifies—and then commodifies and fetishizes—as the work of art. . . . art gets defined as 'a quality of experience' rather than a collection of objects or a substantive essence shared only by such objects" (*Pragmatist Aesthetics,* 25).

44. Dewey, *Art as Experience,* 146–47.

45. Ibid., 249.

46. Ibid., 45.

47. Shusterman, "The End of Aesthetic Experience," 33.

48. Although Jauss appreciates many aspects of Dewey's approach, he notes that Dewey "assigns the traditional predicates of the beautiful in art to natural phenomena or those belonging to the world of objects. In other words, he projects them onto these phenomena to then demonstrate that they are everyday 'sources' of aesthetic experience. . . . The shortcoming in Dewey's theory is . . . that it maintains the illusion of the objectively beautiful without tracing the aesthetic quality of the objects and phenomena of the everyday world back to the attitude of the observer" (*Aesthetic Experience,* 113).

49. This anxiety is evident in Jauss's critique of Adorno as a champion of ascetic Platonism in *Aesthetic Experience and Literary Hermeneutics.* For a different view that shows the importance of experience in Adorno's work, see Shierry Weber Nicholsen, *Exact Imagination, Late Work: On Adorno's Aesthetics* (Cambridge: MIT Press, 1967), chap. 1. That the rigid separation of aesthetic from other kinds of pleasure in the Kantian tradition can itself be accused of asceticism from a Frankfurt school position is demonstrated in Robin May Schott, *Cognition and Eros: A Critique of the Kantian Paradigm* (Boston: Beacon, 1988), chap. 11.

50. This is not the place to attempt a serious account of the differences between aesthetic and nonaesthetic objects. Perhaps the best-known defense of the distinction from a phenomenological perspective was mounted by Roman Ingarden, whose work is discussed in Bohdan Dziemidok and Peter J. McCormick, eds., *On the Aesthetics of Roman Ingarden* (Boston: Kluwer, 1989). For a recent extension of his argument, see McCormick, *Modernity, Aesthetics.* See also the different approaches in Goodman, *Languages of Art,* and Genette, *The Work of Art.*

51. For a recent debate over the role of pleasure in aesthetic experience, see Shusterman, "The End of Aesthetic Experience"; Nehamas, "Richard Shusterman on Pleasure"; Shusterman, "Interpretation, Pleasure, and Value."

52. Steiner, *Real Presences,* 154–55.

53. Krieger claims that "the dethroning of the aesthetic object and aesthetic value and the abolition of the aesthetic realm altogether destroy the closed sanctity of such objects as self-fulfilled, instead opening them anew to an immediate relationship to normal experience. With the theoretical disappearance of closure, which is now seen to have been a deceiving myth, all objects, their would-be fictional boundaries dissolved, flow freely into and out of normal experience, now that they are declared no more than a routine part of that experience" (*Arts on the Level,* 55). Such a complaint overestimates the necessity of absolute closure and boundaried immanence in works of art, which ignores the importance of what Genette has called their transcendent potential *(The Work of Art).*

CHAPTER TWO

Armed Assault

Alphonso Lingis

I hate lies, I would not tolerate lies from anybody. I've always been like that, you, Wayne, explain.

What passion finds is the child, and the child in the old man, is the man in the woman and the woman in the man, is the leopard, serpent, mollusk in the man or woman and the man and woman in the bull, swan, crocodile, and octopus.

Billions of tons of salt water coursing around the vast Pacific brush against the south coast of New South Wales, spreading, taking away, spreading layers of glittering sand below the little town of Cronulla, south of Sydney. Sands that were once rocks, that were built into vast coral cities by multicolored polyps, that were demolished by ocean storms, sands that tufts of salt grass hold on to with their roots, that are swept back into the ocean by storms.

You Cheryl were born and abandoned in Cronulla. How extremely improbable is your existence! There had been the chance encounter of that woman with that man—out of the two and a half billion men on the planet, the chance that she pleased him and he her, and the chance that they disrobed and embraced, and then the infinitesimal chance that out of two hundred million spermatozoa repeatedly ejected into her vagina this *one* met with and got absorbed into this ovum. At any turn of the million chance encounters the path is made of, it would have been someone else, and not you, who was born. And perhaps would have been wanted.

Figure 2.1. Wayne and Cheryl. Photograph by Alphonso Lingis.

You Cheryl were adopted by a Swiss couple. They called you Paul. You have a brother, whom you never see. He cannot accept your sexuality. Your foster parents always called you Paul, until a year ago, when—during what was to be their last visit, for they have moved to Queensland, and are very old now—you made them call you Cheryl. They do, however, approve of and love Wayne very much.

You Wayne were born in Belmain, a working-class district of Sydney. The number of atomic particles in the universe is ten to the 67th power. But the number of possible combinations of the human DNA molecule is ten to the 2,400,000,000th power. The odds of being you are one in ten to the 2,400,000,000th power. That it happened that what was born was you was exceedingly unlikely.

For you Wayne to look back to the time before your birth is to look upon an abyss utterly empty of you. Beneath you, behind you, there is nothing that forecast you, demanded you, required you. You feel yourself drifting and bouncing over a desolate field of drifting sand, a silent and deserted field of rocks. Behind you, you feel this void. Before the trees, roads, buildings that exist now because they have existed, you Cheryl cannot shake loose a sense of inner insubstantiality. You exist in temporary defiance of this void.

You have a brother too, Wayne, but were separated from him when your parents divorced and your mother took him, your father took you. One day he sent you to the shops to buy him a newspaper, and when you came back there was five cents missing in the change. He flogged you with a feather duster for almost an hour and a half, trying to get you to admit that you had spent that five cents on lollies. But you hadn't, and you wouldn't say you did to get him to stop. You hate lies. Your father started dating another woman, and you were in the way. He charged you with being uncontrollable and put you, at the age of seven, in a boys' home.

Junk velvets the hard edges of things. It's a silver fog rolling over all the cubicles, partitions, walls, and fences. How long is it that you have been shooting up, Wayne—thirty years? You, Cheryl—thirty years in silver fog? There is plenty of junk around now, but you are on methadone. Wayne too. The maximum dose. You claim it is for the pain. It makes you spacey and hyper. You especially, Cheryl, are always fidgety and skittish. Medical researchers are now saying that methadone is more damaging to the organism than heroin. The idea is to progressively reduce the dosage. You Wayne and Cheryl are still on the max.

Your soul Cheryl is twitches and quiverings in the surge and algae curtains in the stomach, the somber blue intestines, in the liver, the spleen, on the tips of your fingers under lacquered green fingernails. Your soul

Wayne is turbulence and bluster and crystal calm in the blue veins, the slow heavy vermillion blood, the scurrying macrophages, the dense jelly of cells stirring the murmurs from years ago and far away.

You Cheryl are five feet, nine inches tall, big boned, very skinny, skeletal; right off you say your age: fifty-two. Your face is lean, you have high cheekbones. Your face is long, your cheeks sunken, lips are medium thin, your mouth small, delicate. You have very big brown eyes. You have shaved your eyebrows and pencil in lines first thing when you get up. Your hair is thick and fine—brunette turning to blond—cut short, combed to one side. Your very big hands somewhat discolored with bleached, pink fingernails clean and a little long. You have a gold watch with a very big face, man's watch, loose on your wrist. You dress in moss-green jail T-shirt and shorts, much faded, much patched, worn running shoes. About your neck you have a long string of small beads, the kind Filipino kids sell on the beaches. You keep two mirrors on the table; as you work you check your face, touch it up. You are a queen, if in green jeans. For bronze-furred seals in the Antarctic twilight, for nudibranchs crawling over the coral reef, for naked frogs in tropical swamps, beauty is imperative. Why is it that lust demands beauty?

There is something giddy in our relationship with a mirror. Spaced out away from ourselves, our gestures turn into grimaces, our manipulations flailings, our face screwed up by our scrutinizing gaze breaks into laughter. Looking at oneself while laughing turns into a voluptuous vertigo. How we are lustfully drawn to our own mouth that, in the mirror, we see wide open, exposing the wet, lascivious tongue! We stand in front of the mirror looking at our legs chortling, our belly churning with bubbles of laughter, and, unable to stop ourselves, we stroke that belly, run our hands up between our thighs, fall back upon the bed. They fix mirrors on the ceilings and walls around the beds in bordellos.

When you look in the mirror, you Wayne say, you either see your best friend or your worst enemy. You are a little shorter than Cheryl, and about the same age. You have broad shoulders, strong arms, flat stomach, very tanned. When you were outside, you several times ran the marathon. But there are only migraines, nausea, insomnia in that body now. If your body does not shrivel and sink into itself, it is only because you are pumped with steroids. You are wearing a loose moss-green long-sleeved light sweatshirt, light sweatpants—also much faded, much patched, and new good-quality sneakers. Your head is round, you have a thick black-brown walrus mustache, your mouth is small, sensual lips. Your mouth is not sunken, although they have pulled out all your teeth. You have clear blue eyes. You look English, with your smooth pasty pale skin, your mustache, your full head of bristle gray hair, cut short in back. You are well-groomed, very particular about your appearance. You wear two small silver rings in your left ear. You wear a silver chain with a Masonic cross. On your left hand, you wear four rings, one on your right. You Wayne are handsome. Handsome and impish. You have a dry sense of humor. And a hellish hot glint in those clear blue eyes.

You are not at all sly. People know you would do anything for a friend. Just ask you. There is nothing you Wayne can't fix. You type résumés for staff people, people bring you their computers from home to fix. You are a sensitive bloke. You are very civilized. You are always very pleasant to the female staff. You are respectful of women, and respectful of Cheryl. Cheryl devotes herself to you, to entertaining you. You treat Cheryl very well.

Males, with their on average greater musculature and on average 20 percent greater size than females, do hard work in agriculture, industry, and construction; they are window washers in the wind sixty floors over the street, firemen climbing a ladder to rescue an invalid from a blazing building, they are marines and professional boxers. They are expected to maintain order and system. They are at least expected to do contracted work, even if something insignificant or trivial has to be found, to pay their own expenses. Lazy chiseling parasitical louts are an affront to their own maleness. But nothing so fevers the mind as a male flaunting all his virile voluptuousness.

In fact, you Wayne adore Cheryl. You say that if she dies you will die with her. You will certainly kill yourself to die with Cheryl.

The voluptuous embrace is necrophilic, bodies collapsing, decomposing, already soaking the sheets and oneself with released inner fluids teeming with nameless and chaotic tinglings, spasms, fluids, musks, micro-organisms. The flames of voluptuous pleasure ignite them as they careen and flare apart, in clothing and the wood of the furniture collecting swampy stains, in the air whose minute spheres of water vapor teem with protozoa, in the soil decomposing into unnameable fungi and bacteria.

You Wayne know more about computers than anybody in the place. You have earned twenty-eight certificates for computer courses. You play computer games a lot. You really get into them. Your moves zap electronic people and things, detonate cars and planes, pulverize whole populations. You're a fighter, Wayne. You have been in and out of institutions since the age of fifteen. Your existence is the piece of bad luck that society found in itself. You never had goals to give you a sense of yourself. Your sense of your individuality comes from being isolated from society in institutions. Throughout your street-kid childhood, you were not, like the rest of us, continually told what not to do, and why not. They didn't tell you why not. One can just see how you would react if some bloke came along and said, Let's rob the bank. Okay, let's go, you would say.

You robbed, but it was petty shit. It was not to change things, to break out and become somebody, only to keep up your habit. Again and again you were caught and sentenced. This is your twenty-third year in prison. Eventually they win, they get it their way. Now you are in the middle of a fourteen-year sentence, for armed robbery. Long Bay Gaol is a maximum-security prison; you are in the company of everything society gets in the way of real shit luck: switchblade stalkers, gangsters, child molesters. Murderers radiant with the blood they have shed who stalk the prison with lewd authority.

Among them you met Cheryl, twenty-two years ago. She'd been in for dealing, stealing. Women subjected to a factory job have a roughness, businesswomen have brusque edges and crisp apparel that repel the cloying eyes of lust. What else did you Cheryl have to do but be beautiful? Prostitution was the only source of wages you ever figured out. You Cheryl and Wayne became lovers ten years ago.

It's you, Wayne and Cheryl, we engage in talk with when we visit the jail—or want to hear about, from those who do. You are delinquents and deviants, and not just victims of society that we have to feel guilty about. Your story is going to be funny—funny peculiar and funny ha-ha.

There are no end of things that one cannot prevent, ward off, overcome, or repair. One got born looking like a dork. One had an abused childhood. One got Oedipally triangulated. One discovered one had a queer gene. One got caught up in a relationship that was hopelessly fucked up. There are so many things that one can do nothing about. Could do nothing about them at the time, can do nothing about them now. So many things that all one can do with is laugh. But one can always laugh. One can laugh at one's having being born with a ruined gene, looking like Olive Oyle or Newt Gingrich, at one's Japanese-size microdick, about death itself. A neurotic is someone who is traumatized, that is, cannot get over these disasters. Cannot laugh. Psychotherapists are hardly any help. How tight-assed they are, by and large! They take everything the neurotic dreams over, broods over, so seriously. Every putdown from earliest childhood, every humiliation. They seal the neurotic in his neurosis.

You've had a lot of fights in your time, Wayne, though you've never been stabbed. You got iron-barred once. The person that did that did live to regret it. You'll cop a lot of shit before you'll explode, but when you explode, you really explode. The first time is accidental, you say, the second time is coincidental; the third time is enemy action. You'll cop shit on yourself; you won't cop shit for Cheryl. If someone upsets Cheryl, then that's it; there's no second chances. No chances at all. There's people in this jail who don't necessarily like you, but they got to respect you for the fact that you'll live and die for Cheryl. In fact, you have more friends than anybody.

There are long scars on your arms, Wayne, from fights, but most self-inflicted. Your hands and arms are covered with tattoos. On the bases of the fingers of your left hand, the letters L O V E. A tattoo you made on yourself, using a sewing needle stuck on the end of a toothbrush handle and activated by a motor you took out of a Walkman—decidedly you are very good at things mechanical!—keeps on your right arm your love for Diane Darling, who had been a star performer at a transvestite cabaret on Kings Cross and who died of AIDS in jail. You don't consider yourself a poofter, nobody else takes you for a poofter; they think: it's jail sex. Cheryl though fifty-two calls herself a girl, calls herself a queen. She has small plump breasts. She has had, long ago, her testicles removed. But you Wayne adore Cheryl. And in this, in your adoration of Cheryl, you are getting your own way in something at last!

On your right arm, Wayne, you have a large cross, with "In Memory." Your uncle was a biker, finally crashed and smashed both his knees. When he died, you were not allowed to go to the funeral. In jail, doing a tattoo is cited as bodily assault, doing a tattoo on oneself as self-mutilation. You did this tattoo, and then went to the warden and told him to cite you. This uncle had taken you when, at the age of eleven, you got out of the boys' home, and put you to work in his carnival. You worked the Ferris wheels, cars, roller coasters. You traveled with the carnival all over Australia. Carnivals have a bad reputation: people think there will be fights and they have to lock up their daughters. One does have to use force: when a couple of blokes come up for a ride, they are not inclined to put down their cigarettes and beer bottles. So you got into fights.

Lust and adoration are violent. A force employed on us becomes violence only when it violates our inner space, what we call our person—our separate and discontinuous existence, source of its own acts, responsible for what we ourselves say and do. The adoration that breaks out of us violates our integrity and breaks up our individuality. To be smitten by love is to be not simply wounded, but shattered. Your adoration Wayne is the inner experience of being violated in sexual contact, and of violating Cheryl. Your love, Cheryl, is a craving to be violated.

The ocean fog has settled in the stones of Long Bay Gaol for a hundred years. The foul breath of caged men and women has settled in those stones. The toilets are ceramic bowls without partitions to separate the stink of one's man's shit and sweat from another. You Cheryl are fanatically housebound. You have amazing energy. You are high on washing and folding your and Wayne's laundry. Laundry is always happening.

You get up very early. You like to be maternal. You busy yourself darning socks, mending and altering the clothes of the men, skinny mother of brutes. You vacuum all the floors of the education department. You take the vacuum to the apartment and vacuum it until there is not a wisp of dust lodged in any corner. You call the cell "the apartment." It is but six feet wide, ten feet long. There is a bed bolted to the wall, a toilet, a sink, a jug, a Walkman. The cells are all open to the corridor, with only iron-bar gates.

Many people really dislike you. The staff, but also inmates. You are sneaky. You steal stuff people are using. You are a two-faced bitch. We have to be careful about what we say around you; you will blab about it. You trade in gossip. Whether we are a new inmate or just a visitor, you will have heard all about us before we get there.

To be incarcerated is to not have any life outside. There is nothing to an inmate but his inner life. To be on top of all the gossip is the way to touch, probe, grip on to the inner lives of others, who have only inner lives. Gossip is only way one has in jail to have an intense inner life, penetrating and sizzling with pleasure. Gossip is a pleasure. Pleasure of pursuing prey, of intervening in melodramas, intellectual pleasure of ingenuity and cunning.

The consummate feminine look is that blasé look, that vaporous look, that impudent look, that cold look, that look of looking inward, that dominating look, that voluptuous look, that wicked look, that sick look, that catlike look, infantilism, nonchalance, and malice compounded.

You Wayne insist that Cheryl be treated with respect, and you are violent enough to insist. Because Cheryl still has her penis, she could be housed in the men's section, and with you Wayne. The authorities like homosexual couples forming—it reduces the general aggression in the jail.

Harmoniously married couples outside spend at least eight hours a day apart, at their jobs. You Wayne and Cheryl are locked in a six-by-ten-foot cell together all but five hours a day. But when you are working at your jobs, you are still together. Because Cheryl's a woman in a men's maximum security jail, it's not safe for her wandering around alone. If you hear a scream, you know where the scream's coming from, you know where to go. Sometimes you Wayne are with Cheryl twenty-three hours one day; the other hour you are at some office working on a computer—and as strange as it seems to people, you miss her for that hour! I hate it, you say. I hate it.

Why is it that it is the jeering or derisive remark about our sexual identity, appearance, behaviors, or words that smarts most? Why do we so easily turn being called peculiar into being distinctive, being called eccentric into being exceptional, but when abnormal means abnormal in our sex it is so demeaning and mortifying? How transparent we are to one another in our lusts!

You Cheryl became a woman at the age of fifteen. You trained to be a registered nurse. You were caught stealing drugs, and dismissed. You drifted to Kings Cross, where part of joining the scene was drugs. You did heroin, speed, cocaine and bennies, LSD. You're not into pot. You performed as a female impersonator in the cabarets of Kings Cross—Les Girls, Simone, Candy. Back then you had toured the jails. Carlotta now acts in the weekly show on TV called *Beauty and the Beast.* She still writes you, twice a year, sends you the programs of shows. The numbers drag queens do depend entirely on surprise, their effects momentary. Surprising the aggressor with a put-down so witty he finds himself unable not to laugh at himself. The master in Oriental martial arts is one who catches the lunge of the adversary and throws him with the force of his own blow. Zen and the Art of Drag.

You Wayne and Cheryl are the top of the heap. You are very sharp on people. You see what is going on. You can make things happen. You do the clerical work for the education program. You earn twenty-four dollars a week. Money is clout; the ordinary prisoner can earn but eleven or thirteen dollars a week. You get real coffee or chocolate biscuits, sometimes, from the staff. You also get conversation about the outside world. You even contribute to decisions—for example, about how the money is spent in the education program. Just now you Cheryl are in charge of some repairs and painting that is being done in the wing. You love organizing people. You would have been a very successful businesswoman. You and Wayne are very chummy with the superintendent. You can put in a good word for a bloke if his parole is coming up.

The only thing you Wayne and Cheryl have ever held to is honesty. You believe that a real relationship—not just a relationship like yours, but even a relationship between two good friends—can't last if there's not total honesty at all times. Honesty has always been a thing for you all your lives. It's something you never got from your families, so it's something you've already demanded from your friends and the people around you. In my time, you Wayne say, I've probably met ten to fifteen thousand people in jail these many years that I've been here. Out of those there's probably a hundred that would say I'm their friend; out of that hundred, there's probably sixty that I would call my friends; out of that sixty, twenty that I would say that I know they're honest and upfront with me and I trust them implicitly, and out of that twenty there are five that I would die for or kill for.

Lust arises by contact and spreads by contagion, making us transparent to one another. We find ourselves aroused by feeling the warm thigh of the dozing passenger next to us on the bus, as we are not aroused by the warm vinyl of the bus seat. During rush hour when we are standing in a packed subway car, we feel in a ripple of excitement someone's fingers lightly brush the inside of our thigh. Jean Cocteau drew a picture of an aroused penis and labeled it: the part of a man that never lies. Whatever the educated, disciplined, decent mind may say, the penis stiffening, the labia and clitoris throbbing with blood and excitement and pleasure affirm, Yes I like that, yes he or she is my kind, yes I am attracted to him and her.

You Wayne and Cheryl have used your clout with the staff to get disinfectants strong enough to kill HIV, for use with needles. For there is heroin enough for all in the prison, supplied, of course, by the screws for those eleven or thirteen dollars the prisoners can earn. You Wayne and Cheryl have also insisted that a condom dispenser get installed, but which they then mounted on the wall next to the officers' quarters. So guys have to expose their intentions to the officers, and expose themselves to their shouts and jeers.

There is the pleasure of doing difficult work well, the pleasure of keeping a tight ship, the intellectual exhilaration of solving real problems by the use of the mind. There are pleasures that are productive and instructive. Voluptuous pleasure is laughable pleasure. The awkward thrashing of people copulating, not keeping track of their own limbs, provokes laughter. Already the gleam of eagerness and desire in the eyes provokes teasing and giggles.

Is there any pleasurable activity, any activity that arouses laughter more than sex and eroticism? So much the more incongruous couplings, nonfunctional couplings. Didn't everyone who first tried cross-dressing or golden showers—hey, everyone who first tried oral or anal sex—do it because it was a gas? And an outrage.

The serious discourses of psychotherapists, sociologists, and ethicists rehearse the meaningfulness of the sexual encounter. The moment of voluptuous pleasure must be subordinated to the finality of reproduction. It must be subordinated to the finality of society. It must be subordinated to the wholeness of a relationship, that of the lovers who are persons. If he and she take seriously this discourse, the one who indulges in deviant practices—masturbatory, same-sex, cross-dressing, cross-age, cross-color, cross-species, machinic—will be sealed in earnestness, having to find these practices meaningful for him- and herself. He and she will have to assert that he and she indulge in these practices in order to find fulfillment. And yet don't we really think that the one thing to regret in life is to have not dared, that the one thing one will never regret in life is to have made a fool of oneself for love and for sex?

The working-from-within-the-system seventies, the yuppie eighties, the neoliberal nineties passed you by. You Wayne and Cheryl are sixties counterculture freaks. You are survivors—more than survivors, you are fighters. You are real activists. You write letters to politicians. You are not just working in the education program for the money and the influence; you are both very firm in your dedication to education. You fight causes. You have a mission.

When in 1985 the prison services discovered that they had three HIV-positive inmates, they segregated them. When you Wayne learned that Diane Darling was in the AIDS unit, you went to the high ranker in the jail and asked if you could go in there and talk to her. They said no, that they wouldn't have people going back and forth. But you insisted. Eventually they let you go in. You told her that if she ever needed to talk, or cry, or scream, you would be there. Six months later Head Office started what they called the AIDS Task Force—a group of civilians to enter the jail to educate inmates about HIV. They appointed you the first AIDS peer educator. You and Cheryl ran the HIV-AIDS and Hep C committee for almost six years. Every year you put on a different event for World AIDS Day.

Your old crony Ashleigh from the Kings Cross cabarets got herself arrested and with you Cheryl organized the Long Bay Cowgirls. You sewed up an extravagant, theatrical frock for yourself.

It's with the other transsexuals that you Cheryl are having your own way in something. You give a lot of support to those who end up in the jail. One who was sinking rapidly had a great fear of dying alone. How envious she was of you and Wayne, who will die together. You accompanied her all the way while she was going nowhere, you were there, with her, when she died.

No police force could hope to prosecute and incarcerate all thieves, addicts, and perverts. Every convict is an expiatory sacrifice who suffers his or her life for all.

Chance excites us, quickens the will. In heading off to the back alleys and wastelands where our heads are exposed to the blows of chance, we know in exhilaration what we have received by chance, what we are by chance.

Love is awakened only by chance. It flares up out of the merest coincidence. Love is abruptly ignited in impasses and traps in which one finds oneself immobilized. It is the combustion of interpenetrating dreams of bodies collapsed and dysfunctional copulating. It is the blinding incandescence of luck in the most squalid, the most sordid circumstances, the worst luck. Nothing is more contrary to love than to exercise the reckoning mind so as to exclude adverse chances.

Shit happens. You Wayne and Cheryl have been HIV-positive for ten years. You Wayne were stabbed by a patient while you were a sweeper in the clinic. A few weeks later you Cheryl were in the hospital with anorexia; in the middle of the night two men who were HIV-positive raped you. About the same time, you both contracted hepatitis C. For the past eighteen months you Wayne have had full-blown AIDS symptoms. You have bowel cancer. Shit happens. In 1993 you had come down with so many opportunistic infections, Cheryl, they gave you at best six months to live. It was then that they discovered that the virus was replicating not in your blood but in your bone marrow. There was only one other such case reported—in the United States. Shit happens.

You Wayne have a chest infection. Your skin is breaking out with sarcoma scabs. The ones that are on your backside, it's like sitting on boils. When you take off your underpants for the night, it rips the scabs stuck to them. You Wayne and you Cheryl take everything very methodically: We will have to deal with this . . . you say. And then, later, you say: We will have to deal with that. You each day defy the plague. You are very courageous. You savor each day you are alive. The level of energy you produce is a manifestation of your will. You keep each other alive. You Cheryl say, Whatever keeps us together even twenty-four hours. Even one hour. You are allowed to see a prison doctor every five weeks. You said to him, Listen, I will keep myself alive whilever Cheryl needs me. I will not allow myself to die whilever Cheryl needs me. I don't need your drugs to do that. I have the will in me, the love that I have for Cheryl in me, to keep myself alive whilever Cheryl needs me. But everybody knows the moment one of you dies, you'll both die.

When you get sick, Wayne, you see how it affects Cheryl: she hates to see you sick. That makes you feel guilty, because it really worries her. Quite often you'd be sick, and you'd try not to show it, for Cheryl's benefit. But then you chastise yourself, because the biggest and the best part of your relationship, you think, is the honesty. And you think, Well, if I try and hide it from Cheryl, then I'm not being honest with her. So, you tell her when you're sick. But sometimes you think, Well maybe she doesn't need to know. She just had a bad deal today. But then you think that if you knew that Cheryl was feeling this bad and didn't tell you, you'd be very upset with her. It's a big thing with you, honesty.

You Wayne continue to protect Cheryl. A lot of people think that no one'll touch Cheryl, no one'll rape Cheryl because she's got AIDS. But there are men who think they can't get AIDS from forcing Cheryl to give oral sex to them. Some think that unless they ejaculate inside her, they are at no risk. There are those who think there is no risk if they use a condom. But a number of people have approached you over the months and asked you for your blood! Some people want our blood, you say, because they believe if they get AIDS it can help them get out of jail a little bit earlier. Some people believe that it can at least help them get some privileges. Some people want our blood because they want to commit suicide. Other people want to square up on somebody they don't like. Most times you Wayne take him apart and say, Fuck off! Never ask me that again! But with a close friend, it's not that simple. One said: Come off, Wayne, you're playing God with my life.

Cancers, putrescent infections, blindness, madness, agonizing pain await people dying of AIDS. Those who care for them, those who love them leave their bedside, to go to the other room to get food, to answer the telephone, to receive visitors, they go out to buy groceries and do the laundry. They can, when they can no longer endure to keep watch, slip out of the room. They are not locked in a six-by-ten-foot cement cell all the weeks and hours, all the days and the nights of the infections, the despair, the agony, the delirium, the dying.

We are attached to our separate existence, improbable and irreplaceable, but would we be if we were not certain that we could just as well laugh at it? In taking our ambitions, our values, and our achievements seriously we turn ourselves into idols, which we cannot help fearing will soon be covered with graffiti and pigeon shit. In laughing tenderly over our awkward and bungling adolescent horniness, in guffawing over our melodramatic love affairs, we become attached to them and to ourselves.

What else can we do, do we do, but laugh when we face the improbability of our birth, the ludicrously squalid death we are headed for, the filthy corpse in a dank hole our vaunted and incomparable existence is going to turn into? This laughter at the I, at the demand the I makes in love, laughter over one's birth, over one's death need not be ironic or bitter. It can be as light as the laughter with which we greet the pompous assertiveness of a bumblebee, a frolicsome mouse choosing to give birth to her babies in Long Bay Gaol.

The two men who raped you, Cheryl, are both dead now. May they rest in peace, you say. You went to the funeral service for them. Forgive and forget, you say. Just forget, you say. One would have to remember and forgive everything, from the day you were born and abandoned. Cheryl cannot change who she is, you Wayne say. It's one of the things you love so much about her.

How lucky I am! you Cheryl think. How lucky I have been! How lucky to have met Wayne. How lucky not to die alone, like the other transvestites. How lucky to have quality life. The level of energy you keep up is the energy of this defiance and exhilaration.

Love attaches to the abyss. It is hate that circumscribes its own identity. Tell me whom you hate and I will tell you who you are. Tell me whom you love and I will know as little about you as before.

One day an old flame of yours, Cheryl, appeared in the prison. For weeks how anguished you were—there had now suddenly appeared to you one last chance to know a great passion before you die. Although you realized that leaving Wayne would kill him, Wayne said nothing whatever about what he quickly understood was going on. Finally you understood your great passion made of violence, adoration, and lust is Wayne.

And then one day the prison authorities summoned you Cheryl and presented you with your release. You were led back to the cell, you packed your green prison clothes in a state of pounding agitation. The gates of Long Bay Gaol closed behind you. They gave you a small sum of money; it was not enough to buy a real gun. You took a perfume bottle, practiced holding it and your hand wrapped in a scarf. It was a little after midday; you handed to the cashier a piece of paper on which you had written: This is a holdup. Give me $200. On the back of the paper you had written: your name, your address, your phone number, your jail number. And: P.S. Don't call until 9:30; I won't be ready. By nightfall you were back with Wayne. You tell him how, shrieking with drag queen laughter.

CHAPTER THREE

Reinventing the Wall

Looking into Zaha Hadid

Kay Bea Jones

Among the most provocative characters on the international architectural scene, Zaha Hadid plays protagonist in the search for contemporary forms and ideas. Iraqi-born but located in London ever since she attended the Architectural Association there, Hadid has put forth bold visions for new space. Her winning 1983 proposal for the Peak, a men's club in Hong Kong, drew attention to her colorful multidimensional site graphics that favor the vertiginous, the urban bird's-eye view, and floating angular vistas (see Figure 3.1). The very atmosphere appears to vibrate around vaguely visible forces, which in turn seem to destabilize the surrounding context. The Office of Zaha Hadid (OZH) has built Vitra fire station and *LF one* (landscape formation) for the *Landesgartenschau* international garden show, both in Weil-am-Rhein, Germany (Figures 3.2 and 3.3). OZH's Mind Zone for London's Millennium Dome was contracted by competition. Advancing explorations in contemporary building materials, the installation was planned to last only one year. Hadid's relatively few constructions are the fruits of enormous design research, as recorded in the 1998 monograph *Zaha Hadid: The Complete Buildings and Projects.*[1] Just as baroque space employed but destabilized the harmonies of Renaissance order, Hadid's spaces expand the bounds of Cartesian space and alter modern rules for figural form. Is she positioned as the Piranesi of the twenty-first century, more influential for her renderings than for her realized constructions, or is she a master builder in waiting?

Figure 3.1. Zaha Hadid, *Slabs (Hong Kong from "the Peak")*. Painting. Copyright Zaha Hadid. Reprinted with permission.

Figure 3.2. Zaha Hadid, *Vitra Fire Station, Weil-am-Rhein.* Landscape painting, aerial view. Copyright Zaha Hadid. Reprinted with permission.

Figure 3.3. Zaha Hadid, *Landesgartenschau.* Photograph by Hélène Binet. Reprinted with permission.

Print media have featured Hadid as part of an English avant-garde with roots in Russian constructivism, yet certain assumptions implied by this positioning require interrogation.[2] What characteristics of modern form and social culture persist in her work, and where does she break from the past? Specifically, what has become of the status of the built object through her buildings and drawings, and what perceptual phenomena emerge? As her built work becomes accessible, we may discover what optical consciousness links her design process to the ultimate experience of her architecture. What is occasionally addressed and is of uncertain interest is that Hadid, as a female practitioner, has achieved renown among a male subset of intellectual architects. She is frequently perceived as aggressive and difficult (as are some male prima donnas), yet one wonders about the basis and depth of those perceptions. Hadid has spoken little, if at all, of a tradition she seeks to kill off to make way for her new vision, common rhetoric among cutting-edge types. One would like to infer that self-confidence in her ideas and talent frees her from such posturing and defensiveness.

In the eyes of some beholders, Hadid's works in progress may look out of place, aggressively innovative yet vaguely familiar. As public symbols, her proposals for the Cardiff Opera House (1994–96), the 42nd Street Hotel facade, the Prado Museum Extension (1996), and the London Habitable Bridge (1996) provoke uncanny notions of the contemporary new and its modus operandi. Each challenges relationships between a century of modern ideas and the psychosocial dilemma of modern architecture by leaking interiors and masses into the public realm. Her expressive and very personal kind of drawing displays her unique vision.[3] Her twisted and bent abstraction of Hong Kong and the Weil-am-Rhein pavilion site seem to infiltrate their existing cities. The Peak proposal was entered in an international competition for the design of a men's club. Hadid has described her formal response to the problematic club program as "geological," one in which the elevated site is neither fortified nor allowed to be private, but where instead "by opening the Peak you really negate the idea of a men's club."[4] Hadid has gained acclaim for her groundbreaking visions beyond mainstream architecture. Tangentially identified with the male-dominated neo-avant-garde, she is an anomaly among a group whose politics are less overt than those of their forefathers, but who are similarly devoid of female leaders. As Hadid has achieved recognition, has her gender been an issue? Recently, her project for the Cincinnati Contemporary Art Center has led journalists to note that she will be the first women to design a major American art gallery. As Hadid, long popularized among the stars of the cutting edge, begins to claim major commissions, she is positioned to renew questions of the feminine and females in architecture. Will she make room for an emerging feminist avant-garde? Might her design work and tactics provide for a neomodern engagement with feminist practices and theories? Are texts of body or constructions of gender visible in her form making? Or are we witnessing an exchange of feminist postmodernism for neomodernist postfeminism? To examine Hadid's architecture, built and proposed, is to consider not only the social status of architecture, but also the impact of design on various social milieus.

A close reading of the language of Hadid's projects requires an understanding of her formal and intellectual ground, particularly compared with that of some of her neomodernist counterparts. For example, the persistence of phenomenal space composed of glass walls, dematerialized boundaries, and gravity-defying tectonic members recurs in current experiments such as those featured by Terry Riley in two recent MoMA exhibitions, *Light Construction* and *The Un-Private House.*[5] Reflecting so many modern icons of the first half of the twentieth century, glass is again the material of choice for certain domestic and public buildings, but the critical problem of transparency remains a ruse. Surprisingly absent from both MoMA shows, Hadid's work speaks the neomodern language that Riley seeks to define with his international assemblage. Perhaps indeed the modern lineage of father to son is more apparent in the works of Herzog & de Meuron, Rem Koolhaas, and others who build upon a priori ideas of Mies van der Rohe, Le Corbusier, and the constructivists. A deeper look is required to understand the social and political modern conditions that such neomodern statements reinforce, alter, or transcend. As postmodern criticism has challenged ideologies perpetuated by modern forms, including the linearity of Enlightenment history, positivist progress, and the universal subject, neomodern architecture cannot remain neutral. Some criticism is plagued by the very dialectical opposition that poststructuralism eschews, when the glass house stands in for the withering of domestic privacy and attempts to provide affordable housing are blamed for a failed social project. What seems apparent in the recent *grands projets* and works by Tschumi, Koolhaas, Herzog & de Meuron, Ando, Ito, Libeskind, and others is a renewed interest in the quintessential struggle for purity, the modern desire to privilege the concept in its distilled if idiosyncratic form over all else.

What may distinguish Hadid's work from that of other renowned neomodern architects is its hybrid nature. Her IBA housing project in Berlin combines a tower with a base of terrace houses over shops that shape the street front. Although her material composition, plastic form, and apartment interiors for the urban ensemble appear fresh and stand out in their context, the complex diagram is assembled from familiar types. A courtyard for the interaction of residents is separated from the public street, and the building both stands out and sublimely fits into its neighborhood. Hadid's contribution to a larger urban whole does not depend upon reinventing the city or producing a manifesto to redefine the idea of urbanity. Like many of her contemporaries, she works with knowledge of precedence but relies on the tactics of formal patterns rather than the strategies of the first-generation modern masters.

Four Modernisms

If we recognize the persistence of modernity in light of spatial responses to sociocultural needs and desires, we must acknowledge both successes and failures among buildings that employ abstraction and borrow from the avant-garde. A critical look uncovers myths buried in complex relationships that inspire the will for architectural novelty. If establishing one's identity on the scene requires staking out new ground, innovation has certain value. Yet in defining provenance and evaluating degrees of innovation, we will benefit from some sorting of the strategies of proper modern methods. In short, we observe multiple modernisms.

If we accept criticisms initiated in response to the problems of the posthumanist subject and technological determinism, we see that the international style unconsciously sought solutions for a universal human condition without recognizing diverse populations, climates, or geographies. What resulted was a fracture in the false clarity with which the modern movement has been synthesized and unified. I propose for purposes of critical interrogation the presence of four modern subsets, each keyed to a primary motivating ambition and generally targeted to high or low cultural imperatives.

"Oppositional modern" (high) architecture is theoretically oriented and intended to oppose a prior norm. What distinguishes a building in this category is the architect's fundamental positioning of the design *against* a social, political, or formal condition. As an idea becomes a building, the reactionary stance remains as both catalyst and product. The Lever House and the Seagram Building located across from each other on Manhattan's Park Avenue defy (albeit without violating the zoning envelope) the code-induced pattern of the continuous urban edge, drawing attention to each corporate identity.[6] Opposition to place emerges, for example, in Peter Eisenman's Wexner Center for the Arts at Ohio State University in Columbus, which, however photogenic, is conceptually and actually leaky.[7] Through scale play, the preexisting Jeffersonian grid became the architect's formal device, putting pressure on the central Oval and adjacent auditoriums, resulting in deflection, a kind of thorn in the side of the existing campus hierarchy and public space.

"Economic modern" (low) architecture defines the subset of modern buildings that are value engineered to be cost-effective and efficient. The economic myth of modern construction has unfortunately affected large areas of American cities. On the contrary, aesthetically sublime modern architecture is usually quite expensive. Modern architecture's attempt at literal transparency is rarely attained, given that comfort and commodity call for tinted glazing, which results in reflection or obscurity. When no aim beyond frugality informs formal principles, craft and design development are often sacrificed. Neither artful nor socially ambitious, visionless structures produced in factorylike corporate design offices to populate desolate downtowns and define freeway outer belts deserve much of the criticism aimed at modern architecture.

"Pure modern" (high) architecture specifies a third category of intervention that varies in scale, cultural location, and building type, but is grounded in principle and aesthetic desire and exemplifies phenomenal modern experiments.[8] Talented reactionary architects begin by posing challenges to existing cultural and formal expectations and seek novel forms and facades to express social and political changes. Through deep inquiry and artistic vision, some architects have built works that transcend the polemical to fabricate an architecture of their time, and herein lies the distinction between "pure" and "oppositional" architecture. Project constraints consciously addressed have served architects who have formulated integral physical solutions for thoroughly considered problems. Even as provocateurs, early Mies van der Rohe, Alvar Aalto, and Louis Kahn sustained balance among function, symbol, and craft, ultimately integrating all three. Serious attention to multiple social and programmatic goals positions these works in a different category than that defined by shock value or available funding.

Finally, there is "social modern" (low) architecture, perhaps the most complex realm of design to distinguish. By theorizing the entire problem in situ, designers beget forms that are often so well knitted into their cultural landscapes that they may not stand out in their physical contexts.

If economic limitations or formal desires call for restraint, resultant buildings may not be readily noticed or celebrated for purely aesthetic merits. Transparency of a different sort unveils the social program that motivates expression in modern architecture.[9] Social modernism may not immediately appear as innovative architecture, first, because of variations on possible formal themes, especially where the contribution of good design is not primarily visual; and second, because the project may contribute less obviously to the collection of images noted as modern. Planning or land-use programs such as the Appalachian Trail, the TVA, greenbelt housing, and national park shelters represent initiatives that required collaborations between architects and other allied professions. Visionary social ambitions to achieve the utopian aims of a new society were grounded in the everyday lives of families and workers.[10] Not all modernists held the perception that the high art of architecture and daily life were mutually exclusive.

At the level of the dwelling and the suburb, modern stylism bamboozled the middle class into a way of life marked by social separation and gender isolation. Essentialist economics fostered an antiaesthetic modern architecture, one that has proliferated. Modern buildings made clients believe they would get more for less, when in fact they got what they paid for. Coincident with the modern movement in architecture was a cheapening of aesthetic values. Bernard Tschumi, Rem Koolhaas, and other Hadid contemporaries have called into question the part of architecture called *program, function,* or *events,* and have noted the unstable relationship between space and its uses. This research into reconceptualizing the definition of the use and users of public and private space has revived interest among high-art architects in the social practice of contemporary architecture.

Feeding functionalism, two positivist myths have persisted to generate pathological patterns of growth in the city. First, the social utopian dream of an expanding middle class led to suburbs with reduced densities at the expense of the city. Second, within urban centers, the ordering capacity of the Cartesian grid placed control in the hands of planners and developers with a predilection for the god's-eye view. Both myths fostered the veneration of technology in an ambience where scientific information was privileged over humanist and historic interest. By mythologizing rationality and its mute formal orders, the most cerebral architecture aiming to become high art disqualified sensual, expe-

Figure 3.4. Furniture from 24 Cathcart Road: office of Zaha Hadid. Reprinted with permission.

riential, material, and perceptual sectors, and so risked becoming merely angry architecture. Architects engaged in the critical practice of new or neomodern architecture reflect psychoanalytic criticism of modern society and those architects who shaped it, and, like Hadid, present alternatives to form as a dominant means of control.[11]

Hadid's liberated domestic space is evident in her 1986 renovation of an international-style London residence at 24 Cathcart Road (Figure 3.4).[12] By introducing a storage wall and furniture of her design, Hadid makes the modern living room a landscape for the human body. The experimental showroom grew out of designs for previous urban residences for which she aimed "to create a weightlessness, freedom from the stress of public life."[13] One must touch and lounge on her artful objects in order to caress their textures and absorb their rich colors. A curvilinear yellow couch seat is placed near the wall, which supports its white undulating backrest and from which the seat is detached. How can one imagine sitting up straight in her "red sofa" or her eggplant-chroma V-crested chair at 24 Cathcart? "Wave sofa" and "whoosh sofa" are bent to let several occupants look at one another in conversation. Resting on Hadid's furniture, one's body gives way to directions other than those dictated by the forces of gravity.

Several critics have identified Hadid's work, especially in its emphasis on porous urban walls, as serving to define this liberating new modern architecture.[14] Transcending surface perceptions of ornament and object-oriented mass, tectonic fetishes, and icons of myopic totalizing vision, the essence of new architecture alters the literal frame of reference. By establishing connections between inside and outside, between the building and the ground, the city and the world beyond the object, Hadid brings questions of culture and its users into the frame. Hadid's built works erase myths of economy and functionalism and replace them with multifunctionality, creating spaces informed by inhabitants and providing respite from the overrationalized "big plan."

Beyond Modern Models

Philosopher Gianni Vattimo was early to proclaim the end of a modernity he identified with classical or "strong," rationally dominant models of consciousness. Various social forces, he argues, have generated a transition to new patterns of order characterized by "weak thought," or *pensière débole,*[15] a model of consciousness

> linked to what, in philosophy and epistemology of recent years, is commonly referred to as the "crisis in classical reason," or rather the "weakening" of the strong ontological categories of metaphysics. It is a question instead, or as well, of a highly concrete and specific process of multiplication of social forces, and of a general weakening of the horizons within which design occurs.[16]

Vattimo recognizes that actual social forces have borne greater imperatives than imagined or desired utopian social aims envisioned by autocratic powers. He targets functionalism, the basis for modern architecture's essentialism, as a source of dogmatic control, especially in plan-based design that is obsessed with highly articulated and rigorous distribution of functions. When organizational simplification is used to legitimate the work of the architect, inhabitation is suppressed and one can hope at best for a derivative aesthetic proposal; functionalism "is reassuring but also extremely inadequate or even 'violent' with respect to the multiplicity, the multifaceted nature, and the 'proximity' of existence. Like many forms of legitimation invented by the rationalist mentality, it is ineffective."[17]

Hadid is no prisoner to function or overrationalized formalism. Her projects privilege expressive form over the legibility of deterministic orders or a functional continuum of program-driven spaces.[18] She has suggested that architectural modernism is an unfinished project, especially at the scale of the city. Her desire for "lightness" and floating, release from forces of gravity, brings physical liberation from the building site by opening the ground. *LF one* demonstrates her ground in flux. She extends movement continuously across the local landscape with walls, ramps, and a stair guiding passage into an eight-thousand-square-foot exhibition pavilion that is, by virtue of her pedestrian networks and section design, tied into the ground. The result is a dynamic interior and exterior landscape rather than a static monument. Seeking productive analogies in land forms, Hadid softens the buildings' edges and smoothes transitions between spaces while blurring the break from inside to outside. Her compressed space celebrates the primary activity of motion, recalling the assertion of Walter Benjamin that architecture is fundamentally experienced by the masses in a state of distraction.[19]

Hadid's work invites looking beyond stylistic imagery to the spaces she invests with sensation and movement in the production of social space. Reaping benefits from criticism about the disjunction between psychological estrangement or social isolation and modern architectural ideals, many recent architects have generated new interventions that draw from and sometimes mimic aesthetic models characteristic of compelling modern architecture. To sort out contemporary trends that shape aesthetic environments for the purpose of this inquiry requires clarification of the parameters of symbolic form. Not all building types have the same opportunity for architectural expression. If the aim is to comprehend the perpetuation of new ideals beyond the negation of modernist authority, we ought to focus on those urban building types best positioned to demonstrate the zeitgeist. Buildings least bound by complex function are best situated to respond to aesthetic intentions. It may seem obvious that environments designed primarily as works of art offer the greatest freedom of expression, but those designed to feature other artifacts are not without functional and symbolic expectation. Such iconographic galleries present the dilemma of vessel versus monumental artifact. In such buildings, physical and social function cannot be deemed insignificant, although they may be rendered invisible. Neither does a reduction of pragmatic constraints guarantee a more aesthetically successful architecture. Art centers, especially those dedicated to contemporary arts, have shaped the struggle to define new aesthetic form since Frank Lloyd Wright's controversial spiral for the Guggenheim Museum overlooking Central Park. By breaking the rhythmic continuous edge of Fifth Avenue along the park and providing only curved interior walls viewed tangentially upon descent, the uptown Guggenheim presented challenges to curators and earned distinction as the first gallery to defy function.

When the main program prerogative is to create the locus for new art, the architect is doing much more than marking a blank slate. Art galleries function by disrupting one's experience of the day-to-day routine; they are formally malleable because they seek to awaken the dormant senses of every visitor. Not to be confused with the time-bound "museum," a product of three centuries of Enlightenment legacy and designed for the categorization of "knowledge," the contemporary gallery looks to the future that it serves to shape and foreshadow. When successful, contemporary art centers provide a bellwether for the next sublime, for

> to encounter a work of art (or indeed to acquire historical knowledge), is to experience in the imagination forms of existence and ways of life different from the one in which we have become immersed in our own concrete everydayness. As we grow older, we all narrow our horizons of life, specializing in one thing or another and enclosing ourselves within a particular circle of friendships, interests and acquaintances. Aesthetic experience leads us into other possible worlds, and we are made to realize the contingency and relativity of the "real" world in which we live.[20]

Two art centers by the Office of Zaha Hadid are suggestive in relation to Vattimo's formulation of aesthetic experience. They may also make room for a feminist conception of avant-garde architecture either between or beyond existing modernisms. The successes of both as buildings or works of art are impossible to assert prior to the opportunity to experience them as completed works. However, it is possible to consider the relation between stated intentions and Hadid's unique visualizations before evaluating the faits accomplis. Hadid employs drawing and model abstraction to articulate spatial ideas throughout the design process; her chosen point of view is not fixed and represents her interpretation of the surrounding cityscape. Characterized by her use of black background fields with apparent interior light sources, brilliant color harmonies, projections on canted planes, and converging parallel lines, Hadid's dark graphics have helped her to win competitions and earn commissions. She has been successful in convincing jurors to accept radical and unfamiliar, even threatening, formal gestures for public works.

If some of the best neomodern architecture oscillates between nondiscrete "pure" and "social" subsets of modernism, how do appropriate design tactics embrace the ground, the user, and the city? One recognizes the necessary complexity of any critical model for aesthetic evaluation that looks beyond what is initially or immediately observed. Early international-style modernism and avant-garde art movements (futurism, cubism, constructivism) idealized novelty, but for different reasons. What relation to the past is inherent in "being new"? To eliminate the baggage associated with images of the past, some avant-garde movements proposed acts of total erasure. Yet demands for origins and cultural connections only increased as old urban areas were erased and markings of time disappeared. Manfredo Tafuri preceded new historians in practicing historical analysis aimed at forging intellectual connections between a past not bound by time and sequence and the symbolic potential of new architecture. He recognized that architecture is conceived as the transmitter of information, yet often with too little concern for those receiving its messages. Tafuri theorized the notion of "experimentalism" to assign provenance for novel interventions that deeply contradicted the avant-gardes, whom he described as "affirmative, absolutist and totalitarian":

> They claim pre-emptorily to build a brand new context, taking for granted that their linguistic revolution not only implies but actually "realises" a social and moral upheaval. When Picasso states, "I don't look for, I find," he expresses perfectly the assertive character of the avant-gardes. Those who *look for* must, more or less, work on existing material, choosing,

> assembling and disassembling. But avant-gardes ignore *existing materials.* For them nothing is taken for granted or a priori. Their constructive act is radical, with Malevich's "pure desert" as its symbol.[21]

Whereas modernism as a movement has benefited from positioning intangible ideas and critical reflection before constructing tangible buildings, avant-garde or neo-avant-garde architectural agendas have lost their cogency by privileging ideology over architectural principles.[22] Many avant-garde critiques, written and built, have been shown to lack methodology and rigorous analysis. They often fall victim to the indeterminate banality of new versus old or kill-the-father nihilistic dualisms. Although Hadid's work has been called avant-garde, the term oversimplifies her intentions when viewed from Tafuri's standpoint, which stresses the relation between a metalanguage and the critical image.

Perhaps assuming an intellectual affiliation between Hadid and radical neoconstructivists causes more confusion than clarity. Her work may more appropriately be understood as *experimentalist* and independent of trends. She does not claim to eliminate the old or build an entirely new context, but instead revises the perception of ground before working in it, as shown in her site renderings. Political and tabula rasa agendas seem to interest her less than designing for the broader spectrum of a liberated human experience. Her descriptions and drawings appear to depict Vattimo's definition of design practice: "Designing is to some extent 'readjusting'—readjusting the project continually and in dialogue with a multitude of ever-changing social forces responsible for decisions; and, at the same time, readjusting what already exists."[23]

Two Projects

The municipality of Rome sponsored an invited international design competition for a new Center for Contemporary Art (Centro per le Arti Contemporane [CAC]), with the winner selected in February 1999.[24] Fifteen teams of architects were selected, from among the original 273 submissions, to propose an institutional structure for new art located north of Rome's historic center. Beyond the nucleus of Rome, the area sited along the north side of the Via Guido Reni is near Renzo Piano's new auditorium, Pier Luigi Nervi's Palazzetto dello Sport, and the 1960s Olympic village, renovated in 1999 by Aldo Aymonino. Currently the site includes existing military barracks whose industrial sheds were offered up in the competition brief for either reuse or complete replacement.

The area is characterized by a hybrid collection of evolving contemporary, modern, and nineteenth-century interventions.

Zaha Hadid's winning Roman CAC proposal reuses only two of the existing barracks and fills the rest of the site with delineations in plan, section, and roofscape that resemble superimposed rail tracks gesturing in several directions. Describing the form as an "urban graft," the architect is deliberate about maintaining new structures lower than the buildings surrounding the site.[25] Simultaneously, construction is under way for Cincinnati's Contemporary Art Center, which also draws from specific characteristics of its downtown locale. It is more than coincidence that finds this woman the protagonist of both new centers for contemporary art. Both proposals are civic interventions that unearth linkages, absent in most contemporary museums, between gallery interiors and public streets. Hadid may be among the first architects to succeed in producing space with movement that suppresses the gallery as object icon to redefine its finite imagery.

Hadid has grounded her proposal for the Roman CAC within its physical site. Her own conception for the strategy begins with a reading of the vertical rise of the neighborhood. She presents the new center as an "urban 'graft,' a second skin on the site, effecting the ground to become new soil. Yet it ascends to grow massive when necessary."[26] The building is conceived from the outside in to create a "quasi-urban field, a 'world' in which to plunge."[27] She describes the new center as "porous," designed to connect internal with external circulation beyond the bounds of the building envelope. Movement of visitors is conceived as a force to weave spaces across the grain of the site. The spaces within and outside produce the building's mass, understood as born of the "drift" of path vectors. In Cincinnati, Hadid's gesture invites entry from the public street, this time on a vertically oriented corner site. Her "urban carpet" for Cincinnati originates on the downtown intersection and becomes a stepped ramp inside, moving seamlessly from the reception desk onto the sequence of galleries occupying eight floors. Horizontal or vertical energies are exploited to reinforce her interpretation of the innate forces on each site, and to facilitate the flow of gallery volumes and daylight. Pronounced differences in concepts and formal proposals for the two contemporary art centers reveal a critical component of Hadid's architecture: she is not locked into a fixed image, but driven by an interpretation of context and by her own sensitivities and creative energies.

Hadid's proposed open spaces, with interiors defined to avoid closure, can be understood as modern motifs. Her use of glass is informed by a tradition of the minimum boundary. Glass curtain walls let support structures be revealed while removing the finite portal that might constrict the path. But glass rarely functions as a completely transparent surface, and the overoptimism about economic progress and the universal subject once symbolized by the medium has been repeatedly criticized.[28] In "Transparency: Literal and Phenomenal," Colin Rowe and Robert Slutzky expose superficial myths of modernism by looking beyond the formal qualities in the works of early modern masters.[29] Since that work was first published in 1964, numerous revisionists have reexamined the relation between modern material and facade fixation, finding modern space to be more complex psychologically than previously perceived, its phenomenal layers serving as signifiers that directly influence human social relations. And because exterior glazing is often not transparent at all, the aim and affect of the expressive modern curtain wall has been challenged, in particular by Anthony Vidler:

> Literal transparency is of course notoriously difficult (as Pei himself admitted) to attain; it quickly turns into obscurity (its apparent opposite) and reflectivity (its reversal).... Why then transparency in the first place? To make huge cubic masses, monumental forms, urban constructions of vast scale—disappear? A crisis in confidence in monumentality?[30]

Vidler sees through the positivist reflection on modern transparency to challenge unbecoming ambiguities in the works of contemporary radicals, but neomodern appropriation of curtain walls and abstract glazed surfaces is not fully illuminated by his critique. Hadid is not naive about the aesthetics of glass and, with her Cincinnati CAC, appears to confront Vidler's questions. Never does her monumental intervention appear shy or attempt to disappear; instead, her use of glass is a statement of presence and connection. In the Cincinnati proposal, her spaces are activated by voids and thrusting volumes that differentiate the Walnut and Sixth Street facades.[31] Exterior glass surfaces may be translucent, reflective, or opaque, with fragmented massing scaled by Hadid's own abstract volumes, which become repetitive elements of measure within her system, rather than depending upon windows and doors for scale.

In Rome, Hadid uses theater metaphors and considers architecture a necessary component in the "staging" of art. She directs her attention to the set designed for new art by reconceptualizing the gallery wall. She separates surface from structure, a tactic that opens spaces and allows walls to be either suspended or floor supported, yet always mobile and versatile. She writes, "Against the traditional codification of museum 'wall,' as the privileged and unchangeable vertical armature to show paintings, or as the defining element in discreet space for building order alignment, we propose a critical revision toward its emancipation. The 'wall' becomes the versatile motor to stage exhibition effects."[32] Beyond containing fixed space, the liberated wall may become projection screen, canvas, curtain, or window on the city, and takes its cues from the function and users of the gallery. For Hadid, the design for the antiwall grows out of the need to rethink the identity of the contemporary art museum:

> The utopic space of modernity has fed the white "neutrality" of most museums of the 21st century. Today this attitude must be placed in discussion, not for foolish negation, but for the necessity of architecture to continue its own critical relationship with contemporary aesthetic and social ideas. Since every absolute value about the actual thoughts of the presentation of art has been indefinitely placed on hold, we prefer to orient ourselves toward the idea of "maximumization of exposure."[33]

Hadid's reconsideration of the role and form of the wall sheds light on the palimpsest of surface ornament that often draws attention away from the space. Essential qualities that are effected by the interdependence of surfaces—wall, ceiling, and floor—cannot be shown through orthographic projections or perspectival representations with static viewpoints. The role of the fixed wall in making proportionate and scaled space is known experientially, "by use and by perception, or rather, by touch and sight," according to Walter Benjamin.[34] Ancient golden means, Japanese tea house tatami, Palladian ratios, and Le Corbusier's regulating lines share common design methods in following laws of harmonic proportion. Mies van der Rohe's Barcelona Pavilion introduced blurred and moving boundaries of space through careful construction of interactive transparent, opaque, and columnar definitions of overlapping space with horizontal symmetry. With a tight hold on compositional structure, the architect remains in control. Modernism radically refined the complexity of the wall by abstracting its surfaces, but it nonetheless maintained the wall's role in forming well-proportioned, finite compositions. As Hadid's walls begin to oscillate and become dislodged in space, aesthetic criteria for evaluating spatial proportions are also destabilized.

Here, in Vattimo's words, "'Other' possibilities of existence are realized before our very eyes.... To live in this pluralistic world means to experience freedom as a continual oscillation between belonging and disorientation."[35]

In contrast to the rigidity and stark palette of Miesian modernism, Hadid's gestures are expressive. For visitors to move through the galleries as she intends requires that she replace their expectations with open-minded engagement, even of unfamiliar spaces and systems. Having chosen to give up or work against bound rooms and framed views, she relies on haptic and visceral sensitivities over the intellectualization of geometric proportions or other theoretical rigors. Her plans for the Rome CAC are drawn from vector courses that crisscross between primary roads. She borrows bends from the shape and orientation of the entire site. Where open spaces are superimposed and "filament-like paths" converge or collide, escalators connect floor levels on a slant, while elevators bury the vertical link. Hadid's spatial drift, grafted into place, allows for malleable rooms choreographed by curators cum designers and by spectators participating in reaction to changing exhibits.

In Rome, the vector drift motif becomes a way to organize space by extruding similar volumes. These serpentine extrusions are then subdivided with a structural system linked to skylight patterns that appear in section drawings as exposed beams. The repetition and interference of lines that drop from above allow the ceiling to become a porous surface. If the CAC is built as drawn, light will plunge through the parallel beams, with the angle of the sun recorded as it changes, depending simultaneously on the ground angle of the bar of space and the time of year. The interiority of this system is distinct from the majority of facade-focused monumental galleries.[36] Unlike the first Guggenheim, Marcel Breuer's Whitney Museum, or Frank Gehry's recent galleries at Bilbao and Minneapolis, Hadid's Rome CAC as proposed allows for no memorable facade or object image. Visitors slip into a void from the Via Guido Reni under a projecting gallery bar and turn ninety degrees to enter the building through an undulating surface bathed in light. Hadid states in her competition brief that she intends a different kind of exhibition space from the type that modern "object" museums engendered. She prefers plunging into an anonymous "world" to producing a "signature object" with baggage that weighs it down.

Hadid's critique of the "signature object" draws attention to the flow of pathways in both of her contemporary art centers. Each proposed sequence invites entry without placing the building on a pedestal. Classical monuments celebrated entry with a big gesture, and thereby did not democratically welcome all members of a class-stratified society when a grand stair created a physical and symbolic obstacle. Premodern monumental museum facades act as billboards to signify cultural icons.

Several late-modern works have challenged that language and its message. Alternatives to traditional thresholds and ascents can be found in the entry sequences of both New Haven galleries by Louis Kahn. Kahn designed his 1951 art gallery as an addition to the existing Yale University gallery. The blank exterior wall on Kahn's public entry facade is composed only of brick and horizontal limestone string courses with an entry approach parallel to the sidewalk. Visitors quietly slip in through extruded glazing aligned with the old Yale art gallery. The solid street facade disguises the hidden connection to the inner courtyard. The elegance and grace of the spaces held inside are neither revealed to the street nor allowed to compete with the existing gallery. When Kahn received the commission for the British Art Gallery directly across the street nearly twenty years later, he created another understated facade and entry sequence. He gathered the cultural activity away from the street life (which was accommodated in the base of the museum in the form of storefronts) through a voided corner to draw visitors into an interiorized monumental sequence. As Kahn's movement pattern grew in sophistication, his material palette and ornamental motifs became more refined.

Hadid's sensitivity to context and movement is every bit as sublime as Kahn's, while her poetic language is arhythmic and perhaps speaks with a louder voice. Unlike Kahn's hidden museums, Hadid's buildings do not shy away from having an identity on the street. Her visualization of these urban links is often difficult, engaging, mystical, and abstractly sublime. Like Piranesi's prison drawings, her depictions serve as critical tools to communicate intangible ideas and her commitment to a new vision. She fosters a preference for interiority porous to the exterior, without the monument anxiety that Vidler fears. By privileging open-ended space over the formal object-icon, she challenges conventions by proposing alternative material compositions and tectonics, and opens the door to a novel civic-social architecture. Perhaps this constitutes a feminist way to build: inclusive, nonhierarchical, and multiple, directing formal innovation at social integration. Except for her separation from myths of origin and male parentage in her neomodern motifs, Hadid is not alone in searching for a buildable expression for heterogeneity and multiplicity realized in architectural space. The centrality of feminist critical theory to contemporary architecture seems everywhere apparent, especially as the practice of everyday life is understood as a nonauthoritarian, evolutionary reaction—a taking advantage—that infiltrates the pores of contemporary mythology.[37] By smoothing over imbalances and misperceptions of the status quo, she opens a new space. Whether or not Hadid publicly declares her feminist values is far from the point. Her work, when completed, promises to realize potential (and long overdue) environmental transformations inspired by feminist critical theory. As an individual creative artist, Hadid has the talent and chutzpah to redefine the cultural symbols of our day.[38] The greater feminist "problem" in architecture remains the subject: who gets to practice.

Ultimately, Hadid's proposed work serves the total human condition. Her liberated space characterizes Vattimo's poststructuralist prediction of a world well-ordered, with less fixity and determinacy, and more varied voices, than the past modern one:

> Nihilistic philosophers such as Nietzsche and Heidegger (but also pragmatists like Dewey or Wittgenstein), in demonstrating that being does not necessarily coincide with what is stable, fixed and permanent, but has instead to do with the event, with consensus, dialogue and interpretation, are trying to show us how to take the experience of oscillation in the postmodern world as an opportunity of a new way of being (finally, perhaps) human.[39]

Several questions remain about how to evaluate the work of this woman within the realm of contemporary ideas. It seems as though she has elected to let her buildings, free of inappropriate stylistic or political associations, provide phenomenological answers. She has remained relatively free of the club model of fraternal organizations, through which architects of both genders have sought fame by association. Yet Hadid has emerged as a force with an attitude through her exhibited drawings, her success in international competitions, and her buildings. She has avoided defining herself as a liberal, cultural, or contextual feminist as a way of assigning her formal values in architecture.[40] She eschews categorization, but her prominence on the scene, an overwhelmingly male one, positions Hadid critically. As the first woman to design major contemporary art centers, she will receive much scrutiny. Although characterized as a willful individual, she nonetheless credits her collaborators even as she expresses without apology her sensibilities and determination.

Feminism's critique of unquestionable "genius" and of master models with elusive knowledge bases in architecture is complicated. Hadid may well be considered one of those guys, preferring the identity of artist and iconoclast to revealing her secrets and leaving vulnerable her innermost desires. Yet artistic creativity is not always suited to collaboration, and one must at times be willing to take individual responsibility for that which is different and threatens the status quo. Such risk taking is necessary in the current world, in which men still hold the political capital and financial authority and dominate the profession.[41] Without apology, Hadid uses her skill to revise the existing terrain, then creates a place for herself in it. Formally, the two art centers discussed here situate Hadid's work in the realm of a contextual feminist practice and illustrate her oscillating spaces and determination for change. Her personal authorship, which establishes a subjective sense of beauty and insists on haptic over intellectual comprehension of space and the inclusiveness of her vision, will inform an architecture that enriches the experience of everyday life and that responds to Vattimo's conviction that "if any significance is left to the project in this world, it is linked to the loss of the certainties of the plan, to the assumption of chance, impermanence, and spontaneity; which means of openness and risk."[42] The realization of her two art centers will help to open that space and make room for more women in the front lines of radical public architecture. One fervently hopes that she will have the chance that Piranesi did not to concretize her visions beyond paper.

Notes

1. Aaron Betsky, *Zaha Hadid: The Complete Buildings and Projects* (New York: Rizzoli, 1998).

2. In reviewing Hadid's Cincinnati CAC (Contemporary Arts Center), Joseph Giovannini wrote: "A student of the Russian avant-garde, Hadid also conceives buildings as socializing agents in the city: characteristically, her buildings are generously open to the street, with which they establish reciprocal relationships." More often, Hadid is cited as a member of the neo-avant-garde, especially since her work with

Rem Koolhaas at OMA and for her "vanguard architectonic language" ("Hadid's Midwest Coup," *Art in America,* February 1999, 41).

3. In an interview with Jeffrey Kipnis in the Ohio State Knowlton School of Architecture Baumer Masterclass Seminar in October 1998, Hadid stated: "I really think of another kind of world . . . to explore these kinds of spatial differences, I could not use the same method of drawing. The drawing of plan and section just didn't do anything. So therefore, the importance of the drawing was the way it informed the work of the idea of distortion, the projection, seeing the building in different views allowed it to see beyond the boundary of the project which I think was also very significant."

4. Hadid stated during the Kipnis interview (see note 3), "I could never do a men's club." Kipnis interpreted her response to the problems of the acropolis-like setting and the private club program by noting, "You're basically using the language of modernism to open back up that form of resistance."

5. Catalogs for both exhibitions document the curator's intent. See *Light Construction* (New York: Museum of Modern Art, 1995) and *The Un-Private House* (New York: Museum of Modern Art, 1999), both distributed by Harry N. Abrams, Inc. The director's foreword to *Light Construction* indicates that the show "presents a broadly-based view of the direction of contemporary architecture in the last decade, cutting across cultural, aesthetic and technological boundaries" (6).

6. Although formally novel in their contexts, the curtain-wall skins and public sequences of these two high-rises do not contribute to a more vital street life. One of the most powerful portraits of the Seagram Building, by Ezra Stoller, looks past the building through the glass revolving doors to see the McKim, Mead, and White–designed club across the street, suggesting perhaps that the Seagram can all but disappear.

7. For Eisenman's theoretical explanations of "atopos" and "scaling," see Peter Eisenman, *House X* (New York: Rizzoli, 1982); and Eisenman, *Wexner Center for the Visual Arts* (New York: St. Martin's Press, 1989). See also Margaret Soltan, "Deconstruction and Architecture," in *Reconstructing Architecture: Critical Discourses and Social Practices,* ed. Thomas A. Dutton and Lian Hurst Mann (Minneapolis: University of Minnesota Press, 1996).

8. Some great buildings that have brought renown to the architects for which they are known serve to illustrate "pure modern" architecture: Otto Wagner's Post Office Savings Bank, Asplund's Stockholm Library, Mies van der Rohe's Barcelona Pavilion, Alvar Aalto's Villa Mairea, Gerrit Rietveld's house for Truus Schroder, Le Corbusier's Villa Savoye and Swiss Pavilion, Giuseppe Terragni's Casa del Fascio, Carlo Scarpa's Querini Stampalia, Louis Kahn's Exeter Library and Kimball Museum, and Frank Lloyd Wright's entire domestic oeuvre and both Taliesens.

9. This body of work is exemplified by social housing from the 1920s in Amsterdam and Frankfurt, the American greenbelt housing of Howard Wright and Clarence Stein, the art deco movement of democratic entertainment in cinemas and hotels, and planned communities at Pullman, Illinois; Radburn, New Jersey; and Mariemont, Ohio.

10. Thoughtfully, albeit simply, designed kindergartens, auditoriums, settlement houses, schools, churches, and pocket parks, but especially housing alternatives to urban tenements, furnished new expressions and planning strategies to meet the desires of modern society.

11. See sequential texts by Anthony Vidler, *The Architectural Uncanny: Essays in the Modern Unhomely* (Cambridge: MIT Press, 1994), and *Warped Space* (Cambridge: MIT Press, 2000). In the latter, Vidler introduces "leitmotivs of avant-garde art" to point out what he considers to be the pathologies of modern space and its creators: "The vocabularies of displacement and fracture, torquing, twisting, pressure and release, void and block, *informe* and hyperform that they developed are still active today, deployed in work that seeks to reveal, if not critique, the conditions of a less than settled everyday life" (1).

12. See Betsky, *Zaha Hadid*, 30–31 (for the 24 Cathcart Road residence) and 170 (for furniture designs).

13. See ibid., 18–19, for designs for the Irish Prime Minister's Residence and for 59 Eaton Place. Hadid discusses her distribution of program elements and her choice of materials to, in effect, make space appear to float.

14. Betsky writes: "One might say that Zaha Hadid is a modernist designing lofts tied to technological cores as a celebration of the new. Hadid has no truck with typologies, applied orders, implied assumptions or gravity: she believes that we could and should build a better world, one marked by freedom, above all else. We could be liberated from the past, from the constraints of social convention, from physical laws, and free of our bodies" (ibid., 6).

15. Gianni Vattimo, *The End of Modernity: Nihilism and Hermeneutics in Postmodern Culture*, trans. Jon R. Snyder (Baltimore: Johns Hopkins University Press, 1991). Vattimo develops *pensière débole*, or weak thought, freed from the modernist quest for foundations or origins, and aims to define postmodernism by finding its connection with modernism.

16. Gianni Vattimo, introduction to Pietro Derossi, *Modernism without Avant-Garde*, Lotus Documents 13 (Milan: Electa, 1990), 10.

17. Ibid., 9.

18. Architects use the term *program* as both noun and verb. The thing specifies the necessary square footage to be assigned per function and prescribes required adjacencies. The verb is the act of creating the specifying document.

19. Betsky, commenting on Hadid's body-centered modern, notes: "She does not invent new forms of construction or technology; she shows us a world in new ways by representing it in a radical manner. She finds the roots of modernism in the dissolution of both subject and object and draws them onto the stage of the modern landscape, which she shapes as the place in which we can go boldly wandering" (*Zaha Hadid*, 6–7).

20. Gianni Vattimo, *The Transparent Society*, trans. David Webb (Baltimore: Johns Hopkins University Press, 1992), 10. Vattimo applies the notion of "transparency" with the same postmodern skepticism as many contemporary architects, as a symbolic model for an open, self-conscious society.

21. Manfredo Tafuri, *Theories and History of Architecture*, trans. Giorgio Verrecchia (New York: Harper & Row, 1980), 104.

22. For further discussion of the complex relationship between modernism and the avant-garde, see Peter Burger, *Theory of the Avant-garde* (Minneapolis: University of Minnesota Press, 1984).

23. Vattimo, *The Transparent Society*, 12.

24. For a full explanation of the competition program, process, jury, and invited participants, see Francesco Garofalo, *Arte Futura: Opere e progetti del Centro per le*

Arti Contemporanee a Roma, published by Ministero per I Beni e le Attivitá Culturali, Sopritendenza Speciale Arte Contemporanea (Milan: Electa, 1999).

25. Zaha Hadid and Yahuda Safran, "Space-Craftmanship Skin Pele," *Prototypo* 3 (February 2000): 74.

26. Garofalo, *Arte Futura,* 60–67. The English translation of Hadid's project description in the 1999 competition and exhibition catalog is my own.

27. Ibid., 60.

28. Arthur Danto writes: "Glass today is a social partition that divides many dwellers from the homeless, those whose powerlessness is double. Deprived of the house as *domus,* their impotence is multiplied by their lack of the house as shelter. As dwellers without where to dwell, the homeless are at the farthest edges of humanity. They are mirror images of us whose meaning resides in our means" ("Abide/Abode," in *Housing: Symbol, Structure, Site,* ed. Lisa Taylor for the Cooper-Hewitt Museum [New York: Rizzoli, 1982], 8).

29. Colin Rowe and Robert Slutzky, "Transparency: Literal and Phenomenal," in *Transparency* (1964; reprinted, Basel, Switzerland: Birkhäuser, 1997).

30. Vidler, *The Architectural Uncanny,* 220.

31. Visit the Cincinnati Contemporary Art Center Web site at www.spiral.org to take a "virtual tour" of the proposed building and to access interviews with Hadid and museum director Charles Desmarais.

32. Hadid, quoted in Garofalo, *Arte Futura,* 62.

33. Hadid, quoted in ibid., 62.

34. Walter Benjamin, "The Work of Art in the Age of Mechanical Reproduction," in *Illuminations,* ed. Hannah Arendt (New York: Schocken, 1968), 240. Benjamin was interested in the perpetual human need for shelter. In the same passage, he continues: "For the tasks which face the human apparatus of perception at the turning points of history cannot be solved by optical means, that is, by contemplation, alone. They are mastered gradually by habit, under the guidance of tactile appropriation."

35. Vattimo, *The Transparent Society,* 10.

36. Skylighted galleries by Louis Kahn, Gae Aulenti, and Renzo Piano suggest diverse examples of technical precedent for Hadid's proposal, with Piano's Menil Collection museum in Houston and Beyeler Foundation Museum in Switzerland as most similar. The development of Hadid's pronounced ceiling system will be a defining factor in her gallery spaces, and current representations are too schematic to discuss.

37. See Michel de Certeau, *The Practice of Everyday Life,* trans. Steven Rendall (Los Angeles: University of California Press, 1984). For architectural applications of theories of everyday life, see Mary McLeod, "Henri Lefebvre's Critique of Everyday Life: An Introduction," in *Architecture of the Everyday,* ed. Steven Harris and Deborah Berke (New York: Princeton Architectural Press, 1997); and Mary McLeod, "Everyday and 'Other' Spaces," in *Architecture and Feminism,* ed. Deborah Coleman, Elizabeth Danze, and Carol Henderson (New York: Princeton Architectural Press, 1996). For additional readings on feminist theories and practices of architecture, see Diana Agrest, Patricia Conway, and Leslie Kanes Weisman, eds., *The Sex of Architecture* (New York: Harry N. Abrams, 1996); Leslie Kanes Weisman, *Discrimination by Design: A Feminist Critique of the Man-Made Environment* (Chicago: University of Illinois Press, 1992); Beatriz Colomina, *Sexuality and Space* (New York: Princeton

Architectural Press, 1992); and Beatriz Colomina, *Privacy and Publicity: Modern Architecture as Mass Media* (Cambridge: MIT Press, 1994).

38. Feminist critical theory and feminist criticism of architecture are diverse practices. In this essay, I have suggested postmodern thought that illuminates and serves to situate Hadid's practice. Although feminist critics have raised valid concerns about the postmodern built environment concerning issues of land use, ecofeminism, economic imperatives, and the distribution of public resources, those issues are peripheral to Hadid's chosen practice, which focuses on redefining public, contemporary urban symbols within global culture.

39. Vattimo, *The Transparent Society,* 11.

40. Sherry Ahrentzen has clarified feminist architectural postures according to feminist theory as follows: "a liberal feminist stance ... claims that differences between sexes should not occur and maintains that women should have the same opportunities and rights as men. The second stance, variously called cultural feminism, or feminist standpoint, acknowledges differences and celebrates rather than discounts or marginalizes women's experiences. Contextual feminism attempts to dislodge the centrality of the sex difference argument, but does not deny the social existence of difference. Rather its focus is on recognizing those social conditions that make difference matter and on creating new spaces, relationships, and identities emanating from altered contexts" ("The F Word in Architecture," in *Reconstructing Architecture: Critical Discourses and Social Practices,* ed. Thomas A. Dutton and Lian Hurst Mann [Minneapolis: University of Minnesota Press, 1996], 72).

41. According to Ahrentzen, "Peter Eisenman lamented the absence of young architects and women speakers at a recent ANYone conference that was intended to provoke 'changes in the possibilities of architecture.' He claims that the risks of engaging in such challenge are too great for women who still have not become established or have not been accepted into the profession. Thus, he is suggesting (unknowingly?) that one must become part of a club before one can challenge it" (ibid.).

42. Vattimo, introduction to *Modernism without Avant-Garde,* 13.

CHAPTER FOUR

Pleasures Incarnate

Aesthetic Sentiment in the Nineteenth-Century Work of Art

Judith Stoddart

Victorian sentimental narrative painting has long served as a kind of baseline against which a sophisticated modern aesthetic can be measured. The overt legibility of narrative painting is taken as a sign of its participation in the mass consumption of art against which modernism reacted. Its sentimentality is read as a naive eliding of moral and aesthetic categories, an error brought into sharp focus by the modernist refusal of moral commentary in art. So, for example, Marcia Eaton, in a survey of attitudes toward sentimentalism, laments the blurring of "ethical and aesthetic considerations" implicit in the term. Sentimentality, she argues, displays a "gap between feeling and an appropriate" aesthetic response; it is inherently "*deceptive*" because we are "taken in by" an overly moralized depiction of the world. E. D. H. Johnson betrays a similar impatience with the ethical imperative at work in early-Victorian sentimental genre painting; this lapse in aesthetic decorum, he argues, simply "invalidates" much of the art in the period. Like certain of their eighteenth-century predecessors, British artists in the nineteenth century "too often falsified truth of observation by making it serve a moral message designed to widen the appeal and heighten the significance of [their] subjects."[1] This kind of commentary clearly relies on theories of the pure artistic gaze propounded in the *l'art pour l'art* movement and amplified in modernist aesthetics. Victorian sentimental art, so the usual story goes, is based on assumptions about the interrelations of aesthetics, ethics, and everyday life that were delegitimated in the course of the nineteenth century.

Even as some modernist art has been taken to task for its rejection of ordinary experience, sentimental art has never fully reemerged from its classification as subaesthetic. Recent exhibitions of realist and Pre-Raphaelite canvases have celebrated the Victorians' social vision, as long as it remains, in the words of a curator of the 1997 National Gallery exhibit *The Victorians, British Painting 1837–1901,* "distinctly highbrow": "We certainly have not tried to recreate the exhibitions of Victorian painting held by the Victorians themselves," the exhibit catalog explains, "abundant as they were in what Nathaniel Hawthorne called . . . 'little pathoses and fancynesses.'" The criteria for inclusion in the exhibition—technical "refinement," resistance to ready interpretation, ambiguity—would have pleased late-Victorian aesthetes, so perhaps it is not surprising that most of the paintings exhibited came from the second half of the century. Decadent critics considered subjectivity displayed as impressionistic perceptual distortion to be revolutionary; subjectivity as emotional exaggeration was simply embarrassing. So, one historian of Victorian art in Britain has concluded, the early part of the nineteenth century is best passed over as an unfortunate period in which "those painters . . . who produced the most readily comprehensible narratives, or could satisfy the most widely experienced of the simpler emotions, were naturally held in the highest estimation" by the nouveaux riches who had no regard for recognized rules of good taste.[2]

Craftsmanship, artistic control, and detachment: these characterize a properly aesthetic attitude against which bathetic sentimentalism is measured. In fact, where sentimentalism has been recuperated in recent criticism, it is posed in stark opposition to modern touchstones of aesthetic value. In this feminizing discourse, so the argument goes, feeling, emotion, and mundane experience make their claim on the public imagination. "Modernist detractors of Victorian painting," one art historian has recently argued, "see only sentimentality where contemporary critics saw a complex orchestration of emotional response"; expecting to be affected by sentiment, Victorian viewers "were less inhibited than modern art viewers."[3] But such accounts of sentimental art, whether sympathetic or critical, proceed by describing as self-evident the characteristics of the object under scrutiny. A typical instance is the treatment of Thomas Hall's genre scene *One Touch of Nature makes the whole World Kin* (1867) (Figure 4.1). In one account it stands as a documentary record of "the enthralled response" of popular audiences to contemporary painting;

Figure 4.1. Thomas P. Hall, *One Touch of Nature makes the whole World Kin*, 1867.

the painting functions as evidence of the childlike, feminized, sentimental viewing experience. In a slightly more complicated reading, another critic recognizes, in part at least, the cultural work represented in this image of viewing, saying that the painting acts as a "celebration of the transparency of naturalistic art and the success of nineteenth-century genre in mobilizing sentiment in the interests of a cohesive social order."[4]

In both cases the painting is taken as a record of the immediacy of the interaction between the audience and painting, although to somewhat different ends. That such an image could be said to record transparency at any level points precisely to the ways in which we have continued to regard the sentimental as an uncritical, instinctive emotional response. What this painting foregrounds is, rather, the constructedness of the sentimental response. The title suggests that these urban viewers (so identified by the omnibus in the background) are reacting to a landscape painting; in the familiar formula of the period, disparate city dwellers are momentarily united by their admiration for the beauties of nature, the realm, as the grouping suggests, of feminine and childlike pleasures. That the women and children show the strongest connection to the scene (the connoisseur on the left analyzes, the gentleman in the back keeps his distance, the drayman notices the omnibus driver's call, to which the rest are oblivious) only reinforces the seemingly spontaneous response. But what the painting also emphasizes is that this is not, in fact, a "touch of nature" to which they respond, but a commodified object displayed in a shop window. Although at first we might be tempted to see the audience *in* the canvas as a mirror image of the audience looking *at* the canvas, the frame that seems to prop up the group in the window decisively separates our gaze from theirs, as do the table and the post on the right. And that separation is crucial for understanding the effect Hall is after.

The spectator occupies two possible positions in relation to the work. One is that of the artist, whose eye frames the crowd on what looks like an easel, turning the different classes into one pleasing tableau, in the manner of the images hanging at the top of the picture. That is, what "makes them kin" is less their response to the painting they observe than the artist's ability to turn them into a sentimental grouping, to provide the naturalistic touch that transforms the transient and everyday into a static, harmonious aesthetic whole. Hall's painting, then, is not itself a sentimental genre scene (which relies on the seeming absence of "aesthetic" technique in its effort to make an immediate connection between the audience and the image). It depicts the construction of the sentimental genre scene and casts the sentimental as a privileged perspective created by the eye of the artist.

The second possible position of the spectator in Hall's painting complicates even further any notion that this is a picture about the innocent, natural enjoyment of art and suggests yet another way of approaching sentimentality in the period. Located inside the shop, the spectator is allied with the perspective of the art dealer, who eyes this audience as prospective customers, a view emphasized by the inscription of "bank" on the omnibus at the top of the grouping. Although they probably are not potential buyers of the painting itself (with the exception of the connoisseur, who, significantly, is *not* looking at the painting appreciated by the rest of the crowd), they do represent the varied and growing audience in the period for cheap reproductions. The image enjoyed by the unskilled eye of everyone from the street sweep to the women to the middle-class gentleman is passed over by the trained eye of the well-to-do man on the left, who examines more closely the image propped lower in the window. Is the joke on him, the man too cultured to appreciate a simple natural scene? Or is it on the uncritical admirers of a mere touch of nature, on the group that becomes a stock set of representatives of the varied social classes that purchase engravings and periodical reproductions? In the latter case, the sentimentality of the assembled spectators might function as a send-up of these new consumers of culture, who represent the collapse of commercial and aesthetic value indistinguishable by them but easily spotted by the art dealer anxious to turn a profit. The art dealer, like the omnibus driver, arranges for the transport of all classes. In this reading, the two possible perspectives converge, for the artist turning out images for a profit cannot be distinguished from the art dealer operating from the same motives. Such a treatment would make this painting fit comfortably into the late 1860s, when some painters refused to show their works in the crowded exhibition rooms of the Royal Academy, where engravers were busily at work reproducing visitors' favorite paintings for distribution. Instead, several young artists chose to exhibit their paintings in private settings visited only by more educated audiences.

My interest in this essay lies in how sentimentalism negotiated between the popular and the aesthetic at a moment when these distinctions seemed anything but settled. In the early nineteenth century, few representations of Victorian viewers of art suggest the orderly and codified responses seen in Hall's work. What was the process by which heterogeneous spectators like those in Hall's painting became transfixed by the aesthetic gaze? Sentimentality, I want to argue, offered important strategies for mediating the relationship between emerging ideas of an embodied viewer—the spectator regarded as a site of physical sensation that was felt to be inherently temporal, shifting, diverse—and the traditional claims of art's special social status. Early Victorian sentimental art evoked a mode of aesthetic response with potentially unsettling political implications, as some contemporaries recognized. My test case for this view of sentimentality will be Richard Redgrave's *The Sempstress* (1844), a canvas often taken as exemplary of the genre. Appealing to sensual pleasures, yet yoking them to recognized codes of aesthetic value, such a work deftly performs and contains anxieties about art in a democratic age.

I would also like to suggest one explanation for why modern viewers have taken the sentimental gaze as self-evident, to such an extent that we can mistake an obvious construction of it for the real thing. Like the viewers in Hall's painting, we are conditioned to be enthralled by the artwork, to grant its status as a fetish that can compensate for the triviality of the everyday. Although some critics have exposed the artificiality of that attitude and dated its inception roughly to the period in which Hall produced his painting, art criticism proceeds by assuming the autonomy of the single image, separating it out from either social or artistic context. It is a mode of viewing of which some early-Victorian painters and art critics could only dream, confronted as they were by audiences who could not be made to stand still, who were not in awe of a work of art, and who saw paintings in conditions in which one work was pressed tightly against another from ceiling to floor. "The language of painting," one contemporary critic lamented, had "lost its divinity"; a new generation of spectators regarded even acknowledged masterpieces as "soulless . . . embellishments . . . as mere antique curiosities."[5] These were not leisured viewers contemplating treasures in their studies or in museums. They were middle- and working-class audiences who regarded art as the equivalent of window shopping or going to the theater, as a brief amusement during an afternoon's holiday. Not only were they provokingly peripatetic in taking their aesthetic pleasures, their movement prompted some observers to recall emerging theories of perception, which stressed the instability of an aesthetic experience lodged firmly in the flesh.

Seen in this context, sentimental art becomes more than a byway in art history against which modernism rebels. It looks like an influential means of representing and responding to new ways of seeing. If we ignore the very moment at which the field of art accommodated changing cultural and perceptual conditions, we can hardly recognize how those conditions are in turn coded within works we call modern. By dehistoricizing the modernist gaze and failing to connect it to the period out of which it evolved, we simply replicate in our own practice its apparent hermeticism. Recognizing the modes of seeing at stake in this formative aesthetic moment makes it possible for us to trace important connections between such seemingly disparate images as Redgrave's *The Sempstress* and J. M. W. Turner's *The Angel Standing in the Sun* (1846). The latter has too often been taken as an early proclamation of the modernist position, a declaration of "perceptual autonomy, an exalted announcement of the ungroundedness of vision."[6] Read through the codes of sentimentality I will sketch out in the following pages, this apparently unsentimental canvas reveals a quite specifically grounded version of aesthetic experience. Through my treatment of two seemingly incompatible paintings, I will suggest how this chapter of art history has the potential to unfix our own constructions of the connections between popular and privileged perspectives, and between art and everyday life.

Epistemological shifts in contemporary philosophy and the sciences reverberated through British discourses on the arts in the early 1840s. Distinctions between subjective and objective vision and between experiential and ideal perception had come under attack in recent physiological research. The resulting uncertainty is captured in the work of British philosopher and historian of science William Whewell, a champion of Kantian theories of a priori conceptions who found it increasingly difficult to resist scientific evidence that seemed to bear out British empiricism. In his grand synthesis of the state of epistemology in the 1840s, *The Philosophy of the Inductive Sciences,* he treads a fine line between the sensationalism supported in some physiological research and the idealism that had bolstered British reflections on the arts since Coleridge. "No apprehension of things is purely ideal," he admits; at the same time, "no experience of external things is purely sensational." The difficulty of the resulting position—neither entirely here nor there—left art critics struggling to mark out a "science of taste" that would, in the words of a writer in the *Athenaeum,* separate out "archetypal ideas" that were "universal in the nature of man" from "what is divergent and particular to individuals."[7]

As Martha Woodmansee has demonstrated, physiological accounts of aesthetic experience had been floated earlier in the century; what had changed was the ballast that associationist theories in particular had received from other fields. "Our minds," Archibald Alison had written in his popular *Essays on the Nature and Principles of Taste* (reprinted throughout the 1830s and 1840s), "instead of being governed by the character of external objects," can read into them "a character which does not belong to them." Alison's aesthetic sensationalism gained new force from biological studies in the 1820s and 1830s that suggested not only that perception was firmly grounded in organic processes but that a Cartesian mind/body dualism could no longer be sustained. The changing intellectual climate meant that Francis Jeffrey's "Essay on Beauty," which was first published as an 1811 review of Archibald Alison's *Essays,* looked remarkably current when it was recast as the 1842 *Encyclopaedia Britannica* entry on the subject. Arguing against the universality of aesthetic principles, Jeffrey formulated a theory of taste that fits both with the populist political rhetoric of the forties and with some strands of physiological argument. "There is scarcely any class in society which could not be shown to have peculiar . . . perceptions of beauty," Jeffrey argued in support of a situational aesthetics, "because they have associations with external objects, which are peculiar to themselves, and have no existence for any other persons"; taste is a matter of personal feeling, and "all tastes are equally just and correct, in so far as each individual speaks only of his emotion."[8]

What had been in Jeffrey a typically romantic celebration of emotional experience as opposed to an overly rationalized and regularized explanation of taste evolves at this juncture into a rather different set of issues. Science, feeling, and popular taste were increasingly allied in public discussions of the arts. Scientific empiricism was not necessarily the enemy but more often the ally of those who urged that art's role was to stir the passions of the populace. Where Jeffrey confidently evoked the category of emotion, critics now had trouble pinning down distinctions among intellect, feeling, and sensual experience. In one essay devoted to explaining, in the manner of Jeffrey, a fundamentally democratic theory of aesthetic experience, *ideas, sensations,* and *feelings* are used as interchangeable terms, and they are employed to describe both the impressions all viewers will receive from a painting and the idiosyncratic element of individual acts of viewing. Some "objects confessedly affect all men alike," this critic argues, thus testifying to the existence of sentiments that are "universal in the nature of man"; at the same time, these effects are only felt by "well-organized" natures, whose capacities have been "cultivated" according to conventional notions of feeling and taste. According to his or her unique physical makeup and to the specific circumstances of his or her act of viewing, each individual will be "differently affected" by a painting, and thus all "affections are entitled to an equal respect." On the other hand, "the main end of art" is to be "consonant to the feelings of the sensitive and the educated."[9]

This jumble of early-nineteenth-century ideas about vision and taste is characteristic of writing about art in the period. The notion that taste or aesthetic value was timeless and universal had to be defended at a moment when many claimed that not only style and subject matter but also judgment and appreciation were constrained by locale, economic conditions, and political configurations. If there were no fixed principles to redirect British painting, one writer suggested, perhaps exploiting these constraints would at least produce something distinctive. By consulting the tastes of the "crowds that linger around" the National Gallery "on our annual holidays," British painters might receive the necessary "impulses" to address the question of the day: What "is to be the theme" of a truly "national art"? "The greatest geniuses," countered a writer in *Fraser's,* were never constrained by their audiences; they "invariably burst through the circumstances influencing those around them," intent only on pursuing "those principles which are founded on the immutable laws which govern the world." The field of art should be understood as hermetic, impenetrable to contamination by the public gaze. In fact, the public could hardly be said to be engaged in any kind of aesthetic transaction; the ability to "see" a work of art was possible only for "minds previously cultivated . . . by continual observation of such works themselves." Taste and judgment operated within a closed system. Artists who consorted too closely with the body politic had only themselves to blame if they produced paintings "better suited to a brothel than to instruct the people in the real uses of art to a nation." To concede that artists should satisfy something called "public taste," agreed the *Blackwood's* art critic, was to admit that the fine arts never had been "in their true position"; such an admission would mean sacrificing aesthetic value to the fancies of "diseased ignorance."[10]

Such metaphors of contagion by contact bring to the surface precisely what many commentators on the arts were attempting to suppress: the growing emphasis on the ways in which the perception of art was tied to tangible bodies. If eighteenth-century British accounts of the aesthetic tended, in Terry Eagleton's assessment, toward "a steady undermining of the mind in the name of the body," in the 1840s it became unclear whether this sort of head/heart, mind/body separation could be sustained. Not only did critics engage in a battle over whether aesthetic experience was a matter of feeling and sensation or an "intellectual pursuit . . . to be intellectually understood," the various sides were themselves in disarray over whether such a difference existed, whether feeling designated something existing in the artwork or in the eyes of the beholder, and whether those eyes were guided by culture or nature, ideal forms or physical impulses. "Taste," as an *Athenaeum* writer put it, now appeared to be neither a rational construction nor a transcendental ideal, but "altogether an affair of sensation; and its laws are, and can be, no other than those of the living machines of which sensation is the attribute. The theory of taste is part of the natural history of man," a history that seemed to be unfolding in the public galleries even as he wrote. While art critics struggled to redefine the proper practice and theory of art, the mass audiences visiting museums and public exhibitions in the hundreds of thousands during the 1830s and 1840s pushed for a changing of the aesthetic guard. Retreading the old ground no longer satisfied these culture consumers. With "the awakening of the mental and moral faculties" of a hitherto "rude, uneducated populace," commented one observer, the fine arts were now bound to follow a new "pathway, as it were, through a vast and hitherto unexplored country." Mapping out this terra incognita proved difficult in the absence of fixed aesthetic rules. Critics and artists attending exhibitions of paintings confronted not dispassionate spectators, but passionate, opinionated viewers who demanded to know "*how* one man's taste is not as lawful as another's."[11] In some contemporary accounts of exhibitions in the period, these viewers functioned as all too graphic reminders of the unsettling potential of embodied perception.

The combination of changing theories and altered practice precipitated a sense of crisis of the field of fine art in the 1840s, a period contemporaries characterized, in the charged European rhetoric of the moment, as "a revolution." If the field was not prepared to reform itself, warned a popular journal, there were "tens of thousands" of viewers who were prepared to "impel . . . [it] forward" by "an application of force from without."[12] These pressures came to bear in particular on the annual Royal Academy exhibitions, where roughly a quarter of a million heterogeneous visitors each summer judged the latest productions of

Figure 4.2. From *Illustrated London News,* 20 May 1843, 338.

the art world.[13] Despite the Academy's official sanctioning of the works hung in a given year, this scene of viewing was anything but "officialized" in the manner of a modern museum, where a "ritual separation of subject and object" is enforced through a series of regulations and rules.[14] A representation of visitors to the 1843 exhibition from the *Illustrated London News* (Figure 4.2) marks the difference between the relation of viewers to the artwork in this location and the orderly transaction figured in Hall's painting twenty years later. Here there is no mutual point of admiration; even the gazes of figures apparently within the same family groupings (husband, wife, and children in the center and on the far right) are turned in different directions. Several of the viewers are not even looking at the paintings (the skeptical working figure in the cap on the right side of the image, with his back turned resolutely to the wall, and the woman with the fatigued expression near the center).

The point is not simply that the works crammed together on the walls compete for attention. That was also the case at the exhibition in Westminster Hall the same year (Figure 4.3), an event orchestrated by the government to promote British art. The *Illustrated London News* engraving of the Westminster exhibition endorses the official line that the fine arts could build a cohesive national culture. Contained within this clearly sacralized space, the visitors move in cohesive groups, most looking up-

Figure 4.3. From *Illustrated London News,* 8 July 1843, 17.

ward and standing fixed before particular images from Britain's national history. The gestures of nearly every spectator correspond to those of figures on the walls, illustrating the civic discourse surrounding the Westminster exhibition: through the act of viewing works of art, individuals would learn to see themselves not as individuals, but as citizens engaged in a common public history.

Against such a vision of public harmony, the engraving of the Royal Academy exhibition highlights particularity of expression and gesture. Each visitor in the crowded room is engaged, paradoxically, in an individualized act of viewing. Moreover, looking in this representation is not an isolated act of the eyes (except in the case of the children in the foreground, who appear stunned by the spectacle around them), but a process involving the movement of the body. Whereas in the Westminster exhibition engraving the circulating figures seem frozen in place, the Academy engraving attempts to capture movement, bustle, the restless press of bodies continuing through the seemingly endless line of doorways. If anything is lifeless and static here it is the paintings, a point brought out by the disillusioned commentary of the *Illustrated London News,* where the engraving appeared. After "loung[ing] . . . with the common crowd," the paper's critic condemned the year's offerings as "common-place," lamenting the way in which art had been too much affected by the whims of a "rambl[ing]" audience. What he had seen at the exhibition was not art that enforced attention and subdued the crowds into proper acts of viewing: "The eye is not arrested here, dazzled there, fixed anywhere, by prominent indications of mind-mastery."[15] The proper relationship between art and its audience had been inverted: art is frozen in place by the popular gaze. There is no seemly separation between subject and object in this kind of transaction. Not only do the spectators fail to display a properly aestheticized response to the artworks, the man on the far left of the engraving seems about to commit the ultimate faux pas: he starts to reach out as though to touch the painting in front of him, imagining that he stands, as the height of the work might lead him to think, on an equal footing. As the engraving intimates, the paintings on the walls are pushed to the margins of contemporary life, occupying a space not sacred but, as the rambling activity of the "mediocre class" indicates, a mere extension of the everyday.

This annual spectacle of viewing, which was supposed to reinforce art's special status in its display of works by members of the Academy, was seen as symptomatic of the aesthetic chaos plaguing the field. In the widely reviewed *Hand-Book of Taste, or How to Observe Works of Art* (1843), the scene at the Royal Academy is made exemplary of the problems inherent in the theory and practice of spectatorship. "Do not permit yourself to be deceived," the handbook warns, by the mode of viewing experienced there, "where every thing is seen through a false medium, distracted as the eye must be by the bustle of company, the gaudy dresses, the glitter of frames upon the wall." Art should be contemplated apart from such distractions, or mere vision would be confused for a genuine aesthetic experience. Viewers needed to learn the difference between looking through the body and appreciating with the mind, for "the vision, unaided by education or other intellectual endowments, is no longer a sufficient guide to the spectator," whose attention is all too inclined to wander. Untrained looking remained too much an individual affair, affected by physical organs, prey to "seduction" by showy paintings that catered to the mere "visual gratification of the observer." Taste was, to be sure, partly a product of physical processes as recent scientific discoveries had demonstrated, but among men of "well-regulated minds, and of sufficient experience and education," it was agreed that taste was also one of "those things which can be submitted to rule." Part of the mark of good taste was knowing how to control one's body and to limit one's impulse of physical engagement with external stimuli. Spectators must learn to stand still, to fix their gaze, and to let the artwork "transmit" its power to them. True aesthetic engagement meant not attempting to size up the work, but permitting oneself to be "act[ed] upon" by it.[16] If it was no longer possible to ground taste in a realm of either emotion or reason set apart from the stimulation of the body, the only possible response, according to this handbook, was to chasten the body and to enforce a series of rules. How else could one explain, as a writer later in the period wondered, how "the sensuousness of the hungry ploughman enjoying his slice of bacon is sublimated into the poetic rapture of Keats with a ripe peach melting in his mouth?"[17]

Richard Redgrave, an associate of the Royal Academy in the 1840s and a seminal figure in organizing national art education and the new national museums, campaigned for a different way of understanding the relation between popular enjoyment and educated aesthesis. In his many lectures on art, he attempted to sift through the shifting aesthetic ground. Perception, Redgrave insisted, is "entirely empirical" and inseparable from physiological processes; there "may be a difference in degree, there is none in kind" between popular and educated experiences of the work of art. There were indeed identifiable rules that could be taught to art's new audiences, but these were not the product of an innate sense or superior reason on the part of some viewers. Rather, they represented a "cumulative stock of experience," a Lockean legacy "which had it to be separately gathered by each individual, life would be wasted in preliminary study."[18] Although he never recognizes it as such, what Redgrave works out is an organicist idea of aesthetic knowledge that resonates with Auguste Comte's positivist epistemology of the same period.[19] The cumulative experience of individuals formed a national store of knowledge continually modified by specific encounters with works of art; this store was what was known as taste. Redgrave insisted on the local and limited nature of this body of experiences, influenced, as all empirical sensation must be, by race as well as by physical and social environment. Taste was, in effect, the movement between particular and general—a give-and-take between personal and accumulated experience—but it was never generalizable into a fixed, universal ideal. As a practicing painter, Redgrave felt no need to move beyond particular transactions with an artifact to posit an aesthetic universal; for him what counted was the relation between the spectator and the image on the canvas. This concern allowed him to work out a version of aesthetic experience that sounds remarkably modern, and certainly much less defensive than those of many of his contemporaries.

Yet despite his empiricist leanings and his insistence on the affinity of perception in all classes, Redgrave was not ready to give up altogether on the autonomy of the work of art. In a statement that recalls the guidelines in *The Hand-Book of Taste,* Redgrave outlines an ideal scene of viewing. "To be seen with pleasure," he asserts, paintings "must be considered as pictures . . . they should . . . not be in close juxtaposition, but be enclosed, isolated, and surrounded, if with a surface decoration at all, with one which is quiet, unobtrusive, and giving repose and rest to the eye—if they are to be enjoyed either by the poor man in his cottage or the rich man in his hall."[20] Although in context Redgrave is addressing the fashion of converting images into items of household decoration such as wallpaper, his recommendation does resonate with contemporary discussions of the conditions at the Royal Academy, including his own discussions on other occasions. Redgrave's audience would not have been likely to encounter his own popular paintings outside the Academy; for more than fifty years he was a regular contributor to the annual exhibitions. But if his works had never been displayed in isolated surroundings, many of them enact the mode of viewing he describes here. In particular, *The Sempstress* (Figure 4.4), first exhibited in 1843, exemplifies such an act of aesthetic appreciation while accommodating it to Redgrave's empirical theories. Through this image he deftly negotiates the perceptual chaos of the 1840s. Exploiting physical sensation and emphasizing the sensual experience of art so alarming to many contemporaries, he then stabilizes the viewing eye. At the same time, he explores the fading boundary between the everyday and the properly aesthetic only to reinscribe it by demonstrating the priority of the latter. If the figure of the sempstress is a seemingly realistic image of a kind familiar from the illustrated newspapers of the day, Redgrave frames it so as to highlight the fact that this "must," as he says in his lecture, "be considered as [a] pictur[e]," the production of an academician. In order to sustain effects both of intimacy and of aesthetic distance, Redgrave draws on the emerging codes of Victorian sentimentality.

The differences between an early sketch of *The Sempstress* and the surviving version from 1846 (which appears, from engravings of the original, to be nearly identical to it) show how this image evolved from a

Figure 4.4. Richard Redgrave, *The Sempstress,* 1846. Forbes Art Gallery.

straightforward illustration of Thomas Hood's poem "The Song of the Shirt." In the sketch, the lighting highlights the shirt (the focus of Hood's title); in the painting, the lighting emphasizes the sempstress's body, falling at its brightest point on her neck and breasts. The lower half of her body in the sketch is covered by the shirt and a dark shadow. Here, Redgrave moves the table to the far right, awkwardly manipulates the position of the sempstress's front leg, and calls our attention to the placement by altering the lighting to include her knee. The stippled brushwork of the painting reinforces the artist's appeal to her body language; contemporary reviewers commented on the almost tactile experience of viewing the painting.

In an English genre tradition that usually traded in gentle domestic or pastoral scenes, Redgrave produces an image with a directly sensual appeal. The Dutch style and coloring of the painting would only have augmented this effect for his contemporaries. Although paintings by Dutch masters were widely collected in the first half of the nineteenth century, they were also made to stand in many accounts of the period for a tradition that had "utterly abandon[ed] the power to teach for the art of pleasing." "George IV. was the appropriate fosterer," remarked one critic in the ultimate Victorian moral put-down, "of the taste for Dutch pictures."[21] The sempstress's red dress and her iconic resemblance to the solitary, penitent Magdalen of the Dutch tradition, reinforce Redgrave's attempt to exploit the viewer's physical response. She also recalls, of course, images of the annunciation, but in her case there would be no question of immaculate conception. The implied connection between her line of work and prostitution was common in writings of the period.[22] The spectator is called on to approach this image, at least in the first instance, through an emphatically embodied form of vision.

Judging by the language of his critics, Redgrave's painting draws on a dangerous version of aesthetic experience. It was clearly linked by those who disliked it with the growing anxiety in the art world about the effect of the embodied spectator. Thackeray, for example, who had often expressed support for popular participation in the Academy exhibitions, as well as for Redgrave's earlier paintings of working women in distress, complained that *The Sempstress* played too clearly to the lowest common denominator. His harsh review of the work performed the critic's duty, as he saw it, "to shake any man roughly by the shoulder who seems dangerously affected by art." A writer for the *Athenaeum* used Redgrave's painting as a perfect example of art's tendency to provoke only "the power of feeling and association, which varies with every individual." And those who praised *The Sempstress* did so precisely for this effect of intimate interchange with the viewer.[23] For all of these critics, the "sentimentality" of the painting—a word used in nearly every instance to characterize this relationship with the spectator—is linked not just to an affective reaction, but also to a physical one. In other words, the work dramatizes for these reviewers the interconnection of emotion and physiological sensation current in contemporary aesthetic debates.

I have explored at some length elsewhere this reading of the painting.[24] What concerns me here is the way in which Redgrave contains the embodied response so as to make his painting exemplary of the transformation from what James Clifford has called "an excessive, sometimes even rapacious" relation to art objects into the "rule-governed, meaningful desire" so characteristic of late nineteenth-century museum culture.[25] The spectator's first point of attraction in the painting is obviously the female figure, but, as most in Redgrave's audience would have recognized, this scene is part of a sentimental narrative genre that demands that all details of the canvas be read. That is, it provokes the eye to wander and invites the active participation of the audience in constructing the meaning of the painting, replicating the habits of viewing that so bothered contemporaries. But as Thackeray noted in his critique of *The Sempstress,* something here does not fit with the conventional turn this movement should take. Unlike the works of the English master of the genre, Hogarth, or the paintings of Redgrave's popular contemporaries Frith or Mulready, the details do not lead to any complications or commentaries on the subject at hand. So while the eye may be prompted to be active, the mind is not, particularly for an audience who had no need to decode a narrative so familiar to members of every class: Hood's poem had, as one Victorian put it, become "something of a folk song . . . sung about the streets by poor people," printed on cotton handkerchiefs, reprinted on ballad sheets and nearly every newspaper. Thackeray ironically dismisses the details of the room (the clock, the medicine bottles, the flickering light, the view out the window) as "vast labours of intellect," meaning, of course, that they are just too obvious, mere accessories to the story, not enhancements of it.[26]

Thackeray identifies a significant departure from convention in this case. The details function, in fact, to arrest the narrative development of the painting, because Redgrave is after a quite different effect. The objects in the room, while connected to the story, also draw our attention away from it by the manner in which they are treated. The most obvious example is the grouping of pots, pans, and the water jug and basin on the left side of the painting. Although the jug and basin exist in the early sketch, they are behind the table; here, with the addition of the shelf of pans above them, they form a distinct ensemble in an area of the painting separated from the central figure by the large shadow cutting across the canvas. The relation of the objects to the figure is primarily one of coloring, lighting, and brushwork; the treatment of the jug echoes that of the sempstress's dress. The same kind of tactile engagement provoked by the figure is repeated here in the case of the material object, but because this area of the canvas functions as a clearly arranged still life, our reaction is somewhat different. The sensuous response is abstracted from sensual pleasure—this is not a still life of food or flowers but of inanimate objects—and focused on the elements of composition and artistic treatment. The link between the jug and the figure, then, prompts us to move from our first reaction of physical pleasure to aesthesis.

Other details in the painting work in related ways. The window, for example, while reinforcing the narrative (another sempstress presumably works in another attic window), functions as an allusion beyond the story to one of the characteristic devices in early Netherlandish paintings.[27] The treatment of the room around the sempstress is an assemblage of such academic references. And the figure herself, as I have already noted, recalls the religious iconography both of the penitent Magdalen and of the Virgin Mary of the annunciation. If the subject of Redgrave's painting has the status of a folk image, his treatment of it takes it out of the realm of the everyday and into the realm of the fine arts. Unlike realist paintings of the 1850s, his canvas does not celebrate the beauty of common subjects, but the skill of the educated eye that can transform the commonplace into a work of art.[28] This purpose comes through in the treatment of vision within the painting. Part of the pathos of the figure of the sempstress comes from the difference between her position and those of the iconographic figures she resembles. There is no light dawning on her upturned face to indicate that she has achieved a spiritual vision. As the view out the window emphasizes, she cannot see beyond the bounds of her own situation—even what looks to be outside merely replicates the scene within. This clearly bothered one of the many reinterpreters of Redgrave's painting, Anna Blunden, who changed the view to include a prominently displayed church steeple.[29] If any salvation occurs here, it is only the salvation by the artist, who is able to transform the mundane into the beautiful, to stop time (as the frozen clock movement indicates) against the movement of nature (represented in the dawning of the sun) and to give the sempstress an immortality that will last beyond the death predicated in the narrative.

The *Athenaeum* critic of the 1844 exhibition complained that *The Sempstress* was "too sentimental" because the canvas achieved only "a sort of theatrical and elegant sorrow."[30] Such a comment seems appropriate to the kinds of stage-managed effects I have been describing, for what Redgrave appears to be after is a picture that incites an affective and physical response in the first instance and then carefully guides the viewer to a different relation to the subject altogether. Like Hall's *One Touch of Nature makes the whole World Kin,* this painting foregrounds the artist's construction of the sentimental perspective. Like Hall, Redgrave emphasizes rather than dissimulates aesthetic technique to manipulate the relation between the audience and the canvas. As Thackeray noted, Redgrave does not intellectualize this image; such a treatment would not be consonant with Redgrave's insistence on the empirical nature of aesthetic experience. In its attempt to move between the viewer's immediate, embodied response to the painting and his or her ability to connect it to a series of iconographic and figural allusions, the work approximates Redgrave's notion of an accumulated stock of aesthetic experiences that links particular and general. But his painting is immediately accessible only to a certain degree. As the dark table in the foreground indicates, we are not to imagine that we can simply step into the image; we stand at a certain remove, at a point firmly outside the canvas. This is, as Redgrave stressed in his ideal scene of viewing, a picture, one we are meant to stand in front of, to allow our eye to wander across, but only within the parameters of the frame. The elements that contain the spectator's initial response to the image also control the eye's propensity to stray across the walls of the Royal Academy from one image to the next. Redgrave corrects for the viewer who is unable to articulate between disparate images until, in a moment of visual surfeit, the pictures become simply so much decorated wall paper. The objects in the sempstress's room, as Redgrave recommended in the optimal setting for a painting, isolate and surround the central figure, clearly marking her off from whatever distractions hang nearby.

After attracting the desiring eye, *The Sempstress* offers it "unobtrusive" spots of "quiet" and "repose," transforming enjoyment to admiration of effect. Aesthetic sentiment does not represent in this instance a collapse of subject and object, a too-close relation between spectator and painting. Nor does it indicate the inability of the artist to achieve perspective. In *The Sempstress* Redgrave employs sentimentality to engage an audience as they are perceived at a particular historical moment and then uses it to put them in their place.

At first glance, Turner's *The Angel Standing in the Sun* (Figure 4.5), exhibited at the Royal Academy two years after Redgrave's painting, seems to have little to do with the contemporary controversies of the 1840s. Anything but visual equilibrium appears to be at work here. Not only does the brilliance of the canvas (now much faded, as all of Turner's canvases are, from their original coloring) prompt an instinctive backing away from the work, the historical figures within the canvas have all turned

Figure 4.5. J. M. W. Turner, *The Angel Standing in the Sun,* 1846. Copyright Clore Collection, Tate Gallery, London/Art Resource, New York.

their heads away from the glare. On the one hand, this doubling of effect—viewers mimic the action of the painting's subjects—challenges the separation of audience and object by drawing the spectator into the subject of the painting. On the other hand, it has been taken by many modern critics to be Turner's way of signaling his distance from and disdain for his audience and announcing the "revelatory force in true art."[31] Unlike Redgrave's painting, this image seems to give the viewer little assistance in relating to its cryptic subject: it is emphatically not a painting of everyday life. From Ruskin, who disliked this picture, to a modern museum guidebook, critics have treated it as a fantastic product of Turner's private imagination. "Probably painted in Turner's studio," the guidebook comments, "as it has no reference to external details."[32]

And yet we can assume from nineteenth-century accounts of Turner's practice that *The Angel Standing in the Sun* was not painted in his studio at all, but on a wall of the Royal Academy exhibition rooms. Turner notoriously used the varnishing days before the opening of the exhibition to create his compositions and color palettes. One eyewitness commented on how the artist would arrive with little more than a monochrome sketch and then transform it into a visual display of colors that would distract from any other paintings in the room. Turner deliberately heightened his tones to compete with paintings in the same room and had even been known on one occasion to tone down part of a rival's picture.[33] Like Redgrave, Turner painted with a keen awareness of the conditions and habits of viewing prevalent at the annual Academy exhibitions. Not only was he aware of them, his name had become synonymous with the dangerous aesthetic theory that appealed too much to the visual gratification of the observer. The "judicious" critic could only "grieve," the *Edinburgh Review* lamented, that he produced paintings for the exhibition that were designed to "captivate the admiration of those 'barren spectators'" who admired mere effect. *The Hand-Book of Taste,* while not mentioning Turner by name, took pains to point to his work as exemplary of the very worst errors of contemporary aesthetic theory and practice. The distracted spectators at the exhibition were all too likely to respond to a painting "tone[d] ... for the express purpose of attracting attention" by "casting its neighbour into shade." Pleasure, the *Hand-Book* reminded its readers, should be only a "moderate impression ... produce[d] upon our organs." Pleasurable sensations should not be confused with those that produced too strong an effect, exciting a visual stimulation beyond the rules of good taste. A picture of this type was merely painful, like in kind (in a clear reference to several of Turner's recent pictures) to "looking fixedly upon the sun."[34]

If Turner had committed this error before, he certainly flaunted it again in *The Angel Standing in the Sun,* where the glare spreads across the canvas in a wash of yellows, golds, and reds. While certain critics of the day were insisting that the value of an artwork amounted to more than the viewer's visual perception of it, in this painting the visual effect of the image seems difficult to separate from the image itself. That is, the subject of Turner's picture is allied to the viewer's reaction to it: it chronicles the effect on the body of this revelatory sun. Several art historians have elaborated on Turner's familiarity with contemporary theories of embodied vision and emphasized the way in which both the form and content of *The Angel Standing in the Sun* seem to illustrate such theories.[35] Grounded as these accounts are in the intellectual climate of the period, they tell only one side of the story. Like readings of the painting that cast the figure of the angel as a self-portrait, they approach the work as a kind of romantic lyric, a transcription of Turner's own mental or perceptual experience. But this is not a work that was meant to be overheard, as it were. It was dialogically engaged not only with the works around it but in a specific scene of viewing. The scientific and aesthetic theory that informed Turner's work could not by the 1840s be easily abstracted from the contemporary debates about the cultural politics of spectatorship. Turner neglected the stability of his medium because, as he made clear, the images he exhibited at the Royal Academy were made for the occasion; as one contemporary commented when trying to find an analogy for Turner's mode of painting in situ, these works were "more like some of the transformation scenes at the pantomimes than anything else."[36] They were the performance art of their day, made to be experienced as a theatrical event within the spectacle of the exhibitions.

Art historians' neglect of this context and their overemphasis on Turner's theoretical bent has made *The Angel Standing in the Sun* seem more idiosyncratic than it really is. For example, when Jonathan Crary suggests that Turner uses the angel, "an object with no referent in the world," as "a sign of the inadequacy of conventional means for representing the hallucinatory abstraction of his intense optical experiences," he neglects the fact that the angel does refer to an existing history of representations in the world of art.[37] Its conventionality explains the slight resemblance between its face and that of Redgrave's sempstress: both are drawing on iconographic expressions and gestures. *The Angel* is a much more conventional image in many ways than those Turner had exhibited in previous years. The figures are nearly all recognizable biblical characters familiar to his audience, and ones that had been the subjects of paintings for centuries (Adam and Eve, Judith with the head of Holofernes). As some reviewers noted with relief, the accompanying passages in this case are from Revelation and Samuel Rogers, not, as in the case of so many of his recent productions, from Turner's own obscure poetic production, the *Fallacies of Hope.* Like the companion painting exhibited the same year, *Undine Giving the Ring to Masaniello* (a subject of two popular London stage productions in the period), the apparent subject of *The Angel Standing in the Sun* is accessible to a wide range of viewers. Moreover, the use of the circular format so characteristic of Turner's painting also seems more conventional here than in a painting such as *The Snowstorm* (1842): in Michelangelo, Rubens, Rembrandt, through to Turner's contemporaries such as John Martin, Francis Danby, and Washington Allston, a circular format is employed in similar scenes of biblical judgment.[38]

Although this is not, then, a scene of the everyday, it is a scene that would not have been unknown to Turner's viewers, and one that would not have surprised them as the subject of a painting exhibited at the Academy. What is surprising is its departure from certain generic expectations. First, the canvas is cabinet size (30 inches square, only slightly larger than Redgrave's painting), an inappropriate match to the epic scale of the subject. As Redgrave commented in his catalog for the Sheepshanks Gallery of contemporary British art, these proportions were standard for sentimental genre scenes: they indicated the status of a picture as "a home delight," as "suited to our private residences" and depicting "subjects . . . such as we can live by and love."[39] On approaching Turner's painting, his audience would expect to see this kind of livable subject, so prevalent, as many contemporaries complained, at the Royal Academy exhibitions; up close, they would find an epic subject cut down to size. The joke—at the expense of both genre scenes (despite its physical accessibility, this subject is certainly not calculated to inspire home delight) and epic (this is, after all, one of the grandest biblical epics of them all, as Michelangelo's *Last Judgment* famously displayed)—depends on the movement of the spectator, advancing, sizing up, and attempting to accommodate the expectations of the eye to its actual experience.

The painting's size and subject would have prompted contemporary spectators to indulge their habit of searching for the narrative. As in Redgrave's image, the details of the story from the book of Revelations are all there (the vultures, the chained serpent, the angel with the sword), and, as in Redgrave, these elements frustrate the viewer's effort to make them add up to anything more than what they appear to be. Here again the painting provokes the eye to wander (emphasized in this case by the circular form) and seems to invite the active participation of the audience in constructing its meaning. As in *The Sempstress*, the move to narrative is shut down. This is perhaps one of the reasons Ruskin so disliked the painting; unlike the earlier canvases that he had praised for linking excursive sight to an intellectual process of association, *The Angel Standing in the Sun* resists explanation.[40] The more one tries to sort out details, the more irrelevant they seem to be; for example, the flask in the bottom right-hand corner, apparently added at the last minute, appears to be there simply as an aesthetic object, perhaps in reference to a painting exhibited nearby (a kind of relational move in which Turner often engaged), but not to anything else in the painting.[41] The recognizable figures never fully materialize, remaining, as a reviewer noted, at the level of pictographs rather than actual portraits.[42]

What the painting initiates is movement for the sake of movement, not for the sake of tracing a discernible narrative or symbolic thread. At the exhibition of the previous year, a reviewer had complained about Turner's tendency to create canvases before which the spectator must shift from one viewpoint to another. One could never quite stand still in front of one of his images, the reviewer stated; one constantly had to move around searching for "the exact distance at which nothing becomes something." This only exacerbated the general restlessness of the "uninitiated" who never had learned to stand at the proper distance from a painting. *The Angel Standing in the Sun* is too small to provoke so much bodily movement, although its brightness does prompt a retreat after the more intimate distance suggested by its size. Rather, it seems to substitute the wandering of the eye for the wandering of the body, to move the eye through endless, dizzying circles, an effect only increased by the lack of depth that would allow for an escape in the distance. While the glare makes it difficult to stare at the painting, the form makes it difficult to look away. The eye is caught in a kind of extended *frisson,* a prolonged indulgence in what one writer called in his review of the Academy show that year, the "sin" of the "sensual elements of gratification."[43]

Like *The Sempstress, The Angel Standing in the Sun* was associated by contemporaries with materialist theories of the aesthetic. Both paintings were faulted for a showy appeal, a sense of staged spectacle that would make the viewer mistake visual stimulation for aesthetic effect. And it is in exploiting this contemporary idea of the dangers of sentimental projection—a lack of distance, or sense of identification between perceiver and artwork—that both are able to contain the desires of the audience. Because of his interest in art education, Redgrave takes this project seriously, turning his painting into a kind of template for the proper way to view art. Turner, on the other hand, seems content to treat his canvas as, at one level, an extended joke on contemporary habits of viewing. A reviewer remarked of this painting that it could only be regretted that "no controlling influence exerts its genial restraint" over the work's form or coloring.[44] What the reviewer looked for was a properly contained, recognizably aestheticized image. What Turner offers instead, in the spirit of earlier criticisms of his exhibiting practices, is a version of the old child's game of "made you look." In a painting calculated to catch the audience's eye the moment they enter the room, to outglare the showy array of gilded picture frames and bright dresses circulating at the exhibition and to draw the spectator to stand before it, Turner in effect chastises the spectator for his or her willingness to be led astray. Once the image catches the viewers, it keeps them contained within the frame, challenging them to break out of the circle and move on. Where Redgrave forestalls a too-proximate relation between subject and object by emphasizing privileged perspective, Turner reaches the same end by different means. If the observer is inclined to equate the artwork with his or her perception of it, the artist shows himself a master at manipulating perception: the viewing subject does not control the object, but quite the reverse. The artwork regains its mastery over the audience, but not, as in earlier theories of art, through its elevating effect. This possibility is briefly invoked by the subject of Turner's painting, but quickly subordinated to a very different sense of mastery. In the ultimate sentimentalist ploy, Turner creates a painting that controls the subject by playing on the registers of the body.

Notes

1. Marcia Eaton, "Laughing at the Death of Little Nell: Sentimental Art and Sentimental People," *American Philosophical Quarterly* 26 (1989): 273, 274, 276, 275; E. D. H. Johnson, *Paintings of the British Social Scene from Hogarth to Sickert* (London: Weidenfeld & Nicolson, 1988), 202, 129.

2. Malcom Warner, *The Victorians, British Painting 1837–1901* (Washington, D.C.: National Gallery of Art, 1996), 14; John Steegman, *The Rule of Taste from George I to George IV* (London: Macmillan, 1968), 184.

3. Caroline Arscott, "Sentimentality in Victorian Painting," in *Art for the People: Culture in the Slums of Late Victorian Britain,* ed. Giles Waterfield (London: Dulwich Picture Gallery, 1994), 72.

4. Johnson, *Paintings of the British Social Scene,* 187; Arscott, "Sentimentality in Victorian Painting," 76.

5. "Report from the Select Committee on Fine Arts," *Blackwood's* 50 (1841): 589; George Wallis, "The Improvement of Popular Taste in the Fine Arts," *The People's Journal* 3 (1847): 9.

6. Jonathan Crary, *Techniques of the Observer* (Cambridge: MIT Press, 1990), 143.

7. William Whewell, *The Philosophy of the Inductive Sciences,* 2d ed., 2 vols. (London: Parker, 1847), 2:653; Sir Charles Morgan, "Of Certainty in Taste," *Athenaeum* (2 November 1834): 806.

8. Martha Woodmansee, *The Author, Art and the Market: Rereading the History of Aesthetics* (New York: Columbia University Press, 1994), 130–36; Archibald Alison, *Essays on the Nature and Principles of Taste* (New York: Harper, 1844), 450; Francis Jeffrey, "Essay on Beauty," in *Contributions to the Edinburgh Review* (New York: Appleton, 1873), 28, 38. For a summary of the physiological studies of vision in the early part of the century, see Crary, *Techniques of the Observer,* chap. 3.

9. Morgan, "Of Certainty in Taste," 806.

10. "The Prospects of British Art," *British Quarterly Review* 2 (1845): 478, 477; "On Aesthetical Criticism as Applied to Works of Art," *Fraser's* 28 (1843): 73, 74; [John Eagles], "Sir Joshua Reynolds's *Discourses,*" *Blackwood's* 52 (1842): 767.

11. Terry Eagleton, *The Ideology of the Aesthetic* (Oxford: Blackwell, 1990), 60; [Eagles], "Sir Joshua Reynolds's *Discourses,*" 768; Morgan, "Of Certainty in Taste," 804; "The Prospects of British Art," 466; "Art and Its Interpreters," *Chambers's Edinburgh Journal* 18 (1853): 331. For attendance figures in museums in the first decades of the century, see Bernard Denvir, *The Early Nineteenth Century: Art, Design and Society 1789–1852* (London: Longman, 1984), 19.

12. "The Progress of Art," *Westminster Review* 41 (1844): 92; supplement, *Art Union* 6 (1844): 153.

13. Attendance figures are taken from *Great Victorian Pictures* (London: Arts Council of Great Britain, 1978), 17.

14. Didier Maleuvre, *Museum Memories: History, Technology, Art* (Stanford, Calif.: Stanford University Press, 1999), 100.

15. "The Royal Academy," *Illustrated London News* 2 (1843): 328.

16. Fabius Pictor, *The Hand-Book of Taste, or How to Observe Works of Art,* 2d ed. (London: Longman, 1844), 117, 15, 13, 14, 19, 12–13.

17. Philip Gilbert Hamerton, "Notes on Aesthetics," *Portfolio* (1879); reprinted in *Portfolio Papers* (London: Seeley, 1889), 173.

18. Richard Redgrave, "An Introductory Address on the Methods Adopted by the Department of Practical Art," in *Addresses of the Superintendents of the Department of Practical Art* (London: Chapman & Hall, 1853), 72; Richard Redgrave, introduction, *The Sheepshanks Gallery* (London: Bell & Daldy, 1870), 7; Richard Redgrave, *On the Necessity of Principles in Teaching Design* (London: Chapman & Hall, 1853), 6. See also Redgrave's longer explanation of the empirical process of aesthetic knowledge in "An Introductory Address," 43–44.

19. In his *Cours de philosophie positive* (1830s–1850s), Comte was working through the collapse of Cartesian dualism to construct a theory of knowledge based not on the stability of reason, but on the consolidation of acquired knowledge into an organic system of general ideas.

20. Redgrave, *On the Necessity of Principles,* 23–24.

21. [John Eagles], "De Burton on Pictures," *Blackwood's* 58 (1843): 426; "Royal Academy Exhibition," *Illustrated London News,* 16 May 1846, 319.

22. See, for example, Mayhew's interviews with sempstresses in *The Unknown Mayhew,* ed. E. P. Thompson and Eileen Yeo (London: Merlin, 1971), 141. Christina Walkley, in *The Ghost in the Looking Glass: The Victorian Seamstress* (London: Owen, 1981), reviews sermons and political tracts that deal with the doubtful morality of the figure.

23. William Makepeace Thackeray, "May Gambols" (1844), in *The Works of W. M. Thackeray,* 26 vols. (London: Smith, Elder, 1886), 25:196; "Royal Academy," *Athenaeum* (18 May 1844): 461. For an example of a positive review that links *The Sempstress* to a more populist view of aesthetics, see supplement, *Art Union* 6 (1844): 153–75.

24. Judith Stoddart, "Tracking the Sentimental Eye," in *Knowing the Victorians,* ed. Suzy Anger (Ithaca, N.Y.: Cornell University Press, 2001).

25. James Clifford, *The Predicament of Culture* (Cambridge: Harvard University Press, 1988), 218.

26. Walker Jerrold, *Thomas Hood: His Life and Times* (New York: Lang, 1909), 367; John Clubbe, *Victoria's Forerunner: The Later Career of Thomas Hood* (Durham, N.C.: Duke University Press, 1968), 152; Thackeray, "May Gambols," 199.

27. For an explanation of this convention and an example of its use, see Jill Dunkerton, Susan Foister, Dillian Gordon, and Nicholas Penny, *Giotto to Dürer: Early Renaissance Painting in the National Gallery* (London: National Gallery, 1991), 244.

28. In Pierre Bourdieu's account of French realist art in the nineteenth century, realism also turns out to be less about celebrating the common than about affirming the specialness of art: "It is not sufficient . . . to rehabilitate . . . base or mediocre subjects; a power must be affirmed that belongs to art to constitute everything aesthetically by virtue of form." Pierre Bourdieu, *The Rules of Art: Genesis and Structure of the Literary Field,* trans. Susan Emanuel (Stanford, Calif.: Stanford University Press, 1995), 106.

29. Anna Blunden, *The Song of the Shirt* (1854). For discussions of the reinterpretations of Redgrave's painting throughout the century, see T. J. Edelstein, "'They Sang the Song of the Shirt': The Visual Iconology of the Seamstress," *Victorian Studies* 23 (1980): 183–210; and Walkley, *Ghost in the Looking Glass.*

30. "Royal Academy," *Athenaeum,* 459.

31. Jack Lindsay, *Turner: The Man and His Art* (London: Granada, 1985), 154. Elizabeth Helsinger recognizes this parallel between the audience and the subjects of the painting in *Ruskin and the Art of the Beholder* (Cambridge: Harvard University Press, 1982), 243. Ronald Paulson claims that these figures are images of Turner's contemporary reviewers; see *Literary Landscape: Turner and Constable* (New Haven, Conn.: Yale University Press, 1982), 91.

32. Giuseppe Gatt, *Turner* (London: Thames & Hudson, 1979), 39. For Ruskin this canvas, along with several of Turner's late works, showed his increasing isolation from the outside world. *The Angel Standing in the Sun,* Ruskin wrote in 1857, displayed "distinctive characters in the execution, indicative of mental disease" (*The Works of John Ruskin,* ed. E. T. Cook and Alexander Wedderburn, 39 vols. [London: Allen, 1903–12], 13:167).

33. George Leslie, *The Inner Life of the Royal Academy* (1914; reprint, New York: Blom, 1971), 145–48. John Gage recognizes how central exhibition conditions were to the development of Turner's late palette; see his *Colour in Turner: Poetry and Truth* (London: Studio Vista, 1969), 172.

34. G. F. Waagen, review of *Works of Art and Artists in England, Edinburgh*

Review 67 (1838): 397; Pictor, *Hand-Book of Taste,* 117, 20. Turner exhibited some of his most dramatic images of the sun in the year in which the *Hand-Book* was published, including *A Venetian Scene (St. Benedetto, looking toward Fusina)* and *Light and Colour (Goethe's Theory): the Morning after the Deluge.*

35. Crary explores the affinities between Turner's sun paintings and Gustav Fechner's descriptions of the eye as a sun (*Techniques of the Observer,* 141–43). James Hamilton, in *Turner and the Scientists* (London: Tate, 1998), finds a parallel closer to home in the writings of Turner's friend, the chemist Humphry Davy (173–74).

36. Leslie, *Inner Life of the Royal Academy,* 146.

37. Crary, *Techniques of the Observer,* 143.

38. Gage explores briefly Turner's borrowings from Danby and Martin (*Colour in Turner,* 97, 186). Allston's *The Angel Uriel in the Sun* was exhibited in England in 1811.

39. Redgrave, introduction, *Sheepshanks Gallery,* 2.

40. See Helsinger, *Ruskin and the Art of the Beholder,* chaps. 3 and 8, for Ruskin's readings of Turner's paintings through his notion of what Helsinger terms "excursive sight."

41. On the late addition of the flask, which altered the final shape of the painting, see Martin Butlin and Evelyn Joll, *The Paintings of J. M. W. Turner,* 2 vols. (New Haven, Conn.: Yale University Press, 1977), 2:243.

42. *Spectator,* 9 May 1846; cited in ibid., 2:244.

43. *Athenaeum* (17 May 1845): 496; "A Gossip about the Royal Academy Exhibition," *Illustrated London News,* 9 May 1846, 317.

44. *Athenaeum* (9 May 1846): 480.

CHAPTER FIVE

Caravaggio's Secrets

Leo Bersani and Ulysse Dutoit

On at least two occasions in his work, Caravaggio offers us his head. In a particularly lurid version of self-oblation, Caravaggio painted his own features on the bloody head of Goliath being held by the hair at arm's length, thrust by a victorious David toward the viewer, in the Galleria Borghese representation of that biblical episode. To judge from several other paintings, Caravaggio seems to have found in decapitation a nearly irresistible aesthetic appeal. Not only have two other versions of David with Goliath's head been attributed to Caravaggio, there is also Judith in the very act of cleaving through Holofernes' head with the latter's sword, St. John's partially severed head in the Malta painting *The Decapitation of St. John the Baptist,* the same luckless saint's head being dropped onto a platter held by Salome in the London version of *Salome Receiving the Head of St. John the Baptist* (a third version of this episode, now in Madrid, has also been attributed to Caravaggio), and, finally, the Medusa head, mouth agape and eyes opened wide in terror, originally painted on a parade shield held in the hand of a life-size equestrian sculpted figure in the Medici armory, and now itself removed from that original body and on view at the Uffizi in Florence. But in the other self-portrait we have in mind—the early *Bacchino Malato*—the painter's head rests firmly enough on a provocatively curved shoulder, and what we are being offered in that head, what is directed toward us, could be read as an erotically soliciting gaze.

We want to propose a certain interpretive itinerary from this gaze of the Bacchus self-portrait to the decapitated Goliath-Caravaggio. Let's begin by attacking head-on, so to speak, the trap set for us by images of decapitation. The psychoanalytic association of decapitation with castration has become an interpretive reflex; many people are inclined to take that connection for granted without ever having been instructed to do so by Freud's short piece on the Medusa head. And yet, while we will be acknowledging the irresistible nature of that interpretation—irresistible in large part because Caravaggio himself appears to be proposing it pictorially—we will also be arguing for the need to interpret castration. Far from being the final term in a reading of Caravaggio's images of decapitation, castration is "illuminated" by decapitation, by a cutting off of that part of the body where interpretation itself originates, without which we would never see decapitation as castration. Without *our* heads, we would not be speculating about what the heads in Caravaggio's paintings may "mean," and one way to make us lose our heads—to ruin any confidence we might have about "knowing" him, or, as we shall see, about the very possibility of knowledge—is for Caravaggio to decapitate himself, to thrust toward us (as David thrusts Goliath's head toward the spectator) a bodiless head that can no longer say or mean anything, that can no longer be read.

If Caravaggio finally adopts that extreme solution to what he seems to have anticipated as centuries of interpretive promiscuity in front of his work, he began by seductively inviting the spectator to read him. His paintings repeatedly initiate the conditions in which a visual field more or less urgently solicits and resists its own symbolization. Caravaggio frequently paints the act of looking—a looking at times directed outside the painting, toward the spectator, and at other times taking place among the figures within the represented scene. Among the former, much attention has been given to those in which a boy appears to be looking more or less provocatively toward the spectator. We are thinking of the *Boy with a Basket of Fruit*, the *Bacchino Malato* (both from the mid-1590s and both in the Borghese Gallery in Rome), the Uffizi *Bacchus* from a few years later, and the Berlin *Victorious Cupid* (c. 1601–2). The poses and the looks in these paintings have generally been recognized as erotically provocative, an accurate enough description if we mean by that a body in which we read an intention to stimulate our desire not only to contemplate it but to approach it, to touch it, to enter into or to imagine some form of intimate physical contact with it. What has been called a perplexing, even indecorous nudity (Cupid's position, for example, exposes not only his genitals but also the cleavage of his buttocks), bared shoulders, enticing smiles or half smiles, sensuous parted lips—given all this, and in spite of important variations among the works just mentioned, it seems plausible to say that Caravaggio has painted a series of sexual come-ons.

The come-ons are, however, somewhat ambiguous. In two of the paintings, the *Bacchino Malato* and *Boy with a Basket of Fruit*, the erotic invitation is qualified by a partially self-concealing movement of retreat. The Bacchus self-portrait (Figure 5.1) is at once exhibitionist and self-concealing: if the shoulder is enticingly curved, the movement of the entire arm closes in on the body, which it could be thought of as thereby concealing or protecting from the very advances it simultaneously invites. Also, the boy's flesh has a greenish hue (which accounts for the designation of the *bacchino* as *malato*), and this adds a repellent and repelling note to the provocation. The provocation and the withdrawal are, however, quite evidently poses, which should make us hesitate to see either the self-exposure *or* the self-concealment as natural, or as psychologically significant. The curious inclusion of a section of the youth's spread legs invites us to reconstruct the moment before he turned his head to the right and positioned his arm raising the bunch of grapes to his lips. Since this is a self-portrait, we might imagine the painter, sitting in front of his canvas, not yet having turned toward the mirror in which he will see himself as he will paint himself, posing as Bacchus. The model's identity is, however, irrelevant to the effect of Caravaggio's reminder that this Bacchus is a model who has just been posed *as* Bacchus. There is something grossly natural about those thematically irrelevant knees; they emphasize, by contrast, the youth's role-playing with the rest of his body. Thus there is already, even in this very early painting, an ironic comment on the double movement we will qualify as erotic: the soliciting move toward the viewer and the self-concealing move away from the viewer. It is, we will argue, the movement away that fascinates, indeed that eroticizes the body's apparent (and deceptive) availability. The latter is at once put into question and sexualized by the suggestion of a secret, although the exaggerated artfulness of the entire operation in the *Bacchino Malato* makes of that very suggestion only one element in a nonerotic process of aesthetic design. It is as if this remarkable work included a warning about the reading it also crudely solicits and frustrates.

Figure 5.1. Caravaggio, *Bacchino Malato* (Sick Bacchus), c. 1593. Galleria Borghese. Alinari/Art Resource, New York.

Furthermore, not only may the whole thing be nothing but a pose, but the very setting that supports the pose also works against its erotically provocative nature. What is this half-naked youth inviting us to see? His genitals (unlike those of Cupid in *Amor Victorious*) are hidden, and yet they are also visible. More exactly, they are repeated as something else: as the folded sash, and as the two peaches alongside the extended bunch of grapes on the table. Look at my sex, Bacchus seems to be saying, which is not one. It is the sensual pleasure I'm offering you, but it is *elsewhere,* it can perhaps be anywhere, inaccurately replicated in forms that substitute a visual sensuality for a concealed sexuality. The look that would center *our* look is itself decentered by such displacements, as well as by a certain incompleteness in the entire scene: both the wreath of ivy leaves around the youth's head and the bunch of grapes on the table end somewhere outside the painting. The self-withdrawing pose we originally noted could, then, be thought of not only as a partial concealment of the provocatively exposed body, but also as a redirecting of the viewer's solicited look to objects of undecidable identity (the phallus-sash, phallus-fruit) as well as to a space beyond the painting's frame (a visible space out of our field of vision.)

The most compelling other center of interest in the painting is, however, the table. Formally, its horizontality contrasts with the vertical positioning of the youth's upper body (a contrast repeated, in small, in the way the two peaches are lying on the table.) With its heavy, stonelike quality, this mass of matter more closely resembles the tombstone jutting out at us from *The Entombment* than it does a table, and it brings into the work a threat to life more unsettling than the greenish hue of Bacchus's flesh. This is the unnameable finality of inorganic matter, unnameable because it can't be described, as the boy's sickness or death can, as the result of a process, the end of a history. The stony table brings into the *Bacchino Malato* the impenetrable enigma of matter that does nothing but persist, for all time, in its deadness. Nothing could be more different from the psychic enigma perversely proposed by the boy's smile and pose, although a certain affinity between the sickly youth and dead matter is suggested by the repetition of the greenish gray of the youth's face in the table's surface. By juxtaposing the self-concealment perhaps inherent in the erotically soliciting pose with a radically other order of being, Caravaggio posits a mode of connectedness that, as we shall see, he richly elaborates elsewhere: the relation of the human body not to a more or less enigmatic human intentionality, but rather to a vast family of materiality in which community would no longer be a function of reciprocal readings of desire.

But Caravaggio's main emphasis in these early works—an emphasis that will allow him to make the move just described—is on the apparently unfathomable nature of the erotic. Like the double movement of

Figure 5.2. Caravaggio, *Boy with a Basket of Fruit,* 1593–94. Galleria Borghese. Alinari/Art Resource, New York.

the youth's body in the *Bacchino Malato,* the tensed curve of the wrist in *Boy with a Basket of Fruit* (Figure 5.2) suggests a drawing of the basket toward the boy and away from the prospective buyer, at the same time the painting fosters the illusion that we are looking at an offering. What is the boy offering us—the basket of fruit he seems to be claiming as his, or the highlighted right shoulder that is in effect pushed toward us? By implication, this question makes the open mouth undecidable: Is the fruit vendor offering his merchandise, or has the mouth been opened to make the alluringly tilted head more enticing, thereby shifting the merchandise from the lush but partially withdrawn basket of fruit to the vendor himself? And yet it is of course easier to look at the basket of fruit as something we might possess than at the boy who, by looking directly at the viewer, reflects and resists the invasive gaze that would "take him in." He has only to look at us to remind us that the erotic gaze is itself invasive as well as inviting. His looking at us protects him from our looking at him. The invasiveness is, however, illusory on both sides. What we primarily see in looking at the fruit vendor's eyes is an emphatic point of light in his left eye. We are looked at by that light, and, as Lacan has said in his seminar "The Gaze as *objet petit a,*" what that light "paints" in the depths of our eye is not an object or a "constructed relation," but rather that which is "elided in the geometrical relation—the depth of field, with all its ambiguity and variability, which is in no way mastered by me."[1] The eye is not a point of perspective from which we can look out at, measure, and appropriate the world. Like the fruit vendor's eyes, the viewer's eyes are penetrated by a luminosity that has the ambiguous shimmering of a jewel, a luminosity that, from a cognitive point of view, illuminates nothing. The eye is an unreadable transparency (a fact made viscerally evident by the opening shot of Beckett's *Film,* in which Buster Keaton's glaucous eye, occupying the entire screen, is at once obscenely exposed and wholly impenetrable). The erotically provocative pose transforms the otherwise neutral unreadability of the eye into a willful reticence, as if we were being solicited by a desire determined to remain hidden. Let's note, finally, that the eye's brilliant opacity in *Boy with a Basket of Fruit,* which repels the look it solicits, is the principal element in a complex system of double movements. The fruit, which would otherwise be the passive object of an appetitive attention, is being withdrawn. What the boy thrusts toward us is the unreadability that keeps us at a distance. The one part of the basket's contents that has escaped the boy's protective embrace—the leaf in the lower right section—could be thought of as the most unambiguously available element in the painting, but it is limp and faded, thereby highlighting, by contrast, the inviting ripeness of both the rest of the basket's contents and the boy himself.

In the paintings just discussed (and we would have to add the distancing effect, in the *Victorious Cupid,* of Cupid's slightly mocking, self-controlled smile—in sharp contrast to the immodest full frontal spread of his naked body—as well as the absence of part of that otherwise fully exhibited body, especially the left arm hidden behind the curiously contorted pose), erotic soliciting is countered by a movement away from the solicited viewer, a holding back that complicates the idea of erotic availability. Or rather it is perhaps because of the movement away that we identify these looks and these poses as erotic. Inherent in this sort of erotic invitation is a concealment, and the concealment generates both what we recognize as the erotic invitation and possibly our own eroticized response to it. Sexiness advertises an availability that is somewhat opaque. The erotic here is a function of the noninterpretable address.

We should emphasize "here" because the word could of course be used to describe an invitation without concealment. In Bataille, for example, it refers to an unqualified openness—an availability uncomplicated by any reticence or secretiveness. Any such reticence might be the sign of an individuality resistant to that "communication" in which, for Bataille, the boundaries that define and separate individuals no longer exist. In this state of radical indistinctness, psychic and physical being is reduced to pure openness; being has become a receptive hole. While Caravaggio appears to "consider" this type of address, or solicitation, he seems comparatively indifferent to a wholly nonresistant openness. Even the frequently open mouths in Caravaggio's work—think of the boy rushing away at the right of the scene from the martyrdom of St. Matthew, as well as the boy bitten by a lizard—are more frequently figured as a defensive cry against the world than as a readiness to be penetrated or invaded. What seems to interest Caravaggio more is a body at once presenting and withdrawing itself—a somewhat *enigmatic* body. The distinction between nonerotic and erotic address might be not that the latter solicits greater intimacy, fewer barriers between persons, but that it solicits intimacy in order to block it with a secret. Erotic address is a self-reflexive move in which the subject addresses another so that it may enjoy narcissistically a secret to which the subject itself may have no other access. The subject performs a secret, which is not at all to say that he or she has any knowledge of it.

We might say in passing that the critical gaze of identifying these portraits as homoerotic (an argument based explicitly for some critics on the presumed feminine nature of an erotic tease or, somewhat more credibly, on the Renaissance association of androgyny with homosexuality or bisexuality), *and* identifying Caravaggio himself as homosexual or bisexual, gets rid of what we take to be the greatest originality of these paintings: their intractably enigmatic quality. Caravaggio's enigmas are not meant to be read. At least since Oedipus, the enigma in Western civilization is an epistemological challenge. Its unreadability is fantasized as provisional, and, far from blocking knowledge, it holds forth the promise of new knowledge, of expanding the field of epistemological appropriations. Caravaggio resolutely rejects opportunities for such expansions. The distinction between homosexual and heterosexual reduces erotic soliciting to a sexual identity. It makes the soliciting look transparent: homosexuality is the unveiled secret, the truth thanks to which, as the Proustian narrator says of Charlus when he discovers that the baron's desires are for other men, "everything that hitherto had seemed... incoherent became intelligible, appeared self-evident."[2] Now we "know" Charlus, just as we would presumably know Caravaggio better if we could confidently identify his works as homoerotic and Caravaggio himself as homosexual. The secret is an accident—or a defense that can be broken down—on the way to knowledge. Caravaggio's enigmatic youths propose something quite different: the secret is inherent in their erotic appeal, although there may be nothing to know about them. A provocative unreadability is presented as an occasion that might lead to a sexual arousal. Sexual identities, however probable, deprive these works of their erotic charge. Caravaggio's enigmatic bodies have not yet been domesticated by sexual—perhaps even gendered—identities.

We are interested in Caravaggio's work as a visual speculation on the meaning and the conditions of knowledge. We infer this speculation from Caravaggio's experiments with relationality. One such experiment seems to propose the erotic enigma as defining the terms of a relation, as that which might stimulate us into initiating connectedness. But even in his early paintings, that blocked connectedness is juxtaposed with other possibilities, possibilities that encourage us not to be satisfied with a relationality grounded in the erotic secret—and, more generally as we shall see, with forms of intersubjective knowing that assume a hidden unconscious.

Other versions of the insistent look can be seen in works in which Caravaggio places the solicited subject within the painting. Now the center of interest is a look apparently anxious to decipher another look or another presence. From this perspective, we will briefly discuss two very different paintings: *The Gypsy Fortune Teller* and *The Calling of St. Matthew*, both of which not only demonstrate the range of Caravaggio's imagination of the soliciting gaze but will also help us to unfold the complex logic of both looking and secrets in Caravaggio. There are two versions of *The Gypsy Fortune Teller*, one in the Louvre and the other in the

Capitoline Museum in Rome.[3] The Louvre painting is generally praised for what Mina Gregori calls "its refined composition, its uniformly high quality of execution, and its more accurate description of the psychological relationship between the figures." The painting is, for Alfred Moir, "an elegant satire of human folly," and, for Gregori, the moral message of both versions is "the pitfalls that a youth might encounter." Not only is the generally less appreciated Capitoline version poorly preserved, it is also recognized as having the instantaneous character of a hastily drawn street scene Caravaggio would have copied directly from life. But it is precisely the "finished" quality of the Louvre version (with, for example, its rich play of light and shade, its more elaborate gesticulatory motifs) that, in our view, makes it inferior to the Capitoline work. There is more going on in the carefully painted Louvre scene, and more of an attempt to define the narrative. We are given a psychological anecdote: "the radiant . . . pretty and transparent" youth, as Moir describes him, more baby-faced than in the other version, conscious of the gypsy's attentions, perhaps trying to look indifferent, with the "sly and complacent" gypsy girl perhaps watching the youth's face for the effect of "her suggestive caress of the mount of Venus" on his palm (or, as Giulio Mancini suggested, around 1620, for a sign of his awareness that she is stealing his ring).[4]

In the Capitoline version (Figure 5.3), the young man's face is prominently on display, obviously there in order to be seen (his head is in a forward position, whereas the girl appears to be retreating slightly toward the background), at the same time as his features are expressive of nothing more than that positionality—that is, their availability to another's gaze. Unlike the fruit vendor and, to a certain extent, the young man in the Louvre version of the same subject, the Capitoline nobleman is not marketing his own desirability. The erotically soliciting gaze of the other male figures we have looked at would at once complicate and deproblematize this curiously blank look. The very suggestion of a secret operates less as a barrier to communication than as part of a familiar code that defines a communication as erotic. What the secret is—or whether a secret even exists—is irrelevant to the intelligibility given to a relation by the mere appearance of a secret. The Capitoline nobleman's facial expression is at once more superficial and more challenging. The gypsy's calculations appear to have been defeated by that physiognomic puzzle; her search into the boy's destiny has shifted from

Figure 5.3. Caravaggio, *The Gypsy Fortune Teller*, 1593–94. Musei Capitolini. Alinari/Art Resource, New York.

what is now her inactive hand (no longer probing the secrets of his palm, as in the Louvre version of the same subject) to her extraordinary spying look—as if she had come to realize that his "secret" is not in the lines of his hand but in his look, a look impersonally directed toward her, as if she were nothing more than an accident, or a punctuation, in some larger indefinite space. It would be her mistake to read him as critics have read the painting—as having psychological intentionality. His blank or, better, disinterested availability to her gaze raises what can only be, for the fortune-teller, an anguishing question: How are the two connected? Her professional answer, so to speak, would have been that she can see and speak (pre-dict, say ahead of time) his narrative extensions into his future. But his look suggests other types of extension: not toward her as a psychologically or socially individuated presence, but toward her as an occasion for formal extensions of his own physical presence (the upper part of her outer garment, for example, prolongs the diagonal shape of his sword). The fortune-teller is spying on the young man's face as if his face had the decipherable lines of his palms. But we see her perhaps beginning to realize that there is nothing to read there, that his "secrets" are all visible, and that she herself contributes to

Figure 5.4. Caravaggio, *The Calling of St. Matthew,* 1600. St. Luigi dei Francesi. Alinari/Art Resource, New York.

that visibility, to what Merleau-Ponty would call the fragment of being radiating from him within the universal flesh of the world.[5] We are, then, beginning to see that the concealment spoken of earlier can perhaps be demystified, or that art can displace the secrets of the fascinating gaze, thereby redefining the terms of, and the responses to, a fascinated interrogation of that gaze.[6]

It is also a question of the interpretation of a soliciting look in one of Caravaggio's most remarkable religious paintings, *The Calling of St. Matthew* (1600; Figure 5.4). Here, however, the soliciting is wholly unambiguous. It is Christ beckoning to Matthew to follow him. But the painting satirizes such unidirectional invitations. Christ's eyes are veiled, his outstretched hand seems somewhat deformed and points rather limply at Matthew,[7] who prolongs the gesture by pointing—more forcefully than Christ himself does—perhaps toward himself, perhaps toward the figure just to his right. Rather than the fascinated perception of a visual enigma, Matthew and especially the boy to his left leaning toward him are both looking with a detached, perhaps ironic puzzlement at the darkened, pictorially unimpressive source of this intrusive calling. Matthew, the story tells us, will follow Christ, but Caravaggio has chosen to paint the moment before, the moment of suspension, of the slightly shocked response to a soliciting presence that weakly but unambiguously asks for nothing more interesting than that he be followed. In what may be a commentary on the unseductive nature of *that* invitation, the young man with his back to us appears to be looking elsewhere, somewhere beyond Peter and Jesus, to another source of light. His turning in that direction could be read as the beginning of a movement responsive to that other call, to a source invisible in this painting but that implicitly criticizes the represented caller as a visible element denying the invisibility, or the latency of the visible, to which he belongs. The youth in *The Gypsy Fortune Teller* says: Recognize my anonymous visibility. Christ implicitly proclaims: Recognize me as the center to which all things return. The Christian version of the soliciting presence is a repression both of the erotic secret and of what might be called an impersonal narcissism. In this calling that cannot go unheeded, that is at once enfeebled but perfectly clear, Caravaggio has painted Christ, and Christianity, as an antierotic and antimetaphysical defense. Christianity fosters the illusion of intelligible messages and of readable bodies.

Caravaggio paints two kinds of concealment. The one to which we have devoted most of our remarks so far is designated through an eroticized address, and it is read as enigmatic desire. The other is spatial, although only partly visible within the painting; it is the "concealment" of an unmappable extensibility of being. To speak adequately of the first type of concealment invites a psychoanalytic look, perhaps the most refined interpretive look we have. Merely by positing the notion of an enigmatic subject, we have placed ourselves on psychoanalytic ground. Indeed, Jean Laplanche has recently located the category of the enigma at the very point of emergence of what might be called the psychoanalytically constituted subject. He has spoken of an original and unavoidable seduction of the child by the mother—a seduction inherent in the very nurturing of the child. The seduction in no way needs to be intentional, for, as Laplanche puts it, "the adult world is entirely infiltrated with unconscious and sexual significations of which the adult too does not possess the code." Adult sexuality is implanted in the child in the form of what Laplanche calls an enigmatic signifier—that is, a message by which the child is seduced but that he or she cannot read.[8]

Laplanche speaks of the seductive address mainly as an account of the structural formation of the unconscious: primal repression would be the making unconscious of those elements in the enigmatic signifier that infants cannot "metabolize"—that is, those they are incapable of understanding through some form of symbolization. But the seductive address may be more general than that: *an ego is erotically solicited into being.* The seductive address Laplanche speaks of is, we suggest, embedded in the very calling forth of the infant's being as an independent subjectivity. Relationality constitutes being. In *Arts of Impoverishment,* we speak of Beckett's *Company* as a literary figuration of this originary soliciting of the human subject. In Beckett, the address is vocal: it is represented, or remembered, as someone on his back lying in the dark hearing an unlocatable voice summoning him to identify as his own the life he is being told about. Human subjectivity, Beckett implies, is always a response to an address; there is no presocial, solipsistic "I." The injunction to be, to have a life, is an injunction to answer a call; a human organism becomes a human subject only by recognizing and participating in a linguistic or a gestural sociality. The originating of a human being is the originating of relations.[9]

But we have to go further than this and ask about the nature of the being constituted by relationality. It is how we read the summons, the seduction, the soliciting that determines what or who we are. The inability to decipher the enigmatic signifier constitutes us as sexual beings, that is, beings in whom desire or lack is central. It may seem peculiar to speak of desire as an epistemological category, and yet we would argue that desire as lack is constituted, originally, as the exciting pain of a certain ignorance: the failure to penetrate the *sense* of the other's soliciting—through touch, gesture, voice, or look—of our body. This failure is itself dependent on more fundamental reading: the reading of the soliciting as a secret. The secrets of the unconscious may be nothing more than the introjection of the secrets the other involuntarily persuades us to believe he or she holds without allowing us to read them. The withheld being with which the other addresses us is the other's desirability.

To modify the way in which the human being is addressed would be to modify the relationality that constitutes the human as we know it. Like all painting, Caravaggio's work is about forms of connectedness in space. In painting his portraits of erotically provocative boys, it is as if Caravaggio experienced—or reexperienced—the fascination of the original seduction. For a painter, this experience was perhaps inevitably one of constricted space. The enigmatic signifier structures a relation as fixed gazes—not only the gaze of the one being seduced, but also the gaze of the seducer, who is himself (or herself) seeking in the curious and subjugated look of the other the secret of his (or her) own seductive power. But his work also allows Caravaggio to experiment with a gaze diverted from a space circumscribed by a mutual fascination. The young nobleman in *The Gypsy Fortune Teller* raises the possibility of spatial interests not defined or directed by the imaginary secrets of the other. Perhaps the exploration of this possibility requires a suspension of strictly human interests, a removal from those existential contexts in which paranoid fascination is the human subject's spontaneous response to the other's soliciting (or even interested) gaze.

Caravaggio effects this removal by a betrayal of his subjects. The historical configurations of these subjects are reproduced in his painting, but at the same time the subjects appear, for the first time, as models of a relationality within which their historicity dissolves. The relations that emerge from this shift of register reformulate both intersubjectivity and metaphysics. Caravaggio is a crucial figure in the history of a suspicion fatal to the procedures and the confidence of philosophy: the suspicion that truth cannot be the object of knowledge, that it cannot be theorized. More exactly, the notion of truth itself is a consequence of the primacy given to knowledge. And knowledge "misses" being; it comes, so to speak, when we cease to remember that being happens not as a demonstration but as a kind of showing. To adopt a Heideggerean inflection, we might say that Being "shines" in art.[10] In Caravaggio, this shining is literally rendered by that peculiar light that seems not to be projected on bodies from some locatable external source, but rather originates within the bodies themselves. The light emanating from Caravaggio's figures is the sign of their transformation from merely historical persons to ontological cartographers: Caravaggio re-presents them—which means here that he presents them for the first time—as mapping modes of being. Caravaggio's paint is the metaphysical X ray that compels us to see particular histories and particular myths as *instituting relationalities.*

The particular displacement that interests us here is the move from the erotic—which, with its emphasis on an enigmatic signifier, institutes the unconscious and places a problematic of knowledge at the center of human relations—to another mode of connectedness between bodies. *The Gypsy Fortune Teller* is an early confrontation between these two systems; the extraordinary *St. John the Baptist with a Ram* in the Capitoline Museum in Rome (Figure 5.5) pictorially elaborates on this nonerotic sensuality *and* suggests, in Caravaggio, a certain anxiety about it.

As in *The Gypsy Fortune Teller,* one figure appears to be looking intensely at another; if the youth in *The Gypsy Fortune Teller* returns that look with indifference (he is more of an exposed surface than a participant in this visual pseudodialogue), St. John turns frankly away from the ram, directing his half smile toward us. Thus it seems plausible to align him with the *Bacchino Malato* and *Victorious Cupid,* and even to refer to him, as Alfred Moir has, as "a pagan little tease, uncontaminated by Christian sentiment," addressing the viewer with erotic provocation.[11] Indeed, the painting clearly displays the double character we have associated with the erotic address: the nude youth half reclining with legs spread, and the right arm extending away from us, as if protecting or concealing something from our view. But the effect of provocation, and of an erotic secret, is significantly modulated here. There is, first of all, the gentle intimacy between the boy and the animal. If the extended arm is protecting anything, it is the ram it embraces, a gesture repeated, in the opposite direction, by the ram's head turned toward, almost touching, the boy's face. We begin to see the possibility of a new sort of address (or rather, this time, of exchange), one in which the faces do not become readable but where the very gesture of concealment is performed as a physical *contact* rather than as a provocatively isolating move. Furthermore, the contact here is between species; the youth may be turning his head toward us not to address us erotically, but rather in order to draw our attention to his intimacy with the ram. This possibility does not in itself make his look less ambiguous: To what, exactly, is it that we are being invited? How is the invitation different from the one the *bacchino* appears to be asking us to accept?

The answer lies, we suggest, in the displacement of a secret. The enigmatic signifier Laplanche describes refers us to an unconscious sexual secret, to those words, looks, objects, and scenes with which the child, unable to interpret them, created an unconscious. The mystery that shattered us into sexuality is by definition unfathomable; in its original form, it can never be dredged up from the unconscious and worked through

Figure 5.5. Caravaggio, *St. John the Baptist with a Ram,* 1602. Pinacotecha Capitolina. Alinari/Art Resource, New York.

(like, say, the oedipal conflict, which is a secondary repression, less profound than the uninterpretable primary repressed material). The enigmatic signifier that is the stuff of primary repression is inherently unknowable. What Caravaggio proposes in *St. John the Baptist with a Ram* is a restaging of a scene of erotic provocation in which excitement would no longer be a function of an impenetrable subjectivity. The possibility of reading the youth's smile as a provocative sign of that subjectivity is forestalled by the multiple fanlike structures in the painting, structures that open out into a purely external space. Several versions of this fanlike movement create an interior framing circle: the red drapery, the ram's horns, the boy's legs, and the leaves of the plant in the bottom right corner (frequently a charged position in Caravaggio's work). The scene thus opens out, centrifugally, in various directions, countering the centripetal pull of the youth's gaze. Only the boy's right arm traces a single direction, but its gesture is extended by the tree in the upper right corner and ends somewhere outside the painting's frame, thereby making its destination somewhat indeterminate. Nudity here signifies very differently from the sense it projects in *Victorious Cupid.* There the frontal pose, the well-lighted genitals, the centered pelvis, and the suggestive glimpses of Cupid's buttocks all encourage us to sexualize the gaze; the sexual nature of the message is confirmed by the prominence of the emblems of sexuality. In *St. John the Baptist with a Ram,* the sexual nature of the enigmatic gaze is problematized by the comparative insignificance, pictorially speaking, of those same emblems. The only dead part of the painting is the youth's genitals and the shaded area of his body just above his genitals. Even the boy's spread legs have to be read less as an erotic provocation than as merely one in a series of fanlike structures opening outward, away from the boy's body. Three of these structures could also be read on a single vertical line, from the plant to the legs to the horns, a movement in which the most explicitly sexual element of the picture becomes a minor episode on the way. And yet the provocative address, with the suggestion of a secret (what do the youth's smile and gaze mean or intend?), has by no means disappeared. The persistence of the enigma, and the shift in its sense, are both nicely figured in the ram's horns. Inwardly, they confine space and point to the youth's face, thus confirming his gaze and smile as the painting's narrative center. But in their outward spread, the horns denarrativize the picture, extending the youth away from himself, connecting him, as the other fanlike structures do, to a realm of being he cannot contain, where there are no borders or figures, no beginning or end. This, then, is the youth's secret, one not of interiority but rather of indefinite extensibility, a secret of unrepresented, and unrepresentable, ontological affinities. The fact that the smile, the look, and the pose that designated that secret continue to be identifiable as erotically provocative does, however, suggest that this sublimation of the erotic signifier may be an eroticized reexperiencing of it. In psychoanalytic terms, the renewed research into the trauma of an enigmatic sexuality dissipates the hidden sexual content of the trauma while reasserting its sexual energy. Painting makes visible the sensual grounds of a metaphysical fantasy.

That move is, however, made at a certain expense. If, as we have been arguing, this painting suggests that Caravaggio's youth, for all his centered presence and insistent gaze, is not to be found or, more exactly, contained within this painting, then perhaps his look might be read as a call, an appeal. It is not the peremptory call of Jesus, summoning Matthew to follow him on his pastoral mission in the world. No—the youth's arm is pointed away from us, toward those spaces where he is already, and his head could perhaps be read as an appeal from behind his arm, from a region he can no longer leave. Join me, although where I am is somewhere between two realms of being, between my physical, individuated existence and my being as a disseminated connectedness throughout the universe—a betweenness concretely figured in the painting by a casual, poignant, and haunting intimacy between two species. The transfer of being represented here exacts a price, one obliquely referred to by the anomalous creases under the youth's eyes—as if the transfer of ontological register had *taken time.* Since the empirical individual does not age into the ontological, the time evolved must be the time of the artist's own work—more specifically, the time he needed to rework the erotic enigmas he addressed to himself, to resituate their traumatic effect from an individual unconscious to the spaces at once discovered and reinvented in painting. The concealment deployed in time is both an effect of working time and, perhaps, the imaginary time it would take to follow the trajectory of spatial being. The creases under the eyes of Caravaggio's youth are the anticipatory effect of the time it would take him to rejoin his metaphysical being, a journey to which he must sacrifice his youth and, perhaps, his very life.

It is, however, not the youth with a ram but the painter himself that, quite appropriately, Caravaggio represents as having made that ultimate sacrifice. In drawing his own features on the decapitated head of Goliath, Caravaggio could be thought of as saying to us: In this painting I offer you my head. Or perhaps: In painting (not just in *this* painting), I lose my head. Painting is the decapitation of the artist. It is part of the great

Figure 5.6. Caravaggio, *David with the Head of Goliath,* 1609–10. Galleria Borghese. Alinari/Art Resource, New York.

originality of *David with the Head of Goliath* (1605–6, or 1609–10; Figure 5.6) that Caravaggio enriches rather than reduces the sense of his work by encouraging us, pictorially, to equate this decapitation with castration. The point of David's sword is invisible; it disappears into David's genital area. What we see of the sword is parallel to David's outstretched arm, at the end of which we do of course see something: Goliath's bloody head. So the gesture of the sword is repeated above, as if the unseen violence on the phallus (from which David appears to be withdrawing his sword, as he withdrew it from Goliath's neck) could, as it were, become presentable when it is repeated as decapitation. This of course suggests that Goliath's head is David's phallus, or, to extrapolate, that Goliath's head is the version of himself that David sacrifices in his self-mutilation. In addition to the implied parallelism between David's phallus and Goliath's head, other similarities encourage us to think of the two figures as one. The white drapery on David's torso falls like a head of hair, and the hanging lower part has a shape somewhat similar to the lines of blood flowing from Goliath's invisible neck, lines to which the flowing drapery is also parallel. Also, David's right ear is red; this is a curious repetition in the upper left section of the color of the blood in the lower right section. Finally, it is as if this act of violence had made David somewhat androgynous: there is the Madonna-like melancholy with which he contemplates the severed head, and the curiously expansive volume of the lower part of his body, as if an ample skirt had been thrown around David's hips.

Castration-decapitation has left David in a state of betweenness, not only between gendered identities but also between existential violence and what Caravaggio appears to conceive of as the aesthetic consequence of that violence. David the castrator-decapitator holds his arm forth as a painter might in front of his canvas. In Goliath's head, David-Caravaggio has painted his own castration. That is, Caravaggio has symbolized it through his own severed head, thereby making visible, for us, his interpretation of a fantasy of castration. For if decapitation "hides" a castration fantasy, the latter is not a final term: only decapitation gives us the full sense and, even more important, the profound but ambiguous appeal of castration. Only Caravaggio's head tells us, exactly, what he has lost in sacrificing the phallus. Decapitation is the meaning of castration, for sexuality is originally implanted in the head; the phallus does the bidding of fantasy, sexuality is a *cosa mentale.* In Caravaggio's work, the head, as we have seen, is the principal carrier of erotic messages. Here, however, is a head being offered to us much less ambiguously than the head of the *bacchino malato* or that of St. John with a ram, but it is also a head that can no longer address us. This is a head without secrets, and therefore without a message; decapitation is Caravaggio's extreme solution to the human head as a traumatically enigmatic signifier.

Nothing is concealed behind those dead eyes, eyes that can no longer provoke us erotically. Or perhaps there is a message in Caravaggio's severed head, but it can only be one about interpretation. In cutting off his head Caravaggio forestalls a reading of his work that, however, he also invites in many of his paintings. The thrusting of his head toward the viewer is, to use Frank Stella's expression for this image, an extraordinary act of "pictorial will."[12] It violently removes us from the interpretive level at which concealment has to be thought of as nonspatial (that is, when it is a function of a constitutively inaccessible and unrepresentable unconscious), and in so doing the severed head makes the very identification between decapitation and castration interpretively irrelevant. For Caravaggio, the discovery of what we have called a disseminated spatial concealment—an extension of being also unrepresentable yet nonetheless congenial to the spatiality of painting—seems to require an amputation not only of the sexual but also of life itself. Whereas *The Gypsy Fortune Teller* and *St. John the Baptist with a Ram* suggest that the ontological can be sensually charged, *David with the Head of Goliath* theorizes, so to speak, the impossibility of that conjunction. This extraordinary—and extraordinarily self-destructive—work posits the incompatibility of existence and being. Caravaggio dies a terrible death as a victim of his metamorphosis into art. But much of this work raises the question of whether that death was necessary—a question almost unspeakably poignant if we see in David's expression a melancholy attachment to what he has *de*tached, a belated recognition that there are life-sustaining and even self-expansive modes of losing your head.

Notes

1. Jacques Lacan, *The Four Fundamental Concepts of Psycho-Analysis,* ed. Jacques-Alain Miller, trans. Alan Sheridan (New York: W. W. Norton, 1978), 96, 86.

2. Marcel Proust, *Remembrance of Things Past,* trans. C. K. Montcrieff and Terence Kilmartin, 3 vols. (New York: Vintage, 1982), 2:637.

3. Caravaggio scholars (most notably, Denis Mahon and J.-P. Cuzin) have questioned the attribution of the Capitoline *Fortune Teller* to Caravaggio. In 1951, Mahon wrote that the composition of the Capitoline painting "is in every detail more flaccid than the Louvre version, ... [it] is 'Caravaggio made easy,' without the peculiar accent, without the spice." Given this reaction to the picture, it is hardly surprising that Mahon concluded that it was the work of "a superficially clever and relatively early imitator." Denis Mahon, "Egregius in Urbe Pictor: Caravaggio Revised," *Burlington Magazine* 93, no. 580 (1951): 234.

On the basis of radiographic examination of the Capitoline *Fortune Teller,* Michele Cordaro reattributed it to Caravaggio. See Cordaro, "Indagine readiografica sulla 'Buona Venture' dei Musei Capitoline," *Ricerche di Storia dell'Arte* 10 (1980): 101–6. For a brief history of the debate around the Capitoline version and an account of the painting's cleaning and restoration in the mid-1980s, see Marisa Elisa Tittoni Monti, "*La Buona Ventura* del Caravaggio: Note e precisazioni in margine al restauro," and Elena Zicieri and Claudio Caneva, "Relazione tecnica di restauro e analisi, *Caravaggio: nuove riflessioni,*" both in *Quaderni di Palazzo Venezia* 6 (1989): 179–97.

4. Mina Gregori, in the catalog for the exhibition *The Age of Caravaggio* (New York: Metropolitan Museum of Art; and Milan: Electa, 1985), 215, 220; Alfred Moir, *Caravaggio* (New York: Harry N. Abrams, 1982), 52; Giulio Mancini, *Considerazioni sulla pittura,* ed. A. Marucchi, 2 vols. (Rome: Academia Nazionale dei Lincei, 1956–57), 1:109. In her catalog essay, Gregori argues for a relation between *the Fortune Teller* and certain features of the *commedia dell'arte,* and, more generally, "a tradition of theater-related genre painting" (215–16).

5. See Maurice Merleau-Ponty, *The Visible and the Invisible,* ed. Claude Lefort, trans. Alphonso Lingis (Evanston, Ill.: Northwestern University Press, 1968), esp. chap. 4.

6. It should be mentioned, however, that the youth's advantage is social as well as ontological; indeed, one could maintain that the social is posing as the ontological. We would, however, argue that the type of visibility the youth proposes is the first step in a democratizing of their relation, in what might be called a spatially motivated democratizing.

7. The gesture does, of course, as others have pointed out, also evoke Adam's inert outstretched hand in Michelangelo's *Creation.*

8. Jean Laplanche, *Seduction, Translation, Drives,* ed. John Fletcher and Martin Stanton, trans. Martin Stanton (London: Institute of Contemporary Arts, 1992), 188. See especially the section "The Kent Seminar" and the essay by Laplanche from which the quoted passage is taken, titled "The Drive and Its Object Source: Its Fate in the Transference."

9. See Leo Bersani and Ulysse Dutoit, *Arts of Impoverishment: Beckett, Rothko, Resnais* (Cambridge: Harvard University Press, 1993), chap. 1.

10. For Heidegger, "self-concealing being is illuminated" in art. "This shining . . . is the beautiful. *Beauty is one way in which truth occurs as unconcealedness.*" Martin Heidegger, "The Origin of the Work of Art," in *Poetry, Language, Thought,* trans. Albert Hofstadter (New York: Harper & Row, 1971), 56.

11. Moir, *Caravaggio,* 92. Noting, as others have, that the youth "lacks a halo and the Baptist's traditional attributes, the cross and the scroll, and that a ram rather than a sheep is shown," Mina Gregori also finds that "the pose and the somewhat perplexing nudity of the youth . . . are difficult to reconcile with the ostensibly religious subject"; *The Age of Caravaggio,* 300. Creighton Gilbert has recently argued against the identification of the youth in this painting as St. John the Baptist. Gilbert renames the painting *Pastor friso* (Phrygian Shepherd), and he interprets the shepherd as a classical allusion to Paris. The painting is, in Gilbert's view, a critique of Annibale Caracci's *Paris and Mercury* in the Galleria Farnese in Rome. See Creighton Gilbert, *Caravaggio and His Two Cardinals* (University Park: Pennsylvania State University Press, 1995), chaps. 1–7.

Walter Friedlander discusses Caravaggio's *St. John the Baptist with a Ram* as one of "two cases of persiflage directed at Michelangelo," the other being *Victorious Cupid.* The Michelangelo work of which St. John is a "travesty" is the ignudo above the Erythraean Sibyl on the Sistine Ceiling. Walter Friedlander, *Caravaggio Studies* (Princeton, N.J.: Princeton University Press, 1995), 89–91.

12. Frank Stella, *Working Space* (The Charles Eliot Norton Lectures 1983–84) (Cambridge: Harvard University Press, 1986), 103.

Part II
Aesthetics in Social Contexts: Economies and Ethics

CHAPTER SIX

The Moral Content of Nabokov's *Lolita*

Susan Bordo

In his afterword to *Lolita,* Nabokov wrote that his book had "no moral in tow."[1] An industry of postmodern criticism, seizing on this statement and encouraged by Nabokov's own scorn (lavished on Dostoyevsky, among others) for literary sentimentality and high-mindedness, has developed around *Lolita*'s supposed absence of morality. The book has nothing to do with incest or child abuse, we've been told; it's about the death of meaning, the logic of games, it's a stylish experiment with language. These critics forget that Nabokov insisted in postpublication interviews that *Lolita* had a "high moral content,"[2] and that his wife, Vera—to whom the book was dedicated and who lived her life in the service of Nabokov's art—made it clear that in her understanding of the book, at least, having no moral in tow was hardly equivalent to having no moral point of view. "Lolita discussed by the papers from every possible point of view except one: that of its beauty and pathos," she complained in her diary about the early reviews. "Critics prefer to look for moral symbols, justification, condemnation or explanation of HH's predicament. . . . I wish, though, somebody would notice the tender description of the child's helplessness, her pathetic dependence on monstrous HH, and her heartrending courage."[3]

Vera suggests—and her husband's own literary criticism corroborates—that for Nabokov what distinguishes effective art from pedagogical schmaltz is not the absence or presence of moral attitude but the means by which it is delivered to the reader: through the subtle emotional power of imagery rather than the heavy-handed persuasion of ideas. Believing this, the Nabokovs would surely find a bitter irony in the cultural career of *Lolita*—a career that over the intervening years has generated and installed a set of images, particularly of its heroine, that seem more inspired by cultural archetypes and ideological agendas than by the details of the novel, and that have virtually usurped those details in the popular imagination.[4] Tender? Helpless? Heartrending? Dependent? After Adrian Lyne's film of *Lolita* was screened for a preview audience, one woman said to screenwriter Stephen Schiff, "I guess you called her Lolita because she was really kind of a Lolita, huh?" Rough translation: "She was a sexy little slut, wasn't she?" (or, as *Webster's* more decorously puts it, "precociously seductive girl").

For the previewer of Lyne's film, as for many others nowadays, the very name Lolita is not even recognized as having its origins in Nabokov's fictional twelve-year-old; rather, it exists as an all-purpose signifier for the underage sexual temptress—and she is anything but helpless and dependent. From references to Amy Fisher (the "Long Island Lolita") to Anna Kournikova (the "Lolita of Tennis"), the appellation Lolita is grabbed by journalists when they want to suggest sexual knowingness and artfulness. Twelve-year-old victims of incest are never called Lolitas. We employ the term, as Katie Roiphe does in her memoir of her self-described "Lolita-like" affair with her high school teacher[5]—to emphasize the erotic power of young, sexy teenagers.

Such casual cultural uses of the term do not pretend any kind of literary fidelity to Nabokov's character, of course. Both films of *Lolita*—Stanley Kubrick's (1962) and Adrian Lyne's (1998)—on the other hand, do. Lyne, indeed, makes a great point of the faithfulness of his version.[6] Yet both, as I will argue in detail later, fall prey to (different versions of) an inflated, ideologically driven mythology about Lolita's "power." And so, too, does Pia Pera's *Lo's Diary*, which claims to "fill the void left by the enigmatic but fundamentally passive figure onto which Humbert projected his fantasies."[7] Pera, unlike Vera, views Nabokov's Lolita as a voiceless presence, seen exclusively through Humbert's eyes, whose subjectivity is ignored by Nabokov and must be supplied—that is to say, invented—by twentieth-century feminists. For Pera, that means creating a Lolita who is a fully conscious, scheming sexual agent, not at all a helpless "victim" of Humbert's lust.

Leaving issues of Lolita's sexual agency aside for the moment, Pera surely has a point about the novel, which is told entirely in Humbert's voice and which rarely provides a window onto Lolita's thoughts or feelings. It could be argued, without much strain, that Vera's empathic reading is wishful (or perhaps overly maternal) thinking rather than an accurate representation of what Vladimir actually gave the reader. My own position is somewhere in between. Neither Lolita's loneliness nor her "heartrending courage" is nearly as prominent as Vera would like it to be (nor, perhaps, as Vladimir intended it to be.) But *Lolita* is not merely Humbert Humbert's diary, either. The novel doesn't preach or offer a pedagogy. But it does have a moral point of view—"argued," true to Nabokov's notions about art, in perfectly selected details, sometimes poignant, sometimes repellent, always precise.

Those details, on my reading, reveal neither that Humbert is a monster nor that Lolita is a temptress. Rather, Humbert's moral failing (a failing that many of us share, although perhaps to a lesser degree of self-abandon) consists in his trying to realize the fantasies of imagination, memory, and desire—in themselves beautiful and soul feeding—in the body of an actual human being. It is not in Humbert's arms, but in the realm of "aurochs and angels, the secret of durable pigments, prophetic sonnets, the refuge of art"[8] that Lolita belongs—as Humbert ultimately recognizes. For although finding a child achingly beautiful, being sexually shaken by that beauty, even enshrining it in words and images, is not monstrous, forgetting that she *is* a child—not a sexual equal, whatever her precocity—is.

Ironically, the failure to distinguish between fantasy figure and child is at the heart of both Kubrick's and Lyne's interpretations of *Lolita,* each of which is more a Geiger counter of a particular cultural zeitgeist than an attentive reading of the novel. The same might be said of Pia Pera's "power-feminist" reinvention of Lolita. Kubrick's fiercely antisentimental, satiric emphasis reflected very well a time in which the avant-garde's energies were directed against 1950s conformism, puritanism, and Norman Rockwell Republicanism. Lyne's version, which attempts to rehabilitate Humbert and depict an "equal balance of power" (as Lyne has put it) in the relationship, reflects and speaks more to contemporary concern—coming from sources as diverse as the men's movement, antifeminists such as Rush Limbaugh, and "third-wave" feminists like Pera—to rescue gender politics from the clutches of whining, male-bashing "victim-feminists."

In this chapter I explore the complex conversation that has existed between Nabokov's *Lolita* and postwar culture, focusing on Kubrick's and Lyne's movie adaptations as exemplary of how and why Nabokov's "moral content" got mangled in that conversation, but also briefly discussing scenes from *Eyes Wide Shut* and *American Beauty,* mass-media representations of the nymphet, and other contemporary "participants" in that conversation. Throughout—and often in counterpoint to Kubrick's and Lyne's interpretations—I offer my own understanding of what Nabokov was trying to accomplish in his novel; my aim is not only to provide an interpretation that reveals the "moral content" of *Lolita,* but to suggest why it is both relevant and still unnerving, even in 2003.

Kubrick's *Lolita:* Censorship, Sixties Cynicism, and the Issue of Lolita's Body

"How Did They Ever Make a Movie of 'Lolita'?"

Seizing an opportunity that they couldn't resist, some critics replied to that provocative question, posed on billboards and in the trailer to Stanley Kubrick's 1962 film version: "They didn't." Sue Lyon is too mature, too curvy, they complained; Peter Sellers's Quilty takes up far too much of the movie. Pauline Kael, always on the alert for high-art clubbiness and elitism, accused her colleagues of "fake erudition," of demonstrating that they had read the book by complaining of the movie's departures from it—and perhaps that was true for some reviewers.[9] But for many of my generation, Kubrick's movie was the original, Nabokov's novel a palimpsest. That is, we read Nabokov through Kubrick. Indeed, I am convinced that until Adrian Lyne radically rewrote the story in 1998, Kubrick's interpretation virtually dominated the popular cultural imagination and understanding of the book.

Nabokov is a writer who is lavish with details, all of them chosen with acute consciousness and art, and compacted with meaning. So it's not surprising that when Kubrick offered him the job of translating *Lolita* from novel to screenplay, he at first felt only "revulsion" at "the idea of tampering with my own novel."[10] The idea was completely abandoned—albeit, as it turned out, temporarily—when he and Vera heard of plans to appease the censors by having Lolita and Humbert marry at the end. Eventually, however—with the assurance that this ending would not be required—Nabokov agreed, and his name is listed in the credits. But in fact, little of Nabokov's work made it into the final version of the film—"only ragged odds and ends," as the author commented in the foreword to the published version of his screenplay.[11] He pronounced Kubrick "a great director" and the actors "magnificent," but told his son Dmitri that watching the movie was like being a patient in an ambulance, watching the scenery go by, powerless to change it.[12]

Kubrick, too, was not happy with the film, in particular with the compromises that he had to make to comply with Hollywood's powerful Production Code during a decade often referred to as the "plague years" of Hollywood self-censorship. (He confessed years later, "Had I realized how severe the [censorship] limitations were going to be, I probably wouldn't have made the film.")[13] One big problem was the representation of Humbert, whose wicked scheming is as monstrous as it is comic. Throughout much of the novel, Humbert, while discoursing elegantly about childhood loves and nymphet charms, in fact behaves like a lecherous and manipulative scumbag. At the beginning of his relationship with Lolita, he constantly schemes ways to fondle her surreptitiously without her knowing (at one point, he even steals "the honey of a spasm," that is, has a covert orgasm, while Lolita remains oblivious; 59). The night they begin their cross-country journey, he drugs her so he can pleasure himself while she's unconscious. Later in the relationship, he badgers, terrorizes, and bribes her with money into dispensing her sexual favors. In 1962, none of this could be included in the film, nor could Kubrick have Humbert's narrative voice-over engage in musings of an explicitly lascivious nature.[14]

Still, Kubrick insightfully recognized that it was crucial that changes made with the censors in mind not work to rehabilitate or soften Humbert in the eyes of the viewer. He knew that Humbert isn't Humbert if there aren't abusive aspects of his behavior that he (Humbert) recognizes are "objectively" horrible, but nonetheless indulges in and describes with sardonic, urbane wit. Kubrick solved the problem (as Nabokov did in his own screenplay) very intelligently, by using the relationship between Humbert and Lolita's mother, Charlotte (rather than Humbert's sexual proclivities), to expose the "hidden" Humbert: the selfish, callous—even cruel—schemer behind the kindly, civilized professor of literature. Reading Charlotte's pathetic written declaration of love for him, he laughs uproariously (in Nabokov's screenplay, he does a jig). After Charlotte (played by Shelley Winters) is conveniently killed by a car, he relaxes contentedly in the bath with a "rapturous swig of Scotch" (as Nabokov described the detail, one of those added by Kubrick that the author praised as "appropriate and delightful"). James Mason's Humbert, who fit to a tee the physical descriptions of Humbert in the novel—dark, ruggedly handsome, but in a suave European mode—embodied smooth, surface civility and secret, guilty unease to perfection. The division between his public face (polite, refined, urbane) and his inner life (wriggling, poisonous worms squirming through his brain) is written on his face in virtually every scene.

The choice of curvaceous, strikingly pretty blond teenager Sue Lyon for the title role—a selection made with the censors in mind—was less fully satisfactory. Employing a twelve-year-old actress was out of the question, of course. But so, too, was even using an actress who *looked* like she was twelve. We were still pre-Twiggy in 1962. Calvin Klein had not yet imported the tight buns and taut muscles of gay male aesthetics into the commercial realm, and Audrey Hepburn's flat-chested Holly Golightly was just a tiny, new blip on a screen filled with compact but hourglass-shaped Gidgets and Tammys. An undeveloped female body, Kubrick feared, would scream to the Production Code Administration: "This is a *child* having sex with a middle-aged man." Sue Lyon's Lolita—her actual age fifteen and her "literary" age upped to fourteen—had a body that looked like it had been enhanced by estrogen for some time. The script also gave her a fourteen-year-old's life—high school proms, steady boyfriends—along with the banal sexual knowingness of a teenager.

Lyon was not entirely off the mark. She did bring a bored, know-it-all smirk to the role, like one long "puh-lease!" that actually turned her beauty to advantage, suggesting it was something she hadn't yet grown into and giving it an eerie cast, like a preteen version of JonBenet Ramsey, painted to be years older than her age for a pageant. Sometimes her physical shtick—when she plopped down bored on the couch, or munched on Humbert's bacon as she sauntered lazily up the stairs, or mugged, stealthily popping gum—seemed just right. But her body—its shape, its movements, the sense of consciousness it projected—was far from that of a child, an alteration that might have seemed innocuous, perhaps even desirable, to a moviemaker intent on establishing her sex appeal within the limits of the Production Code, but an essential error for the serious reader of the novel, a major distortion, not only of the character of Lolita, but of the nature of the appeal her body (and her diffident sexuality, which I discuss later) holds for Humbert Humbert.

The nymphet's allure is very particular. To the lover of the nymphet, as Humbert assures us, conventional female beauty is irrelevant, even an obstacle to desire; ordinary little girls, indeed, may be far more "comely." The ineffable but bodily signs of the nymphet are announced, instead, by her catlike facial bone structure and slim legs: "the slightly feline outline of a cheekbone" and "the slenderness of a downy limb" (19). A few pages later, Humbert adds to this first brief description (introduced in a generic discussion of the nymphet) through a reminiscence of a young prostitute, chronologically past it at sixteen or seventeen, but still bearing the bodily signs of her former nymphage in her "immature body," "her hips no bigger than those of a squatting lad" (23). The nymphet has no curves. In Nabokov's descriptions, her bones always outstrip her flesh. She's a colt. Her "agile, giggling legs" (52), with their "schoolgirl thighs" (41), lope around, doing their tomboy thing, while the nymphet-lover trembles and swoons.

To translate Lolita's body into contemporary imagery, it's less like that of a healthy, muscular Nike teen and more like—indeed strikingly like—that of the undeveloped waif of the fashion pages, with whom Lolita also shares a certain glazed-over detachment. The waif is cool, bored, barely awake. So, much of the time, is Lolita. Her smile, we are told, "hung in its own remote flowered void, so to speak, or wandered with myopic softness over chance objects" (260). When she exposes her crotch (which she does often), it's out of carelessness or lack of shame rather than sexual exhibitionism. Her "guileless limbs" (56), as Humbert describes them, are innocent of their erotic power. Unlike that of the fashion models, Lolita's carelessness is not entirely an act. She's still a kid. She's not yet developed a woman's hyperconsciousness of being observed. Yes, she apes the gestures of movie stars, but her still-boyish body wears those efforts awkwardly. When she puts on lipstick, it's smudged and overdone. Her hygiene is poor; she rarely washes her hair, and "the only sanitary act she performs with real zest" (47) is brushing her teeth. Yet Humbert loves her "brown fragrance" (42) and dirty jeans.

In the book, then, Humbert is drawn to Lolita's twelve-year-old body, with its "narrow white buttocks" (127) and "puerile hips" (39), its "thin, knobby wrist[s]" (56) and "beautiful boy-knees" (111), precisely for its immaturity. He's repelled by "that sorry and dull thing, a handsome woman" (68), and views even the "average coed" (with her "heavy low-slung pelvis" and "thick calves") as a "coffin of coarse female flesh" (159). Although he acknowledges that Charlotte is quite attractive by ordinary standards, he is personally revolted by her "heavy hips" and "round knees" (as well as her "pitifully ardent" nature; 68–72). As Lolita approaches thirteen, Humbert realizes that in just two years or so her nubile nymphet limbs could be well on their way to the hideous, inexorable fate of developing womanly heft. He recommends that she diet: "The tour of your thigh, you know, should not exceed seventeen and a half inches. More might be fatal." (He adds, for the reader: "I was kidding, of course" [191]; Nabokov knows he was not.)[15]

New Yorker critic Pauline Kael, in defense of Kubrick's film, dripped particular scorn on those critics who remarked on how mature Sue Lyon looked. She suggested they needed to visit a local grade school: "Have the reviewers looked at the schoolgirls of America lately? The classmates of my fourteen-year-old daughter are not merely nubile; some of them look badly used."[16] But Kael forgets that when Humbert first sees his Lolita in the novel she doesn't look "badly used" at all. She looks like a child of twelve—more precisely, she looks like another child of twelve, named Annabel and described with many Poe-like allusions, with whom Humbert had fallen in love on the Riviera when he was a boy himself. That child died, and Humbert had been haunted by her "seaside limbs and ardent tongue" (17) ever since. When he sees Lolita kneeling in her mother's garden (kneeling, not sunbathing seductively as in the film), Humbert feels, with "the impact of passionate recognition" that "it was the same child—the same frail, honey-hued shoulders, the same silky supple bare back, the same chestnut head of hair. . . . I saw again her lovely indrawn abdomen where my southbound lips had briefly paused; and those puerile hips on which I had kissed the crenulated imprint left by the band of her shorts" (38–39).

Am I making too much of a few extra curves? I don't think so. Getting Lolita's body right seems to have mattered very much to Nabokov. He gives us plenty of information, even her approximate measurements at age twelve, when Humbert first spied her in her mother's garden: "Hip girth, twenty-nine inches; thigh girth (just below the gluteal sulcus), seventeen; calf girth and neck circumference, eleven; chest circumference, twenty-seven; upper arm girth, eight; waist twenty-three; stature, fifty-seven inches; weight, seventy-eight pounds; figure, linear" (100).[17] Nabokov did not regard such statistics as droll window dressing. In preparing to write *Lolita,* he carefully recorded statistics chronicling the gently ascending weights of young girls of various heights as they advanced in age from twelve (beside "57 inches, 82 lb." is recorded "four lb. more than Lolita") to thirteen ("84 lb.") to fourteen ("86 lb."), and then a rude leap to 104 pounds at fifty-nine inches, age seventeen (Lolita's age at her death.) Ages fifteen and sixteen are not listed; instead, a blank column separates fourteen from seventeen, an empty but decisive abyss between the end of the body's possibilities of nymphdom and that triple-digit, absolute boundary of womanhood.[18]

Nabokov is not alone in marking one hundred pounds as a steep fall from grace; my anorexic students do, too. When I reread the novel after a decade spent researching and writing about young women's feelings of shame about their bodies and about the cultural images that inspire that shame, that fact struck me forcefully.[19] I thought of the students who had written in their journals of their disgust—very much like Humbert's—at their own bodies plumping out into womanhood, despising the heft of a thigh, the jiggle of loose buttocks, the thick calves, the "coffin of female flesh," nursing a secret pride over the bones that poke out from their elbows, knees, collarbones. I thought of their revulsion over their hungers (for sex, for comfort, for food), as self-critical of what they saw as their own excessive desires as Humbert was of the adult woman's. I thought of the physical poses they often struck, arms folded over their chests, the toes of their long, slim legs pointed inward, the sleeves of their sweaters covering their hands, emerging from hiding only to offhandedly push back the hair usually falling in their eyes.[20]

Nabokov, of course, was an artist, not a sociologist or cultural theorist. Nonetheless, he had extraordinary precision and subtlety as a cultural observer. With his keen eye and ear for detail, he now seems uncannily prescient in giving Humbert a taste for undeveloped, coltish beauty that's hardly an eccentricity anymore. Humbert didn't acquire that taste from fashion magazines. But it could be argued that fashion itself was only giving form to something already in the cultural air when it began to celebrate the woman-who-is-not-yet-a-woman. When Nabokov wrote *Lolita,* that "something," while not yet embodied in mass-media images of waifs and nymphets, was arguably foreshadowed in a new spirit of ridicule and rebellion against the Charlottes (read: conventional wives and mothers) of postwar culture and what many men (and a bit later, young women) began to view as the prison of their domestic domain.[21] As just one marker of this rebellion, note that *Playboy*—a magazine for which Nabokov frequently wrote—made its first appearance in 1953 with a strident editorial (written by Hugh Hefner) issuing insults against "woman" and declaring independence from the tyrannies and entrapments of wives and mothers-in-law. In place of "woman," Hefner offered the playmate. Her body was far from androgynous, of course. But psychologically, Hefner assured his male readers, she was a child: fresh and fun loving, without sexual demands of her own, happy to be "played" with by daddy (and ruled by him; Hefner virtually ran the lives of the young women who worked for him.)

Lolita, of course, was not just psychologically a child but *really* a child—and Nabokov rightly objected, when shown Sue Lyon's picture, that she didn't look enough like one. Kubrick reassured him that she "could be easily made to look younger and grubbier" for the part.[22] He didn't keep his promise. When we first see Lolita in what is arguably the most famous scene in the movie, she's a bikinied beach-blanket Dolly, all soft curves, sunbathing in the backyard. She knows how to wiggle across a room. Her makeup is expert, her hair Breck-girl coifed. As she sprawls across the bed in the Enchanted Hunters Hotel, where Humbert and she have intercourse for the first time, we see that she is wearing spike heels! Take the gum out of her mouth, and she and James Mason are a pretty attractive couple—a fatal flaw not only for understanding the sexual aesthetics of the pedophile (why would Humbert, who has nothing but contempt for the body of a grown-up woman, desire a child who looks like one?) but for what Nabokov called the "moral content" of the story.

Moral *content.* Not message. Not lesson. *Content.* Nabokov, I believe, is being as precise here as in any other of his choices of language. The moral point of view of *Lolita* is conveyed not through explicit argument (hence Nabokov was correct in claiming that the book has "no moral in tow"), but through a juxtaposition and friction between details that we are (in theory) "free" to judge morally however we see fit, but that are nonetheless chosen with enormous care to elicit the emotional response Nabokov desires the reader to have. So, on the one hand, we are given Humbert's obsessional projections, in which a fictional category of femaleness—called the nymphet and elaborately described by Humbert in several swooning passages—allows Humbert to view Lolita as an "elusive, shifty, soul-shattering" charmer around which no man can be safe, a "little deadly demon" of "fantastic power" (18–19).[23] On the other hand, the pubescent banalities with which Nabokov details Lolita's habits—the movie magazines, the pop jargon, the lust for cheap trinkets and roadside attractions as Humbert and Lolita drive across country together—give us Lolita as child, with the mentality and inexperience of a child. A child whose stepfather's penis is much, much bigger than anything adolescent Charlie offered at camp, a child who is convinced—because Humbert tells her so—that she will be sent to reform school if she tells the police about his kidnapping of her, a child who performs fellatio for money so she can squirrel away enough to run away from her stepfather.

Being a child, of course, does not mean being an angel. Lolita taunts and sulks and connives; she has a smutty mouth. But it is adolescent rebellion rather than sexual provocation that drives her crudeness. She may talk flippantly to Humbert about her "murdered mummy," but she also devours sentimental novels about self-sacrificing mothers and brave little daughters and cries herself to sleep at night—every night. This is the sort of detail Vera Nabokov has in mind in insisting on the "pathos" of Lolita's loneliness—a loneliness to which Humbert is largely indifferent, except as it interferes with his own desires. He hears her cry every night; why doesn't he run to comfort her? "I always preferred the mental hygiene of noninterference," he explains later. But, "squirming and pleading" with his memory, he is forced to recall, too, that "it was always my habit and method to ignore Lolita's states of mind while comforting my own base self" (261).

Nabokov, however, is not Humbert, and although he, too, is guilty—as author—of ignoring Lolita's states of mind (as moving as they are, details that provide a window onto Lolita's own experience are few and far between), his attitude toward her situation is far from indifferent. Over and over, he calls on us to look squarely, consciously, clearly at the violations Humbert causes in the service of his created dreamworld, as wc are made aware of the disjunction between Humbert's engorged fantasies and the child-life of the youngster he's screwing, who'd rather be (and should be) eating a hot fudge sundae. Lolita's body, which Humbert loves for its immaturity, is also a constant reminder to the reader that this is not a May-December romance but a grown-up man lusting after a child. Make Lolita too womanly, and you risk invoking another kind of narrative altogether—the age-old, same-old story of Eve's responsibility for Adam's sin. Kubrick may not have meant it to happen, but his film does drift in this direction, and Sue Lyon's (that is to say, Kubrick's) Lolita, with her stacked little body, teasing smirk, and trampy vamping, comes pretty close to baby Eve.

The archetype would have been mitigated had Kubrick insisted on including any of the vignettes from the novel that bring Lolita's misery—her pain over her mother's death, for example—to the forefront. But in Kubrick's *Lolita,* one good sobfest and dead mommy is forgotten. (Humbert, to calm her down, promises her a brand-new hi-fi and all the latest records, and apparently the bribe works.) The same scene in the novel, significantly, ends with Lolita sobbing *despite* Humbert's having plied her with gifts all day. Emphasizing Lolita's sadness and loss would not have jibed, of course, with the film's dedication to inflecting the "dark" with the comic; it would have altered the overwhelmingly ironic, anti-sentimental character of the movie. We were at the dawn of the sixties—a period dominated by a rebel male ethos, both in the emerging student politics and in the arts—and cool, cynical iconoclasm was hip. The old legalities were still in place (in 1962, the same year that *Lolita* was released, Lennie Bruce got busted for saying "motherfucker" in a comedy routine), but everything suggestive of soft, domestic, or "feminine" values was in for a beating—by Mailer, Bruce, Kesey, Mark Rudd, Stokely Carmichael, and others. (Betty Friedan's *Feminine Mystique* was also published in 1962, but it wouldn't be until the late sixties that feminism made any dent in the cultural politics of the decade.) Kubrick may not have been able to defy the censors with literal or visual material that broke the code, but like many other savvy filmmakers before him—those, for example, who managed to playfully sneak homosexual themes and images into "straight" movies—he could certainly misbehave through attitude.

In doing so, he was not radically out of touch with one side of Nabokov. The irreverent aspects of *Lolita* were there to be mined from the novel, and they meshed very well with the emerging sensibility of the period. Many, in fact, credited *Lolita* as a turning point in encouraging, as F. W. Dupee put it, "the fading smile of the Eisenhower Age to give way to a terrible grin."[24] But so, too, are there elements of a very different nature in the novel, elements that look backward (as Nabokov does in *Speak Memory*) to a lost paradise rather than forward (as for the young, American rebels) to a clean break with the past. After Lolita has run away, Humbert cleans out his car: "My Lolita! There was still a three-year-old bobby pin of hers in the depths of the glove compartment. There was still that stream of pale moths siphoned out of the night by my headlights" (267). It's a perfect, small poem about the irrevocable pastness and continuing presence of the imprints of intense love—much too elegiac to be included by Kubrick.

Kubrick also omits any reference to Humbert's love of Annabel and his lyrical remembrances of boyish bliss past. Humbert was morally ruined, of course, by attempting to reincarnate those memories in a new relationship with a living twelve-year-old girl, and the novel does not "excuse" him because of his history. (Nabokov makes his disdain for that sort of psychological argument clear in the book.) But the Annabel memory does reveal a core of beauty at the center of the poisonous apple. Humbert, for Nabokov, although not for Kubrick, is not simply a charming monster with a thing for little girls, but a relic of a less dispose-all culture, tormented by what might be described as an exquisite hypersensitivity to beauty, excruciatingly pained at its passing, unable to let it go. He may joke about disposing of Lolita when she's past her nymphage, but actually, he's a man who can't even throw her bobby pin away. And when he finally does see her again, pregnant and married and "only the faint violet whiff and dead leaf echo" of her nymphet self, he realizes that he stills loves her: "No matter, even if those eyes of her would fade to myopic fish, and her nipples swell and crack, and her lovely young velvety delicate delta be tainted and torn—even then I would go mad with tenderness at the mere sight of your dear wan face, at the mere sound of your raucous young voice, my Lolita" (253).

Lyne's *Lolita:* Nice Humbert, Orgasmic Lo, and Nineties Sexual Politics

Like the publication of the novel on which it is based, the premiere of Lyne's adaptation, which aired first on the Showtime ("No Limits") cable television channel, then was released in theaters, was a long-anticipated, controversial event. The film had been spurned by U.S. distributors for nearly a year while it played in various cities in Europe,[25] and Lyne, complaining of the tyrannies of political correctness in America, had created the expectation of new levels of sexual candor in the depiction of the Lolita-Humbert relationship. He proudly pointed out that Nabokov's novel, published in Paris in 1955, also had to wait for acceptance in the United States. Viewers expecting graphic sex or skin were undoubtedly sorely disappointed, for Lyne's film, accommodating the Child Pornography Prevention Act of 1996, has none of that. Neither has it any of the wicked humor of the novel, or of Kubrick's earlier film.

From the opening credits, Lyne's film announces an interpretation that is virtually the mirror image of Kubrick's. Kubrick's opening credits are both transgressive and ironic: a close-up of Lolita's foot as Humbert (unseen except for his hand) painstakingly paints her toenails with polish, while Nelson Riddle's ersatz Rachmaninoff piano music wrings its heart in the background. Kubrick's tongue is in his cheek from the start. Lyne's movie, in contrast, begins (and pretty much remains) in nostalgic, dreamy, soft focus, as Humbert, having just murdered Quilty, eyes brimming with tears, virtually in a swoon, drives his car down a country road. Mist is everywhere, both visually and musically, as Ennio Morricone's minimalist, elegiac, lyrical score (no overblown romantic crescendos in Lyne's film) plunks little teardrops of notes here and there. A voice-over skips the first paragraph of the novel ("Lo—lee-ta: the tip of the tongue taking a trip of three steps") to begin on the more nostalgic, tender note of the second: "She was Lo, plain Lo in the morning, standing four feet ten in one sock" (11).

"Did she have a precursor?" (11). In Lyne's film, yes. The actress playing Annabel looks to be about eighteen and straight off the pages of *Glamour* magazine, complete with fashionable straw hat and pretty camisole, which she unbuttons seductively in front of a watching Humbert. In cinematography, the episode is even more drenched in Old World vapors than the rest of the movie. The relationship, however—unlike the clumsy, fevered, mutual groping that occurs in the book between twelve-year-old Annabel and thirteen-year-old Humbert—is something from Showtime's late-night *Red Shoe Diaries* (minus the complete undress and coupling, of course). It is a boy's fantasy—not a boy's memory—of a first sexual encounter. As soon as I saw Annabel's breast curves, her languorous body as she stretches on the beach, her sultry glances from beneath lidded eyes, I knew that something fatally wrong was going to happen in this movie.

Critics have lavished much praise on screenwriter Stephen Schiff's liberal use of exact quotes from the novel. Nabokov's narrative of the Annabel episode was apparently not enough, however, to make the exculpatory point that Schiff wanted, so he supplied some very non-

Nabokovian language of his own to drive home a psychological "motivation" for Humbert's later behavior. "Whatever happens to a boy the summer he is fourteen can mark him for life," we are told portentously at the outset of the Annabel episode. (Yes, Lyne decides to make Annabel fourteen, too—even though public morality would presumably find nothing shocking about a twelve-year-old and a thirteen-year-old necking in the sand.) Then, at the end: "The shock of [Annabel's] death froze something in me. The child I loved was gone, but I kept looking for her long after I'd left my own childhood. The poison was in the wound, you see, and the wound wouldn't heal." This contemporary theory of Humbert as a wounded child, passively suffering the poison of unhealed hurts, is the film's dominant understanding of him—it suffuses Jeremy Irons's portrayal, which has nothing wicked, scheming, or even mildly lecherous about it.

Irons plays Humbert as a man who's simply tragically in love with the wrong woman and doesn't know what to do about it. Around her, he's not only haunted by boyhood memories, he's as shy, awkward, and tentative as a boy himself, gazing at her like a love-struck puppy, and never, ever trying one illicit fondle (never even contemplating one) until she "seduced" him at the Enchanted Hunters. (Lyne, like Kubrick, conveniently omits Humbert's drugging of Lolita the night before.) Unlike Nabokov's Humbert, Lyne's Humbert wouldn't dream of groping Lolita without her consent. Yes, he does rape Lolita in an act of fury—after she has provoked and taunted him—but there is not a single scene in which Humbert is portrayed as the initiator of erotic relations with her.

Lyne, Schiff, and Irons all stress, in a documentary called *The Lolita Story*, that they felt it important that the audience *like* Humbert, that they find him (as Schiff puts it) "appealing, although he is a monster." I agree with the theory. "Humbert is all of us," Elizabeth Janeway declared in her 1958 review of the novel, insofar as he underlines "the essential, inefficient, painstaking and pain-giving selfishness of all passion, the greed of all urges, whatever they may be, that insist on being satisfied without regard to the effect their satisfaction has upon the outside world."[26] But in fact there's nothing greedy or monsterlike in the slightest about the Humbert that Lyne, Schiff, and Irons have created.[27] Unlike Kubrick's Humbert, he doesn't even have much of a sleazy side with Charlotte (doesn't contemplate her murder, for example, as both Nabokov's and Kubrick's Humberts do). When Melanie Griffith as Charlotte screams the words at Humbert—"You're a monster!"—it seems excessive, although Humbert's vile diary is in her hand. On his part, Irons just stands there like a helpless, trapped little boy (in the same scene in the Kubrick film, you can see James Mason's mind turning, trying to devise a clever way out even as Charlotte shrieks).[28]

And Lolita? Lyne, unlike Kubrick, gets the body part right (or perhaps it might be fairer to say that by 1998 the cultural milieu had altered sufficiently to permit him get it right). And on the face of it, his film *seems* to break some important ground that Kubrick feared to tread in the depiction of the title character. Fourteen-year-old Dominique Swain was cast, controversially, in the title role. She doesn't look twelve (and Lyne, following Kubrick, has aged the character to fourteen), but she does have a leggy, lithe body that is more faithful to the Lolita of the novel. In 1998, her shape is also more conventionally feminine—for females of *all* ages—than it was when Sue Lyon played the role. So, presumably to make her look more like a child, Lyne loads her with accessories that ostentatiously advertise her girlhood: old-fashioned plaits wrapped around her head, retainers on her teeth, milk mustaches, oversize pajamas.

Ladies and gentleman of the jury, don't be seduced by this artfulness! Lyne's Lolita is a child only when she's guzzling milk in front of an open refrigerator, or crying into her pillow at night, or rolling a jawbreaker around in her mouth. When she's after sex or money, she's all woman. In one scene, she's sitting across the room from Humbert, trying to convince him to let her be in the school play. A knowing look passes over her face, and she crawls over to where he is sitting in a rocker and begins rocking the chair with her foot. "I have a right to be in a play," she pouts. "Not if I say you don't," he replies. She moves her foot to caress his inner thigh. "You like that. . . . You want more, don't you? Well, I want things, too. . . ." She expertly moves her hand up his thigh, her finger inching toward his crotch. "I think my allowance should be two dollars. . . ." (Still closer to his groin; by now, she has him virtually in the palm of her hand, so to speak. "God yes," Humbert agrees.) ". . . and I get to be in the play."

Lyne's Lolita is a highly passionate girl, too, and—although she's deeply wounded and cries like a baby when Humbert smacks her across the face in anger—appears to get turned on by a little sexual violence. In the scene alluded to earlier, Humbert rapes her, inflamed by the sight of her, her lips smeared with scarlet, apparently having returned from a date with another lover. Lolita tries at first to lie, but when she realizes he's not buying it, she gives up playing the innocent and smiles provocatively, a bag of bananas that Humbert's just bought her dangling from her hand, in a quintessential "she's asking for it" moment. As he throws her on the bed and enters her, she becomes sexually excited, giving him ardent, deep tongue kisses, then alternately cackling wildly and swooning with pleasure at his rough treatment.

Viewers unfamiliar with Nabokov's *Lolita* (or whose memories of the book have been dimmed by time) are unlikely to recognize that Nabokov's heroine never behaves anything like this.[29] Never lasciviously creeps across a floor, expert fingers making their way to Humbert's crotch. Never has an orgasm on Humbert's lap. Takes no pleasure in being raped. Yes, the novel's Lolita is careless, experimental with her body. But sex with adolescent Charlie (at summer camp) had hardly "roused" her (127); she thought it was a kid's game, "part of a youngster's furtive world, unknown to adults." Lolita had done the deed, but her sexual consciousness was still that of a child. And yes, in the book Lolita does barter sex for money. But it's always Humbert who initiates things, Humbert who does the begging, the pleading. Lolita, in Nabokov's words, merely exploits "her power to deny" him. This "drop in Lolita's morals" (as Nabokov, oozing irony, has Humbert describe it) occurs only after she has been with Humbert for some time, continually badgered by him for her favors (167–68).

As far as Lolita's own sexual passion with Humbert goes, in the novel it never even takes off, let alone reaches the heights we see in Lyne's film. In fact, there's no evidence that she is sexually responsive at all. Humbert describes her as his "Frigid Princess," who invariably preferred a "Hamburger to a Humburger," and at best would tolerate his caresses when promised money or presents. "Never did she vibrate under my touch," he recalls (152). For Humbert, who is revolted by the "pitifully ardent" passion of mature women, Lolita's sexual diffidence is a large part of her appeal. "There she would be," he recalls fondly, "a typical kid picking her nose while engrossed in the lighter sections of a newspaper, as indifferent to my ecstasy as if it were something she had sat upon, a shoe, a doll, the handle of a tennis racket, and was too indolent to remove" (151).

Lyne and Schiff take *this* image of Lolita reading the funny papers, oblivious to Humbert's mounting passion, and convert it into an atmospheric, hazy, sun-streaked romantic idyll in which Lolita, sitting on Humbert's lap, is overcome with sexual excitement and appears to have an orgasm. An earlier version, using a body double, had gone even further, showing her body arched in ecstasy, Humbert inside her from the rear. That one had to be replaced when the Child Pornography Prevention Act of 1996 ruled it illegal not only to have a minor engage in "sexually explicit conduct" for a scene, but also to make it *appear* as if a minor is engaging in such conduct. The final version of Lyne's movie, appeasing this law, is (as one reviewer put it) "shot innocently from the neck up." Apparently, depicting a child having an orgasm while sitting on daddy's lap doesn't count as "sexually explicit conduct" as long as the genital regions are offscreen. But why show Lolita having an orgasm at all? In the comparable scene in the novel, Lolita not only has no orgasm of her own, but she is oblivious to Humbert's orgasm, much to Humbert's relief. "Blessed be the lord, she had noticed nothing!" he exults. He prides himself on the fact that he "had stolen the honey of a spasm without impairing the morals of a minor" (58–59).

What's going on here? Kubrick's physical maturation of Lolita, as we've seen, was to appease the censors. An orgasmic Lolita, in contrast, seems to be deliberately and provocatively upping the sexual ante, in defiance both of the novel and of some notion of public morality or sexual politics. In this regard, the comments that both Lyne and Schiff have made about their conception of the Humbert-Lolita relationship are illuminating—and astounding, to an attentive reader of the novel. Lyne has said he wanted to portray an "evenly weighted battle of the sexes," and Schiff that he viewed Humbert and Lo as "a couple—a very odd couple, to be sure, but a couple nonetheless . . . testing each other, confounding each other, and, yes, loving each other."[30] Evenly weighted? An odd but loving couple? These notions are utterly foreign to Nabokov's novel, and in their rhetorical insistence ("a couple nonetheless"; "and yes, loving each other") sound suspiciously like an answer to the contrary position that a relationship between a twelve-year-old and a forty-five-year-old can never be one of equality, is by its nature one of exploitation. In challenging this—which Lyne and Schiff seem intent on doing—Lolita's invented orgasm figures prominently. It's harder, as Lyne and Schiff surely understood as they tried to adapt Nabokov's details to their May-December conception of the relationship, to see an orgasmic

Lolita, swooning on her stepdad's lap, as a less than willing and equal partner in the relationship. By the same token, it's harder, too, to think of Humbert as a selfish predator, taking advantage of the power difference between them. At the very least, he's a pleasure-giving predator, a politically correct pedophile.

But who holds the position Lyne and Schiff are out to refute (conveniently altering key details of Nabokov's novel in order to do so)? Feminists, of course. Or, at least, popular images of "second-wave" feminists (such as Kate Millett, Susan Brownmiller, Robin Morgan), who, according to now commonly held caricatures, are grim, puritanical scolds who see male predators at every office watercooler, at every frat party, behind the doors of every faculty office. Few public figures have done anything to dispute these caricatures; rather, the forces perpetuating them have grown increasingly diverse—from the tirades of Rush Limbaugh, Camille Paglia, and Christina Hoff-Sommers to antifeminist polemics in popular magazines such as *Esquire,* to "men's movement" reclaimers of ancient male warrior archetypes. In the 1990s, "third-wave" and "power" feminists joined the fray, with Naomi Wolf charging that the second wave not only demonized men but also demeaned women by viewing them as defenseless victims of male predation. Wolf tagged her predecessors "victim-feminists" and her own position "power-feminism," appealing to a new generation's need to redefine itself as sexier, savvier, less complaining, more male loving, and better "assimilated" to the dominant culture than their mothers' generation of feminists.[31]

For many young feminists, the centerpiece of the new agenda was an insistence on the sexual agency and potency of women—*all* women—even in relationships of seemingly dangerous inequality. They seemed oblivious to the fact that their version of female agency was often simply the ability to manipulate men sexually. Katie Roiphe, for example, who became briefly famous for insisting that the very notion of "date rape" is largely a feminist concoction, describes her "power" in her affair with her thirty-six-year-old high school teacher (when she was sixteen) in this way: "He felt guilty. I had something he wanted. . . . He and I bargained over each act of physical intimacy like hagglers in an open market, and in the course of that bargain, I learned a kind of sexual control that would stay with me for the rest of my life."[32] The same conception of power is evident in *Lo's Diary,* journalist Pia Pera's reimagining of

Lolita from Lolita's point of view. The following is Pera's version of the "honey of a spasm" scene. Unlike in Nabokov's version, Lolita *knows;* it's Humbert whose ignorance is exploited.

> I feel that trunk of his swelling, bigger and bigger. He goes on singing, endlessly, now slow, now fast, very fast, then he turns red and, fighting for breath, mangles the words. It's a waste of time to try to correct him by singing along—by now he's out of time, in the sense that he's all in my power.... I'm all hot inside, I'd like to hug and kiss him without all these pretenses, but I'm going to wait till the next move; for now I pretend nothing's happening, and go on biting my apple.... at every crunch he rocks more quickly, throwing his head back as if he's on a swing, and then tries to act normal so I can't tell how excited he is, until only the core is left, and since I feel sorry for him for not being able to just take what he so desperately wants—to hold me tight against him, crush me—I throw the core in the fireplace and end up right on top of him, against that hard little stick, and then I start humming along with him again.... I press against him, until he holds me still, interrupts the nursery rhyme, and, all trembling, forgets to keep up his pretense. I feel weird, too, I melt, and something goes by without my really seeing it, a whir of swift wings, it disappears in an instant and we sit there looking at each other, all blushing, not knowing what to do. I'd like to curl up and wrap myself in his arms. It would be nice but then he'd get scared; I'll put off my courage lesson till another time—you can't insist on everything at once. Luckily the telephone rings, and I run to answer it. He takes advantage of this to get up and go to the bathroom, and when he finally comes back I'm in the garden. He looks around confused and satisfied, maybe he hasn't yet realized what happened to him: that I seduced him. That now he's mine.[33]

It may sound very contemporary, until one recalls that images of women as the mighty controllers of male sexuality have an ancient and enduring lineage in our culture. And as to its "feminism"—it wasn't that long ago that some lawyers were still defending child molesters on the grounds that the little girls had seduced them. I'm not denying, of course, that women are sexual beings, with desires as strong as men's. But that's precisely why some men turn to little girls. Humbert is excited by Lolita's innocence, not her sexual proficiency—and by the fact that he can intrude, unnoticed, into her child's world while he remains keenly aware of "the secret system of tactile correspondence between beast and beauty—between my gagged, bursting beast and the beauty of her dimpled body in its innocent cotton frock" (57).

Whether it's politically correct or not, the fact is that Nabokov's Lolita barely exists as a "sexual agent" for Humbert—an essential fact that is lost in Pera's rush to make Lolita the mastermind of the relationship. The way she *does* exist for him, as he himself puts it, is as his "own creation" (59), his fantasy nymphet, whose reality he continually "solipsize[s]" in favor of his own imaginative construction. That's the only way he can feel free to molest her. He's a civilized man, after all, and knows that one doesn't have sex with children. But with Lolita "safely solipsized" (while on his lap, let's not forget) and Humbert carefully modulating his behavior so that his mounting excitement, and his erection, remains concealed from her, the stiflingly domestic suburban den vanishes, to be replaced by a "self-made seraglio" in which the beast in man can release itself without fear of "ridicule or retribution," where he is no longer "Humbert the Hound, the sad-eyed degenerate cur clasping the boot that would presently kick him away," but "a radiant and robust Turk, deliberately, in the full consciousness of his freedom, postponing the moment of actually enjoying the youngest and frailest of his slaves" (57–59).

Solipsize. Humbert's own word for his behavior toward Lolita—in the same scene in which Pera paints him as a clueless, aging boy-toy—is stark and ugly, which is exactly how Nabokov wants us to see it. He wants us to remember that the power difference between adult and child is the essence of the pedophile's pleasure—and of the violence done to the child. But is it necessary to portray Lolita as utterly victimized, without any agency of her own, in order to remain faithful to this essential insight? Nabokov doesn't think so, and neither does Nancy Jones, whose feminist reworking of *Lolita* is as determined as Pia Pera's to give Lolita her own voice and story. Her Lolita (called Molly, which is also the title of the book) is hardly passive in her relationship with her stepfather, yet Jones is careful to remind us continually that the fact that Lolita may have technically "seduced" her stepfather—that is to say, initiated their first act of sexual intercourse—does not make him any less the exploiter of her innocence. As Molly's childhood friend Betsy reflects, having read Molly's diary of her life with "Richard Richard" (Betsy's discovery of the diaries is the central narrative device of Jones's novel):

> Molly did seduce her stepfather. She gave no details of the seduction in her journal, but I imagine her tossing off her nightgown and panties as Ava Gardner might have discarded a boa. Molly never tanned deeply, but

> her skin acquired a pinkish, golden hue, as if, like a ripening peach, she has absorbed something of the sun itself.
>
> In summer, when we took our baths together before my mother put us to bed, Molly would bat her eyes and blow soap bubbles at me from her end of the tub. We sat face-to-face, our backs and buttocks against the cold porcelain, our legs straddling each other's rosy, slippery legs. Once, Molly pressed her feet and toes against my vulva, which she kneaded unconsciously, rhythmically, as she lathered herself with soap.
>
> I imagine his anticipation as she straddled him; perhaps he held his breath as I did then, in disbelief. No doubt, his face grew hot, and deep within him something stirred, something urgent and forbidden.
>
> After our long-ago bath, that night under the covers, I lay quite still, knees clenched and bent almost to my chest, troubled by the wet, insistent throbbing between my legs. Molly was asleep, unaware and unconcerned. Sometimes when we climbed the basketball standards, the cool, smooth metal rubbed against our panties and produced the same sensation I felt that night, but I never connected it with the flint-against-steel friction between Bogey and Bacall.
>
> Richard Richard knew, however—he knew. When his twelve-year-old stepdaughter draped herself across the bed, unbound hair spilling across his lap, he knew what caused him to take the small hand caught in the tangle of silky mane and clasp it to his groin. When she knelt before him, explored his mouth with her tongue as she undid the buttons of his shirt, he knew why his breathing slowed and halted as he drank her in. When she took his sex in her hands and pumped it gamely, he knew why it leapt and quivered between her fingers. He knew all this and more.
>
> He knew everything that she did not.[34]

Jones's novel is much truer to Nabokov's *Lolita* than Pera's. And, as far as films go, Sam Mendes and Alan Ball's *American Beauty* (1999) is more the moral descendant of Nabokov's *Lolita* than Lyne and Schiff's *Lolita.*[35] At a turning point in *American Beauty,* forty-two-year-old ad exec Lester Burnham (Kevin Spacey), having fantasized about having sex with his daughter's friend Angela (Mena Suvari) for several months, is finally in a position to make the dream come true. If ever there was a "sexy little slut," Angela is it. She continually brags, crudely and often cruelly, about her extensive sexual experience and attractiveness to men. She flirts shamelessly with Lester. Listening in at his daughter's bedroom door, he has overheard her speculating about the size of his dick and telling Jane that if he built up his arms and chest she'd "totally fuck him" (he immediately digs up his old set of dumbbells and begins exercising). One night, as Lester comforts Angela after she's had a bad fight with Jane, everything suddenly becomes possible. He tells her how beautiful he finds her, and he kisses her. Willingly, she lies back on the couch and allows him to pull her jeans off, caress her legs and face, unbutton her blouse. And then, with Lester barely believing that he is actually going to do what he has dreamed of for so long, she tells him it's her first time—and everything reconfigures. This is not the mythically carnal creature of his fantasies, he realizes; this is a nervous child.[36] And Lester tends her as such, drying her embarrassed tears, making her a sandwich, reassuring her of her desirability but no longer able to act on it.

Humbert Humbert, of course, goes for the Humburger rather than the sandwich. But Vladimir Nabokov wrote *Lolita,* not Humbert Humbert. It is Vladimir Nabokov who gives Humbert a voice, Nabokov who constructs the architecture of the whole and fits the details he has chosen within it. And Nabokov refuses to allow the reader to share Humbert's mythical view of Lolita's sexual power. For Nabokov—as for Lester Burnham—the sobering fact is that Lolita is a child. Lyne's Lolita, in contrast, hasn't awoken from Humbert's dream.

Postscript: *Lolita* in an Empire of Images

When Nabokov wrote *Lolita,* it could be imagined that a taste for the waif was the province of a special sort of pedophile. Today, one doesn't have to loiter around schoolyards in order to catch an illicit glimpse of a twelve-year-old, her body in an unknowingly revealing or sexually piquant posture. Just open a fashion magazine. The models themselves may not be minors, but the careless poses they strike with their skinny, long-limbed bodies could be illustrations for a coffee-table edition of *Lolita.*

Sometimes these representations go too far and are recognized to be bordering on "kiddy porn." In 1995, Calvin Klein was forced, submitting to public protest, to yank a series of CK perfume ads from television and magazines. In these ads, the models were arranged with long legs spread, underwear exposed, their bodies "coded" as those of children (finger in mouth, little denim skirt). They didn't seem sexually knowing or artful; their legs were spread awkwardly, as though they weren't posing for pictures but caught unawares. The boys did not look like models at all, but like "real" children, creating the impression that the photographer had happened upon the actual world of the child and was peeping into it. In the television versions of the ads, this feeling was intensified by the voice of an (unseen) adult photographer, telling the child to take off her jacket, turn this way or that, while she performed for him guilelessly, awkwardly.

Klein, in defending the ads, argued that none of the models were actually children, as though this settled any moral qualms about the ads.[37] This kind of argument is not uncommon in our culture. Unlike Nabokov, we are not much inclined to tunnel deep into the content and meaning of the images that obsess us, whether as sexual fantasies or as blueprints for girls' bodies (and souls). Instead, we focus on the ethics of the images' production—the ages of the actresses and models employed, whether they have been made to diet for their jobs, and so on. Taken to task for their role in promoting eating disorders, the designers scoff and claim it's "just fashion" and point out—often lying to us—that the models eat like horses.[38] The parents of children who participate in kiddy beauty pageants think they've covered themselves ethically if their little girls claim to enjoy the pageants. And Adrian Lyne boasts to *Premiere* magazine about how well he protected Dominique Swain, by putting a pillow between her body and Jeremy Irons's (then he turns to the interviewer, his face alight with excitement over the scene: "It's sexy, isn't it?").[39]

It's very rare that popular culture exposes or interrogates (rather than simply reproduces) our fantasies about Lolita-like girls. I believe that this is one reason *American Beauty* seemed fresh and innovative. There's a striking scene, too, in Kubrick's posthumously released *Eyes Wide Shut* (an appropriate title, in the context of this discussion)[40] in which seventeen-year-old actress Leelee Sobieski appears as the daughter of a costume shop owner from whom socialite doctor Bill Harford (played by Tom Cruise) wants to rent a hood and mask, in order to attend a mysterious orgy he's heard about from a pianist pal of his. In the middle of the business transaction, the shop owner hears a giggle coming from behind a sofa in a back room and discovers his daughter dressed only in panties and bra. She has apparently been entertaining two nearly naked Japanese businessmen, who claim, when the girl's father rages at them for having "no sense of decency," that they were invited "by the young lady." "Young lady?" the father bellows, "This is my daughter! And couldn't you see that she's a child?"

Sobieski has the face of a cherub in the film, and although her small breasts are developed, she has a slight, linear body that—particularly because her head is rather large in proportion to her torso—seems barely beyond childhood. Many people found her two fleeting appearances to be the only truly transgressive moments in the film. (In her second scene, we discover that the shop owner's moral outrage is a sham, and he's actually quite willing to rent out his daughter's favors.) For me, in the midst of studying *Lolita* in all her incarnations, it was almost as though Kubrick, in 1999, was showing us a bit of what his Lolita might have been like, had he been freer—and perhaps gone psychologically deeper—when he made his 1962 film. The two brief scenes with Sobieski were more unnerving than *Eyes Wide Shut*'s sinister orgy scenes, more erotically alive than the much more extensive footage of Nicole Kidman's toned and tidy body. How could such a body seem transgressive in any way? Sobieski, not yet grown into (or cosmetically altered into) the perfect proportions of Hollywood norms, seemed to have popped into the celluloid world from the real one—where nasty things do indeed happen to little girls.

In what I have elsewhere called "our empire of the images," the processings of the dreamworld are voracious, however; just a few months later, my issue of *Movieline* arrived with Leelee on the cover, glamorized and confidently sultry in a low-cut black dress.[41] The pictures inside revealed the same coltish body as in *Eyes Wide Shut,* but in poses more assertively, smoothly provocative than her giggling, nervous presence in the film. The images were not disturbing, as Sobieski's childlike appearance in the movie is, but presented the familiar, reassuring cultural archetype of the knowing, pubescent temptress. Such images do not jar us into moral wakefulness; rather, they lull us into comfort with the eroticization of immature bodies.

This, then, is a call not for censorship, but for consciousness. Nabokov was not a moralist, and neither am I. At many points in Nabokov's *Lolita,* we are encouraged to empathize with, identify with Humbert. It's not monstrous to be haunted by dreams of youthful bliss, to feel stifled by the conventions of domestic life, to be drawn to a fantasy of beauty that will heal the soul of its compromises. Nabokov knows that it's a possibility for all of us to fall in love with our own projections and forget the real person in front of us. But at the same time, he recognizes that it's ruinous not to look squarely, clearly, consciously at our created dreamworlds, their erasures of reality, the consequences of the letting those erasures get out of hand. In an empire of images, I would add, we need to apply that critical consciousness to our collective fantasies, too.

Notes

1. Vladimir Nabokov, *Lolita* (New York: Berkley, 1955), 286. Page numbers for further quotations from this source appear in parentheses in the text.

2. Andrew Field, *VN: The Life and Art of Vladimir Nabokov* (New York: Crown, 1977), 306.

3. Quoted in Stacy Schiff, *Vera (Mrs. Vladimir Nabokov)* (New York: Random House, 1999), 236.

4. During the past forty-eight years, the novel has been translated into twenty languages and has sold more than fifty million copies.

5. Katie Roiphe, "Upfront: The End of Innocence," *Vogue*, January 1998, 38, 40, 46.

6. *Lolita*, dir. Stanley Kubrick (MGM, 1962); *Lolita*, dir. Adrian Lyne (Showtime Productions, 1998).

7. Pia Pera, *Lo's Diary* (New York: Foxrock, 1999), quote from jacket flap.

8. Nabokov, *Lolita*, 281. Pera's book is perhaps best known for having inspired a copyright infringement lawsuit by Dmitri Nabokov, a suit that ultimately held no legal water but that resulted in Farrar, Straus & Giroux's abandoning plans to publish the book. Pera ultimately resolved the feud with Nabokov by allowing him to print a (nasty) preface to her published book, recounting the whole affair in the light in which he saw it.

9. Pauline Kael, "Lolita," *Partisan Review* (fall 1962).

10. Vladimir Nabokov, *Lolita: A Screenplay* (New York: Vintage, 1961), vii. Nabokov admitted that had he gone into writing for the stage or screen, he would have "applied a system of total tyranny, directing the play or picture myself, choosing settings and costumes, terrorizing the actors . . . and, in a word, pervading the entire show with the will and art of one individual" (x).

11. Ibid., xii.

12. Brian Boyd, *Vladimir Nabokov: The American Years* (Princeton, N.J.: Princeton University Press, 1991), 466.

13. Quoted in ibid.

14. For example, thinking about Lolita's inevitable maturation, Humbert plots that either "I would have to get rid somehow of a difficult adolescent whose magic nymphage had evaporated" or "with patience and luck I might have her produce eventually a nymphet with my blood in her exquisite veins, a Lolita the Second, who would be eight or nine around 1960, when I would still be *dans la force de l'age*." He even contemplates the possibility of "Dr. Humbert practicing on supremely lovely Lolita the Third the art of being a granddad" (158–59). At times in the novel, Humbert does become sharply but briefly morally aware, only to have the impulse pass as lust mounts again. After their intercourse at the Enchanted Hunters Hotel, for example, an expression of pain passes across Lolita's face as she settles in the car, and Humbert suddenly sees what has happened in a light other than as the fulfillment of his fantasies: "This was an orphan. This was a lone child, an absolute waif, with whom a heavy-limbed, foul-smelling adult had had strenuous intercourse three times that very morning." (The mention of three times is apt to startle even the most jaded reader.) But within a few minutes, Humbert begins to feel "the writhing of desire again" and is plotting ways to put her in a better mood so that he can have her again, parked somewhere on the side of the road (129).

15. Nabokov hints that Charlotte may have been a nymphet herself. The novel tells us that her first husband was twenty years older than she, and in an old album Humbert is able to make out in a picture of Charlotte "a dim first version of Lolita's outline" (72).

16. Kael, "Lolita."

17. One of my students, for a project on Lolita's body, made circles of string for each of these measurements to demonstrate for the class just how "linear" Lolita is. We were all amazed at her slightness.

18. Boyd, *Vladimir Nabokov*, photo of Nabokov's notebook (pages of photos unnumbered).

19. See Susan Bordo, *Unbearable Weight* (Berkeley: University of California Press, 1993); Susan Bordo, *Twilight Zones: The Hidden Life of Cultural Images from Plato to O.J.* (Berkeley: University of California Press, 1997).

20. I might also mention that many of my students with eating disorders, true to the statistics, have histories of sexual abuse—ex-Lolitas trying to find salvation, paradoxically but also logically, by becoming the diffident waifs that our culture has endowed with immunity from hurt.

21. For more on the male rebellion of this period, see Susan Bordo, *The Male Body: A New Look at Men in Public and in Private* (New York: Farrar, Straus & Giroux, 1999), 112–123; Barbara Ehrenreich, *The Hearts of Men* (New York: Anchor, 1984).

22. Nabokov, *Screenplay*, xi.

23. See also Nabokov, *Lolita*, 43.

24. Quoted in Schiff, *Vera*, 236.

25. Celestine Bohlen, "New 'Lolita' Is Snubbed by U.S. Distributors," *New York Times Book Review*, 23 September 1997.

26. Elizabeth Janeway, "The Tragedy of a Man Driven by Desire," *New York Times Book Review*, 17 August 1958, 19.

27. Frank Langella's truly slimy Quilty, robe flapping, stroking his own naked thigh as he promises Humbert "unique erotica" if he spares his life, absorbs all the monster-plasma in Lyne's *Lolita*.

28. Jeremy Irons puts it tellingly when he says in *The Lolita Story* that Humbert's character demonstrates that "nice people do terrible things." Humbert Humbert—a "nice person"? Tormented, yes. Brilliant, yes. Ultimately filled with heart-wrenching regret, yes. But nice? Nabokov, I believe, wants us to achieve identification with Humbert less cheaply, not by realizing that he's "nice people" (just like the rest of us) but by confronting the fact that the rest of us aren't so nice either. Maybe an Englishman can imagine niceness as a possibility, even a desirability, for human nature. But for a Russian like Nabokov (it is one area where he would be in accord, I think, with Dostoyevsky), "nice" just doesn't cut it. We don't get to the depths of the human soul, its capacity for good *or* evil, through "nice." *Seeing*—truly, honestly seeing—requires sacrificing the illusion that any of us is "nice."

29. I was startled to see, however, that almost without exception the reviewers, who presumably have read the novel and ought to take some responsibility for knowing what's in it, remarked on Lyne/Schiff's faithful rendition: a "lavishly faithful production" (James Caryn, "Revisiting a Dangerous Obsession," *New York Times*, 31 July 1998, 28); "almost debilitatingly loyal to Nabokov's novel" (Michael Wood,

"Revisiting Lolita," *New York Review of Books,* 26 March 1998, 9); "careful, even loving, loyalty to the book" (Anthony Lane, "Lo and Behold: Why Can't America See the New 'Lolita'?" *New Yorker,* 23 February–2 March 1998, 182). I can only guess that they were seduced by Lyne's use of charming period details and carefully chosen, lyrical quotations.

30. Stephen Schiff, *Lolita: The Book of the Film* (New York: Applause, 1998), xvi. He certainly succeeded in confounding Michael Wood, who wrote in the *New York Review of Books* that the orgasm scene in the movie "seems relatively healthy, since it's only sex, and both are enjoying themselves. I know it isn't healthy, and I don't think it is once I remember her age. But I have to make myself remember this" ("Revisiting Lolita," 9–13). Wood wouldn't have this difficulty if he went back to read the book. The idea of Hum and Lo mutually pleasuring each other (*The Joy of Sex,* perhaps, on the bookshelf behind them) is utterly at odds with Nabokov's depiction of the relationship, which (as I hope my quotations in the first part of this essay make clear) is about as far from a May-December romance as can be imagined.

31. Naomi Wolf, *Fire with Fire* (New York: Random House, 1993).

32. Roiphe, "Upfront."

33. Pera, *Lo's Diary,* 102–3.

34. Nancy Jones, *Molly* (New York: Crown, 2000), 122–23.

35. *American Beauty,* dir. Sam Mendes (Dreamworks Pictures, 1999). *American Beauty* (which "first started rattling around" screenwriter Alan Ball's head during the Amy Fisher/Joey Buttafuoco affair) makes no explicit references to Nabokov or *Lolita,* yet there are many striking correspondences between *Lolita* and *American Beauty,* both of a "small detail" nature (for example, Lester Burnham's age is forty-two—the same as Humbert's when he first meets Lolita) and in terms of the overall moral and aesthetic vision of the film. Unfortunately, I cannot go into this argument here without making this a much longer essay.

36. This is a slight paraphrasing of Ball's stage directions, which read: "His POV: Angela lies beneath us, embarrassed and vulnerable. This is not the mythically carnal creature of Lester's fantasies; this is a nervous child" (Alan Ball and Sam Mendes, *American Beauty: The Shooting Script* [New York: Newmarket, 1999], 93).

37. Michelle Ingrassia, "Calvin's World," *Newsweek,* 11 September 1995, 60–66.

38. Few ask why so many young girls find the cool detachment, the desirelessness of those skinny bodies so compelling, or why our entire culture is repelled by mature female flesh that has not been tidied by hours at the gym or the nips and tucks of surgery.

39. Rachel Abramowitz, "How Do You Solve a Problem Like Lolita?" *Premiere,* September 1997, 95–98.

40. *Eyes Wide Shut,* dir. Stanley Kubrick (Warner Bros., 1999). Kubrick's screenplay is based on Arthur Schnitzler's novel *Dream Story,* also an appropriate title.

41. Susan Bordo, "In an Empire of Images, the End of a Fairy Tale," *Chronicle of Higher Education,* 19 September 1997, B8. Mena Suvari appeared in a similarly provocative cover shot two months later. In one of the inside photos, she looks strikingly like JonBenet Ramsey.

CHAPTER SEVEN

The Aesthetics of Jewishness

Shelley Winters

Joseph Litvak

> It's safe to say that Pamela [Harriman] would have been appalled by Monica.
>
> One talked in the deep rolling cadences of Winston Churchill; the other, like a Valley mall rat. One gave her men monogrammed silver cigarette lighters; the other, books like "Oy Vey! The Things They Say: A Guide to Jewish Wit."...
>
> "Pamela was so about subtlety and cunning," says Sally Bedell Smith, who wrote a biography of Mrs. Harriman. . . . "Monica plays the game all wrong. Pamela would have taken that job with Bill Richardson, and set herself up as an emissary between the U.N. and the White House. She would never have wanted to work at Revlon."
>
> —Maureen Dowd, in her *New York Times* op-ed column, 11 October 1998[1]

In the second volume of her memoirs, Shelley Winters recalls an "embarrassing" moment during the filming of the 1963 screen version of Genet's *The Balcony*. Doing a scene with Lee Grant, who played her lover, Winters was instructed by the director to surprise Grant by kissing her:

> "Action!" the director yelled. I handed Lee Grant one of my diamond earrings in a sexy way, then, petting her throat, I spoke some of the dialogue and then I gave her a big wet kiss, holding the back of her head. . . . The director yelled "Cut." Lee Grant exploded in anger.
>
> "She ruined my hair," she shouted. "Just ruined it."
>
> She said not a word about the kiss, she just insisted we do it again, and I must kiss her without messing her hair. I refused to do it again. . . . I wasn't embarrassed while kissing her, but I was sort of embarrassed

> afterward. Lee Grant wasn't embarrassed at all and was furious at me because I wouldn't do it again. She had very gooey lipstick on and it got all over my mouth and upper lip. I informed her I was sorry, but no matter how much she begged, I wouldn't kiss her again.[2]

Winters's memoirs have achieved almost canonical status in the genre of kiss-and-tell, but this account of what we might call the Lee Grant incident strikes an uncharacteristic note in the brazen narrative that surrounds it. It is easy enough to explain this embarrassment on the part of an actress and celebrity otherwise proud to exhibit that peculiarly Jewish shamelessness known as chutzpah: in 1963, homosexuality and lesbianism, even of the lipstick variety, represented something of a last frontier of liberal showbiz insouciance, so that when Winters admits her "lack of lesbianism" (428), no one has to strain much to hear the undertone of self-consolation. But there's something about this behind-the-scenes scene, this little drama of actressy "temperament," that I think exceeds the glibly historicist diagnosis of homophobia (not to mention the way the diagnosis produces self-consoling or self-congratulatory side effects of its own). There's something about the *messiness* of the scene, in short, that makes me want to stick with it, with its big wet kiss and its "ruined" hair and its very gooey lipstick, as tenaciously and as embarrassingly, perhaps, as that lipstick of Lee Grant's sticks to Shelley Winters's mouth and upper lip. For if this thespian anecdote has a lesbian subtext, its suggestion of lesbian in-difference,[3] of becoming undifferentiated, that is, from another woman ("As I write," Winters writes, "I'm amazed to realize how my life has been intertwined with Lee Grant's"; 429), is itself intertwined with a suggestion of *Jewish* in-difference, of getting stuck to, stuck on, stuck with another Jewish body, and another Jewish face.

Another is the operative word here. Winters has never denied her ethnicity, and one of the leitmotifs of her memoirs—the first volume of which is titled, *Shelley, Also Known as Shirley*—is precisely the feisty persistence, alongside the glamorous Hollywood movie star named Shelley Winters, of her authentic, irreducible, Jewish self: the streetwise, working-class, left-wing, loud-mouthed, troublemaking, Brooklyn-bred Shirley Schrift. While the family name, Schrift, betokens an unabashed inscription of Jewish identity, the professional alias, Shelley Winters, performs the function of a doubly anglicizing makeover: just as the first (or Christian) name, Winters tells us, pays tribute to her favorite poet, so the last name, although derived from her mother's maiden name, Winter, completes a certain cosmetic work of whitening. When Shelley Winters—I want you to read *Winters* as a verb—Jewishness is not simply effaced, as in some snow job, but rather, in keeping with the ambiguity and ambivalence that characterize the cultural project of assimilation as a whole, palimpsestically preserved, as in some nose job, at once signified and toned down, or, even, signified by *being* toned down.

Which is to say that when Shelley Winters gives Lee Grant—née Lyova Rosenthal, though her nom de guerre echoes the last name of a U.S. president—a big wet kiss, and when, as a result, Winters gets Grant's very gooey lipstick all over her mouth and upper lip, the embarrassment of this sticky situation has as much to do with race as with sex. Or rather, the sexual embarrassment and the racial embarrassment can at no point be unstuck from each other: when Grant and Winters kiss, when their Jewish lips speak together, the messy, sexy consequence of this smooching is not only the smudging of these two heterosexually identified actresses, and of the line separating them, but also a simultaneous melting and thickening of their respective masks as "American" women, a dissolution into gooey Jewishness, in which they risk outing each other as "un-American" to the degree that they both risk becoming reracialized.

The recipient of her costar's big wet kiss, Grant finds out how it feels when Winters begins to thaw. (If Winters comes, as her favorite poet might have said, can spring be far behind?) About the kiss, Winters claims, "Lee Grant wasn't embarrassed at all"; but Grant was sufficiently hot and bothered to have "exploded in anger," if only because Winters had "mess[ed] her hair." Thus warmed up, like chocolate in a double boiler, Grant, at any rate, returns the favor by leaving an incriminating impasto of herself on Winters's face. Incriminating not just because lipstick traces always are, but for a more specific reason as well. For though Winters cultivates a scrupulous vagueness about the circumstances of Lee Grant's career—"she had not worked in films for a number of years," Winters remarks elsewhere (315)—Grant had not worked in films since 1951 because she had been blacklisted, and she had been blacklisted, according to Ephraim Katz, because "her then-husband . . . had been on the blacklist and she refused to testify against him before the House Un-American Activities Committee."[4] Not all of the victims of the blacklist and the red scare were Jews, of course; but enough *were* Jews, and Jewishness was sufficiently interchangeable, in the national imaginary, with un-Americanness *tout court,* that during the fifties and early sixties (what Winters calls "the middle of my century"), red and black could easily have been mistaken for the colors of a race that had supposedly just established itself as neither colored nor a race at all.

Winters doesn't say what color Lee Grant's lipstick was (though some shade of red might be a good guess), and the fact that *The Balcony* was filmed in black and white makes it impossible for us to tell. Or, more accurately: this fact emblematizes the extent to which Jewish American identity, whatever color it was or wasn't wearing in 1963, continued to be defined in relation to African American identity. I am gesturing here toward the influential account of black-Jewish cultural politics by Michael Rogin in his book *Blackface, White Noise: Jewish Immigrants in the Hollywood Melting Pot.* Centering his analysis on the Jewish appropriation of blackface in early-twentieth-century mass culture, and particularly on the seminal instance of Al Jolson's starring role in *The Jazz Singer,* Rogin argues that, for American Jews, "assimilation is achieved via the mask of the most segregated; the blackface that offers Jews mobility keeps the blacks fixed in place."[5] When, near the end of the book, Rogin notes that with the onset of the HUAC investigation, Jews in Hollywood became vulnerable once again, he merely hints at the ironic return of blackface through the blacklist.[6] In more frankly moralistic deployments of his thesis,[7] however, the argument would go something like this: having been granted their precarious yet comforting blanket of wintry whiteness "at the expense of blacks,"[8] an expense made most vivid in the highly charged performance of putting burnt cork on their faces *and then taking it off,* American Jews paid the price for their abjection of African Americans when, in the 1950s, their disavowed racial difference came back to haunt them, with a vengeance.

As Kathy Peiss points out in *Hope in a Jar,* her fascinating study of America's "beauty culture," lipstick is the most problematic of all cosmetics, insofar as it is regarded as the "most artificial," the most apt to recall the sexual provocativeness of "paint."[9] Winters's recollection of kissing Lee Grant has the advantage of underscoring the extent to which lipstick's sexiness can also be a raciness, its sexual provocation a racial one. (One of Peiss's major themes is the racial politics of American beauty culture and the central roles played in it by racially marginal women such as the African Americans Annie Turnbo Malone and Madam C. J. Walker and the Jewish Helena Rubinstein.) *As* paint, that is, especially paint that can get smeared all over someone else's face, Lee Grant's lipstick, I want to suggest, alludes, and alludes all the more disturbingly because "accidentally," to the burnt cork with which an earlier generation of Jewish entertainers would black up so as, paradoxically, to white up. Yet I also want to suggest that, both in its indeterminate color and in its very determinate texture, this lipstick can inscribe Jewishness, like a message scrawled on a dressing-room mirror,[10] as something more materially specific, and more fantasmatically productive, than the mere nonblackness to which accounts like Rogin's would reduce it. Maybe black, maybe red, definitely gooey, Lee Grant's lipstick, which in effect becomes Shelley Winters's lipstick too, presents us with the embarrassing possibility of figuring out just what postwar American culture thinks Jewish "blood" is.

For blood is one of the many substances that, whatever its shade, lipstick—sticking to the lips, painting the mouth, rewriting the labia, arousing and signaling "passion"—metonymically evokes. And if blood—to quote from Winters's 1969 gangster pic *Bloody Mama*—is thicker than water, Lee Grant's lipstick might go to show that Jewish blood is among the thickest. Thanks to its extraordinary gooeyness, moreover, her lipstick also accentuates the way in which any lipstick resembles food, as though inviting one to feast on it, or on the lips it adorns, or on the face and body to which those lips—if I may wax poetic—serve as portals. (Just a few pages into the just-published *Read My Lips: A Cultural History of Lipstick,* coauthored by Meg Cohen Ragas and Karen Kozlowsi, references to lipstick's "rich color, luscious texture, [and] creamy consistency," to "the buttery, vanilla-scented kiss of a glorious Guerlain lipstick," had my mouth watering.)[11] With Grant's lipstick smeared all over her mouth and upper lip, in fact, Winters could almost be sporting a chocolate moustache—not unlike the one she may have worn, in my mind's eye anyway, after indulging in what she tells us repeatedly is her "standard tranquilizer: tuna-fish salad and tomato on rye toast and a chocolate milk shake" (457 and passim). Nothing particularly Jewish about this meal—unless we interpret its tranquilizing efficacy, its excellence as comfort food, as deriving in part from the symbolic fulfillment of a Jewish-liberal wish for racial harmony implicit in the chocolate milk shake, dreamy synthesis of winter's cool and summer's warmth, precursor of Jerry Seinfeld's beloved black-and-white cookie. Nothing Jewish, either, unless the toasted rye bread imparts a certain delicatessen flavor to the other ingredients, conjuring up a culinary tradition in which tuna sandwiches and milk shakes, or egg creams, mean *dairy,* thickness means *schmaltz,* and blood phantasmagorically turns into *borscht.*

That culinary tradition, of course, is also a cultural tradition, or, rather, a set of terms used to describe not just Jewish immigrants in the Hollywood melting pot but, more globally and more damningly, a certain sticky, shticky, boiled-down essence of mass culture itself. As Pierre Bourdieu has pointed out, schmaltz—rendered chicken fat—metaphorically defines the peculiarly unwholesome medium, the gooey atmosphere of sentimentality and facile pleasure, in which most nonelite cultural production supposedly takes place.[12] As for borscht, the fabled belt to which it gave its name may designate a geographically specific entertainment network that has vanished, along with its audience and personnel and historical moment, but this lost object, it seems, somehow refuses to *stay* lost, resurfacing as the bad object, the generalized middlebrow bilge, the vulgarly stereotypical commercialism, from which the most ambitious—that is to say, the most easily embarrassed—Jewish cultural critics and cultural practitioners still can't dissociate themselves fast enough.[13]

It won't come as much of a surprise to you, I suspect, to learn that, despite Shelley Winters's aggressive, and indeed well-founded, claim to be A Serious Actress, those ambitious critics, when they turn to consider her career, tend to see her as swimming in just such unsavory soup. In one of the cruelest comments on Winters's work, Pauline Kael, reviewing her Oscar-nominated performance in *The Poseidon Adventure* (1972), wrote: "Shelley Winters . . . yearns to see her grandson in Israel and makes endless jokes about her bloated appearance. (She's so enormously fat she goes way beyond the intention to create a warm, sympathetic Jewish character. It's like having a whale tell you you should love her because she's Jewish.)"[14] Kiss me: I'm Jewish. If this command is seldom heard anymore, it's because Kael has hardly been alone in refusing to obey it. For with the occasional anachronistic exception, like Fran Drescher's proletarian *belle juive,* Jews in American mass culture, almost never construed as sexually desirable, can no longer even aspire to whatever compensatory lovability they may once have enjoyed. Television commercials for the Olive Garden restaurant chain beckon us with images of zesty, old-world Italian familialism. But while Italian Americans constitute the "good" white European ethnic group, the warm, lip-smacking appeal they are permitted (or required) to project stands in sharp contrast to the popular image of the Jews, who, insofar as they are supposed to control the culture industry, must appear in it as little as possible, lest, their lips gooey with schmaltz and borscht and chocolate egg creams and chopped liver, they give too visible a face to the slickness and sickness that critics from left, right, and center agree in regarding as a bloated mass culture's virtual lifeblood. (Even the all-American status of the bagel remains questionable: as recently as a year ago, ads for McDonald's and Lender's bagels were busy de-Judaizing their product—softening and lightening it, making it look gentler and more Gentile—for the New England market.)

So when a whale tells you you should love her because she's Jewish, you can only recoil in disgust—I'm following through Kael's logic here—not just because she's a whale, not just because of the fat in her, but because of the fat she's in: the oily, oozy, viscous mass that seems her very element, and that threatens to become yours if you let her near you. Let me try to describe Winters's big scene from *The Poseidon Adventure,* the movie about an ocean liner that turns belly up, and the *Titanic* of its day, as Winters observed in a 1998 interview.[15] Gene Hackman, who plays the leader of the small but stellar group of surviving passengers, has gotten lost trying to swim through a corridor to the ship's engine room, and now Winters's enormously fat character, poignantly named Belle Rosen, having produced a necklace proving that she was once "underwater swimming champ of New York for three years running," and having leaped into the water to rescue Hackman, swims back to the surface with him:

> BELLE: You see, Mr. Scott? In the water, I'm a very skinny lady. [She suddenly cries in pain, and her face becomes contorted. It's obvious that she's having a heart attack. She falls back into the water. Hackman's character dives in and carries her to the surface again, pulling her onto a platform.]
>
> BELLE [stunned and speaking haltingly]: I guess I'm not the champion of the Women's Swimming Association anymore.
>
> SCOTT: Hold on, Mrs. Rosen. Just hold on.
>
> BELLE: Mr. Scott, enough is enough. Please let me go. [She produces a necklace bearing the Hebrew word chai.] Give this to Manny. Tell him he has to give this to our grandson. You see, that's the sign for life. [Her breathing and speech are becoming more labored.] Life . . . always

> matters very much. [She hiccups and blinks, then her face goes blank; it's clear that she's dead.]
>
> SCOTT [sobbing and hugging her]: Oh, God!

To Pauline Kael and her dry-eyed kind, it might seem as though the water through which Winters swims, by virtue of her swimming through it, had turned into so much chicken soup: chicken soup whose ostensible life-enhancing powers are negated by the globules of fat that float on its surface, waiting to congeal in the cultural bloodstream like the cholesterol that causes Belle Rosen's fatal heart attack (we have seen her pilfering dessert from her husband's plate, for which she must be punished, as surely as the character played by Stella Stevens must be punished—also by death—for calling her "old fat-ass"). That is, Winters's character's last words—"Life always matters very much"—are contradicted, mockingly inverted like the ship itself, by the lethally bathetic conditions of genre, style, and performance, the vast Hollywood ocean of bad taste and deadly commercialism, in which they have their very being. One must have a heart of stone not to laugh at the death of Belle Rosen. Better: one will end up with a heart of stone if one doesn't laugh at her death, since anyone who would swallow it unironically risks the same petrifying cardiac disaster that befalls her.

Life always matters very much. Brandishing the Hebrew word *chai*—"that's the sign for life"—Winters brandishes as well the condensed version of secularized Judaism circa 1972: call it the *Fiddler on the Roof* version, to invoke the mainstream artifact that the Jewish intelligentsia still most loves to hate.[16] But what do we make of the confusion of necklaces, whereby the one with the Hebrew word and the one with the swimming medal seem to have been melted together? Is Jewish showbiz wisdom, or the showbiz representation of Jewish wisdom, somehow equivalent to a preternatural talent for subaquatic sports? Even after decades of assimilation in America, Jewish athletic ability continues to go unrecognized, and in late-twentieth-century American mass culture, Jews, apparently still suffering from that old Freudian (not to say Shelleyan) lack of oceanic feeling, continue to be enlisted in an invidious vaudeville routine in which, cast as figures of uniquely venal intellectuality, they play the part of a corrupt and corrupting Culture opposite African Americans' masquerade as Nature.[17] In this context, it is somewhat startling, then, to encounter, in the chapter of Horkheimer and

Adorno's *Dialectic of Enlightenment* titled "Elements of Anti-Semitism," an association of Jews both with what the authors call "our animal prehistory" and with that particular adaptation to nature that the authors theorize as the benign form of "mimesis."[18] Bringing to the surface the deep structure of anti-Semitic psychology, Horkheimer and Adorno write:

> There is no anti-Semite who does not basically want to imitate his mental image of a Jew, which is composed of mimetic cyphers: the argumentative movement of a hand, the musical voice painting a vivid picture of things and feelings irrespective of the real content of what is said, and the nose—the physiognomic *principium individuationis,* symbol of the specific character of an individual, described between the lines of his countenance. The multifarious nuances of the sense of smell embody the archetypal longing for the lower forms of existence, for direct unification with circumambient nature, with the earth and mud.[19]

Shelley Winters interpreting the American Jew as great white—or not so white—whale, Lee Grant's lipstick now resembling mud: going against the stereotypical grain, these would be examples of a happy, or at least utopian, affinity between Jews and nature, which is at the same time, for Horkheimer and Adorno, an affinity between Jews and mimesis.

But as critics like Miriam Hansen and Martin Jay have shown, *mimesis* is a highly ambiguous term for Horkheimer and Adorno. "In the context of the culture industry," Hansen observes, "the concept of mimesis is obviously dominated by the negative connotations of both an unreflected mimicry onto reified and alienated conditions and the misguided aesthetic investment in imitation."[20] Because the culture industry itself, even when ruled by the likes of Rupert Murdoch and Ted Turner, is still thought to be a Jewish conspiracy ("And so people shout: Stop thief!—but point at the Jews"),[21] anti-Semitism also gets to feed off this negative mimesis, whereby the muddy lipstick on the Jew's face takes on yet another layer of significance: "As far as mass culture is concerned," Adorno writes, "reification is no metaphor: it makes the human beings that it reproduces resemble things even where their teeth do not represent toothpaste and their care-worn wrinkles do not evoke cosmetics."[22] That "cosmetics," as Hansen points out, decorously stands in for *Laxativ* in the original German text has the indecorous effect, for us, of dirtying the toothpaste, of adding an excremental tinge to the already gooily overdetermined lipstick on the Jewish face.[23] Instead of rubbing your noses in this particular "negative connotation," however, I want it to conjure up the even greater offensiveness of the lipstick that mass culture would inscribe on *everyone's* face, permitting not a single consumer to escape the reifying, alienating taint of "looking Jewish." For if lipstick is the most culpably sexual of cosmetics, isn't it also the most culpably fetishistic of commodities, the one that, sticking to you, at the very borderline between your inside and your outside, not so much becomes you as makes you become it? Doesn't lipstick, in its tantalizingly liminal quasi-edibility, blur the boundary between the consumed object and the consuming subject? Isn't lipstick, rather than the etymologically obvious candidate (namely, mascara), therefore the literalization, the symptom par excellence, of mass culture as mask culture, where everybody, regardless of race, gender, or sexuality, has to put on what I will be so vulgar as to call Jewface?

"The model of aesthetic vulgarity," Adorno remarks in his *Aesthetic Theory,* "is an advertisement showing a chocolate-eating child who winks as though it had been caught in the act."[24] But then, a few sentences later: "The archetype of modern vulgarity is the smiling poster model, an ad for Toothpaste International, whose feminine splendour is not for real—as the prankster will attest who blackens those all-too-brilliant teeth, thereby innocently blabbering out the truth about the bogus splendour of culture."[25] It is as though the chocolate-eating child had itself melted into the smiling poster model, who, making things even messier, melts as well, as her all-too-brilliant teeth, seeming to have been painted with chocolaty lipstick, decay into the candy that would rot them, or the rot that would candy them. (I'm delighted to learn, from *Read My Lips,* that there are lipstick companies named Hard Candy and Urban Decay.)[26] An excessively, suspiciously shiny whiteness degenerates into dark goo; a hard, glittering feminine splendour gets bogged down in its own bogusness. In the regime of aesthetic vulgarity administered by, indeed identical with, the culture industry, everybody, especially the consumer, is a model working for Toothpaste International. More precisely, everybody is an assimilated Jewish movie star, whose incandescent "brilliance," as much the razzle-dazzle of the commodity as the glow of brainpower, is virtually programmed for meltdown—not because the sentimentalism of the melting pot into which we've all been thrown contrives to make us soft, but because sentimentalism names the condition in which the reified hardness required of each and every consumer, the cynical shrewdness whereby each and every customer proves to be a *tough* customer, necessarily produces its own apparent undoing, in the deliquescence, the mimetic, assimilative plasticity, equally required for successful social adaptation: when the going gets tough, every tough cookie knows how to imitate a marshmallow, just as every chewy bagel knows how to go soft as a jelly donut.[27] As Miriam Hansen, explicating Horkheimer and Adorno, puts it: "As hieroglyphic signs, the characters of film and television rehearse the compulsive assimilation of human beings to the commodity. In the very assertion of individuality, every face, every smile congeals into a mask, a grimace."[28] Assimilating and congealing and assimilating, melting and hardening and melting, thawing and freezing and thawing again, the subject of mass culture moves in an endless cycle of liquidity and solidity, of soupy summers and chilly winters, caught in a constant state of *engoomment* that, once again, I will be so vulgar—or is it so compulsive?—as also to term an endless state of *enjewment.*[29]

So while Winters, by the time of *The Poseidon Adventure,* had congealed into the Jewish mother enjoining us to *enjoy,* the lipstick episode nine years earlier, when she was still operating under the code of Hollywood "sultriness," already has the capacity to bring tears to our eyes. Not only does it undermine the distinction between a "good," prehistorical, *soft* mimesis on the one hand and a "bad," reified, *hard* mimesis on the other: it also reminds us that, if every one of us is a star—incessantly, compulsively modeling ourselves on the characters of film and television—being a star is no piece of cake. Indeed, it is much more like a scoop of ice cream—a scoop of ice cream going in and out of the freezer, over and over. Never is Winters more chilling, accordingly, than when she seems to assume her most vanilla flavor—when, instead of playing one of the grimacing Jewish-mother roles that have become signatures of her middle and late career (her stock-in-trade as a "supporting" actress), she puts on, for instance, the bland face of WASP gentility, as in what may be her most brilliant performance: her impersonation of Charlotte Haze in the first film version of *Lolita* (1962). Although any child knows that the novel on which the film and its more recent successor are based has pedophilia as its scandalous subject, no one, as far as I can tell, has noticed the *other* scandal of Stanley Kubrick's cinematic adaptation: I mean the scandal of Winters's interpretation itself, which implicitly makes Jewishness "universal"—not in the wary, evasively "humanitarian" mode of, say, the fifties stage and screen versions of *The Diary of Anne Frank* (in the latter of which Winters, incidentally, had appeared four years earlier, winning the first of her two Oscars for her performance), but, rather, in the vulgar mode of a prankster innocently blabbering out the truth about the bogus splendor of culture.

Early in the film, Winters's Charlotte is meeting James Mason's Humbert Humbert, newly arrived in West Ramsdale, New Hampshire, and looking to rent a room in her house; as she shows him the room, she sings the praises of the town, punctuating her performance by taking drags from a cigarette stuck in the cigarette holder she elegantly wields:

> CHARLOTTE: We're really very fortunate here in West Ramsdale. Culturally, we're a very advanced group, with lots of good Anglo-Dutch and Anglo-Scotch stock. And we're very progressive.... [She leads Humbert into the hallway, picking up a stray sock.] Excuse the soiled sock. [Throwing the sock into a drawer, she notices his attention to some piece of kitsch.] I see that you're interested in art. In that case, in that case, you really must see the collection of reproductions I have in my bedroom. [Gliding into the bedroom, she points to a picture on the wall.] My Dufy. And there's my little Van Gogh. Monet. Is Madame Humbert...?
>
> HUMBERT: There is no Madame Humbert. We are divorced.
>
> CHARLOTTE: Oh...
>
> HUMBERT: Happily divorced.
>
> CHARLOTTE: When did all this happen?
>
> HUMBERT: About a year ago, in Paris.
>
> CHARLOTTE [dreamily]: Oh, Paris... Frahnce... Monsieur. You know, monsieur, I really believe that it's only in the romance languages that one is able to really relate in a mature fashion.... In fact, I remember when the late Mr. Haze—
>
> HUMBERT: The late Mr. Haze?
>
> CHARLOTTE: Yes, he's passed on.
>
> HUMBERT: Oh.
>
> CHARLOTTE: When we were on our honeymoon abroad, I knew that I'd never felt married until I heard myself addressed as *señora.*
>
> HUMBERT: You were in Spain?
>
> CHARLOTTE: No, Mexico.

"I was enchanted with Charlotte and very proud of her," Winters writes. "Kubrick had the insight to find the areas of me that were pseudointellectual and pretentious. We all have those things in us" (348). The outrageous confection that is Winters's Charlotte *is* enchanting; even hard-boiled Pauline Kael could find it in her heart to write: "Shelley Winters's Charlotte is a triumphant caricature, so overdone it recalls Blake's 'You never know what is enough until you know what is more than enough.'"[30] (Kael knows her Shelley better than her Blake.) Part of the enchantment, as with any caricature, comes precisely from the overdoing of what is usually underdone; and since, as Ralph Lifschitz, I mean Ralph Lauren, would tell you, what is usually underdone, what, in American culture, epitomizes underdoing itself, is still the quietly tasteful Protestant mystique, the hazy aura enwreathing those who come from good Anglo-Dutch and Anglo-Scotch stock, the triumph of Winters, egged on by her Jewish director, consists in making the stock sticky, in thickening the haze, until it achieves the consistency of one of the "prize-winning pastries" of which Charlotte later boasts. Winters's triumph is all the more deliciously "ethnic" for the diegetic absence of any Jewish signifiers. Indeed, it constitutes the triumph of Jewishness as the aesthetic vulgarity of pure form: form shamelessly in excess of its occasion, form as the agglutinative process of *overdoing it.* At its best, according to Horkheimer and Adorno, Jewish mimesis resembles "the musical voice painting a vivid picture of things and feelings irrespective of the real content of what is said." Winters's enchanting performance in *Lolita* goes even further, painting a vivid picture of gentility itself as an inherently vulgar, latently "Jewish" disrespect for content. Performing gentility, that is, as a practice of refinement, the point of which is to filter out all vulgar matter—the way a plastic cigarette holder would impose a certain distance between the lips and the butt—Winters performs the inevitable failure of that gentility, which never inhales more pseudointellectuality, pretentiousness, and vulgarity than when it tries not to.

Gentile or Jew, we all have those things in us: we are all cigarette holders, consumers and commodities at once. And the enchantment of this discovery has indeed to do with the musical voice of an actress who, as few people remember, appeared on Broadway in *Oklahoma!* and would later star in *Minnie's Boys,* the musical biography of the Marx brothers. Keeping up her "culturally advanced" patter ("Frahnce," "monsieur," "madame," "Excuse the soiled sock"), Winters's Charlotte speaks, or sings, the language of the New Hampshire hausfrau with what I can only call a Jewish accent. In other words, it doesn't seem entirely accurate to say that Winters *has* a Jewish accent: colored blond—and therefore better able to pass as a white Protestant—Winters gets further protection from her vocal colors, which, though hinting of the Brooklyn upbringing on which she so often and so proudly insists, much more powerfully recall the strains of her native St. Louis, so much so that her former voice teacher, Alice Hermes, can pronounce this brutal verdict: "Shelley Winters speaks badly—she has lower-class Midwest speech."[31] On the one hand, of course, this "bad speech" is the secret of Winters's extraordinary success and professional longevity, the mark of that sacred American averageness by means of which she has melted into the mainstream, in a career stretching from her 1943 screen debut in *Cover Girl* to her role as the television grandmother of the neo- or would-be Shelley Winters known as Roseanne. On the other hand, however, Winters's "bad speech" betrays the tendency of melted Jewishness to coagulate, producing potential blockages in the very mainstream to which it has assimilated itself—or worse, producing the mainstream *as* blockage. For if Winters lacks, along with what she would consider lesbianism, what America most readily recognizes as a Jewish accent—the blood-curdling, Yiddish-inflected New Yorkese of entertainers from Fanny Brice to Howard Stern—the badness of her speech cannot, pace Alice Hermes, simply be attributed to lower-class Midwesternness. In addition to the "defects" of class and region, what is perhaps less a Jewish accent than a Jewish *grain* (as Roland Barthes might have said) makes itself heard in Winters's voice—not just as a lush repertoire of whines and whimpers, or just as the harsh effects of nasality and dentalization that, as my bar mitzvah coach once pointed out to me, characterize Jewish speech from coast to coast, though all of these things are undeniably *in* that voice, but also as an almost literal impediment of the tongue, an ethnic thickening or slurring that, by definition hard to define, suggests nothing so much, to my ears, anyway, as peanut butter, or chocolate, or lipstick, stuck to the roof of her mouth.

Or, to put it differently: Shelley Winters is a Method actress. Lest you think that the entire essay boils down to this rather unremarkable conclusion, let me ask if we're sure what a Method actress is. Method actresses, and actors, especially the actors, are famous, of course, for "speaking badly" (Marlon Brando is automatically the name on everyone's lips)—for mumbling and muttering to such an extent that the Method in question now seems to come down to a caricature of itself, to a crude technology of inarticulateness. Winters herself observes, more neutrally: "I hesitate when I speak naturally and I have irregular breathing and speaking patterns" (461). In his book on Method acting, and on the history of the Actors Studio, the temple of the Method, Foster Hirsch implies a connection between the Method as a potentially "mannerist style," with its "battery of verbal and physical hesitancy that's Studio shorthand for neurotic agitation," and the "immigrant fear" that possessed the Method's founders, a fear that, like the language of Clifford Odets, on whose plays the Method nourished itself, had a distinctly "Jewish flavor."[32] To be sure, Method acting can hardly be said to constitute an exclusively Jewish affair—not when its most celebrated practitioners are figures like Brando, James Dean, and Montgomery Clift. But what if one were to write an alternative history of Method acting, which is to say of acting in America, which is to say, in turn, of American mass culture, focusing instead on a group of exemplary female performers, like, say, Shelley Winters and Lee Grant? By doing so, one might arrive, for instance, at a better grasp of the hesitancy that is the hallmark of the Method's neurotic antistyle. Criticized even by Lee Strasberg, the Method's head rabbi, for "fussing around . . . too much,"[33] Winters does seem at times a veritable bundle of nerves. But if her nervousness betokens the immigrant fear that still courses through her blood, that nervousness is bound up with a nerviness, yes, with a chutzpah, that testifies, atavistically, irregularly, and discordantly, to an immigrant talent for making a fuss, even for making a mess, for revealing the fear circulating through the national bloodstream as a whole. On Winters's lips, at least, what might sound like mere inarticulateness, that is, is really a labor of disarticulation: an embarrassing method for making *all* American speech sound bad, by exposing the glutinously tongue-tying implications of a universally required cultural fluency.

Speaking badly, then, Winters models a Jewish mannerism of bad manners, a formalism of bad form—not just aesthetic vulgarity, but an aesthetics *of* vulgarity. At the heart of this aesthetics is precisely that lipstickiness that, among other embarrassments, prevents one from speaking precisely. Think of Shelley Winters, fresh from kissing Lee Grant, as smearing her gooeyness all over the smiling face of America—even as getting that gooeyness, that mama lotion, inside the smiling American mouth, from which it thus seems to issue as the smile congeals into a grimace. This particular messing around, I've been trying to suggest, is

Winters's "earthy" way, especially when she plays non-Jewish characters, not just of making Jewishness universal, but of showing how universal Jewishness already is. Indulge my sentimentality, however, as I end by returning to Winters as Jewish mother, apparently unadorned by lipstick, or by makeup of any kind, yet teaching us a thing or two about the Hollywood melting pot, which Jews not only go into, but even cause to boil over, so that its contents spread out, lavalike, across the whole cultural landscape. In 1975, at the end of Paul Mazursky's bittersweet autobiographical film *Next Stop, Greenwich Village,* she gives this advice to her son, the Mazursky figure, who has come to say goodbye to her in her shabby Brooklyn apartment as he leaves for California to be in a movie:

LARRY: Mom, please. No crying.

MRS. LAPINSKY: Promise me you won't get a big head. And promise me you'll always remember where you come from. Remember, your grandmother, how she got out of Poland? They had to sneak across the border in a wagon covered with potatoes. And the guards, they stuck bayonets into the sacks. That's where you came from. Oh, I almost forgot [opening the refrigerator]. Apple strudel for the plane.

LARRY: What am I gonna do with apple strudel on a plane?

MRS. LAPINSKY: You'll eat it, that's what you'll do with it!

LARRY: So long, Mom. [He moves toward the door.]

MRS. LAPINSKY: Sweetheart? Larry?

LARRY: Yeah, Mom?

MRS. LAPINSKY: Listen, if you ever actually meet Clark Gable, tell him that your mother loved him all of her life. And she saw every picture he ever did.

LARRY: I'll tell him.

MRS. LAPINSKY [becoming more anxious]: Uh, Larry, write!

LARRY [trying to leave]: I will.

MRS. LAPINSKY: Would you promise you'll write every day?

LARRY: I promise, Mom.

MRS. LAPINSKY: And you'll call once in a while? You know, that's why we put a phone in.

LARRY: I'll write every day, and I'll call every other day. How's that?

MRS. LAPINSKY: Larry? [dramatic pause as a sly smile lights up her face; then, she says, carefully and seriously] Be a good actor. [He leaves, and so does her smile, as she blinks back the tears.]

Somehow, the moment seems unusually rich when Winters's Mrs. Lapinsky (a name I want to pronounce both as *Lip*inski and as Lewinsky) delivers her parting shot: "Be a good actor." In the final scene of this film about worshipping at the Actors Studio, Winters's Jewish mother could almost be an acting teacher as well. (Winters herself has in fact had a significant secondary career as a "moderator," or teacher, at the Actors Studio.) You can, if you wish, hear the admonition to be a good actor as an admonition to stick it to those who would stick bayonets into potato sacks. But then, watch Shelley Winters's "goo-goo eyes" as they well up with tears,[34] see those bayonets turning into lipstick tubes, and tell me if you don't want her to let you have it, right in the kisser. Tell me, in other words, if she doesn't look more glamorous than ever.

Notes

1. Maureen Dowd, "F.O.B.'s: Femmes of Bill," *New York Times,* 11 October 1998, 4:17.

2. Shelley Winters, *Shelley II: The Middle of My Century* (New York: Simon & Schuster, 1989), 428–29. Page numbers for further quotations from this source appear in parentheses in the text.

3. On the theory of lesbian in-difference, see Teresa de Lauretis, "Sexual Indifference and Lesbian Representation," *Theater Journal* 40 (May 1988): 155–77.

4. Ephraim Katz, *The Film Encyclopedia* (New York: HarperCollins, 1994), 548.

5. Michael Rogin, *Blackface, White Noise: Jewish Immigrants in the Hollywood Melting Pot* (Berkeley: University of California Press, 1996), 112.

6. Ibid., 251–68.

7. See, for instance, Andrea Most, "'We Know We Belong to the Land': The Theatricality of Assimilation in Rodgers and Hammerstein's *Oklahoma!*" *PMLA* 113 (January 1998): 77–89.

8. Rogin, *Blackface, White Noise,* 100.

9. Kathy Peiss, *Hope in a Jar: The Making of America's Beauty Culture* (New York: Henry Holt, 1998), 154–55.

10. I allude to an anecdote Winters relates about replacing Bette Davis in the Broadway production of *Night of the Iguana*; *Shelley II,* 399.

11. Meg Cohen Ragas and Karen Kozlowski, *Read My Lips: A Cultural History of Lipstick* (San Francisco: Chronicle Books, 1998), 10.

12. Pierre Bourdieu, *Distinction: A Social Critique of the Judgment of Taste,* trans. Richard Nice (Cambridge: Harvard University Press, 1984).

13. See, for instance, Daniel Boyarin, *Unheroic Conduct: The Rise of Heterosexuality and the Invention of the Jewish Man* (Berkeley: University of California Press, 1997), 39–40: "Knowing nothing of eastern European Jewish literature or 'high' culture, of *Edelkayt* or the *mentsh,* [John Murray Cuddihy] imagines an *Ostjude* constructed more or less in the image known from the Borscht Belt"; or see R. B. Kitaj's explanation of why he doesn't like Marc Chagall, cited in Sander Gilman, *Love +*

Marriage = Death and Other Essays on Representing Difference (Stanford, Calif.: Stanford University Press, 1998), 165: "My reasons are hard-nosed and wholly unoriginal—the usual suspects: Pont Neuf prettiness and the French cuisined shtetl schmaltz of those long years from some damn good early modernist Yiddishkeit to the Riviera showbiz of his later wholesale trade."

14. Pauline Kael, *For Keeps: Thirty Years at the Movies* (New York: Penguin, 1994), 476.

15. The interview took place in May 1998 on Tom Snyder's *Late Late Show.*

16. For instance: "There is, it seems, sufficient evidence to make it plain that the notion of the pale, thin, side-curled, studious *Yeshiva-Bokhur* as erotic object for young women is not a mere nostalgic construction à la *Fiddler on the Roof*" (Boyarin, *Unheroic Conduct*, 69); or: "From public mosaics in the center of Chicago to his evocation in the self-consciously romantic musical *Fiddler on the Roof*..., Chagall had come, by the time of his death in 1985, to represent 'Jewish art' in the post-Shoah Diaspora. It is a visual world that has come to be the stuff of kitsch sold today in Jerusalem's tourist shops" (Gilman, *Love + Marriage*, 164–65).

17. I have in mind a virtual topos in contemporary television drama of the most self-consciously "literate" kind: in episodes of such shows as *The Practice* and *Law & Order,* an expert witness, whose Jewishness is nowhere explicitly identified but everywhere implicitly signified, is exposed as a greedy professional fraud; in the episode of *The Practice,* this fraudulence emerges all the more egregiously in contrast with the fiction of an African American truth untainted by money, rhetoricity, or ambition.

18. Max Horkheimer and Theodor W. Adorno, *Dialectic of Enlightenment,* trans. John Cumming (New York: Continuum, 1993), 187.

19. Ibid., 184.

20. Miriam Hansen, "Mass Culture as Hieroglyphic Writing: Adorno, Derrida, Kracauer," *New German Critique* 56 (spring/summer 1992): 54.

21. Horkheimer and Adorno, *Dialectic of Enlightenment,* 174.

22. Theodor W. Adorno, "The Schema of Mass Culture," in *The Culture Industry: Selected Essays on Mass Culture,* ed. J. M. Bernstein (London: Routledge, 1991), 82.

23. Hansen, "Mass Culture as Hieroglyphic Writing," 54.

24. Theodor W. Adorno, *Aesthetic Theory,* ed. Gretel Adorno and Rolf Tiedemann, trans. C. Lenhardt (London: Routledge & Kegan Paul, 1970), 340.

25. Ibid., 341.

26. Ragas and Kozlowski, *Read My Lips,* 71.

27. On Jell-O as an overdetermined signifier in the context of Jewish American cultural politics, see Marjorie Garber, "Jell-O," in *Symptoms of Culture* (New York: Routledge, 1998), 141–50.

28. Hansen, "Mass Culture as Hieroglyphic Writing," 54.

29. I mean also to signal here the psychoanalytic concept of "enjoyment" or *jouissance.*

30. Kael, *For Keeps,* 42.

31. Quoted in Foster Hirsch, *A Method to Their Madness: The History of the Actors Studio* (New York: Da Capo, 1984), 232.

32. Ibid., 221, 230, 87.

33. Quoted in ibid., 135.

34. Kael, *For Keeps,* 678.

CHAPTER EIGHT

Theorizing Popular Practice in Eighteenth-Century Aesthetics

Lord Kames and Alexander Gerard

Maureen Harkin

> Nothing more rigorously distinguishes the different classes than the disposition objectively demanded by the legitimate consumption of legitimate works, the aptitude for taking a specifically aesthetic point of view.
>
> —Pierre Bourdieu, *Distinction*, 1984

Eighteenth-Century Aesthetics and Nonelite Audiences

The impact of various forms of cultural studies and new historical inquiry in recent years has generated much new interest in popular culture and aesthetic practices in the eighteenth century. From Robert Darnton's work on popular French culture to John Brewer's studies of consumerism in England, a new impetus to consider nonelite forms of cultural practice has become evident in many recent literary-historical eighteenth-century studies.[1] There has been less interest, however, in pursuing how Enlightenment writers and theorists themselves understood the aesthetic experience of those involved in such practices, how they represented the experience of the lower-class or otherwise marginalized subject of popular aesthetic practice. The fact that the crowd at the popular spectacle, or the mass audience for the popular book, presented a challenge variously accepted or suppressed in the emerging discourse of Enlightenment aesthetics still remains on the periphery of recent critical attention, and analyses of actual Enlightenment theories of nonelite aesthetic response are still wanting.

Nonetheless, theorized accounts of the forms of noncanonical taste predate Bakhtin, Barthes, Williams, and their heirs, even if driven by quite different motivations. In fact, this philosophical interest in the reactions of diverse groups outside a mainstream or middle-class norm is an almost inevitable consequence of the turn in eighteenth-century aesthetics from a consideration of external objects to a concern with the aesthetic response of the subject.[2] This emphasis on response rather than object in Addison, Hume, Burke, Kames, Gerard, and the rest raises the issue of who the audience or audiences are for the aesthetic spectacle. Correspondingly, these Enlightenment theories of legitimated or elite preferences are variously confronted, disturbed, or haunted by the presence of an other, variously identified as uneducated, corrupt, foreign, or feminine taste. This is the theme, for example, that runs through the whole "standard of taste" argument best known from Hume's account, where the troubling fact of mass deviations from a standard of approved taste is most frequently canvassed.[3]

To put this another way, problems of establishing standards of taste inevitably shade into problems of constructing subject and community identity, implicitly acknowledging, if not legitimating, a wide range of possible social variations. Eighteenth-century British writers on aesthetics—and especially the Scottish authors discussed here—in their attempts to acknowledge and contain differences in audience and preference, essentially take on the project of demonstrating how a bourgeois-dominated social order can still generate the conviction of shared interests and sentiments that it requires for its survival. It is in acknowledgment of this historical task that Terry Eagleton has argued that the very emergence of Enlightenment aesthetics as a separate discourse is a symptom of the historical shift from feudalism and absolutism, with their dependence on constraint and displays of authority, to a bourgeois social order whose ultimate binding forces are "habits, . . . sentiments and affections"—marking aesthetic response as a site rich in potential for generating social unity and the discourse on aesthetics as a privileged place for the imaginings of social formations and their hierarchies.[4] This newly sharpened sense of the social stakes of the dynamics of response to various aesthetic performances, the importance of generating or regulating sentiment on the social margins, is manifest in eighteenth-century writings on aesthetics.

I do not want to suggest, however, that aesthetics can be understood simply as a form of hegemony.[5] Such an explanation tends to direct attention away from actual variations in response and toward a more monolithically conceived dominant or elite experience. Eagleton's account, despite an attentiveness to the issue of class that sets it apart from the older tradition of works on British aesthetics by writers such as Samuel Monk and Walter Hipple,[6] nonetheless continues this tradition in its tendency to lead discussion of the historical task of eighteenth-century aesthetics back toward a more or less exclusive concern with a bourgeois male subject: a subject no longer thought of as unproblematically representative or universal, perhaps, but still largely assumed to be unchallenged in its dominance.[7] In this concern with the bourgeois subject, the problem of the experience of the more diverse, more marginalized, and potentially more resistant subjects of actual eighteenth-century discourse—at least the version of them that surfaces in contemporary works on aesthetics—continues to be overlooked.

In short, the framing of the work of eighteenth-century aesthetics as essentially proclaiming the cultural dominance of the bourgeoisie prematurely suppresses the possibility of class-based and other differences of response that is present as a problem, and at times a real threat, in some of the most compelling works of mid-eighteenth-century British aesthetics. In what follows, I will discuss these presences of "the plurality," as Kames terms them, in the now curiously neglected treatises of Lord Kames and Alexander Gerard that treat these matters at greater length. I wish to show that the consciousness of a popular or crowd response as an inescapable fact in theorizing aesthetic response in these two authors marks a new stage of historical self-consciousness. Their characterization of such response in terms of compulsive imitations and repetitions on one level may well simply instantiate what E. P. Thompson has called the "spasmodic view of . . . the common people," that is, the notion that these agents act from the simplest, least self-conscious motives and can be patronized if not dismissed.[8] But their collective force, nonetheless, is to undermine the assumption that the response of the educated bourgeois or upper-class subject is the only one that need be taken note of.

In so doing, Gerard and Kames offer an account of aesthetics that can be characterized as antisublime on this as on a number of other counts.

This may partly explain a certain neglect of Gerard's and Kames's work: the sublime, after all, has been accorded the status of dominant category and "principal event" of eighteenth-century British aesthetics by modern scholarship.[9] Anyone examining such studies of the connections between aesthetics and the social order in eighteenth-century Britain over the past fifteen or twenty years cannot fail to be struck by the high priority given to the various discourses of the sublime, from Addison on. The interest in Burke's *Philosophical Enquiry* in particular has tended to dominate discussions of the relations between aesthetics and social formations in the period.

Yet there is, on the face of it, something rather contrary about this privileging of the discourse on the sublime as the exemplary site to pursue discussions of aesthetics, the subject, and the social order in the eighteenth century. To begin with what is well-known, there is a marked tendency in eighteenth-century British versions of the sublime, from Addison through Baillie, Burke, and Blair, to reformulate the classical concept and category of the sublime, transforming it from a rhetorical and social event into an intense but solitary experience of the relationship between self and external nature. The Longinian rhetorical sublime, an effect of exchange between orator and auditor, is recast as a heightened experience of the subject's own depth of response and superior powers of apperception.[10]

Although Burke introduces the complementary category of the beautiful as an aesthetic of the social and discusses sympathy and imitation as the phenomena that ultimately bind society together, a certain unease is evident in these passages on the relation of the social and the aesthetic. Sympathy, or the imaginative reconstruction of the situation of others, and the imitation that Burke links to it are cornerstones of social life in Burke's account. At the same time, they pose the threat of sameness, a collapse of all social hierarchy and difference:

> The second passion belonging to society is imitation, or, if you will, a desire of imitating, and consequently, a pleasure in it. This passion arises from much the same cause with sympathy [the first passion belonging to society]. As sympathy makes us take a concern in whatever men feel, so this affection prompts us to copy whatever they do.... This forms our manners, our opinions, our lives. It is one of the strongest links of society.... if men gave themselves up to imitation entirely, and each followed the other, and so on in an eternal circle, it is easy to see that

> there never could be any improvement amongst them. Men must [then] remain as brutes do, the same at the end that they are at this day, and that they were in the beginning of the world. To prevent this, God has planted in man a sense of ambition, and a satisfaction arising from the contemplation of his excelling his fellows in something deemed valuable amongst them. It is this passion that drives men to all the ways we see in use of signalizing themselves, and that tends to make whatever excites in a man the idea of this distinction so very pleasant. (*Philosophical Enquiry*, 49–50)

Burke's stigmatizing of sympathy and imitation as marks of brutish lack of ambition, mere herd behavior, signals the wildly different valuation of an aesthetic associated with the crowd, the "numbers from all parts" who crowd to plays and spectacles (48), and the sublime understood as an aesthetic of individuation and ambition.

The sublime, in short, is a manifestly bourgeois aesthetic that assumes an educated and male subject and values the solitary and distinctive as opposed to the devalued concepts of imitation and sympathy that Burke identifies with lower-class social and aesthetic response. The sublime experience of "a sense of inward greatness" (51) is generated by a subject, fascinated with his own inner depths, who essentially stages his own experience in a natural scene emptied of any contending authorial power. The subject of the sublime is by definition one of a distinct, privileged group of viewers, not a universal one. All this would suggest, then, that the discourse of the sublime is not the place to look for a sustained and developed account of how eighteenth-century thinkers engaged with the relationship between aesthetic experience and social formations. It is, rather, the discourse on the aesthetics of sympathetic imitation—a response that Burke expels, and demonizes, as the antisublime sentiment of the mob, the death of difference and individuation—that far more centrally concerns itself with the aesthetic experience of a variety of subjects beyond the educated and leisured class.

The writings on sympathy and aesthetics of Burke's close contemporaries, the midcentury Scots theorists David Hume, Henry Home, Lord Kames, and Alexander Gerard, all published within a few years of Burke's *Enquiry*, were well-known to the same audience, although their canonical fortunes have diverged sharply since then. Hume's essay "Of the Standard of Taste," the central articulation of midcentury concerns about the variations of taste, is the only one that remains widely read. As part of this project is one of returning largely neglected texts to discussion, I shall confine my comments primarily to an account of Kames and Gerard. In general terms, however, all three works are distinguished by their attentiveness to the need to theorize the aesthetic experience of both the subjects traditionally privileged in aesthetic inquiry *and* an emerging mass public, and thus offer a more compelling account of what is at stake in a field here acknowledged to be fractured along lines of gender, class, and other forms of difference. Their aesthetics center (as sublime discourse does not) on elaborating the impulse to sympathetic emulation—the imaginative or actual re-creation of certain textual effects or situations on the part of the reading or viewing subject, not the experience of intensity or personal interiority. All three identify sympathetic imitation as a central issue, precisely because it is understood as the most powerful force, automatic and more or less uncontrolled, driving response among nonelite audiences: women, the young, and, especially, lower-class audiences. Sympathetic repetition or imitation is sufficiently powerful, in fact, that all three enshrine an opposing critical detachment as an ultimate value and marker of correct—that is, educated—taste. In these works the sense of the potential overthrow of the subject's rational control of his or her response that is so constitutive a part of the Longinian sublime and still present in Burke is accepted as a common effect of aesthetic response but regarded with suspicion as a sign of vulnerability or susceptibility, now that it is identified with a differently classed subject. Although they differ considerably in emphasis and argument, the antisublime aesthetics of Kames and Gerard are important in their guiding assumption that the complex social act of sympathetic emulation, rather than the individual transport of the sublime, is the most compelling and significant form of aesthetic response for the mass of respondents.

Gerard: Rhapsodic Repetition

Gerard's *Essay on Taste* was the prize-winning entry in a competition sponsored by the Select Society of Edinburgh in 1756, but was first published, in London and Edinburgh, in 1759, just two years after Burke's *Enquiry*.[11] Two further editions appeared in 1764 and 1780.[12] Gerard's long essay is laid out in three parts on seven "simple principles" of taste that he identifies (the sense of beauty, novelty, sublimity, and so on), the formation of taste, and its social importance or usefulness. I will have to eschew a systematic account of Gerard's treatise here and its relation to precursor texts by Baillie, Hogarth, and others.[13] My goal is instead to show how the responses of repetition and emulation, which Gerard identifies as characteristic of lower-class or uneducated audiences and as troubling instances of a general tendency to meaningless reiteration in the aesthetic sphere, are nonetheless now acknowledged as central facts in the scene of aesthetic response. Although Gerard shows the same concerns as Burke about the tide of repetition he identifies as lower-class response, his account signals the necessity of engaging with it as a force that can no longer be excluded.

Gerard describes the members of this mass audience as sharing the common trait of being too easily affected by what they see or hear, offering no resistance to texts. The *Essay* is thus typical of that strain of eighteenth-century writing on new forms and audiences, especially the novel and its readers, that manifests intense anxieties about the seductive effects of reading on excessively sensible or susceptible readers—those unprotected by education or temperament from being swayed by textual representations or suggestions.[14] Most commonly for Gerard this refers to female readers, but also includes foreigners and, most threateningly, lower-class readers (*Essay,* 86–87, 119–20, 128, 200–201). Their response is represented as a predisposition to repeat what they have heard, either in the text itself or from critical commentators, lacking as they do any other modes of response.

What is the specific nature of this threat of such unprotected encounters with texts? The answer to this question is most fully developed in the context of Gerard's account of the importance of precision in textual response. Here Gerard argues that his ideal, the possessor of a taste correctly proportioned to its object, escapes being overwhelmed by powerful texts by the conversion of a private, nonverbal experience into analytic discourse: by the transformation, that is, of the reader into the generator of a new, specifically critical, verbal text. He thus accords with Hume's arguments in "Of the Standard of Taste": the mark of true taste is essentially the ability of the reader to translate an aesthetic experience into critical response.[15] This translation, however, is not achieved through simple approbation or condemnation; it must make certain critical distinctions:

> Extravagance [in "commending and blaming"] proceeds . . . from an incapacity to distinguish and ascertain, with precision, different degrees of excellence or faultiness. Instead of forming an adequate idea of the nature of beauty or deformity, we go beyond all bounds of moderation; and when we want to express our sentiments, can do it only in general terms, tumid and exaggerated. If we are displeased, we signify it, with the inveteracy of a *Dennis,* in terms of general invective; and, without explaining the causes of our disapprobation, pronounce it poor, dull, wretched, execrable. If we are pleased, we cannot tell, with what, how or why; but only declare it fine, incomparable, with the unmeaning rapture of an ancient rhapsodist, who, without understanding the principles of art, or the sense of an author, like a madman, really agitated by the fury which the poets feigned, could recite or praise them with such vehemence as transported himself, and astonished his auditors. (*Essay,* 113–14)

And Gerard continues with a long and richly detailed footnote identifying the discussion of the rhapsodes of ancient Greece in Plato's *Ion* as the *locus classicus* for a critique of such repetitions.[16]

The nature of the danger posed by these encounters—inexact praise?—may still appear somewhat obscure, but residing in Gerard's figures is the specter of mob discontent and violence, "go[ing] beyond all bounds . . . and . . . agitated by fury," evoking an atmosphere of riot and civil uprising and, inevitably, suggesting the events of 1745.[17] Like Plato's Socrates, who aligns the rhapsode and poet alike with those bacchantes and dangerous throngs possessed by the gods,[18] Gerard thus appears to stigmatize intensity of response as an irrational force, but with the further suggestion that such irrational enthusiasms are, in a modern scene of mass exposure to cultural performances, no longer accepted social and cultural facts but more dangerous political forces.

Thus it is unsurprising that, like Hume, Gerard ranks skill in formulating an exact critical response to a given text much higher than and, indeed, in opposition to an intensely felt response. The ability to construct a considered argument is not an event subsequent to the nature of aesthetic experience, but a transformation of it, one that puts the reader of true taste in a position of strength, that is, in the position of an author. The possession of critical language functions as a sign of the rescue of the subject from the overwhelming, magnetic force exerted by the author on the rhapsode and by the rhapsode on his listeners. Armed with a set of models with which to compare a given performance, a critical framework and terminology, the authoritative reader is proof against the "transports" and astonishment that reduce the untrained reader to cries of, precisely, "incomparable" (*Essay,* 113–14). The ability to put proper bounds to the effects and pleasures of texts is then achieved by a form of critical rewriting, which, at its most powerful, is able to convert even "inferior beauties" to flaws (120). Anticipating Macherey, Gerard's notion of criticism could be "summed up as a value judgment in the margin of a book: 'could do better.'"[19]

Where Gerard differs from Burke, of course, is in his sense of this critical audience as no longer dominant but rather a beleaguered minority. Even the most unambitious authors and texts have the capacity to mesmerize the majority of readers, and most scenes of reading will be ones in which these readers are reduced to a state of "blind, enthusiastic feeling." Hence the sense of menace implicit in Gerard's figuring of the rhapsodic crowd. Despite the shrinkage of the vocabulary of too-susceptible readers, their speech (a melange of repetitions of the words of the author and unreasoning exclamations of pleasure or distaste) is not restrained but rather excessive, a verbal gush. The characteristic speech of these rhapsodes and other ignorant but powerfully impressed readers is prolix, going far beyond what is appropriate ("*moderation*" "forming an *adequate* idea of the beauty or deformity"of the text; *Essay,* 113–14), as well as unreasoning. The subject thus abandoned to the suggestions of the text marks this both by a lack of new or original speech and an excess of words—by a kind of repetition compulsion in which, to use Freud's terms, "a thing which has not been understood inevitably reappears."[20] Gerard presents this almost demonic form of repetition as a basic drive, toward the kind of sameness and nondifferentiation gestured to by Burke and posited by Freud as an instinct to reiterate and "restore an earlier state of things."[21] This drive is only barely countered and contained in an influential but nonetheless small minority who hold these compulsive forces at bay.

Gerard's responsiveness to the fact of new reading publics, in utilizing the terms of sympathetic relation (text and simple, rhapsodic reiteration) for description, functions in fact as an opportunity for elaborating exclusionary rules of reading practices. Nonetheless, Gerard's fascination with a kind of rhapsodic reiteration that seeks pleasure rather than critical authority testifies to the strength of the threat posed to his normative schema by sympathetic readers.

Kames: Compulsory Emulation

Samuel Johnson's opinion of Kames's *Elements of Criticism* was recorded by Boswell in 1769, some years after its first publication: "The Scotchman has taken the right method in his *Elements of Criticism.* I do not say that he has taught us any thing; but he has told us old things in a new way."[22] Johnson's comment reveals just how perfectly expressive of orthodox opinion the *Elements* was understood to be in the decades after its publication, an orthodoxy further evidenced in the book's extraordinary success, going into eight authorized British editions alone between 1762 and 1805.[23] The *Elements* has a special status among midcentury works on aesthetics as one of the most widely circulated treatises on aesthetics of its day; now it is hardly read.

The length and scope of Kames's treatise, which runs to more than twelve hundred pages in the first edition, also makes a claim for its being the most thorough, not to say exhaustive, treatment of aesthetics and audience at midcentury. More comprehensive in range than either Burke or Gerard,[24] the book defies quick summary (perhaps the motivation behind Goldsmith's riposte to Johnson, "It is easier to write that book than to read it").[25] Kames's method is to proceed with copious illustration and example, one reason for the book's length. The book falls into two unequal parts, the first two chapters elaborating a psychology of a generalized subject of aesthetics, with the subsequent chapters being devoted largely to an analysis of general aesthetic principles (sublimity, novelty, uniformity, and the like) and descriptions of the functioning of particular arts. I will focus here on two major features of Kames's work: his delineation of the aesthetic experience of the lower orders in relation to a ruling class and his confident conviction, arrived at through his distinctive reformulation of the notion of sympathetic emulation, that aesthetic experience will invariably "inforce *[sic]* submission to government" by all social groups.[26]

The account given in *Elements of Criticism* of the link between aesthetic experience and the social order, at least regarding "the generality," is that aesthetic performances simply provide one way among others of displaying the inevitability of social hierarchies. Kames repeatedly characterizes the aesthetic experience of the typical uneducated viewer as simply a form of political domination. According to Kames, the experience of any form of the arts, from literature to gardening, is a more or less direct means for the reproduction of a community understood as a stable social hierarchy: the arts unfailingly produce direct benefits in the form of social control. The text, which has some ambition as a work of ethics, also lays out a rudimentary system of morality based on "the sympathetic emotion of virtue," which bestows great influence upon good example by "prompt[ing] us to imitate what we admire" (*Elements,* 1:70–75). In this schema, sympathetic emulation is central, and reliable; subjects emulate, more or less involuntarily, approved behavior and shun the bad. There is no corresponding "sympathetic emotion of vice."[27] But Kames's remarks on sympathetic imitation in ethical practice remain schematic and of lesser interest, precisely because they do not engage with difference or conflict. It is the field of aesthetics that Kames nominates as the privileged arena in which the fact of class difference is acknowledged and managed, and where Kames's understanding of sympathy as a kind of involuntary imitation of approved models is most evident.

Before exploring how this works in effect, I should note how class difference in aesthetic response is thus acknowledged, and indeed made a focal point, in the *Elements,* but at the same time coexists with a notion of "spontaneous consent" to the values of the dominant group.[28] As aristocrat, major landholder, and judge, Kames occupied a position near the top of the Scottish social hierarchy that accounts for some of the complacency with which he views social division.[29] But even by eighteenth-century standards of assumptions about sympathy with the wealthy, Kames's confidence that the landowner's point of view can be shared or understood is striking.[30] This is often evident in his unself-conscious identification with other landowners and collectors in his examples, for instance, in his choice of the example of "another's property indented into my field" to illustrate the unease caused by incomplete or interrupted series (*Elements,* 1:365–67). The effect this produces in the text is a peculiar combination of attentiveness to difference and an extraordinary lack of concern about the possibility of resistant audiences, deviant readings, or challenges to critical or social authority.

A notable example of this confident conservatism in action is Kames's transformation of the problem of the standard of taste into what he clearly regards as a less complicated issue, the question of acknowledging the difference of taste between one social class and another. Kames's solution to the problem of differing preferences is to pose it as one of varying levels of taste between more and less socially powerful groups, rather than as a question of differences between equally competent judges or disputing authorities (*Elements*, 3:356–62). Thus the problem is converted into the simpler one of recognizing the social authority of those who, being most familiar with "the more elegant pleasures" (3:361), are ostensibly in a position to appreciate fully the merits of Homer, for example, while lower-class readers acknowledge their own lack of qualification as judges (3:361). Upon this division of society into those possessing delicacy of taste and those without rest the foundations of social hierarchy and stability:

> Nature . . . hath wisely and benevolently filled every [social] division with many pleasures; in order that individuals may be content with their own lot, without envying the happiness of others: many hands must be employ'd to procure us the conveniencies of life; and it is necessary that the different branches of business, whether more or less agreeable, be filled with hands. A taste too nice and delicate, would obstruct this plan; for it would crowd some employments, leaving others, not less useful, totally neglected. In our present condition, happy it is that the plurality are not delicate in their choice. They fall in readily with the occupations, pleasures, food, and company, that fortune throws in their way; and if at first there be any displeasing circumstance, custom soon makes it easy. (3:354–55)

This tendency to resolve the philosophical question of the standard of taste inherited from Hume by means of understanding variation of taste as a simple function of social position is typical of Kames. Avoiding a direct statement that the level of taste varies according to the relative wealth and leisure of a given individual, Kames rather suggests that these useful toilers actively cooperate with "fortune" in finding their way to less agreeable stations in life by some inherent lack of delicacy. Taste is inseparable from class status, but it is not the product of class-determined access to education; instead, it is the mark of the ability to profit from such circumstances that justifies a privileged status. This kind of move, resolving and recuperating all variation into simple means for distinguishing one class from another, is just the sort of thing Walter Hipple had in mind when he described Kames's "philosophical vice" of providentially resolving all potential conflicts.[31] Nonetheless, Kames's frank class-taste equivalence here has the virtue at least of requiring that he then provide his reader with some sketch of just how these lower-class readers and spectators—those who are not delicate in their choice—participate in aesthetic experience.

Kames is unusually candid about what is at stake in questions of aesthetics: keeping up social and political hierarchies. His vision of the field of aesthetic experience is as the privileged means by which the individual subject and entire classes are reconciled to their assigned places in the social structure. The experience of the various arts in Kames has as its primary social function reproducing submission to the rules of the established social order—an oddly proto-Althusserian scene of the interpellation of the subject, where the subject is hailed, recognizes that he or she is being addressed, and, by this recognition, accepts the identity and terms by which he or she is thus called.[32] In this scene, *all* spectators' responses are understood as being limited to a recognition of social order and their place in it; yet the process has different consequences for those with limited education and experience of the fine arts. For these subjects, a kind of involuntary emulation of the models offered to them is always and invariably the occasion for the exercise of a useful auxiliary form of government power. This is in fact what distinguishes their response from the reasoned criticism of the upper-class critic.

The mechanics of this process are most succinctly laid out in Kames's chapter on gardening and architecture, in which he describes these latter as practices whose usefulness in raising approved social sentiments is enhanced by the fact of their accessibility to the uneducated Scots populace. In concluding his chapter, Kames reiterates his claim about the helplessly emulative position of this audience in the face of the simplest artifacts presented by metropolitan power:

> It is observed above of gardening, that it contributes to rectitude of manners. . . . It is observed in Scotland, that even a turnpike-road has some influence of this kind upon the low people in the neighbourhood. They become fond of regularity and neatness; which is display'd, first upon their yards and little inclosures, and next within doors. A taste for regularity and neatness thus gathering strength, comes insensibly to be extended to dress, and [finally] even to behaviour and manners. (*Elements,* 3:350)

The ability of the network of Scottish turnpike roads to effect a kind of imitation on the part of Scottish peasants presents this transformation of landscape as having an irresistible force of example. This borrows from and extends Hume's, and indeed Gerard's, argument in claiming that for those without the means for discursive or physical resistance, a compulsive imitation of models of taste or behavior is the only option. The significant point of difference between Gerard and Kames, however, is clearly the absence of anxiety connected to the forms of lower-class aesthetic repetition, and this derives from Kames's concept of the aesthetic message.

That message renders the apparent simplicity of this putative drive to emulation somewhat deceptive. What informs this account of spruced-up yards and neatened dress in particular, and Kames's discussion in general, is its reliance on threat. In the Scottish scene Kames invokes, the building of turnpike roads was largely motivated by the necessity of quickly transporting troops in case of uprisings, part of a series of post-1745 regulations designed to suppress Scottish independence and, indeed, difference (other laws specifically prohibited traditional Scots highland dress, forms of association, and language).[33] Thus the existence of these roads offers, in addition to a model for the emulation of the "low people," a reminder of the forces that can be mobilized by metropolitan power to compel uniformity of response.[34] It is this context that allows Kames to read sympathetic emulation of the aesthetic artifact as a repetition that is reliable, a means of reproducing "submission to the rules of the established order."[35]

What is distinctive in Kames, then, is his version of the kind of message the aesthetic spectacle delivers and the thoroughly controlled form of emulation it initiates among its most marginalized viewers. Kames's account of the peculiar salience to lower-class viewers of the social forces implicitly mobilized in the display of the aesthetic artifact in one stroke accounts for and eliminates the possibility of difference in response. It is the implied presence of real force that has the only real social agency. Hence the fine arts provide a model, but even more, an *incentive,* for reconciling lower-class members to their assigned place in the social structure, and this assures their general acceptance of models of taste along with other social regulations. In Kames's confidence that such sympathetic emulation of aesthetic models is in every sense compelled and predictable, the function of the fine arts as a virtual arm of government empties out the very issue of social difference as a problem.

Aesthetic experience in Kames's schema does not provide a means to challenge or reimagine the subject's position in social relations, but essentially restates that position. Hence the effects of imitation by weak or vulnerable readers are not a matter of anxiety for him. The concerns of Gerard, Hume, and other less serenely conservative writers—that sympathetic imitation might be directed toward different ends, might be a more subversive social force—is quite foreign to Kames. His account of the workings of lower-class aesthetic experience offers an alternative to elite response, but assumes the continued dominance of that elite.

The Aristocracy of Culture?

We began with the claims of Bourdieu and Eagleton—that the "aesthetic point of view" was the surest mark of class distinction and that the aesthetic is largely reducible to ideology, a form of political dominance. The *Elements*' confident assumption that literary and aesthetic practice affirms but cannot transform a social reality seems to anticipate some of the major recent arguments of such critics on the complicity of aesthetics with political oppression. The work of Bourdieu, in particular, with its detailed accounts of class-based differences in taste and arguments that aesthetic preferences mark and perpetuate upper-class hegemony, makes him a distant heir to Kames, despite their being on opposing sides of the class conflict both describe. Bourdieu's complex calculus of social and educational capital positioning the subject in a given social rank of course maps a terrain divided into far more numerous and subtle gradations of class fractions than the terrain of either Gerard or Kames, but this richness of detail at the level of classification only serves to highlight the single claim at the center of Bourdieu's work: that the domain of the aesthetic generally serves to maintain class hierarchies.[36]

Yet the contrast between the kinds of preferences Bourdieu discerns among his respondents (whose concerns, for example, center far more on realism versus formal experiment than on eighteenth-century questions of emulation)[37] and those of the hypothetical subjects of Kames and Gerard also reveals the differences between these aesthetic systems and the historically contingent nature of aesthetic experience. This shifting and indeed elusive quality to aesthetic experience suggests the possibility that the aesthetic always remains to some extent a space of uncertainty and indirection, a site where links with the political and ideological are not always straightforward,[38] and where ideological categories may be unsettled and challenged. What I hope to have shown here, in describing two Enlightenment models of the social function of aesthetics, as well as the *Elements*' prefigurings of more recent arguments from the left concerning the political appropriation of the aesthetic, is something of this unpredictable variety and meaning of aesthetic response in any given context. If sympathetic repetition as a mode of response associated with lower-class viewers is feared as mob behavior by Gerard and, conversely, seen as guarding fixed class positions by Kames, it is difficult to say which model has the greatest persuasive or explanatory force for actual aesthetic experience circa 1760. What we can say is that their attempt to incorporate diversity of aesthetic response marks a new acknowledgment in British writing on aesthetics of the pressures of different audiences and peoples.

For all their differences, Kames and Gerard both focus on textual repetitions or reenactments, inscribed on the body or in the behavior of lower-class respondents, and thus insistently link aesthetic experience to the contemporary political scene. In the post-Union, post-1745 Scottish context of these works, where British parliamentary control had been extended deep into the practices of everyday life, these bodily traces recall the many tangible forms of political domination then exercised over the Scots populace. The alternately unruly and subjugated crowds of *An Essay on Taste* and *Elements of Criticism* clearly evoke those of recent Scottish and British history, and incarnate some of the deep anxieties concerning the relationship of Britain to its own Gaelic fringes. The sense of the significance of the crowd and its challenge to narrowly conceived theories of taste gives the work of Kames and Gerard an odd eloquence on forms of power and powerlessness on the social margins.

Notes

1. See, for example, John Brewer and Roy Porter, eds., *Consumption and the World of Goods,* (London: Routledge, 1993); John Brewer and Susan Staves, eds., *Early Modern Conceptions of Property* (London: Routledge, 1996); Robert Darnton, *The Great Cat Massacre* (New York: Basic Books, 1984); Robert Darnton, *The Forbidden Best-Sellers of Pre-Revolutionary France* (New York: Norton, 1995); Erin Mackie, *Market à la Mode: Fashion, Commodity, and Gender in "The Tatler" and "The Spectator"* (Baltimore: Johns Hopkins University Press, 1997); and John Brewer, *The Pleasures of the Imagination: English Culture in the Eighteenth Century* (New York: Farrar, Straus & Giroux, 1997).

2. See George Dickie's argument on the eighteenth-century shift from the formulation of objective notions of beauty in earlier philosophical inquiry into literary and aesthetic value to a concern with the viewer or reader in *The Century of Taste: The Philosophical Odyssey of Taste in the Eighteenth Century* (Oxford: Oxford University Press, 1996), 3–5.

3. David Hume, "Of the Standard of Taste," in *Essays, Moral, Political and Literary* (rev. ed.), ed. Eugene Miller (Indianapolis: Liberty Classics, 1987), 226–49. See the discussion of Hume's acknowledgments and evasions of the class qualifications assumed in aesthetic judgments in Richard Shusterman, "Of the Scandal of Taste: Social Privilege as Nature in the Aesthetic Theories of Hume and Kant," *Philosophical Forum* 20 (1989): 211–29.

4. Terry Eagleton, *The Ideology of the Aesthetic* (Oxford: Basil Blackwell, 1990), 19–20.

5. The possibility of challenge offered by aesthetic experience to social norms should not be prematurely closed off. See, for example, George Levine's critique of Eagleton and discussion of recent work on aesthetics and ideology in his "Introduction: Reclaiming the Aesthetic," in *Aesthetics and Ideology,* ed. George Levine (New Brunswick, N.J.: Rutgers University Press, 1996), 11–13, 17–22.

6. Samuel Holt Monk, *The Sublime: A Study of Critical Theories in XVIII-Century England* (New York: Modern Language Association, 1935); Walter Hipple, *The Beautiful, the Sublime and the Picturesque in Eighteenth-Century British Aesthetic Theory* (Carbondale: Southern Illinois University Press, 1957).

7. Eagleton does guardedly acknowledge the possibility of the liberatory potential of the aesthetic, but essentially gives a history of its consistent use as a form of political domination. See *The Ideology of the Aesthetic,* 26–28, 31–69.

8. E. P. Thompson, "The Moral Economy of the English Crowd in the Eighteenth Century," *Past and Present* 50 (1971): 77–136.

9. As Ashfield and de Bolla acknowledge in their introduction to *The Sublime: A Reader in British Eighteenth-Century Aesthetic Theory,* ed. Andrew Ashfield and Peter de Bolla (Cambridge: Cambridge University Press, 1996), 1.

10. See, for example, John Baillie: "[Longinus] has entirely passed over what the *Sublime* is. . . . the *Sublime* in *Writing* is no more than a Description of the *Sublime* in *Nature*. . . . That Object only can be justly called the *Sublime,* which in some degree disposes the Mind to this *Enlargement* of itself, and gives her a lofty *Conception* of her own *Powers.*" John Baillie, *An Essay on the Sublime* (1747; reprint, Los Angeles: William Andrews Clark Memorial Library, 1953), 3–4. See also Edmund Burke, *A Philosophical Enquiry into the Origins of Our Ideas of the Sublime and the Beautiful,* ed. J. T. Boulton (1757; reprint, Notre Dame, Ind.: University of Notre Dame Press, 1968), 1, 51. Page numbers for further quotations from this source appear in parentheses in the text.

11. Alexander Gerard, *An Essay on Taste* (1759; facsimile edition, Menston, Eng.: Scholar, 1971). Page numbers for further quotations from this source appear in parentheses in the text.

12. The 1780 edition was an expanded edition, incorporating a new essay, "Of the Standard of Taste."

13. There has been little modern discussion of Gerard's work. For the most significant recent accounts, see Peter de Bolla, *The Discourse of the Sublime: History, Aesthetics and the Subject* (Oxford: Blackwell, 1989), 72–92; and Dickie, *The Century of Taste,* 29–54. Earlier accounts are given in Hipple, *The Beautiful, the Sublime and the Picturesque,* 67–82; and in Monk, *The Sublime,* 109–13.

14. The field is too vast to do more than simply indicate its better-known monuments. Signal instances include Samuel Johnson, *Rambler* No. 4, 31 March 1750; Charlotte Lennox, *The Female Quixote* (1752); James Fordyce, *Sermons to Young*

Women (1766); and Hannah More, *Strictures on the Modern Female System of Education* (1799). See the review of sources in Ioan Williams, *Novel and Romance 1700–1800: A Documentary Record* (New York: Barnes & Noble, 1970).

15. If the untrained taste "pronounce the whole in general to be beautiful or deformed, it is the utmost that can be expected; and even this judgment, a person so unpractised will be apt to deliver with great hesitation and reserve.... [The authoritative critic, conversely,] can pronounce, without danger of mistake, concerning the merits of every performance." Hume, "Of the Standard of Taste," 237.

16. "Socrates proves, from the concessions of his antagonist [Ion the rhapsode], that neither did his sentiments proceed from true taste, from a vigourous perception of the beauties he recited, nor his encomiums from judgment, from a critical skill in the principles of beauty. He therefore, in his usual strain of irony, resolves both into an unaccountable agitation of spirit, proceeding either from madness or from inspiration; and with great humour compares the several muses to as many magnets. The muse inspires the poet, without any agency or knowledge of his; he in the same manner conveys the inspiration to his rhapsodist, and he to its attentive hearers; just as the loadstone *[sic]* by its imperceptible and unaccountable influence, attracts a ring of iron, that a second, and that a third" (Gerard, *Essay on Taste,* 113–14).

17. And also riots like the 1736 Porteous Riots in Edinburgh. See Paul Langford, *A Polite and Commercial People: England 1727–1783* (Oxford: Clarendon, 1992), 45–46. On the frequency and violence of riots in eighteenth-century Britain, see George Rude, *The Crowd in History 1730–1848* (New York: John Wiley, 1964), 33–65.

18. "Like the priestesses of Bacchus... a poet is [only] able to write poetry... [when he] has no longer command of his intellect." Plato, "The Ion," in *The Works of Plato,* ed. Thomas Taylor and Floyd Sydenham (Frome, Somerset: Prometheus Trust, 1996), 5:424.

19. Pierre Macherey, *A Theory of Literary Production,* trans. Geoffrey Wall (London: Routledge & Kegan Paul, 1978), 15–16.

20. Sigmund Freud, "Analysis of a Phobia in a Five-Year-Old Boy," in *The Standard Edition of the Complete Psychological Works of Sigmund Freud,* ed. and trans. James Strachey (London: Hogarth, 1953–74), 10:122.

21. Sigmund Freud, "Beyond the Pleasure Principle," in *The Standard Edition of the Complete Psychological Works of Sigmund Freud,* ed. and trans. James Strachey (London: Hogarth, 1953–74), 18:7–64, esp. 34–43.

22. Entry for 16 October 1769 in James Boswell, *Boswell's Life of Johnson,* ed. R. W. Chapman (Oxford: Oxford University Press, 1953), 414–15.

23. In addition, many other unauthorized, abridged, and American and foreign editions were issued from the 1770s through the nineteenth century. See the discussion of the book's reception and subsequent history in Helen Whitcomb Randall, "The Critical Theory of Lord Kames," *Smith College Studies in Modern Languages* 22, nos. 1–4 (October 1940–July 1941), esp. 69–88, 137–39.

24. As de Bolla notes; although, as he observes, Kames's habit of working by constant reference to textual examples creates an impression that "one is reading 'Criticism' rather than aesthetics." De Bolla, *The Discourse of the Sublime,* 92.

25. Boswell, *Life of Johnson,* 414.

26. Henry Home, Lord Kames, *Elements of Criticism,* 3 vols. (1762; facsimile edition, New York: Johnson Reprint, 1967), 1:iii. Page numbers for further quotations from this source appear in parentheses in the text.

27. Kames explicitly argues this; ibid., 1:73–74.

28. "Spontaneous consent" is Gramsci's phrase. See Antonio Gramsci, *Selections from the Prison Notebooks,* ed. and trans. Quintin Hoare and Geoffrey Nowell Smith (New York: International, 1971), 12.

29. For biographical details, see Ian Simpson Ross, *Lord Kames and the Scotland of His Day* (Oxford: Clarendon, 1972); William C. Lehmann, *Henry Home, Lord Kames and the Scottish Enlightenment* (The Hague: Martinus Nijhoff, 1971); Arthur McGuinness, *Henry Home, Lord Kames* (New York: Twayne, 1970).

30. On the strength of sympathy with the wealthy, see David Hume, *A Treatise of Human Nature,* 2d ed., ed. P. H. Nidditch (Oxford: Clarendon, 1978), 362–71; Adam Smith, *The Theory of Moral Sentiments,* ed. D. D. Raphael and A. L. Macfie (Oxford: Oxford University Press, 1976), 50–52, 179.

31. Hipple, *The Beautiful, the Sublime and the Picturesque,* 107.

32. This summary relies on Judith Butler's in her discussion of Althusser's theory of interpellation in *The Psychic Life of Power: Theories in Subjection* (Stanford, Calif.: Stanford University Press, 1997), 106–31. See Louis Althusser, "Ideology and Ideological State Apparatuses (Notes Towards an Investigation)," in *Lenin and Philosophy and Other Essays,* trans. Ben Brewster (New York: Monthly Review Press, 1971), 127–86, esp. 170–77.

33. See Ross, *Lord Kames,* 55–58.

34. Kames's thinking here again foreshadows Althusser's model of the mix of ideology and repression in the category of "ideological state apparatuses," which includes literature and the arts. See Althusser, "Ideology and Ideological State Apparatuses," 142–45; Gramsci, *Prison Notebooks,* 12.

35. These are Althusser's terms. See Althusser, "Ideology and Ideological State Apparatuses," 132.

36. Pierre Bourdieu, *Distinction: A Social Critique of the Judgment of Taste,* trans. Richard Nice (Cambridge: Harvard University Press, 1984), 11–18, 23, 101–15, and passim.

37. Ibid., 32–35.

38. See Levine, "Introduction," 17.

CHAPTER NINE

The Labor Theory of Beauty

Aesthetic Subjects, Blind Justice

Douglas Mao

That the beautiful have it better is hardly a secret. Common wisdom has long held this truth to be self-evident, and study after study has confirmed that more attractive people make more money, win more esteem from their peers, even inspire more evident affection in infants. Who has never granted preferential treatment to the better-looking? Who has never felt a twinge of guilt about doing so? And who has never, under the provocation of this twinge, wondered whether there may not be some friction between our admiration of human beauty and our aspiration to live justly? To be sure, few of us will put this train of uncertainties high on the list of moral perplexities worth pondering (if indeed anybody has made such a list since the days of George Eliot), and some may deny outright that they have ever confronted it. Yet I feel no hesitation in insisting, right up front, that such denials will never prove wholly true, that indeed everyone from modeling agent to mother superior has experienced some shading of such an anxiety at one time or another. The essay that follows is, in a sense, about some of this anxiety's implications—for the field of aesthetics, but also for a broader politics, insofar as a political dimension inheres in the utopian longings encoded in everday life. The first section concerns the relationship between beauty and subjectivity in early aesthetic inquiry; the second and third, to which the first may be regarded as a lengthy preface, concern historical and contemporary understandings of the relations among beauty, labor, and desert.

Even those who would demur at the claim that everyone has felt anxious about preferring the beautiful may agree that questions about the relation between justice and human beauty are more pressing today than they have ever been before. One writer who seems to think so, or at least to think that others think so, is Elaine Scarry: in her recent *On Beauty and Being Just,* she argues that a praiseworthy but misapplied feeling for justice has been responsible for beauty's disrepute among humanities scholars for the past two decades.[1] I will return to Scarry's claims below, for the moment noting only that the turn Scarry detects seems to bear on, and to originate in, certain habits of thought and arenas of controversy peculiar to the end of the twentieth century. For one thing, public discourse in the United States today is marked by a convergence between unprecedentedly explicit condemnation of inequalities arising from factors such as race, gender, age, and sexual orientation (on the one hand) and (on the other) unprecedentedly relentless broadcasting of the benefits that accrue to the physically beautiful and that may be withheld from the unlovely or plain. Recalling also that techniques for improving appearance are more varied, complex, and radical than ever before, we may even say that one of the minor collisions currently defining American existence lies in a confrontation between advertising campaigns stressing how attractiveness is everyone's opportunity and legislative and educational campaigns waging war on "lookism." At the very least, we can observe that this kind of conflict represents a highly visible manifestation of a long-standing tension between the claims of beauty and justice.

Certainly, the strains in the relationship between the two have been growing more and more apparent since the emergence of aesthetics as an area of intellectual inquiry two and a half centuries ago. Cautious though we need to be in constructing historical trajectories of values, it remains fair to say that since the Enlightenment, the promotion of justice has grown more and more tightly affiliated with the promotion of greater equality in the distribution of social goods, and that legitimations of inequality have grown less and less plausible as belief in the divine or natural sanction of human hierarchies has receded into the realm of the ideologically untenable. Beauty, on the other hand, has more and more firmly come to be associated with luxury, surplus value, and elitism; for although it has always been obvious that the wealthy and powerful have ampler access to beautiful things and better training in discrimination, the complicity of taste with domination has only slowly emerged as a staple of critical reflection on the arts. The culminating phase of this development may be said to have commenced in the 1970s, with the rise of a critique that discerns in the aesthetic a stronghold of last resort for the impulse to hierarchize human beings and moves to show how taste is not merely intertwined with social elites but a constituent of the very possibility of class.

Here I allude to the influential line of argument initiated by Pierre Bourdieu in *Distinction,* his 1979 study of cultural consumption patterns in France. "The detachment of the pure gaze" of aesthetic evaluation, Bourdieu argues,

> cannot be dissociated from a general disposition towards the world which is the paradoxical product of conditioning by negative economic necessities—a life of ease—that tends to induce an active distance from necessity.
>
> . . . Taste classifies, and it classifies the classifier. Social subjects . . . distinguish themselves by the distinctions they make, between the beautiful and the ugly, the distinguished and the vulgar, in which their position in the objective classifications is expressed or betrayed. . . .
>
> . . . art and cultural consumption are predisposed, consciously and deliberately or not, to fulfil a social function of legitimating social differences.[2]

If Bourdieu's work seems to fit more and more neatly into current trends in American theory and criticism, the reason lies not only in the direct influence it has exerted, but also in the fact that it so clearly seems to participate in the demystification of "culture" that has become one of the central projects of intellectuals in the United States in recent years. Indeed it would seem, given the plasticity and pervasiveness of this demystification, that the aesthetic eye's entanglement with elites would have hummed as an undertone through many kinds of discussions about art, its institutions, and its audiences even if that eye's exclusionary operations had (somehow) managed to escape explicit consideration.[3]

It is worth pointing out, moreover, that the other critique of pleasurable gazing most important to contemporary cultural analysis also turns on a certain incompatibility between beauty and justice, although it has little to do with competitive cultivation or restrictions of access to cultural capital. The line of argument I have in mind here is that of Laura Mulvey's well-known 1975 essay "Visual Pleasure and Narrative Cinema," in which Mulvey explicitly sets out to "destroy" that scopic pleasure of Hollywood film wherein "women are simultaneously looked at and displayed, with their appearance coded for strong visual and erotic impact so that they can be said to connote *to-be-looked-at-ness*."[4] Mulvey's point is not quite that pleasure qua pleasure is always to be regretted (no serious thinker after utilitarianism has been able to afford labeling as a categorical antihedonist, after all), but rather that the pleasure of cinematic looking in its pre-utopian, mainstream mode enforces what we might describe as a radical inequality between two classes of persons, men and women: "In a world ordered by sexual imbalance, pleasure in looking has been split between active/male and passive/female."[5] In Bourdieu, Mulvey, and critics drawing upon them, the gaze figures as an appropriate site of inquiry into the work of domination by virtue of its exclusivity and its mastery—and also, implicitly, by virtue of its centrality in a world devoted to the image, a world that indeed *recognizes* itself as governed to an unprecedented degree by visual culture.

Will anything strike us as missing from these formulations, however, if we consider them in relation to the culture of the image as such? Regarded from this angle, what they seem most notably to omit is attention to the highly charged mythology of reward surrounding those involved in the production of images, above all the celebrities whose faces and bodies provide those images' fundamental material. This is hardly to insist that Mulvey's short piece *should* have taken up the question of celebrity culture at length, of course, and it is certainly not to place such a demand on Bourdieu, who operates in a very different field. It is to suggest, however, that the two theoretical approaches that have governed recent scholarly inquiry into relations of beauty, justice, the gaze, and hierarchy do not offer us much help in coming to terms with what may be the most inventive relegitimation of social hierarchy to emerge in the United States in the twentieth century. The idea of treating celebrities as a social group whose forms of privilege might be compared to those of historically defined classes is, of course, riddled with theoretical and practical pitfalls; but even if it is not true that media-marketed persons form a coherent elite in their own experience, there can be no question about the public's widespread attunement to the possibility that celebrities reside at the pinnacle of the social hierarchy, or about the media's intensification and exploitation of this attunement.

Viewed from the perspective of the United States in 2003, in other words, Bourdieu's 1979 French text may seem most quaintly out of touch in its faith that the ruling caste is defined by a form of taste keyed to (putatively private but clearly public) consumptions of Schoenberg, rather than one oriented toward (putatively discreet but finally spectacular) appearances in Prada. And although the foregoing points scarcely compromise the Mulveyan form of analysis (which turns less on the abjection of the woman who appears in the film than on the filmic gaze's construction of a certain subjective disposition), they do complicate it in meaningful ways. For it is not only that, as Mulvey herself notes, "the cinema has distinguished itself in the production of ego ideals as expressed in particular in the star system";[6] it is not only that the woman on screen, as powerful agent, may elicit an ambivalent identification from the male viewer. It is also that outside the darkness of the theater, the formerly gazing subject will inevitably be reminded that the lead actress belongs to the wafer-thin upper tier of modern society known as celebrities, whereas he belongs to the gigantic lower known as the rest of us—and will recognize, at some level, that this situation obtains precisely *by virtue of* the star's appearance as viewed rather than viewer.

Quite apart from its way of complicating the meaning of the gaze, then, the ascent of celebrity culture offers another compelling reason to inquire into the relation between physical beauty and distributive justice. If it is true that our own era's most distinctive renaturalizing of hierarchy turns upon a division between those who have their images widely disseminated and those who do not, and if it is also true that the "beautiful people" are indeed frequently marked by physical comeliness, then the time has never been more ripe for philosophical reconsideration of the rewards of what my university library's catalog, at least, indexes as "personal beauty." Mulvey and Bourdieu are clearly right in implying that a critique of the conditions of visual and other aesthetic pleasures constitutes an important contribution to a reimagining of the possibilities for social justice; to this we might add, however, that under the sign of the culture of the image, theoretical inquiry into the beauty of persons as persons—*as well as* representations—may be not less but more relevant than it has ever been before. And it is under this conviction that the following essay proceeds.

Beauty and Subjectivity

We might begin by recalling that the field of aesthetics has not always trained its gaze so exclusively on the work of art: in his *Aesthetic Theory*, Theodor Adorno memorably decries the fact that since Schelling, "aesthetic interest has centered on artworks," and reminds the reader that while "natural beauty" is "now scarcely even a topic of theory," it "was still the occasion of the most penetrating insights in [Kant's] *Critique of Judgment*."[7] Demarcated more or less consistently as the domain of inquiry into the "nature of the apprehension of beauty and other perceptual qualities of intrinsic value,"[8] aesthetics originally embraced not only the beauty of nature to which Adorno points but also *human* beauty, although the elision of interest in the latter came still earlier, and can indeed be discerned within the arc of Kant's own career. In his 1764 *Observations on the Feeling of the Beautiful and Sublime,* Kant follows Edmund Burke in taking as the archetype of beauty the beautiful woman: the third of his four sections, on "the distinction of the beautiful and sublime in the interrelations of the two sexes," commences with the observation that woman is properly named the "*fair sex*" and rightly "known by the mark of the beautiful," whereas men "could make a claim on the title of the *noble sex,* if it were not required of a noble disposition to decline honorific titles and rather to bestow than to receive them."[9] In the *Critique of Judgement,* published twenty-six years later, however, Kant limits his consideration of human beauty to a few problematic pages falling at the close of a demonstration that a pure judgment of beauty can never be made in accordance with an ideal.

We will turn to the more extensive treatment of human beauty to be found in the earlier Kant and in Burke shortly, but it is worthwhile first to pause over this vexed moment from the (more influential) third critique, which finds Kant at once raising and evading some difficult questions bearing directly on the problem of beauty and justice. In this section, Kant argues that ideals always depend upon a sense of perfect fitness for a determined purpose, which means that there can be no ideal of a flower (because the objective purpose of the flower is unclear), or of a house (because the purpose of a house is understood, but the details that would define the *best* provision of shelter are unclear), or of anything else in the universe—except the human being. As the "only being which has the purpose of its existence in itself," the person "alone of all objects in the world" is "susceptible of an ideal of *beauty*." And yet because the purpose of human existence is a *moral* purpose, a difficulty arises:

> The visible expression of moral ideas that rule men inwardly can . . . only be gotten from experience; but to make its connection with all which our reason unites with the morally good . . . visible as it were in bodily

> manifestation . . . requires a union of pure ideas of reason with great imaginative power even in him who wishes to judge of it, still more in him who wishes to present it.[10]

It is hard, if not impossible, to determine with certainty the relation between external bodily contours and internal moral ones; and in any case, Kant will observe next, the human moral ideal will permit "no sensible charm to mingle with the satisfaction in the object."[11] Appreciation of the human moral ideal thus seems to purge itself of the sensuous fabric—at once the basis for and the object of aesthetic judgments—after all, which is to say that no judgment of human beauty can constitute a *pure* judgment of *beauty* alone. And given that human beauty has already been shown to be the *only* beauty that we could even for a moment have imagined susceptible of judgment according to an ideal, it must be that no judgment in accordance with an ideal can be a pure judgment of beauty. To take up ideals at all is to leave the domain of the purely beautiful and enter into the realm of concepts.

In presenting this section of his argument, Kant intimates that he raises the question of human beauty less for any interest it may hold on its own than for its assistance in clinching his argument about ideals. Yet this intimation is surely disingenuous, for a complete omission of the question of human beauty from the *Critique* would have been striking on at least two counts. First, there was Kant's own stress on the beauty of women in his earlier *Observations,* utter neglect of which in the later work would surely have demanded some explanation. And second, there was the fact that the relation between external appearance and inner morality had been a vital topic of discussion in Germany, France, and England since the 1775 appearance of Johann Caspar Lavater's *Physiognomical Fragments,* which promoted the idea that physiognomy could be practiced in a wholly scientific manner—that with training one would be able, infallibly, to discern an individual's inner excellence from his or her external features.

Kant would explicitly, if ambivalently, address physiognomy in his 1798 *Anthropology from a Pragmatic Point of View,* where he admits that "there is a characterization by physiognomy," yet also declares that this characterization "can never become a science" and dismisses as "absurd" the contention that God would have "joined a beautiful body with a good soul in order to commend the person He created to other people."[12] Yet Kant speaks to the question of physiognomy no less significantly (and ambivalently) in the section of the third critique that we have been considering. We have already seen him remarking that great imaginative power would be required in judging of the visible expression of inward moral ideas, and at another moment—notably exiled to a parenthetical clause falling in the middle of a footnote—he offers the qualified endorsement "(*if* it may be assumed that external nature expresses the proportions of internal)."[13]

There may be a characterization by physiognomy, but it can never be a science: Kant seems compelled to admit the possible falsity of the assumption that beauty without mirrors beauty within, while at the same time wanting to avoid prolonged consideration of this assumption's flaws. But why would such a consideration be dangerous? The reason becomes obvious once we step back to consider what the *Critique* as a whole sets out to accomplish. Should it be the case that outer beauty in no way corresponds to inner or moral beauty, Kant would have to concede that the particular ethical subject is in practice bound to an aesthetic object (its body) whose virtues or lack thereof bear no relation to that subject's ethical life—a state of affairs that would pry apart the linkage between ethics and aesthetics that it is the very business of the *Critique* to affirm. The conclusion that there is finally no meaningful connection between physical charms and moral excellence might not be logically impossible to integrate into the *Critique,* but it would certainly make the work's central enterprise feel shakier—especially for those who tend to approach philosophy in a Kantian style, a style in which analogies do an enormous amount of work in securing (or unsettling) faith in the pertinence of the conclusions reached by more rigorously abstract analysis.

Thus Kant's reason for diverting attention from the weaknesses of the expressive theory; but what is it that compels him to endorse the theory only weakly rather than strongly in the first place? What prevents him from simply affirming the superior goodness of beautiful persons? As Kant himself suggests when he (partially) ridicules Lavater in the *Anthropology,* the answer is simply the evidence of day-to-day experience. We constantly encounter disparities between comeliness and goodness in those we meet, and no matter how much we would like to believe beauty the reward or expression of virtue, the evidence of a basic disconnection between the two is everywhere at hand. Or as Georg Christoph Lichtenberg, one of the angriest critics of Lavater's "rash and devastating notion that the most beautiful soul inhabits the most beautiful body, and the ugliest soul occupies the ugliest body," demanded in 1777, "Are not all history books and all large cities full of beautiful villains?"[14] (Even in the section of the *Critique* that we have been examining, Kant pauses to wonder why, if the outer conforms to the inner, we should regard as most beautiful those whose features are closest to, rather than farthest from, the mean. Resolutely analogical at this point, he muses that the most extreme moral excellence should, in theory, correspond to some extreme of facial or bodily form; and yet we tend to name as beautiful the one who conforms most nearly—within the parameters of his particular race—to an average compounded from the thousands of persons we have seen in our lives, the dull middle rather than the great.)[15]

Kant does not address the question of how, in practice, we treat those we perceive as more beautiful, of course, and it is certainly hard to imagine the Kantian moralist endorsing any pronounced or extensive favoritism toward the fair of feature or form. Still, to the degree that Kant retains an investment in the expressive theory of beauty, he must appear to license any preferential treatment of the beautiful that might reasonably follow from their probable moral superiority. This was precisely what Lichtenberg found so pernicious about the *Physiognomical Fragments*; in justifying his attack on Lavater, he wrote of wanting "to prevent people from practicing physiognomy for the advancement of brotherly love in the same way that, in earlier times, people scorched and burned for the advancement of the love of God."[16] As Lichtenberg's anxiety reminds us, it is not enough to aver that outer beauty expresses inner goodness and then move on, as though belief in such a connection has no consequences. On the contrary, it is precisely this question of real effects in the treatment of persons that renders the judgment of human beauty a more immediately ethical matter than any judgment of a work of art. Although the latter may be the recipient of our benefits, favors, or attentions in several senses, it cannot *experience* being preferred or being rewarded as human beings can. It cannot in the strictest acceptation be a recipient of justice or a victim of injustice, whereas most of us would agree that in certain situations, at least, some injustice may attend the extension of preferential treatment to more attractive persons.

Most of us today, that is; but what of Kant and other early writers on aesthetics? What will strike us forcefully, if we peruse Kant's *Observations* or Burke's 1757 *Philosophical Enquiry into the Origin of Our Ideas of the Sublime and Beautiful,* is that the question of the right by which the beautiful receive greater admiration, let alone that of the possible injury done to the less beautiful, never arises. In the case of Burke, this omission follows almost necessarily from an initial insistence that beauty's evolutionary origin lies in a human requirement of heterosexual monogamy. As man, unlike other animals, is not designed to "live at large," writes Burke,

> it is fit that he should have something to create a preference, and fix his choice; and this in general should be some sensible quality; as no other can so quickly, so powerfully, or so surely produce its effect. The object therefore of this mixed passion which we call love, is the *beauty* of the *sex.* Men are carried to the sex in general, as it is the sex, and by the common law of nature; but they are attached to particulars by personal *beauty.*[17]

One can hardly imagine a defter way of evading questions of fairness while yet admitting that beauty inspires preference for the beautiful. Burke does not actually claim that each individual woman's beauty will appeal uniquely to some one individual man, but the implication resonates so strongly (and sweetly) through the passage that objections premised on any quantifying of beauty (some have more, some have less) will sound impertinent and crude. Nor will Burke be deterred by the evident fact that many will wish to enter into social relations with more than one beautiful person. By a device similar to the one just noted, he recuperates this state of affairs as an intimation of *each* such relation's praiseworthy uniqueness:

> I call beauty a social quality; for where women and men, and not only they, but when other animals give us a sense of joy and pleasure in beholding them . . . they inspire us with sentiments of tenderness and affection towards their persons; we like to have them near us, and we enter willingly into a kind of relation with them.[18]

Whether nonbeautiful persons and animals are not also entitled to tenderness, affection, and relation—let alone whether they are harmed by the preferential direction of such feelings toward the beautiful—does not come into question. The only subjectivity of interest here is that of beauty's admirer ("*we* like to have them near us").

Not irrelevant to this passage's evasion of the question of preference is a certain slippage on the matter of gender. Burke at first appears to locate beauty solely among women ("Men are carried to the sex in general... by the common law of nature; but they are attached to particulars by personal *beauty*") but immediately thereafter allows that both women and men may be beautiful. In this, he inaugurates a line of thinking that will persist throughout the *Enquiry*, according to which both women and men may be beautiful, but women are clearly *more* beautiful, and woman the beautiful sex. Rebutting the claim that the determinant of human beauty is proportion, for example, Burke will aver that "both sexes are undoubtedly capable of beauty, and the female of the greatest; which advantage I believe will hardly be attributed to the superior exactness of proportion in the fair sex," while in countering the proposition that beauty comes from fitness he will remark, "If beauty in our own species was annexed to use, men would be much more lovely than women; and strength and agility would be considered as the only beauties. But to call strength by the name of beauty... is surely a strange confusion of ideas, or abuse of words."[19] Of his many statements in this vein, perhaps the most notorious is the one in which he affiliates beauty (in contrast to sublimity) with the weakness that makes women charming and grandfathers more lovable than fathers: "Where it is highest in the female sex, [beauty] almost always carries with it an idea of weakness and imperfection. Women... learn to lisp, to totter in their walk, to counterfeit weakness, and even sickness. In all this, they are guided by nature. Beauty in distress is much the most affecting beauty." And whereas the "authority of a father... hinders us from having that entire love for him that we have for our mothers," we "generally have a great love for our grandfathers, in whom this authority is removed a degree from us, and where the weakness of age mellows it into something of a feminine partiality."[20]

When it comes to the gendering of beauty, the Kant of *Observations* is happy to follow Burke fairly closely. We have already seen him opening the third section with the claim that women are the beautiful sex, whereas "we [men] could make a claim on the title of the *noble sex* [könnten wir auf die Benennung des edlen Geschlechts Anspruch machen], if it were not required of a noble disposition to decline honorific titles and rather to bestow than to receive them." He continues:

> It is not to be understood by this that woman lacks noble qualities, or that the male sex must do without beauty completely. On the contrary, one expects that a person of either sex brings both together, in such a way that all the other merits of a woman should unite solely to enhance

> the character of the beautiful, which is the proper reference point; and on the other hand, among the masculine qualities the sublime clearly stands out as the criterion of his kind [unter den männlichen Eigenschaften das Erhabene als das Kennzeichen seiner Art deutlich hervorsteche].[21]

Once again, beauty is appropriate to both sexes, but more so to women, for whom it plays the role of focal virtue taken by nobility in men.

Yet there is another asymmetry in play here. Although Kant is pleased to describe women as beautiful and to name some masculine activity sublime, he clearly prefers to call men *themselves* not sublime *(erhaben)* but noble *(edel)*. The aesthetic feminine quality, in other words, can comfortably be applied to female persons as well as things, whereas the aesthetic masculine quality cannot so readily be applied to male human beings. The discrepancy arises not so much from a fortuitous difference in usage, however, as from a more broadly consequential asymmetry in eighteenth-century treatments of subjectivity. In texts like Kant's and Burke's, beauty and sublimity *both* preferentially belong to objects rather than subjects,[22] but beauty seems less at odds with the human case because the tendency of the discourse is to install female persons in the situation of perceived object rather than perceiving subject.[23] Eighteenth-century writing virtually never ventures the possibility that the universal or presumptive human subject might be other than a masculine one, in fact, and vacillates strikingly on the question of whether women's capacity for subjectivity is not more partial or more doubtful than men's.[24] It is the exposure of just this vacillation that resides at the heart of the century's most comprehensive feminist document, Mary Wollstonecraft's *Vindication of the Rights of Woman* (1792), where it takes the form of a demand that moralists, philosophers, and educators decide once and for all whether women have souls—and that if the question be decided in the affirmative, women be given the same opportunities for moral improvement that men enjoy.

In Burke's and Kant's aesthetic treatises, moreover, the propensity to beauty seems inversely proportional to competence in moral undertakings. According to Burke, the "softer" virtues allied with femininity and beauty (such as "easiness of temper, compassion, kindness and liberality") are "of less immediate and momentous concern to society, and of less dignity," than sublime and masculine ones, although they win our affections much more readily: "Those persons who creep into the hearts of most people, who are chosen as the companions of their softer hours," he notes, "are never persons of shining qualities, nor strong virtues. It is rather the soft green of the soul on which we rest our eyes, that are fatigued with beholding more glaring objects."[25] For Kant, meanwhile, "The virtue of a woman is a *beautiful virtue,*" whereas that "of the male sex should be a *noble virtue,*" which means, as it turns out, that the ethical demand upon women is to behave *less* ethically, but more intuitively and aesthetically, than men. In the very next sentence, Kant explains in Rousseauvian tones that women

> will avoid the wicked not because it is unright, but because it is ugly; and virtuous actions mean to them such as are morally beautiful. Nothing of duty, nothing of compulsion, nothing of obligation! Woman is intolerant of all commands and all morose constraint. They do something only because it pleases them, and the art consists in making only that please them which is good. I hardly believe that the fair sex is capable of principles. . . . But in place of it Providence has put in their breast kind and benevolent sensations, a fine feeling for propriety, and a complaisant soul.[26]

As Christine Battersby points out, Kant does not deny that women have a moral capacity, but he does suggest, in the *Observations* and in his later writings, that they "have a duty to remain outside the sublime." While for Kant "women are . . . not incapable of becoming 'persons' in the full sense," they "have no duty to do so," and indeed bear a kind of responsibility to refrain.[27]

Thus if the unequal distribution of beauty provoked much less anxiety in Burke and Kant than it will in us, this is so in part because for them beauty is essentially the property of an object—an understanding not perturbed by the case of women's beauty because *insofar as* a woman is beautiful she is conceived (for the purposes of this kind of discourse) not as a subject in her own right but as the object of some perceiver's admiration. Questions about the rewards that attend corporeal beauty, in other words, do not interest Kantian or Burkean aesthetics because there is, for all intents and purposes, *no such thing as a physically beautiful or unbeautiful subject,* although there are physically beautiful and unbeautiful human beings. This is not to say that Burke and Kant could rigorously defend omission of the question of the rewards of comeliness if pressed. The point is rather that their basic disposition in treating of beauty would make such pressing sound strange, even where the benefits that may accrue to the beautiful seem to hover in the background of discussion (as in Burke's stress on how beauty fixes the feeling for the sex in general to one particular object, which so clearly encodes the question of women's dependence on marriage for financial provision).[28]

It is worth recalling here that if Burke and Kant limited discussion of the benefits of beauty to the side of the beholder, they could hardly have defended this limitation as natural or intrinsic to philosophical treatment of the topic: in the *Symposium,* after all, Plato had taken pains to comment upon the benefits of beauty-inspired love both to the beloved and to the lover. At the same time, however, we might notice that the Platonic instance confirms rather than disrupts what we have just observed to be an association between philosophically relevant benefits and the capacity to enjoy subjectivity in the fullest sense. In the *Symposium,* after all, the object of admiration is not the woman but the youth, and the benefit at issue is nothing other than a kind of training for the eventual assumption of full personhood. It was precisely the fact that the youth would eventually turn into a man that made pertinent both *objections* to the relationship of lover and beloved (a subject in the fullest sense is being misused) and *defenses* of it (the older lover is preparing the subject for maturity). Nor is this question of ethical training and example irrelevant to the eighteenth century: as Wollstonecraft's demand for equal opportunity in moral development reminds us, the telos of the human is a moral telos throughout the writing of the period.

In the next section of this essay, we will turn to a related aspect of beauty's removal from active subjectivity, its dissociation from labor, by way of seeing more specifically how recent developments in the relation between personal beauty and justice have come to unsettle understandings prevailing since the origin of aesthetics. First, however, we might take a moment to think about how the beautiful or unbeautiful subject does in fact break into Western discourse. Wollstonecraft's protest against the reduction of moral beings to pretty toys will again lead the way inasmuch as it calls attention to how aesthetics' want of interest in the relation of justice to personal beauty was both supported and undermined by other discourses centered on women—discourses in which the piety that the best men will choose their mates based on moral excellence was balanced by the acknowledgment that less admirable ones would base their selection on more superficial charms. Fictions of the period, especially fictions written in English, everywhere admit the latter (hard) fact even while embracing the former faith: here *Pamela* and *Clarissa* meet, in spite of the divergent fates of their heroines, and the point carries forward to Jane Austen and beyond. If certain kinds of representations thus place the physically beautiful subject at their centers, moreover, these same venues also—occasionally—make room for her sister, the subject who suffers for lack of physical beauty in spite of her moral stature, as in the case of Eugenia from Fanny Burney's *Camilla* (who, like Esther Summerson in *Bleak House* and Lady Castlewood in *Henry Esmond*, has been disfigured by smallpox).

By this point, the reader familiar with nineteenth-century fiction will be looking ahead to those narratives *(Jane Eyre, Villette, Bleak House)* in which the plain or disfigured woman takes center stage; and indeed one could make the case that it was primarily through the novel that the physically less beautiful subject at last came into her own—especially if one focuses on writing in English. Savaging the pre–George Eliot British novel in *The Way of the World*, Franco Moretti complains that in contrast to its Continental counterparts, this form adheres with painful fidelity to the fairy-tale paradigm in which no gray areas intervene between good and bad, and in which the virtuous protagonist is at the denouement "recognized for what he has always been," the lowly peasant for a handsome prince. This is the stuff neither of moral complexity nor of intelligent readers' interest, as far as Moretti is concerned, and yet it does contain the germ of an important democratic impulse. For what Tom Jones, Waverley, and Jane Eyre turn out to have a right to is "not only a vast rural estate, or a nice sum of money, or a title" but "their very identity—better yet, their identity as *people endowed with rights.* They had been deprived, we could say, of the right to have rights: restoring it to them is nothing more than an act of justice." The effort of these novels, Moretti remarks, is to show "that *everyone*—bastard child, woman, drunk, fugitive, pauper—has the right to tell her/his side of the story, to be listened to and to receive justice."[29]

Of all the texts Moretti considers, the one that receives the most contemptuous dismissal is *Jane Eyre*,[30] in part because its heroine's insistent description of herself as "plain" resonates with the aspect of the democratic disposition that most sets Moretti's teeth on edge: the allegedly pervasive English habit of favoring the common and the normal, "the socially 'neutral' and thus potentially universalistic" semantic sphere.[31] Whatever its accuracy or deficiencies, Moretti's claim is instructive for us because it suggests how fictions like *Jane Eyre* did indeed orchestrate a certain affiliation of the normal to the less beautiful, or at least a marginalization of the beautiful. If, as Moretti notes, the polished Blanche Ingram becomes "the cut and dried alternative" to the protagonist with whom we perforce identify,[32] this strict dichotomy means more than that Brontë extends an English suspicion of excellence as monstrosity into a new sphere. It means also that the experience of lacking beauty becomes as discursively shareable as any—becomes legible *as* a human experience, as it were, virtually for the first time. This is not to deny that the *very* beautiful, the hubristically beautiful, have been suspect since antiquity, but it is to take note of the wide gap between Kant's *Observations,* wherein the beautiful woman supplies the norm, and *Jane Eyre,* wherein the deprivations attendant on plainness are presented as meaningfully problematic. And it is to suggest, more broadly, that the nineteenth-century English novel—supported by that powerfully polysemous adjective *plain*—proved crucial in introducing the subjectivity of the less beautiful into representation.

Is there a difference, however, between claiming that *Jane Eyre* shows how a want of physical beauty may cause pain and claiming that it and its kindred fictions mark the discursive emergence of the physically less beautiful subject? What Moretti does not quite say, although the point is implicit in his argument, is that when the bastard child, woman, drunk, fugitive, or pauper is restored to his or her rights, restoration is premised on the implication that said character is not *in essence* the disreputable thing in question and would not like to be—that the "true" identity of each is an identity *as citizen,* stripped of contingent features like bastardy, drunkenness, flight, poverty, and even (although more problematically) femaleness. It is this that makes Jane's eventual acceptance of her own possible attractiveness crucial to her tale, which is finally not the story of the physically less beautiful subject granted her prerogatives, but that of the beautiful subject restored to rights after a period of imprisonment in the physically less beautiful casing, the frog revealed as a princess after all. If justice is served when Jane is revealed to be "endowed with rights," in other words, the message of this event is not that the profoundly or authentically plain have rights, but rather that there are no profoundly or authentically plain people. The belief that grounds *Jane Eyre*—and the belief that surely grounds most people's feelings about their own appearance and merits—is that in the deepest, most essential core of one's being, one is beautiful no matter what. Plainness or ugliness is a mistake in the eye of the beholder. The truth of one's subjectivity is always beauty, and beauty always the truth.

Laboring to Be Beautiful

There is more to the story of human beauty and justice than this business of mistaken identity, however. The problem is not only that some people, or many people, will be distracted from one's essential beauty by some contingent (bodily) plainness; it is also that those who are very beautiful on the outside may seem in no meaningful way to have earned that beauty—may seem unjustly rewarded for what is, after all, a pure gift rather than anything of their own invention. Meditation on any human asset can give rise to something of this confrontation with fortune's arbitariness, to be sure, but personal beauty is especially provoking because it seems virtually the only quality rewarded for its mere existence, quite apart either from the effort expended by its bearer or what it accomplishes beyond its own radiance. General intelligence, a fine mezzo-soprano voice, even a knack for predicting fluctuations in global markets: these capabilities are honed in practice and training and garner their rewards only after application, whereas beauty, to our moral disquiet and sometimes our bitter resentment, seems to assume its prerogatives without effort—to constitute one of those données of the life narrative, one of those accidents of birth, that after all count for so much even in a democracy.

In other words, the privileging of the beautiful can sometimes seem a grotesque anachronism, a holdover from some earlier mode of thinking that finds social goods rightly distributed not when there is a proportion between reward and labor but when assets accord with naturally or divinely ordained position. Even in that foundational text of modern thinking about distribution, Rousseau's 1755 *Discourse on Inequality*, this point emerges with striking clarity, although more because of something Rousseau notably omits than because of anything he explicitly says. Reconstructing the prehistoric events that long ago set the stage for the present unhappy conditions of civilization, Rousseau associates the very earliest glimmerings of inequality as such with differences in physical attractiveness: imagining the first fixed social organizations, he writes, "Young people of opposite sexes live in neighbouring huts, and the transient intercourse demanded by nature soon leads . . . to another kind of relationship, no less sweet and more permanent. People become accustomed to judging different objects and to making comparisons; gradually they acquire ideas of merit and of beauty, which in turn produce feelings of preference."[33] When, a few paragraphs later, he comes to consider how inequality gained its first *substantial* foothold in human society, however, he notably fails to mention beauty as a differentiating factor. Hierarchies arose, he supposes, not because everyone admired or esteemed the strong, the adroit, and the ingenious, but because "the stronger did more productive work, the more adroit did better work, the more ingenious devised ways of abridging his labour."[34] It was only through the medium of labor, as far as Rousseau can discern, that differences in natural gifts could have been transformed into differences of rank. Thus the reason beauty can have no place among the practical origins of inequality is that its possibilities do not appear to be realizable through toil. If Rousseau's genesis of inequality, like the biblical Genesis, has two beginnings, this is so because what would otherwise seem the most immediately hierarchizing of human qualities proves immune to mediation by work.

Rousseau was not the only eighteenth-century philosopher to presuppose an antipathy between loveliness and effort: the incompatibility between beauty's serenity and labor's traces is often remarked in writings of the period, and indeed nowhere more plainly than in the Burkean and Kantian explorations we have just been considering. In expounding on the virtues of the sublime in the *Philosophical Enquiry,* Burke notes that its "delightful horror" is to the mental plane what "common labour" is to the physical, where labor ("a surmounting of *difficulties,* an exertion of the contracting power of the muscles") is salutary less because of what it accomplishes than because it remains the best remedy for evils like melancholy, dejection, and despair, which arise from "a state of rest and inaction." Beauty, on the other hand, is associated with the "positive pleasure" caused by a diminishing of tension: it "acts by relaxing the solids of the whole system," as we can discern from the fact that when "we have before us such objects as excite love and complacency," the head reclines, the eyelids partly close, the hands "fall idly to the sides," and all is "accompanied with an inward sense of melting and languor." It is not only that the sublime dwells on the great and fearsome whereas the beautiful affiliates itself to the small and pleasing; it is also that the sublime dwells with effort, whereas beauty makes its home in rest.[35]

As we might expect, the early Kant remains broadly faithful to this distinction even as he rewrites its particulars to suit his own installation of the moral at the heart of philosophical inquiry. Near the beginning of the third section of the *Observations,* he avers that beautiful actions "display facility, and appear to be accomplished without painful toil," whereas "strivings and surmounted difficulties arouse admiration and belong to the sublime":[36] beautiful moral behavior is characterized by ease, opacity to interpretation, and a failure to prove quite fully moral after all, which is why it remains rightly associated with that ideally non-laboring, mysterious, and amoral creature known as woman. And while it would clearly be absurd to dissociate labor wholly from the work of art (which is, after all, a made thing), Kant insists that artistic beauty, like beautiful feminine behavior, will appear antipathetic to slavish rule following and strain. With regard to poetry, he remarks that "nothing tires more than laborious craftsmanship," just as in the *Critique of Judgement* he will affirm that beautiful art will seem as if a piece of nature—something that we feel obscurely to abide by rules where yet we can detect "no trace of the rule having been before the eyes of the artist and having fettered his mental powers."[37] The "beautiful arts," he continues (in that later work), "must necessarily be considered as arts of *genius,*" because genius is precisely that

> innate mental disposition *(ingenium) through which* nature gives the rule to art. . . . the author of a product for which he is indebted to his genius does not know himself how he has come by his ideas; and he has not the power to devise the like at pleasure or in accordance with a plan, and to communicate it to others in precepts that will enable them to produce similar products. (Hence it is probable that the word "genius" is derived from *genius,* that peculiar guiding and guardian spirit given to man at his birth, from whose suggestion these original ideas proceed.)[38]

If physical beauty and the capacity to perform beautiful actions are gifts rather than acquisitions, so too is the ability to produce the very most beautiful things, which partakes both of personal beauty's apparent freedom and of its positioning beyond the reach of effort alone. Genius and beauty, that is to say, are both structurally aristocratic.

This last point was certainly not lost on that singular late Kantian Oscar Wilde, who near the beginning of his own moral tale about beauty has Henry Wotton tell the still impressionable Dorian,

> You have a wonderfully beautiful face, Mr Gray. . . . And Beauty is a form of Genius—is higher, indeed, than Genius, as it needs no explanation. It is one of the great facts of the world, like sunlight, or spring-time, or the reflection in dark waters of that silver shell we call the moon. It cannot be questioned. It has its divine right of sovereignty. It makes princes of those who have it. . . . People say sometimes that Beauty is only superficial. That may be so. But at least it is not so superficial as Thought is. To me, Beauty is the wonder of wonders. It is only shallow people who do not judge by appearances. The true mystery of the world is the visible, not the invisible.[39]

Again, it is no accident that Henry compares human beauty to a sovereign holding divine right *and* to givens of the physical world: what links human beauty, natural beauty, and aristocracy is their antipathy to explanation. To disclose how a thing's beauty originates in mere adherence to certain rules, or to trace the genealogy of a member of the hereditary ruling class back to a pre-aristocratic moment, will be to undo a substantial part of the magic. And this murdering by dissection will prove especially swift where labor enters the picture. For the eighteenth- or nineteenth-century observer, the most damaging aspect of an unveiling of technique could well be the revelation of a work's debt to dreary effort, just as the most dangerous cut to the armor of social position would be the discovery of a fortune's or title's origins in work.

It is perhaps not surprising, then, to find that the poet who gave the twentieth century its most brilliant reformulation of the adage *Ars est celar artem* is also the last major British or Irish writer to mount a serious defense of the privileges of aristocracy:

> We sat together at one summer's end
> That beautiful mild woman your close friend
> And you and I, and talked of poetry.
>
> I said "a line will take us hours maybe,
> Yet if it does not seem a moment's thought
> Our stitching and unstitching has been naught.
> Better go down upon your marrow bones
> And scrub a kitchen pavement, or break stones
> Like an old pauper in all kinds of weather;
> For to articulate sweet sounds together
> Is to work harder than all these and yet
> Be thought an idler by the noisy set

> Of bankers, schoolmasters, and clergymen
> The martyrs call the world."
> That woman then
> Murmured with her young voice, for whose mild sake
> There's many a one shall find out all heartache
> In finding that it's young and mild and low.
> "There is one thing that all we women know
> Although we never heard of it at school,
> That we must labour to be beautiful."[40]

As in Kant, both the beauty of poetry and human beauty are allergic to the traces of effort, and as in Wilde the third member of the triad that also embraces beauty and genius is aristocraticness, or rather dislike of the philistine middle class. What differentiates Yeats's statement from Wilde's, of course, is that rather than delighting in the unearned mystery of beauty (or the mystery of beauty's unearnedness), it protests that the beautiful woman and the powerful poet also labor—that banker, schoolmaster, and clergyman are wrong in despising them for idleness. Yeats, in other words, defends the privileges of beauty and genius by at once admitting that these must appear free gifts and insisting that in truth they are strenuously earned. He employs, that is to say, the very argument at the heart of the old Tory defense of the aristocracy, the claim that the aristocrat properly understood was not exempt from labor, but rather bound by the task of maintaining social cohesion and protecting the least fortunate from want (not to mention exploitation by the commercial classes—a point here suggested by Yeats's effort to align poet and pauper against the professional middle).

If there is a sense in which "Adam's Curse" (or for that matter Henry Wotton's exhortation) speaks directly to public feeling about justice and hierarchy in contemporary democracies like the United States, it would depend upon the fact that the most visible equivalent of an aristocracy today is defined by a peculiar combination of beauty *and* labor. In the American imagination, celebrity is rarely completely unearned: the British royal family and those who marry into it clearly constitute the major exception (last residue of the old system) proving the rule that public devotion is in most cases secured by talents realized through effort, as for example acting and singing. Present-day celebrity can no more afford to appear parasitic than could aristocracy as such after the eighteenth century. At the same time, however, celebrities, if they are to *be* celebrities, ordinarily must not be perceived as having gotten where they are *solely* on the basis of hard work. To be as magical as demanded, they need the defining accident of birth that used to be called star quality—a je ne sais quoi, over and above the relevant talent, that usually incorporates a high degree of physical charm. The neo-aristocracy of celebrity, then, is at once more rooted in visible labor than old-style aristocracy *and* more dependent on the birth-gift of physical beauty; and we may even be tempted to hazard that part of the work of beauty on this front is to fill the void of wonder left when birth alone is no longer a plausible ground for social prominence.

But is beauty alone ever enough to make a star? And if one of the open secrets of all that media buzz, spin, and hype is that it is, what are the consequences for a public that hews irregularly but tenaciously to certain democratic ideals respecting desert? One of the most fascinating turns taken by celebrity culture in recent years has consisted in the rise of a figure who tips the balance so strongly away from visible effort and toward simple beauty that she (or he) threatens to test the limits of public tolerance for the culture itself. This figure—whose image is everywhere projected, whose power to earn is everywhere remarked, and whose capacity to call forth resentment is part of her (or his) mystique—is of course the fashion model, especially as magnified in the form of the supermodel, origin of a newly intense recognition of the economic benefits of physical attractiveness. The point of irritation is not that the model may have an income as high as that of other celebrities, but rather that income and fame seem predicated on a minimum of labor (ceaseless fashion industry proclamations about how hard models work notwithstanding) and on a superficiality that Wilde may have found endearing but most Americans are trained from the earliest age to mistrust. There are already, in fact, signs of a backlash: reporting on women's magazines' increasing tendency to put nonmodel celebrities on their covers, the *New York Times* has quoted one expert's opinion that the public views models as "one-dimensional," as "offer[ing] no substance, just beauty," and another as complaining that models have somehow lost the personalities they had during a golden age of just a few years ago.[41]

If the famous movie or rock star seems happily to wed active earning with that certain something that makes for greatness, in other words, the famous model seems to do what the beautiful person always does, but more spectacularly and potentially more infuriatingly—that is, call attention to the fact that life under a democracy is hardly life under a system that rewards hard work and minimizes inequalities of birth. (Usually less visible than models, possessors of immense inherited wealth do this much less reliably, of course.) Such an effect is neatly captured in a 1998 episode of the Texas-sited animated sitcom *King of the Hill,* in which young Bobby Hill plunges into the world of husky boy fashion modeling after being "discovered" in a clothing store for larger-size children. Bobby's mother supports his modeling career, but his father, Hank, objects; matters come to a head when Hank discovers that Bobby has been using his modeling earnings to pay the middle-aged next-door neighbor to do his household chores. What troubles Hank is not so much modeling's famous disconnection from heterosexual masculinity (although anxiety in this area figures as an important subtext elsewhere in the episode) as its apparent removal from anything that might be called honest labor. That a boy of nine can afford to have "his" domestic tasks performed by a much older man simply because he has the look that husky boy modeling wants seems the sign of some basic failure of correspondence between effort and reward, an affront to the conviction that working hard and playing by the rules are the paths to success.[42]

The belief that reward will come in proportion to effort is found more commonly in the homilies of parents and politicians than among the articles of faith actually held by grown-up Americans, of course, but the conviction that this proportion *would* obtain in a truly just society has not, for all that, ever been less than pervasive in the postwar United States. As Jennifer Hochschild's fascinating 1981 study *What's Fair?* suggests, a "norm of investments"—the view that "community members deserve rewards in proportion to what they put into the community"—almost always plays some part in contemporary Americans' feelings about social justice, although it will usually be found variously admixed with other distributive principles.[43] A certain basic rightness about the idea of equal reward for equal effort is acknowledged by virtually all of the Americans Hochschild interviewed for her project, even those strongly guided by the most leveling or hierarchizing of distributive principles: at the former extreme, the norm of "strict equality"; at the latter, the norm of "ascription," or distribution according to traits "such as age, sex, race, class, or religion."[44]

Borrowing Hochschild's terms, we can say that what makes the ascent of the supermodel so vaguely but consistently troubling is its affiliation with ascriptive differentiation, the principle of distribution regarded with most suspicion by those committed to specifically democratic ideals—which may mean (depending on the context) either a circumscribed group of progressives or virtually all Americans. For people like Hank Hill, the favoring of the beautiful that seems a harmless fact of life in most situations may, in the case of the model, seem to subvert the ideals for which their country stands, because it entangles part of capitalism's claim to legitimacy (its compatibility with a norm of investments) with an antithetical mode (the norm of ascription). For a more actively progressive politics, meanwhile, preference for the beautiful can seem of a piece with the other ascriptive norms that have always constituted the root, if not indeed the essence, of social injustice. Insofar as it is indeed a quality set by birth, is degree of loveliness or ugliness any less objectionable a distributive principle than race or gender?[45] And might we not expect a theoretically consistent progressive politics to try to broaden the struggle against ascriptive differentiation to encompass discrimination on the basis of beauty?

We might expect this, and in fact we have seen it. For it is precisely as the fruit of a resolution to carry the fight against norms of ascription onto new terrain that we need to understand the campaigns against "lookism" mounted since the early 1980s, which constitute something like the doctrinal or dialectical antithesis of the supermodel apotheosis occurring in the same years. Even those quickest to mock anti-lookism have recognized that its goal is finally to enfranchise yet more persons hitherto marginalized by ascriptive norms, and that its guiding principle has been a constituting of the less good-looking as a group whose rights of equal opportunity (in housing and employment, for example) must be held sovereign by any democracy worthy of the name. Where anti-lookists and their critics have differed is on the questions of whether physical appearance is primarily a matter of birth rather than personal agency and whether, in either case, it should be subject to leveling legal intervention.

These differences became sharply apparent following what may have constituted the acme of anti-lookism's legislative success: the 1992 passage, by the Santa Cruz (California) City Council, of a sweeping anti-discrimination ordinance that includes "personal appearance"—height, weight, hairstyle, and style of dress are mentioned—among the qualities that landlords and employers are forbidden to use in evaluating applicants. (Dubbed the "purple hair ordinance" after one author of the bill observed that people with purple hair have faced discrimination, the measure does allow employers to "enforce cleanliness and grooming standards for 'reasonable' business purposes.") Then "believed to be the most far-reaching 'anti-lookism' statute in the United States," the ordinance was roundly denounced for sending the message "that you don't have the right to make judgments on people based on their choices and actions," in the words of James Lileks of the Minneapolis *Star Tribune,* and elicited a torrent of warnings, from the right and center, about the tide of political correctness allegedly engulfing the United States.[46] Some readers on the academic left, meanwhile, found in the measure unnerving testimony to "politicized identity's imbrication in disciplinary power," as Wendy Brown put it in a 1993 essay. For Brown, the measure aims, disastrously or at least disagreeably, "to count every potentially subversive rejection of culturally enforced norms as themselves normal, as normalizable, and as normativizable through law."[47]

Notably absent from such reactions has been substantial interest in whether this kind of legislation is sponsored by a feeling for justice on which many might, after all, find common ground. This omission is attributable in part, of course, to the framers' apparent deafness to the notion that different degrees of responsibility might apply to different aspects of appearance—an invitation, if ever there was one, to scolding by libertarians and left radicals alike. Surely, however, the omission also owes a great deal to the fact that serious engagement with the problem of ascriptive differentiation almost always leads to the grim conclusion that it is impossible to live perfectly justly after all. Is prejudice against a person whose weight is excessive because of a recognized medical condition (whatever that may mean) less defensible than prejudice against a person who simply likes to eat too much? The question is troubling because, as we well know, there is nothing "simple" about the desire to eat too much. If it were easy to cease overeating, almost everyone would. Once such a discussion commences, moreover, it quickly comes to our attention that very few people would choose to be unattractive rather than attractive, unloved rather than esteemed, stupid rather than clever, or even lazy rather than energetic, which implies in turn that there is a not wholly meaningless sense in which people are really not responsible for their own deficiencies. If we begin by questioning too strenuously the validity of preference for the more attractive, we will soon—so it seems—be forced to question the justice of preference for the intelligent, the interesting, the hardworking, the kind.

Just this anxiety flickers at the moment in *On Beauty and Being Just* when Elaine Scarry—concerned to show how beauty promotes rather than comes to blows with our sense of justice—turns to the problem of desert. "Sometimes," she writes, the undeservingness of beautiful persons

> is urged on the grounds that their beauty is natural: such persons were born with it, lazily inheriting it through no labor or merit of their own. (This argument is not very strong since so many things we unembarrassedly admire—great math skill, a capacity for musical composition, the physical agility of a dancer or speed of an athlete—entail luck at birth.)[48]

Exactly so, we might counter, but what if we should find not that our admiration for the mathematically gifted erases our anxieties about preferring the beautiful, but rather the reverse—that unease about our reactions to beauty leads to important questions about all human gifts?

Not wishing to mount a defense of ascriptive norms, Scarry is left with two principal means by which to salvage beauty for justice, both of which notably evade the question of whether it is right or wrong to prefer beautiful persons. The first strategy, which harks back to Burke and Kant and which Scarry prefers through most of her essay, is to redirect attention to the subject perceiving beauty and away from effects on the beautiful (or unbeautiful) perceived. Most of *On Beauty and Being Just* consists of reminders that the feeling for beauty is, with respect to the perceiving consciousness, life-giving, energizing, provocative of the desire to be educated, and so on. The second strategy is directed much more locally at what Scarry herself names "the problem of lateral disregard, the problem that whatever benefits accrue to an object through its being the focus of our attention are not being equally enjoyed by nearby objects in the same class."[49] In her very phrasing of the problem ("object" and "attention" rather than "person" and "reward"), Scarry moves to diminish its seriousness as a matter of distributive justice; but in order to dispose of it fully she invokes the insight that beautiful persons and things exert a "pressure toward the distributional," inspiring us to care for and attend to things that resemble them, including less beautiful ones.[50] This claim speaks so aptly to our sense of what makes beauty worthwhile, of course, that even the grumpiest of anti-aesthetes would be embarrassed to deny it wholly. And yet it is important to see that it speaks not at all to the questions of *justice* that arise when a person is selected for a job on the basis of looks rather than relevant skills, or even when one believes oneself passed over, in love, in favor of someone more beautiful of feature but less deserving of affection.[51]

Scarry could, of course, have made a perfectly reasonable and convincing case that beauty is double-edged, an incitement to justice that also raises profound difficulties for those who wish to live justly, but *On Beauty and Being Just* will accept no such halftones: impelled to clear beauty of every charge, it turns those who critique some of its tendencies into pleasure-hating "opponents."[52] Why so monolithic a defense? The answer surfaces most concretely in a footnote, where Scarry observes that "over the last fifteen years, many students, even the brightest and most good-hearted among them, have (as a result of the general prohibition on beauty) spoken in their papers about the way a poet or novelist reifies a garden or a flower or a beautiful bird by his or her lavish regard."[53] If acute distress attends the discovery that beauty and justice might come into conflict, the reason is partly that appreciation of loveliness can seem one of the last points of resistance to a culture of complaint that (in the view of some) wants to render all pleasure illicit in the end. In such a context, the feeling for beauty appears as one of the last fragments of humanity surviving the ravages of modernity, one of the last indications that some people do not (as Frank O'Hara put it in a rather different context) totally *regret* life.[54]

Scarry's concern is the more noteworthy because a similar solicitude has emerged in the very discourse that, with anti-lookist initiatives, constitutes recent decades' most notable reaction against the American obsession with physical appearance: a vigorous feminist critique of what Naomi Wolf has dubbed "the beauty myth." Undertaken in books such as Robin Lakoff and Raquel Scherr's *Face Value: The Politics of Beauty,* Ellen Zetzel Lambert's *The Face of Love: Feminism and the Beauty Question,* Nancy Friday's *The Power of Beauty,* and Wolf's *The Beauty Myth* itself, this reexamination dwells less on the possible injustice of preference based on physical appearance than on the disproportionate (and often hugely destructive) burden of beauty placed on women specifically—on the ways in which women's tethering to standards of attractiveness from which men have largely been exempt impedes gender equality. What is remarkable about these modestly revisionary texts, however, is that while none doubts that the gender imbalance of the beauty burden is wrong, all are characterized by a decided, indeed an impassioned, resistance to the proposition that we might sacrifice our admiration of physical beauty by way of creating a more just society. "Without beauty, or without the ability to love it," Lakoff and Scherr conclude in a typical passage, "we would be isolated and sad in a bleak and unforgiving world. We have to find a way... to preserve our enjoyment of beauty... without resentment and without obsession."[55] For these writers, beauty can and must be recuperated through a collective project of new understanding, a learning to appreciate in a way that would be more open, more flexible, and finally more democratic. In the new order thus proposed, no person need be unbeautiful, because outward beauty would be an expression of love and acceptance of self and others, not a sign of enslavement to the competitive urge.

The forces against which these writers most directly position their work are marketing strategies whose unattainable standards lead women to hate their bodies. It may therefore be cause for either celebration or dismay that the most visible responses to this line of critique have appeared in advertising itself, which has lately seemed to assault the beauty myth in order to sell beauty-enhancing products. In recent years, Oil of Olay has been promoted on television by middle-aged women who say that they have no interest in looking like teenagers; posters and postcards for the Body Shop have borne (over an illustration of a decidedly Boteroesque Barbie doll) the slogan, "There are 3 billion women who don't look like supermodels and only 8 who do... love your body"; and the New York–area gym Crunch has been sold without beautiful bodies but *with* an actor dressed in a rabbit suit whose adventures end in the trademark slogan "No Judgments." Most immediately revealing of what is at stake, perhaps, is an ad for hair color, frequently aired in late 1997 and early 1998, in which Jane Seymour contrasts relationships and career decisions, which are big things, to getting rid of a little gray, which is a very little thing: "It's just a little box of hair color," she concludes, which seems to mean that beauty is no big deal.[56]

Of course Seymour is not saying that we need not worry about beauty, but that we need not worry about worrying about beauty, and it is on this distinction that the new marketing crucially turns. The implication of the spot is not that we are allowed to stop caring about how we and others look, but that beauty is so easy to obtain that the decision to participate in the competition—to succumb to rather than to fight the beauty myth—should prompt no moral anguish. If being beautiful, or at least relatively more beautiful, just takes a little effort, then you have only yourself to blame if you are not beautiful, and indeed others may rightly blame you for your laxity. Women must no longer be held to impossible standards of appearance, but the effortless application of a little box of dye is surely not so very much to ask; to repine at so tiny a demand is to court the absurdity that personal appearance is utterly beyond one's control (precisely the message that so many commentators found in the Santa Cruz measure). Even if we cannot all be *most* beautiful, we can all try to look our best. Beauty is a matter of personal responsibility and effort.

What makes this line of reasoning seem more plausible today than it has seemed in any previous era, clearly, is that opportunities for undertaking the beauty effort have expanded so dramatically in recent decades. To continuously evolving and improving cosmetics, grooming techniques, and plastic surgery have been added, as we are all aware, an arsenal of body-shaping regimens predicated on new forms of the diet pill and diet plan, as well as a thriving traffic in (and culture of) home exercise equipment, fitness centers, private gyms, and personal trainers. Even as anti-lookism and exposés of the beauty myth have reiterated the moral that judging by physical appearance is not fair, in other words, new developments in the technology of making-beautiful have made it possible to rationalize a preference for beautiful people with new vigor, on the understanding that attractiveness is more than ever a matter of effort and that those who make the effort deserve the rewards they receive. Within this transformation, the new exercise technologies play perhaps the defining role, because they present in distilled form the promise that physical and quantifiable work will be transformed into beauty directly. And in so doing, of course, they clinch a rapprochement between the once antipathetic terms of beauty and labor, a rapprochement that must count as one of the most fascinating yet least discussed changes in American habits of thinking to emerge in the postwar era.[57]

If Kant avoided an unsettling disjunction between the ethical and the aesthetic by assuming an expressive correlation between virtue and beauty, then many contemporary Americans will be more likely to deal with the moral dilemmas attendant on comeliness by assuming a correlation between laboring to be beautiful (regarded as a possible moral imperative) and bodily results. Under this labor theory of beauty, the idea that effort is rewarded mutates rapidly into the assumption that effort is *always* rewarded, and that one may praise the lovely and blame the ugly without invoking ascriptive norms. Nor, it must be said, does this point bear only on dieters and spin class regulars. The blanket assault of beauty advertising via print, television, and Internet means that even those uninterested in refashioning their bodies, even those suspicious of the too-obviously pumped, tanned, and dyed, will be exposed regularly to affirmations that lack of beauty may legitimately be stigmatized as the deserved result of a want of effort, a failure of application analogous to the indolence of the "deservedly" poor.

Thus although it would not be wrong to understand the rise of gym culture (scene of relaxation and health, but also of competition-inflected labor) as a further infiltration of capitalist instrumentality into the sphere of what used to be "leisure," there may be more at stake in the explosion of beauty technologies than grammars of reification and commodification alone can fully compass. To say that its new affiliation with labor is just what beauty needed to obtain a new legitimacy, as it were, is to notice that this affiliation defuses precisely the anxieties about equality, reward, and personal responsibility provoked by anti-lookist campaigns—campaigns legible, as we have seen, as the latest attempt to extend egalitarian enfranchisement to a set of persons never before conceived as a group with rights in need of protection. From this point of view, the ascent of the labor theory of beauty furnishes another example of how, in a society torn between meritocratic and egalitarian ideals, *a rhetoric of effort can curtail discussion of the forms and meanings of equality,* and (in a slightly different register) of how *devotion to what seems a norm of investments can in fact help to preserve discrimination along ascriptive lines.*

Taken out of context, of course, claims like these can easily be made to sound paranoid and silly: the only noncrazy answer to the question, Is gym culture out to undermine the very foundations of progressive politics? will be no. The assertion is not, however, that new technologies of making beautiful and new conceptions of beauty constitute deliberate political interventions. It is rather that (whatever their origins) they exert important effects on ethical and aesthetic beliefs from which they might at first seem quite removed, beliefs that sometimes do have real effects in the political sphere. To situate the new avenues of self-improvement within a history of the relation between beauty and labor is not to impute to makers of Nautilus machines an intention to halt the progress of freedom, any more than demystifying the beauty myth means claiming that feminine beauty is no more than a conscious male conspiracy to enslave half the human race. It is, however, to suggest that when we feel a certain uneasiness about beauty's rewards we always gesture (if faintly) to the possibility of a more radically just society. And it is to wonder, on the other side, whether the logic according to which we recuperate minor preferences might not be the same one that leads us to disavow the utopian urge, to doubt that a just society can ever be brought to birth.

Effort Visible

Is this quite all, however? Is it right to say that the labor theory of beauty helps us to rationalize a preference for what remains a contingent corporeal quality, something ultimately separable from subjectivity as such? Or does the foregoing discussion imply a more complicated relationship among subjects, labor, and beauty?

By way of answering this question, we might turn briefly to one of the more influential meditations on social justice of the late twentieth century, Michael Walzer's 1983 *Spheres of Justice: A Defense of Pluralism and Equality,* and specifically to an intriguing moment falling in Walzer's last chapter but two. Having tried for much of his polemic to show how equality might be saved from its friends as well as its enemies (the preface opens, "Equality literally understood is an ideal ripe for betrayal"),[58] Walzer turns, in the section that will interest us, to the question of "recognition," and specifically the problem of "public honor and individual desert." A footnote to the main discussion, at this point, includes the single significant mention of human beauty to be found in the book:

> But do people deserve the rewards that come not because of some achievement but because of some state of being? Is the winner of a beauty contest *honored?* The organizers of contemporary beauty contests seem to have a dim and embarrassed sense that the winner would not be honored were she chosen merely for her natural endowments, for they have introduced a variety of "talent" criteria. Honor is (for us) the recognition of an action; and displaying one's physical beauty or, for that matter, announcing one's noble birth and blood does not qualify as an action in the proper sense. It is necessary to use one's endowments in some socially valued way. But it's obviously not difficult to imagine societies founded on different conceptions of honor.[59]

It should be obvious that this treatment will encounter difficulties in situations where the labor theory of beauty has come to preside. If, as seems increasingly to be the case in the United States, physical beauty is perceived to be the result of (more or less consciously competitive) effort, then display is no longer the only "action" associated with it, and might perhaps be honored as other accomplishments are. Still, Walzer's point will hold good to the extent that the fashioning of corporeal beauty fails to be "socially valued" in the sense that achievements providing pleasure or instruction beyond themselves are. No one yet seems quite ready to "honor" the supermodel in the way that people honor artists, scientists, or political leaders. (On this last point, however, see Naomi Campbell's recollection, on the 15 July 1998 broadcast of *The Late Show with David Letterman,* of her audience with Fidel Castro. On being introduced to Campbell's fellow model Kate Moss, it seems, Castro honored Moss with the observation that she had started the "revolution" of the "little models.")

What lends Walzer's footnote special interest, however, is that it falls in the midst of a consideration of the very questions about contingent attributes and subjectivity that the anti-lookist argument seems inevitably to invite. In the next paragraph of his main text, Walzer writes:

> Advocates of equality have often felt compelled to deny the reality of desert. The people we call deserving, they argue, are simply lucky. Born with certain capacities, raised by loving or exacting or stimulating parents, they then find themselves living, quite by chance, in a time and place where their particular capacities . . . are also valued. For none of this can they claim any credit; in the deepest sense, they are not responsible for their own achievements. Even the effort they expend, the painful training they undergo, is no evidence of personal merit; for the capacity to make an effort or to endure pain is, like all their other capacities, only the arbitrary gift of nature or nurture.

By way of refuting this argument, Walzer stresses that justice must be understood to operate among persons, and that the capacities and experiences in question are simply not separable from personhood. The egalitarian claim just described is, Walzer writes,

> an odd argument, for while its purpose is to leave us with persons of equal entitlement, it is hard to see that it leaves us with *persons* at all. How are we to conceive of these men and women once we have come to

> view their capacities and achievements as accidental accessories, like hats and coats they just happen to be wearing? How, indeed, are they to conceive of themselves? . . . We don't encounter other people as moral and psychological blanks, neutral bearers of accidental qualities. It isn't as if there is X and then there are X's qualities, so that I can react separately to the one and the other. The problem that justice poses is precisely to distribute goods to a host of Xs in ways that are responsive to their concrete, integrated selves. Justice, that is, begins with persons. More than this, it begins with persons-in-the-social-world, with goods in their minds as well as in their hands.[60]

One need not partake of postmodern discomfort with the positing of "concrete, integrated selves" to find this argument a little limited, if not disingenuous. It will be enough to notice that although Walzer's take may work well as a prescription for what socially administered justice should be, it does not speak adequately to feelings about justice as we commonly experience them. For Walzer's argument to satisfy us completely, we would have to believe that all the people who have ever thought, "How unjust that my sister got the brains in the family," or, "In a just universe, I would be more attractive," are simply mistaken about the nature of justice. We would have to believe justice irrelevant to what we often experience as a contingent relation between the subject who suffers, desires, and needs (on the one hand) and the abilities that may garner that subject relief, satisfaction, and reward (on the other).[61] Were it to rise from its footnote to the main body of Walzer's text, beauty would trouble Walzer's argument, because it has seemed for so long something less integral to the self than a capacity, yet more integral than a possession. Can we truly feel right about declaring that the energetic deserve the honoring to which their effort leads, whereas the beautiful do not deserve any honoring that might arise from their looks? Walzer's retreat to the ground of personhood notwithstanding, it is clear that the basis for his distinction between what may be honored and what may not be rests very precisely with effort after all. Those natural capacities amenable to combination with effort we honor, but we do not honor those that stand apart from effort, as for example the effortless beauty that we find in *Spheres of Justice* and Rousseau.

The curious implication of Walzer's reasoning, then, is that evaluation of persons conducted with an eye to justice as such must finally privilege one quality, disposition to effort, above all others. Or, more exactly: Although Walzer's scheme does not make effort the only criterion for true desert, it does make effort the necessary condition of all deserving. And thus if it is also true that the "problem that justice poses is . . . to distribute goods to a host of Xs in ways that are responsive to their concrete, integrated selves," then the self *as a subject of justice* is in a crucial sense defined, prior to the introduction of any other qualities, by its effortfulness. Before the eyes of justice, in this view, one is what one does, or at least what one tries in good faith to do, and the self is better described as an origin of activity than as a center of contemplation, yearning, or delight. Such an understanding—which, it must be said, operates powerfully in most contemporary American thinking about justice—comes very near to constituting the subject as a producer, an origin of projective activity not merely manifested in its works but (here some strains of capitalist individualism converge with Marx) finally defined by them.

In calling attention to the way in which effort comes to govern subjectivity, Walzer's remarks illuminate those further complexities of the labor theory of beauty alluded to above, and to which we can now turn. For if the subject of justice is understood primarily as a productive subject, the "earning" of a beautiful body will not mean that the earner has acquired just another asset wholly unrelated to selfhood; it will mean rather, or also, that this person has made manifest on his or her frame the critically defining quality of disposition to effort. Under this scheme, that is to say, earned beauty once again becomes an expression—but not, as in Kant, an expression of general moral health. Rather, it becomes an expression of that determining effortfulness that seems to exist only in its expression and yet at the same time, paradoxically, to reside at the very heart of one's being. The claim that beauty is only skin deep, long a ground for objecting to preferential treatment of the beautiful, thus loses much of its force. No longer a quality randomly distributed to deserving and undeserving souls alike, physical beauty becomes one of the preeminent signifiers of that basic desert belonging to the subject disposed to produce.

Of course, no one unreservedly subscribes to the idea that the true self is the self-who-produces; and even if everyone did, the foregoing would hardly imply that beauty's rewards should cease to prompt dismay and resentment. Most would remember (for one thing) that beauty is not *all* labor, that there remain those accidents of birth and aging that provide the material on which moisturizing, plucking, toning, dieting, and surgery go to work. Nor does the foregoing imply that beauty marketing's recuperation of anti-lookist discourse has utterly foiled progressive attempts to expand the category of equality, or that efforts (feminist and otherwise) to disseminate a less narrowly competitive understanding of beauty are doomed. It does suggest, however, that we will likely go wrong if we adhere to the intuition that in emphasizing *mediation* (by labor), the labor theory of beauty must further weaken the belief that outside expresses inside. On the contrary: in a postaristocratic environment, as we have seen, effort will normally replace birth as the measure by which the self (qua subject of justice) is "known" by others, and in so doing will tend to install itself at the heart of personhood. If aesthetic subjects are now more fully aesthetic objects than they have ever been, therefore, this means more than that Cartesian dualism has recently been subject to strain, more even than that postmodern culture's premium on visuality has allowed surface to infiltrate the realm of interiority in new ways. It means also that the adoption of labor as the currency of justice may now be serving not to diminish, but rather to enhance immeasurably, the power of the image.

Notes

1. Elaine Scarry, *On Beauty and Being Just* (Princeton, N.J.: Princeton University Press, 1999).

2. Pierre Bourdieu, *Distinction: A Social Critique of the Judgement of Taste,* trans. Richard Nice (Cambridge: Harvard University Press, 1984), 5–7.

3. It must be added, however, that very few of those who have drawn on Bourdieu share the unrelenting hostility to the aesthetic articulated in *Distinction.* For the Bourdieu of this text, the aesthetic embraces none of the redemptive possibility claimed for it even by other ready demystifiers such as Terry Eagleton, but rather remains thoroughly absorbed in the work of subordinating the working class, from which it is always finally withheld: "It must never be forgotten that the working-class 'aesthetic' is a dominated 'aesthetic'" (41).

4. Laura Mulvey, "Visual Pleasure and Narrative Cinema," in *Film Theory and Criticism,* 4th ed., ed. Gerald Mast, Marshall Cohen, and Leo Braudy (New York: Oxford University Press, 1992), 748, 750.

5. Ibid., 750.

6. Ibid., 749.

7. Theodor W. Adorno, *Aesthetic Theory,* trans. Robert Hullot-Kentor (Minneapolis: University of Minnesota Press, 1997), 61. Why this disappearance, according to Adorno? "Natural beauty vanished from aesthetics as a result of the burgeoning domination of the concept of freedom and human dignity, which was inaugurated

by Kant and then rigorously transplanted into aesthetics by Schiller and Hegel; in accord with this concept nothing in the world is worthy of attention except that for which the autonomous subject has itself to thank" (62).

8. Peggy Zeglin Brand and Carolyn Korsmeyer, "Introduction: Aesthetics and Its Traditions," in *Feminism and Tradition in Aesthetics,* ed. Peggy Zeglin Brand and Carolyn Korsmeyer (University Park: Pennsylvania State University Press, 1995), 4.

9. Immanuel Kant, *Observations on the Feeling of the Beautiful and Sublime,* trans. John T. Goldthwait (Berkeley: University of California Press, 1960), 76.

10. Immanuel Kant, *Critique of Judgement,* trans. J. H. Bernard (New York: Hafner, 1951), 69–70, 72.

11. Ibid., 72.

12. Quoted in Robert E. Norton, *The Beautiful Soul: Aesthetic Morality in the Eighteenth Century* (Ithaca, N.Y.: Cornell University Press, 1995), 206.

13. Kant, *Critique of Judgement,* 72; emphasis added.

14. Quoted in Norton, *The Beautiful Soul,* 198.

15. Kant, *Critique of Judgement,* 70–72.

16. Quoted in Norton, *The Beautiful Soul,* 197. Lichtenberg's phrasing is not as exaggerated as might appear. At one point in *Physiognomical Fragments,* Lavater envisions a social reorganization under which the ugliest—and thus most morally susceptible—children would be transferred from mainstream society (and the care of their parents) to a special preserve free of "extraordinary enticements to vice" (quoted in Norton, 209).

17. Edmund Burke, *A Philosophical Enquiry into the Origin of Our Ideas of the Sublime and Beautiful* (Oxford: Oxford University Press, 1990), 39.

18. Ibid.

19. Ibid., 89, 96.

20. Ibid., 100, 101.

21. Kant, *Observations,* 76–77; and Immanuel Kant, *Vorkritische Schriften,* vol. 2 of *Immanuel Kants Werke* (Berlin: Bruno Cassirer, 1912), 269.

22. Kant would famously revise this position when treating the sublime in the third critique itself, concluding that we are mistaken when in ordinary speech we refer to the sublimity of the boundless ocean or the starry firmament. Sublimity, Kant decides, "does not reside in anything of nature, but only in our mind, in so far as we can become conscious that we are superior to nature within, and therefore also to nature without us" (104); the word "sublime" should properly "only be applied to a state of mind, or rather to its foundation in human nature" (121). In thus neatening the messy triad of beautiful-sublime-noble into a cleaner binary, Kant distances himself from the meditations on feminine beauty that render the *Observations* less adequate as an account of *all* human beings' perceptive faculties; at the same time, however, he widens the theoretical gap between the feminine, passive beautiful and the masculine, active sublime.

23. Burke installs beauty squarely in the object: "Beauty is, for the greater part, some quality in bodies, acting mechanically upon the human mind by the intervention of the senses"; *Philosophical Enquiry,* 102.

24. See, for example, the case of Hume, to which Carolyn Korsmeyer turns in considering how acknowledgments of gender differences imperiled the universal subject of the judgment of taste. Carolyn Korsmeyer, "Gendered Concepts and

Hume's Standard of Taste," in *Feminism and Tradition in Aesthetics,* ed. Peggy Zeglin Brand and Carolyn Korsmeyer (University Park: Pennsylvania State University Press, 1995), 55–63.

25. Burke, *Philosophical Enquiry,* 100–101.

26. Kant, *Observations,* 81.

27. The phrasing is Battersby's. Christine Battersby, "Stages on Kant's Way: Aesthetics, Morality, and the Gendered Sublime," in *Feminism and Tradition in Aesthetics,* ed. Peggy Zeglin Brand and Carolyn Korsmeyer (University Park: Pennsylvania State University Press, 1995), 92–93, 96. Jane Kneller notes that in Kant, taste and femininity align in several crucial respects: the two "share the common aim of furthering human culture" and are at moments granted the status of ends in themselves, only to be resubordinated at last "to individual morality and masculinity, respectively." Jane Kneller, "Discipline and Silence: Women and Imagination in Kant's Theory of Taste," in *Aesthetics in Feminist Perspective,* ed. Hilde Hein and Carolyn Korsmeyer (Bloomington: Indiana University Press, 1993), 180–81. Tom Furniss, meanwhile, observes that in Burke the sublime "acts as a means of staving off the devastating effects of beauty—which needs to be resisted because it is at once the primary vehicle of civilization and that which perpetually threatens to undermine it." Tom Furniss, *Edmund Burke's Aesthetic Ideology* (Cambridge: Cambridge University Press, 1993), 38.

28. At one juncture in the *Observations,* Kant does refer to something like the physically unbeautiful subject, but even here he makes a point of stressing the opposition between beauty and nobility and seems uncertain about how to relate subjectivity to existence as a beautiful or unbeautiful being: "Finally age, the great destroyer of beauty, threatens all these charms; . . . gradually the sublime and noble qualities must take the place of the beautiful, in order to make a person always worthy of a greater respect as she ceases to be attractive. In my opinion, the whole perfection of the fair sex in the bloom of years should consist in the beautiful simplicity that has been brought to its height by a refined feeling toward all that is charming and noble. Gradually . . . the reading of books and the broadening of insight could refill unnoticed the vacant place of the Graces with the Muses, and the husband should be the first instructor. Nevertheless, when the epoch of growing old, so terrible to every woman, actually approaches, she still belongs to the fair sex, and that sex disfigures itself if in a kind of despair of holding this character longer, it gives way to a surly and irritable mood" (92).

29. Franco Moretti, *The Way of the World: The Bildungsroman in European Culture* (London: Verso, 1987), 205, 213.

30. At one point, Moretti upbraids Jane for refusing to stay with Rochester after Bertha's appearance: "Why does it *never* occur to her that perhaps this is just the situation in which her celebrated humanity could really prove its worth?" (ibid., 188). Further on, he mocks the narrative requirements that lead Jane "to learn a remote and disagreeable language like Hindu" (203), thus economically imputing to Brontë a xenophobia endemic to her island nation.

31. Ibid., 190.

32. Ibid., 188.

33. Jean-Jacques Rousseau, *A Discourse on Inequality,* trans. Maurice Cranston (Harmondsworth: Penguin, 1984), 113–14.

34. Ibid., 118.

35. Burke, *Philosophical Enquiry,* 122–23, 135, 103.

36. Kant, *Observations,* 78.

37. Ibid., 52; Kant, *Critique of Judgement,* 149–50.

38. Kant, *Critique of Judgement,* 150–51.

39. Oscar Wilde, *The Picture of Dorian Gray* (London: Penguin, 1985), 45.

40. William Butler Yeats, *In the Seven Woods: Being Poems Chiefly of the Irish Heroic Age* (Dundrum, Ireland: Dun Emer, 1903), 18.

41. Alex Kuczynski, "Trading on Hollywood Magic," *New York Times,* 30 January 1999, C4.

42. A similar note of distress is sounded by Judith Martin (Miss Manners) in a book derived from her John M. Olin Lecture at Harvard. In the United States today, Martin remarks, no rung of the social ladder "commands universal respect, unless it is that of celebrity, that super-category based on the lucky accident of having become conspicuous for whatever reason, good or bad. Perhaps that is because it skips over the old work ethic, which seems too slow and tedious now that everything depends on it. It isn't the climbing Horatio Alger whom we admire now, but the sitting Lana Turner, who is discovered at the drugstore counter and rewarded for simply being—whatever it is that she is." Judith Martin, *Common Courtesy* (New York: Atheneum, 1985), 55. Remembering that Lana Turner eventually had to act, we may, of course, prefer to switch the example to that of model Rachel Williams, allegedly discovered in an elevator.

43. Jennifer L. Hochschild, *What's Fair? American Beliefs about Distributive Justice* (Cambridge: Harvard University Press, 1981), 52. Similarly, if we survey the major paradigms of distributive justice articulated by postwar American philosophers (John Rawls, Michael Walzer, Robert Nozick), we find that although none chooses reward for investment or effort as the foundational principle of justice, all admit the intuitive justness of such reward and note that it will be crucial to the day-to-day functioning of any just society.

44. Ibid., 52.

45. That the question of beauty is never completely separable from the question of gender will be obvious to just about everyone, regardless of political or philosophical disposition; for one aspect of this issue, see the discussion of the "beauty myth," below. That the intersections between questions of beauty and questions of ethnicity are no less complex, manifold, and fraught will also be clear to anyone familiar with the histories of (to name just a few candidates) colonialism, eugenics, advertising, and art. Yet the degree to which aesthetic responses continue to shape race relations remains underappreciated, where admitted into public discourse at all.

46. James Lileks, "Equality for the, uh, Different," *Star Tribune* (Minneapolis), 19 January 1992, metro ed., 25A; David Landis, "Anti-lookism Law," *USA Today,* 14 January 1992, final ed., 1D; "'Ugly' People Now Protected in the Land of Beautiful People," *Toronto Star,* 28 May 1992, metro ed., B1.

47. Wendy Brown, "Wounded Attachments: Late Modern Oppositional Political Formations," in *The Identity in Question,* ed. John Rajchman (New York: Routledge, 1995), 212.

48. Scarry, *On Beauty and Being Just,* 78.

49. Ibid., 65–66.

50. Ibid., 67, 81.

51. Scarry advances a still less persuasive third line toward the close of the book, arguing that beauty and justice are intimately related because both depend on a cognition of symmetry. Given that (as Scarry herself admits) symmetry has not always been held to be the defining characteristic of the beautiful, we may wonder why beauty should be invoked at all here—why we should not rather say that symmetry provides all the sensuous analogue of justice that we need. Even granting that beauty is fully relevant, however, one might ask what significance the analogy between justice and beauty ultimately carries, given Scarry's own insistence that it is really *no more than* an analogy.

To this, Scarry replies that "in periods when a human community is too young to have yet had time to create justice . . . beautiful things . . . hold steadily visible the manifest good of equality and balance" (ibid., 97). Quite apart from its unironic evocation of reifying (not to say ethnocentric) narratives of the Progress of Civilization, this formulation is troubling because it implies that there are only two kinds of society, just and unjust, and that we live in a just one. Certainly, Scarry cannot mean that we live in a perfectly just world wherein there remains nothing left to do; and yet the bare intimation of such achieved harmony supports her book's larger effort to make questions about the injustices attendant on beauty sound strident and irrelevant. The relentlessly celebratory tone of *On Beauty and Being Just* has its costs, among them foreclosure of the kind of debate about *systemic* injustice that writers like Bourdieu and Mulvey (whatever their faults) so provocatively initiate.

Scarry steadfastly refuses to name any names in her book, but if critics like these are among the "opponents" of beauty to whom she alludes, then it must be said that she misrepresents their social critiques when she rewrites them in thoroughly individual terms—and that after this translation, little more is required to make them sound absurd. (Who would not find ridiculous the claim "that a human face or form or a bird or a trellis of sweet pea normally suffers from being looked at" [59]?) In Scarry's formulation, every question of beauty begins and ends with the individual perception, unfolding in isolation from determining contexts and from the consequences of systematic repetition. In perhaps the most telling moment in the book, she declares that if "our responses to beauty are alterable, culturally shaped," then "we are at liberty to make of beauty what we wish" (74), thus dexterously eliding the difference between a collection of individuals who may individually reform their values and the "we" of a society in which what beauty connotes must be changed through polemic, debate, education, and possibly legislation—any of which will likely be as painful as they are interesting.

52. Ibid., 60.

53. Ibid., 127.

54. The text is "Meditations in an Emergency." Frank O'Hara, *The Collected Poems of Frank O'Hara,* ed. Donald Allen (Berkeley: University of California Press, 1995), 197.

55. Robin Lakoff and Raquel Scherr, *Face Value: The Politics of Beauty* (London: Routledge, 1984), 283. Other sources: Ellen Zetzel Lambert, *The Face of Love: Feminism and the Beauty Question* (Boston: Beacon, 1995); Nancy Friday, *The Power of Beauty* (New York: HarperCollins, 1996); Naomi Wolf, *The Beauty Myth* (London: Chatto & Windus, 1990).

56. In a campaign that takes the commodification of anticommodification perhaps as far as it can go, commercials for Master Card first show articles of purchase along with their price tags, but end by reminding the viewer of the pricelessness of

some intangible human good related to the narrative built around the articles. One ad in this series pairs cartoon characters with the makeovers that would solve their cosmetic problems (Droopy Dog is captioned, "Face Lift: $3,000"), but in the final moments an ecstatic Fred Flintstone floats above the message that "being happy with who you are" is "priceless."

57. This is not to say that beauty and labor shared no close ties earlier in the century. In *Venus Envy,* her recent history of cosmetic surgery, Elizabeth Haiken shows that cosmetic procedures, initially developed to repair war injuries, first gained a foothold as an elective practice when "surgeons and the American public accepted the idea that a man's appearance was crucial to his economic status"—and specifically the view that a returning soldier with a deformity might experience unwarranted difficulties in gaining employment. The premise quickly spread to embrace other kinds of workers: "If appearance was crucial for a man who needed to support himself (and perhaps others as well), why not for a single woman or widow? What about a wife, the continuance of whose homemaking career might well depend on keeping her husband from straying to a younger woman? What about actors, dancers, and movie stars, whose livelihood really did depend upon their looks? And what about the millions of Americans . . . who were . . . becoming increasingly convinced that their appearance played a key role in determining their access to the good things in life?" Elizabeth Haiken, *Venus Envy: A History of Cosmetic Surgery* (Baltimore: Johns Hopkins University Press, 1997), 32–33, 103–4.

58. Michael Walzer, *Spheres of Justice: A Defense of Pluralism and Equality* (New York: Basic Books, 1983), xi.

59. Ibid., 259–60.

60. Ibid., 261. Walzer's is only one of scores of attempts, by philosophers of distributive justice, to deal with the problem of gifts of birth. See, for just two brief examples, John Rawls, *A Theory of Justice* (Cambridge: Harvard University Press, 1971), 100–108, 310–15; and Eric Rakowski, *Equal Justice* (Oxford: Clarendon, 1991), 107–19.

61. This is one reason Richard Rorty's effort to rethink the subject as subject of suffering is so extremely important; it is also why dismissals of this rethinking as mere epiphenomena of a culture of complaint are inadequate. Slavoj Žižek, in high anti-PC gear, in *The Metastases of Enjoyment: Six Essays on Woman and Causality* (London: Verso, 1994): "Victimization is thus universalized; it reaches from sexual abuse and harassment to the victims of AIDS, from the cruel fate of the homeless to those exposed to cigarette smoke. . . . It is part of the public image of a movie or rock star to have his or her favoured victim: Richard Gere has the people of Tibet. . . . Philosophy itself was quick to contribute to this universal victimization: in his *Contingency, Irony and Solidarity* (Cambridge: Cambridge University Press, 1989) Richard Rorty, *the* philosopher of liberal-democratic pluralism, defines man as such as a potential victim, as 'something that can be hurt'" (214).

CHAPTER TEN

Sinthom-osexuality

Lee Edelman

Sinthom-osexuality: inelegant neologism, grafting, at an awkward join, the sounds of French and English with a hyphen, like some scrap of cord to bind what seems discordant. If this word without a future seeks a hearing here it is not to play for time but to assert itself, instead, *against* futurity, against its propagation, insofar as it would designate an impasse in the passage to the future and, by doing so, would pass beyond, pass *through*, the saving fantasy futurity denotes. Can "saving," though, be right to name a future that, whatever else it holds in store, is sure to hold our deaths? The fantasmatics of futurity, compelling us to dwell within a social space imagined to survive when we do not, promotes imaginary suture *in the face of death*, promotes the living pledge of generation as a shield against the ego's destined end. Thus we are saved (that is, preserved, conserved, congealed in our identities) by fantasy, which writes us into scenic space until we seem to permeate that space itself—a space wherein "the subject," as Lacan points out, though "frequently unperceived, . . . is always there."[1]

Is *always* there. Turned into setting, into mise-en-scène, the enduring subject of fantasy takes the place of place itself so that the subject's disappearance as an *actor* in the scene need signal neither loss of presence nor the absence of that consciousness by which it "knows" itself. As Slavoj Žižek puts it: "In [fantasy] I find myself reduced to the evanescent point of a thought contemplating the course of events during my absence, my non-being."[2] To be there, *always*, though unperceived, to inhabit the space of perception as such and thus to become the disembodied witness to one's absence, to one's very disembodiment—doesn't this fantasy imagine a reality effectively guaranteed, not threatened, by the logic of temporality, guaranteed by our faith in a "course of events" that is certain to continue upon its course in due course when we are gone? And isn't it, then, an effort to fill what Lacan calls the void or the lack in the Other—the emptiness that makes it the meaningless prop on which the reality effect of consistency and meaningfulness relies—through our stopgap identification with that uninhabited place of the gaze, through the optimism of this fantasy for which we are compelled to opt: the fantasy of a future for the sake of which we give our lives in order thereby to animate the place of what otherwise remains unable to see our reality into being?

Sinthom-osexuality, by contrast—denied and denying the seductive appeal that fantasy thus exerts, refusing the pledge of futurity that mends all tears, however mean, in reality's dress with threads of meaning (attached as they are to the eye-catching sequins of sequence, and thus of *con*sequence)—presents us with fantasy turned inside out, the seams of its costume exposing reality's seamlessness as mere seeming, the fraying knots that hold each sequin in place now usurping that place. The *sinthome,* for Lacan, as a name for the inexpressible singularity of the subject's existence, the particular way that the subject knots together the real, the imaginary, and the symbolic, is more than just an etymological antecedent of what we know as *symptom;* it denotes the archaic and inchoate basis of the subject's relation to the drive by designating the template of its access to *jouissance.* It defines, that is, the condition of which the subject itself is a symptom: the meaningless relation to enjoyment that animates the subject beyond all fantasy, the knot by which the subject is bound to its constitutive libidinal career such that the subject can never manage to get over itself, as it were. Impervious to analysis, the *sinthome* as stupid enjoyment, as the irreducible node of senseless compulsion on which the coherence of the subject rests, connects us, Lacan insists, to the real, to the order of the incognizable upon which we stumble time and again—an order linked, in turn, to the death drive, about which Lacan insists in the seminar devoted to the question of the *sinthome:* "The death drive, it is the Real insofar as it can only be thought as Impossible, which is to say that each time it shows the tip of its nose, it is unthinkable."[3]

As the site at which the all-sustaining fantasy of futurity confronts the violence of a *jouissance* that rends it precisely by rendering it in its relation to the drive, *sinthom*-osexuality specifies the "sin" with which the "homosexual" continues to be charged as that of figuring a threat to the subject's faith that its proper home is in meaning, a threat made real by the homosexual's construction in the image of a radically despiritualized "home": the *sinthome* as the senseless machinery that shapes the subject's *jouissance.* I mean to suggest that homosexuality, as a cultural figure or trope, as the hypostatization of social fantasies that designate the field of force that queerness seeks to name, has been made, in more than one sense of the word, to embody *sinthom*-osexuality. It continues, therefore, to be thought as a threat to the logic of thought itself to the extent that it figures, as *sinthome* of a heterosexually elaborated symbolic order, the access to unthinkable *jouissance* beyond every limit of pleasure, a *jouissance* that would, in fantasy, put an end to fantasy as such, and thus put an end to futurity too by reducing the assurance of meaning in fantasy's promise of unbroken continuity to the meaningless circulation and repetitions of the drive.

We can hardly escape the cultural fantasy that figures gay sexuality, and with it the defining importance of the sexual to the experience of gay sexuality, in intimate relation to a fatal, and even murderous, *jouissance*—that figures gay sexuality, as I have suggested, as its *sinthome.* While Andrew Cunanan, for example, held the media in a rapt fascination that seemed to partake of *jouissance* itself, Gary Bauer, of the Family Research Council, pronounced that "those who practice homosexuality embrace a culture of death," and Peter A. Jay, a regular contributor to the *Baltimore Sun,* echoed this phrase (a commonplace in the conservative discourse of the antiabortion movement) and drew what seemed to him an obvious connection to the murderous rampage of Cunanan: "For half a century at least, male homosexual life in the United States has been a culture of death.... Sooner or later, a product of that culture was going to take violence on the road.... There will be other young men who have come face to face with the knowledge that their own lives are blighted and doomed... and now want to experience the rush of killing *in more traditional ways.*"[4] Concurring in the notion that murderousness inhabits the gay male's traditional, if antifamilial, repertoire of values, Larry Kramer, writing in the *New York Times,* commented several years ago on what he hoped would signal a transformation of gay culture: "Allowing sex-centrism to remain the sole definition of homosexuality is now coming to be seen as the greatest act of self-destruction.

There is a growing understanding that we created a culture that in effect murdered us, and that if we are to remain alive it's time to redefine homosexuality as something far greater than what we do with our genitals."[5]

But can anyone, including Larry Kramer himself, really think that such a redefinition, however intent on covering up the realities of "what we do with our genitals"—a redefinition that might define us as "artistic," perhaps, or as a "gentle, loving people," or maybe just as possessing a fabulous instinct for color and style—can anyone think such a redefinition would alter the dominant fantasy within which our meaning is always a function not only of what we *do* with our genitals but also, and even more tellingly, a function of what we *don't* do: a function, that is, of the envy-, fear-, and anxiety-inducing fixation on our freedom from the necessity of translating the corrupt, unregenerate vulgate of fucking into the infinitely tonier and sacramental Latin of procreation? It's not, after all, mere coincidence that Gary Bauer's description of homosexuals as "embrac[ing] a culture of death" follows, in his view logically, from his meditation on the spiritual meaning that quickens the month of June: "Traditionally, June is a month jam-packed with weddings," he observes, "a time to celebrate the abundance of God's love and His special plan for procreation. 'Male and female He created them,' the Book of Genesis says, and through this natural pairing of one man and one woman a family is created and the hope of a new generation is carried forward."[6]

"A family is created": like Freud's "a child is being beaten" (which no doubt will follow in the fullness of time), the phrase strategically elides the particularities of agency. No fucking could ever take place here, for all such possible nastiness is borne away with the fantasy of futurity secured as "a new generation is carried forward." The child of the two-parent family thus proves, paradoxically, that its parents *don't* fuck; and on its tiny shoulders weighs the burden of maintaining the fantasy of a time to come when meaning, at last made present to itself, no longer depends on the fantasy of its attainment in time to come. So while June remains the privileged season for Bauer and his flock to extol what they see as the "hope of a new generation," it's always open season on those who fly in the face of this mandate that they "suffer the little children" and who, as a consequence, compel the world to brood upon the abyss, an occupation less appealing, it seems, than cooing over the cuteness of the fledgling brood in the nest—less appealing, that is, unless one is able to coo and brood at once, like opponents of women's abortion rights who whip out their fetal photos like so many snapshots from family albums and brandish them all the more fervently when the fetus, after abortion, is both most childlike and most brutalized. Such allegedly life-affirming acts of morbid fetishization, acts that reveal implicitly the morbidity of fetishization as such, are by no means outside the central currents of social and cultural discourse. To the contrary, they allow us access to the very logic that drives that discourse: a logic not for June alone but truly for all seasons, and never more visible, despite its Albric's cloak of benevolent futurism, than in the season in which, throughout the West, we are ordered, each and every one, to attend to the birth of the Child.

Take, for example, Tiny Tim—or even, with a nod to the spirit of the late Henny Youngman, "Take Tiny Tim, *please!*": his "withered little hand," as if in life already reaching from the stillness of the grave, keeping us in a stranglehold as adamant as the "iron frame" supporting his "little limbs";[7] his "plaintive little voice" (99) refusing any and all complaint, the better to motivate thereby its massive media magnification in the echoes of which, year in and year out, God blasts us, every one; his "little, little" (125) figure parading its patent vulnerability with the all-too-sure conviction of embodying the ruthless spiritual uplift, the obligatory hope for the future to come, imposed by the celebration of Christmas, "when its mighty Founder," as Dickens is pleased to put it, "was a child himself" (104); his "patient and . . . mild" (125) disposition so thoroughly assuring the utter humility of its coercive self-display that his father with "tremulous" voice recalls how profoundly Tiny Tim "hoped the people saw him in the church, because he was a cripple, and it might be pleasant to them to remember upon Christmas Day, who made lame beggars walk, and blind men see" (94).

Very pleasant indeed. And more pleasant by half than remembering who made lame beggars lame—and beggars—and all those blind men blind. But then *A Christmas Carol* would have us believe that we know the answers to any such questions—know them as surely as we know who would silence the plaintive note of that little voice and require that the "active little crutch" (94) kick the habit of being leaned on. The inexplicable sufferings of the world, smoldering through the text like its dense brown fog, rise, in the story's logic, like acrid smoke from a sodden faggot—rise, that is, from the one whose stingy, reclusive, and anti-communitarian ways express themselves fully when he stands exposed, and exposed not least to himself, as that criminal by criminals themselves reviled: as the dreaded pedocide. "Secret, and self-contained, and solitary as an oyster" (46), Scrooge may evoke the traditional iconography of the miser as filtered through the lens of a liberal critique of industrial capitalism, but the sins of the countinghouse count for little until they are made to account metonymically for the death of that little, little child for whose threatened absence from the merrymaking of Christmases Yet to Come the jury need not even leave the box in order to find Scrooge guilty as charged of what the indictment would no doubt characterize as "futuricide" by "hum-buggery."

Others, more invested than I in practicing a form of queer theory intent on setting the record straight about authors or characters who are not, might point to Scrooge's resistance to marriage in favor of partnership with another bachelor businessman, Jacob Marley, whose name he declines to paint over even after his partner's demise and to which he answers thereafter as readily as he answers to his own—"it was all the same to him" (46); they might point to the anality implicit in the text's depiction of that partnership and cite the lament of Marley's ghost that he never allowed his spirit, in life, to rove "beyond the narrow limits of our money-changing hole" (61); they might point to the ghost's remark to Scrooge, "I have sat invisible beside you many and many a day" (63), or to Scrooge's comment on the bond that once connected him to his fellow apprentice, Dick Wilkins, "He was very much attached to me, was Dick" (75); they might even point to the charwoman's representation of Scrooge as a "wicked old screw" (115) who deserved to have all his worldly goods stolen from the very bed of his corpse because, as she puts it derisively, he wasn't "natural in his lifetime" (115); and having adduced such passages, those critics might claim that Scrooge could use a rainbow flag, not a Christmas tree, with which to spruce up his home. In proposing that Scrooge be viewed, instead, as a central literary embodiment of *sinthom*-osexuality, I have no interest in revealing some sexual identity encoded in the text, but want, instead, to address the elaboration of a cultural fantasy linking Scrooge to the fate of Tiny Tim as surely as the *sinthome* is linked to the historical consistency of the subject, or as queer sexualities are linked to the conceptual coherence of heterosexual desire.

Scrooge, as a bachelor in a text that declares "a bachelor . . . a wretched outcast" (103) while pointedly, and therefore defensively, describing the narrator himself as "man enough" (82) to be turned on by Belle's beautiful daughter, registers from the outset a mode of enjoyment alien to that of the community at large and alien, more significantly, to the idea of community itself. "It was the very thing he liked," Dickens tells us of Scrooge's disengagement from every customary act of social intercourse. "To edge his way along the crowded paths of life, warning all human sympathy to keep its distance, was what the knowing ones call 'nuts' to Scrooge" (47). However nutty this seems to make him in the eyes of those he encounters, the pleasure Scrooge takes, what turns *him* on, comes in part from refusing to use his nuts to drop acorns from the family tree; indeed, his every enjoyment partakes of the logic of such a refusal, of the pleasurable pain of a negation so great that he almost seems to refuse the very warm-bloodedness of mammalian vitality, as if, like a textbook-perfect example of the death drive according to Freud, he aimed to return to the icy, inert immobility of a lifeless thing: "The cold within him froze his old features, nipped his pointed nose, shrivelled his cheek, stiffened his gait; made his eyes red, his thin lips blue; and spoke out shrewdly in his grating voice. A frosty rime was on his head, and on his eyebrows, and his wiry chin. He carried his own low temperature always about with him; he iced his office in the dog-days; and he didn't thaw it one degree at Christmas" (46).

Place beside this a passage from Lacan's seminar on the *sinthome* in which he writes, with regard to the foreclosure of meaning in the real: "It sets everything on fire, the Real. But it's a cold fire. The fire that burns is a mask, if I might put it this way, of the Real. The Real of it is to be looked for on the other side, the side of absolute zero."[8] Scrooge, like an incarnation of the Real's cold fire nearing absolute zero, threatens a shutdown of life's machinery by exposing it *as* machinery, by denying the spiritualization that bathes it in the warmth of symbolic meaning. This refusal to embrace the genealogical fantasy that braces the social order cannot, as *A Christmas Carol* makes clear, be a matter of public indifference, for the point of the tale, and therefore the point of its status as the text that enjoys the distinction, above all others in our literary canon, of a ritual repetition that supplants as much as it supplements the season's more sacred rites, is that Scrooge and the *sinthom*-osexuality he might be said to embody threaten, by their refusal to participate in the realization of futurity, the fantasy structure that undergirds reality itself.

"Keep Christmas in your own way, and let me keep it in mine," Scrooge advises his nephew, Fred; "Keep it!" the nephew counters, "But you don't keep it." "Let me leave it alone, then" (48), his exasperated uncle responds. But neither nephew nor text is allowed to consent to leave Scrooge alone to leave Christmas alone, since Christmas here stands in the place of the obligatory collective reproduction of the child, the obligatory investment, that is, in the social as the *order* of the child, demanding collective assent to the truth that the child exists to make flesh. Or demanding, instead, that such collective assent dialectically be affirmed by naming, humiliating, and then, at its whim, redeeming the one who refuses it—affirmed, that is, by the structural mandate that he who refuses the child *be* refused, providing the occasion for communal access to the negativity of a *jouissance* for which, as its embodiment, he must, in the first place, be reviled. If, as the terroristic adage of our culture's long children's hour proposes, "it takes a village to raise a child," then, we might add, it takes, albeit perversely, a villain too: a Scrooge, a *sinthom*-osexual, on whom to project the force of the death drive, the obtrusion of the Real, that never can be acknowledged as the engine driving the reproduction of sociality itself.

The pleasurable fantasy of survival (Tiny Tim, as Dickens's last-minute addition to the manuscript tells us, does "*NOT* die"; 133), requires, therefore, more than anything else, the survival of a fantasy: the fantasy, for instance, that Tiny Tim, futurity's fragile figure, does *not* excite an ardent fear—or is it a fearful ardor?—to see him, "as good as gold . . . and better" (94) at last cash in his chips; the fantasy, in fact, that Scrooge, not we, must answer for such a fantasy; and, equally self-serving, the fantasy, perhaps most pleasurable of them all, that the pleasure we get from Scrooge's "salvation" through punitive abjection shares nothing with the sadomasochistic enjoyment Scrooge embodies in the text. *A Christmas Carol* thus engages a truth about the nature of neighborly love far removed from the surfeit of communal goodwill its conclusion so cloyingly enshrines. Scrooge, the self-denying miser—living alone, and in darkness, on gruel—extends to his neighbors, unneighborly as it no doubt makes him seem, the same self-denying enjoyment to which he consents to submit as well. In this he enacts the negativity that Freud and Lacan both discerned in the stricture to love one's neighbor as oneself; he unleashes, that is, *as the love of his neighbor*, the force of a primal masochism like that of the superego asserting its imperative, "Enjoy!" What might seem to bespeak narcissistic isolation from everyone around him—his self-delighting stinginess, his solipsistic rejection of creature comforts for others as for himself—instantiates, then, a death drive opposed to the ego and the world of desires, expressing, instead, the will-to-enjoyment perversely enshrined in obedience to the superego's insatiably masochistic demands. Thus Scrooge's death, when revealed by the spirit of Christmas Yet to Come, far from rescuing Tiny Tim, assures his death as well; for the miser's grave, like a black hole, fully realizes the negativity, the cruel enjoyment, the neighborly love, to which he was devoted: the triumph of the death drive in the reification of the fatality he always was. Scrooge's persistence, therefore, *as* Scrooge, as the unrepentant *sinthom*-osexual he has been throughout the tale, must be understood as determining that there will be no future at all. For Scrooge makes Christmas Yet to Come, like the spirit who ushers it in, nothing but a "spectral hand and one great heap of black" (111)—makes it, in other words, the perpetually empty place of the Other's gaze, the traumatic obtrusion of the Real well evoked by the specter's "Unseen Eyes" (113). As "Scrooge" thus names the "wicked old screw" (115) who screws, or fucks with, the future, so *A Christmas Carol*, like the *sinthom*-ophobic culture it reflects, must, to preserve the fantasy that lives only with our Tiny Tims, give a turn of the Scrooge that turns him toward the promise of futurity by turning him into "a second father" (133) to the boy who "did *NOT* die" (132). With this act of conversion worthy of so-called ministries of hope that promise "life" to those grown sick to death of being queer, *A Christmas Carol* resurrects Scrooge and Tiny Tim at once by liberating the Santa the *sinthom*-osexual would deny.

Only thus can queers escape the charge of embracing a "culture of death" and earn the right to be viewed as "something far greater than what we do with our genitals." *A Christmas Carol,* with striking clarity, spells out just how we may gain that "right" when we learn that Scrooge, now family-friendly and blissfully pronatalist, had—alas, poor Marley—"no further intercourse with Spirits, but lived upon the Total Abstinence Principle, ever afterwards" (134). We may, by accepting this peter-less principle, be tolerated as the "social equals and responsible citizens" that Larry Kramer and others would have us become; like Scrooge we may thus be reborn as "second father[s]" to the future, permitted to perform our part in the collective adoration of the child and thus to reinforce the fantasy condensed in Tiny Tim. But we might, instead, do well to recall that Lacan, toward the end of his teaching, held that by moving beyond the fundamental fantasy that engages analytic interpretation, one confronts the meaningless spur or nub of one's access to *jouissance,* the Thing that holds the drive, indecipherably, in a fixed rotation around it; and faced with this spur, this *sinthome,* itself the limit of analysis and outside interpretation, the subject, Lacan proposed, must consent to identify at last with *it.* Make no mistake, then: Tiny Tim survives at our expense, as the endless perpetuation of the threat that he *might* die. *Sinthom*-osexuality, of which it is always said that it will be the death of him, must oblige by showing that Tiny Tim is always already dead, mortified into a fetish, animated only by the collective dream, the fantasy wherein he *doesn't* rise up and say to us, reproachfully, "Father, don't you see I'm burning?"

Given that there isn't now, and hasn't been, much doubt about who killed him, why not at last claim kinship with the Scrooge who, unregenerate, declines to grasp the future in the figure of the child for whose protection *as a concept,* as the sign of our accession to imaginary wholeness, everything, by force if force is needed, must give way? Scrooge, however, repudiates Scrooge lest Tiny Tim should die, so this murderous Scrooge—the Scrooge whose determination to embody his *sinthome* Dickens, like his character, refuses in the end—must be looked for elsewhere, in a figure, for example, like Monsieur the Marquis in Dickens's *A Tale of Two Cities,* a man whose very face is no more animated than a death mask save for "two compressions, or dints" where his nose was "pinched at the top of each nostril" and these, the sole indication of his vitality, "persisted in changing colour sometimes, and they would be occasionally dilated and contracted by something like a faint pulsation; then they gave a look of treachery, and cruelty, to the whole countenance."[9] The fatality of the drive evinced by these faint pulsations becomes quite literal when the carriage in which he is riding drives over a child in a Paris street. Unmoved by the father's desperate shrieks, the Marquis surveys the sullen crowd that circles like "rats come out of their holes," and then, evincing the inalienable narcissism, the anticommunal enjoyment that marks the future-killing queer, declares, "It is extraordinary to me... that you people cannot take care of yourselves or your children. One or the other of you is for ever in the way. How do I know what injury you have done my horses?"[10]

In the Dickensian version of talion law, the Marquis, like the child he runs over, must die, while Scrooge, converted to futurism by the ominous figure of futurity itself, is granted the very gift of life he gives to Tiny Tim, but granted it only insofar as he devotes that life *to* Tiny Tim, becoming a "second father" by renouncing the fatal self-enclosure as which reproductive sociality condemns whatever refuses to mirror back its imaginary form. For the *sinthom*-osexual's narcissism is a narcissism unto death, exposing a duality or division internal to narcissism itself. The pervasive contempt, for example, reserved for whatever gets called "narcissistic" permits the ego-sustaining enjoyment—in effect, the narcissistic reassurance—of identifying with the social opprobrium directed at anything "narcissistic," an opprobrium that might, in the absence of such identification, bear down on us as well. Just as the projection of the *sinthome* onto those condemned as *sinthom*-osexuals enacts reproductive futurism's own *sinthomatic* drive, so the *sinthom*-osexual's association with narcissistic satisfaction, when considered in light of the self-satisfied—or, better, self-satisfying—abjection of narcissism itself in all forms of dominant discourse, expresses a recognition, deeply buried though it may be, that narcissism bears within it something at odds with its libidinal investment in the ego as a form. Narcissism, one might say, like the concept of *jouissance* in Lacanian theory, must be understood to designate two contradictory states, one of which serves precisely to defend against access to the other. Laplanche and Pontalis observe that Freud himself proposed two strikingly different readings of narcissism, arguing first that it marked the subject's cathexis of the ego as an object and later insisting on the priority of an objectless narcissistic state.[11] Hypostatized in his final theory as primary and secondary narcissism, these different renditions of narcissistic libidinal cathexis split narcissism in two at the point where the question of the object emerges, and therefore where the question of the ego's privilege *as an object* is at stake. Primary narcissism acknowledges no separation of ego and id, and consequently it carries into the heart of all subsequent elaborations of narcissistic love a resistance to the ego's autonomy, a reminder of something other than the empire of imaginary form; secondary narcissism, on the other hand, makes an idol of the ego, but only by means of imaginary identification of the ego with the other, an identification that secures the fixity and the coherence of the ego's form and necessitates subsequent efforts to defend the ego's formal integrity.

We might then propose, in the manner of Lacan, the following formula to express the logic of the narcissistic dynamic: *narcissism is always a narcissism of the Other.* By this I mean not only that it is always the Other whose truth the indictment of narcissism would punitively expose, but also that narcissism bespeaks the styling, the eroticized ascription to the ego of recognizable and therefore of defensible form, only insofar as narcissism is always already, which is to say primally, invested in the nondifferentiation of the ego and the id, in the unsymbolizable real of the drive that imperils the ego as object. Hence the first paradox of narcissism: it loves the Other too well, beyond all reason, beyond all pleasure, even unto death. And from this there follows its second paradox: that narcissism, construed as an erotic investment in the ego it cathects, as a libidinal relation by means of which the self would secure itself, comes nonetheless, for psychoanalysis as well as for the culture at large, to name a Scrooge-like self-containment linked to sterility and death, a refusal to move outward or forward toward engagement with the Other, a denial of the vital energies by which the social is sustained.[12] Oh, and did I mention that Freud's first reference to narcissistic investment occurs in the context of theorizing the origins of gay male sexuality?[13]

Not, of course, that we needed to wait for Freud to make this connection: doesn't Plato's Athenian Stranger already suggest as much in the *Laws,* when, notwithstanding his stated belief that "somehow every one is *by nature* prone to that which is likest to himself," he insists that "the intercourse of men with men, or of women with women, is *contrary to nature*"—and contrary to nature despite the fact that such practices, scorned for self-indulgence, enact what the Athenian himself describes as the "lawless *natures*" of men.[14] With this paradox, akin to those informing our understanding of narcissism, the Stranger reads as unnatural submission to the lawlessness of one's nature, and he does so by suggesting that an erotics of the same invariably leads toward death insofar as its practice involves "intentionally destroying the seeds of human increase."[15] Nature is less the ground for deciding the question of same-sex desire here than the stake in a struggle to appropriate the "natural" for the purposes of the state; it is produced, that is, as the stylized effect of a statist ideology that operates by installing pro-procreative prejudice as the form through which desiring subjects assume a narcissistic stake in a future that is, as the Stranger implies, the *state's* and not their own.

Hence his insistence not only on laws that "would master the soul of every man, and terrify him into obedience," scaring the subject straight just as Dickens's spirits terrified Scrooge, but also on enshrining, by naturalizing, various socially inculcated values, components of what Freud will define as the ego-ideal, "sanctioned by custom and made law by unwritten prescription."[16] If the narcissism associated with homosexual desire thus becomes, for Plato no less than for Freud, the basis for social survival by being turned *against* itself—undergoing transvaluation from primary to secondary, from deadly to vital, only insofar as it dissociates itself, at least nominally, *from* itself and from the *sinthom*-osexuality that absorbs the identity it disavows—then perhaps, at this particular millennial moment of no escape from the ideological tropism turning our eyes toward the light of a future that glitters before us like a hypnotist's watch,[17] we might ask just how and to what effect the primal negativity, the fatal self-enclosure that Scrooge casts off for the sake of Tiny Tim, *returns*, albeit in altered form, as the driving force behind the logic of reproductive futurism.

And how better to engage that question than by turning to consider a text that turns our thoughts to the holiday following Christmas, and the birth of the sacred child, by a week to provide a secular repetition of futurity's repeated birth: a text that turns on the unexpected arrival of a new year's baby who turns, in turn, a single, miserly, miserable man, a bachelor properly linked with those I've been calling *sinthom*-osexuals, away from his backward turn of mind, from the sterility of his behindsight, toward the prospect of a future in which his narcissism finds its proper stake at last. For who could evince more pointedly the deathly shriveling of vital forces through the closed economy of a backward gaze than Eliot's Silas Marner, whose very name sounds the drawn-out sigh, "alas," of a mourner perpetually turned toward the past as he licks the wounds of his endless grief—or endlessly grieves in order to have the more reason to lick his wounds. But as Eliot's narrative skein unravels, Raveloe's weaver will be purged of "the repulsion [he] had always created in his neighbors" as a result of "his general queerness," and he'll be woven into the social text insofar as he gives up his worship of gold for the golden curls of the child that he finds on his hearth, precisely on New Year's Eve, as the assurance of futurity.[18]

Not that Eliot depicts this golden child as a golden calf; that role, of course, is assigned instead to Marner's hoarded coins, to the gold that, before it vanishes, "kept his thoughts in an ever-repeated circle, leading to nothing beyond itself" (125). The child he discovers on New Year's Eve and names Hephzibah—Eppie, for short—leads him, though, or so we are told, away from the worship of those false gods, away from his narcissistic delight in the stacks of coins he would touch with his hands or those he was wont to imagine "as if they had been unborn children" (21). And unborn children they might well be, for the refusal of proper engagement with the social that leads him to lavish love upon these figurative "children" alone keeps him from the heterosexual productivity that would literalize and reverse the figure. Like Scrooge, for whom a future in which he fails to ward off Tiny Tim's death could only be one that realizes his own constitutive deathliness too, Silas Marner evokes, in his miserly self-containment, as the following passage makes clear, a threat not only to his own well-being but to the social order's as well—a threat, that is, to its *future,* for the assurance of which nothing does the trick like the beauty of a child: "In old days there were angels who came and took men by the hand and led them away from the city of destruction. We see no white-winged angels now. But yet men are led away from threatening destruction: a hand is put in theirs, which leads them forth gently towards a calm and bright land, so that they look no more backward; and that hand may be a little child's" (131). If Silas becomes, in his own meek way, a pillar of the social order instead of, say, a pillar of salt, it is only because the threat of that salt, with which Eliot has no beef, cures him; at the moment, that is, on New Year's Eve when he opens his cottage door to look to the past instead of the future, clinging to the chance of his money's return rather than looking ahead, Eliot depicts him as if he *had* in fact suffered the fate of those who turn ass-backward to look toward Sodom. With his hand on the latch of the still-open door, "he was," Eliot tells us, "arrested"—though not, of course, by a Raveloe vice cop, but rather by one who must be viewed as a *nice* cop, by the authority, that is, of the author who figuratively punishes his narcissistic idolatry in order to lead him, ever so "gently to a calm and bright land" beyond, that is, into the future as such. Toward that end she has him "arrested . . . by the invisible wand of catalepsy" so he stands "like a graven image, with wide but sightless eyes" (100).[19] In this state of suspended animation, appropriate emblem of the *sinthom*-osexual's threatened suspension of animation itself, Marner, become the image of the lifeless images to which he gives his life, is given another chance for life, a prospect of rebirth, and given it in the form of the child who crawls through his open cottage door with all the salvific contrivance befitting a diaper-clad deus ex machina.

But the narrative machinery that draws this diminutive deity to the weaver's door is engaged, paradoxically, to effect his rescue precisely from the "ever-repeated circle," the lethal compulsion to repeat, that the narrative figures *as* machinery. His solitary years have turned him into an extension of his loom, which "as he wrought in it without ceasing, had in its turn wrought on him, and confirmed more and more the monotonous craving for its monotonous response" (42), and that loom is defined, explicitly, as a machine for reproducing sameness, thus advancing itself as a figure for the machinelike insistence of the *sinthome,* or even for its embodiment in *sinthom*-osexuality: "The livelong day he sat at his loom, his ear filled with its monotony, his eyes bent close down on the slow growth of sameness in the brownish web, his muscles moving with such even repetition that their pause seemed as much a constraint as the holding of his breath" (21). The novel that bears Silas Marner's name may recoil from the weaver's enactment here of something inhuman—automatic, mechanistic—that seems to reduce the human subject through subjection to its drive, may recoil or draw back from the turning back toward the sameness that, like Sodom, makes us worth no more than our salt, but no less than "recoil" can escape the trace of the *cul* from which it derives can the novel escape repeating the weaver's mechanistic repetitions at his loom.

For the text plots its likeness to that machinery in the machinery of its plot. As justly, then, as Silas Marner, accused of theft in Lantern Yard, could say to his onetime friend, William Dane, "You have woven a plot to lay the sin at my door" (14), so might he charge George Eliot with similar weaving of her own—a weaving that may lay at his door the sin of getting caught in the sameness of the web he weaves "like a spider" (16), out of himself, but that also lays at his door, and quite literally, the child intended to free him from its primally narcissistic snare. What, after all, are the odds that a nearsighted man, still mourning the theft of his gold, would suffer a cataleptic fit in his doorway on a frigid New Year's Eve at the very moment that a golden-haired child, attracted by the light from his open door, should toddle away from the corpse of her mother, frozen in the snow onto which she had fallen in an opiated haze, and settle herself before the hearth where the nearsighted man, his cataleptic seizure now past, could mistake her hair for his gold? Whatever the chances, it's Chance alone, the god of novelistic contrivance, that thus gives Marner his second chance; which is worthy of mention since Eliot explicitly opposes Chance to nature, excoriating those who rely on it as prone to narcissistic indulgence: "Favourable Chance is the god of all men who follow their own devices instead of obeying a law they believe in.... The evil deprecated in that religion [of Chance], is the orderly sequence by which the seed brings forth a crop after its kind" (74).

And here is the nub of the matter: *Silas Marner* poses its fiction as serving to forward this "orderly sequence" of reproductive futurity, whose privileged emblem, the child, it deploys as a figure of naturalization: a figure, to be sure, of *nature,* but one that reads nature as a figure, or, still more scandalous, as a cathected form, a style of social relation: a style that Marner must adopt *as* nature and one that the novel, however fantastic the narrative means by which it brings this about, must represent as "orderly," as part of the natural order, and, therefore, as *prosaic* and not a style, an imposition, a formal machinery, at all. "Eppie," the novel insists, "was an object compacted of changes and hopes that forced his thoughts onward, and carried them far away from their old eager pacing toward the same blank limit—carried them away to the new things that would come with the coming years" (125). At the dawn of a new millennium what could possibly seem more certain than that those coming years will come? That the movement of life is forward? That those who embrace "the same blank limit"—narcissistically, repetitively—destroy, as Plato understood, "the seeds of human increase"? But if narcissism is, as I've argued, always a narcissism of the Other, if the weaver's repetitive turnings back speak less to his self-enclosure than to a self-negating openness to the Otherness of things, then the nature the novel poses in opposition to that narcissism, the nature borne by the newborn, has no use for the Other at all. Just as the seed supposed to offer escape from the *sinthom*-osexual's self-enclosure, his narcissistic repetition, necessarily brings forth a crop, as Eliot notes, *after its kind,* so the weaver's love for Eppie, supposed to open him to difference, more precisely, as we soon discover, "blent them into one" (130), preparing the way for Marner's wholly canonical, but nonetheless self-deconstructing, representation of what we're invited to read as pedocentrism's triumph over narcissism: "I've come to love her as myself" (181). He comes to love her, that is, not only in the way he had formerly loved himself, but also in a way that allows him, through her as figure, to love himself still. Why marvel that such a triumph repeats what it poses as passing beyond? Old Mr. Lammeter at the end of the story tells us all we need to know about the real relations secured by nature's stylization in the image of the child: "Things look dim to old folks; they'd need have some young eyes about 'em, to let 'em know the world's the same as it used to be" (182). To "know the world's the same": reproductive futurism, consecrated though it may be to heterosexual norms of difference, undertakes *repetitively* to perpetuate such a sameness, intent on transforming the Other into the image of itself, intent on maintaining the fantasy space in which it will *always* be there. Narcissism, though, condemned as sameness, takes in and takes on, perhaps too well, the Other it loves to death, pushing beyond and against its own pleasure, driving instead toward the end of forms through the formalism of pure drive. Freud, as the century just ended began, may have told us that parental love "is nothing but the parents' narcissism born again,"[20] but the ostensible self-evidence, throughout our culture, of the difference between narcissism on the one hand and the care and nurturing of a child on the other, between figures of *sinthom*-osexuality and the *sinthomatic* drive to produce and abject them, makes clear, as the twenty-first century starts, that what is finally at issue in the production of the child and the futurity it serves to figure, for Scrooge, for Silas Marner, and for all of us as well, is the *style* by which a culture enacts its *sinthome* by disavowing it.

And lest we lose sight, as these final reminders of Tiny Tim and little Eppie rise before us once more, of how we are all of us victimized by the vulnerability of the figural child, blackmailed by the blight of its future that *sinthom*-osexuality portends, let me end by recalling the "Fourteen Words," the credo by which loyal members of various U.S. white separatist organizations affirm their commitment to racial hate: "We must secure the existence of our people and a future for white children."[21] So long as "white" is the only word that makes that credo appalling, *sinthom*-osexuality, despite itself, has a future after all.

Notes

1. Jacques Lacan, *The Four Fundamental Concepts of Psychoanalysis,* ed. Jacques-Alain Miller, trans. Alan Sheridan (New York: W. W. Norton, 1981), 185.

2. Slavoj Žižek, "'The Thing That Thinks': The Kantian Background of the *Noir* Subject," in *Shades of Noir*, ed. Joan Copjec (New York: Verso, 1993), 222.

3. Jacques Lacan, *Le Sinthome* (typescript of Seminar 23, 1975–76, University of Texas at Austin), 134. The translation is mine. The original reads, in its fuller context: "Ce que Freud souligne de cette mort, si je puis m'exprimer ainsi, la Triebe, d'en faireun Trieb; ce qu'on a traduit en français par, je ne sais pourquoi, la pulsion, la pulsion de mort, on n'a pas trouvé une meilleure traduction, alors qu'il y avait le mot dérive, le pulsion de mort, c'est le Réel en tant qu'il ne peut être pensé que comme Impossible, c'est-à-dire que chacque fois qu'il montre le bout de son nez, il est impensable."

4. Gary Bauer, "Family Research Council Fundraising Appeal Letter," 2 June 1997, on-line at http://www.bridges-across.org/ba/frc970602.htm. Peter A. Jay, "After the Holocaust, Still Playing with Fire," *Baltimore Sun*, 20 July 1997, emphasis added.

5. Larry Kramer, "Gay Culture, Redefined," *New York Times*, 12 December 1997, A23.

6. Bauer, "Family Research Council."

7. Charles Dickens, *A Christmas Carol*, in *The Christmas Books*, Vol. 1 (Harmondsworth: Penguin, 1985), 97, 94. Page numbers for further quotations from this source appear in parentheses in the text.

8. Jacques Lacan, *Le Sinthome*, 130. The translation is mine. The original reads: "Le feu, c'est le Réel, ça met le feu à tout, le Réel. Mais c'est un feu froid. Le feu qui brûle est un masque, si je puis dire, du Réel."

9. Charles Dickens, *A Tale of Two Cities* (New York: Vintage, 1990), 113.

10. Ibid., 114.

11. See the entry for "Narcissism" in J. Laplanche and J.-B. Pontalis, *The Language of Psycho-Analysis*, trans. Donald Nicholson-Smith (London: Hogarth, 1983), 255–57.

12. Consider in this regard Freud's discussion of the "narcissistic" nature of both the germ cells and malignant neoplasms in *Beyond the Pleasure Principle*, in *The Standard Edition of the Complete Psychological Works of Sigmund Freud*, Vol. 18, ed. and trans. James Strachey (London: Hogarth, 1986), 50. Later in the same text Freud asserts: "Our argument had as its point of departure a sharp distinction between ego-instincts, which we equated with death-instincts, and sexual instincts, which we equated with life instincts. (We were prepared at one stage to include the so-called self-preservative instincts of the ego among the death instincts; but we subsequently corrected ourselves on this point and withdrew it.)" (53).

13. In a note added in 1910 to *Three Essays on the Theory of Sexuality*, Freud evokes narcissistic object choice to describe male homosexuals who, identifying with their mothers, "take *themselves* as their sexual object" (*Three Essays on the Theory of Sexuality*, in *The Standard Edition of the Complete Psychological Works of Sigmund Freud*, Vol. 7, ed. and trans. James Strachey [London: Hogarth, 1986], 145).

14. My quotations from Plato are taken from the Benjamin Jowett translation of *The Dialogues of Plato* in *Great Books of the Western World*, Vol. 7 (Chicago: Encyclopedia Brittanica, 1952), 707, 646, 736; emphases added.

15. Ibid., 737.

16. Ibid., 737, 738.

17. One instance of the doxa insisting on the galvanic property of the infant: trying to describe the enduring appeal of "punch bowls" at a party, Amanda Hesser

writes, "People gravitate toward punch bowls and surround them, as they do a newborn" ("Dip into the Past," *New York Times,* 15 December 1999, D1).

18. George Eliot, *Silas Marner: The Weaver of Raveloe* (Harmondsworth: Penguin: 1996), 77, 83. Page numbers for further quotations from this source appear in parentheses in the text.

19. At the same time that Marner suffers his cataleptic rigidification, Molly, Eppie's mother, succumbs to a death described in a similar way: "The complete torpor came at last" (ibid., 108). The parallel between the two might be carried further insofar as her opium addiction defines her ensnarement by a repetition compulsion equivalent to Marner's virtually narcotic integration into his machine.

20. Sigmund Freud, "On Narcissism: An Introduction," in *The Standard Edition of the Complete Psychological Works of Sigmund Freud,* Vol. 14, ed. and trans. James Strachey (London: Hogarth, 1986), 91.

21. Attributed to David Lane, this "credo" has become the slogan for a variety of white supremacist groups. See, for example, the information provided on the Anti-Defamation League's Web site at http://adl.org/hate_symbols/numbers_14words.asp.

Part III
Aesthetic Subjects: Bodies, Minds, Identities

CHAPTER ELEVEN

The Combinatorial Aesthetics of Neurobiology

Barbara Maria Stafford

This essay reopens the question of the psychobiology of aesthetic responses that preoccupied nineteenth-century art theorists from Humbert de Superville to Charles Henry.[1] Specifically, I want to consider associational or interweaving perception in conjunction with the "new philosophy of mind" that has emerged in response to major computational developments in neurobiology. I will be arguing against the narrow tendency, evident in cognitive science and disciplines influenced by it, to equate consciousness solely with linguistic capabilities. High-order images, like cross-linking works of art, exhibit how our polarized perceptions of the world are processed as representations in various areas of the brain, become recombined, and then are analogically unified through "cross-modal matching."[2] To demonstrate the importance of networked spatial relations in the construction of self-awareness, I want to wrestle with two conundrums.

The first was identified by Francis Crick (among others) as central to providing a systematic account of higher-order consciousness. He spoke of the enigma of how different stimuli to different portions of the brain become married, as if by enchantment, to produce a single, unified somatic experience of an object within an existential subject.[3] The second puzzle emerges from problems of assessing the role played by qualia in determining a sense of self.

Briefly, I want to recuperate the sophisticated workings of analogy as a cross-cortical model for mental combination, for the fitting of bits and pieces of experience together. In this postmodern age of difference, the subtle varieties of likeness and the delicate art of making connections bridging distant elements have been lost. The cubist portrait–still lifes of Braque, Gris, and Picasso, as Pierre Reverdy remarked, show how subjectivity exists in interaction with a world characterized by spatial flux, not rigid geometries.[4] The enfolding of an inner self, the four walls of a room, and the outside world demonstrate the French poet's conviction that consciousness comes into being just as objects come into being: because of their relations. Just as a mental and bodily engagement moves detached things closer to one another, we become aware of awareness only in the drive toward attaining connectedness, during that expenditure of psychic and physical energy forcing disparate things to converge. The in-betweenness of assemblage, those body-object amalgams composed of tossed scraps and found objects, reveals the stunning spectrum of relocatable patterns available to human subjectivity.

Collage, as the process of transforming ephemera by cutting and pasting it into momentarily stable configurations, is, therefore, a particularly effective technique for capturing the chimera of consciousness in action. Originating with the cubists and expanded by the dadaists and surrealists, this "gluing" of transitory detritus extends into montage, film editing, and, now, computer manipulation. Compounding incongruous parts and provisionally joining farfetched elements in space and time break duality-establishing boundaries, whether in art or in science.[5] Anticipating the cross-kingdom fusions fabricated by Berkeley's David Ow, welding together the genetic substance of a firefly and tobacco to form phosphorescent plants, artists such as Hannah Hoch merged, substituted, and mutated aspects of one species of imagery into another.

More recently, Suzanne Anker's installation piece *Zoosemiotics* (1993) used a large glass vessel filled with water set in the middle of a room to magnify silvery sculptural simulations of animal chromosomes distributed on the wall in random, mostly circular order. The abstract mirroring performed by the beaker selectively coalesced the X shape of the chromosomes (found in one specific cell), changing them into miniature bodies dancing on the curved sides of the globe and swimming within the transparent liquid. This optical compression, anthropomorphization, and transformation of linguistic grids and codes into cavorting figures offers a striking parallel to the selective fashioning of graffiti-like experience into a coherent self by the mind. Similarly, in Orshi Drozdik's process piece *Erythrocytes* (1988), the stationing of a convex lens mounted on a rod and sited in front of a sea of sculptured cells invites individual viewers to unify, personalize, and internalize an anonymous body's microphenomena. I am suggesting, then, that the brain's "binding" capacity, no less than gene splicing or blood chemistry, can be externalized for scrutiny precisely in those aesthetic situations when it abruptly juxtaposes or tightly links variegated experiences.

Crick's formulation of the "binding problem" restates the great epistemological riddle of abstraction. Here, I must venture into a short excursus. In the second chapter of *Body Criticism,* titled "Abstracting," I argued that there were two major strands of cognitive compression or selective epitomization running through Western thought: one, a purist, minimalist, so-to-speak Mies van der Rohean "modernist" view, which saw the mind as dissecting sensations to arrive at a geometric Absolute; and a second, prismatic, synthetic, Frank Gehryean, if you will, "postmodernist" view, which envisioned the mind stitching chaotic appearances together, placing novel findings in contact with existing knowledge so that the old is simultaneously constructed and deconstructed by the new.[6] It may help to imagine such mental sorting and combining of contrary visual information as a process akin to Henry James's differential refraction of uniquely marred personae through the translucent sides of a golden bowl. That beautiful, but subtly cracked, crystal goblet served the novelist as a single, but shattering, focalizing object capable of revealing his motley characters' more or less flawed temperaments, their healthy or unhealthy consciousness. This Janus face of abstraction—as both quintessence and chromatics—captures the brain's preferential mechanism in action, able to eliminate some neuronal groups while strengthening others and so allowing us to learn over time.[7]

Box art (from Marcel Duchamp's *Boite-en-Valise* to Lucas Samaras's glass, fur, or needle-lined coffers and compartments) represents an intensification of collage practices. It, too, divides all physical existence into the hard-edged container and the always-escaping stream of the contained.[8] Resembling the brain in the fact that an amazing, even paradoxical, variety of things can be stored, conserved, memorialized, but, above all, gathered and transmuted within its confines, the box is the epitome of a malleable universe finely adjusted to the contradictory emotions of its owner.

The enigmatic vitrine constructions of Joseph Cornell, in particular, capture the dreamlike nature of human consciousness: ever present and ever in the past. In Cornell's phrase, these "toys for mathematicians" enshrining different levels of imagery precipitate mental voyages flowing backward and forward in time and across space. Deeply personal to the artist, these haunting environments also touch museum-goers by provoking a flow of explicit and implicit memories.[9] Indifferent or fleeting castoffs—like vanishing sensations—are alchemically metamorphosed into cherished, enduring objects for every man and woman. These perishables preserved within a sheltering receptacle do for vision what the madeleine did for fragrance. We become aware of a transparent wine glass, an agate marble, a Victorian doll, a sky chart, or the blued-over engraving of a Medici portrait before we *think* it. One can say of these volatile, qualia-laden reliquaries what Proust claimed for his tea-steeped biscuit: "But when from a long-distant past nothing subsists—still... the smell and taste of things remain poised a long time, ready to remind us... in the tiny and almost impalpable drop of their essence, of the vast structure of recollection."[10]

The olfactory epithelium and the limbic system, that oldest part of the brain from an evolutionary standpoint, remind us that receptor cells fire messages that, in turn, transmit signals flooding us with love, desire, sorrow, joy, and rage. The confounding ways in which scents, savors, sights, and sounds manage, in Kipling's words, to make our "heartstrings crack" raise the other pressing question the new mind researchers, no matter their camp, agree requires resolution. How does the brain produce a cohesive consciousness from physical substances that waft, caress, vacillate, shimmer, or drift outside of us and yet touch and alter us internally? A key, and much-disputed, factor in the process of cognitive binding is precisely the mysterious role played by qualia.

No one demonstrated better than Joseph Cornell that molding the welter of the passions into manifestly organized compositions is one of the greatest and most haunting achievements of the visual arts. In *Taglioni's Jewel Casket* (1940), he created a blue-velvet-lined wooden box that ceremonially presents a crystal necklace elegantly draped above a rising tide of glass cubes. One of a series of works titled *Homages to the Romantic Ballet*, it bears an inscription in Cornell's hand affixed to the inside lid:

> On a moonlit night in the winter of 1835 the carriage of Marie Taglioni was halted by a Russian highway man, and that enchanting creature commanded to dance for this audience of one on a panther's skin spread

> over the snow beneath the stars. From this actuality arose the legend that to keep alive the memory of this adventure so precious to her, Taglioni formed the habit of placing a piece of artificial ice in her jewel casket or dressing table where, melting among the sparkling stones, there was evoked a hint of the atmosphere of the starlit heavens over the ice covered landscape.[11]

By giving palpable shape to intense emotions, Cornell unforgettably turned indescribable intimacies into publicly shareable analogies. This age-old search for material equivalences to match the qualitative feel of elusive inner states fueled the pursuit of color correspondences (a peculiarly romantic quest engaging Goethe to Delacroix). It continues to drive research into how people are affected by distinctive odors (an old question, underlying the development of the perfumer's blending skill as well as early-modern medical therapies directed against airborne contagion). It remains evident in the desire to find visual or verbal parallels for the gamut of tactile pressures the body can undergo (think of Diderot's struggle to inventory Chardin's veiling glazes and textured strokes or the Marquis de Sade's encyclopedic itemization of erotic palpations). And it lives on when we try to articulate the gustatory pleasures (famously classified by Brillat-Savarin) arising from rolling delicious flavors around the tongue and over the palate.

Historically, such hard-to-systematize sensations posed, and continue to pose, a major difficulty for many scientists and philosophers, from Isaac Newton to the British empiricists, up to and including Gerald Edelman. Given that, presumably, no two people experience these secondary qualities or characteristics (as Shaftesbury notably termed them) exactly alike, how do such variable subjective conditions fit into a *general* theory of consciousness? This isomorphist quandary—taking similarity to mean exact copy (and here, I think, an art historical perspective on the range of gradations possible between an original and a replica is especially pertinent)—has led Daniel Dennett, for one, to deny the existence of inner mental states altogether. His is a slightly softer version of Paul and Patricia Churchland's robotic model of the brain as computer or information processor, a position that reduces that organ to rapid-fire neuronal operations performed in parallel.[12] Ironically, in spite of the reliance by numerous brain researchers on conspicuous connective metaphors such as "nets" and "maps" to describe perceptual categorization, this computational theory does not satisfactorily explain how vision, anatomical structure, the nervous system, and a shifting external milieu interact to form a sustaining and sustained psychic architecture that is also fluidly developmental.

Modern philosophy from Descartes forward has quantified certainty, that discursive activity of mathematics asserting that nothing has been introduced by the actual operation of the intellect that it cannot fully identify. In other words, the claim is that nothing is being added or subtracted, equated or changed without the mind's active warrant that no mistake either has occurred or is possible. To ensure the maintenance of *exact* identity, mathematical vigilance of this sort admits only a small set of valid transformations. Discursive certainty, as opposed to the proportional adjustments typical of analogy, is a matter of stating specifically how things are staying the same and precisely how they are being altered.[13] The Cartesian legacy to the computational philosophy of mind, I believe, is thus twofold. First, it always raises doubts in the face of ambiguity—that is, when things are not clear and distinct. This wariness, together with the application of an anatomizing method, continues even when, *by their very nature* (like synaesthetic qualia), the phenomena in question cannot be clear and distinct both because they are nuanced and because they permeate one another. Second, a debilitating Pyrrhonian skepticism accompanies the realization that the contents of the mind have somehow become transformed and that this shift cannot be *completely* identified and *wholly* articulated through measurement. To obviate the resulting corrosive doubt, the measurements became so fine grained that they "nanotechnologize" the phenomena observed, dissecting complex, engulfing experiences into fragmented microminiatures.

I offer as a counterexample to such militant quantitative rationalism the recent work of Bill Viola. One of the leading artists currently working in video and sound installations, he uses innovative multimedia technologies to explore sense perception as an avenue to embodied self-awareness. Created in 1994, Viola's *Stations* comprises five channels of video projection accompanied by strangely unnerving underwater sounds. Five cloth screens are suspended from the ceiling of the unlit gallery. Large slabs of polished black granite are placed flat on the floor touching the screens. Five gently swaying figures, submerged head downward, have their vertical reflections individually righted on the highly polished, tombstonelike horizontal surfaces. At random intervals, the projected bodies glide out of the frame, leaving the vacated space shadowy and silent. Suddenly the male and female figures take turns plunging back into view with a brilliant splash of noise and flare of light that momentarily blazes in the gloom.

In describing *Stations,* the artist commented that "an initial surface appearance of eerie, serene beauty resides over a deeper disturbing aspect of muted violence and disorder, with the disrooted, isolated, free-floating bodies evoking an eternal state between dream and death."[14] In an earlier piece, *Reflecting Pool* (1977–80), various figures were not drowned, but hovered in midair above the concentric ripples of a deep, mirroring spring concealed within a lush forest. Like the magical artifacts trapped within Cornell's nocturnal boxes, Viola's tranquil or agitated dark water contemplatively envelops the beholder, drawing her or him experientially downward into the normally unseen well of consciousness. Significantly, video plastically models mutable and nebulous sensations in a way that artificial intelligence systems or smart machines do not. As a "softer," unfurling technology, video constitutes a participatory medium coterminous with our own dissolving imaginings, wants, sensations of mortality and eternity. The monumental scale, wavy motion, and elemental rhythm of *Stations*'s nudes—spanning youth to older age—fuse in uncanny synchronization with the growth, change, and endings of the viewer's inner life.

Not just the present but the past also offers an untapped repertory of sophisticated imaging strategies demonstrating the complexities of physically, mentally, emotionally, and spiritually connecting as we dive beneath our own and others' surfaces. This topic, as far as I can tell, remains largely unaddressed in the social scientific and scientific literature on consciousness, with the exception of recent suggestive work on categorization and metaphor.[15] A fuller understanding of art's ability to create harmony out of life's discontinuities would help to account for those as yet noncomputed characteristics of the mind: namely, how it is able to bring distant things into contiguity and the mutuality, not identity, of human feelings.

I want to add three further reflections to current discussions about the new mind. First, consciousness appears to be inherently visual. Fundamentally about representation, it involves developing a visualizable self-image over time, permitting us to see and feel ourselves as standing both apart from and inside our surroundings.[16] The coherence associated with self-awareness—lasting for longer or shorter periods—becomes evident not so much through the invocation of the Cartesian language of automata, pulleys, and now wiring, transistors, and software, but in the production of fugitive or lasting patterns of relations. In that sense, consciousness becomes real only insofar as consciousness is desired. The practical production of a unified and graspable display of self results from the selective correlation of many different representations distributed over widespread areas of the brain.

Appositely, this palpably connective neurological language has a symbolic counterpart in the talismanic thaumaturgy used by Greco-Egyptian temple priests to invoke the ineffable oneness of the divine presence through a divisible material object. What might appear an improbable comparison, in reality, embeds the enigma of not-so cerebral bonding within a Darwinian competitive universe of animal appetites and the carnal biology of natural selection. Simultaneously, the startling correlations made by the "new mind" can also be situated within an ancient procreative and sexualized system of divination, of antithetical powers and reproductive potencies springing from physical attraction.

I am conjuring up the neo-Platonic and gnostic cosmos of magical correspondences, the oracular realm of spellbinding sympathies in which all things possess vertical and horizontal linkages arcing across the three kingdoms of nature. Synesius, Iamblichus, Proclus, and much of the late Roman world also looked for visible portents connecting the corporeal to the incorporeal domain. Mediating omens were thought to bring about liaisons between tangible objects—stones, gems, pieces of bone—and a higher, intangible psychic dimension. Not surprisingly, given that there is something mysterious about the art of healing, the alliance between magic and medicine has a long history in the West. During the Renaissance, Marsilio Ficino's (1433–99) translation of the just-discovered *Corpus Hermeticum,* as well as works by Plotinus, propagated the view that the wise physician could control disease by directing astral influences into the sick body.[17] Talismans, amulets, and charms enhanced his receptivity of planetary influences and so helped uncover elaborate sympathies existing between the terrestrial and celestial zones. This interconnected universe of correspondences remained in place until severely compromised by the derision of the Enlightenment. Jaucourt, in his medical articles written for Diderot's and D'Alembert's *Encyclopedie,* mocked the doctrine of pictorial signatures and its attendant belief in the binding capacity of incantatory artifacts joining the greater and lesser worlds, the exterior and the interior realms.

While easy to ridicule from a rationalist standpoint, the theory of sympathies and antipathies was fundamentally concerned to explain how dramatically different sensory phenomena could be collected, recollected, and internalized as part of one's own noetic substance. Finding or inventing a similar kinship between visible sign and invisible or remote meaning determined the abrupt juxtapositions typical of a baroque cabinet of curiosities (Figure 11.1), the segmented, miniature-lined compartments of a Ching dynasty treasure chest, and the imaginative leaps from the ordinary to the extraordinary elicited by box art of the sort that inspired Joseph Cornell (Figure 11.2). Paradoxically, it also characterizes the computationalists' identification (not approximating resemblance) of brain with consciousness, their desire for a direct, unmediated link between an originating material organ and the epiphanic presence of an elusive, singular awareness.

This brings me to my second point. It seems more fruitful to situate the binding problem within the context of philosophical and rhetorical analogy than within that of quantitative certainty. Alternately praised or vilified from Plato to Aquinas, Mill, and Wittgenstein, analogy seems a more apt concept for getting at the complexly designed ways in which first-person phenomena hang together than the computer-derived "interface." The fashionability of the latter term already presupposes that the brain functions like a special sort of apparatus.[18] One current dictionary defines an interface as "the collection of components which connects the analogue and digital computers to each other and controls and converts the data." As early as 1837, however, the adjective *interfacial* emerged in crystallography texts to describe the surface energy, tension, polarization, and absorption occurring between two faces of a crystal.[19] One may well ask, What is the appropriateness for brain research of importing into its organic precincts a word that alludes either to the intercommunication between two or more pieces of dead equipment or to that between the several planes of inert minerals?

The nonsentient implications of this geologic metaphor were extended in more recent times by Marshall McLuhan. His analysis of loudspeaker telephones or electrical "intercoms" now governs, I believe, the computational notion that a whole set of confrontational systems (much like

Figure 11.1. Jean Varin and André-Charles Boulle, *Cabinet on Stand*, c. 1675–80. The J. Paul Getty Museum, Los Angeles. Reprinted with permission.

Figure 11.2. Artist unknown, *Ballerina Sand Box,* c. 1890. Photograph reprinted by permission of Richard Balzer and Associates, Inc.

Duchamp's mechanical betrothals, Picabia's graphically sexed male and female machine-portraits produced for the pages of Stieglitz's *291*—replete with flirtatious lightbulbs, phallic sparkplugs, and clock springs dipped in ink—or Rebecca Horn's darkly erotic cyborgs) possess streamlined components that *really do* couple in a devicelike way.[20]

If it is true that human cognition is inherently modular, then it must give birth to correspondences. Analogy's efficacy consists not simply in communicating what already exists, but, like consciousness, in visibly bringing forth what, in fact, it communicates. Recall that in its ability to make things actually get together, analogy resembles the affinity-producing efficacy of a charm or amulet. Generative powers of attraction—rather than the mechanistic and chance riveting of chaotic assemblages into a functioning system—belong to a magical domain of metamorphoses where imaginings take on flesh. The coming together of opposite ideas is a creative function akin to sexual reproduction in that a third, new and unifying, individual arises from two distinct and separate beings. Ironically, then, this supposedly outmoded realm of corporeally conceived liaisons is more biologically up-to-date than the current model of awareness that has it resulting from the asexual merger of cybernetic hardware. The joining of differences by discovering or generating similarities—whether at the macro or the micro level—even coincides better with the fundamental premise of evolutionary theory that the earth's species, including *Homo sapiens,* arose through divergence from a common ancestor. Darwin's explanation that diversity was wrought by natural selection over millions of years is based on a principle not only for separating but for assimilating very different kinds of organisms.

This emergent dimension of analogy prevents the "new mind" from being absolutely severed from the "old mind." Specifically, it succeeds in illuminating John Searle's view of sentience as a set of intricate interlocking sensations that almost pragmatically arise in the brain in response to the interactions of its many parts. It also lends support to Roger Penrose's thesis that our understanding exceeds any computer because a computer only uses algorithms (that is, sets of precise rules that specify sequences of actions to be taken in order to solve problems or prove propositions).[21] This position has been much attacked because, it is argued, computational cognitive science does not require that people comprehend the lengthy and incredibly complicated programs employed to solve cognitive problems. But the issue (and here I also differ with Penrose) is not whether we do or do not understand the rules we use to arrive at mathematical (his example) or other conclusions but, rather, how we can be made to see or become aware of the somatic operations we undergo while we are in the process of experiencing them. As I have been suggesting, making these intricate and intuitive procedures visible constitutes the entire history of art. Moreover, by taking us back up the Darwinian ladder of evolution to the associative origins of human thought, analogy offers a nonalgorithmic technique for binding the known to the unknown, expressed in terms of similarities and antitheses. Learning, in this developmental scheme, arises not from a chain of reasoning but from a dynamic back-and-forth motion among choices that embrace the entire universe in their scope.

The limitations of algorithms for ascertaining what and how we know leads to my third point, also concerning the operations of analogy and its pertinence for understanding brain functioning. It remains questionable whether scientists can simulate on computers, the way they simulate tornadoes, the suppleness of encompassing cognitive processes. Indeed, is the machine-ideal of replication, copy, and digital reproduction adequate for the mystery of self-imaging that goes on inside us? The joining impulses of analogy, on the other hand, enact in another medium and in an external space those leaps and springs of the mind that elude computational modeling yet lie at the heart of human awareness. According to the analogical system, the mind acts like spreading fingers, grasping and sweeping together various things. The aesthetic counterpart to this tangible reaching for affinities, while acknowledging divergences, is verisimilar illusion. Unlike the manufacture of delusively exact simulations, viewer-adjusted illusion arises from the painter's skill in juxtaposing the chromatic manifold. Seen from a specific vantage point or from a particular perspective, such approximating compositions momentarily persuade the beholder that different sorts of phenomena can physically coexist within an imaginative or mentalized realm.

Baroque poetics—steeped in the neo-Platonic and gnostic doctrine of emanations, founded on a graduated descent from the macrocosm to the microcosm and sloping uninterruptedly downward from the One to the many—are characterized by just such a search for vertical and horizontal junctures suturing all portions of the cosmos. It is the Piranesian capriccio predicated on analogy, therefore, that most nearly resembles the unpredictable, staglike jumps of neurons, leaping along global reentry pathways, darting in and out of memory, fleeing toward and away from categories.

Most recently, Umberto Eco satirized the early-modern "excess of wonder" that led an Agrippa of Nettesheim or an Athanasius Kircher to engage in maniacal processes of Hermetic semiosis, encouraging any similarity to be exploited.[22] But unlike the interpretive extremes typical of postmodern deconstructionism, the classical theory of analogy does not claim that, for the healthy mind, everything means almost anything or necessarily possesses a similarity to everything else. Besides, and contra Eco, analogy has something specific to add to the electronic computing revolution and to the so-called death of linear thinking.[23] The computer's nonsequential capacity to arrange data first in this way and then in that has an important precursor in Leibniz's *ars combinatoria.* This hieroglyphics of manipulable characters was simultaneously an analogical method for spurring mental invention and a parallel processing model of the abstracting powers of intelligence demonstrating that human beings can think about more than one thing at a time.

To conclude: my point has been twofold. Historical examples showing the brain at work practically instantiate both the durable and the mutable processes of human cognition in ways that the new computational philosophy of consciousness—couched in terms of classifier systems, algorithms, and neural networks—has rendered opaque to ordinary comprehension.[24] More significant is that these elaborate compositions also reveal what the computer cannot, that is, the ongoing ritual of conscious and unconscious elaboration itself. Thus a baroque cabinet of curiosities, like an English landscape garden, is not merely a secret museum and an idiosyncratic receptacle for seducing a private audience; its sensory array of precious fragments, freestanding ruins, ceremonial devices, and cult artifacts concretely enacts the juxtapositive impulses of the intellect. Although forging links always occurs within a given cultural milieu, it also transcends the limits of any particular environment to exhibit the designs by which the mind *generally* creates affinities. I have been proposing uses for the past, then, so that people will not blindly trust hidden or automated maneuvers they cannot possibly understand without the assistance of a commonsense analogy linking neurophysiology to life situations.

Far from positing an indeterminate and limitless relativism, appropriate analogy encourages us to accept the fit between two disparate things only if we understand the second thing to follow from the first based on our prior experience. By establishing geometric relations of proportionality, equivalences, and nuanced degrees of resemblance among heterogeneous objects, it permits the comparability of not just individual but human patterns of awareness and action. Instead of insisting on a literal isomorphism between the brain's nanoprocesses and anatomized qualia—which does not do justice to the larger, holistic intertwisting of ideas with affect—analogy places these unlike phenomena (receptor cells and felt experiences) into relation. As currently defined, the heart of the problem of consciousness lies in the flagrant contrast or clash between organ and awareness. How does one satisfactorily reconcile the paradox of a disembodied brain as scientific instrument and conglomerate of dissected processes with the everyday ambiguities, unfixed meanings, enchaining and mingling of displacements, transformations, compressions, and hidden affinities we somatically experience as sentience?

Art, I have been suggesting, assists in locating a point of contact between a juxtapositive mass of precisely firing neurons and our cloudy inner atmosphere. It pictures both the hardwiring in compositional action and the perplexing weather within, enabling us to analogize visually a concordance between matter and thought. Every work of art consists of parts that are modified or even inverted by the contexts into which they are placed. Collage, assemblage, and grotesques, especially, *display* contradictions in a kind of double exposure on their surfaces, forcing us to see the arbitrariness of the copula and the magnitude of the required reconciliation. Revitalizing forgotten or, if remembered, despised analogy, then, might help us discover not only how the mind seeks out and connects linear with nonlinear arrangements, or manages to synthesize the vast quantities of data with which we are increasingly inundated, but how, time and again, it binds our shifting, compound selves into a single self in moments of consciousness.

Notes

1. See Barbara Maria Stafford, *Symbol and Myth: Humbert de Superville's Theory of the Absolute Signs in Art* (Cranbury, N.J.: Associated University Presses, 1979).

2. Ellen Dissanayake, *Homo Aestheticus: Where Art Comes from and Why* (New York: Free Press, 1992), 166.

3. Francis Crick, *The Astonishing Hypothesis: The Scientific Search for the Soul* (New York: Scribner, 1994).

4. Jennifer Pap, "'Entre quatre murs': Reverdy, Cubism, and the Space of Still Life," *Word & Image* 12 (April–June 1996): 181.

5. Suzanne Anker, *Gene Culture: Molecular Metaphor in Visual Art,* exhibition catalog (New York: Plaza Gallery, 1994), 2.

6. Barbara Maria Stafford, "Abstracting," in *Body Criticism: Imaging the Unseen in Enlightenment Art and Medicine* (Cambridge: MIT Press, 1993).

7. For a full exposition of these ideas, see Barbara Maria Stafford, "Recombinancy," in *Visual Analogy: Consciousness as the Art of Connecting* (Cambridge: MIT Press, 1999).

8. Walter Hopps, "Boxes," *Art International,* 20 March 1964, 38.

9. Daniel Schacte, *Searching for Memory: The Brain, the Mind, and the Past* (New York: Basic Books, 1996).

10. Marcel Proust, *Swann's Way,* trans. C. K. Scott Moncrieff (New York: Modern Library, 1956).

11. Quoted in Alex Migelon and Norman Laliberte, *Art in Boxes* (New York: Van Nostrand Reinhold, 1974), 84.

12. See, for example, Patricia Smith Churchland, *The Mind-Brain Continuum: Sensory Processes,* ed. Rodolfo Ilinás and P. S. Churchland (Cambridge: MIT Press, 1996).

13. Carl Page, "Symbolic Mathematics and the Intellect Militant: On Modern Philosophy's Revolutionary Spirit," *Journal of the History of Ideas* 57 (April 1996): 238.

14. Bill Viola, *Stations* (1994), exhibition handout (Los Angeles: Lannan Foundation, 10 July to 22 December 1996).

15. See, for example, Douglas Hofstadter, *Fluid Concepts and Creative Analogies: Computer Models of the Fundamental Mechanisms of Thought* (New York: Basic Books, 1995), esp. 205–67; Ronald McClamrock, *Existential Cognition: Computational Minds in the World* (Chicago: University of Chicago Press, 1995), esp. 132–34.

16. See Antonio Damasio, *The Feeling of What Happens: Body and Emotion in the Making of Consciousness* (New York: Harcourt, Brace, 1999).

17. Martha Baldwin, "Abracadabra or Magic in Medicine," in *Abracadabra: The Magic of Medicine,* exhibition catalog (London: Wellcome Institute for the History of Medicine, 1996), 12–13.

18. This technological annihilation of the body's space receives support from information theory and cognitive science; see Albert Borgmann, "Information, Nearness, and Farness," in *The Robot in the Garden: Telerobotics and Telepistemology in the Age of the Internet,* ed. Kenneth Goldberg (Cambridge: MIT Press, 2000), 91.

19. Ivan Illich, "Guarding the Eye in the Age of Show," *Res* 28 (Autumn 1995): 47.

20. Marshall McLuhan, *Understanding Media: The Extensions of Man* (New York: McGraw-Hill, 1964); Elizabeth Legge, "Thirteen Ways of Looking at a Virgin: Francis Picabia's La Saint Verge," *Word & Image* 12 (April–June 1996): 227. Also see the excellent essay on early-twentieth-century gendering of machines by Caroline A. Jones, "The Sex of the Machine: Mechanized Bodies in Early Modernism," from the session "The Body" at the conference "Histories of Science/Histories of Art," 4 November 1995.

21. John D. Searle, *Mind, Language and Society: Philosophy in the Real World* (New York: Basic Books, 1998). See also Roger Penrose, *The Large, the Small, and the Human Mind* (Cambridge: Cambridge University Press, 1997).

22. Umberto Eco, *The Limits of Interpretation* (Bloomington: Indiana University Press, 1995).

23. James Bailey, *After Thought: The Computer Challenge to Human Intelligence* (New York: Basic Books, 1996).

24. This reduction of animal behavior to patterns goes back to cybernetics and the epistemological structure of technology as knowledge. See Carl Mitcham, *Thinking through Technology: The Path between Engineering and Philosophy* (Chicago: University of Chicago Press, 1994).

CHAPTER TWELVE

Cloth Wounds

Queer Aesthetics of Debasement

Kathryn Bond Stockton

It is surprising that shame can adhere to forms of beauty, especially to the contours of beautiful cloth. (Women wrapped in beautiful clothes may betray the vanity said to be their shame. Men who rush to their own cloth beauty likely suffer a woman's vain shame.)[1] It is more surprising to learn, from certain novels, that this debasement clinging to beauty can make the wearer of beautiful garments a martyr to clothes.

What can it mean to be martyred for clothes—to believe in your clothes as you suffer from clothes, to bear the wounds that come with clothes, even to give up your very self (but what would that mean?) for the cause of your clothes? O vain shame. So-called homosexual fictions—from fictional lesbian autobiographies, without any claim to aesthetic density, to the high modernist camp of Genet, aesthetic texts of such dense weave, such lyric sheen—lend a range of intricate answers.

As an initial foray into martyrdom, I will sample novels from three distinct histories, offering twentieth-century martyrs as diverse as those of the mannish lesbian of Great Britain's twenties, American butches and femmes of the sixties, and even the sailors of postwar France. These remarkably various fictions specify, remarkably, not entirely various logics. Taking up the cause of clothes, as if clothes are a dangerous rite that they would defend, all three novels imagine scenes of sacrifice. However, in ways we might not expect, sacrifice is joined to sexual fantasy. The throwing of oneself outward in sacrifice merges with the goal of being caught by other arms—a sexy pietà. This odd motion of throwing and being caught calls our attention to something odder still. Clothing, in these novels, is a throwing and a catching, a centrifugal force. In the act of clothing, one is thrown outward into cloth arms (the arms of one's clothes), caught and held as a public gesture, in the social field. Clothing is this act of public self-betrayal, by which one seems to reveal onself. But could clothing also be a social self-enclosure, a kind of pietà? Could clothes offer a kind of social holding, a social self-hoarding, as odd as that may seem, of one's humiliation at the hands of something loved?

If so, we are likely to see a debasement freed from its command performance as either oppression or subversion, or, in the now-familiar critical sense, both-at-once. The debasements in these novels will not trace the logic of debasement as subversion, broken selves as radical selves, or the strategic miming of debasement as undoing or failing to undo political and economic arrangements. Rather, these debasements are at least a partial calling out from the subversion/oppression calculations of recent "theory." The thrust of the debasements I will be exploring (queer acts of clothing) is a turning toward forms of sociality that use humiliation for their own designs—attraction and aesthetic delight. Although this debasement might sound familiar from Leo Bersani's smart formulations, my own stress on a *social* embrace makes a different kind of move than Bersani's strong stress on the anticommunal nature of sex as self-debasement. Recall that Bersani (through Freud and Bataille) defines the act of sexual pleasure as "self-shattering," "a kind of . . . self-debasement," in which "the sexual itself [is] the risk of self-dismissal," and, therefore, "ascesis."[2] All of this leads Bersani, even in his readings of Genet, to celebrate "solitude" as the proper goal of the "anticommunal, antiegalitarian, antinurturing" nature of sex.[3]

By contrast, I will argue for the social nature of sartorial sacrifice. These are social actions (these self-debasements) that do not create harmonious communities of similarly identified same-sex queers. They create, instead, a kind of social solitude for people who are set, in some deep measure, apart from each other—but in an apartness they create together and in which they are "held" (sometimes sexually by a lover, sometimes mentally in someone else's mind, in any case materially). I want to scout these unusual forms—what I will call "the social holdings" (as if they might be hoarded)—of self-debasements. How do they unfold? According to our novels, from three different histories, that depends dramatically on how one negotiates the wounds that come with cloth.

The Cloth of Woundedness

There are many ways to be hurt by one's clothes:

- A psychic wound may emerge from wearing certain clothes, as if one's thoughts show a certain cut of cloth.
- A woman's genital "wound" (à la Freud) may be announced or dismissed by one's clothes, calling out on "every woman's" garment a vagina; on "every man's" garment, escape from this sorrow.
- Some may hand out bodily wounds to those who wear "unnatural" clothes, wounds that themselves may be worn as clothes: a bruise, for example, as a kind of purple cloth.
- Finally, perhaps most intriguing of all, one may suffer the divine humiliation of devotion to fabric: a sailor, for example, may feel a coat of "coal dust on his body, as women feel, on their arms . . . the folds of a material that transforms them into queens."[4]

These are cloth wounds—which makes both Freud and the dictionary wrong (or simply defensive) when it comes to cloth. The dictionary tells us clothes are designed to cover, protect, or adorn the body, slyly saying nothing of their flagrant penchant for revealing, wounding, or debasing the body that they pretend to cover.[5] Moreover, we are told that "cloth" is related to the Old English *clitha,* meaning "a poultice": a soft moist mass, of flour or herbs, applied to a sore or inflamed body part.[6] By this rendering, cloth is seen as a solace for sufferings, not as an agent, as cloth also is, for a wounded appearance.

Freud, for his part, adheres to a covering. Recall that at the end of his essay "Femininity" (1933), Freud imagines pubic hair as a natural model for human clothing, because it covers and conceals a woman's genitals. Here is the "unconscious motive," Freud tells us, for women's contribution (their only contribution) to civilized development: plaiting and weaving, which, of course, only "imitate" Nature's invention of the pubes.[7] "The step that remained to be taken," says Freud, in the passage from pubic hair to clothes, "lay in making the threads adhere to one another, [since] on the body they stick into the skin and are only matted together." In other words, as it solves the problem of sticking, cloth is a greater adherence to a covering.

What is being covered? Not a person's body in any simple sense. Not, even more particularly, the genitals. Freud is more specific still. What is being covered, in Freud's own phrase, is "genital deficiency"—his essay is on "femininity," after all. Indeed, what has led Freud to pubic hair and cloth is his last, rushed, ragbag discussion of "a few more psychic peculiarities of mature femininity": vanity and shame. Peculiar, indeed, is the feminine adherence of one to the other, shame to vanity, vanity to shame, so that they would appear to wear each other's clothes. As it happens, one is a cover for the other. "The vanity of women," Freud famously informs us, is "a late compensation for . . . original sexual inferiority." Vanity, in other words, is fancy-pants shame, which "has as its purpose," says Freud, "concealment of genital deficiency." Yet this is no real concealment at all. Vanity is calling out: "Look at my cover." By Freud's rendering, in spite of what he claims, clothing is not primarily concealment; it is not primarily a more attractive version of its model, pubic hair. Clothing, rather, is bold revelation, a cover turning inside out: it reveals the *category* (male or female) of the person's genitals it purports to cover. On "every woman's" sweater, a vaginal wound.

If I have offered the fictions of Freud—lacking in all subtlety and cloaking historicity, when it comes to clothes—it has been to dramatize how Freud gets something right in this case when he is wrong. He stresses clothing's concealments, unconvincingly, even as he rightfully points to its displays. Additionally, whether rightly or wrongly, Freud, by implication, fingers display of genital shame as "civilization's" strong investment in gendered clothes (different clothes for women and men). Yet this lack of historical regard (stressing clothing's universal operations) does not keep Freud, in 1933, just five years past Radclyffe Hall's *The Well of Loneliness,* from his own peculiar timeliness. I think it would even be fair to say that Freud and Hall were voicing something in much stronger terms than were their contemporaries: not just the sociopolitical disadvantage attached to women's clothes, but the bodily and psychic wounding that may powerfully adhere to them.

Even the psychoanalyst J. C. Flugel did not put the matter of clothes so starkly in his famous treatise *The Psychology of Clothes* (1930), launched from a series of talks he gave for the BBC in 1928—the year in which *The Well* was banned.[8] Flugel had no theory of wounding. True, he argued to abolish fashion in favor of some kind of uniform dress (which would level differences), and he himself theorized clothes (in a move Freud intensified) as satisfying two "contradictory tendencies" (those of "decoration" and "modesty"). This makes clothes resemble, Flugel said, the neurotic symptoms of people who suffer "attacks of . . . blushing" as they negotiate between the states of "shame" and "exhibitionism," so that "clothes resemble a perpetual blush upon the surface of humanity." Yet, in spite of this theory of blushing, Flugel had no theory of wounding.[9]

Nor exactly did New Women writers have any such theory of clothes wounding women, although they were grappling with what women's clothes mean and limit.[10] (Constraints on women's freedom of movement, the fit of women's clothes to their jobs, and sartorial limitations to cultural authority were central issues here.) Rather, it was when debates about New Women got replayed, in the so-called second wave of feminism, especially, most clearly, among historians of the 1980s, that feminist talk about some New Women's cloth wounds emerged.[11] Feminist historians, at that moment, sought to understand both the various motives and the stakes attached to New Women's refusal of women's clothes. Some historians predictably championed those New Women (Woolf, for example) whom they imagined "adopted male dress as a self-conscious political statement," believing that "clothes are cultural artifacts, lightly donned or doffed."[12] They explained with less ease (what they referred to as) the "Mannish Lesbian" of the 1920s, a New Woman whose costume change was not so easy, and whose "symbols [thus] acquired a second, darker message . . . public condemnation, social ostracism, and legal censorship."[13] It was left to those more sympathetic to this figure to explain the Mannish Lesbian's refusal of women's clothes as a sign that she bravely symbolized "the stigma of lesbianism (just as the effeminate man is the stigma-bearer for gay men)."[14]

What interests me is this mention of "stigma." Notice the assumption that a woman *refusing* women's clothes would find herself (still) bound up with a wound—more pointedly, a stigma. (*Stigma:* "a distinguishing mark burned or cut into the flesh, as of a slave or criminal"; "marks resembling the crucifixion wounds of Jesus"; "a mark, sign, etc. indicating that something is not considered normal or standard.")[15] This sort of stigma would seem to be the sign of "lesbianism" pure and simple. Refusing women's clothes may publicly reveal one's sexual preference for other women's bodies, thus resulting in a stigma. But can we put the emphasis the other way around? One's public preference for other women sexually can make the public see—and see, perhaps, in a whole new way—something about some women's refusal of women's clothes. What might the reading public never have had put before them, in any large way, before the public banning of Hall's *The Well of Loneliness* that so publicized Hall and her protagonist as "the mannish lesbian"? Something perhaps deeply known by many women. A different kind of shame than the presumed "stigma" of "lesbianism" (although there was surely that). What *Well*'s readers might well have confronted is the shame some women have historically felt (not the discomfort, not the displeasure, but, really, the shame) in having to wear women's clothes, a kind of psychic debasement that runs so deep it seems in excess of a simple preference for wearing men's clothes. Moreoever, this shame could eerily match, and therefore newly emphasize, the psychic debasement that *men* in Hall's time were asked to feel in relation to women's clothes on themselves ("Imagine a man in a dress like that," says Captain Ramsey in *The Well of Loneliness*, "too awful to think of—"). Otherwise, Stephen, the novel's mannish lesbian, could not feel such shame in women's dresses. Discomfort, yes. Even a sense of diminished pleasure. But not the humiliation she feels.

What might this psychic debasement—as pictured in Hall's *The Well of Loneliness*—say about a deep-seated stain on the meanings attached to "normal" women's clothes, even to their acknowledged beauty? This strong reaction to women's adornment—as expressed in the voice of a character who must contemplate these clothes upon herself—amounts to *a hate for what she also loves*, for what she would admit is beautiful but also both wounding and debasing. What may be desperately alluring at arm's length—women's clothes and their acknowledged beauty—may be debasing if put upon oneself, even in the eyes of so-called normal men who love "normal" women. Beauty, in this way, may be seen to be a wound. Or, to put it differently, in *The Well of Loneliness*, and, then, distinctively, in *Stone Butch Blues* and Genet's *Querelle*, it is queer to know a cloth wound when you see one.

It is even stranger to negotiate cloth wounds through the act of martyrdom. This is what we have yet to see and understand. In the novels I examine here, in this essay, there are full-scale scenes of sacrifice, all involving clothes. These scenes of martyrdom clearly offer something beyond a symbol for queers' social stigma in the obvious sense. The question is, what, exactly, do they offer? Here another writer comes into view—Georges Bataille—one likely thoroughly read by Genet, although he was also writing at the same time as Hall (and, like Genet and Hall, writing from a background in Catholic thought).[16] Bataille is heuristically interesting on sacrifice; his essays make us see what questions we could ask of a martyrdom to clothes, and further how this sacrifice goes hand in hand with fantasy.

Sacrifice, at times, can sound in common parlance like a dour religious act, mired in resignation to a bad reality. Not so for Bataille. Briefly, Bataille, in *Theory of Religion,* deems "religion's essence . . . the search for lost intimacy."[17] Lest this "intimacy" sound too immediately relational or sexual, we should realize that this is a call to "the intimacy of the divine world," whose chief feature is its "unreality," its separation from "real relations" and the "world of things."[18] Religion, one could say, is a search for the intimacy of unreality. In fact, it is the main function of sacrifice to destroy "an object's real ties" by drawing "the victim out of the world of utility" while delivering her or him to a world of "unintelligible caprice," thus giving sacrifice "an appearance of puerile gratuitousness."[19] Question 1: Could sacrifice surrounding clothes, whatever that might look like, be depicted as destroying, at least in some respect, a person's "real ties" to the world of utility?

We have said this destruction has a fanciful nature, in Bataille's view—taking one toward both caprice and unreality. Now we must see that sacrifice is also tied to a movement, in Bataille's rendering, so often tied to fantasy. Here I mean a casting of one's self outside oneself (in fantasy, a mental leap) so as to break not just with one's reality, but also with one's "individuality," according to Bataille.[20] With the act of sacrifice, Bataille is saying, such casting turns physical and, of course, violent. In fact, this break with one's individuality lies at the heart of the sacrificial urge, according to Bataille, and constitutes the intimacy of sacrificial violence. In his lurid essay "Sacrificial Mutilation and the Severed Ear of Vincent Van Gogh," Bataille proclaims that automutilation (the chopping off of one's finger, for example) reveals what's at stake in religious sacrifice: the need to externalize the self, to throw oneself out of oneself, to disrupt the homogeneity of the self, whether by the sacrifice of animal proxies (a religious cop-out) or the madman's chopping off of his ear.[21] Question 2: Could clothing be creatively rendered as both an act of fantasy *and* an act of sacrifice, allowing one to throw oneself, to feel oneself as a kind of thrown self? Our selected fictions, to be sure, are going to show that a martyrdom to clothes is a happy self-betrayal, for when you give up loneliness to make yourself a character, by means of either fantasy or cloth, you give yourself away. But are you caught and held?

The Cloth of Loneliness

Arguably the most famous "lesbian" novel, Hall's *The Well of Loneliness* (1928), answers no: one is not embraced in a martyrdom to clothes. Sadly, in *The Well,* fantasy fails. Sacrifice fails. The novel's martyr, as we are going to see, is left in the singular posture of refusing her wounded women's clothes. As any reader of the novel will remember, *Well* begins and ends with intense salvific scenes. The novel's heroine, Stephen Mary Gordon (who carries in her name a gendered cross between a famous church martyr and one who wraps a martyred son in arms), is born on Christmas Eve and bears, as another character puts it, the "outward stigmata of the abnormal—verily the wounds of One nailed to a cross."[22] Yet, in what seems a cross-dressing pun, Stephen, the novel's most loyal cross-dresser, wears the martyr's "cross" on her clothes. Whether she dresses as a woman or a man, she is unable to shake cloth wounds.

Realize, to begin, that for all of its pains, the novel is actually shockingly flat—at the level of the sentence (no sentence will transport you) and even at the larger level of its plot (which is, more or less, a story of impasse). This very flatness has clearly aided those who, since 1928, have wished to read the novel as fairly "factual"—to find in *The Well* a historically accurate portrait of the second-generation New Woman (her lesbian lust announced by her clothes) or to find a fiction "still true" to butch women, and thus one easily altered on spec.[23] Consider, for example, that, according to a recent oral history of a lesbian community *(Boots of Leather, Slippers of Gold),* Hall's French twist on 1920s British aristocracy was stretched to cover its readers' lives in the American fifties factory town of Buffalo, New York.[24] Truly, *Well* has proved a crossover text of vast proportions, rivaled now only by *Stone Butch Blues* (1993), which allows its readers to universalize the lives of 1960s Buffalo lesbians.

None of this intrigue surrounding historicity is beside the point. The power of *The Well*'s sentimental realism, its relentless portrait of a cross-dressing Christ, is for me its "clothemes" (to coin a comic word), that is to say, its mythemes (as Roland Barthes would call them)—its myths surrounding clothes. I believe these clothemes are somewhat detachable from the specific plotlines that engage them, but, as they emerge in different plots and other histories, they are largely altered.

Here is what I mean. In *The Well of Loneliness,* strutting, deflating, tearing cloth, and shedding tears (all involving clothes) are the central clothemes, one might say, all of which resurface in *Stone Butch Blues* to a similar logic but different effect. For in *The Well*, at the dawning of these clothemes (at least in novel form), fantasy sputters; sacrifice fails. There is, finally, only loneliness. Especially at the novel's start, other than her clothes, there are no arms of a public sort to catch a humiliated Stephen in embrace. Further into *Well*, there are no social holdings (no public structures), at least of the sort that Stephen can trust, to make her self-humiliation into solitude. Later, we learn: "As long as she lived Stephen never forgot her first impression of the bar known as Alec's—that meeting-place of the most miserable of all those who comprised the miserable army. . . . who, despised of the world, must despise themselves beyond all hope, it seemed, of salvation" (387). Even early on, the heroine's martyrdom looks like a sacrifice gone awry. She succeeds only in sacrificing clothes.

I refer, of course, to the tragicomic scenes at the start of the novel in which first love, first clothes, and first wounds all stick together in a first plot block. Stephen has fallen for the housemaid Collins, as nursery stories have "stirred her ambition":

> She, Stephen [age seven], now longed to be William Tell, or [Lord] Nelson, or the whole charge of Balaclava; and this led to much foraging in the nursery rag-bag, much hunting up of garments once used for charades, much swagger and noise, much strutting and posing. . . . Once dressed, she would walk away grandly . . . going, as always, in search of Collins, who might have to be stalked to the basement. (19)

Stephen courts Collins dressed as a boy—Lord Nelson, in particular, that famous martyr from the Battle of Trafalgar. Collins, for her part, laughs at Stephen and appears distracted, because she is suffering from housemaid's knee. Seeing, perhaps, that masculine clothes cannot bear any comedy, that they shrink from laughter and suggestions of vanity, Stephen finds herself "thoroughly deflated," dressing up "as Nelson in vain," "and must tear off the clothes she dearly loved donning, to replace them by the garments she hated" (20).

Cut away from this scene for a moment. Before we return to its real fascination—Stephen's bid for martyrdom—realize two things. Stephen, in moments, is clearly attracted to Collins's *debasement* (sometimes in the basement), "since despising, [Stephen] could still love her": "Watching her, Stephen felt unhappy and embarrassed, not so much for herself as for Collins; and this feeling increased, so that thinking about her made Stephen go hot down her spine" (18). Debasement, we are shown, is perfectly seductive on someone else—as is a "soft" "dress" (which Stephen "very much wanted to remember") that a beloved of Stephen's later wears (a dress "so soft that it had easily torn"; 141). The kind of debasement that Stephen herself is forced to wear ("the garments she hated") is a different matter altogether. Stephen takes it hard—what she feels in her clothes—beginning in this scene: "How she hated soft dresses and sashes, and ribbons, and small coral beads, and openwork stockings! Her legs felt so free and comfortable in breeches" (20). This motif of comfortable freedom fades from later passages, giving way to stronger laments: "I *hate* this white dress and I'm going to burn it—it makes me feel idiotic!" (37). "She stood there an enraged and ridiculous figure in her Liberty smock. . . . the bow [in her hair] sagged down limply, crooked, and foolish" (52).

Return, now, to the scene of Collins's knee. How striking that Stephen, dressed as a girl (in her "hated" girls' clothes), starts to act the martyr. She even tries to take on a wound not her own. It's a funny scene (a martyr seducing at the tender age of seven) in a novel hardly noted for either camp or wit. Nightly she cries in "an orgy of prayer":

> Please, Jesus, give me a housemaid's knee instead of Collins. . . . Please, Jesus, I would like to bear all Collins' pain the way You did. . . . I would like to wash Collins in my blood. . . . This petition she repeated until she fell asleep, to dream that in some queer way she was Jesus, and that Collins was kneeling and kissing her hand, because she, Stephen, had managed to cure her by cutting off her knee, with a bone paper-knife and grafting it onto her own. The dream was a mixture of rapture and discomfort, and it stayed quite a long time with Stephen. (21, 22)

For all of these elaborate dreams of sacrifice, Stephen's fantasy of grafting Collins's damaged knee onto her own is not a sacrifice she can perform. Just as sadly, this fantasy collapses into Stephen's loneliness instead of solving it. And so, as she cannot come to wear Collins's knee in this way, Stephen, yet again, changes her strategy. Getting mad at Jesus ("You don't love Collins, Jesus, but I do"; 22), Stephen cries, "I've got to get housemaid's knee my own way—I can't wait any longer for Jesus!" (23). However, this bid for attaching her heart to a wounded knee makes a cloth wound more than anything else, which redounds upon herself:

> The nursery floor was covered with carpet, which was obviously rather unfortunate for Stephen. . . . All the same it was hard if she knelt long

> enough. . . . Nelson helped her a little. . . . She would think: "Now I'm Nelson. I'm in the middle of the Battle of Trafalgar—I've got shots in my knees!" But then she would remember that Nelson had been spared such torment. . . . [Still] there were endless spots on the . . . carpet, and these spots Stephen could pretend to be cleaning. . . . Enormous new holes appeared in her stockings, through which she could examine her aching knees. . . . this led to rebuke: "Stop your nonsense, Miss Stephen! It's scandalous the way you're tearing your stockings!" (22, 23)

Earlier, Stephen had failed to extract the needed power from Nelson's clothes, which had led to Stephen's tearing them. Now her failure to elicit any wound from him (somehow he's a martyr without a wound to lend her) leads to different rips as she comically copies the movements of her servant, making her the figure of a carpet-cleaning Christ. As this savior, Stephen only succeeds in revealing, metaphorically and literally, the wound that sits on her women's clothes ("enormous new holes appeared in her stockings"). Moreover, because the invert child has scandalously torn her feminine garments, wounding a woman's proper cover, and has succeeded in tearing her skin, the head servant orders Collins to lie, to tell the child her knee is getting better from these efforts so that Stephen will stop them. This fabrication, which even Stephen questions, is emblematic for the book as a whole. Nothing is solved by the logic of wounding. Collins, according to conventional rhythms, consorts with a footman, while Stephen's martyrdoms are mainly productive of exile and tears:

> [Stephen] sobbed as she ran . . . tearing her clothes on the shrubs in passing, tearing her stockings and the skin of her legs. . . . But suddenly the child was caught in strong arms, and her face was pressing against her father. . . . she crouched here like a dumb creature that had somehow got itself wounded. . . . "I'm going to send Collins away tomorrow; do you understand, Stephen?". . . Bending down, [her father] kissed her in absolute silence—it was like the sealing of a sorrowful pact. (28, 29)

Gone is the purpose behind her wish for sacrifice: to be held by Collins *and* her own boy's clothes; really, to be held in her masculine clothes. Even this final wrapping by her father is no solution. (Her father later dies; her lover, Mary, leaves, when Stephen sends her away to a man.) It only closes off this first plot block, which repeats in different fashions throughout Hall's *Well,* recycling unmistakable clothemes of loneliness.[25]

The Cloth of Communal Adherence

Out of the nineties there arrives a solace for loneliness. In Leslie Feinberg's *Stone Butch Blues,* loneliness seems taken up and transformed in the space that Stephen Mary Gordon never trusted: the lesbian bar. Shot through with its nostalgia for community—fifties and sixties bar life in Buffalo, along with labor struggles in a string of city factories—*Stone Butch Blues* begins, even so, with a lonely letter. It has been written at the story's end, to a lover lost at the story's middle, although it is placed at the story's start: "Dear Theresa, I'm lying on my bed tonight missing you . . . hot tears running down my face . . . as I have each night of this lonely exile."[26] It could almost appear that *Stone* is picking up where *Well* left off; as if, years after sending her away, Stephen is writing to her great love, Mary, to reminisce about a lost community.

And yet what has changed between these novels' settings, between the loneliness of *The Well*'s late 1920s and the bracing sociality of *Stone*'s 1960s, is something very 1993 (the year *Stone* was published). Call it *feminist* butch relations. I refer to the unforeseen phenomenon, still under way, of a feminist affirmation of the once dirty secret of a lesbian history: femme-butch relations, which relied on "gender roles" later so heavily critiqued by many feminists. This affirmation, sometimes with a dose of nostalgia, takes many forms; among them, as one could readily imagine, is a reading of these couples as deconstructing pairs.[27] But I am more struck by Feinberg's sense of sacrifice: the way in which her butch, who is physically wounded due to her clothes, wears her resultant gashes and burns for the sake of her femme, who wears women's clothes. This is a social working out of women's wounds, as we are going to see, and one in which the presence of the femme (even as the letter's worshipped ghost) makes all the difference.[28] True, gone is Hall's Catholic discourse, but not its sense of martyrdom. And now, unlike the setting in *Well,* there are social structures—an erotic system, even—that can turn debasements toward a social self-enclosure. This is even a fantastic self-betrayal: a feminist fantasy of *in*equality, a fantastic embrace of differential roles. Indeed, as if to underscore its fantasy structure, the novel's lonely letter is a form of pillow talk to a lost great love, but pillow talk remembrance of the (good old) raids of the 1960s, when butches were beaten up by the cops. Here is a memory of a raid on a bar:

> That's when I remember your hand on my belt, up under my suit jacket... where your hand stayed the whole time the cops were there.... "Stay with me baby, cool off," you'd be cooing... like a special lover's song sung to warriors. The law said we had to be wearing three pieces of women's clothing.... I never told you what they did to us down there [in the jail]... but you knew.... We never cried in front of the cops.... Did I survive?... only because I knew I might get home to you.... You bailed me out.... You gently rubbed the bloody places on my shirt and said, "I'll never get these stains out."... You laid out a fresh pair of white BVD's and a T-shirt for me and left me alone to wash off the first layer of shame. I remember it was always the same.... you would find some reason to come into the bathroom.... In a glance you would memorize the wounds on my body like a road map—the gashes, bruises, cigarette burns. Later, in bed, you held me gently.... You didn't flirt with me right away, knowing I wasn't confident enough to feel sexy. But slowly you coaxed my pride back out.... You knew it would take you weeks again to melt the stone.... You treated my stone self as a wound that needed loving healing. (8, 9)

Here are *Well*'s recognizable sentiments: pride, swift deflation, sorrow, and a palpable longing for embrace. Again, we as readers are held to the novel by an intricate chain of interlocking clothemes. Overall, we see how the members of this couple reveal their culture's (violent) investment in gender-differential clothes for men and women ("The law said we had to be wearing three pieces of women's clothing"). In the face of this investment, we see how this couple wears their sexual deviance. They even wear it as something shared between them—a deviance that neither can sustain on her own. In *unequal* ways, they are marked by the discipline and punishments of gender.

The femme's deviance is strangely unmarked when she's on her own. Dressed as a woman, she can't be seen for the deviant she is, because she blends, passes, and wears the expected wound of her gender, *as is expected,* on her clothes. The butch, by contrast, looks to be refusing the women's clothes that, for herself, she feels as a wound (even though she clearly loves her lover to wear them). Yet it is by this act of refusal that she gives herself away to her lover and the law. For when, sartorially, she throws herself from her woman's wound in her fantasy dress-up as a "man" (or, more precisely, as a masculine woman), she is seen by the law, but is also lit up for her femme's attractions to gender clichés (warriors wearing BVDs as their heroics turn them into stone).

The femme herself, through these very clichés, also crosses expectations. The fabricated "man" she is choosing to love is a "failed" authenticity busted by authorities. It is for this "failure," we are led to believe, the butch's position as a not-man, that the femme loves the butch. This is in part because this "failure" allows the femme to be demanding, political, protecting ("you bailed," "you rubbed," "you laid," "you held"—the bulk of the verbs belong to her). And indeed, it is the femme who springs the butch from jail and supports the butch financially when, because of her appearance, the butch loses employment. The femme advocates for the one who would not like to walk in her shoes.

Just as literally, the law becomes a character in these scenes of sacrifice—the cops invading, intruding, and forcing the butch to wear the clothing that signals the "normally feminine" wound that women (are asked to) wear as cloth (the rule: three pieces of women's clothing).[29] If the butch refuses (refuses women's clothes), she is sent to jail and beaten—made to wear on the surface of her skin (gashes, bruises) the wound she refuses to reference with her clothes.

As if she is a macho Christ, the butch takes the role of wearing of these wounds. Around these wounds she forms a "stone." This is the mark of emotional hardening that is a monument to felt humiliation. The femme's vocation, in relation to these wounds (which, complexly, mirror her own), is to catch a thrown self, a self thrown in sacrifice, a self dramatically externalized and ruptured, and then to "melt the stone"—in essence to be the holder and dispenser of tears. The femme melts the stone so the butch can decide not to take it anymore—but not to take it anymore "again and again." For here's the rub: the femme melts the stone so the butch can go back, again and again, to encounter the law ("it was always the same"). Together, what they advocate is a repetition of wounding and refusal at the hands of their clothes (the femme wears the cloth wound, the butch fights the cloth wound, the cops intervene, the butch wears the skin wound . . .). All of this puts them about the business of holding, as a couple, a psychic wound they never would have made each other wear.[30]

The Cloth of Curve

Stone Butch Blues may be a rather unimaginable lesson in how to have a feminist fantasy—how to imagine two women addressing the shame of their clothes by returning, in sacrificial cycles, to a beating. Genet's *Querelle* (1953) is more circular still, proposing the queer's devotion to fabric (his wish to be held, as it were, by his clothes) as an elegant, self-embracing shame. This is shame not just because it resembles women's vanity, but because it points toward other men's arms. The wish to be held by one's own clothes is a wish to be held by arms that both are and are not one's own. Wraparound shame that comes from the thrill of men's tightly wrapped clothes is tightly tied, moreover, to sacrificial scenes. Sacrifice is a kind of wrapping in *Querelle*. It mimes the act of clothing by being a throwing of oneself from oneself that allows the subject to touch back upon himself as if he were a set of arms different from his own.

Amazingly, the fighting in *Querelle* is as oddly self-reflexive as the clothing. In this novel set in the seaside city of Brest, destroyed by bombs in World War II—a novel about sea and sailors, sailors in port, workmen and sailors, and the dark circuitry between cops and criminals, who are sailors—fighting is a way of calling arms upon oneself.[31] Even the act of murder in the novel, performed by a sailor in glamorous clothes, is revealed to be self-sacrifice. This is hinted at by the title *Querelle*, taken from the self-reflexive French verb, *se quereller*, "to pick a fight," as if one's fight is with oneself. Killing can be self-reflexive in war: a soldier's state-sanctioned murder of other soldiers like himself may, at any time, turn back upon himself as his state-ordered death (the command that he sacrifice himself for his brothers). In Genet's novel, the link between this turnaround and clothing's wraparound is forged by fantasy. In *Querelle*, fantasy is central to narration, as is always the case in Genet. (The novel is narrated by a "we" who address themselves to "inverts.")[32] Here, however, sexual fantasy is even fabrication of the most communal and literal sort: the actual filling of an outfit by the narrators. Counter to what novel readers might expect (starting with a character, who is then gradually described by a narrator), Genet's storytellers begin with clothes. They fantasize a fighting man in clothes they wish to wear. They launch him as a character in what they start to tell. They sacrifice their insides (their thoughts, their desires) in order to throw themselves outside themselves in this act of clothing.

Indeed, we begin on the edge of their fantasy: the sailor's uniform "cradles the criminal, it enfolds him," "envelops him in clouds," "in the tight fit of his sweater, in the amplitude of his bell-bottoms" (4). This is an outfit the narrating "we" would like to fill out—ideally, with themselves. And so they do. They fabricate a sailor from themselves:

> Little by little, we saw how Querelle—already contained in our flesh—was beginning to grow in our soul, to feed on what is best in us, above all on our despair at not being in any way inside him, while having him inside ourselves. . . . (We are still referring to that ideal and heroic personage, the fruit of our secret loves.) . . . to become visible to you, to become a character in a novel, Querelle must be shown apart from ourselves. (17, 18)

Querelle is not just sweater and pants. As a walking fantasy, Querelle is a state of mind that gets externalized. Indeed, by making narration fabrication, the filling of a sailor's suit, the narrators ostentatiously betray themselves. They reveal hidden desires inside themselves in order to throw themselves outside themselves, making Querelle a desire they can cling to—and now a concept to "get inside." That they imagine their fantasy man to be a murderer seems only right, for this lets him take a more virile route to their own self-sacrifical position, as if virility bends to their fantasy. For when Querelle's murders turn into sacrifice, he can be seen to put his virility at the service of their wish for passivity, to share with the narrators a longing to be caught in glamorous arms: those of a body or a dangerous weapon or a beautiful cape.

It is this very concept of the wraparound that grounds the narrators' devotion to fabric, their interest in tightly fitting sweaters as a social self-enclosure. The novel's only invert, Lieutenant Seblon, even wears their fantasies on his sleeve, for the cops to see:

> Before the two police officers had left [his] cabin, the Lieutenant wanted to put on his cloak of navy blue, and then did so with such coquetry—which he at once, and clumsily, corrected—that the total effect was not of just "putting it on",—that would have been far too manly, but rather that of "wrapping himself in it"—which, indeed, was the way he thought of it himself. Again, he expected embarrassment, and he made up his mind (once more) never to touch a piece of material again in public. (92)

But, of course, he does. In fact, he becomes the novel's poster boy for divine humiliation, betraying (in the sense of revealing) that the fantasy filling up Querelle is a man's secret wish to be surrounded. Here is the lieutenant on the subject of protection, blowing vanity's cool cover to uncover sacred shame:

> When I became an officer, it wasn't so much in order to be a warrior, but rather to be a precious object, guarded by soldiers. Which they would protect with their lives until they died for me, or I offered up my life in the same manner to save them. It is thanks to Jesus that we can praise humility, for he made it into the very characteristic of divinity.... Humility can only be born out of humiliation. Any other kind is a vain simulacrum. (265)

The lieutenant knows that just as he and his soldiers wrap around to meet each other, playing, interchangeably, savior and saved, the soldier's protection is a social embrace, now making weaponry, like his cloak of navy blue, a sign of erotic self-revelation: a dead giveaway.

So we read that the lieutenant, who "took care never to be caught counting the stitches of any imaginary needlework... [n]evertheless... betrayed himself in the eyes of all men whenever he gave the order to pick up arms, for he pronounced the word 'arms' with such grace that his whole person seemed to be kneeling at the grave of some beautiful lover" (24). Here, in the graceful lining of the sentence, lies the lieutenant's wish for embrace, betraying both his loneliness and his longing for a lover-at-arms. Earlier, he mused:

> After having been so overwhelmed by the loneliness to which my inversion condemns me, is it really possible that I may some day hold naked in my arms... those young men whose courage and hardness place them so high in my esteem?... My tears make me feel soft. I melt. (8, 9)

No wonder the narrators' fantasy man, Querelle, feels depressed when he contemplates faggots. For he must be seen to shun such softness so he can be hard for the narrators' fantasy. Yet he is made to wear his shunning as a shawl:

> [This] quite depressing thought [about faggots] generated, up his spine, an immediate and rapid series of vibrations which quickly spread out over the entire surface of his black shoulders and covered them with a shawl woven out of shivers. (88)

For the narrators who have crafted it, Querelle's depressing thought about faggots their own self-debasement, as if they are wrapping themselves in a shawl of delicious shame, going both fabric soft and orgasmic in a quick spread of shivers.

Their self-envelopment, via Querelle, their sense of being dangerously surrounded, is even more fluid after his homicides. Here is Querelle flowing out of himself, then flowing back to fill himself, after killing a sailor like himself:

> Querelle grabbed [Vic] by the throat.... As Vic had the collar of his peacoat turned up, the blood... ran down the inside of his coat and over his jersey.... The murderer straightened his back. He was a thing.... Beautiful, immobile, dark thing, within whose cavities, the void becoming vocal, Querelle could hear it [himself as a thing] surge forth to escape with the sound, to surround him and to protect him. (61)

Here, of course, is that all-important wrapping: a kind of surround sound. Then, Querelle, after a pause, "snorted twice... moved his lips so that Querelle might enter [himself], flow into [his own] mouth, rise to the eyes, seep down to the fingers, fill the thing [himself] again" (62). Querelle is doing what the narrators do, both in fantasy and clothing: flowing out of themselves to surround themselves. He is how they hear themselves. He is even how the narrators see themselves, sexually surrounded and sacrificed.

In fact, unexpectedly, Querelle seeks sexually to sacrifice himself after killing Vic. The murder is his alibi for this act of martyrdom. To "wash him[self] clean," he seeks to be buggered by the owner of a brothel (a man named Nono). "This would be capital punishment," we read, a "sacrificial rite" (68). "It came... from an imperative that had issued from within himself"; "his own strength and vitality were ordering him to bend over" (72). Odder still, this sacrifice commences with a curious act of clothing. At the moment of Querelle's "self-execution," Querelle and Nono surprise each other by performing "a perfectly synchronized" gesture that indicates their mutual experience of wearing sailors' belts that buckle at the back—a sign of "their submission," say the narrators, "to the glamor of the naval uniform" (73). Submitting to this "glamor" in the sacrificial act, Querelle receives a genital wound. He is opened, like a sailor's belt, at the back. But notice the fanciful terms of this sacrifice. Nono, penetrating, "was holding Querelle with seemingly the same passion a female animal shows when holding the dead body of her young offspring—the attitude by which we comprehend what love is: consciousness of the division of what previously was one... while you yourself are watching yourself" (75). Here in the strangeness of the animal metaphor are those breaks from real relations and from individuality that Bataille predicts. Nono, as a mother in an animal pietà, is watching how, in sacrifice, an animal proxy is thrown from oneself (as part of oneself) in loving division. Then, as if the figure of the cop is required for this fantasy, too, making this holding (Nono's holding) a public display, we read next: "Querelle felt floored by the full weight of the French Police Force: . . . [a cop's] face was attempting to substitute itself for that of the man who was screwing him. Querelle ejaculated onto the velvet" (76). In *Querelle,* this kind of layered sociality makes debasement possible: the fantasy of French police, held in the face of a single cop, superimposed on a brothel owner's visage. By this eccentric setup, sacrifice passes through the martyr onto cloth. This is a gorgeous giving up of the ghost, as if, at the height of his crucifixion, Christ had climaxed on a lush altar cloth (and lived to tell the tale).

Realize, now, that the novel ends by returning to a pietà, one in which Querelle, then the lieutenant, plays the role of Christ. Actually, by a set of intricate ploys, Querelle bequeaths martyrdom to the lieutenant. With Querelle's help, the lieutenant accuses himself of a crime in order to aid a young man in jail.[33] This allows Lieutenant Seblon to wrap himself in the humility that he believes defines divinity. Cloth is required to mark this shame, largely because any wound to the cloth (even a stain) makes one aware of a uniform's glamour, thus showing outwardly how humility can mark divinity. So the lieutenant, on a tryst, in a thicket, happens to lie, belly down, on some waste, staining his uniform coat in the process:

> Shame went right to work on him. . . . In the mist . . . he still glimpsed the gold of the braids on his cuffs. As pride is humiliation's child, the officer now felt prouder than ever. . . . From this particular spot in Brest . . . a light breeze, gentler and lovelier than the petals of Saadi's roses, spread the humility of Lieutenant Seblon over the . . . world. (265–66)

Fittingly, this staining is the prelude to an ending, joining the lieutenant to the fantasy, Querelle. Their farewell is a scene of embrace, such as the lieutenant and the narrators have longed for. Now the fantasy hands his legacy back to his creators so they can possess it. In fact, Querelle, almost playing the faggot, is sending the lieutenant off to sacrifice himself:

> The officer pulled the sailor's head toward him, and Querelle rested his cheek on Seblon's thigh. . . . Then [Querelle] got up, throwing his arms round the officer's neck, and . . . riding the crest of a wave of femininity from god knows where, this gesture became a masterpiece of manly grace. . . . Querelle smiled at the thought of drawing so close to that shame from which there is no return, and in which one might well

> discover peace. . . . this phrase formed in his mind, saddening in all that it evoked of autumn, of stains, of delicate and mortal wounds: "Here's the one [Lieutenant Seblon] who will follow in my footsteps." (274)

Then the lieutenant, as if he is answering, although this is later and he is in custody: "I shall not know peace until he makes love to me, but only when he enters me and then lets me stretch out on my side across his thighs, holding me the way the dead Jesus is held in a Pietà" (275). This imagined wrapping in arms (the lieutenant, finally, getting held) forms the obvious climax of a fantasy—the narrators' fashioning of an animated garment. It forms as well Genet's fantastic fusion of the novel's divine humiliation with the humiliation of devotion to fabric. By this juncture, fantasy has turned the invert reader away from persecution toward a pietà that insulates, as does a cloak, the strangely self-embracing queer. This is a betrayal that reveals a secret grace:

> Thus [Lieutenant Seblon] dreamt of wearing a wide black cape, in which he could wrap himself. . . . Such a garment would set him apart, give him a hieratic and mysterious appearance. . . . To wear a pelerine, a cape. . . . In such a garment I would feel rolled up inside a wave, carried by it, curled up in its curve. The world and its incidents would cease at my door. (191–92)

As you will have guessed, the character and the novel named "Querelle" are such a cape: something any invert, to assuage her loneliness, can crawl inside and read like a book.

The Curve of Cloth

These are things these novels say about the curve of cloth. Actually, recent critics of fashion—many of them feminists—seem to understand that clothes (from the start of plainstyle for men in the nineteenth century—at least for white men of nonethnic cultures) operate a debasement aesthetic. Material meant to decorate, seen as aesthetic enrichment for the body, can visit debasement upon the wearer, even as the wearer may think she's being praised.

Queers rip the veil from this game of cloth. As the novels discussed above show, rushing to or from their clothes, queers unveil some unspoken agreements. "Men" (of the middle-class plainstyle variety) may not, by definition, have wounds on their clothes, but, still, they cannot wish strongly to be held by them. Clothes harm them least when they cease to behold them. Aesthetic recognition of even manly garments (one thinks of the lieutenant) may turn men toward the dangers of debasement. "Women," by contrast, who turn from cloth beauty may be supplied with substitute wounds (a skinned knee and formidable loneliness in Hall's *Well*; in Leslie Feinberg's *Stone Butch Blues*, gashes, burns, and pursuit by police). Only by such supplied debasements, in these novels, can they be let off the hook of aesthetics. Such is the shame at times attached to beauty. But, as I say, fashion theorists know this much. What they don't know is a martyrdom to clothes—what I have termed a pietà, a certain social holding of one's humiliation at the hands of something loved.

By these novel portraits we can ask ourselves why sacrifice appears in queer aesthetics. One reason must be obvious: a queer aesthetic that uncovers the shame that is so attached to beauty is likely to seem sacrificial if it wishes to hold onto beauty. The effort boldly to value shame (always a curve) is central to the legacy of a martyred god (as Hall knows and Genet lampoons, in his serious way). Shame, theologically, but so, too, aesthetically, is a kind of blush in the face of beauty. Shame can be a way of pointing at the glamour (by definition, "a seemingly mysterious and elusive fascination") that must in part escape us; even, by definition, must amaze us, causing, in Genet, a "submission to the glamor of the naval uniform."

More important, at least for this essay on these novels, clothing mimicks the action of sacrifice; it is the site of social sacrifice. The subject-in-clothes is cast to a realm outside itself—to a kind of "unreality," according to Bataille. Clothing, of course, would seem to contradict this; and, in some respects, it does. The subject-in-clothes seems, if anything, thrown to a public all too real, caught and held by a social world that, traditionally, has been devoid of caprice in its gender prescriptions. Here, however, is the insight of our novels: if the act of clothing is this public self-betrayal, in a known social field, clothing can also be a move toward self-enclosure inside the wrap of fantasy. When clothes seem inappropriate to wearers—for example, butch women adopting men's clothes—they discernibly signal a body broken from established versions of "real relations." As a result, the social field must hold, and behold, this wearer as one humiliated, cast beyond its reach. The question then arises of how the subject bears humiliation and her seeming break from the larger social field, even as she's held, on public display.

This is where the contexts of our novels are so telling. *Well's* negativity over social shame seems to stem from its Catholic groundings—ironically, the very source of Stephen's martyrdom—and its suggestion that the lesbian establishments of the 1920s (particularly for members of the British aristocracy) were sad places of humiliated loneliness. Consequently, there can be no holding of humiliation that is anything but loneliness. There is no pietà for Stephen in her clothes. By contrast, of course, *Stone Butch Blues*, which upholds the labor union and the lesbian bar as sites of productive failure and shame, shows a pietà of a striking sort. The couple, sartorially split from itself, is a fascinating figure for the holding *by* one's clothes. Each reads her shame from the other one's arms, so that their holding becomes humiliation at the hands of something loved. Beyond the enclosure of something like Feinberg's fantasy of bar life, Genet concocts the dreamscape of a military fog. Here, as we have seen, in the narrators' fantasy of beautiful Querelle, or in something simpler like an officer's cape, public self-betrayal of a dangerous sort is what the martyr risks. But this is a gamble for very large stakes, as I have been arguing all along. This is a wager for a kind of a social holding that begs no pity: the social solitude of a beautiful shame.

Notes

1. These are cultural stereotypes this essay will engage. From the outset, one should notice their narrowness—for all of their broad and sweeping generality. That is to say, they presume the reign of plainstyle for Euro-American men, of largely white and nonethnic cultures, largely beginning in the nineteenth century. They also presume a bourgeois, middlebrow preference for plainstyle. To gauge the extent to which they may still operate as forceful American cultural stereotypes, at least by the end of the 1990s, see Malcolm Gladwell, "Listening to Khakis: What America's Most Popular Pants Tell Us about the Way Guys Think," *New Yorker*, 28 July 1997, 54–65. Gladwell explores "the roundabout way [required] to sell a man a pair of pants," since "the man in the middle [of the economic spectrum] . . . probably isn't comfortable buying clothes at all" (55). Taking a look at the Dockers campaign (beginning in the fall of 1987), along with other spin-offs (Haggar ads, for instance), Gladwell examines "the notion of khakis as nonfashion-guy fashion" (56), which "lure[s] men . . . with the promise of a uniform," "so as not to scare them" (57). The point of these ads was "to talk about [fashion] in such a coded, cautious way that no man would ever think Dockers was suggesting that he wear khakis in order to look *pretty*" (62), since if a man "knows he is attractive and is beautifully dressed—then he's not a man anymore. He's a fop. He's effeminate" (62). Quentin Crisp adds to these views by filling in the picture for the period at the start of this study: "The

men of the twenties," Crisp writes, "searched themselves for vestiges of effeminacy as though for lice. They did not worry about their characters but about their hair and their clothes. Their predicament was that they must never be caught worrying about either.... the symbolism of clothes was recognized by everyone. To wear suede shoes was to be under suspicion" (*The Naked Civil Servant* [New York: Holt, Rinehart & Winston, 1968], 21–22). In many respects, my essay engages three novel portraits of what options fall to those queer people who feel the force of these stereotypes.

2. Leo Bersani, "Is the Rectum a Grave?" *October* 43 (winter 1987): 217, 222.

3. See ibid., 215; and Leo Bersani, *Homos* (Cambridge: Harvard University Press, 1995), 151–81.

4. Jean Genet, *Querelle*, trans. Anselm Hollo (New York: Grove, 1974), 88. Page numbers for further quotations from this source appear in parentheses in the text.

5. The modesty/protection/decoration trinity (with varying emphases placed on each) is the single greatest theme in the voluminous history of commenting on clothes. Nearly all studies relate themselves to these three "fundamental motives" (as J. C. Flugel deems them) for human clothing; see J. C. Flugel, *The Psychology of Clothes* (New York: International Universities Press, 1930). Studies of clothing in the context of consumption (Veblen, most obviously), and even of fashion as a system, also route themselves along this axis, although "decoration" is the category they expand in any number of social, political, and semiotic ways. As one would expect, commentary on the fashion system comes the closest to claiming that we are damaged by clothes. For a sampling of the range of texts that address the meanings and the motives behind human clothing, consider the following: Thomas Carlyle, *Sartor Resartus*, ed. Kerry McSweeney and Peter Sabor (New York: Oxford University Press, 1987); Herbert Spencer, *Principles of Sociology*, vol. 2, pt. 4 (New York: D. Appleton, 1896–97); Thorstein Veblen, *The Theory of the Leisure Class* (New York: Penguin, 1987); Georg Simmel, "Fashion," *American Journal of Sociology* 62 (1957): 541–58; Louis Flaccus, "Remarks on the Psychology of Clothes," *Pedagogical Seminary* 8 (1906); Knight Dunlap, "The Development and the Function of Clothing," *Journal of General Psychology* 1 (1928): 64; Hilaire Hiler, *From Nudity to Raiment* (London: Foyles, 1929); Bernard Rudofsky, *Are Clothes Modern?* (Chicago: P. Theobald, 1947); Lawrence Langner, *The Importance of Wearing Clothes* (Los Angeles: Elysium, 1991); Roland Barthes, *The Fashion System*, trans. Matthew Ward and Richard Howard (Berkeley: University of California Press, 1990); Elizabeth Wilson, *Adorned in Dreams: Fashion and Modernity* (Berkeley: University of California Press, 1985); Pearl Binder, *Dressing Up, Dressing Down* (London: Allen & Unwin, 1986); Ruth P. Rubinstein, *Dress Codes: Meanings and Messages in American Culture* (Boulder, Colo.: Westview, 1995); Juliet Ash and Elizabeth Wilson, eds., *Chic Thrills: A Fashion Reader* (Berkeley: University of California Press, 1993); Jane Gaines and Charlotte Herzog, *Fabrications: Costume and the Female Body* (New York: Routledge, 1990).

6. These definitions are taken from *Webster's New World Dictionary*, 3d college ed.

7. Sigmund Freud, "Femininity," in *New Introductory Lectures on Psychoanalysis*, ed. and trans. James Strachey (London: Hogarth, 1974), 132. All further quotations from Freud are from the same page.

8. On the atmosphere and events surrounding the banning of *The Well of Loneliness*, see Vera Brittain, *Radclyffe Hall: A Case of Obscenity?* (New York: A. S. Barnes, 1969).

9. Flugel, *The Psychology of Clothes*, 20–21. From reading Flugel, one is reminded that, apart from Freud, the vast majority of clothes commentators address themselves to "shame" generally. That is to say, although they all recognize sex and gender differences as critical to the meaning of clothes and to the development of fashion systems, they do not assign differential shame to the fact of men or women wearing clothes. Flugel, for example, discusses "modesty" and "decoration" (in Freud, "shame" and "vanity") as a compromise made by both sexes: "Clothes serve to cover the body, and thus gratify the impulse to modesty. But, at the same time, they may enhance the beauty of the body, and, indeed, as we have seen, this was probably their most primitive function. When the exhibitionistic tendency to display is thus lured away from the naked to the clothed body, it can gratify itself with far less opposition from the tendencies connected with modesty than it could when it was concentrated on the body in the state of Nature. It is as though both parties were contented with the new development, the compromise involved becoming in consequence a relatively stable one.... In fact, the whole psychology of clothes undergoes at once a great clarification and a great simplification, if this fundamental ambivalence in our attitude be fully grasped and continually held in mind" (21, 22).

Even where Flugel comes close to implying differential shame—for example, where he addresses men's removal of their hats in church, in contrast to women keeping theirs on ("the assumption is that clothes are a sign of disrespect in man, but nakedness a sign of disrespect in woman"; 104), his discussion veers off toward a different kind of point about exhibitionism. And although he invokes at several points "the castration complex," and at times in ways that indicate he must be assuming differential shame, his mentions of it never break out in the direction of a wounding attached to or worn on clothes (see 28, 30, 42, 102, 105, 120, 121). The closest he comes to direct statement is in his chapter titled "Individual Differences." Discussing the type of person who seems supremely overconfident in his choice of clothes, Flugel comments: "Such little evidence as I possess points to the excessive satisfaction with clothes being a compensation for an extreme intolerance of the naked body, an intolerance that is itself founded on a strong castration complex. If this should prove to be generally true, it would seem that persons of this type (all that I have so far met are of the male sex) cling desperately to a satisfaction in clothes, because these, in virtue of their phallic symbolism, give reassurance against the fear of phallic loss" (102).

10. For starters, one could consult writings by Jane Addams, Charlotte Perkins Gilman, Mary Wooley, Gertrude Stein, Virginia Woolf, Djuna Barnes, and Natalie Barney.

11. A famous pair of articles may be taken as an index to these debates. See Carroll Smith-Rosenberg, "Discourses of Sexuality and Subjectivity: The New Woman, 1870–1936," in *Hidden from History: Reclaiming the Gay and Lesbian Past*, ed. Martin Duberman, Martha Vicinus, and George Chauncey Jr. (New York: Meridian, 1989) (a revision of her final chapter in *Disorderly Conduct*, 1985); and Esther Newton, "The Mythic Mannish Lesbian: Radclyffe Hall and the New Woman," in the same volume (a revision of her essay in *Signs* from 1984). What makes these essays especially intriguing as a pair of essays representing split views is their common origin: a paper coauthored by these women in 1981, which itself appeared in French under the title "Le Myth de la lesbienne et la femme nouvelle," in *Strategies des femmes* (Paris: Editions Tierce, 1984).

12. Smith-Rosenberg, "Discourses of Sexuality and Subjectivity," 276, 279.
13. Ibid., 279.
14. Newton, "The Mythic Mannish Lesbian," 283.
15. *Webster's New World Dictionary,* 3d college ed.
16. For commentary on the largely antagonistic relationship between Bataille and Genet, see Edmund White, *Genet,* trans. Anselm Hollo (New York: Grove, 1974), 360, 397–98, 565. Especially germane is this observation: "Sadly, he [Bataille] and Genet had so much in common (a love of Sade, Gilles de Rais, Nietzsche, a taste for violence, steely eroticism and Catholic pomp) that they *should* have appreciated one another, but there is evidence of personal animus" (398).
17. Georges Bataille, *Theory of Religion,* trans. Robert Hurley (New York: Zone, 1992), 57.
18. Ibid., 44.
19. Ibid., 43, 45.
20. Ibid., 51.
21. Georges Bataille, "Sacrificial Mutilation and the Severed Ear of Vincent Van Gogh," in *Visions of Excess: Selected Writings, 1927–1939,* ed. and trans. Allan Stoekl (Minneapolis: University of Minnesota Press, 1985), 67. The madman's automutilation boldly illustrates the elements of sacrifice previously mentioned, especially those that link to fantasy: the destruction of real ties, the link to unreality, the draw out of utility, the restoration to unintelligible caprice. Bataille furnishes this example in his essay: "In the days that preceded the automutilation, he drank several glasses of rum or cognac. He still suspects that he was influenced by the biography of Van Gogh, in which he had read that the painter, during a spell of madness, had cut off his ear and sent it to a girl in a house of prostitution. It was then that, walking along the Boulevard de Menilmontant on December 11, he 'asked the sun for advice, got an idea into his head, stared at the sun to hypnotize himself, guessing that its answer was yes.' He thereby seemed to receive approval. 'Lazy man, get out of your sorry state' it seemed to be telling him, through thought transmission. 'It did not seem very hard,' he added, 'after contemplating suicide, to bite off a finger. I told myself: I can always do that'" (61–62).
22. Radclyffe Hall, *The Well of Loneliness* (New York: Anchor, 1990), 246. Page numbers for further quotations from this source appear in parentheses in the text.
23. Of course, these portraits can be overlapping categories. Esther Newton, in "The Mythic Mannish Lesbian," may be bridging both views. Consider these statements: "Cross-dressing for Hall is not a masquerade. It stands for the New Woman's rebellion against the male order and, at the same time, for the lesbian's desperate struggle to be and express her true self" (290). "*The Well* has continued to have meaning to lesbians because it confronts the stigma of lesbianism—as most lesbians have had to live it. . . . [The] reason for *The Well*'s continuing impact . . . is that Stephen Gordon articulated a gender orientation with which an important minority of lesbians still actively identify, and toward which another minority is erotically attracted" (282–83).
24. See Elizabeth Lopovsky Kennedy and Madeline D. Davis, *Boots of Leather, Slippers of Gold: The History of a Lesbian Community* (New York: Penguin, 1993), 9, 34, 328–31. For other indications of *Well*'s influence, see Una Troubridge, *The Life and Death of Radclyffe Hall* (London: Hammond, Hammond, 1961); Vern Bullough and Bonnie Bullough, "Lesbianism in the 1920s and 1930s: A Newfound Study,"

Signs 2 (summer 1977): 895–904; Blanche Wiesen Cook, "'Women Alone Stir My Imagination': Lesbianism and the Cultural Tradition," *Signs* 4 (summer 1979): 719–20.

25. The novel ends, of course, with Stephen's grandest sacrifice. Concerned to preserve Mary's future as a potentially normal woman, Stephen fakes her unfaithfulness to Mary, which sends Mary off, as Stephen plans, to the arms of Martin. (As another character puts it: "Aren't you being absurdly self-sacrificing?"; 433.) To be sure, Hall's novel draws to a close not with the assurance of salvation but with an odd kind of demon possession: "Oh, but there were many, these unbidden guests.... The quick, the dead, and the yet unborn—all calling her.... Aye, and those lost and terrible brothers from Alec's, they were here, and they also were calling: 'Stephen, Stephen, speak with your God and ask Him why He has left us forsaken!' She could see their marred and reproachful faces with the haunted, melancholy eyes of the invert" (436). The novel concludes with Stephen's unanswered plea to God: "We believe.... We have not denied you.... Acknowledge us, oh God.... Give us also the right to our existence!"

26. Leslie Feinberg, *Stone Butch Blues* (Ithaca, N.Y.: Firebrand, 1993), 5. Page numbers for further quotations from this source appear in parentheses in the text. Quite intriguingly, the novel's opening letter is so self-sustaining that it appears in Joan Nestle's edited volume *The Persistent Desire: A Femme-Butch Reader* (Boston: Alyson, 1992) as (what looks like) an archival document, presented with the title, "Letter to a Fifties Femme from a Stone Butch," by Leslie Feinberg. I assumed that it *was* archival until the publication of *Stone Butch Blues*. Ann Cvetkovich (see note 27, below) has noticed this oddity too. The phrase "fifties femme" is even confusing, since the protagonist of the novel, Jess Goldberg, is born in 1949 and thus frequents lesbian bars in the 1960s and 1970s.

27. On femme/butch as an erotic system, see the essays in Sally R. Munt and Cherry Smith, eds., *Butch/Femme: Inside Lesbian Gender* (London: Cassell, 1998), especially the essay by Ann Cvetkovich, "Untouchability and Vulnerability: Stone Butchness as Emotional Style." See also Sue-Ellen Case, "Toward a Butch-Femme Aesthetic," *Discourse* 11 (fall 1988/winter 1989): 55–73; Nestle, *The Persistent Desire;* Teresa de Lauretis, *The Practice of Love: Lesbian Sexuality and Perverse Desire* (Bloomington: Indiana University Press, 1994); Judith Halberstam, "Lesbian Masculinity or Even Stone Butches Get the Blues," *Women and Performance* 8 (1996): 61–73; Sally R. Munt, *Heroic Desire: Lesbian Identity and Cultural Space* (London: Cassell, 1997).

28. The acknowledgments to *Stone Butch Blues* are quite telling on this score. From the way Feinberg thanks the femmes in her life, we are asked to recognize the femme as demanding, critical, political, protecting, and even seminal: "You demanded that I write this novel"; "if I couldn't take criticism from a femme I wouldn't be here today telling this story"; "[you] consistently spoke up to defend butch lives as well as [your] own when voices like mine could not be heard"; "the thoughtfulness you brought to the editing was an extension of your political sensitivity"; "your commitment to this book—from planting the seed to midwifing its birth ('Push, push!')—flowed not only from your passionate beliefs but from your long history of political organizing." This is the voice of a feminist butch.

29. As it happens, it is not at all clear there was any such rule. Kennedy and Davis note in *Boots of Leather:* "According to Professor Nan Hunter of the Brooklyn College Law School, no such law exists (personal communcation, January 1992). It is her guess that a judge in a particular case made a ruling that two or three pieces

of clothing of the 'correct' sex negated male or female impersonation and that set a precedent used by law enforcement agencies" (411).

30. From a cross-comparison with *Boots of Leather, Slippers of Gold,* the oral history of this same community (also published in 1993), the *novelistic* work of *Stone Butch Blues* might become apparent, particularly its wonderfully worked-out investment in wounds as communal refusal of the cops. Although I don't want to ride this point too strongly and thus appear to correct a novel with an oral history, and although it may be that the bars in the late 1960s or the bars in Canada (where at least one raid takes place) showed a different picture than the Buffalo bars of the 1950s, it appears, if *Boots* is accurate, that there were very few raids in the fifties and very few bars in the 1960s. Police harassment, according to *Boots,* was largely directed at black lesbians and cross-dressing men of various races. White lesbians, according to these sources, took their beatings mostly from each other or from their attempts to "expand their territory" into other bars. See Kennedy and Davis, *Boots of Leather,* 41, 42, 46, 56, 63, 74, 90, 92–98, 127–28, 145–47, 149.

31. Although the novel's setting is named as Brest—and Genet appears to want us to know this—the novel, hung quite literally in a fog, gives no clue to historical setting or event. Even so, given the fact of Brest's wartime destruction, along with the novel's date of publication (1953), one can imagine that Genet's first readers could better appreciate that the novel's setting is a fantasy Brest. On the circumstances surrounding Genet's composition of *Querelle,* see White, *Genet,* 288–94.

32. One could regard this narratorial "we" as the royal "we" of a singular narrator; I am purposely deciding to take the "we" more literally—as a plurality.

33. We read in the novel: "The fact that the cop had recognized his generosity spurred the Lieutenant on to further sacrifices. It elated him.... He [the Lieutenant] became more and more attached to the young mason, in a mystical and specific way" (209, 210). As a matter of fact, this young mason, named Gil, who has murdered his coworker, is, quite dramatically, the victim of a cloth wound. He is the object of a cruel joke perpetrated by the queer bully Theo, whom he later kills in rage. The joke is this: Theo has gone through Gil's laundry bag and found a pair of his dirty briefs ("slightly soiled with shit and blood at the back"); when he lays them out on Gil's bed, they attract flies, along with the attention of all the other masons, who have gathered around to taunt. They use the cloth wound to suggest to Gil that he is open at the back.

CHAPTER THIRTEEN

Embodying Culture

Dorian's Wish

Audrey Jaffe

Here, from the middle of *The Picture of Dorian Gray* (1891), is Dorian Gray's recollection of his famous wish: "He had uttered a mad wish that he himself might remain young, and the face on the canvas bear the burden of his passions and sins; that the painted image might be seared with the lines of suffering and thought."[1] But his actual words (at the novel's beginning) are these: "If it were I who was always to be young, and the picture that was to grow old!" (49). Dorian's identity inheres in—is made of—the contrast and active interchange between the novel's constructions of beauty and ugliness; interpretations of the novel tend to rest on the meanings attributed to each. Yet it has never been noted that the moral weight the picture comes to bear during the course of the novel—the meaning Dorian himself attributes to it—is far removed from the initial whimsy that brings it into being. Dorian's wish for an exchange is itself exchanged, his original, impulsive desire for youth and his aversion to aging replaced by a morally charged scenario in which the picture becomes the bearer of "passions and sins." But this exchange is actually true to the novel's economics of degradation, since, as the portrait alters, what matters is not the type of action committed—not the kind of "degradation"—but rather (as if such matters are codifiable, and self-evidently so) the amount. The picture pictures accumulation, displaying not the detail of experience but the fact of it: we can't know, from looking at it, "what happened"—as the history of the novel's reception (and the insistent need to decode the changing image) suggests.

For Dorian, sin, old age, suffering, even "thought" are rendered equivalent in a generalized picture of degradation that looks like this:

> The cheeks would become hollow or flaccid, yellow crows' feet would creep round the fading eyes and make them horrible. The hair would lose its brightness, the mouth would gape or droop, would be foolish or gross, as the mouths of old men are. There would be the wrinkled throat, blue-veined hands, the twisted body, that he remembered in the grandfather who had been so stern to him in his boyhood. (153)

Or maybe this:

> Lying on the floor was a dead man, in evening dress, with a knife in his heart. He was withered, wrinkled, and loathsome of visage. It was not until they examined the rings that they recognized who it was. (264)

The speculations of the first passage ("the mouth would gape and droop") are, for all intents and purposes, fulfilled by the second. And yet as the picture reduces all degradation to a common currency—the currency of ugliness—it exposes the surprising presumption, given the subtleties of taste Dorian comes to embody, that when it comes to ugliness there is no question of taste, at least for Wilde's readers. In this sense the picture and the book express a widely shared fantasy about ugliness. Age and sin, the novel's circulation of ugliness terms ("hideous," "horrible," "wrinkled") suggests, are interchangeable not only with one another but also with other forms of the "loathsome," such as the figure of the "horrid old Jew" who owns the theater in which Sibyl Vane performs or the grandfather of whom Dorian has "hateful memories."

Dorian's beauty similarly lacks specificity. Like his ugliness, which attaches itself indistinguishably to the figures "old" and "Jew," it both evokes and denies affiliation. And despite the possibility of claiming affiliations for it—Eve Sedgwick, for instance, contrasts Wilde's middle-class Irishness with Dorian's aristocratic Englishness, whereas for Linda Dowling, Dorian's beauty has a Hellenic textual history[2]—within its immediate social and cultural context the novel's ideal of beauty ("gold hair, blue eyes, rose-red lips") constitutes an evacuation of meaning: it is meant to signify nothing other than beauty itself. Thus binding together ideal of beauty with exchangeable images of degradation, the novel forecloses its own celebration of insincerity as a multiplication of personalities into a stark division and accountability: the difference between beauty and ugliness.

Dorian's relation to his picture has, of course, been theorized in many ways, not least powerfully within the moral framework the novel itself provides. But the abstraction of Dorian's identity in an economy of appearances as well as the novel's special status in the history of homosexual identity allow for another kind of interpretation, one that attends to the relationship between cultural identities and the forms that come to embody them. For the difference between beauty and ugliness per se participates in the underlying binarism of contemporary identity politics, a construction that depends less on specific details of identity than on the positive or negative valuation of identities: on the positing of desire or its absence. Identity politics—like *Dorian Gray*—resolves what might be a multiplicity of identities into a choice between identities, in the form of a difference between self and other. And this difference, I wish to argue here, reflects the condition of belonging or not belonging to a group. Indeed, it is precisely because of the congruence among the ideologically constructed identities of the late nineteenth century, the image making of identity politics, and *Dorian Gray*'s figuration of identity as an interplay between valued and devalued images of the self that, in Wilde's novel, "we may catch the early strains of an identity politics whose anthem will eventually become loud enough to make itself heard even on Saint Patrick's Day."[3]

Dorian Gray illuminates, in several ways and with relevance to several different discourses, the aesthetic dimension of modern and contemporary identities. Attributing moral significance to the blots and marks the picture accumulates, the novel makes of a paradigmatic aesthetic difference—that between beauty and ugliness—a paradigmatic cultural drama that finds its echo in contemporary formulations of cultural and political identity. The difference between Dorian's original wish and his memory of it, for instance—the difference between an impulsive expression of the desire not to age and a moral narrative about sin and retribution—encapsulates the transformation of inchoate experience into moral narrative that characterizes the formation of cultural narratives.[4] In the drama Wilde's novel makes out of the difference between beauty and ugliness—the danger of discovery, the obsessive checking and rechecking of the picture, the adventures in "low life" whose meaning Dorian confirms on the surface of the portrait as soon as he lives them—the formation of cultural identity appears as the moralization or rationalization of aesthetic choices: choices whose meaning might be revealed in, or might just as well be hidden by, the face one chooses.

My argument situates *Dorian Gray* in the context of late-nineteenth-century ideologies that may be viewed as precursors of a modern symbolic politics of identity, ideologies in which the individual is with increasing frequency imagined as a member of a group. Relevant here is the Foucauldian account of a shift from action to essence in the formulation of nineteenth-century identities. But more useful is the model of nationalism, which serves as a general model of identity from the nineteenth century onward and accounts to some degree for both the affective passion and the dominant trope of male bonding in *Dorian Gray.* Nationalism, like identity politics, positions identity as the culmination of a narrative of desire and an effect of group membership; in it, desire for the latter—membership in the group—is indistinguishable from desire for the former, for identity per se (thus the relevance of Julia Kristeva's description of nationalism as a condition in which "to be" is "to belong").[5]

Neither person nor, exactly, character, Dorian is, the novel tells us, a "type": the "visible symbol" of the age (49). And, it has followed, the novel's critics have taken Dorian—and/as Wilde himself—to be a preeminent figure for and prefiguration of aesthetic culture and, more recently, modern male homosexual identity. But what happens at the intersection of character and cultural embodiment? What does it mean to imagine a culture "in the form of a person"?[6]

Toward the end of the nineteenth century, historians and theorists of sexuality agree, the shaping activities of medicine and law codified a variety of activities and modes of being into an identity. In the formulations of some critics, "what happened" is that at the end of the century homosexual persons, and homosexual culture, became visible.

> In the final week of April 1895 Oscar Wilde stood in the prisoner's dock of the Old Bailey, charged, in the dry words of the indictment, with "acts of gross indecency with another male person." . . . The prosecutor for the Crown explained to the jury in more vivid terms what this meant: Wilde and his co-defendant had joined in an "abominable traffic" in which young men were induced to engage in "giving their bodies, or selling them, to other men. . . ." Wilde answered these charges, as is well known, in a speech of sudden and impassioned energy. Passionately defending male love as the noblest of attachments, a love "such as Plato made the very basis of his philosophy, and such as you find in the sonnets of Michelangelo and Shakespeare," Wilde called it "pure" and "perfect" and "intellectual" . . . his superb self-possession and ringing peroration so electrifying that the courtroom listeners burst into spontaneous applause. . . . The applause of Wilde's listeners marks the sudden emergence into the public sphere of a modern discourse of male love

> formulated in the late Victorian period by such writers as Walter Pater and John Addington Symonds and Wilde himself, a new language of moral legitimacy pointing forward to Anglo-American decriminalization and, ultimately, a fully developed assertion of homosexual rights.[7]

> Thus, although Basil's painting is entirely exterior to the text, it provides the reference point for a mode of representation that admits the visible, erotic presence of the male body.[8]

> When Basil Hallward confesses his love for Dorian Gray, those who dwell under contemporary signs of Hellenism cannot help but hear the opening notes of their own song: "[A] while ago I went to a party... after I had been in the room about ten minutes... I suddenly became conscious that someone was looking at me.... When our eyes met, I felt that I was growing pale. A curious sensation of terror came over me, I knew that I had come face to face with someone [who]... would absorb my whole nature, my whole soul.... I have always been my own master; had at least always been so, till I met [him].... Something seemed to tell me that I was on the verge of a terrible crisis in my life."[9]

Offered as originary moments in the instantiation of modern male homosexual identity, these scenes (and the critical frames in which they are situated) may also be regarded as illustrations from a cultural history under construction. Moments at which homosexuality is said, with some suddenness, to become visible, they also demonstrate cultural identity's imaginary status: they are opportunities for identification, places where the self may, imaginatively, be located. Not just moments in the history of a cultural identity, that is, these are mirror scenes for the constitution of one, delineating for reader, spectator, consumer, and critic what I wish to call the imaginary body of culture. For rather than announcing that a particular identity has currency, visibility bestows that currency, and what "currency" means, in this sense, is availability for identification ("His attraction to Dorian Gray appears as nothing other than the first act of the now well developed drama of self-realization *we* call coming out").[10] Indeed, these scenes encapsulate a necessary moment in the constitution of an identity politics. Inscribing the new and attractive visibility of the subject as visibility itself, they register the transformation of a degraded image into an idealized one, or into a figure in whom, at least theoretically, anyone might see him- or herself. For, paradoxically, to enter into visiblity is to give up some degree of cultural difference at the very moment that one claims it: to enter into a common realm in which images of cultural identity circulate. As theorists of the visible from Jean Baudrillard to Kaja Silverman have reiterated, rather than registering the emergence into public light of something already in existence, visibility *is* that something, signaling the inseparability of identity from representation.[11] Cultural identity is, precisely, an identification with culture itself, with a generalized form of identity imagined as cultural embodiment.

Franco Moretti, Werner Sollors, and others have described a shift in constructions of identity during the eighteenth and nineteenth centuries from the (more or less) given to the invented. Invoking Benedict Anderson's idea of "imagined communities," for instance, Sollors describes the way in which, following the American and French Revolutions, "the immediate connectedness of the aristocracy was replaced by a mediated form of cohesion that depended, among other things, on literacy and 'national' (and ethnic) literatures." Literature and the circulation of printed texts in general, Anderson argues, assist in the formation of communities circumscribed less by birth or territorial boundaries than by their members' shared knowledge.[12]

Imagined communities, of course, require imagined identities—identities not limited (as the communities are not) to categories of nationality or ethnicity. Dowling's history of the Oxford movement, for instance, which uncovers the homosocial codings of the Oxford Hellenistic tradition, both reveals the embedding of one culture in another and details the making of a new culture, a new group identity, out of an already existing tradition. Yet although Dowling traces "the role of Victorian Hellenism in legitimating 'homosexuality' as an identity," what remains unelaborated in her account and elsewhere is the relationship between the (previously uncodified) individual and the (now codified) group, as the formation of a new identity is the formation of new identities, the invention of "homosexuality" the invention of individuals now deemed "homosexuals."[13] If such formations require new identities, that is, they also require the inculcation of desire for those identities—and, as a corollary, of a desire so seemingly fundamental that it tends to remain beneath the level of analysis: the desire for identity itself.[14]

In response to a literary-critical tradition oblivious to the homosexual or homosocial content of literary texts, recent readings have been devoted to the act of decoding. In the case of *The Picture of Dorian Gray,* the goal has been to return the novel to its specific historical and sexual context, reading against what Sedgwick calls the "alibi of abstraction": the abstract moralism, the evacuated sexuality, of the novel's once-standard interpretations.[15] Yet the abstractions on which the novel relies, the empty terms of its codings, and above all the definitive binarism on which it depends remain unavoidable; it is, after all, the affiliation between the aristocratic male body and the abstraction "beauty" that allows for the text's general currency. Regarded as one of modern male homosexual identity's most important icons, Dorian Gray is also a paradigmatic cultural image: an image that, making no secret of its desirability, defines its culture's requirements for beauty (hence its class determination, aristocratic, and its national one, English). Dorian symbolizes his era in more ways than one: his beauty is no more idealized within the context of his coterie than it is in Victorian England generally, and it is the abstractness of that beauty—the protean significance of his cultural ideality—that enables not only him but the novel itself to "pass." Returning some degree of abstraction to the novel's interpretation, therefore—and returning to the abstractions on which the novel relies—I wish to locate desire for Dorian, and Dorian's desire, within a more inclusive eroticization of identity, one in which Dorian's wish to "be" his picture reveals identity itself, here allegorized as culture's visible form, as one of the modern subject's most sought after objects of desire. Thus the late-nineteenth-century ideology that, following Foucault's logic, is said to have redefined self in terms of sexuality—the ideology in which "who I am" becomes "what I want"—is here reimagined with ontology as desire's subject, so that what is "wanted" is, precisely, "who I am": identity itself.

Jeff Nunokawa writes that the achievement of Wilde's novel was to give modern homosexual identity a human face.[16] And indeed, the novel accomplishes this in precisely the kind of narrative sleight of hand that, belying the direction of the narrative itself, enables Nunokawa's comment to pass without eliciting the obvious questions: How, exactly, "human"? More compellingly, which face? The conversion of loss into gain that the novel effects—the way the enduring image of the beautiful Dorian emerges from an ostensible narrative of decline—resembles what might be called the conversion narrative of identity politics: Dorian dies into representation, his beauty prefiguring what Dowling refers to as the current wide acceptance of homosexuality by the dominant culture, functioning as a kind of projection into the future, an invitation to the transformation of the image of homosexuality itself.[17] The novel's erotics, I thus wish to suggest, is finally a cultural one, its language of sexual desire supporting a narrative of cultural desire, a desire for cultural embodiment. Dorian's wish is a wish for beauty, but Dorian's beauty is a figure for the desirability of a certain modern configuration of identity: for the achievement of identity as a place in a cultural narrative.[18]

In his book on the politics of American identity, *Our America,* Walter Michaels takes aim at what he calls the essentialist bias of all accounts of cultural identity: the way in which, in his words, these accounts "understand culture as a kind of person."[19] To understand culture as a kind of person is, for Michaels, to tie actions to essence, identifying oneself with ancestors whose experiences and memories one did not share. To no good end, cultures are imagined to possess identities, argues Michaels, and inherent value is (therefore) attributed to their survival.

But how is it that a set of practices (Michaels's definition of culture) comes to be identified with personhood? How do habits acquire the nimbus of identity? Why is the sum more than its parts? (Or, how is it that "modern homosexual identity" comes to acquire a "face," and what does it mean that it does?) One answer might lie in Foucault's discussion of the way late-nineteenth-century medical and juridical discourses transformed practice into identity, making "possible the formation of a 'reverse' discourse: homosexuality began to speak in its own behalf, to demand that its legitimacy or 'naturality' be acknowledged, often in the same vocabulary, using the same categories by which it was medically disqualified."[20] To a certain extent this formulation begs the question, since rather than explaining personification, it personifies—"homosexuality began to speak in its own behalf." But it nevertheless suggests a formulation similar to the one I am advancing here: that desirable images of cultural identity emerge in response to, and are inseparable from, what Judith Butler calls the "injurious term" that gives a particular identity its name—the term that, in the Althusserian scenario of interpellation, calls it into being.[21] And it suggests, too, via the rhetoric of personification, the role the group plays in this identity-forming narrative: that it is possible to speak on one's "behalf" only once identity has been defined in mutual terms, as something shared with others.

If we pursue the implications of Foucault's narrative, in which conflicting images of identity exist in necessary relation to one another, then Wilde's picture-painting scene—the scene in which Dorian recognizes himself "as if for the first time"—begins to resemble a positive alternative to the Althusserian scenario in which the subject is hailed as a subject of the law. Indeed, the scene seems itself to constitute a response, in the form of a counternarrative, to the question Butler poses about Althusser's scenario: "Why should I turn around?"[22]

> The lad started, as if awakened from some dream. "Is it really finished?" He murmured, stepping down from the platform.
>
> "Quite finished," said the painter. "And you have sat splendidly today. I am awfully obliged to you."
>
> "That is entirely due to me," broke in Lord Henry. "Isn't it, Mr. Gray?"
>
> Dorian made no answer, but passed listlessly in front of his picture, and turned towards it. When he saw it he drew back, and his cheeks flushed for a moment with pleasure. A look of joy came into his eyes, as if he had recognized himself for the first time. (48)

For Butler, the offer of identity is itself compelling: the subject turns, despite his or her ostensible guilt, because identity is an offer that cannot be refused. Wilde's version, imagined as response or resistance to the Althusserian scene, reproduces its form but not its content: Dorian's response to the picture enacts a fantasy of self-hailing in which the self answers to its own desire rather than to the admonitory call of the law. What seems important, then, is not the problematic and perhaps undecidable status of the self that turns (must not that self—so the question goes—already be a subject in order to turn?), but rather the similar structures of these dissimilar scenes: the way both Althusser and Wilde figure the production of identity as a turn toward it, both imagining identity as that which, in a narrative of desire, one moves toward. What compels and confers identity, in these scenarios, is nothing other than the desire for it.

And that desire, once again, is the desire to belong. For the self hailed here, as in Althusser, is not, nor can it be, self-appointed; rather, it is the effect of the existence of the group, or—as Butler puts it—of society. For if, as Butler suggests, the desire for identity is the desire to be constituted socially, then identity must take shape as the image of social life.[23] And so it does in *Dorian Gray.* In a discussion preceding Dorian's arrival, Lord Henry Wotton and Basil Hallward discuss the partial nature of their own and others' identities: one possesses intellect and talent, another beauty, another wealth ("Your rank and wealth, Harry; my brains, such as they are—my art, whatever it may be worth; Dorian

Gray's good looks"). Dorian, in this conversation, is said to possess only beauty: "He is some brainless, beautiful creature, who should always be here in winter when we have no flowers to look at" (25), and when he appears he is indeed depicted as not yet in possession of an identity—he is empty of and available for one. Yet at the end of this scene—the scene in which Basil paints the famous portrait—Dorian possesses all the qualities Henry, Basil, and formerly Dorian himself possessed individually. Indeed, the apparent fluidity of identity boundaries in the painting scene is arrested by the emergence of Dorian's identity as the only one that counts (there are three bodies here, but finally only one identity), and he is constructed not only as an image of the others' desire but as an embodiment of their very qualities: of Basil's images and Henry's words.

As Lee Edelman has argued, Wilde's novel inscribes identity in a narrative of desire.[24] From the novel's initial representations of Dorian as beautiful vacancy and potential, to the look that comes into the lad's face that Basil had never seen there before (41), to Dorian's "recognition" of himself in the portrait, identity is something Dorian achieves in the picture-painting scene, and it is the result not just of his own wish, but of the combined yearnings of all three characters. In these scenes, the group is imagined as a body, with each member possessing some aspect of the whole, and Dorian is the projected image of that whole—a composite body. It is this wholeness that he "recognizes . . . as if for the first time" in the picture, this wholeness that makes the picture the place he wants to occupy. Desire for Dorian—including Dorian's desire for himself as picture—is desire for the imagined wholeness of the group. Indeed, it is the impossibility of distinguishing between desire for a particular individual and desire for cultural embodiment that Dorian's wish to change places with the picture defines and that defines the picture of Dorian Gray.

Thus when Dorian's image appears on the canvas, the very picture of Basil's desire for him and of Henry's influence, not only does the novel dramatize what Ed Cohen has called the inscription of homoerotic desire, but it also allegorizes the emergence of cultural identity per se as an effect of triangulated desire. It is the *idea* of culture that takes shape here in, and as, an imaginary body, and the idea of the group—of the self as an idealized projection of others—that enables the replacement, or at least the overlapping, of the injurious name with the beautiful face. If in Althusser's narrative the policeman's call is the call of the dominant culture, defining the respondent as guilty before the law, Wilde's alternative scenario offers the reverse fantasy, or the subject's fantasy of reversal: an allegory of being interpellated as an object of desire. Collapsing the difference Freud wished to maintain (in his discussions of homosexuality) between desire for and possession of the other, it suggests a fantasy of such perfect identification with the other that the other turns out to be, for better or worse, the self.[25]

This scenario perhaps explains why it is that identity, even when, if not especially when, imagined as one's own, must often (if not always) be constituted with reference to an external image.[26] For in producing Dorian's idealized image, the painting scene allegorizes the element of desire that transforms practice into personhood. A set of practices does not constitute a culture; only a set of practices endowed with meaning and value does. And such a set of practices, as Michaels's argument suggests, necessarily takes an embodied form: culture is always what someone else (even, as *Dorian Gray* makes clear, one's own self imagined as someone else) is doing. Culture is not a "set" of practices but rather a reading of them, an interpretation that unifies disparate practices, attaching meaning to action and in this way individualizing it, with the idea of the individual—of actions performed by someone—giving coherence to the activity of the group. Dorian Gray thus figures in this argument as an exemplary image of a person who is also an embodiment of culture—an embodiment of a particular culture, to be sure, but also an allegory for the way culture in general takes shape "as a kind of person."

But what kind of culture, and what kind of person? The rhetoric of exchange—specifically, of changing places—that informs Dorian's wish and structures his story further reinforces the importance of the idea of culture to the imagining of modern identities. And here the narrative of identity politics gives way, at least briefly, to that of cosmetology—to the very real (no longer magical, that is) issue of choosing a face.

Dorian wishes, of course, for both faces, the beautiful and the ugly—not for just one or the other, but rather for the exchange between them. And his desire is fulfilled not only by the beautiful face but by the ugly one, with its marks and blotches, as well—and by the way each supplements the other, each suggests meanings the other fails to provide. For despite the exchangeability of images discussed earlier in this essay, Wilde's novel does attribute value to ugliness. As part of the narrative culminating in Dorian's death, the picture evinces the temporality he rejects:

it ages, wrinkles, degrades. But it also reflects a process of accumulation: the portrait turns sin into gain by rendering it visible. This is, after all, where Dorian's actions appear, where his experience accumulates like capital. Like a miser visiting his wealth, Dorian obsessively checks his profits, and each blotch and wrinkle challenges the novel's moralizing with an equally compelling logic of accumulation. Despite the absence of individuality that the novel's general representation of ugliness suggests, then, the accumulation of marks on the picture's surface does suggest the possibility of individuality: here, at least, something is happening. Why, then, is it not a pretty picture?

In the Murad advertisement shown in Figure 13.1 (an advertisement for a wrinkle-removing cream for women and an implicit updating of the Dorian Gray scenario), the lines on the woman's face are replaced by—are, indeed, visible only as—the advertiser's lines, labeled with the contents of a cultural narrative (and directed toward both the woman's image and its audience—"the day *you* totaled the car"). The projected replacement of one face with another replaces one narrative with another. The face (and, indeed, the identity of its owner) is in fact figured as a kind of map, each mark rendering "invisible" experience visible, denoting a site at which something happened. But of course rather than simply rendering the invisible visible, the marks denote the absence of anything but cultural narrative; the map, like Dorian's hideous portrait, figures the indistinguishability of authentic self and cultural projection.

Since identity becomes visible only when marked as cultural narrative, both identities—the ugly (or less desirable) and the beautiful—appear as pictures. The fantasy, and the parallel in contemporary culture (and an important element of the *Dorian Gray* scenario), is that one can participate in (embody) cultural values without giving up one's "real" self. Here, as in Wilde's novel, the "ugly" self occupies the position of the real and is similarly imagined as detachable: that to which one necessarily refers, one's undesirable face is also that which one need not (but for the grace of God, and plastic surgery) own. Notably, the ugly face is the particularized one, whereas the attractive face is generalized, the latter's evacuation of experience rendering it available for a spectator's projections. The femininity of the Murad ad's Wildean revision is thus relevant to the novel's construction of Dorian's identity, for the visual cues that conventionally invite spectatorly identification and fantasy—that re-

Figure 13.1. Murad advertisement.

sult in a spectator's perception of blankness and availability—are in our culture, as in Wilde's, denoted feminine.[27]

What happens, then, to the self one does not want to be—the self whose identifications the subject refuses? The advertisement relies for its persuasiveness on its ability to appeal to a spectator who wants to erase, but also values, experience's marks: with its labels insisting on the very debilities the cream is to erase, the ad suggests not exactly (or not only) the effacement of experience, but rather its dematerialization or internalization. Like the picture of Dorian Gray, it offers the spectator an opportunity to embody the cultural ideal yet simultaneously possess an alternative, authentic self—not exactly keeping the body that records that experience, but rather (although perhaps with less energy than one devotes to actively maintaining, or attempting to achieve, the culturally idealized body) preserving it as mental picture: maintaining the memory of such a body. Dorian's obsessive return to his hideous image—the way he commits his "sins" in a spirit of scientific inquiry, in order to gauge their effect on the picture (124); the way he finds himself, inexplicably, "enamoured" of it (135)—suggests a similar desire for a self that isn't picture-perfect, a self one can call one's own. For the attraction of the ugly self is the lure of authenticity—of the cultural authority granted the idea of the true self. Read thus, as a narrative about a choice of cultural narratives, Wilde's novel may appear to be less about sin—either in general or any particular variety—than about the eroticization of particular images of cultural identity and of the idea of cultural identity itself.[28]

The idea of culture invests a single person's actions with the identity, the shared meaning, of the group; put another way, in cultural identity, the identity of the group is discernible—made palpable—in a single person's actions. Culture, according to this logic, is always embodied, always a matter of value manifested in someone's appearance, someone's place. Indeed, as a matter of imagining the other as a person with whom one can, and would like to, as Lord Henry himself wistfully suggests, change places ("I wish I could change places with you, Dorian"; 256), cultural identity collapses person into place; identity becomes a cultural position, a place one can occupy. And just as culture depends on the illusion that a practice is more than a practice, so too does changing places substitute being for doing, so that culture makes itself, and reproduces itself, by substituting identity for practice, imagining practice in embodied form. *Dorian Gray*'s scenario of "changing places" short-circuits a scenario of imitation (I do what you do) with a scenario of identity (I become you, put myself in your place) in which identity, seemingly kept intact, in fact is revealed as nothing more than a function of place. Pictured outside the self, the identity one wants—which one wants because it is pictured—appears knowable and available for occupation. (In the world according to *Dorian Gray*—the world, the Murad ad tells us, we still inhabit—there is always a more desirable version of "you" out there.) "Changing places" replaces narrative and temporality with substitution and magic, exchanging a condition of desire in which identity is always slipping away with one in which identity is to be had for the asking—or the wishing.

Even as it is said to signal the new visibility—the emergence into public light—of late-Victorian homosexual culture, then, *The Picture of Dorian Gray* allegorizes the general desire that transforms practice into culture, that marks the difference between practice and culture. Culture appears here as a structure in which practices have meaning precisely because, and only because, someone else is performing them.[29] Why is it, I have asked of Foucault's account of nineteenth-century identities, that individuals not only accept the terms of their medicalization, but take on those identities, begin to speak "in their own behalf"? The eroticization and idealization of group identity in the projection of an imaginary body figures culture's invitation to spectators to recognize themselves—and seek to place themselves—in a symbolic structure not of their own creation. Dorian's beauty signals the illusory achievement of an identification with culture itself; it is the beauty of identity as wish fulfillment, a fantasy of experience invested with value. Desire for Dorian captures the lure of cultural narrative as the context in which, at a historical moment that is ours as much as Dorian Gray's, self-recognition can and does take place. Identity as this novel figures it—and, I have suggested, contemporary identity politics does as well—is the imagined occupation of a place in a cultural narrative, a place that takes visible form as an imaginary body whose identification with the group gives new meaning to the visual fullness of the Lacanian imaginary. Put simply, there are too many people in it.[30]

Diana Fuss has defined identity politics as "the tendency to base one's politics on a sense of personal identity—as gay, as Jewish, as Black, as female."[31] But this definition classifies as personal what are obviously terms of group affiliation, terms whose appropriation guarantees visibility in the symbolic realms of culture and politics. In the model I have described here, "identity politics" is reconceived, on the model of late-nineteenth-century ideologies, as the creation of a desirable identity, its crucial mechanism the projection of that identity in an imaginary body. Identity politics is, precisely, the attempt to bestow value on culturally devalued identities; it transforms ugliness (a particular identity as perceived by the dominant culture) into beauty (that same identity, as projected in response by the group so named), and its mechanism is the transformative power of the image of the group. In the "identity" of identity politics, the individual and the group function as reflexes and projections of one another—mutually constitutive images—with the group functioning as the engine of the desire for identity, the body out of which individual bodies are made. That same desire for visibility—without, of course, the accompanying political concern—is manifest in the desire to inhabit a spectacularized, mass-produced version of beauty. In both cases, cultural identity takes shape as an implicit opposition between images of ideality and degradation; in both, identity is constituted as an exchange between identities—identities imagined, finally, as different versions of the self.

The body imagined as desirable, I have suggested, is the body of culture: the projection of culture as an imaginary body. Such a formation depends not just on the desirability of particular identities, but on the positing of identity itself as desirable; that with which everyone must identify, it is also that which everyone must desire. Thus embodied, identity presents itself as something to be desired, something to be wished for, something others could imagine being. Imagining identity as a body whose place a spectator may wish to occupy, and as a person with whom one might like to change places, Wilde's novel renders visible the element of desire out of which cultures are made.

To return, then, to Michaels's problem with the personification of culture: the problem (if it is one) is not that we imagine culture as a person, and that we could have it some other way. The problem, or the issue, is that culture *is,* essentially, the imagining of the self in another's place (or, as in *Dorian Gray,* simply in another place), a fantasy of participating in an experience that has meaning precisely because it is—at least figuratively—someone else's. This logic both explains and resituates what I would call our own culture's persistent *Dorian Gray* fantasy: the nagging suspicion that one's true self is really somewhere—if not, indeed, somebody—else.

Notes

1. Oscar Wilde, *The Picture of Dorian Gray* (Harmondsworth: Penguin, 1985), 119. Page numbers for further quotations from this source appear in parentheses in the text.

2. Eve Kosofsky Sedgwick, *Tendencies* (Durham, N.C.: Duke University Press, 1993), 151; Linda Dowling, *Hellenism and Homosexuality in Victorian Oxford* (Ithaca, N.Y.: Cornell University Press, 1994), 150.

3. Jeff Nunokawa, "Homosexual Desire and the Effacement of the Self in *The Picture of Dorian Gray*," *American Imago* 49 (1992): 313.

4. My sense of the way experience becomes cultural narrative, as argued here, is indebted to Walter Michaels's account of cultural identities in *Our America* (Durham, N.C.: Duke University Press, 1995). I refer to the transformation of events, actions, or choices (such as, for instance, the eating of matzoh or the not-eating of pork) into identity-producing narratives. A version of this may be seen in Foucault's narrative about the construction of homosexuality as an identity, as well as in Linda Dowling's discussion of the formation of a homosexual cultural tradition. Michel Foucault, *The History of Sexuality*, vol. 1 (New York: Vintage, 1980); Dowling, *Hellenism and Homosexuality.*

5. "Subjectively, the issue of 'national' identity is that indistinct domain of psychic and historical experience which transforms identity into belonging." Julia Kristeva, "Proust: In Search of Identity," in *The Jew in the Text: Modernity and the Construction of Identity*, ed. Linda Nochlin and Tamar Garb (London: Thames & Hudson, 1995), 140.

6. Michaels, *Our America*, 80. Eve Kosofsky Sedgwick discusses "reading *Dorian Gray* from our twentieth-century vantage point where the name Oscar Wilde virtually *means* homosexual" in *Epistemology of the Closet* (Berkeley: University of California Press, 1990), 165; see also Nunokawa, "Homosexual Desire"; Ed Cohen, "Writing Gone Wilde: Homoerotic Desire in the Closet of Representation," *PMLA* 102 (October 1987): 801–13.

7. Dowling, *Hellenism and Homosexuality*, 1–2.

8. Cohen, "Writing Gone Wilde," 806.

9. Nunokawa, "Homosexual Desire," 312.

10. Ibid., emphasis added.

11. See, for instance, Jean Baudrillard, *Simulations* (New York: Semiotext[e], 1983); Kaja Silverman, *The Threshold of the Visible World* (New York: Routledge, 1995).

12. Werner Sollors, *The Invention of Ethnicity* (New York: Oxford, 1989), xi; Franco Moretti, *The Way of the World* (London: Verso, 1987); Benedict Anderson, *Imagined Communities: Reflection on the Origins and Spread of Nationalism* (London: Verso, 1985).

13. Dowling, *Hellenism and Homosexuality*, 31.

14. Foucault's work has, of course, explored in detail the means by which subjectivity is produced through techniques such as confession and self-examination. My concern here lies closer to the problem Judith Butler explores in *The Psychic Life of Power: Theories in Subjection* (Stanford, Calif.: Stanford University Press, 1997) when she asks what causes us to desire our own subjection (see 102).

15. Sedgwick, *Epistemology of the Closet*, 164.

16. Nunokawa, "Homosexual Desire," 313.

17. Dowling, *Hellenism and Homosexuality*, 31. Dowling locates Wilde at the origin of "the modern emergence of homosexuality as a positive social identity" (xvi). She also implicitly recognizes the role played by the group in transforming homosexuality's image: "Such writers as Symonds and Pater and Wilde . . . find the opening

in which 'homosexuality' might begin to be understood as itself a mode of self-development and diversity, no longer a sin or crime or disastrous civic debility but a social identity functioning within a fund of shared human potentialities, now recognized *as* shared" (31).

18. It is, of course, important that the paradigmatic representation of this desire is figured as the difference between beautiful and ugly male bodies. In *Epistemology of the Closet,* Sedgwick argues that many significant late-nineteenth-century concepts take the male body as their metaphorical shape: "In the development toward eugenic thought around and after the turn of the century, reifications such as 'the strong,' 'the weak,' 'the nation,' 'civilization,' particular classes, 'the race,' and even 'life' itself have assumed the vitalized anthropomorphic outlines of the individual male body and object of medical expertise" (178). I want to emphasize both the cultural specificity of *Dorian Gray*'s images and what might be called the novel's will to abstractness: the way the opposition between beauty and ugliness encapsulates the binary construction of identity in identity politics.

19. Michaels, *Our America,* 180.

20. Foucault, *The History of Sexuality,* 101.

21. "Called by an injurious name, I come into social being, and because I have a certain inevitable attachment to my existence, because a certain narcissism takes hold of any term that confers existence, I am led to embrace the terms that injure me because they constitute me socially" (Butler, *The Psychic Life of Power,* 104). "Existence," in this formulation, is the same as being constituted socially: life is equated with cultural life, with existing within the context of the social group.

22. Ibid., 108.

23. Ibid., 104.

24. Lee Edelman, *Homographesis: Essays in Gay Literary and Cultural Theory* (New York: Routledge, 1994), 17.

25. For a discussion of this issue in relation to Freud's construction of homosexuality, see Diana Fuss, *Identification Papers* (New York: Routledge, 1995), 12, 19.

26. The clearest formulation of this is Lacan's mirror scene, in which self-recognition involves the reflection of the self as mediated by the gazes of others. See Jacques Lacan, "The Mirror Stage," in *Écrits: A Selection,* trans. Alan Sheridan (New York: W. W. Norton, 1977), 1–7.

27. See Natalie Angier, "Nothing Becomes a Man More than a Woman's Face." *New York Times,* 1 September 1998, B6.

28. Even as the medical/juridical establishment creates a type, Dowling suggests in *Hellenism and Homosexuality,* a cultural tradition for that type emerges deliberately and self-consciously, using as its framework another, previously existing tradition. The form that the "coded counterdiscourse" (xv) of homosexuality takes, in Dowling's reading, supports my formulation of culture as always someone else's at the same time that it deconstructs the idea of an "original" tradition by suggesting that traditions always emerge in discourse with one another.

29. This formulation is obviously indebted to René Girard's idea of triangular desire. See René Girard, *Deceit, Desire, and the Novel: Self and Other in Literary Structure,* trans. Yvonne Freccero (Baltimore: Johns Hopkins University Press, 1965), chap. 1.

30. See note 26, above.

31. Diana Fuss, *Essentially Speaking* (New York: Routledge, 1994), 103.

CHAPTER FOURTEEN

Bad Taste, the Root Evil

I. A. Richards and the Postnational Subject

Howard Horwitz

Formalism and Basic English

Was I. A. Richards the first postcolonial theorist? The answer to this question is undoubtedly no, but the question is not as absurd as it may at first seem. His efforts over forty years to spread C. K. Ogden's Basic English, an 850-word world language, makes him arguably the first transnational, indeed postnational, theorist. Basic English belonged to an extensive movement in the early decades of the twentieth century to develop an artificial language, like Esperanto, to serve as a world language. Basic English was a successful example of the movement, with branches in twenty-five countries, including China, by the late 1930s. Basic English translations of books ranging from the Bible to Plato to Shakespeare appeared, along with introductions to various topics by authors such as William Empson. Winston Churchill and Franklin Delano Roosevelt commissioned feasibility studies of Basic's possible government use.[1] Richards promoted Basic English to rally support for the United Nations, and more broadly to convert people from thinking of themselves as national citizens, a habit of mind that Richards engenders to violence and imperial domination. Basic English seems a curious vehicle for Richards's political idealism, given that he ascribed the political and cultural crises of his lifetime largely to citizens' inability to comprehend the complexity and "resourcefulness" of language, so fundamentally ambiguous that readers and auditors must attend primarily to shifts in the meaning of words.[2] Reducing a language to 850 words would seem an unlikely device for enhancing our sensitivity to ambiguity, yet Richards espoused Basic English as a model way to cultivate such sensitivity.

The Basic English project recasts Richards's critical theory. As the inaugurator of critical methods that evolved into the New Criticism, Richards is often nowadays impugned as a formalist who reduced literature to what Wellek and Warren later called its "aesthetic function." To the formalist, the meaning of literature subsists entirely in the way it exploits "the resources of language." Wellek and Warren thus extol literature (or any work of art) as "an object of knowledge *sui generis* which has a special ontological status." Literature is a "mode of existence," exhibiting "identity" or "unity" between its "content" and its "form," a unity that intimates the unity of experience and that readers can apprehend by attending to structure.[3]

New Criticism's focus on the formal, specifically linguistic, properties of texts supposedly neglected the contexts in which literature is produced and criticism is undertaken. Such formalism, we tend to hold, generates criticism that is ahistorical, hence apolitical, and thus by default conservative.[4] Critics today wish to avoid even the appearance of formalism. We deny that the form of an artifact alone embodies that artifact's meaning. Instead, we generally affirm, the meaning or significance of an artifact emerges in relation to some larger context or framework, usually history, psychology, economics, gender relations, class relations, or cultural politics generally. Regarding writing as an exemplary social activity, our avowed antiformalism thus permits criticism to be revisionary, reshaping the contexts in which it is performed.

Richards, too, viewed writing (and also reading) as a profoundly social act,[5] as scholars such as Richard Ohmann, Terry Eagleton, and Gerald Graff have shown.[6] Beginning with his seminal work of the 1920s, from which New Criticism evolved and English studies acquired the shape it still largely possesses, Richards proclaimed that the fate of culture depends upon how we read. Culture is in chaos, Richards lamented; we are poor readers afflicted with "disorganized," "disordered" sensibilities. "Bad taste and crude responses are not mere flaws in an otherwise admirable person," Richards declared in his groundbreaking *Principles of Literary Criticism* (1925). "They are actually a root evil from which other defects follow."[7] To save culture from disorder, Richards sought to forge reading subjects duly responsive to art and its ambiguity.

Bad taste, the root evil. As literary scholars, we should be so lucky; for then our enterprise might be more highly valued. With its elementary moral analogy, the idea that bad taste is the root evil may now seem a quaint idea—at least inside the academy. Yet Richards secured respect and funding for literary studies precisely by stressing the political import of taste. Poetry—and, more important, how we "use" poetry—is the emblematic "means of ordering our minds."[8] The poet uses words, Richards writes in *Science and Poetry* (1926), "*as a means of ordering, controlling and consolidating*" experience. Therefore, proclaims a well-known maxim in the peroration of this volume, poetry "is capable of saving us, . . . of preserving us or rescuing us from confusion and frustration."[9] Poetry fulfills its salvific office only when accorded the kind of attention it demands. "The quality of the reading we give" poetry measures "the degree in which we can order ourselves" (*Practical,* 327, 329). This ability to order ourselves symbolizes our ability to order culture, and Richards therefore urged at the end of *Practical Criticism* (1929) the appointment of Chairs of Significs, who would be better equipped than scholars from competing disciplines to understand fundamental principles of social order (314).

Richards taunted aesthetic theory for its inadequate account of meaning, by which he meant the psychological ordering that constitutes experience and that art consummates. He sought to develop a theory of interpretation or theory of criticism (*Practical,* 316; *Principles,* 10) adequate to this process along with "educational methods" to enhance readers' "discrimination," meaning their own psychic ordering (*Practical,* 3). Richards's term for proper psychological ordering is *satisfaction,* and this political economy of satisfaction is the basis not just of aesthetic pleasure, but of all value, which is the true subject of the critic. Value, for Richards, involves maximal coordination of mental impulses, or "appetencies." Aesthetic satisfaction is valuable because it provides the foundation for ordered cultural economies.

If Richards's efforts inaugurated a movement training readers to construe meaning only by performing technical operations upon the form that art takes, Richards himself was no formalist of this sort. He repeatedly reminded his readers that language is ambiguous and must be apprehended as it shifts about in specific contexts. No technical operation works for all contexts, he insisted. Instead, readers must vigilantly examine ambiguity, or "Multiple Definition,"[10] the recurring shifts in meaning.

Basic English was intended to train readers' sensitivity to ambiguity, which is to say, to develop taste, which would include active cultivation of cultural diversity.[11] Like his theory of interpretation generally, however, Basic English accomplishes this goal by resorting to a formalism, which I will call ontological idealism, far more fundamental than any formal technique we might associate with the New Criticism. In many practical ways Richards remains our forebear. Obviously his focus on close reading still underpins our pedagogy. But also, Richards's efforts to spread Basic English and thereby engender citizens who do not identify themselves with a singular cultural or national regime prefigure recent attempts by theorists such as Homi Bhabha to understand the way the "ambivalence of language" discloses the ambivalence underlying the idea of nationality. For Bhabha, the ambivalence of language disarticulates the ideology of nations and our subjectification by that idea,[12] thus permitting new "forms of cultural identity and political solidarity" not grounded in national or even finally ethnic identity.[13] If Richards's most political work does anticipate current critiques of national identity, it is worth examining whether or not key contemporary literary theory has sloughed off Richards's deep formalism. Richards sought to promote satisfaction and "order" in selves and the social order. Today we increasingly value art and criticism for their capacity to unsettle selves and cultural orders. Dissatisfaction is the new order of the day, but even while promoting a new affect for the subject, a new taste, efforts to reimagine the subject refurbish Richards's ontological formalism.

The Two I. A. Richardses

For Richards, the office of the critic/teacher is to forge subjects who experience a particular kind of pleasure in art (and hence in any experience). Richards doubts the value of most persons' experience. Recall the idiosyncratic "protocols" or short interpretive essays that Richards, in *Practical Criticism,* asks his hapless students to write about anonymous poems. His students' responses are wildly impressionistic, often missing the basic grammatical sense of poems. No doubt this experiment illustrates Richards's point in *Principles of Literary Criticism* that any phenomenon, even simple objects, "can arouse in different persons and in the same person at different times extremely different states of mind." Such "variety of response" (9) indicates that persons consist of "a welter of disconnected impulses." Amid this welter, "always some impulse, or set of impulses . . . interferes, or conflicts, with others" (183, 46). This interference among impulses renders individuals unable to regulate their conduct and social interactions. In the tradition of Plato's *Republic*, which Richards later translated into Basic English,[14] Richards is allegorizing the relation between psychology and the state. The order (or disorder) of the mind symbolizes the ordering of the state. Richards defines identity as "a system of interests." Experience involves "disequilibrium" or "perturbation" among our constitutive interests. The question is whether experience will involve incessant disequilibrium, and hence the welter that precipitated the Great War, or resolve into equilibrium (*Sciences*, 30, 26, 28).

Richards held out some hope that equilibrium could be achieved by formal interpretive techniques. As the experience of art is for Richards emblematic of mental economy and finally political economy, a formal interpretive method seems an attractive mechanism for governing the psychic and social orders. Richards tries most directly in *Practical Criticism* to develop a formal method to remedy his students' bewilderment. Bewilderment, however, seems virtually inevitable, because language is inherently ambiguous. Cultural arbiters "dread . . . the bewilderment that might ensue if we recognised and investigated the inevitable ambiguity of . . . verbal formulae" (320). Richards stressed throughout his career the ineluctable ambiguity of language. Words mean only in context; meaning is "the interactions of words with one another."[15] As he wrote in the chapter on Basic English in *Interpretation in Teaching* (1938), "any word's meaning [depends] on the other words present with it and on the purpose which, together, they are attempting to fulfill."[16] Consequently, the meaning of words "shifts" with each subsequent word in a series.[17] Nor does word order in itself manifest the purpose of the speaker or writer; the same series of words can express different purposes. In sum, because words are "linked with all . . . words and phrases in an unimaginably multifarious manner,"[18] all words are instances of Multiple Definition, the (shifting) linguistic situation confronting all interpreters.

The reason for the fundamental "indefiniteness" or "indefinition" of language is the metaphorical nature of language and also thought.[19]

Metaphor is not just a poetic technique for arousing emotions, but the basic principle of abstraction by which we apprehend what Richards and Ogden call "sign-situations."[20] "Thinking is radically metaphoric"; it works through analogy, "by which a sign stands for (takes the place of) an instance of a sort. To think of anything is to take it as of a sort (as a such and such)."[21] Signs do not correspond to their referents, and so all thought as well as language is a form of translation (a point Richards ponders at length in *Mencius on the Mind*). Because thought and language are indefinite, metaphoric, forms of translation, forms of noncorrespondence, signs must be ambiguous. The inherent ambiguity of language renders "correct understanding . . . a triumph against odds. We must cease to regard a misinterpretation as a mere unlucky accident" (*Practical*, 315).

Fortunately, ambiguity is "systematic," and Richards can therefore envision "a reasoned general technique for construing" (*Practical*, 323, 294). Richards's formal method involves breaking what he calls "total meaning" into four "contributory meanings"—sense, tone, intention, aim (*Practical*, 173–81). When in doubt about the meaning of an utterance or line in a poem, the reader identifies one of these elements and then uses this understanding as the basis for determining the other components and finally the total meaning.[22] This procedure is formalist in the familiar sense: it presumes that meaning is construed by attention to the inherent properties of language and literary form. Richards's method fails, however. Richards himself asserts numerous times that the four contributory elements of meaning are inseparable and hard to distinguish, since they always work in "combination" (*Practical*, 176–77). If the four contributory meanings are commingled, then no one of them can be isolated as a foundation for determining the others.

Take the example of irony. An ironic remark means something different from the dictionary meanings of its individual words. Hence identifying the apparent "sense" of an ironic remark can only be misleading, because the meaning of the ironic utterance positively departs from the dictionary meanings of its words. Nor can identifying the tone help a reader understand the so-called sense of the utterance, for sense and tone here are identical. The sense of the utterance *is* its ironic tone. In general, to have an account of tone is already to have an account of sense and intention, indeed of the entire utterance. We can conclude that Richards's formal method is utterly circular: one must already have an interpretation of an utterance in order to specify its tone, sense, and so forth. Attention to Richards's four contributory meanings provides no help in understanding any of the others, and finally the so-called total meaning, because these categories, really, don't exist. There is no total meaning, only meaning.

As I suggested above, Richards intuits this fact, discussing often the inseparability of the (finally illusory) contributory elements. Richards therefore abandons his systematic endeavor throughout much of *Practical Criticism.* Although he often heralds a systematic technique for construal, he stops attempting to describe one. During the bulk of *Practical Criticism,* Richards largely ignores his method and extols instead what we might call "unsupported" taste. This mode of reading overcomes the primary obstacle to correct interpretation: habit. Readers tend to impose preconceptions upon texts, and they therefore do not read them but traffic in "stock responses" (chap. 5, 223–40; chap. 8, 275–87). Readers must surrender their preconceptions. Such a reader, "unprovided by any such criteria, theories and principles, often feels himself distressingly at a loss before a poem." This unencumbered reader faces "too sheer a challenge to his own unsupported self" (296). But only such an unsupported self can "triumph against odds" to perform "correct interpretation" (315). One might think that without principles to restrain preconceptions, readers' interpretations will be entirely stock responses. Yet the unsupported self triumphs over ambiguity precisely for having perilously dispensed with preconceptions. Once purified of a structure of beliefs—with belief defined as distorting preconception—the reader can develop "a little pertinacity [in] . . . examining our intellectual . . . instruments" (314).

Richards's criterion for interpretive success now becomes "the quality of the reading" rather than its mere "correctness" (*Practical,* 327). Gerald Graff has argued that Richards's "denial of the validity of principles" renders him unable to verify interpretations and the value of poetics.[23] Graff's analysis is logically correct, but perhaps misses the point. "Quality" of interpretation does not here supersede "correct" interpretation but rather encompasses it. The Ricardian aesthetic subject, by transcending the ordinary mode of perception (habits!), is now able to examine the criteria of judgment that formerly shaped, and thus skewed, interpretation. The unsupported reader is able to study the principles of ambiguity itself. This is what it means to have taste.

Satisfaction and Being

Taste redeems experience "from being a mere welter of disconnected impulses" by inducing equilibrium among the subject's interests (*Sciences,* 34). Richards calls this condition satisfaction, and it exists when waste is eliminated from the political economy of identity.[24] In a "wasteful [mental] organization," some appetencies are "thwarted or starved" when others are realized (*Sciences,* 36; *Principles,* 52). In ordinary mental economies, appetencies compete haphazardly; each "interferes, or conflicts, with others" (*Principles,* 46). Experience therefore involves perpetual conflict, because the very components of experience by definition negate each other.

Notably, Richards does not seek to replace the language of impulse and appetency, adapted from experimental psychology.[25] But he did believe that the psychological economy for satisfying appetency is incompletely systematized and therefore inefficient (*Principles,* 46). Adapting a widespread anxiety about waste and inefficiency in the period (exhibited by figures as disparate as Thorstein Veblen and F. W. Taylor), Richards abhors waste because it offends the mind, whose "function is to coordinate"; "a growing order is the principle of the mind" (*Principles,* 50). By definition, however, the diversity of impulses composing mind makes competition among appetencies inevitable. "Every systematization in the degree to which it is stable involves a degree of sacrifice." Appetencies imply opportunities for action, and so each impulse satisfied means that a "price [is] paid in opportunities foregone." Richards gauges the success of mental economies "by the extent of the loss, the range of impulses thwarted or starved" (*Principles,* 52). Richards thus advances a Benthamite economy of mind:[26] the greatest good for the greatest number of appetencies. Mind "attempts[s] to organise impulses so that success is obtained for the greater number or mass of them, for the most important and the weightiest set" (*Principles,* 46). That which is "valuable . . . will satisfy an appetency without involving the frustration of some equal or *more important appetency*" (*Principles,* 48). "The most valuable states of mind . . . involve the widest and most comprehensive co-ordination of activities and the least curtailment, conflict, starvation and restriction" (*Principles,* 59).

People of refined sensibilities possess such a well-coordinated psychic political economy, and can function more widely or fully, to use Richards's terms.[27] They

> are those fortunate people who have achieved an ordered life, whose systems have developed clearing-houses by which the varying claims of different impulses are adjusted. Their free untrammeled activity gains for them a maximum of varied satisfactions and involves a minimum of suppression and sacrifice. (*Principles,* 53)

Three apparent paradoxes attend Richards's characterization of his optimal aesthetic subject, which is to say optimal subject. First, by suppressing numerous impulses, refined subjectivities experience "a *maximum* of varied satisfactions." Although Richards seeks coordination of response, he is not opposed per se to variety of response. He indeed craves variety, but ordinarily the mind entertains variety so unsystematically that it cannot be said to respond variously but only haphazardly. Only a nervous system "in a high state of vigilance" can value variety and respond discriminatingly to it (*Principles,* 181, 184). Second, the fortunate few, who suppress so well conflict among appetencies, surprisingly experience "a *minimum* of suppression and sacrifice." Richards is describing effects here. The well-ordered mind negotiates the claims of rival appetencies so well that it does not feel that satisfying one appetency curtails others; indeed, quantitatively more impulses are available to experience. Richards can therefore happily submit a third paradox, in which the vigilant nervous system feels "free" and "untrammeled" rather than, well, vigilant. The satisfied person has "the feeling of freedom" (*Principles,* 235). Richards does not use the term *freedom* here in a metaphysical way. Derived from psychologists like Charles Sherrington and William James, freedom means the feeling "of relief" (*Principles,* 235) from having incessantly to resolve conflicts among competing appetencies.

An important question remains: How does the disordered subject become ordered (tasteful)? Significantly, the formalism that Richards helped develop—attention to the form and language of the poem, to metaphor and other figural language, to paradox and its resolution—does not finally help otherwise disordered readers and viewers apprehend and acquire art's economy. Because of "the amazing interdependence of our words," which makes "language . . . very like a society" (*Basic,* 65; *Page,* 103), meaning is context specific, and no formal method can anticipate the possible variety of linguistic contexts. Therefore, as Richards writes in *How to Read a Page,* "In general, all the reader has . . . is his ability to see how a passage hangs together" (65). Fortunately for humanists, poetry itself cultivates the capacity to coordinate appetencies and is thus indispensable to "free, varied and unwasteful life." "In ordinary life a thousand considerations prohibit for most of us any complete working out of our response," Richards writes. "But in the 'imaginative experience' these obstacles are removed" (*Principles,* 237). "The ordinary man suppresses nine-tenths of his impulses, because he is incapable of managing them without confusion." The poet's "superior power of ordering experience" makes available to him a far greater range of impulses, until he expresses "completeness of . . . response." Freed from the narrow pathways of habit, the artist enjoys "greater plasticity" of response (*Principles,* 243–44).

Art cultivates plasticity of response (good taste) through a kind of natural transmission. The poet "brings order out of chaos" because he is "concerned with the record and perpetuation of the experiences which seem to him most worth having" (*Principles,* 61). *Perpetuate,* a term adapted from the post-Darwinian discourse still entering the language during Richards's formative years, is a curious notion to apply to the effect of poetry. In what sense can art be said to *perpetuate* experience? The idea that art perpetuates experience suggests for one thing that for Richards art is not mimetic. *The Meaning of Meaning* explains that no mode of reference, not even so-called statements, is mimetic. Reference "is not a question of matching between images." Thoughts or propositions do not "copy" or "represent" "the things to which the reference points."[28] Art, therefore—which Richards calls "pseudo-statement" only because it does not imitate or correspond to phenomena—is judged by "its effect in releasing or organizing our impulses and attitudes" (*Sciences,* 60).

Although a poem does not imitate an object or activity, it should represent the experience of a phenomenon. The poet selects words

> because the interests whose movement is the growth of the poem combine to bring them, just in this form, into his consciousness *as a means of ordering, controlling and consolidating* the uttered experience of which they are themselves a main part. The experience itself, the tide of impulses sweeping through the mind, is the source and the sanction of the words. They represent this experience itself, not any set of perceptions or reflections." (*Sciences,* 33)

This passage indicates what it means to say that poetry perpetuates the experience it represents. Here, the "experience itself," not the poet, selects words; the "interests [in] movement" bring the words to mind. Poetic pseudostatements, then, perpetuate experience because in them experience perpetuates itself. Aesthetic representation is perpetuation. The words, although no doubt abstracted from the experience, "represent" the experience insofar as they transmit it.

Poetry perpetuates a specific mode of experience, aesthetic experience, that epitomizes the mind's tendency to order. Aesthetic experience itself elicits words that consolidate the experience they partially compose. The aesthetic, for Richards, actively seeks to control the movement (perturbation) that constitutes it. Poetry and the poet therefore quite naturally display order; the experience perpetuated is the activity of ordering. Here emerges a deeper formalism than that of any formal method. Whatever the apparent subject of art, all aesthetic experience has finally the same content, that of ordering. The content of aesthetic experience is its form: the activity of ordering. And this formal quality of aesthetic experience perpetuates itself in the reader. The tasteful reader experiences the process of ordering itself. Ordinarily, experience involves a "metaphorical distance," "a gap between what knows and what is known." In aesthetic experience, this gap "can close down to nothing. What the mind then knows is its own activity—KNOWING becomes BEING" (*Page*, 178).

Emancipation from Words

By such perpetuation poetry saves us from confusion, which is to say poetry saves us from ourselves. By ordering appetencies, aesthetic experience converts bewilderment into satisfaction, thus converting "ordinary" subjects into aesthetic subjects. Once art has redeemed the psychic economy, appetencies lose their identity as appetencies, no longer needing to be singularly satisfied. Key features of the self are superseded, specifically preconceptions, but habit generally, the very framework in which experience occurs. Despite his debt to William James, who insisted upon and even lauded the indispensability of habit to identity,[29] Richards frequently laments the way habit frames new experiences. The poet's activity, in contrast, "outwits the force of habit; the impulses he awakens are freed, through the very means by which they are aroused, from the inhibitions that ordinary circumstances encourage" (*Principles*, 244).

Richards must be entertaining another of his paradoxes here, for can an impulse travel a pathway that is not habitual? Richards's sources in experimental psychology postulated that habit structures the interaction among impulses. Richards objects that such neurological guidance "abbreviates" responses (*Principles,* 244). The term *abbreviate* makes sense here only if impulse begins undirected and is then compromised by being directed. But what could an undirected impulse be, since impulses by definition move and movement entails direction? Richards resolves this contradiction by concocting impulses exempt from movement. Recall that the poet's superior power of ordering experience frees him from having to suppress nine-tenths of experience in order to avoid confusion. "Impulses which commonly interfere with one another and are conflicting, independent, and mutually distractive, in him [the poet] combine into a stable poise" (*Principles,* 243). Poetry perpetuates this equipoise in the attuned reader.

> The equilibrium of opposed impulses, which we suspect to be the ground-plan of the most valuable aesthetic responses, brings into play far more of our personality than is possible in experiences of a more defined emotion. We cease to be oriented in one definite direction; more facets of the mind are exposed and, what is the same thing, more aspects of things are able to affect us. To respond, not through one narrow channel of interest, but simultaneously and coherently through many, is to be *disinterested* in the only sense of the word which concerns us here. (*Principles,* 251)

Richards's disinterested aesthetic subject, although constituted by impulse, is freed from the effects of impulse, freed from orientation. Only when deconstituted as an impulsive subject can the subject understand and evaluate value. Only when removed from or freed from oneself, that is, can one become truly oneself and have taste.

Ironically, Ricardian taste is finally a mode of discrimination that does not discriminate. Richards's disoriented subject, for whom knowledge has become being, has no knowledge with which to discriminate. When the metaphorical gap in knowledge is overcome, Richards affirms, "we may wonder if [the subject] still 'knows,' whether . . . 'know' here [is] a useful word." Richards believes that cessation of knowing is an ideal condition "toward which . . . the whole universe strives" (*Page,* 178). Here is the true formalism, which we can call the ontological idealism, of Richards's aesthetic theory. It holds that the capacity for critique depends upon the formal character of the subject. A subject is a function not of its beliefs and actions but of its mode of mental activity, its mode of being, a feature of subjectivity not produced within culture, indeed not produced at all. Richards asks of the subject, Are its impulses in movement or at equipoise? Does it know phenomena or simply experience itself? Richards's ontological formalism explains why he does not even register what strikes me as a crucial contradiction in his argument. He complains that untrained readers are both disorganized (a welter of responses) and habitual, or too organized. Yet being too organized (habitual) amounts for Richards to being disordered, because the real culprit here is culture, which is to say specific values, orientation.

Richards must finally discount as well a key form of orientation, of which the literary critic would seem most solicitous: language. Our relation to language is, of course, utterly habitual, which we might call idiomatic. Certain words seem to fit together; linguistic associations abound. But readers may therefore impose idiosyncratic associations upon word series. Thus Richards heralds in *Practical Criticism* "an intelligence perfectly emancipated from words," who will recognize ordinary discourse as routine, poorly understood rhetorical "manoeuvres" (325). Because "interconnections" and "interactions" among words and the mental associations that constitute the meaning of words render language ambiguous, Richards explains in *How to Read a Page,* only "thought freed from words might see all these interrelations together" (186). One might reasonably ask, How can someone emancipated from words have any understanding of words? Richards himself sympathized with this question,[30] but the equipoise that Richards envisions must be freed from words, as from all concrete forms of experience, from all orientation.

Richards's view of the aesthetic subject informs his view of education. Despite his abhorrence of waste, Richards disavows advancing any "special ethical idea" (*Principles,* 51). Richards's implausible disavowal is crucial to his project, which involves improving culture by overcoming acculturation. The Ricardian teacher advances no special ethical idea because training in equilibrium occurs through poetry itself. Since poetry perpetuates valuable experience, reading and teaching merely provide poetry the opportunity to perpetuate itself. Richards himself would agree that such a view smacks of crude philosophical realism. He ridicules those "who define communication as the actual transference of experience." Such a view involves the "transcendental consideration" "that minds interpenetrate and mingle" (*Principles,* 175). Nevertheless, Richards's theory of communication involves a radical form of transference: experience transfers itself. If we understand language—if we understand ourselves—through language, our ideas are in danger (the greatest danger of all) of being susceptible to vagaries of habitual association.[31]

It is in order to control the self (and its constitutive political economy) by transcending the self, Richards declares, quite fantastically, that the poem itself perpetuates equilibrium in the tasteful reader. The poem must be experience perpetuating itself, with the poet merely its corporeal vehicle and the reader an inchoate organism in which the aesthetic experience induces order. On this view, poems, value, aesthetics, subjects are modes of being without particular content. They can therefore be culturally efficacious because valuable art perpetuates no specific value but the very constitution of value, the equipoise of ordered experience. Particularity of impulse—orientation—disturbs psychic political economy precisely by making it specific. Poems perpetuate the mind's innate (but obstructed) tendency to order rather than specific values like Catholicism or hedonism or radicalism.

Transcending the Nation

Richards's ontological idealism, in which persons and ideas are disembodied, seems inconsistent with his notion that aesthetic experience perpetuates itself. "Perpetuate" is a corporeal activity, and indeed stems not only from post-Darwinian discourse but from nationalist discourse of the day. Whether or not experiences perpetuate themselves, species do. During this period, social scientists and members of the elite classes complained that the finest of the species were not perpetuating themselves in sufficient numbers. "Perpetuation," that is, comes most specifically from eugenics discourse, ubiquitous in the period, with its protests that the lower classes were outbreeding the so-called artisan classes, what we now call the professional and managerial classes. Eugenists sought to regulate breeding patterns to order the melange of social interaction.[32] Thus Richards could quite inveterately define his theoretical and pedagogical objectives, and in particular the goal of Basic English, as enabling persons (more precisely, their ideas) to "breed a better race of ideas" (*Basic,* 115).[33]

Richards's aesthetics mutes the generally abominable racism of eugenics discourse. He writes: "The disparity among the states of mind recognised as good by persons of different races, habits and civilizations is overwhelming" (*Principles,* 44). The eugenist premise here is that different races exhibit different character traits. Yet Richards does not make invidious distinctions among racially specific character traits, and indeed he applauds the disparity they represent.[34] Likewise, liberal eugenists such as Havelock Ellis in Britain and Luther Burbank in the United States sought to maximize each race's best traits by encouraging the most "fit" (whatever this term might mean) of each race to breed (and the "unfit" to exercise patriotic restraint).[35]

Richards responded to disparity a bit differently. In principle, disparity of response is indispensable to maximal psychic economy (satisfaction); yet disparity of response was in practice excessive, threatening (to continue the eugenist conceit) to waste not only individual appetencies but the best appetencies of the nation. Richards's model of aesthetics and education was meant to coordinate disparate appetencies in the nation (whose managerial class he was training). He promoted Basic English as the best mechanism for achieving maximization of response. Basic English, then, fulfills Richards's hopes for his theory of interpretation, overcoming particularity of meaning, bewilderment at ambiguity, and particularity of identity, finally of national identity.

Nations and Peace, a 1947 volume written in Basic English that Richards hoped would advance the cause and objectives of the United Nations, explains the peril of national identification. Nationhood, for Richards, is truly, to use Benedict Anderson's term, an "imagined community." Citizens have internalized narratives of national development and imagine what Anderson calls "communion" with compatriots they will never meet and with whom they may have little in common. Nationhood, that is, is a mode of identification, involving "a conception of personhood."[36] Nations, Richards writes, "are kept up by feelings."[37] These feelings posit an analogy between ourselves and the nation, imagined as an extension of "a common living place," whose sovereignty protects our individual sovereignty. The nation "is greater than we are. At the same time it is ourselves. If it becomes greater we seem to become greater ourselves. A wound to it seems a wound to ourselves" (*Nations,* 8, 24–25). This identification through the nation is sustained largely through what Anderson calls "the *attachment* that peoples feel for the inventions of their imaginations."[38] As Richards formulates the point in Basic English, national identification involves "pictures" we hold of the past and of our relation to that past and to others who putatively share it. "Our pictures of our own nation and of other nations are chiefly made up of feelings" (*Nations*, 27).

Nationalist feelings inevitably involve aggression, however. Nations arise semiotically, against other nations: "The power of any nation changes with the powers of other nations." Precisely because they need to confirm their sovereignty, nations view themselves in competition with other nations, and so the feelings sustaining nations are "chiefly fears of and pressures from other nations" (*Nations*, 30, 29). Particular nations therefore behave like a "special interest" among all nations (*Nations*, 76), and we can see that Richards's view of international relations parallels in macrocosm his view of identity as a political economy among perpetually interacting interests (or appetencies). These interactions may well be harmonious, but they start as competitive. Appetencies and interests seem so autonomous that identity is best understood as a mode of foreign policy. Richards distinguishes two mental economies in his 1926 *Science and Poetry*, one "a kind of Treaty of Versailles," the other "a League of Nations." The Versailles mental economy, which Richards brands "Tradition," "assign[s] frontiers and spheres of influence to . . . different interests, . . . based chiefly upon conquest." In this mode, interests compete for scarce resources, one prospering by vanquishing others. The League of Nations mental economy is not "a new balance of power, a new arrangement of conquests," phrases suggesting that conflict among interests is only temporarily suspended. Instead, the League of Nations economy is "the moral ordering of the impulses," "a new order based on conciliation, not on attempted suppression" (*Sciences*, 40).

In this "new [mental and world] order," specific interests cease to exert specific influence. In the new order, citizens no longer identify themselves with nations, but are "supranational," as Richards put it in *Basic English and Its Uses* (1943). Such an identification supersedes notions like "international" and "foreign affairs," which, like the Treaty of Versailles mental economy, involve "mutual restraint" among competing entities. Supranational citizenship involves "purposes transcending those of any nation" or alliance (*Basic*, 12–13).[39] Richards's supranational political economy mirrors his ideal of satisfaction, in which impulses, although yielding to others, experience no restraint. In Richards's supranational model, "planetary citizens" or "universal citizens" belong to the "United People of the earth," under a World Government, yet experience no restraint upon any singular national identification. A citizen of the UP feels no less a citizen of Russia or the United States (*Nations,* 157). Note a common feature of both planetary citizenship and the mental economy of satisfaction. In the supranational model, one becomes an ideal national citizen by "transcending" the interests forming national identification; likewise, satisfaction realizes impulses precisely by transcending them. In both cases, specific impulses or interests become substantless, generating no conflict because exerting no influence on mental or political economy. Impulses, interests, identities, and finally nations are fully realized only when derealized.

Basic English promotes the psychological economy effecting the supranational ideal. Basic English will unite the world by furnishing a common language and thus the "techniques for a common culture" (*Basic,* 44). Richards advocated Basic English rather than Esperanto or ido precisely because it is based on an actual language that many already use and many more will inevitably learn. Against charges of linguistic imperialism,[40] Richards stipulated that a common language "neither can nor should be imposed by one nation . . . upon others."

> It must carry no implications of intellectual, technological, or other domination. . . . We can guard against this danger only by conceiving a world language in a truly planetary spirit—as a universal medium, not as an extension of the sphere of influence of some one pressure group. (*Basic,* 11)

Basic English avoids linguistic imperialism, and succeeds as a "universal medium," by illustrating the fundamental condition of language, interpretation, and thought: ambiguity, indefinition. Although Basic necessarily involves the "reduction and ordering of the meanings" of words, Richards, unlike Ogden and promoters of other artificial languages, did not regard Basic English as a means to increase precision by eliminating idiomatic nuances (*Basic,* 25).[41] Richards trumpeted Basic English's imprecision. Its imprecision exemplifies the ambiguity of language, the way words (and, for that matter, all thought) are metaphorical, substituting for but not corresponding to referents. Basic English thus attunes readers to the way the meaning of words is not "fixed for all occasions" (*Basic,* 61). Basic English forces us

> to see that a word (or a sentence) works by relating itself in various ways to various other influences in the passage. . . . We cease to think of it as

> an isolated, self-governing addition. We realize instead that it is a component. And with the dissipation of the cloudy magic-charged concept of the proper or true meanings of separated words, the way is open to a fruitful exploration of the structures of meaning.[42]

Working in Basic English, then, is "very nearly a pure exercise *in interpretation.*"[43] It is a universal medium because it provokes users to contemplate the structure of meaning and experience rather than to focus on the meaning of words. Basic English debunks the myth that words have proper meanings, which Richards called the Proper Meaning Superstition. Basic English disabuses readers of the "superstition that every good sentence or paragraph should have one and only one meaning." It alerts us to the multifarious opportunities in language, to the range of possible uses and interpretations of words.[44] Thus Basic's "very limitations" "provoke thought" about linguistic parameters and about the responsibilities of usage, thereby enhancing the "quality of understanding and reflection" (*Basic,* 119, 118). By not purporting to furnish meaning, Basic English "promote[s]" "strict critical examination and questioning of meanings."[45]

Richards calls this effect "freedom" from "blind adherence to rules worked out by others" (*Basic,* 120). Such freedom is again ontological. By sensitizing users to ambiguity, to the multifarious indefinition of words and identity, Basic English's reductiveness frees aesthetic subjects from believing in the meaning of words. Basic English produces Richards's aesthetic subject, who is free because words convey no definite meaning and because language users have no deep commitment to what words mean, as they have no knowledge at all. Basic English functions, that is, by derealizing itself and its users. Words and users both lack definite content. The supranational subject is Richards's aesthetic subject, freed from preconceptions (from its belief structures) because it understands that language does not finally mean. Here, both language and subjectivity exist only as structural principles, without particular content or orientation (and thereby qualifying as universal mediums).

Something Else Besides

As we have already seen, however, that which eschews orientation is not free but rather does not exist. The freedom of Richards's supranational, aesthetic subject is self-negating, because the supranational subject has no definite existence, no orientation. Richards's aesthetic subject can have no guiding beliefs, no definite commitments; and the language in which the subject operates must also eschew orientation. Hence this mode of subjectivity can scarcely be a means for resolving conflict, whether psychological, academic, or political (either domestic or global), because it lacks the equipment (orientation, interests) for even recognizing conflict. It makes no sense to propose such an insubstantial subject as cultivating diversity, one of Richards's stated goals. This subject can have no values nor indeed be a subject.

When we contemporary critics declare our opposition to the formalism that Richards's work spawned, we surely would want to extend the critique to what I have been calling his ontological formalism. We jointly disown the notion of a purified, emptied, autonomous subject—something like the Cartesian subject—partly because this abstract mode of subjectivity, purportedly subsisting independent of social context, seems crucial to the rhetoric justifying structures of domination.

This critique has been especially vital to postcolonial theory, which has undertaken the crucial task of analyzing the relations among nationalisms, political domination, and definitions of subjectivity. Homi Bhabha has measurably advanced efforts to define a subjectivity that is not a function of nationalist, ideological enthusiasms. Bhabha's initial tactic is to debunk myths of the autonomous subject. There can be no subject in equipoise, Bhabha observes. "The very structure of human subjectivity" involves "contradictions and ambivalences" rather than "unity."[46] Bhabha's account of the subject eschews the resolution of conflict that Richards assiduously pursues. Bhabha's subjectivity is "a space" of interminable contest among diverse elements ("Commitment," 24–25). Because any action requires two terms, agent and object, subjectivity involves a "splitting" or "ambivalence," a term Bhabha uses etymologically to mean tending in different directions. The subject (and by extension culture) is neither "*One*" value or category (like class or gender) "*nor the Other... but something else besides,* which contests the terms and territories of both" ("Commitment," 28).

Bhabha's definition of ambivalence resembles Richards's understanding of ambiguity: both conceptions involve Richards's multivalent reference. Bhabha derives the concept of ambivalence from the structure of representation, emphasizing the nonidentity between signifier and signified. Richards, we will recall, derived "ambiguity" from this same idea, and Bhabha succeeds Richards also in reasoning that therefore knowledge and identity are metaphorical. Metaphor involves the "transfer" of meaning from one place to another, and thus always implies the nonidentity between items compared ("DissemiNation," 291). Finally, like Richards, Bhabha extends his analysis by analogy to ideas of nation and national identity. The very impulse to nationhood "lies in the impossible unity of the nation as a symbolic force." An ambivalence structures the idea of nation. Is nation merely a formal (political and administrative) connection among citizens or a deep social (customary) association?[47] The term *nation* bespeaks at once an idealized totalization among citizens and the often contingent, accidental character of citizens' interactions. Thus the idea of nation is ambivalent, pointing in and emerging from bipolar (and contradictory) directions ("Narrating," 1–3).

This structural ambivalence informs any evocation of the nation and implies a "critique of the fixed and stable forms of the nationalist narrative," as well as of any subjectivity affiliated with it. This "structure of undecidability" discloses an "interstitial space" of "cultural hybridity" in which "cultural difference"—a mode of identification that does not long for the self-completion aspired to by totalizing national narratives—becomes imaginable. Because nation and subjectivity are always being constructed and are therefore ambivalent, neither has intrinsic identity or absolute existence. Indeed, "cultural identification is . . . poised on the brink" of a "'loss of identity.'" Traditional narratives of identity, in Bhabha's view, attempt to eschew or recoup this loss. In contrast, "cultural difference is to be found where the 'loss' of meaning enters . . . into the representation of the fullness of the demands of culture" ("DissemiNation," 303, 312, 313, 304, 313).[48]

In Bhabha's view, traditional commitments to identity seek to reconstitute the "space" of identification as a "fullness." Bhabha seeks to go "beyond the multicultural politics of mutual recognition," which possesses a "seductive reasonableness" yet recycles tenacious notions of (desires for) definite identity. Bhabha espouses instead a mode of identification consistent with the structural undecidability of "subjectivity and nation." What he calls "transnational" or "*inter*national" identification recognizes that "the 'other' is never outside or beyond us," but "emerges forcefully within cultural discourse." In registering "the articulation of cultural difference" that displaces (by calling attention to) "the problematic unity of the nation" and subjectivity, this mode precipitates "awareness of the ambivalence of our identifications."[49]

Bhabha's transnational subject seems to reverse the values Richards invests in his supranational subject. It involves movement and multidirectionality, contesting values, whereas Richards seeks equipoise grounding value. But instead Bhabha only inverts Richards's model, reproducing Richards's ontological formalism. Bhabha aspires to formulate a subjectivity that is "postontological," and to speak "of community and communication *without* the moment of transcendence." Transnationality is not a form of "exile," he avers; his exhortation to reconceive agency is not a "plea for unregulated openendedness."[50] Yet despite these disavowals, Bhabha conceives transnationality as the circumvention of identification. Like Richards, Bhabha defines subjectivity, and also agency, as a mode of experience rather than as a constellation of beliefs and behavior. (Indeed, ambivalence undoes such constellations.)

Transnationality/ambivalence abides in the "gaps" and "spaces" in representation—that is, in the nonidentity between signifier and signified that structures all representation. It emerges from the way identification, because not natural, is not absolute, and therefore from the way identity is not itself. If so, then identity is its structure. As Richards's subject is realized through disorientation, identity consists for Bhabha of a "disturbing alienation" (disturbing to the traditional desire for "fullness") "or overpowering of content," content meaning here our beliefs about experience. Ambivalence involves "the erasure of content in the invisible but insistent structure of linguistic difference" (nonidentity between signified and signifier). "The ill fitting robe of language alienates content in the sense that it deprives it of an immediate access to a stable or holistic reference 'outside' itself" ("DissemiNation," 314). If Bhabha's transnational subject is entirely a structural principle—consisting of its alienating mode of identification, which parallels the structure of representation—then it is resolutely ontological.

Like Richards's postnational subject, the ambivalent subject is a mode of being, not possessing knowledge (which would make it an ideological subject), but experiencing instead "a certain relation to knowledge." The ambivalent subject does not know things but glimpses the semiotic (metaphorical) structure of knowledge ("Commitment," 30–31).[51] The ambivalent subject is an aesthetic subject, then, in the most traditional sense; it experiences the fundamental mode of being, in this case any entity's nonidentity with itself. Although he would not use the term, Bhabha, like Richards, exhorts us to a particular kind of taste. We should appreciate our ambivalent mode of existence.

Bhabha's ontological formalism is, like Richards's, also a political formalism, in which the agency and values of the subject are a function of its ontological status. This is surely true of Richards's aesthetic, supranational subject, whose freedom and tolerance stem from its freedom from belief, its disorientation. Likewise, for Bhabha the ambivalence of subjectivity dislodges familiar commitments; it "alienates our political expectations" ("Commitment," 25). Only when alienated from our subjectivity and its orientation—only when being neither ourselves nor the Other but something else besides—are we "free to negotiate" cultural identities. The ambivalent subject is capable of critique and action only because it occupies (or, more precisely, doesn't occupy) an "*in-between* space," exempt from particular definition, having become the undirected ambivalence that constitutes phenomena, whose disorientation is now perpetuated in a subject with no "specific . . . allegiance" ("Commitment," 38, 21). Bhabha thus repeats in a different idiom the metaphysics of Richards's account of the subject. Bhabha's something-else-besides is the later avatar of Richards's equipoise.

The ambivalent, transnational subject follows Richards's equipoise in having, finally, no identity. The "*inter*national dimension" of culture and identification, as Bhabha's italics underscore, is the "space" "in the boundaries *in-between* nations and peoples" (and of course within any single subjectivity) ("Narrating," 4–5). If transnationality is a space between substantive entities or concrete identifications, and if ambivalence is disorientation and the experience of alienation and undecidability, then subjectivity is nothing.[52] Bhabha may describe "ambivalence" as continually in movement, but it has the same characteristics as Richards's aesthetic equipoise—none. "Ambivalence" is prior to definition, to allegiance or commitment. Transnational identity can have no definition, no orientation, lest it recapitulate the purportedly totalizing domination of traditional national identity. Transnational identity is the marker for the "loss of identity" or "loss of meaning" that "traditional" identity is continually trying to recuperate, but that ambivalence exploits by being aware of it.

One wonders what sort of agency such a subject could exercise. If the subject consists of self-alienation, of its awareness of its artificiality, and of its consequent "undecidability," and if the subject is neither one thing nor another, then it possesses no tools with which to negotiate, and the last thing attributable to it is agency. Moreover, if this non-oriented subject could act, what objectives would it pursue, given that its "political expectations" have been alienated? In locating critique in structural disorientation, Bhabha repeats the ontological formalism of Richards's account of citizenship. Bhabha's account of agency is similarly self-negating, because it is realized only if void. Richards himself might have regarded this vision as another immanently resolvable paradox. I regard it as merely a wishful contradiction.

Richards's and Bhabha's idealism is typical of a syndrome scholars find in twentieth-century liberalism. In its effort to avoid political domination and promote justice and impartiality, modern liberalism tries to develop, in the words of Chantal Mouffe, "a neutral conception of citizenship" based on principles of justice that are not functions of anyone's particular values.[53] On this view, liberal pluralism thus negates the capacity to argue or work for substantive values. As Stanley Fish has argued about an array of liberal political theorists, the imperative to impartiality renders the modern liberal able "neither to affirm nor forswear principle."[54] Accordingly, Richards sought to resolve conflict and end domination by divesting the supranational subject of national values and indeed of any orientation, which might conflict with other orientations. Bhabha even more explicitly defines the transnational as a space in-between, international, as if "international" somehow means life without nations, without "allegiance," rather than relations among nations. If this is the "commitment to theory," as Bhabha titles a chapter, it is no commitment at all.

Even the first well-known effort to imagine a transnational identity typifies ontological idealism. In 1916, Randolph Bourne addressed "the failure of the 'melting pot'" model of American identity. "Diverse nationalistic feelings" persisted among immigrant populations, producing conflicts among the groups composing the nation. "Assimilation" made "the memories of Europe . . . more and more intensely real," so that the "more and more objectively American" people became, the "more and more German or Scandinavian or Bohemian" they became, a phenomenon applicable to older Americans as well. To remedy this situation, Bourne proposed that Americans come to conceive of themselves as "cosmopolitan" and "trans-national." This is not "some homogenous

Americanism" but one in which "foreign cultures" remain "distinct but cooperating." Bourne thus urged a "federated ideal" of "integration." Citizens remain "hyphenates"; the different cultures composing citizens "merge but they do not fuse." America can thus become "the first international nation," "the world-federation in miniature," its citizens "transnationals." They enjoy "dual citizenship," Americans who "retain that distinctiveness of their native cultures and their national spiritual slants."[55] The national spiritual slants, however, can retain their distinctiveness yet not generate the conflicts Bourne abhorred, only if their distinctiveness makes no real difference, involves no commitment to any values that might conflict with values of another national slant. Bourne's transnational model of identity resolves conflict by nullifying the particularity of cultural identification. The federated ideal thrives when no particular values remain. If Richards is adapting Bourne's idealism about identity and politics, Bhabha only extends and radicalizes this tradition. Eschewing (indeed alienating) substantive values, Bhabha's political charge is not really a politics but an aesthetics, a taste for a certain conception of subjectivity.

I do not have space here to consider at length how representative Bhabha's postnationalist model may be of postcolonial theory. It is surely the case that many (post-Lacanian) post-Marxists have tried—as liberal theory long has tried—to consider ways in which cultural identification can proceed in what Gayatri Spivak has called postidentitarian rather than ethnic, class, or national terms.[56] Stuart Hall, who also speaks of "the deep ambivalence of identity and desire," calls this idea "diaspora identity," with the culturally specific term *diaspora* standing for the general structure of identity.[57] In practice, this approach to defining identity has virtues. In principle, let me submit, this effort often involves imagining what for Ernesto Laclau and Chantal Mouffe is the "indeterminacy of the social," the "open space" of the social, as if cultural solidarity can proceed only if the categories of identity, agency, and solidarity—the social—have been vacated.[58] Identity (whether individual or social) is surely not absolute, but its contingency does not in itself make it diasporic or, as Mouffe thinks, ambiguous,[59] which are other terms for Richards's indefinition. Identity, if it is anything, is concrete, specific.[60]

One point I have been trying to establish is that notions like the ambivalent or postnational or even perhaps postidentitarian subject recapitulate what we can safely call Richards's "modernism." With respect to Richards—a modernist if anyone was—the term *modernism* involves a complex of associations: the noncorrespondence or metaphoricity of representation, the ambiguity of language, the idealist disorientation of identity, the capacity for agency, supranational or planetary identity. This conjunction of concepts suggests either that Richards was a postmodernist or that postmodernism scarcely exists, having extended rather than deposed the New Criticism. In any event, Richards's aesthetic subject, along with his utopian idealism, is alive and well, and the ontological formalism surviving in Bhabha's work presents no new account of agency, and more likely renders agency impossible.

The complex of associations inherited through Richards is ill founded. It is true that thought as well as language usage is metaphorical, because signs do not correspond to their referents. But this fact renders neither language inherently ambiguous nor subjectivity ambivalent. Ambiguity exists when a specific reference is unclear. The metaphoricity of language would make language inherently ambiguous only if comprehension requires correspondence (identity) between sign and referent. We should not be surprised, perhaps, that Richards, despite his protests, residually sought correspondence as the criterion of validity. But recent homages to the ambivalence or uncertainty of identity retain the same (illusory) criterion. The nonautonomy and contingency of the subject does not make it ambivalent. The term *ambivalent* itself indicates the formalism of the conception. Only if the substance of identity is a function of its structure or ontological status does the fact that subjectivity emerges semiotically—we experience identity not immediately but rather through images of it—constitute psychology or affect and make us "ambivalent." Only if one desires to be an autonomous self could the recognition of nonautonomy affect the status of our commitments. For twenty-five years the humanities, and literary criticism in particular, have been trying to leave behind the premises of the New Criticism. Certainly I. A. Richards's ontological idealism is worth abandoning. Perhaps it is time we did so.

Notes

1. I. A. Richards, *Basic English and Its Uses* (New York: W. W. Norton, 1943). Subsequent references to this work will be cited in the text as *Basic*. Few discussions of Richards's work mention Basic English, and these generally mention Basic in

passing, as an illustration of his supposed mechanistic functionalism. John Paul Russo, in his monumental biography of Richards as a significant influence upon modern culture, gives serious attention to the Basic English movement. He notes Churchill's and Roosevelt's interest in Basic English as an administrative tool, which Richards proudly noted in his writings (see, for example, *Design for Escape: World Education through Modern Media* [New York: Harcourt, Brace, 1968], 53). Russo explains as well how the popularization of Basic eventually fractured Richards's friendship with Ogden. See John Paul Russo, *I. A. Richards: His Life and Work* (Baltimore: Johns Hopkins University Press, 1989), 397–404.

2. I. A. Richards, *How to Read a Page: A Course in Efficient Reading, with an Introduction to a Hundred Great Words* (New York: W. W. Norton, 1942), 22. Subsequent references to this work will be cited in the text as *Page*. Richards wrote this book partly to explain and justify Basic English. Richards encapsulated this view of the mobility of meaning in a 1940 lecture at Yale, "The Resourcefulness of Words," which he developed into *How to Read a Page*. See I. A. Richards, *Speculative Instruments* (New York: Harcourt, Brace, 1955), 72–77.

3. René Wellek and Austin Warren, *Theory of Literature*, 3d ed. (New York: Harcourt, Brace, 1956), 25, 24, 156, 142, 27.

4. For arguments attributing this depoliticized critical dynamic to Richards, as well as to the New Criticism generally, see Paul A. Bové, *Intellectuals in Power: A Genealogy of Critical Humanism* (New York: Columbia University Press, 1986), 39–77; Terry Eagleton, *Literary Theory: An Introduction* (Minneapolis: University of Minnesota Press, 1983), 31, 45–47, 50; Richard Ohmann, *English in America: A Radical View of the Profession* (New York: Oxford University Press, 1976), 75–77. John Fekete has argued that Richards's innovations resulted in "the isolation of the resulting studies from their historical context" by means of a "programmatic mystification of totality" (*The Critical Twilight: Explorations in the Ideology of Literary Anglo-American Theory from Eliot to McLuhan* [London: Routledge, 1977], 35–36). Pamela McCallum has argued that Richards's view of literature, with its distinction between statement and pseudostatement, "inhibit[s] its usefulness for studying unique socio-cultural phenomena" (*Literature and Method: Towards a Critique of I. A. Richards, T. S. Eliot, and F. R. Leavis* [Dublin: Gill & MacMillan, 1983], 87).

5. This point holds, whatever the character of the criticism Richards influenced. But arguably neither did the New Critics pretend to be apolitical; they regarded their cultural politics to reside precisely in viewing literature as a special mode of existence. Even this mode of existence, formal and linguistic though it was, was not independent of contexts. For example, right after they assert that literature consists entirely of "relations between words," Wellek and Warren declare that "the meaning of poetry is contextual." They mean specifically here that "a word carries with it . . . an aura of synonyms and homonyms"; words do not signify independent of the historical context of their usage. Wellek and Warren thus assert, "Nor is the isolation of literature from direct intellectual or social influences tenable" (*Theory of Literature*, 175).

6. See Ohmann, *English in America*, chap. 4; Eagleton, *Literary Theory*, chap. 1, esp. 45; and Gerald Graff, *Professing Literature: An Institutional History* (Chicago: University of Chicago Press, 1987), 167–79. Although largely accepting Bové's critique, Graff does emphasize the degree to which Richards's methods radically al-

tered educational politics by replacing philological models of study with a focus on the effects of texts (177).

7. I. A. Richards, *Principles of Literary Criticism* (New York: Harcourt, Brace, 1925), 60, 62. Subsequent references to this work will be cited in the text as *Principles.*

8. I. A. Richards, *Practical Criticism* (New York: Harcourt, Brace, 1929), 327. Subsequent references to this work will be cited in the text as *Practical.*

9. I. A. Richards, *Poetries and Sciences* (New York: W. W. Norton, 1970), 33, 78. This volume is a reissue of *Science and Poetry* (1926, 1935), with appendixes. Subsequent references to this work will be cited in the text as *Sciences.*

10. Richards's sojourns in China beginning around 1930 confirmed for him the need for systematic study not of univocal meaning but of multiple definition. See I. A. Richards, *Mencius on the Mind: Experiments in Multiple Definition* (New York: Harcourt, Brace, 1932).

11. Typically thorough and illuminating as his treatment of Basic English is, Russo emphasizes Basic as a mechanism for simplifying reference rather than for illustrating how to approach ambiguity. Moreover, Russo terms Richards's efforts to spread Basic a "second career," when in fact Richards worked to further Basic continuously throughout his long career, ever since Ogden developed Basic in the mid-1920s and even after the world language movement fizzled. Richards viewed Basic English as the culmination of his attempts to engage ambiguity. The only treatment of Basic as exemplifying ambiguity with which I am familiar is that of W. H. N. Hotopf, *Language, Thought and Comprehension: A Case Study of the Writings of I. A. Richards* (Bloomington: Indiana University Press, 1965), 118–19.

12. Homi K. Bhabha, "Introduction: Narrating the Nation," in *Nation and Narration,* ed. Homi K. Bhabha (London: Routledge, 1990), 3–4. Subsequent references to this work will be cited in the text as "Narrating."

13. Homi K. Bhabha, "DissemiNation: Time, Narrative, and the Margins of the Modern Nation," in *Nation and Narration,* ed. Homi K. Bhabha (London: Routledge, 1990), 302. Subsequent references to this work will be cited in the text as "DissemiNation."

14. I. A. Richards, *The Republic of Plato: A Version in Simplified English* (New York: W. W. Norton, 1942).

15. I. A. Richards, "The Interactions of Words," in *The Language of Poetry,* ed. Allen Tate (New York: Russell & Russell, 1960), 73.

16. I. A. Richards, *Interpretation in Teaching* (New York: Harcourt, Brace, 1938), 209–10.

17. "The modes and the shifts and changes of meaning recur and recur." Richards, *Page,* 142.

18. I. A. Richards, *So Much Nearer: Essays toward a World English* (New York: Harcourt, Brace, 1960), 175.

19. Richards dedicates an entire chapter in *Interpretation in Teaching* to the indefiniteness of ideas of the "definite." Theorists, he contends, always attempt to identify a definite meaning as an "initial point for surveys." For Richards, their own language exhibits the impossibility of the enterprise (145).

20. I. A. Richards and C. K. Ogden, *The Meaning of Meaning: A Study of the Influence of Language upon Thought and of the Science of Symbolism* (New York: Harcourt, Brace, 1923), chap. 3. Literary scholars will of course note here that Richards

and Ogden are employing the vocabulary we now associate with C. S. Peirce and Ferdinand de Saussure. (They judge Saussure's analysis of the sign to be naive.) But we should note also that the idea that communication operates through signs had long been part of the rhetorical tradition. In his 1783 *Lectures on Rhetoric and Belles Lettres,* still influential through the nineteenth century, Hugh Blair wrote that "the connexion between words and ideas may, in general, be considered as arbitrary and conventional" (*Lectures on Rhetoric and Belles Lettres,* 2 vols. [London: Cadell, in the Strand, 1785; reprint, New York: Garland, 1970], 1:123). In his probably even more current *Philosophy of Rhetoric* (1776), Hugh Campbell similarly observed that "not a natural and necessary, but an artificial and arbitrary connexion" "subsisteth between words and things" (*The Philosophy of Rhetoric,* ed. Lloyd F. Blitzer [Carbondale: Southern Illinois University Press, 1963], 258). Adam Smith's *Considerations Concerning the First Formation of Languages* and Locke's discussion of words as signs in *Essay Concerning Human Understanding,* Book 3, employed similar formulations, which appeared also in work by Richards's immediate predecessors in literary study. In 1893, Barrett Wendell of Harvard wrote that language consists of "arbitrary symbols," meaningful only conventionally ("American Literature," in *Stelligeri, and Other Essays Concerning America* [New York: Scribner's, 1893], 101). "Signification" is conventional, wrote George Lyman Kittredge, also of Harvard and the prominent editor of Shakespeare. "Words are conventional signs," with "no natural and essential meaning," "no character in themselves" (Kittredge and James B. Greenough, *Words and Their Ways in English Speech* [New York: Macmillan, 1901], 219, 221, 224).

21. Richards, *Interpretation in Teaching,* 48–49. I suspect that "metaphor" became Richards's way for thinking about what experimental psychologists of the period called "apperception," meaning the way perception of phenomena proceeds within prior conceptual frameworks. Russo characterizes Richards's view that metaphor exemplifies the noncorrespondence of signs, which he worked out in the early 1930s after visiting China, as his "breakthrough" on metaphor (251–60). The works cited in note 20, above, suggest that he was adapting a long tradition on this matter.

22. In a 1973 volume honoring Richards, Joan Bennett remarks that the value of *Practical Criticism* rests largely with Richards's "fourfold definition of a poem's meaning," which "has proved a valuable guide for readers." "Because of I.A.R.'s influence it is now widely recognised that the ability to respond fully to a writer's fourfold meaning is the most indispensable ability for a student of literature" ("'How It Strikes a Contemporary': The Impact of I. A. Richards' Literary Criticism in Cambridge, England," in *I. A. Richards: Essays in His Honor,* ed. Reuben Brower, Helen Vendler, and John Hollander [New York: Oxford University Press, 1973], 59).

23. Gerald Graff, *Poetic Statement and Critical Dogma* (Evanston, Ill.: Northwestern University Press, 1970), 60, 46.

24. Russo *(I. A. Richards),* McCallum, *(Literature and Method),* and Hotopf *(Language, Thought and Comprehension)* present helpful discussions of Richards's theory of value. Russo does seem to me wrong in distinguishing equilibrium from satisfaction (191).

25. Richards was familiar with the work of, among others, Charles Sherrington *(Integrative Action of the Nervous System),* William James *(Principles of Psychology),* G. F. Stout *(Analytic Psychology),* Alexander Bain *(Emotions and the Will),* James Ward *(The Realm of Ends),* Theodule Ribot *(The Psychology of Emotions),* and John Watson *(Behaviorism),* with whose views Richards differed more than some have

thought, objecting to Watson's prohibition against speaking of consciousness (see "Review of John B. Watson, *Behaviorism*" [1926], reprinted in *Complementarities: Uncollected Essays,* ed. John Paul Russo [Cambridge: Harvard University Press, 1976], 16–23). Richards cites these authors in various venues. McCallum, Hotopf, and, of course, Russo present useful extensive discussions of these influences.

26. See *Principles of Literary Criticism,* 48, 54–55. Richards mentioned often how significant an event to him was Ogden's publication of Bentham's *Theory of Fictions.* Other scholars have discussed the Benthamite logic of Richards's account of mind, Eagleton and Fekete with a very different emphasis. But simply labeling Richards's view "a defective utilitarian theory of value" does not, it seems to me, begin to understand his logic and its implications (Eagleton, *Literary Theory,* 45; see also Fekete, *The Critical Twilight,* 30–31).

27. Ohmann especially, but Eagleton as well, concludes, pace Richards, that the resolution of conflict among appetencies leads to the inability to act, with action rendered undesirable because it indicates, in Richards's term, "perturbation" in the psychic structure (Ohmann, *English in America,* 75, 77; Eagleton, *Literary Theory,* 46–47). Richards's goal, instead, is action, and also versatility of response, under specified psychic conditions.

28. Richards and Ogden, *The Meaning of Meaning,* 60–61.

29. See, for example, William James, *The Principles of Psychology,* vol. 1 (1890; reprint, New York: Dover, 1950), chap. 4.

30. As soon as he imagines the ideal interpreter freed from words, Richards promptly notes: "There are moments when it all seems strangely simple and clear. But that vision would be incommunicable" (*Page,* 186). This problem—that aesthetic satisfaction cannot be communicated and by extension can hardly be experienced—does not dissuade Richards from his project; he barely pauses to raise the question.

31. This is, I think, the reason Richards contends that "the striking of a clock is the cause of our thinking of its striking" (*Principles,* 126). "Cause" seems the wrong word here. The striking of the clock may *occasion* this thought, but only habitual associations make the sound to us like a clock. Yet Richards needs our idea of the sound to be caused by the sound, so that the idea is not a function of habitual association.

32. The literature on the eugenics movement is voluminous; let me cite here just a few reference sources. Probably the best-known history of the movement (deservedly so) is Daniel J. Kevles, *In the Name of Eugenics: Genetics and the Uses of Human Heredity* (Berkeley: University of California Press, 1985). See also Mark H. Haller, *Eugenics: Hereditarian Attitudes in American Thought* (New Brunswick, N.J.: Rutgers University Press, 1963); Diane Paul, *Controlling Human Heredity: 1865 to the Present* (Atlantic Highlands, N.J.: Humanities Press, 1995). For a discussion of some approaches to the study of eugenics, see Howard Horwitz, "Always with Us," *American Literary History* 10, no. 2 (1998): 317–34. For some of the key work advocating eugenics, see Sir Francis Galton (who coined the term), *Inquiries into Human Faculty and Its Development* (London: J. M. Dent, 1883); Karl Pearson, *Nature and Nurture: The Problem of the Future,* Presidential Address before the Social and Political Education League, 28 April 1910, Galton Eugenics Laboratory Lecture Series, No. 6 (London: Dulau, 1910); Charles B. Davenport, *Heredity in Relation to Eugenics* (New York: Henry Holt, 1911). Because of the mathematical techniques they developed in order to measure population patterns, Galton and Pearson are regarded as the

founders of modern statistics. Pearson and Davenport directed the most prominent eugenics laboratories, Pearson at the Galton National Eugenics Laboratory, University College, London, and Davenport at Cold Springs Harbor, Long Island, with funding from the Carnegie Institute and the Rockefeller Foundation. For a typical popularization of eugenist ideas, see Theodore Roosevelt, "Race Decadence" (1911), in *The Works of Theodore Roosevelt,* vol. 12 (New York: Scribner's, 1926), 184–96.

33. No one reading in the social sciences could have missed encountering exhortations to eugenics. At least one of Richards's psychological sources, Theodule Ribot, was an influential figure in the eugenics movement because of his 1879 work *Heredity: A Psychological Study of Its Phenomena, Laws, Causes, and Consequences* (New York: Appleton, 1915).

34. Bové *(Intellectuals in Power)* and Fekete *(The Critical Twilight)* argue that Richards disdains "difference." Yet it is not difference or diversity (of views and conduct) in itself that galls him, but rather its degree of purposiveness.

35. See, for example, Havelock Ellis, *The Problem of Race Regeneration* (New York: Moffat, Yard, 1911); Luther Burbank, *The Training of the Human Plant* (New York: Century, 1907).

36. Benedict Anderson, *Imagined Communities: Reflections on the Origin and Spread of Nationalism,* rev. ed. (London: Verso, 1991), 6, 204.

37. I. A. Richards, *Nations and Peace* (New York: Simon & Schuster, 1947), 27. Subsequent references to this work will be cited in the text as *Nations.*

38. Anderson, *Imagined Communities,* 141. Richards clearly implies, as Anderson will stipulate, the way our "pictures" of ourselves and the nation must to some extent be unconscious, their evolution forgotten (see Anderson, 187–206).

39. Richards again links his view to Bentham, who coined the term *international* but would regard the abiding conflicts of international relations as "man's chief disgrace" (*Basic,* 12).

40. Russo explains these in detail; *I. A. Richards,* 397–404.

41. Ogden thought Basic afforded "minimum vocabulary with maximum efficiency" (quoted in ibid., 399). Similarly, the linguist Otto Jespersen defended artificial languages not based on one extant "national language" because actual languages are too nuanced, too idiomatic. What Jespersen called "interlanguage," although limited in expressiveness, would make for simplified and therefore more efficient communication (see "Introduction: An International Language," in *Selected Writings of Otto Jespersen* [London: George Allen & Unwin, n.d.], 739–40). A perfected interlanguage would be "as easy, clear and rich as possible" ("History of Our Language," in *Selected Writings of Otto Jespersen,* 753).

42. Richards, *Interpretation in Teaching,* 203.

43. Richards, *So Much Nearer,* 252.

44. Richards, *Interpretation in Teaching,* 203.

45. Richards, *So Much Nearer,* 250–51.

46. Homi K. Bhabha, "The Commitment to Theory," in *The Location of Culture* (London: Routledge, 1994), 19, 23. Subsequent references to this essay will be cited in the text as "Commitment."

47. The distinctions informing these questions have of course long been central to Western political philosophy. The problem is Hobbesian, and it is succinctly expressed in Thomas Paine's distinction between Society and Government at the outset of *Common Sense* (New York: Penguin, 1983), 65.

48. Bhabha adapts the phrase "loss of identity" from Julia Kristeva.

49. Homi K. Bhabha, "Editor's Introduction: Minority Maneuvers and Unsettled Negotiations," *Critical Inquiry* 23 (spring 1997): 438; "Narrating," 4–5.

50. Bhabha, "Minority Maneuvers," 437; "DissemiNation," 304; "Minority Maneuvers," 459.

51. Bhabha is undoubtedly alluding here to Louis Althusser's notion that art does not give us knowledge "but what it gives us does nevertheless maintain a certain *specific relationship* with knowledge. This relationship is . . . one of difference." Althusser's distinction here between what art gives us and scientific knowledge is reminiscent of Richards's distinction between statement and pseudostatement. See "A Letter on Art in Reply to André Daspre" (1966), in *Lenin and Philosophy, and Other Essays* (New York: Monthly Review Press, 1971), 222.

52. Let me suggest that this idealism afflicts theoretical invocations of spatial metaphors generally, as in the now proverbial call to "open up a space" for resistance or contestation, a formulation that Bhabha employs in numerous variations. This formulation presupposes that agency exists only when a subject is free from a constituting context, when instead action is possible only within contexts.

53. Chantal Mouffe, *The Return of the Political* (London: Verso, 1993), 7. As he is for many scholars of liberalism, John Rawls *(Theory of Justice)* is Mouffe's exemplary modern liberal.

54. Stanley Fish, "Mission Impossible: Settling the Just Bounds between Church and State," *Columbia Law Review* 97 (December 1997): 2323. Fish includes Mouffe among the liberals.

55. Randolph Bourne, "Trans-National America," *Atlantic Monthly,* July 1916; reprinted in *Randolph Bourne, the Radical Will: Selected Writings, 1911–1918* (New York: Urizen, 1977), 248, 253, 255, 257, 263, 258, 263, 260, 259.

56. Gayatri Chakravorty Spivak, "Poststructuralism, Marginality, Postcoloniality and Value," in *Contemporary Postcolonial Theory: A Reader,* ed. Padmini Mongia (New York: Arnold, 1996), 204.

57. Stuart Hall, "New Ethnicities," in *Black British Cultural Studies: A Reader,* ed. Houston A. Baker Jr., Manthia Diawara, and Ruth H. Lindenborg (Chicago: Univeristy of Chicago Press, 1996), 167; Stuart Hall, "Cultural Identity and Diaspora," in *Identity: Community, Culture, Difference,* ed. Jonathan Rutherford (London: Lawrence & Wishart, 1990), 236.

58. Ernesto Laclau and Chantal Mouffe, *Hegemony and Socialist Strategy* (London: Verso, 1985), 152. Even with her analysis of modern liberalism, Mouffe, too, repeats its idealism when she writes, for example, of the "indetermination that is constitutive of modern democracy," or of the "radical indeterminacy" of power, law, and knowledge. Contingency is not identical with indefinition, but Mouffe thinks this association indispensable to imagining the reformation of culture (*Return of the Political,* 146, 164). Laclau and Mouffe remark, as Bhabha will echo, that critique based on such indeterminacy is indispensable for conceiving the "politically negotiable character of every identity" (*Hegemony,* 104). I would query, however, whether identity is something we negotiate, as in a contract or consumer purchase to which we are party, or instead a condition we experience, within an organizing framework of beliefs, and therefore not subject to negotiation.

59. Mouffe urges readers to acknowledge "the contingency and ambiguity of every identity" (*Return of the Political,* 76). Let me suggest that the terms *contingency* and

ambiguity are neither synonymous nor mutually entailing. All identity is no doubt contingent, existing and acquiring definition only in context. Depending upon context, some signs, although not others, are ambiguous. Ambiguity is a function of context, not ontology.

60. This idea does not mean that the subject is stable or autonomous or unchanging, only that it has definition, by which it is distinguishable from other entities.

Part IV
Rethinking Aesthetics: Secrets and Magic, the Gift and the Child

CHAPTER FIFTEEN

The Gift

Reflections on the Eames House

Beatriz Colomina

The oldest published photograph of the Eames House shows a truck on the site, occupying the place of the house, taking its place, anticipating it. The windshield happens to lie exactly where a glass facade will terminate the building. The steel frame of the house is being assembled from a crane on the back of the truck as it steadily moves down the narrow site carved out between a steep hillside and a row of eucalyptus trees. It is said that this process took only a day and a half.[1]

The Eameses immediately celebrated. A sequence of photographs shows the ecstatic couple holding hands under the frame, then stepping off the retaining wall onto a thin beam suspended like a tightrope across the space, and finally posing in the middle of the beam, still holding hands. Ray has a white bird in her raised hand (Figure 15.1).[2]

The Eameses liked to celebrate things. Anything. Everything. This is not just whimsy, a distraction from the work. It is part of the work itself. Walking along the beam of the house under construction is the beginning of the occupation of the house. They are literally moving in, even if the crafting of the basic fabric of the building was to take almost a year. The house became an endless process of celebration over the course of their lives.[3] When they walk across the steel tightrope before the tent has even been pulled up over the frame, they are launching an intense program of construction through festive play. Every stage of the play is recorded, photographed, and disseminated to an international audience.

Circus, it turns out, was one of their fascinations. When asked in 1970 to give the prestigious Charles Eliot Norton Lectures at Harvard Uni-

Figure 15.1. Ray and Charles Eames on the newly constructed steel frame of their house in Pacific Palisades, California, 1949. Library of Congress, Prints and Photographs Division. Copyright Lucia Eames/Eames Office (www.eamesoffice.com).

versity, Eames concluded the first of his six lectures by presenting a three-screen slide show of circus photographs he had been shooting since the 1940s. The 180 images were accompanied by a sound track featuring music and other sounds recorded at the circus. The theme of the lectures was that "the rewarding experiences and aesthetic pleasures of our lives should not be dependent solely upon the classic fine arts, but should be, rather, a natural product of the business of life itself."[4] Eames turned to the circus because what "seems to be a freewheeling exchange in self-expression, is instead a tightly knit and masterfully disciplined organic accumulation of people, energies and details."[5] In a talk given before the American Academy of Arts and Sciences in 1974, he elaborated on the point:

> The circus is a nomadic society which is very rich and colorful but which shows apparent license on the surface. . . . Everything in the circus is pushing the possible beyond the limit. . . . Yet, within this apparent freewheeling license, we find a discipline which is almost unbelievable.

> There is a strict hierarchy of events and an elimination of choice under stress, so that one event can automatically follow another. The layout of the circus under canvas is more like the plan of the Acropolis than anything else.[6]

In many ways, this is what Eames thought architecture was, the ongoing theatrical spectacle of everyday life, understood as an exercise in restrictions rather than self-expression. The endless photographs of the ridiculously happy Eameses displaying their latest inventions are part of an extraordinarily precise and professional design practice. We see them on top of the frame of their house, "pinned" by metal chair frames, holding Xmas decorations, waving to us from inside a Xmas ball, wearing Easter hats or masks, photographing their own reflections in the house, and so on. In almost all of the early photographs they wear matching outfits, as if to emphasize the performative aspect of their work. The Eameses were very precise about their clothes, commissioning their dress from Dorothy Jenkins, an Oscar-winning designer who did the costumes for many films, including *South Pacific, The Ten Commandments, Night of the Iguana,* and *The Sound of Music* (Ray Eames's distinctive pinafore dresses are even reminiscent of Julie Andrews's dresses in this film). The effect of the Eames costume is the professional couple as a matching set, carefully positioned like any other object in the layout. The uniform clothes transform the couple into a designer object that can be moved around the frame or from picture to picture. It is always the layout that is the statement, not the objects. And the layout is constantly reworked, rearranged.

If design is not the self-expression of the designer, it is the occupant's daily life that leaves its mark on the house. Eames houses used "industrial technology to provide ... an 'unselfconscious' enclosure that would satisfy the essentials for comfortable living. Such a structure could then be made into a personal statement by the occupant, who could fill it with the accessories of his or her own life."[7] All the ephemera of daily living take over and define the space.

For Charles Eames, everything was architecture, from the setting of a table for breakfast to a circus performance. Everybody was a designer. He trusted, sometimes to later disappointment, the choices craftsmen would make.[8] If they knew their trade, he believed, they would know what a good solution was. He respected the individual's capacity to choose well, even if the individual had little experience: "I don't believe in this 'gifted few' concept, just in people doing things they are really interested in doing. They have a way of getting good at whatever it is."[9] Employees arriving at the Eames Office were routinely assigned tasks for which they had no previous experience.[10] It was thought that anybody who applied his or her attention totally, obsessively, to a problem would come up with a good solution, especially if there were many restrictions, such as limited time, materials, or money. Eames spoke nostalgically of his days at the MGM studios, where he often had only one night to make a whole new set out of a limited range of props.

This idea of design as the rearrangement of a limited kit of parts is constant in the Eameses' work. Everything they produce can be rearranged; no layout is ever fixed. Even the formal lectures were sometimes rearranged in midstream. Kits of parts, movable partitions, "The Toy," the plywood cabinets, the House of Cards, the Revell toy house, the Kwikset House—all are infinitely rearrangable. The Eames House is a good example. Not only was it produced out of the same structural components as the utterly different Entenza House (designed by Charles Eames with Eero Saarinen), but the Eames House was itself a rearrangement of an earlier version. After the steel had already been delivered to the site, Eames decided to redesign the house. He put the same set of steel parts together in a completely new way.[11]

The structure exhibits the same logic of rearrangement that will soon dominate its interior. The Eames House blurs the distinction between designer and occupant, accommodating structure and mobile accessories. Where does the work of the designer end and that of the occupant begin in this house? Are the famous colored panels on the facade ephemera (picked up from the history of modern art like the pieces of driftwood the Eameses were always picking up and rearranging) or "unselfconscious structure"? In fact, the colors of the panels were meant to change. Ray said that they chose the cheapest kind of paint from Sears Roebuck so that they could experiment, but the original colors remain.[12] Eventually the panels became fixed in the mind of the architectural community and were taken to be the architecture. But for the Eameses, the real architecture of the house was to be found in their endless rearrangement of collectibles within it. The real space was to be found in the details of their daily life.

Charles constantly reflected on what "quality" makes a good architect. In an interview with Digby Diehl, Eames recalled a conversation he had with Saarinen on the subject: "One of the things we hit upon was the quality of a host. That is, the role of the architect, or the designer, is that of a very good, thoughtful host, all of whose energy goes into trying to anticipate the needs of his guests—those who enter the building and use the objects in it. We decided that this was an essential ingredient in the design of a building or a useful object."[13] The house has to efface itself in favor of the creative choices made by its occupants. Its only role is that of the "shock absorber" that protects a unique and ever-changing lifestyle: "The house must make no insistent demands for itself, but rather aid as a background for life in work . . . and as re-orientator and 'shock absorber.'"[14]

It is difficult not to think of the war. Domestic life can no longer be taken for granted. It becomes an art form carefully constructed and marketed by a whole new industry, a form of art therapy for a traumatized nation, a reassuring image of the "good life" to be bought like any other product. Rather than offer a complete environment to the postwar consumer, the Eameses offered a variety of components with which individuals could construct and rearrange themselves. The Eameses insisted that life is making choices. They left most of them to the occupants, rejecting the role of the artist in favor of that of the industrial designer and catalog distributor.

The idea of the house as shock absorber is also literal. The Eameses devoted a lot of research to perfecting the rubber shock absorbers in their furniture. In the 1946 exhibition of their plywood furniture at the Museum of Modern Art in New York, a rotary device was used to show the strength and flexibility of the rubber shock mount, and a tumbling drum containing the plywood "Eames chair" demonstrated its durability. A house is likewise meant to absorb the eccentric movements of everyday life. In the Eames House, panels shift, furniture moves in and out. It became a kind of testing ground for all the work of the office. Everything moves in the end. Only the basic frame stays still, and this frame is meant to be almost invisible. A necessary prop—no more than that. As Esther McCoy writes in a caption for an image of trees reflected on the glass walls of the Eames House:

> After thirteen years of living in a house with exposed steel frame, Ray Eames said, "The structure long ago ceased to exist. I am not aware of it." They lived in nature and its reflections—and reflections of reflections.[15]

The house dissolved itself in a play of reflections, restless images that immediately caught the eye of the world. The Eames House was published everywhere, exposed, scrutinized.[16] The images multiplied and became the objects of reflection. Their appeal was part of the general fascination with objects in postwar America that extended from pop-up toasters to buildings.

It was beautiful while it lasted. For a brief period, the span of about five years following the end of the war, America seemed to embrace modern architecture. It wasn't, as with the so-called International Style exhibition of 1932, the importation of some European ideas repackaged as a style. It was the development of a whole new mode of operation, one that fascinated Europe in the same way that European models had once fascinated the U.S.A. And it was not just Europe. The war seemed to have opened the frontiers, particularly to the Pacific. The Eames House held a special place in this new geography. Reyner Banham wrote:

> For most Europeans—and some Africans, Australians, and Japanese to whom I have spoken—the Case Study era began around Christmas 1949. By that time the magazine *Arts and Architecture* had achieved a sufficient degree of penetration into specialized bookstores and architectural libraries for the impact of the first of the steel-frame Case Study houses to trigger—as British architect Peter Smithson said—"a wholly different kind of conversation."[17]

That first steel house that Banham refers to was the Eames House, No. 8 of the Case Study House Program, into which the Eameses moved precisely on the eve of Xmas day 1949. The Case Study House Program was, as Banham noted, "overwhelmingly Charles and Ray Eames in foreign perception."[18] That explains why foreigners thought of it as 1949, even if the program had started in January 1945, a few months before the end of the war.

The Case Study House Program was sponsored by the magazine *Arts & Architecture* under John Entenza.[19] The magazine commissioned a number of architects to design one house each as a prototype for a new way of living—the postwar way of living. The assumption was that the soldier returning from war had become a "modern man," a figure who would prefer to live in a modern environment utilizing the most advanced technology rather than return to live in "old fashioned houses with enclosed rooms." The twenty-six houses resulting from this program were not only published in *Arts & Architecture*, they were, for the most part, built. They were open to the public for six to eight weeks before their occupation. Each was to be completely furnished under an arrangement with the manufacturers. Like so many of the houses of the modern movement in Europe, the Case Study houses were exhibition houses. The program was enormously successful both professionally and among the wider public. The first six houses to be opened received almost four hundred thousand visitors.

The program was preceded by two competitions organized by *Arts & Architecture:* the 1943 "Design for Postwar Living" and a second such competition in 1944, sponsored by the U.S. Plywood Association. These competitions encouraged participants to arrive at a "pattern of living for the American worker" and his family. This American worker, it says in the call for entries, "conditioned by the war-time years and including the members of the armed forces, who would become a part of the working population . . . is likely to have an enormous respect for the machine both as creator and as a weapon of destruction . . . and it is very likely that he will not only accept but demand simple, direct, and honest efficiency in the material aspects of the means by which he lives."[20] The Second World War, *Arts & Architecture* implied, provided the context for the acceptance of modern architecture. It was as if the war had educated the taste, the aesthetic sensibility, of the public.

A historical reference for the Case Study houses can be found in Le Corbusier's fascination with the technologies developed during World War I and his dream of an architecture that would "recycle" these materials and techniques into the mass production of houses. This was most obvious in his relationship with Gabriel Voisin, who, after the war, was looking to transform his war aircraft factories by breaking into the building industry.[21]

The Case Study House Program likewise exemplifies the impact of the war on both architectural discourse and the specific techniques and materials employed in the production of housing. On the one hand, the industry was recycling the products and techniques that it had developed and tested at war. On the other hand, and this is what is new, the architects themselves, unlike their European counterparts, had been involved in the development of those military products.

During the war, Charles and Ray Eames had formed a company with John Entenza to mass-produce plywood war products. In 1941–42 they developed a molded-plywood splint for the U.S. Navy to replace a metal leg splint, used in the field, that did not sufficiently secure the leg and so led to gangrene. The Navy accepted the Eames prototype and, with the financial support of Entenza and the help of other architects such as Gregory Ain (who later became involved in the Case Study House Program), designed the equipment needed for mass production, and eventually put 150,000 units into service. In addition, the company designed and developed a body litter, an arm splint, aircraft parts, and other products, all in molded plywood. By 1945 the Eameses were producing lightweight plywood cabinets and molded plywood chairs and tables with the technology they had developed for the military. A photograph of the plywood lounge chair of 1946 shows Charles reclining on it, the position of his leg indicating that he has not forgotten where it comes from. In addition the Eameses produced molded plywood children's furniture, molded plywood animals, and even plywood Xmas decorations cut out of leftover splints. Military and medical equipment had become the basis of domestic equipment.

This obvious displacement from war to architecture can be found throughout the Case Study House Program in more subtle forms. The very idea of standardization, which had been perfected by the military, was very much part of the program's agenda. Every component of the Eames House was selected from a steel manufacturer's catalog and bolted together like a Meccano set.

One is reminded again of Le Corbusier, who in relation to his potential collaboration with Voisin had written (with Amedee Ozenfant) in *L'Esprit Nouveau:*

> Houses must go up all of a piece, made by machine tools in a factory.... It is in aircraft factories that the *soldier-architects* have decided to build their houses; they decided to build this house like an aircraft, with the same structural methods, lightweight framing, metal braces, tubular supports.[22]

From that point of view, the Eames House represents the realization of Le Corbusier's dreams. While Le Corbusier theorized the factory-made house, or at least new materials and building techniques, the houses he managed to build in the meantime used the most conventional techniques. Like Le Corbusier, Charles Eames was an avid reader of catalogs on marine and aviation equipment. He later said about the house that he regretted having "stuck so close to the building industry," neglecting several offers from outside quarters, and that if he were to do it all over again "he might treat this house more as a job of 'product design,' less architecture in the traditional sense."[23]

But how could the house *be* less architecture in the traditional sense? It seems to be one of their plywood cabinets blown up in scale. It is built out of off-the-shelf components, assembled off the back of a truck, in just over one day. It is hard to imagine a more radical gesture. It was precisely its radicality that attracted worldwide attention.

Perhaps nobody was more captivated by the Eameses, and more lucid about their work, than their buddies the British architects Alison and Peter Smithson. In a 1966 *Architectural Design* issue devoted exclusively to the Eameses and prepared by the Smithsons, they wrote:

> There has been much reflection in England on the Eames House. For the Eames House was a cultural gift parcel received here at a particularly useful time. The bright wrapper has made most people—especially Americans—throw the content away as not sustaining. But we have been brooding on it—working on it—feeding from it.[24]

The house as an object, a gift all wrapped up in colored paper. This comment reflects so many of the Smithsons' obsessions, so much of what they saw as new in the Eameses: the attention to seemingly marginal objects (which the Smithsons perceptively understood as "remnants of identity"), the love of ephemera, of colored wrapping paper, and so on.

For the Eameses, gifts were all-important. They maintained that the reason they began to design and make toys (the House of Cards, "The Toy," the masks) was to give them to their grandchildren and the children of staff members and friends. But the concept of gift extends far beyond the toys. Not only were the Eameses extremely generous with their friends (they once paid for airline tickets so the Smithsons could visit them in California), but they understood all their work as a gift. In an interview Charles said: "The motivation behind most of the things we've done was either that we wanted them ourselves, or we wanted to give them to someone else. And the way to make that practical is to have the gifts manufactured. . . . The lounge chair, for example, was really done as a present to a friend, Billy Wilder, and has since been reproduced." Wilder wanted "something he could take a nap on in his office, but that wouldn't be mistaken for a casting couch."[25] In addition to the "nap" chair, the Eameses designed a "TV chair" for Wilder. An article in a 1950 issue of *Life* magazine shows a multiple-exposure photograph of Billy Wilder moving back and forth on the plywood lounge chair of 1946, claiming that it was designed so that the "restless Wilder can easily jump around while watching television."[26]

From the toys to the furniture to the houses (which were either designed for their closest friends, John Entenza and Billy Wilder, or as toys, like the Revell House and the Birthday House designed for Hallmark Cards in 1959), to the major productions (such as the film *Glimpses of the U.S.A.*, which they understood as a token of friendship to the Russians), to their most complex exhibitions, the Eameses always concentrated on what they were giving and how it should be presented. They thought of everything as a gift. Design was gift giving.

No one has understood the Eameses better than the Smithsons. They took it all personally, seeing the Eames House as a gift wrapped in colored paper, the Eames chair as "a message of hope from another planet," and the Eames cards as giving them "the courage to collect whatever pleases us."[27] These gifts transformed their own practice:

> The prettiness of our lives now I attribute to Ray even more than Charles; we would not be buying flower-patterned ties but for the Eames card game. . . . I like to think it is to Ray and Charles Eames we owe the debt of the extravagance of the new purchase. The penny whistle, the Woolworth's plastic Christmas decoration and toy, on to the German pressed metal toy and the walking robots: fresh, pretty, colorful ephemera.[28]

The Smithsons were eager to return the favor. Their special issue of *Architectural Design*, "Eames, a Celebration," was a gift given in return for so many others. They wrote: "The essays on the work of Charles and Ray Eames which make up this issue are very personal, and the impulse behind them was to repay the debt the authors felt they owed to the Eames in a way that would be both pleasurable and useful to the Eames themselves."[29]

The sense of the Eames House as a gift also points to the constant shift in scale in their work: from house to cabinets, to children's furniture, to toys, to miniatures. Even the architectural models are treated like toys, played with by excited architects and clients acting like curious children. Eames once said that in the "world of toys he saw an ideal attitude for approaching the problems of design, because the world of the child lacks self-consciousness and embarrassment."[30] In Eames architecture everything is a toy, everybody is a child. Perhaps this explains the constant presence of children in the photographs of the Eameses' work. When have we ever seen so many children in architecture?

Charles and Ray saw everything through the camera. This explains the astonishing continuity from work to work in so many different scales. If the eye is the eye of a camera, size is not fixed but continuously shifting. They used to shoot at everything. This was surely not just an obsession with recording. There is that, no doubt, but they also made decisions on the basis of what they saw through the lens, as is evident in Ray's description of the process of decision making in the Eames House:

> We used to use photographs. We would cut out pieces from photographs and put them onto a photograph of the house to see how different things would look. For instance—there was a space in the studio we wanted filled. It was between the depth of the floor where it opens for the stairs (this is not so in the house where there is a balcony rail). We wondered what to do. We had some pier pylons from Venice pier (we had wanted to keep something of it to remember it by). Well, we had pictures of it, glued them onto a photo and decided it worked so went ahead and did it.[31]

To remember the Venice pier they take a piece of it with them. This is characteristic of the Eameses, who over the years accumulated an astonishing quantity of objects. The pylons can be seen standing outside the house. But to see if they could keep a memory of the object inside the house they used photographs and collage. Indeed, a photograph of the Venice pier ends up filling the space in the house they had tested using collage.

The photocollage method had already been important to architects of the early European avant-garde. Mies van der Rohe photocollages pictures of the models of his glass skyscrapers onto a photograph of the Friedrichstrasse, glues photographs of landscape and materials to the Resor House drawings, and glues together photographs of landscape, sculpture, and paintings in the project of the Museum for a Small City. The structure of the building gives way to a juxtaposition of photographic images. But it would be important to understand in what sense the Eameses transformed the strategies of the avant-garde. How was the Eames House able to "trigger," in Peter Smithson's words, "a wholly different kind of conversation"? As Smithson wrote:

> In the 1950s the Eames moved design away from the machine aesthetic and bicycle technology, on which it had lived since the 1920s, into the world of the cinema-eye and the technology of the production aircraft; from the world of the painters into the world of the lay-out men. . . . The Eames aesthetic, made definitive in the House at Santa Monica Canyon, California (as the machine aesthetic was given canonical form in the "dwelling unit" in the Esprit Nouveau Pavilion, Decorative Arts Exhibition, in Paris, 1925), is based on an equally careful selection, but with extracultural surprise, rather than harmony of profile, as its criteria. A kind of wide-eyed wonder of seeing the culturally disparate together and so happy with each other. This sounds like whimsy, but the basic vehicle—the steel lattice frame and in the case of the house, the colour film and colour processing in the graphics work, the pressing and mouldings in the case of the furniture—are ordinary to the culture. . . . Charles Eames is a natural Californian Man, using his native resources and know-how—of the film-making, the aircraft and the advertising industries—as others drink water; that is almost without thinking.[32]

This shift from the machine aesthetic to color film, from the world of painting to that of the layout men, from Europe to California, can be traced in the shift between the first and second versions of the Eames House. The first version, the so-called Bridge House, published in *Arts & Architecture* in 1945, seems to be based on Mies's 1934 sketch of a glass house on a hillside. The scheme was rejected in 1947, after Charles went to the Museum of Modern Art to photograph the Mies exhibition, in which the sketch was first made public. Charles must have already known. In fact, he said that he didn't see anything new in the projects that were exhibited, but he was impressed by Mies's design of the exhibition itself. Shortly after his visit to the exhibition, the Eameses came up with a new scheme for their house.

The first version, which Charles designed with Eero Saarinen, faithfully followed the Miesian paradigm in every detail. The house is elevated off the ground as a kind of viewing platform. The sheer glass walls are aimed at the landscape, lined up with the horizon. In the original drawings, published in *Arts & Architecture* in December 1945, we see the occupant of the house standing behind the glass, an isolated figure looking out at the world that is now framed by the horizontal structure. The interior is almost empty. In the model of the house published in March 1948, the only thing occupying the house is the reflection of the surrounding trees, which the Eameses went to considerable trouble to photograph by placing the model on the actual site and carefully superimposing an image of the trees in the foreground. The effect is classic Mies. As in the Farnsworth House, there is a stark elevated interior with at most a few isolated pieces of furniture floating near the glass in a fixed pattern prescribed by the architect.

In the second version the house is dropped to the ground and swung around to hug the hillside. It no longer faces the ocean. The view is now oblique and filtered by the row of eucalyptus trees in front of the long east face. A low wall is wrapped around the patio on the south facade, partially blocking the ocean from the view of someone sitting in the space and focusing attention on the patio as an extension of the house, as an interior. The dominant focus is now in rather than out. The house abandons the Miesian sandwich, where floating slabs of floor and ceiling define a strictly horizontal view. The floor is treated like a wall with a series of frames defined by rugs, tiles, trays, and low tables on which objects are carefully arranged. In fact, floor, wall, and ceiling are treated in a similar way. Not only are they now given the same dimension (the sandwich being replaced by a box), but they start to share roles. Hans Hofmann paintings used to hang horizontally from the ceiling. Ray said that it was necessary to protect them from the strong light, and that she and Charles "would be able to see them well from that position."[33] Many photographs of the house are taken from a very low angle, and we often see the Eameses sitting on the floor surrounded by their objects. The west wall is clothed in birch because they needed something they could hang objects on. On the east wall, much of the glass has become translucent or is wired ("to make people realize it is there")[34] or replaced with opaque colored panels. The sheer surface is broken up with louvers. The occupants can see only fragments of the outside, fragments that have the same status as the objects that now take over the interior. The view is there but restricted to a few of the many frames. Everything overlaps, moves, and changes. The singular unmediated view is replaced by a kaleidoscopic excess of objects.

The eye that organized the architecture of the historical avant-garde has been displaced by a multiplicity of zooming eyes. Not by chance, the Eameses' 1955 film *House: After Five Years of Living* is made up entirely of thousands of slides. Every aspect of the house is scrutinized by these all-too-intimate eyes. The camera moves up close to every surface, every detail. But these are not the details of the building as such; they are the details of the everyday life that the building makes possible.

Le Corbusier also considered film the best medium to represent his architecture. In his movie *L'Architecture d'aujourd'hui,* made with Pierre Chenal in 1929, he moves through the space of his houses (Villa Savoye, Garches, Villa d'Avray) without taking his jacket off. In *House: After Five Years of Living* the Eameses take the opposite approach. Everything, as the title indicates, is about living in the house. The focus is extremely close: flowers, bugs, eggs, pots and pans, crockery. Whereas Le Corbusier includes figures to show the scale, and perhaps to insist that he is just visiting, in the Eames film there are no figures, only traces of ongoing life.

Le Corbusier's film is all horizontal panning—like the modern house, which frames a horizontal view. The Eames film is just a collection of slides. This is consistent with the house itself. It is impossible to focus in the Eames House in the same way that we do in a house of the twenties. Here the eye is that of a TV watcher: not the fifties TV watcher, but closer to that of today's multiple screens, some with captions, all viewed simultaneously. It helps to follow more than one story at once.

To some extent the Eameses pioneered this mode of viewing. They were experts in communication. In 1959 they brought *Glimpses of the U.S.A.* to Moscow, projecting it on the seven screens suspended within Buckminster Fuller's geodesic dome. In the film, 2,200 still and moving images present the theme of "A Day in the Life of the United States." Fuller said that nobody had done it before and that advertisers and filmmakers would soon follow.[35] The Eameses used the technique repeatedly:

> Having come upon the use of multiple images, we exhibited a tendency to find new uses for it. If you give a young boy a hammer, he'll find that everything he encounters needs hammering. We found that everything we encountered needed the multiple-image technique. . . . I used the process with triple slides in the Norton lectures at Harvard, in order to give a depth of view. In each lecture I would talk for five minutes and then show three minutes of imagery, and then talk seven minutes more.[36]

The Eames House is also a multiscreen performance. But Mies is not simply abandoned. Indeed, the house takes an aspect of Mies's work to its extreme. When Eames gave up on the first scheme after seeing the Mies exhibition at MoMA, he did so because he saw something else there. In fact, it was the exhibition technique that inspired him. When he published his photographs of the exhibition in *Arts & Architecture,* he wrote: "The significant thing seems to be the way in which he has taken documents of his architecture and furniture and used them as elements in creating a space that says, 'this is what it is all about.' "[37]

Eames was very impressed by the zooming and overlapping of scales: a huge photomural of a small pencil sketch alongside a chair towering over a model next to a twice-life-size photograph, and so on. He also noted the interaction between the perspective of the room and that of the life-size photographs. The visitor experiences Mies's architecture, rather than a representation of it, by walking through the display and watching others move. It is a sensual encounter: "The exhibition itself provides the smell and feel of what makes it, and Mies van der Rohe great."[38] What Eames learns from Mies, then, is less about buildings, more about arrangement of objects in space. Exhibition design, layout, and architecture are indistinguishable, as Mies had demonstrated in his layout for the magazine *G,* his numerous exhibitions with Lilly Reich, the Silk Cafe, the Barcelona Pavilion, and so on. Eames picks up on the idea that architecture is exhibition and develops it.

Once again, the Eames House takes something from history and transforms it. The house is an exhibition, a showroom, but it is a different kind of showroom from those of the modern movement. The multiple eye belongs to a completely different kind of consumer. It is the eye of the postwar acquisitive society. While Mies is famous for his comment "Less is more," the Eameses said that their "objective is the simple thing of getting the most of the best to the greatest number of people for the least."[39] The glass box gives way to such a density of objects that even the limits of the box are blurred. The role of the glass changes. With Mies, reflections consolidate the plane of the wall. The complex lines of trees become like the veins in marble. With the Eames House, the plane is broken. The reflections of the eucalyptus tree are endlessly multiplied and relocated. Eames even replaces a panel on the south facade with a photograph of a reflection of the trees, confirming that every panel is understood as a photographic frame. Furthermore, the Eameses take photographs of the reflections on the exterior glass, switch some from positive to negative, and reassemble them into a panel. Apparently intended for the house, the panel ends up in the Herman Miller showroom in Los Angeles.

Just as the house is a showroom, the showroom is a house. The Eames House and the showroom for Herman Miller, built at the same time, are in fact the same project. They use the same principles. A light, unself-conscious enclosure, a minimum of architecture, provides a flexible frame for multiple interior arrangements. A wall-size photomural is used to construct the sense of an exterior, complete with patio, garden, trees, outdoor furniture, and a neighboring house. A complete lifestyle is laid out down to the smallest detail of cutlery and table settings. The space is even filled with personal objects: an African leopard and an early American weathervane loaned by Billy Wilder, a Herbert Matter photograph and a Hofmann painting loaned by John Entenza, and so on. Gifts from friends.[40]

The showroom quality of the Eames House is exemplified by its repeated use as the site of fashion photographs. Magazines such as *Life* and *Vogue* insert their models into the building, lining them up with the architecture, even merging them into the interior elements.[41] In this, the house participates in another long tradition of the historical avant-garde. Ever since the first years of the twentieth century, modern architecture has been used as a setting for fashion publicity. In fact, the history of modern architecture is the history of the showroom, the history of a blending of architecture and exhibition. But the Eames House is no longer just a uniform backdrop for fashion designs as discrete innovations. The garments are blended into the fabric of the house, mingling with the objects. The accompanying text bounces back and forth between the "California bold look" of the architecture and the fashion. What is on display in the showroom is the equal status of all kinds of objects. The announcement of Case Study Houses Nos. 8 and 9 in the December 1945 issue of *Arts & Architecture* shows the silhouettes of both the Eameses and Entenza surrounded by the galaxy of objects that define their respective lifestyles. The role of the architect is simply that of happily accommodating these objects.

A photograph of the Farnsworth House under construction shows the lonely figure of Mies with his back to the camera somberly appraising the empty frame (Figure 15.2). His enormous figure cuts a black silhouette into the frigid landscape. With his coat on, he stands like a Caspar David Friedrich figure confronting the sublime. At about the same time, but a world away, the Eameses put on their new outfits, climb into their frame, and smile at the camera.

Figure 15.2. Ludwig Mies van der Rohe at the Farnsworth House construction site, Plano, Illinois, c. 1951. Mies van der Rohe Archive, Museum of Modern Art, New York. Originally photographed by Sharland; reprinted with permission. *Life Magazine* copyright 1954 Time, Inc.

Notes

1. The Eameses said that the structural shell of the Eames house was raised by five men in sixteen hours ("Life in a Chinese Kite: Standard Industrial Products Assembled in a Spacious Wonderland," *Architectural Forum*, September 1950, 94).

2. The first photograph was published in Elizabeth A. T. Smith, ed., *Blueprints for Modern Living: History and Legacy of the Case Study Houses* (Cambridge: MIT Press, 1989), 182, and credited to the Eames Office. The second, in "Steel in the Meadow," *Interiors*, November 1959, 109, is attributed to Jay Connor. The third, reproduced here (Figure 15.1), was printed in John Neuhart, Marilyn Neuhart, and Ray Eames, *Eames Design: The Work of the Office of Charles and Ray Eames* (New York: Harry N. Abrams, 1989), 108; it is attributed to John Entenza.

3. Not by chance, they moved into their house on the eve of Xmas 1949.

4. Digby Diehl, "Charles Eames: Q & A," *Los Angeles Times West Magazine*, 8 October 1972, 14. This interview was later reprinted in Digby Diehl, *Supertalk* (New York: Doubleday, 1974).

5. Neuhart et al., *Eames Design*, 356.

6. Quoted in ibid., 91, from Charles Eames, "Language of Vision: The Nuts and Bolts," *Bulletin of the American Academy of Arts and Sciences* (October 1974): 13–25.

7. Neuhart et al., *Eames Design*, 137.

8. Charles decided to leave the design of a door handle and lock for the home in the hands of a locksmith, "who, he felt, would handle the problem with a degree of sensitivity born of his own training and craftsmanship. He was later horrified to find a large and clumsy fitting placed in an awkward position on the door." John Neuhart and Marilyn Neuhart, *Eames House* (London: Academy Editions, 1994), 56.

9. Charles Eames, quoted in Bill N. Lacy, "Warehouse Full of Ideas," *Horizon*, September 1980, 27.

10. Pat Kirkham, *Charles and Ray Eames: Designers of the Twentieth Century* (Cambridge: MIT Press, 1995), 89.

11. Although many sources insist, following the Eameses, that the new version used only those parts already delivered to the site, with the exception of one additional beam, Marilyn and John Neuhart question this: "A count of the seventeen-foot vertical girders needed for both house and studio yields a total of twenty-two for the first and sixteen for the latter, considerably more that would have been needed for the first version of each. In addition, there do not appear to have been any seventeen-foot girders in the original house. Additional trusses would also have been required to accommodate the reworked plan" (*Eames House*, 38).

12. Ray Eames, interview with Pat Kirkham, July 1983, Box 61, The Work of Charles and Ray Eames, Manuscript Division, Library of Congress. See also Kirkham, *Charles and Ray Eames*, 115–16.

13. Quoted in Diehl, "Charles Eames," 16.

14. Charles Eames, quoted in "Case Study Houses 8 and 9 by Charles Eames and Eero Saarinen, Architects," *Arts & Architecture*, December 1945, 43; also quoted in *Portfolio Magazine*, summer 1950.

15. Esther McCoy, *Case Study Houses 1945–1962* (Los Angeles: Hennessey & Ingalls, 1977), 54. This book was first published in 1962 as *Modern California Houses*.

16. In addition to *Arts & Architecture*, the Eames house was published in *Architectural Forum* (September 1950), *Architectural Review* (October 1951), *Arquitectura* (Mexico, June 1952), *L'Architecture d'aujourdhui* (December 1953), *Interiors* (November 1959), *Domus* (May 1963), and *Architectural Design* (September 1966).

17. Reyner Banham, "Klarheit, Ehrilichkeit, Einfachkeit . . . and Wit Too! The Case Study Houses in the World's Eyes," in *Blueprints for Modern Living*, ed. Smith, 183.

18. Ibid.

19. About the Case Study House Program, see McCoy, *Case Study Houses*, and Smith, *Blueprints for Modern Living*.

20. John Entenza, "Competition: Designs for Postwar Living," *California Arts & Architecture*, April 1943.

21. See Beatriz Colomina, *Privacy and Publicity: Modern Architecture as Mass Media* (Cambridge: MIT Press, 1994), 159.

22. Le Corbusier-Saugnier, "Les Maisons 'Voisin,'" *L'Esprit Nouveau* 2 (November 1920): 214.

23. "Life in a Chinese Kite," 96.

24. Alison Smithson and Peter Smithson, editorial comments in "Eames, a Celebration" (special issue), *Architectural Design* 36 (September 1966): 432.

25. Diehl, "Charles Eames," 17. The Wilder-inspired aluminum frame chaise was first manufactured by Herman Miller in 1968.

26. "A Designer's Home of His Own: Charles Eames Builds House of Steel and Glass," *Life*, 11 September 1950, 152.

27. Alison Smithson, "And Now Dhamas Are Dying Out in Japan," *Architectural Design* 36 (September 1966): 448; Alison Smithson, "Eames Dreams" (paper delivered on the occasion of the opening of an Eames exhibition in Berlin, September 1979), in Alison Smithson and Peter Smithson, *Changing the Art of Inhabitation* (London: Artemis, 1994), 84.

28. Smithson, "And Now Dhamas," 447.

29. Smithson and Smithson, editorial comments, 432.

30. "Eames, Charles," *Current Biography* (New York: Wilson, 1965), 142.

31. Ray Eames, interview with Kirkham.

32. Peter Smithson, "Just a Few Chairs and a House: An Essay on the Eames-Aesthetic," *Architectural Design* 36 (September 1966): 443.

33. "We hung them off the ceiling for two reasons—one was because they needed to be kept away from strong light and the second was because we thought we would be able to see them well from that position." Ray Eames, interview with Kirkham.

34. Charles Eames, quoted in "Life in a Chinese Kite," 94.

35. R. Buckminster Fuller, letter to Ms. Camp, 7 November 1973, Box 30, The Work of Charles and Ray Eames, Manuscript Division, Library of Congress.

36. Charles Eames, quoted in Diehl, "Charles Eames," 14.

37. Charles Eames, "Mies van der Rohe" (photographs by Charles Eames taken at the exhibition), *Arts & Architecture*, December 1947, 27.

38. Ibid.

39. Charles Eames quoted in "A Designer's Home of His Own," 152.

40. "Furniture Show Room by Charles Eames," *Arts & Architecture*, October 1949, 26–29.

41. "California's Bold Look," *Life*, June 1954, 90–97; "California Ideas: Spreading West to East," *Vogue*, 15 April 1954, 60–87.

CHAPTER SIXTEEN

What Is Construction, What's the Aesthetic, What Was Adorno Doing?

Robert Kaufman

Always aestheticize! Surely such a directive, felt to have been the disciplinary refrain of a formalist theory and poetics, was what brought forth Fredric Jameson's now classic counterinjunction:

> Always historicize! This slogan—the one absolute and we may even say "transhistorical" imperative of all dialectical thought—will unsurprisingly turn out to be the moral of *The Political Unconscious* as well.[1]

A great deal of critical theory, since Jameson issued his mandate, has assumed an identity between *the aesthetic* (particularly in its Kantian and modernist versions) and the process of *ideological deformation* of the material, the real, the sociopolitical; ultimately, of the historical. For many critics working during the past two decades from the Marxian or Marxian-derived premises of the "critique of aesthetic ideology," it has been axiomatic that Kantian aesthetics and the art contemporaneous with it establish an essentialist or transcendental ideology of literary-cultural value whose Other, from romanticism through modernism, will be the material, the social, and the historical; whose Other, to formulate it more precisely, will be the critical attempt to engage the material, social, and historical from a political, interventionist standpoint. Meanwhile, the desire to further such critical engagement has kindled the search for an aesthetic different from the classically Kantian or modernist versions and their legacies in hopes of finding an aesthetic more attuned, or at least less hostile, to the materio-historical. Widely propagated notions such as the anti-aesthetic come quickly to mind, summoning up diverse practices in art and theory (not to mention the influential volume of essays collected under that title by Hal Foster).[2] And, of course, recent years have been marked by the intent to coordinate divergent aesthetics (or anti-aesthetics) rather than to promote any single form, structure, style, or mode.

Important as the revisionist project (and a kindred effort in cultural studies) has been, I want in this essay to advance a claim that may seem at odds with anti-aesthetic exploration of artistic and critical history. Put simply, there is good cause to question a foundational assumption here, namely, that Kantian, romantic, and modernist aesthetics *do* ideologically deform the real, the material, and the historical by turning them first into art and then into the latter's ideology. A strong case presents itself that, on the contrary, assumptions or articulations of ideological deformation themselves deform or misrepresent the aesthetic. This deformation or misrepresentation stems from a tendency—tracing itself back at least to the tangled reception histories of Walter Benjamin's "The Work of Art in the Age of Mechanical Reproduction"—to posit an identity between *the aesthetic* and the different (though certainly related) phenomenon of aestheti*cization.* There are various theoretical and methodological grounds on which to distinguish the two phenomena. But given the reliance by much critique-of-aesthetic-ideology criticism on Frankfurt school "critical theory," and given the critique of aesthetic ideology's particular turn throughout the 1990s to the work of Theodor Adorno (amid more widespread renewal of attention across the humanities to the Frankfurt school oeuvre, including a plethora of new Adorno studies), it becomes even more interesting to make the aesthetic's case from within a Marxian vocabulary and syntax, and above all from within Adorno's profound contributions to Marxian-based critical theory.

What I'd like to suggest is that even when approached from Marxian traditions of dialectical criticism—perhaps especially when approached from those traditions, the Adornian most importantly—real doubts arise concerning the validity of the critique of aesthetic ideology's fundamental methodological translation. At issue is a presumptive ability—much asserted, but hardly demonstrated, in contemporary ideology critique—to translate *from* Marx and Engels's anatomy (in *The German Ideology*) of left-wing "Young Hegelian" consciousness philosophy's theory of politics and state power *to* the examination of an ostensibly homologous romantic, aesthetic, or modernist "ideology" of literature and art.[3] Yet, in crucial if sometimes unacknowledged ways, Marxian critical theory traditions (starting with Marx and Engels) have effectively regarded the dynamics of Kantian and modern aesthetics as *anti*-aestheti*cist.* To state this even more polemically: those Marxian traditions proceed at key moments—pace today's critique of aesthetic ideology—on the presumption that *the aesthetic* is *anti*-aestheti*cist,* and that the aesthetic's anti-aestheticizing propensity enables, among other things, the thinking of history and historicization themselves, the very ability to posit, however provisionally, the sort of "transhistorical imperative" that Jameson understandably associates with dialectical thought (and that knows its analogues in deconstructively conceived imperatives to think Otherness).

While Jameson's own writing has been extremely important to various critique-of-aesthetic-ideology critics, his oeuvre is scarcely capable of being wholly or even largely identified with straightforwardly anti-aesthetic revisionism. But because of its enormous influence on Marxian-inflected literary and cultural criticism, and because of its decades-long meditation on the place of ideological demystification within literary-critical activity, it makes sense, in a rethinking of aesthetic ideology and the materio-historical, to treat Jameson's work as exemplary and, it turns out, as a somewhat surprising touchstone. For in the twenty years since *The Political Unconscious* sounded its clarion call for (or its codification of) a return to dialecticized historicism, Jameson has expressed interesting reservations about the overhasty or antagonistic positing of opposition between the materio-historical and the aesthetic. When one traces out the logic of these Jamesonian reservations, some positions begin to take shape that would be hard to square with much of the aesthetic-ideology criticism that regularly cites Jameson. Relevant here are various, recurrent conclusions Jameson has reached or gestured toward: that the aesthetic ought to be distinguished from aestheticization; that the former is, in notable ways, hostile to the latter; and that the ironic denouement of this history within Marxian critical theory—ironic in terms of the analysis laid out in *The German Ideology* and the *Theses on Feuerbach*—may well be that the counterspecter of a new Young Hegelianism appears today not in the guise of commitments to the aesthetic, but, paradoxically, in the ideology of "the material, and materialist criticism" itself. Though the configuration of ideas that I'm invoking becomes visible at charged junctures in Jameson's work, it more clearly echoes a constellation of thought that within Marxian critical traditions finds its most sustained and celebrated exposition in Adorno, generated, as I will show, by Adorno's unique, widely misunderstood attempts to hold fast to the Kantian aesthetic even as he sheds new light upon it. It is therefore no accident that Jameson comes closest to these positions—and also attempts an at least apparent distancing from them—in the fascinating study of Adorno with which he began the 1990s.

Indeed, at a symptomatic moment in his indispensable *Late Marxism: Adorno, or, The Persistence of the Dialectic*, Jameson gets it exactly half right when he characterizes Adorno's *Ästhetische Theorie* (1970) as a series of "guerrilla raids into the *Critique of Judgement*," raids that "turn [Kant's third *Critique*] inside out and rewrite it."[4] Now, Adorno does, in some sense, raid and rewrite the third *Critique*; and Jameson joins a host of critics who have noted that the earlier *Negative Dialectics* is meant to correspond to Kant's *Critique of Pure Reason*, while *Aesthetic Theory* stands, like Kant's last *Critique*, as linchpin and culmination of a constellated critical theory. But Adorno doesn't quite undertake the *Guevarista* forays against an enemy stronghold that Jameson's metaphor implies. Rather, Adorno's reworkings of Kant—into a late-modernist, Left vocabulary—constitute invaluable appropriations and translations that might well be regarded, at least in significant part, as a critical theory formally and phenomenologically indistinguishable from Kant's own accounts of aesthetics and epistemology.

Jameson has good warrant for this attempt to distance Adorno from the figure of Kant; in fact, Jameson's effective apology for Adorno's often apologetic Kantianism repeats, or raises to the second power, Adorno's now elided, now explicit defenses of Kant. We have to do here with one of the latest and more complicated enactments of a much-buried but still-haunting plot within Marxian and Marxian-inflected aesthetics, in which Kant effectively becomes the ghost of the old Hamlet, disappearing with the allegedly materialist dawn but murmuring—to Adorno in particular—"Adieu, adieu, adieu; remember me." This conjuring away or summoning up of the figure of Kant is a maneuver that for Marxism (and the various post-Marxisms) begins with Marx and continues unabated. It is animated by recurrent polemics within Left criticism over whether to regard "Kant" as the figure for a prescriptive, bourgeois-modern theory and practice of desocialized representationalism in aesthetics, politics, and ethics, or as the figure for the negative critical project of understanding the limits of thought and conditions of possibility for philosophy and praxis both.

In what follows, I'll use Jameson's reading of Adorno's reading of Kant as the site from which to examine key features of Kantian aesthetics, features that Adorno deems essential to critical apprehension of and engagement with modernity; I'll be taking Jameson's interpretation as exemplary of notable trends in Marxian and Marxian-influenced theory of the postmodernist period. If space permitted, I'd also want to discuss adjacent critic-theorists who work in different registers or somewhat distinct languages from Jameson's to show that what's at stake in treatments of Kant and Adorno (or Adorno's Frankfurt school colleagues) concerns contemporary theory in ways that go well beyond Marxian or Marxian-oriented methodologies. Here I'll simply note that in a manner substantially parallel to Jameson's distancing of Adorno from Kant, various critics have opposed a Benjaminian constructivism to what is deemed a canonical Kantian aesthetics. In these marshalings of Benjamin and/or Adorno for anti-Kant critique, *construction* or *constructivism* operates as a term meant (along with *materiality, the social, the historical*) to counter what is stigmatized as *formalist, static, self-reflexive, Kantian essentialism.* Thus construction is frequently the place where *Ideologiekritik* rereadings of the Frankfurt school converge with anti-aesthetic theories of social construction, or with plottings of alternative aesthetic theories and practices intended to project defamiliarizing, emancipatory historiographies.[5]

Jameson's 1990 reassessment of Adorno appeared just as another significant wave of Frankfurt school studies (often concentrating on Adorno) was breaking. One thinks—to name only a few—of works by Susan Buck-Morss, Martin Jay, Shierry Weber Nicholsen, Robert Hullot-Kentor, Miriam Hansen, J. N. Bernstein, Russell A. Berman, Richard Wolin, Peter Uwe Hohendahl, and Lambert Zuidervaart (and, more recently, Tom Huhn, Anthony Cascardi, and Beatrice Hanssen). And the critical work has arrived along with the increasing availability of Adorno's and Benjamin's texts in English translation. In Adorno's case, it would be hard to overestimate the significance of Nicholsen's immediately indispensable translations (1991–92) of Adorno's *Noten zur Literatur* and Hullot-Kentor's luminous, long-awaited new translation of *Ästhetische*

Theorie (as well as the fact that under Hullot-Kentor's general editorship, an English-language *Selected Works* is under way).[6]

Jameson's above-quoted comments about Adorno's "guerrilla raids" on the third *Critique* occur amid his own 250-page meditation on Adorno, in which Jameson essentially reverses his earlier preference (hardly concealed in *Marxism and Form* and *The Political Unconscious*) for a Lukácsian-Sartrean, rather than an Adornian, Marxism. In *Late Marxism,* Jameson retrospectively stages his earlier hesitancy about Adorno as a matter of periodization: Adorno's sober and seemingly non-*engagé* dialectic had first been out of step with the explosions of the sixties and seventies, and then unassimilable to the radically populist orientations of theoretical discourse and cultural studies in the eighties. For us today, Jameson convincingly observes, Adorno's relentless refusal of the notion of a secret subversiveness latent within commodified, culture-industry culture—Adorno's insistence that this or that projection of mass-culture radicalism is in reality the profoundly depoliticizing projection of capital itself—this, Jameson lucidly demonstrates, is dialectical tonic for the post–Cold War era of the global market and its privileged ideologeme, the hyperweb technological sublime. One should perhaps go on to quote the recipient of the city of Frankfurt's 1995 Adorno Prize—an artist whom Jameson a few years ago linked intriguingly to Adorno and to reimaginings, not of postmodernism, but of something like a modernism that could come after modernism—"There is the rule. There is the exception. The rule is culture. Culture is a question of rules. It is part of the rules. Exception is a question of art. Everyone speaks the rule: cigarettes, computers, t-shirts, television, tourism, war."[7]

Yet Jameson's powerfully made historical case for a return to Adorno serves to mute the formal, Kantian core in the Frankfurt school aesthetician. It would hardly do to claim Adorno as an anti-Kantian; instead, *Late Marxism* alternates among the guerrilla-raids analogy, a neutral description of Adorno's variations on Kantian assumptions, and, at key moments, a silence about Adorno's having indicated that Kant provides the impetus for some of *Aesthetic Theory*'s most original contributions. (In *Late Marxism*'s wake, Jameson has more or less resurrected his earlier, more explicitly anti-Kant viewpoint, associating Kantian philosophy with neo-Kantian positivism, or locating the value of Kant's third *Critique*—and of aesthetics itself—in the latter's unintentional failures, its inabilities to systematize what Jameson assumes it had determined to systematize.)[8] In another place, one might supplement these responses to Jamesonian analysis with the more scandalous suggestion that Jameson's most acute criticism during the 1990s flowed precisely from *Late Marxism*'s Adornian-Kantian impulses, a suggestion that might befit the critic who for some time has been thought to have succeeded Adorno as the key literary-critical voice in Marxian theory. One thinks not only of Jameson's determination to remain patiently immanent and diagnostic vis-à-vis the postmodern. Relevant too are what various observers have deemed his "unfathomable" accolades for what they had regarded as the antipolitical stance and methodology of works like Walter Benn Michaels's *The Gold Standard and the Logic of Naturalism.*[9] One might point as well to Jameson's calls for an aesthetics that would help develop "a new sensorium" capable of mapping the mode of production proper to what he designates, after the late Ernest Mandel, "the third stage of Capital."[10]

A long-historical view of the Kantian crux in Marxist aesthetics involves consideration of the ways two interrelated figural clusters—which rapidly install themselves at the heart of romantic and nineteenth-century culture—generate key intellectual methodologies (and concomitant notions of sociopolitical agency) for the Marxian critical theory traditions that emerge from the Enlightenment and romanticism; those Marxian traditions for their part will almost ritualistically distance themselves from the two figural constellations at issue. These figural groupings emanate from Kant's entire oeuvre but are located most dynamically in the "interplay" Kant envisions among the *Critique of Pure Reason,* the *Critique of Practical Reason,* and the *Critique of Judgment* (with special emphasis on the last). This returns us to the question of *construction,* because the initial figural grouping involves an anti-essentialist constructivism inherent in Kant's aesthetics and epistemology that is quite distinct from the labor-theory-of-value *productionism* often emphasized in Marxian aesthetics. (That productionism, of course, springs in part from Marxian attempts—starting with the *Theses on Feuerbach* and *The German Ideology*—to conceive "the determining character of the mode of production" nondeterministically, as it were; as a site where agents of production might be imagined not only to produce the products generated by the mode and means of production but also to produce their own agency.) Rather than a Lukácsian (or, at times, a Brechtian-

Benjaminian) transmutation of the metaphorics of artistic "making" into "the dialectical self-making of the working class," Adorno adapts Kant's much less determinate notion of human construction, which in turn will yield a markedly different version of human agency. Meanwhile, the second figural grouping simply involves the combined figures of Kant himself and the Kantian itself.

Commentators have previously observed that for all its own Hegelianism, the Frankfurt school maintains—in certain ways, even foregrounds—a Kantian legacy that distinguishes it from more fully Hegelian theory. Much Frankfurt school work (certainly Adorno's) sees Kantian philosophy's eschewal of totality, its methodological insistence on foundational and irreconcilable antinomy between the intelligible and the empirical, the phenomenal and the noumenal, as the cornerstone of critical theory's elaboration of the nonidentical and of its dedication to concrete particularity. Responding to Lukácsian claims that Kantian philosophy merely instantiates or reproduces "the antinomies of bourgeois thought" (and that a synthesizing theory should dialectically transcend those antinomies), the Frankfurt school holds that Kantian antinomies, while not to be regarded as immutable, at the very least reflect accurately the divisions between life and thought (and the divisions present inside each) under actually existing capitalism and "really existing socialism" both.[11] Still, Adorno's explicit and profound commitment to key aspects of Hegelian thought and procedure, everywhere evident in his oeuvre (famously evident, in fact, in the very syntax of his sentences), has at times made it difficult to see that Kant remains vital to Adorno. There is even reason to believe that when Adorno directly challenges (or rhetorically distances himself from) Kant, he generally seems to be writing from within politically situated occasions where he feels compelled to worry the question of bourgeois formalism. In a cultural-political signification Adorno shares with various Left allies and interlocutors, he often invokes Kant as the sign for bourgeois formalism, even where it is manifest that, logically speaking, Adorno's position is virtually indistinguishable from Kant's. Meanwhile, when Kant is not clearly present in the docket, Adorno can proceed quite happily as a Left Kantian. And Adorno certainly is at pains to defend Kant against Hegel's infamous critique of Kant's "Hebraic" refusal of conceptual totality. The negative dialectic, then—the undoing of dialectical synthesis—can be grasped as Adorno's imagining a history in which Kant follows Hegel and as a return to the seemingly nondialectical moment in order to prevent dialectical reification and positivism. On this view, *Aesthetic Theory* is, as Jameson observes, a rewriting, but a rewriting that moves in a direction opposite to that which Jameson charts. *Aesthetic Theory* rewrites the history of aesthetic theory (and Marxist theory as well), making it spiral from Hegel to Kant.[12]

The claim for the Kantian base of Adorno's (and Jameson's) critical procedures should probably first be pursued by tracing Adorno's recurrent use of the idea of construction, showing that Adorno sometimes explicitly aligns the concept and practice with what he deems its Kantian source and that at other times Adorno explains (and proselytizes for) modernist construction without bothering to mention Kant. Adorno's initial debt is undoubtedly to Benjamin's early insights into the properly modernist movements of artistic constructivism (as well as to Benjamin's early treatments of Kantian theory as the starting point for a radical criticism);[13] from that vantage point, the teasing out of a constructivism inherent in the Kantian aesthetic will begin to look like an attempt on Adorno's part to plot the ways in which the antiorganicism of modernist constructivism stands as a realization, not a refutation, of Kantian aesthetics.

The background sources in Kant that for Adorno establish a penumbra of construction can be schematically presented and then followed through with more textured discussion of Adorno's own work. The place to begin is with an old third-*Critique* chestnut, the Kantian aesthetic's *quasi*-conceptual quality: although the aesthetic looks like conceptual, purposeful, rule-based thought or activity, it quite precisely only *looks like* them, only mimes them at the level of form.[14] Consequently, the aesthetic is formal. But for Kant, such formality is—or becomes—generative. This means simply that within the realm of thought, the aesthetic, rather than being determined by, provides *the form for* conceptual, purposeful thought or cognition. Aesthetic thought-experience remains "free" (at least, relative to more properly conceptual thought) from the preexistent rules assumed to govern conceptual-objective thought (*Judgment*, sec. 5, 54; see also sec. 2, 45–46). In the Kantian lexicon, the aesthetic functions as the site of "reflective" rather than "determinate" judgment.[15] The aesthetic is thus both a boot-up disk for conceptual thought as such (for "cognition in general," as Kant puts it; *Judgment*, sec. 9, 62), and, as Adorno and others will stress, the engine for new, experimental—because previously nonexistent (and therefore, free of status quo–determined)—concepts. The operative notion is that thought determined by society (which is to say, thought determined by society's reigning concepts of itself) can never give a satisfactory, even provisionally true picture of that society. So for Adorno, the Kantian aesthetic will not simply exceed the status quo, the socioconceptual, by affording utopian images of a society yet-to-be. With its quasi-social and quasi-conceptual character, aesthetic experiment—even the most seemingly recondite aesthetic experiment—also provides a prerequisite of critical thought when (if only by negation or in art's negative space) it offers formal means for allowing new (and not necessarily utopian) aspects of contemporary society to come into view.

What aesthetic experiment thus constructs and/or makes available is, among other things, the intellectual and emotional apparatus for accessing, and to that extent the social material of, "the new." Crucially at play is the effective lack of an object in Kant's formulation of aesthetic experience; the subject experiences and "will talk about the beautiful as if beauty were a characteristic of the object and the judgment were logical . . . even though in fact the judgment is only aesthetic and refers the object's presentation merely to the subject" (*Judgment,* sec. 6, 54). This imputation to the object of qualities projected by the subject appears also to work metonymically (as far as Adorno's own constructivism is concerned) with Kant's attempts in the first *Critique* to make a Euclidian figuration of human construction help imply a significant claim: that the human mind's ability to *construct* what Kant calls figural but "true" geometric proofs can establish the possibility of synthetic a priori judgments. Those compass-and-protractor proofs are, Kant emphasizes, figural constructions of analyses not dependent on empirical objects; although geometric proofs do not utilize empirical materials or the objects actually referred to, their figurative constructions nonetheless, Kant underscores, discover truths in relation to the physical world and to the process of analytic/mathematical measurement itself.[16]

Last, and perhaps most important, is the dynamic paradox of judgment on which Kant has premised the success of his third *Critique* and critical philosophy as a whole: the paradox of the simultaneous "demand for agreement," and actual impossibility of achieving consensus, about the beautiful—what from a literary-critical perspective could be grasped as the fictive, and structurally defamiliarizing, character of the

Kantian "demand" (see *Judgment,* sec. 6, 53–54).[17] Aesthetic-ideology criticism tends to see this demand not as a paradox (let alone a dynamic one) or as the disinterested appraisal of beauty that Kant imagines. Rather, the demand is seen as a coercive mandate of cultural-political conformity made not only by an empirical, bourgeois subject, but also, at least allegorically, by the supersubject: the bourgeois state. Yet Kant's celebrated qualification that the judging subject feels *as if* everyone must agree with his or her appraisal is more than a concessionary attempt to build flexibility or conditionality into the scheme. The *as if (als ob)* imparts a fundamentally aporetic character to the entire process of aesthetic judgment. However much the subject feels as if there are grounds for universal agreement with his or her "disinterested" judgment of beauty, he or she simultaneously knows that, in empirical fact, such a presumption cannot possibly be met. (It might be more accurate to say that the subject knows this on the assumption that he or she lacks that delusional "fanaticism" that for Kant characterizes, in a parallel case, misguided attempts to take literally the figurative, speculative, and momentary "identification" with the sublime.)

Kant's theoretical description, in other words, captures a patently fictive—although true, insofar as subjectively experienced—sense of disinterest and agreement. Kant implies that this is an experience of agreement whose self-divided logic weirdly projects the possibility of uncoerced social construction from the very absence of an object, general rule, norm, or standard of taste that would determine the process called the judgment of beauty. Kant figures that possibility of uncoerced social construction as the "*postulate*"—emphatically not as the reality or realization, but simply the "postulate"—of a "*universal voice*" (*Judgment,* sec. 8, 60). The subjective aesthetic experience of feeling that others should (or would, if only they were consulted) share one's judgment (since that judgment is experienced as disinterested, as if it were uncoupled from extant concepts and sociomaterial interests)—this subjective experience is fused aporetically with the conceptual-objective knowledge that, empirically speaking, while other subjects undergo formally similar experiences or thought-feelings, their experiences/thought-feelings actually are attached to substantive judgments different from one's own. This self-divided phenomenological structure is theorized as ground and springboard for a rational, noninstrumentalized, noncoercive constructionism. The implied necessity for such constructionism arises from the constitutive impasse the structure produces; to resort to coercion would immediately and obviously vitiate the subject's initial judgment of beauty because that judgment requires the sense—however subjective and provisional—of disinterest. Coercive or violent attempts to obtain others' agreement might prove the subject's power but would perforce establish that his or her judgment could not be one of beauty, as the need for force reveals interest to be at issue.

Awareness of both the impulse toward and the problematically "fictive" character of agreement, uncoerced interchange, conversation, discussion, and decision making (which of course appears, with distinct tonalities and consequences, in Arendt, Adorno, Habermas, and others) consequently serves as a cornerstone for views that the third *Critique*, rather than commencing an "aestheticist" history of mandated taste and behavior that will issue from an institutionally hegemonic artistic-cultural sphere, instead theorizes via aesthetic experience the grounds of possibility for newly conceived and constructed sociopolitical arrangements.[18] In short, the standards- and convention-eschewing character of the aesthetic, together with its tendency to foster interchange about how and why other subjects would or would not share the judging subject's conceptually undetermined judgment, impels the aesthetic toward an ongoing construction of intersubjectivity. This process is *anti*-aesthetic*ist* in that it springs not only from the eschewal of preexisting beautified or idealized images, conventions, and crystallizations that have already achieved conceptual status, but from a necessary eschewal of determination-by-extant-concepts *tout court.*

Given the centrality and all-informing role of this Kantian schema in Adorno's aesthetics, it is surprising that Adorno's own unique articulation of construction has not received wider attention. The need more fully to address the topic has, to be sure, been registered: Jameson himself has offered a lucid (albeit highly compressed) summary of Adornian construction; more recently, Martin Jay has attempted to think through Adornian construction and the closely related matters of mimesis and expression.[19] Robert Hullot-Kentor, however, is the English-language writer who has paid the most sustained attention to construction. He has noted how factors that might be taken for granted—for example, the title of Adorno's first published philosophical work, *Kierkegaard: Construction of the Aesthetic* (1933)—evidence Adorno's having from the start put construction and its problematic status front and center.

The ambiguity in the title "as to whether the book is a presentation of Kierkegaard's construction or is itself the construction of the aesthetic," is precisely "a claim to know the object from within."[20] Construction also serves to convey that "a true organicity can be achieved only by way of a principle of dissonant composition." Rather than romantically assuming that in a reified world, materials themselves can still count as organic, construction—literary and otherwise—actively reassembles the materials it finds, yet does so only "to achieve the self-expression of the material" and to come "once again closest to the organic."[21] Hullot-Kentor concludes that, for Adorno, construction animates a Benjaminian desideratum, the "ability to form constellations" of critical thought; conversely, absent the process of construction, "knowledge separates from its material" and we enact the history-as-sacrifice-of-subjectivity outlined in *Dialectic of Enlightenment.* Construction stands as a starting point for attempts to fulfill (noninstrumentalizing versions) of Enlightenment.[22]

The unfinished *Aesthetic Theory* (Adorno died in 1969, amid plans for a final revision of the text) gathers and refines ideas about construction that Adorno had been working out for decades; his prior meditations on construction had been built up through ongoing considerations of music, philosophy, and poetics. *Aesthetic Theory* condenses and rearticulates the previous meditations into what Adorno calls "the dialectic of construction and expression." *Expression* is a cognate term for *mimesis,* or, rather, for a mimetic behavior that keeps faith with the truth of human suffering: "In expression [artworks] reveal themselves as the wounds of society" (*Aesthetic,* 237). For Adorno, expression or mimesis emphatically does not mean straightforward imitation or copying; on the contrary, insofar as mimesis partakes of aesthetic quasi-conceptuality, it counters (or balances) conceptual thought's imperial subsumption of particulars under general/universal rules. Adorno understands mimesis as a discovery or enactment of nonidentical, potentially nondominative "affinities," affinities between different concrete particulars, between subjects and objects, subjects and other subjects, subjects and whatever might be adjacent to them; this is what aesthetic representation instantiates and stimulates.[23]

Meanwhile, construction involves the spiritual, intellectual, and/or rational treatment (or handling, configuration, manipulation) of expression's mimetic materials; construction takes them "out of their primary context and transforms them" in the necessary process of the "mediation of expression in artworks through their spiritualization" (*Aesthetic*, 57, 114). While "construction inheres tautologically in expression, which is its polar opposite," at the same time even the most relentlessly constructivist artworks carry within them "the indelible trace of mimesis, on which construction depends" (*Aesthetic*, 100, 138). There is no balanced medium here, no rightly struck harmonious synthesis that can establish a standard or goal; the reality is always that "the aporia of mimesis and construction compels artworks to unite radicalism with deliberation" (*Aesthetic*, 115). In the case of "exemplary artists" (e.g., Schönberg, Klee, Picasso),

> the expressive mimetic element and the constructive element are of equal intensity, not by seeking a happy mean between them but rather by way of the extremes: Yet each is simultaneously content-laden, expression is the negativity of suffering, and construction is the effort to bear up under the suffering of alienation by exceeding it on the horizon of undiminished and thus no longer violent rationality. (*Aesthetic*, 257)

Those commentators who have turned their attention to Adornian construction observe that Adorno intermittently gives the sense, in *Aesthetic Theory* and various late essays, that despite the ongoing interrelationship of expression and construction—the necessity of their asymmetrical interanimation—a certain primacy nonetheless attaches to construction.[24] What the secondary literature has not explained is Adorno's having established a textured and signifying linkage between his constructivism and Kant's: How and why should Kant figure as more than just an aesthetic-theory background source for Adornian construction? Another way to approach the question would be to show (and then wonder about the fact) that in *Aesthetic Theory* and Adorno's late essays, it is—contrary to expectation—decidedly not Hegel who animates Adorno's constructivism (though neither is it exactly the case that a polemic surfaces against Hegel). This is all the more notable in the face of the long-standing, quite accurate consensus about Hegel's importance to Adorno.[25] Logic would seem to dictate that the apparent dynamism of Hegelian cancellation/sublation *(Aufhebung)* should best represent construction, but Adorno moves in the opposite direction. Here one probably could not overestimate the importance to Adorno of the Kantian aesthetic's quasi-conceptuality (or aconceptuality). As discussed above, quasi-conceptuality—which provisionally escapes determination by extant concepts, cognitive objects, norms, and rules—produces the generative impasse of aesthetic experience and judgment (which in turn generates the possibility of construction itself). "In every artwork, and not only in the aporia of the faculty of reflective judgment, the universal and the particular are densely intertwined. Kant touches on this when he defines the beautiful as 'that which pleases universally without requiring a concept'" (*Aesthetic,* 165).[26] On the other hand, Hegelian philosophy's relentless dedication to the conceptual severely undercuts the former's ability to do justice to art and aesthetics, which require immersion in the work's formal, nondiscursive or nonconceptual character: "Kant's emphasis on the work's formal constituents, through which the work becomes art in the first place, does more honor to the truth content of art than Hegel does, who directly intended this but never developed it out of art itself" (*Aesthetic,* 354).[27]

If construction exists in fruitful tension with expression, there is another phenomenon to which it is more ominously related, although neither Adorno nor his interpreters have put it quite this way. The third phenomenon or term that helps clarify the theoretical and historical stakes of Adorno's constructivism (and his invocations of Kant) is *production.* It would seem that part of Adorno's interest in developing constructionist ideas involves the plotting of an alternative to *productionism*—not only to capitalist productionism, but also to what Adorno regards as Marxism's own grim version of instrumental rationality, where what is unduly valued is the objectness of the material product, artifact, or object that has been worked into existence and become "objectively identified" with its ostensibly revolutionary, supersubject maker. In short, we have to do here with the heroic Hegelian- or Viconian-Marxist narrative of the proletariat coming to know itself at the point of production where it creates itself and history until the two terms become fused. In Adorno's eyes, the worker, in the name of the objective identification proclaimed by revolutionary productionism, is him- or herself simply produced as an object.

That Adorno had long worried this question, and pondered a way to articulate within Marxian aesthetics a compelling alternative to instrumental productionism, is evident throughout his writings. And the worry is not only about other people's errors; Adorno is himself committed to aesthetic, sociological, and historical analyses that spring from—and continue to utilize—Marxian thought about modes of production, means of production, and relations of production. As for the history of aesthetics, Adorno is one of those who most brilliantly brings mode- and means-of-production terminology into the work of art itself (in order to describe the latter's making, its internal workings, its commodity-like objectification in the modern era, and, more macrologically, its interactions with society). "Art is modern when, by its mode of experience and as the expression of the crisis of experience, it absorbs what industrialization has developed under the given relations of production. . . . That this modernity is more than a vague Zeitgeist or being cleverly *up to date* depends on the liberation of the forces of production. Modern art is equally determined socially by the conflict with the conditions of production" (*Aesthetic,* 34).[28]

Although committed simultaneously to grasping art in terms of Marxian production categories and to understanding these very notions of social production through the language of aesthetic illumination, Adorno is also capable of asking difficult questions about the inherent tendencies of such terminology. Consider, for example, a lengthy passage from "Sur l' eau," the concluding section of the second part of *Minima Moralia* (the part subtitled "1945"):

> He who asks what is the goal of an emancipated society is given answers such as the fulfillment of human possibilities or the richness of life. Just as the inevitable question is illegitimate, so the repellent assurance of the answer is inevitable. . . . There is tenderness only in the coarsest demand: that no-one shall go hungry anymore. Every other seeks to apply to a condition that ought to be determined by human needs, a mode of human conduct adapted to *production* as an end in itself. Into the wishful image of an uninhibited, vital, creative man has seeped the very fetishism of commodities which in bourgeois society brings with it inhibition, impotence, the sterility of the never-changing. The concept of dynamism, which is the necessary complement of bourgeois "a-historicity," is raised to an absolute, whereas it ought, as an anthropological reflex of the *laws of production,* to be itself critically confronted, in an emancipated society, with need. The conception of unfettered activity, of uninterrupted procreation, of chubby insatiability, of freedom as frantic bustle, feeds on the bourgeois concept of nature that has always served solely to proclaim social violence as unchangeable, as a piece of healthy eternity. It was in this, and not in their alleged levelling-down, that the positive blue-prints of socialism, resisted by Marx, were rooted in barbarism. . . . The naive supposition of an unambiguous development towards increased *production* is itself a piece of that bourgeois outlook which permits development in only one direction because, integrated into a

> totality, dominated by quantification, it is hostile to qualitative difference. If we imagine emancipated society as emancipation from precisely such totality, then vanishing-lines come into view that have little in common with increased *production* and its human reflections.... even the *forces of production* are not the deepest substratum of man, but represent his historical form adapted to the *production of commodities*.... A mankind which no longer knows want will begin to have an inkling of the delusory, futile nature of all the arrangements hitherto made in order to escape want, which used wealth to reproduce want on a larger scale. Enjoyment itself would be affected.... *Rien faire comme une betê,* lying on water and looking peacefully at the sky, "being, nothing else, without any further definition and fulfillment," might take the place of process, act, satisfaction, and so truly keep the promise of dialectical logic that it would culminate in its origin. None of the abstract concepts comes closer to fulfilled utopia than that of eternal peace [Keiner unter den abstrakten Begriffen kommt der erfüllten Utopie näher als der vom ewigen Frieden]. Spectators on the sidelines of progress like Maupassant... have helped this intention to find expression, timidly, in the only way that its fragility permits.[29]

In what seems a quite traditional manner, Adorno offers a recognizably Kantian "purposelessness" meant to stand in opposition to means-driven existence (which here is emphatically identified with modern phenomena of production; the latter has been linked, throughout "Sur l'eau," not only to capitalism, but also to economistic Social Democracy and—most fatefully, however much it goes unnamed—to really existing, Soviet-style socialism). But as consideration of Adorno's historical intertext will show, the passage involves far more than an aesthetic utopianism filled with images of calm and voluptuous drifting.

Our previous discussion explicated Adorno's constructivism within the dynamics of aporetic aesthetic experience (or aporetic reflective judgment). That experience, it should be added, is called forth by the reading (or listening or viewing) subject's engagement with artworks that have issued from the artist's own first-order activity (individual and social) of *making:* the artist's casting expression and construction into relationship. Adorno theorizes the later-stage (reading, listening, viewing) subject's participation as "second reflection," which he conceives as aesthetic experience's evocation of dialectic itself. The reader reconstructs, figuratively speaking, the artist's earlier acts of reflective construction that are now embedded in, and summoned up by, the work (see *Aesthetic,* 19, 26, 139–40, 166–67). The subject in second reflection has the opportunity to engage—via the constructed work of art—historical meaning and its stubborn opacity by way of thought's turn toward the felt opacity of artistic detail. Adorno sees the entire process as a stimulus to the possibility of critical thought and discovery, which is not so much a guarantor of any particular ethics, politics, and/or agency as their necessary prerequisite. Although he offers countless illustrations of construction from the history of the arts, Adorno's favorite, recurrent example is Schönberg.

In language that for our purposes could not be more telling, Adorno highlights Schönberg's "implicit Kantian question," which Adorno characterizes as "radical, without any ontological pseudo-radicalism"; he remarks too that Schönberg's "productive criticism of [every subjective ingredient] interlocks with constructivism."[30] Moreover, it emerges that the "complete construction" Adorno finds in Schönberg's late works (and supremely in the fragmentary opera *Moses und Aron*) exists only in relation to an ephemeral yet insistent, often negatively enacted, expressivity. Adorno traces this constructionist-expressionist history in the arts from figures like Keats and Hölderlin, through symbolism, Valéry, the second Viennese school, and beyond.[31] Such integrally constructed art takes on—in Schönberg, for example—"something of the quality of finger exercises, of studies for works that were never created"; the negational generativity of these constructions lets them function "not [just as] works, but as paradigms of a possible music."[32]

These materials involving Adornian construction and its relation to Kant and aesthetic utopianism—along with overarching questions about Hegelian dialectic and efforts to create a Marxian alternative to productionism—are further illuminated by a consideration of the 1961 essay "Vers une musique informelle" (an essay Adorno wrote just as he made his initial attempt to begin composition of *Aesthetic Theory*). "Vers une musique informelle" considers what was then being called "musique informelle" and has since been deemed the New Music's entry into postmodernism; Adorno discusses John Cage, Olivier Messiaen, Herbert Eimert, and others, particularly in relation to second Viennese school modernism. (Whether the essay's treatment of these "postmodernists" reveals a stance on Adorno's part that is itself "exceedingly postmodern," as Jameson contends, is another matter.)[33] As might be predicted, "Vers une musique informelle" is filled with reflections on the constructionist heritage, but also (as Jameson rightly notes) with a perhaps surprising sympathy for the postmodernists' retreat from late constructivist hyperformalism. Not unexpectedly (and in a way that parallels "The Aging of the New Music," though with a more generous tone), the essay resolves into the notion that the new generation of composers, if they are in fact to create a truly informal music, will paradoxically have to do so by pushing construction further rather than by renouncing it and its animating critical subjectivity. The desideratum of a salutarily informal music, in other words, would be sought through more radical experiments in formal construction, not through renunciation of the latter.

What should now be remarked is that in "Vers une musique informelle," Adorno offers an important suggestion about how we are to read the figure of the Kantian in Adorno's late work, above all in *Aesthetic Theory.* The real clue comes not so much in the essay's scattered and laudatory references to Kant, nor in the complete absence of Hegel (in an essay on music's future, probably the subject closest to Adorno's heart), nor even in the extraordinary diagnosis that "it is only now that we are in a position to appreciate fully the truth contained in the edifice of Kant's *Critique of Judgment.*"[34] Instead, after "Vers une musique informelle"'s careful and sustained discussions of the necessity and radicality of construction and its insistence on construction as the basis of the aesthetic (and hence on new experiments in construction as the basis for aesthetic renewal), the telltale sign surfaces ultimately in the essay's meditative closing lines, where Adorno summons the image of Kant's late essay "Eternal [or Perpetual] Peace" (1795):

> Impossible as it has been to discover what music authentically is, it has been no less impossible to bring wholly authentic music into being. It is better to admit this than to bar the way to it by choosing one type or the other and claiming that it embodies the ominously positive musical ideal. Informal music is a little like Kant's eternal peace [ist ein wenig der ewige Frieden Kants]. Kant himself thought of this as an actual, concrete possibility which is capable of realization and yet is nevertheless just an idea. The aim of every artistic utopia today is to make things of which we do not know what they are.[35]

One realizes with a start that the end of this construction-centered essay—the final phrase of which Adorno would go on to quote in one of *Aesthetic Theory*'s most crucial discussions of construction, expression, second reflection, Kant, and artistic form—is in turn a revisitation of *Minima Moralia*'s 1945 reflection on alternatives to *productionism.* The *ewiger Frieden* evoked at the end of the *Minima Moralia* passage quoted earlier (a passage that had itself "ended" part 2 of that text, the war-ending "1945" meditations) had omitted Kant's name, but was of course the same Kantian idea now explicitly pronounced at the culmination of "Vers une musique informelle."

The confluence allows us to see that the purposeless aesthetic suspension—the stasis—presented in *Minima Moralia*'s "Sur l'eau" gestures toward something more than a state of utopian bliss (although certainly it gestures toward that, too). Kant's well-known proposal for eternal or perpetual peace cannily projects, instead of a substantively focused vision of peace, an ostensibly static solution (a form, formalization, procedures for an international dispute-resolution forum) as a way to end human resort to warfare. Yet, as readers have observed for two centuries, Kant wagers on the idea that "static" formalization might contribute powerfully (and with flexibility) toward creating peace in ways that substantive proposals by themselves cannot. As a recent interpreter of Kant's "Zum ewigen Frieden"[36] puts it, Kant's solution aims to initiate the real concretization of an ideal by initially "subordinating the material principle, or goal, of perpetual peace to the formal principle," and so provide a form that might actually begin "to make the impossible possible."[37] Adorno understands this idea—as its placement at the end of "Vers une musique" attests—as nothing less than construction itself. In other words, the static character of aesthetic suspension is not just a marker of utopian grace and escapist or futurist deferral, nor simply construction's other or prerequisite; it belongs formally *to* construction, to the present-tense activity of constructing the materials for new concepts. The apparent timelessness of the eternal or perpetual here exists as something in construction; meanwhile, the release from focus on a goal (or on productionism's goal, the product) allows for concentration on the problem of construction (of imagining and making the form) itself. The drifting-on-the-water languor of *Minima Moralia*'s "Sur l'eau," whatever else it is, is also the turn to apparent stasis as a method for moving away from the dynamic-seeming but actually rapidly constricting movement of everyone and everything toward the productionist telos of product.

The relatively abstract register of "Vers une musique informelle"'s conjuration of "Zum ewigen Frieden" takes on tone and color when we shuttle back to *Minima Moralia* and forward to *Aesthetic Theory*'s quotation of "Vers une musique informelle" (as Adorno's intertext invites us to do). And in perfect complement to the stasis-as-languorous-grace version of *ewiger Frieden* presented in *Minima Moralia*'s "Sur l'eau," *Aesthetic Theory* brings stasis and construction together in a stunning, but hardly utopian, passage that moves from Haydn to Beethoven, and then to Baudelaire and the writer to whom Adorno was to have dedicated *Aesthetic Theory*, Samuel Beckett. In a more retrospective vein than either "Vers une musique informelle" or *Minima Moralia*, *Aesthetic Theory* locates certain features of stasis in the nineteenth-century "crisis of experience" that Benjamin had stressed in his Baudelaire writings. *Aesthetic Theory* then moves to a dystopian tour de force plotting of the mutual constitution and deconstruction of modern aesthetic stasis and dynamism, exemplified above all in Beckett:

> The dynamic principle, by means of which art was long and insistently justified in hoping for homeostasis between the universal and the particular, is rejected. Even its magic is shorn away by the sense for form; it begins to seem inept.... This experience can be traced back to the middle of the nineteenth century. Baudelaire, the apologist of form no less than the poet of the *vie moderne*, expressed this in the dedication of *Le spleen de Paris*, when he wrote that he can break off where he pleases.... [Baudelaire's] *dégoût* extends to the dynamic principle that engenders the work as autonomous in itself. Since that moment the law of all art has been its antilaw. Just as for the bourgeois nominalistic artwork the necessity of a static form decayed, here it is the aesthetic dynamic that decays in accord with the experience first formulated by Kürnberger but flashing up in each line and stanza of Baudelaire, that life no longer exists. This has not changed in the situation in which contemporary art finds itself.... Process has been unmasked as repetition and has thus become an embarrassment to art. Enciphered in modern art is the postulate of an art that no longer conforms to the disjunction of the static and dynamic. Beckett, indifferent to the ruling cliché of development, views his task as that of moving in an infinitely small space toward what is effectively a dimensionless point. This aesthetic principle of construction, as the principle of *Il faut continuer*, goes beyond stasis; and it goes beyond the dynamic in that it is at the same time a principle of treading water and, as such, a confession of the uselessness of the dynamic. In keeping with this, all constructivistic techniques tend toward stasis. The telos of the dynamic of the ever-same is disaster; Beckett's writings look this in the eye.[38]

Stasis, dynamism, construction (and, clearly, the classically Kantian formulation of "static," formal aesthetic experience, "purposiveness without purpose") all inhere in one another, and in Beckett. If the tone of this minihistory within *Aesthetic Theory* is grim, it is no more a representation of the whole truth than was the utopian, lazy drifting of "Sur l'eau," nor, for that matter, the utopian element in the constructivist image of Kant's perpetual peace that closed "Vers une musique informelle." Lest we miss the complexly intertextual effect, "Vers une musique informelle" carries an epigraph:

> Dire cela, sans savoir quoi.
>
> —Beckett, *L'innommable*

The point is not just that Beckett presides over the essay, as he was to have presided—as dedicatee—over *Aesthetic Theory.* It is that the "dire cela, sans savoir quoi" is, in fact, the aphoristic theme on which Adorno plays variations at the end of "Vers une musique informelle," variations that link Kantian construction to Beckett, the unflinching Beckettian gaze to idealist hopes for perpetual peace, and all to the critical possibility that emerges from concrete construction of something not yet nameable: "to make things of which we do not know what they are." When *Aesthetic Theory,* in its treatment of construction, quotes the final words of "Vers une musique informelle," it thus accesses a constellation Adorno has fashioned—from exemplars of literary and theoretical construction—in order to represent and construct constructivism itself.[39]

What about Hegelian negation? My concern here has actually been not so much with the old question of whether all this constitutes a rejection, a modification, or always *was* the good version of Hegelian Marxism. What seems more interesting is the relevance today of Adorno's translations of Kantian constructivism, when the very currency of an older, even if retooled, critical negativity seems at least temporarily to have been integrated into late capitalism. The particular construction of Kant, Beckett, and the New Music in "Vers une musique informelle" bears out that Adorno seemed to have been invested not so much in forging a critical postmodernism that anticipates Jameson as in an exploration that involved imagining a modernism that might come after modernism (or, better, imagining a nonantiquarian modernism that might succeed postmodernism). This was and is a project involving a new set of coordinates, but also the adaptation of some old ones, not least those of Kantian aesthetics and modernist art.[40] Adorno's late work, expressing concern about the possible loss of art's ability to engender critical thought, rethinks a Hegelian conceptualism that, for all its manifest dialectical movement, has trouble allowing the nonconceptual, or the not-yet-conceptual, ever to emerge.

Meanwhile, a seemingly aestheticist or positivist Kantianism turns out to practice, by dint of aesthetic quasi-conceptuality's vocation to resist external determination by extant concepts, a sustained negation of ruling concepts. Adorno indicates that Hegelian resistance to the nonconceptual is at one with Hegel's condescension to the aesthetic as a source of knowledge. This condescension tends to convert Hegelian negation into its opposite, into an unintentional affirmation (by programmatic negation) of the given. The concern has hardly disappeared since Adorno's death; it is surely what has led Martin Jay to imply that the meaning and viability of Hegelian assumptions and procedures within Frankfurt critical theory (and its various legacies) must yet again be subject to reappraisal in a culture where, as Jay puts it, "Beavis and Butthead have replaced Horkheimer and Adorno as the reigning champions of negation."[41] Indeed, Jameson in an analogous formulation has acknowledged the same phenomenon, remarking the representations today widely proffered amid "the iridescent sheen of consumerist daily life" (and here the most relevant representations would seem to be those announcing the ostensibly passé or pathetically diminished vocations of art and aesthetically inflected critical theory): "The question about poetry after Auschwitz has been replaced with that of whether you could bear to read Adorno and Horkheimer next to the pool."[42]

If there is an Adornian legacy today, it would seem to entail the notion that literature, art, and philosophical aesthetics find their vocation in the critical thought they enable. Adorno's late work undertook to explore and then show how the static—but also charged and generative—phenomenon of purposeless aesthetic experience was at the core not just of the fullness of self-reflexive reflection, nor even of an elsewhere-oriented utopianism, but also of a Kantian-based theory of how Marxian, Marxian-derived, and adjacent critical thought and practice might construct construction—might construct possibilities for critical agency—itself.

Notes

For their responses to earlier versions of this essay, I am greatly indebted to Russell A. Berman, Bill Brown, Adam Casdin, James Chandler, Norma Cole, Frances Ferguson, Martin Gammon, Geoffrey Galt Harpham, Tom Huhn, Robert Hullot-

Kentor, Martin Jay, Michael Kelly, Shierry Weber Nicholsen, Robert Polhemus, Arthur Strum, Daniel Warren, and Alex Woloch. Special thanks to Fredric Jameson for having generously made suggestions concerning an essay that takes issue with aspects of his own interpretations. Any mistakes are my own.

1. Fredric Jameson, *The Political Unconscious: Narrative as a Socially Symbolic Act* (Ithaca, N.Y.: Cornell University Press, 1981), 9.

2. Hal Foster, ed., *The Anti-aesthetic: Essays on Postmodern Culture* (Port Townsend, Wash.: Bay, 1983).

3. For sustained analysis of *The German Ideology*'s textual and interpretive reception histories—and for examination of the critique of aesthetic ideology's founding but highly problematic argument for *The German Ideology*'s applicability to the realm of literature, art, and philosophical aesthetics—see Robert Kaufman, "Red Kant, or the Persistence of the Third *Critique* in Adorno and Jameson," *Critical Inquiry* 26 (summer 2000): 682–724.

4. Fredric Jameson, *Late Marxism: Adorno, or, The Persistence of the Dialectic* (New York: Verso, 1990), 127.

5. See below for Jameson's discussion of construction in Adorno. For an intriguing meditation on Benjaminian constructivism and Kantian aesthetics (in relation to contemporary literature and theory in the context of globalization), see Homi K. Bhabha, "The World and the Home," *Social Text* 31/32 (1992): 141–53; reprinted in *Dangerous Liaisons: Gender, Nation, and Postcolonial Perspectives,* ed. Anne McClintock, Aamir Mufti, and Ella Shohat (Minneapolis: University of Minnesota Press, 1997), 445–55. For Bhabha's further treatment of Benjamin's materialist constructivism vis-à-vis globalized literary-theoretical study, see his *The Location of Culture* (London: Routledge, 1994).

Bhabha's thoughts about Benjaminian constructivism might be usefully juxtaposed with those of a critic not usually paired with Bhabha: Paul de Man. As is well-known, the trajectory of de Man's final two decades went something like this: a movement from profound (if seemingly formal) engagement with Benjamin's 1928 reversal (in the *Trauerspiel* study) of critical priorities between symbol and allegory (a reversal made over against a romantic and modernist poetics complicatedly bound up with Kantianism); to much more explicit invocation of the Left penumbra around Benjamin and Adorno; and finally, toward assimilation of *The German Ideology* to his own reading of the third *Critique,* so that, in de Man's account, Kant and Schiller could emerge as the first card-carrying Young Hegelians. (For Benjamin himself, of course, *Trauerspiel* allegoresis was inseparable from—or was even the basis for—constructivism. For a fuller treatment of de Manian/deconstructive interpretations of Benjaminian allegory, see Kaufman, "Red Kant.") Although not the only place this schema appeared, de Man's 1969 "The Rhetoric of Temporality" perhaps most dramatically announced and propagated the deconstructive revaluation of traditional romantic concepts and terminology, especially the reprioritization of allegory over symbol; see "The Rhetoric of Temporality," in Paul de Man, *Blindness and Insight: Essays in the Rhetoric of Contemporary Criticism,* 2d ed., rev. (Minneapolis: University of Minnesota Press, 1983), 187–228.

Jameson's own mobilization of allegory as a critical concept has probably too readily been treated *apart* from the Benjaminian/de Manian matrices that he often seems to have assumed without fully elucidating. A signal example may have been Jameson's controversial "Third World Literature in the Era of Multinational Capitalism," *Social Text* 15 (fall 1986): 65–88, where the projection of anti-neocolonialist "national allegories" in contemporary Third World literature invoked, in a very compressed and virtually unreferenced manner, Benjaminian/de Manian notions of allegory, but without a patient spelling out of the *Trauerspiel* dynamic that Benjamin had theorized: namely, that allegory represents the broken, ruptured truth of attempts at "symbolic" reconciliation, and hence always signifies its own necessarily nonidentical, "mortified"—but also, critical, available-for-reconstruction—character. (See "Third World Literature," passim, and especially at 73.) It would require another essay to consider whether such a fuller elaboration of the negationalist, nonidentical nature of allegorical representation that Jameson glancingly summons up would answer the challenges Aijaz Ahmad and others have directed toward the analysis of Third World culture offered in "Third World Literature in the Era of Multinational Capitalism." See Aijaz Ahmad, "Jameson's Rhetoric of Otherness and the 'National Allegory,'" *Social Text* 17 (fall 1987): 3–25; reprinted in Aijaz Ahmad, *In Theory: Classes, Nations, Literatures* (London: Verso, 1992), 95–122. See also Jameson's answer to Ahmad's article, "A Brief Response," *Social Text* 17 (fall 1987): 26–27.

6. See Theodor W. Adorno, *Ästhetische Theorie,* ed. Gretel Adorno and Rolf Tiedemann, vol. 7 of *Gesammelte Schriften* (Frankfurt: Suhrkamp, 1970); trans. Robert Hullot-Kentor under the title *Aesthetic Theory,* ed. Hullot-Kentor (Minneapolis: University of Minnesota Press, 1997). Subsequent references to this work will be cited in the text as *Aesthetic.* And see Theodor W. Adorno, *Noten zur Literatur,* 4 vols. (Frankfurt: Suhrkamp, 1958–74); trans. Shierry Weber Nicholsen under the title *Notes to Literature,* 2 vols. (New York: Columbia University Press, 1991–92). Also of importance during the past decade has been the translation of Adorno, *Quasi una fantasia: Musikalische Schriften,* ed. Tiedemann, vol. 16 of *Gesammelte Schriften* (Frankfurt: Suhrkamp, 1963); trans. Rodney Livingston under the title *Quasi una Fantasia: Essays on Modern Music* (London: Verso, 1992).

7. Jean-Luc Godard, *JLG/JLG: Autoportrait de Decembre,* prod. and dir. Jean-Luc Godard, 1994; see also the companion text, Godard's *JLG/JLG: Phrases* (Paris: P.O.L., 1996), 15–19; translation mine. The relevant Jameson essay on Godard is "High-Tech Collectives in Late Godard," in *The Geopolitical Aesthetic: Cinema and Space in the World System* (Bloomington: Indiana University Press, 1992), 158–85. For a salutary analysis of the ways that tensions between mass culture and Frankfurt school theory might be reframed around the possibility of identifying genuinely mimetic and scriptural substrata within various popular-culture texts (an approach that would go beyond celebratory discoveries of subversive subtexts, as well as beyond one-dimensional condemnations of either Frankfurt elitism or popular-culture philistinism), see Miriam Hansen, "Mass Culture as Hieroglyphic Writing: Adorno, Derrida, Kracauer," *New German Critique* 56 (spring/summer 1992): 43–73; reprinted in *The Actuality of Adorno: Critical Essays on Adorno and the Postmodern,* ed. Max Pensky (Albany: State University of New York Press, 1997), 83–111.

8. See, for example, Fredric Jameson, "The Antinomies of Postmodernity," in *The Seeds of Time* (New York: Columbia University Press, 1994), xvi, 2–3, 8, 15–16, 42–43; and Jameson, "Transformations of the Image in Postmodernity," in *The Cultural Turn: Selected Writings on the Postmodern* (London: Verso, 1998), 101–2. (The latter does go some way toward associating Kant with Adorno, to Adorno's detriment; the cited passage makes evident Jameson's belief that Adorno's failure, like

Kant's, is to be remedied by way of Hegel.) The sense that *Late Marxism* had muted Adorno's resistance to Hegelian synthesis surfaced in reviews of the book; although not explicitly articulated through Kant, Eva Geulen's response to *Late Marxism* is representative in this regard; see her review "A Matter of Tradition," *Telos* 89 (fall 1991): 155–66. For a wonderfully ironic review of *The Seeds of Time* that rigorously assesses Jameson's recent work and overall career (and that is animated by questions of judgment and political agency in modernity), see Geoffrey Galt Harpham, "Late Jameson," *Salmagundi* 111 (summer 1996): 213–32. See also, for two bracing and relentless demonstrations of Kantian theory's built-in impasses, which frustrate attempts to derive a politics from the theory itself, Harpham's "Aesthetics and the Fundamentals of Modernity," in *Aesthetics and Ideology*, ed. George Levine (New Brunswick, N.J.: Rutgers University Press, 1994), 124–52; and "So . . . What *Is* Enlightenment? An Inquisition into Modernity," *Critical Inquiry* 20 (spring 1994): 524–56. (All three Harpham essays are reprinted in Harpham's *Shadows of Ethics: Criticism and the Just Society* [Durham, N.C.: Duke University Press, 1999].) For an overview of Jameson's approaches to Kant, see Kaufman, "Red Kant."

9. See the discussion of Michaels's work in Fredric Jameson, "Immanence and the New Historicism," in *Postmodernism: or, The Cultural Logic of Late Capitalism* (Durham, N.C.: Duke University Press, 1991), 180–217.

10. See Fredric Jameson, "Cognitive Mapping," in *Marxism and the Interpretation of Culture*, ed. Cary Nelson and Lawrence Grossberg (Urbana: University of Illinois Press, 1988), 350; see also *Postmodernism*, xx, 3, 35, 53, 400. For an evaluation of Jameson's use of Mandel, and of Jameson's argument for the connection between late-capitalist economics and postmodernist culture, see Martin Jay's review of Jameson's *Postmodernism, or The Cultural Logic of Late Capitalism* in *History and Theory* 32 (1993): 296–304.

11. For discussions of how the Frankfurt school generally approaches Kantian theory, see, for example, Susan Buck-Morss, *The Origin of Negative Dialectics: Theodor W. Adorno, Walter Benjamin, and the Frankfurt Institute* (New York: Free Press, 1977), passim and esp. at 22, 45, 53, 63, 74. See also Martin Jay, *The Dialectical Imagination: A History of the Frankfurt School and the Institute of Social Research, 1923–1950*, 2d ed. (Berkeley: University of California Press, 1996), 46, 52; and Jay, *Marxism and Totality: The Adventures of a Concept from Lukács to Habermas* (Berkeley: University of California Press, 1984), passim and esp. at 46, 48, 244–245; as well as Anthony Cascardi's *Consequences of Enlightenment* (Cambridge: Cambridge University Press, 1999).

12. This may have also been something of a biographical spiral dynamic for Adorno, who felt that his own experience of critical thought all but began when, at the age of fifteen, he started studying Kant at weekly meetings with Siegfried Kracauer, who "brought Kant to life for me. From the beginning, with his guidance, I discovered that the work was not to be read as pure epistemology, as an analysis of the conditions of scientifically valid judgments, but as a sort of encipherment from which the historical situation of the mind could be read, with the vague expectation that something of the truth itself was to be won." Theodor W. Adorno, "Der wunderliche Realist: Über Siegfried Kracauer," in *Noten zur Literatur*, ed. Tiedemann, vol. 11 of *Gesammelte Schriften* (Frankfurt: Suhrkamp, 1974), 388; quoted and translated in Robert Hullot-Kentor, "Foreword: Critique of the Organic," in Adorno, *Kierkegaard:*

Construction of the Aesthetic (1933), trans. Hullot-Kentor (Minneapolis: University of Minnesota Press, 1989), xiv–xv. (The passage also appears in Adorno, "Der wunderliche Realist: Über Siegfried Kracauer," *Noten zur Literatur,* 3:85; *Notes to Literature,* 2:58–59.) See also Buck-Morss's discussion of the importance of the Adorno-Kracauer study sessions on Kant in *The Origin of Negative Dialectics,* 2–3, and Jay's treatment of them in *Marxism and Totality,* 245–46; see too Jay's suggestion that crucial theorizations in *Aesthetic Theory* look back to Kant rather than Hegel (*Marxism and Totality,* 272–73). Adorno's *Drei Studien zu Hegel* is itself filled with surprising returns to Kant: "Hegel praised the greater consistency of Kant's successors in comparison with the abysmal discontinuities of the Kantian system, and he even outdid them in this regard. It did not occur to him that the Kantian discontinuities register the very moment of nonidentity that is an indispensable part of his own conception of the philosophy of identity" (Adorno, *Hegel: Three Studies,* trans. Shierry Weber Nicholsen [Cambridge: MIT Press, 1994], 11). Shierry Weber Nicholsen's *Exact Imagination, Late Work: On Adorno's Aesthetics* (Cambridge: MIT Press, 1997) includes rich treatments of Adorno's cross-wirings of Kant and Hegel; see, for example, her thoughts on reevaluations of Adorno and Kant (18, 231 n. 4).

13. For a provocative revisitation of Benjamin's early relationship to radical versions of Kant, see Howard Caygill, *Walter Benjamin: The Colour of Experience* (New York: Routledge, 1998).

14. See Immanuel Kant, *Critique of Aesthetic Judgment,* pt. 1 of *Critique of Judgment,* trans. Werner S. Pluhar (Bloomington: Indiana University Press, 1987), sec. 6, 53–54. Subsequent references to this work will be cited in the text as *Judgment.*

15. See Kant, "First Introduction" to *Critique of Judgment,* sec. 5 ("On Reflective Judgment"), 399–404.

16. Immanuel Kant, "Transcendental Doctrine of Method," in *Critique of Pure Reason,* trans. Norman Kemp Smith (New York: St. Martin's, 1929), 576–78 ff. For a classic exposition of Kant's turn toward geometry as a basis for implied construction within pure intuition—that is, for Kant's derivation of the activity of geometric figural construction as a ground for notions of *presentation* or *hypotyposis,* for combination, in other words, of the a priori and the concrete—see P. F. Strawson, *The Bounds of Sense: An Essay on Kant's "Critique of Pure Reason"* (London: Methuen, 1966), pt. 5, "Kant's Theory of Geometry," 277–92. While Adorno likewise works from such a base idea (of the importance of imaginative figural construction) out toward various levels of construction and constructivism, he does not associate the idea with geometry, because the latter, for him, tends to signify merely calculative rather than "constructivist" phenomena. To the extent Adorno does connect Kant to geometric discourse, it is to identify Kant's aesthetics—erroneously, and in contradiction to how Adorno treats the third *Critique* when geometry is not explicitly discussed—with a calculative, golden-mean harmonizing that actually corresponds not to Kant's concept of the beautiful, but precisely to its calculative cousin (which Kant terms "the normal," or "standard," "idea of beauty"; see esp. *Critique of Aesthetic Judgment,* sec. 17, 79–84. For an example of Adorno's sometime conflation/condemnation of calculative geometry and Kantian aesthetic "formalism," see his comments about Max Frisch's *Don Juan, or The Love of Geometry,* in *Aesthetic Theory,* 48.

17. For an important analysis of what might be called, in a literary-critical vocabulary, Kant's self-consciously estranging way of characterizing the demand for

agreement, see Hannah Ginsborg, "On the Key to Kant's Critique of Taste," *Pacific Philosophical Quarterly* 72 (1991): 290–313.

18. For differently inflected treatments of the shared grounds for constructionist approaches, see, for example, Kimberly Hutchings, *Kant, Critique and Politics* (London: Routledge, 1996); Onora O'Neill, *Constructions of Reason: Explorations of Kant's Practical Philosophy* (Cambridge: Cambridge University Press, 1989); Dick Howard, *The Politics of Critique* (Minneapolis: University of Minnesota Press, 1988); Anthony Cascardi, *Consequences of Enlightenment* (Cambridge: Cambridge University Press, 1999); Frances Ferguson, *Solitude and the Sublime: Romanticism and the Aesthetics of Individuation* (New York: Routledge, 1992).

19. See Jameson, *Late Marxism,* 169–81; Jay, "Mimesis and Mimetology: Adorno and Lacoue-Labarthe," in *The Semblance of Subjectivity: Essays in Adorno's Aesthetic Theory,* ed. Tom Huhn and Lambert Zuidervaart (Cambridge: MIT Press, 1997), 29–54; reprinted in Martin Jay, *Cultural Semantics: Keywords of Our Time* (Amherst: University of Massachusetts Press, 1998), 120–37. Although not explicitly articulated around the issue of construction, Tom Huhn's "Kant, Adorno, and the Social Opacity of the Aesthetic," in *The Semblance of Subjectivity,* 237–58, offers a wonderful discussion of how Adorno thinks through and revivifies Kant.

20. Hullot-Kentor, "Foreword," xviii. See also Hullot-Kentor's discussion of Adorno's constructionist *style* (xiii–xiv).

21. Ibid., xvii, xiv, xvii.

22. Robert Hullot-Kentor, "Popular Music and Adorno's 'The Aging of the New Music,'" *Telos* 77 (fall 1988): 90–92. This essay is Hullot-Kentor's introduction to Adorno, "Das Altern der neuen Musik," *Dissonanzen,* ed. Tiedemann, vol. 14 of *Gesammelte Schriften* (Frankfurt: Suhrkamp, 1973), 143–67; trans. Hullot-Kentor and Fredric Will under the title "The Aging of the New Music," *Telos* 77 (fall 1988): 95–116. See also the introduction's concluding words: "In *The Philosophy of New Music,* Adorno came to the conclusion that the construction of the material resulted in the loss of expression; what he suggests is more radical construction. Construction is both the ability to manipulate the material and to break it out of the forms in which it has rigidified. The recommendation therefore means: more subjectivity. This is not a request for arbitrariness, but for the freeing of the social forces of production, which in art are forces of expression" (94).

23. See, for example, the comments about aesthetic representation allowing or crystallizing "the affinity of elements that remain unidentified" (that is, that do not merge into a single, dominant identity) (Adorno, *Aesthetic Theory,* 138).

24. See ibid., 24; see too, for example, Jameson, *Late Marxism,* 169, as well as Hullot-Kentor's above-quoted comments from "Popular Music and Adorno's 'The Aging of the New Music,'" that Adorno's response to too much construction (at expression's expense) is "more radical construction."

25. Nicholsen and Jeremy J. Shapiro, for example, are entirely on target when they suggest the representativity of Adorno's attempts in his seminars "to bring out both the relative truth content and the relative limitation of Kant and Hegel in relation to one another, against the background of Marxian, materialist assumptions. Adorno vindicated both Hegel's argument against Kant—that the limitations of reason set by Kant already implied the transcendence of these limits—and Kant's argument for the necessity of something outside the totalizing tendency of thought." See Shierry Weber Nicholsen and Jeremy J. Shapiro, introduction to Adorno, *Hegel:*

Three Studies, xix. With specific regard to the question of construction, see also Hullot-Kentor's explanation that "central to Adorno's construction is a reappropriation of Hegelian mediation" ("Foreword," xviii).

26. The point about quasi-conceptuality and aporetic reflective judgment is one Adorno develops throughout *Aesthetic Theory.* For example: "The logic of art, a paradox for extra-aesthetic logic, is a syllogism without concept or judgment" (136). "Constitutively a protest against the claim of the discursive [the conceptual] to totality, artworks therefore await answer and solution and inevitably summon forth concepts" (i.e, construct "new" concepts) (98). "It is admirable that Kant's aesthetics let this contradiction [art's being aconceptual but seeming to call forth judgments that spring from the conceptual faculties] stand and expressly reflected on it without explaining it away. On the one hand, Kant treats the judgment of taste as a logical function and thus attributes this function to the aesthetic object to which the judgment would indeed need to be adequate; on the other hand, the artwork is said to present itself 'without a concept,' a mere intuition, as if it were simply extralogical. This contradiction, however, is in fact inherent in art itself, as the contradiction between its spiritual and mimetic [constructionist and expressivist] constitution" (97). See too Adorno's statement that construction—in this instance, the construction of form—"provides the mediating category of how art, which Kant considered blatantly nonconceptual, subjectively bears that element of the universal and the necessary that, according to the critique of reason, is reserved exclusively for discursive [conceptual] knowledge" (114).

27. Adorno makes the allegation several different ways in *Aesthetic Theory,* but in each case, baleful consequences flow from Hegel's complete conceptualism. For instance: "Hegel's critique of Kant's formalism ought to have valorized nonformal concreteness. This critique was not, however, within Hegel's purview; it is perhaps for this reason that he confused the material elements of art with its representational content *[Inhalt].* By rejecting the fleetingness of natural beauty, as well as virtually everything nonconceptual, Hegel obtusely makes himself indifferent to the central motif of art, which probes after truth in the evanescent and fragile" (76).

28. Emphasis appears in the original translation to indicate that Adorno himself uses the English phrase *up to date:* "Dass solche Moderne mehr sei als vager Zeitgeist oder versiertes up to date-Sein" (*Ästhetische Theorie,* 57). See, too, the following examples: "[The artist] embodies the social forces of production without necessarily being bound by the relations of production" (43). "The history of art has known moments that are reminiscent of the technical revolution of material production" (59). "To the extent to which a drama—itself a sonatalike product of the bourgeois era—is in musical terms 'worked,' that is, dissected into the smallest motifs and objectivated in their dynamic synthesis, to this extent, and right into the most sublime moments, the echo of commodity production can be heard. The common nexus of these art-technical procedures and material processes, which has developed in the course of industrialization, has yet to be clarified but is nevertheless strikingly evident. With the emergence of intrigue and development, however, commodity production not only migrates into artworks in the form of a heterogeneous life but indeed also as their own law" (223). "A pure productive force such as that of the aesthetic, once freed from heteronomous control, is objectively the counterimage of enchained forces, but it is also the paradigm of fateful, self-interested

doings. Art keeps itself alive through its social force of resistance; unless it reifies itself, it becomes a commodity" (226).

29. Theodor W. Adorno, *Minima Moralia: Reflexionen aus dem beschädigten Leben* (Frankfurt: Suhrkamp, 1951), 206–8; trans. E. F. N. Jephcott under the title *Minima Moralia: Reflections from Damaged Life* (London: Verso, 1974), 155–57, emphases added. Adorno calls the section "Sur l'eau" after a book of Maupassant sketches about sailing.

30. Theodor W. Adorno, "Sacred Fragment: Schönberg's *Moses und Aron,*" in *Quasi una fantasia,* 229. The essay treats *Moses und Aron* as a fragmented tour de force, above all for its dissonant integration of expression and construction.

31. For further discussion of how Keats (together with Hölderlin, Valéry, Schönberg, and others) enters Adorno's critical aesthetics, see Robert Kaufman, "Negatively Capable Dialectics: Keats, Vendler, Adorno, and the Theory of the Avant-Garde," *Critical Inquiry* 27 (winter 2001): 354–84.

32. Theodor W. Adorno, "Arnold Schönberg (1874–1951)," in *Prismen: Kulturkritik und Gesellschaft* (Frankfurt: Suhrkamp, 1955), 213–14; trans. Samuel Weber and Shierry Weber Nicholsen under the title "Arnold Schoenberg, 1874–1951," in *Prisms* (Cambridge: MIT Press, 1967), 171.

33. Jameson, *Late Marxism,* 247.

34. Adorno, "Vers une musique informelle," *Quasi una fantasia,* 319.

35. Ibid., 322. The translation of the final sentence is amended in accord with Hullot-Kentor's rendering of it in *Aesthetic Theory,* wherein Adorno himself quotes that same, final sentence of "Vers une musique informelle"; see *Aesthetic Theory,* 114.

36. See Immanuel Kant, *Kants Gesammelte Schriften* (Berlin, 1911), vol. 8, 341–86; trans. under the title "Perpetual Peace: A Philosophic Sketch," in *Kant's Political Writings,* 2d ed., ed. Hans Reiss (Cambridge: Cambridge University Press, 1970), 93–130.

37. Susan M. Shell, "Cannibals All: The Grave Wit of Kant's Perpetual Peace," in *Violence, Identity, and Self-Determination,* ed. Hent de Vries and Samuel Weber (Stanford, Calif.: Stanford University Press, 1997), 157, 160.

38. For the larger context of this particular engagement with dynamism, stasis, and construction, see Adorno, *Aesthetic Theory,* 222. For a parallel trajectory that culminates with Celan, see Adorno, *Aesthetic Theory,* 321–22.

39. Hullot-Kentor's foreword to *Kierkegaard* conveys this implicitly, citing "Vers une musique" at key moments in its explication of Adornian construction; see "Foreword," xiv, xvii, 146 nn. 21 24, 36.

40. In this light, see Adorno, "Über die geschichtliche Angemessenheit des Bewussteins," interview with Peter von Haselberg, *Akzente* 12 (June 1965): 487–97; trans. Wes Bloomster under the title "On the Historical Adequacy of Consciousness," *Telos* 56 (summer 1983): 97–103. This and a companion interview (Adorno, "Education for Autonomy," interview with Helmut Becker, trans. David J. Parent, *Telos* 56 [summer 1983]: 103–10) are very helpfully introduced by Russell A. Berman's "Adorno's Radicalism: Two Interviews from the Sixties," pp. 94–97. Among his other comments, Adorno cites Rimbaud's "Il faut être absolument moderne" (98)—a line he is often prone to quote (see, for example, *Aesthetic Theory,* 3–4, 33, 93, 192). Yet in the interview, Adorno makes evident that the citation is not part of an aestheticist beautification-of-the-everyday campaign but rather a matter of thinking about possibilities

for affecting social issues and institutions. In taking Rimbaud's dictum seriously, Adorno essentially treats the phrase as part of a genuinely modern art's self-definition (whether in the period of modernism proper or thereafter); that self-definition in turn translates Marx's "ruthless critique of everything existing" into a principle of critical aesthetics. To understand Rimbaud's phrase, Adorno implies, is to see that really modern art offers a vital model for an indispensable task: that of questioning and of imagining new questions.

41. Martin Jay, "Educating the Educators," *Salmagundi* 101/102 (winter/spring 1994): 34; the essay has been reprinted in Jay, *Cultural Semantics,* 108.

42. Jameson, *Late Marxism,* 248. It is worth noting that Jameson's recent *Brecht and Method* (London: Verso, 1998) features markedly increased recourse to a vocabulary of construction (although the phenomenon and term continue to be distinguished from Kantian aesthetics, while *production* and *productivity* command final pride of place). Equally noteworthy are the ways that *Brecht and Method* persuasively refutes recent attempts to claim Brecht for "anti-aesthetic" art and theory.

CHAPTER SEVENTEEN

The Secret Life of Things

Virginia Woolf and the Matter of Modernism

Bill Brown

For Miriam Bratu Hansen

You should be reading this with something in your hands besides this book. And something, really, besides a pencil or a pen. Something like an empty glass, a rubber band, or a paper clip that you can rub between your fingers, that you can twist and bend back and forth. For the idea is to wonder whether—while concerning ourselves with one or another crisis of the subject—we have not been in the midst of another effort to think about the object, if not indeed to liberate material objects. The comic version of this effort would resemble a scene from *Mork & Mindy:* when asked what could have happened to all the sponges in the kitchen, the alien (Robin Williams) proudly announces, "I took them to the river and set them free."

A somewhat more serious version can be found in the work of Jean Baudrillard, who denounces the way that the object, because it is considered "only the alienated, accursed part of the subject," has been rendered unintelligible, "shamed, obscene, passive." Undoing the privilege of the subject is not for him a matter of attending to the subject's fraught, fragile, and divisive constitution. It is a matter of imagining how the "destiny of the subject passes into the object," of naming the object "sovereign," of celebrating the crystal's revenge, indeed "crystal revenge."[1] And yet, of course, the luminous transparency of the crystalline object, its auratic singularity, can only impoverish other objects, material objects, or material understood as itself an object: not shimmering, exquisite crystal, let us say, but glass that is nothing but glass. Is it not the very splendor of the object that allows objects to disappear so readily in

Baudrillard's subsequent work, evaporating into one or another version of the hyperreal?

No less than the tradition he writes against, Baudrillard seems to suffer from what Theodor Adorno called the familiar "allergies to entity," a chief symptom of which is the failure to recognize that there can be no "primeval history of the object," only a history "dealing with specific objects." The passage into materialism, as Adorno came to describe it, requires acknowledging "things" outside the subject/object trajectory, which means thinking sensation in its distinction from cognition. For the "dignity of physicality" is indissoluble in, and not exhausted by, the subject/object relation, epistemologically or phenomenologically understood.[2] Still, if "things" are indeed not exhausted by that relation, it is only in the subject/object nexus where they occur, or where they can be *narrated* as the *effect* (not the ground) of an interaction at once physical and psychological, at once intimate and alienating. To the degree that the "thing" registers the undignified mutability of objects, and thus the excess of the object (a capacity to be other than it is), the "thing" names a mutual mediation (and a slide between objective and subjective predication) that appears as the vivacity of the object's difference from itself. What happens, should we drop the crystal, should it shatter, and should we glance at the bits of glass that, although they are nothing but glass, captivate our attention? What happens when we deauraticize *the* object (that is identifiable only within a fundamentally static structure) and begin again with the vertiginous banality of things—with some sense of the curious thingness of those objects we incessantly if unconsciously touch, the objects we see without ever looking? What if we looked?

In fact, "things" seem to have achieved a new discursive visibility. From the disciplines of anthropology and history, as from the interdiscipline of "material culture studies," important anthologies summon us to attend to things: *The Social Life of Things* (1986), *Material Cultures: Why Some Things Matter* (1998), *History from Things* (1993), *The Sex of Things* (1996). These volumes assume the task of denaturalizing consumer practices, of tracing (both within and between cultures) the *work* of exchange and consumption: the way economic value is created in specific social formations; the way cultural values become objectified in specific material forms; the way that people shape, code, and recode the material object world; the way they make things meaningful and valuable. Just as such analysis exposes the politics that underwrite our most daily acts of exchange, as Arjun Appadurai would have it, so too, in Victoria de Grazia's words, this analysis "responds to the imperative to know about material needs, wants, and desires."[3]

But is it *things* that these volumes constitute as the object of their address? The degree to which the essays trace generalizable circuits of exchange and consumption is the degree to which they can address *no thing at all,* but only objects, if you will allow me to pursue my axiomatic distinction. The sort of objectification that takes place during those operations that produce use value, sign value, cultural capital will never produce a thing. Producing a thing—effecting thingness—depends, instead, on a fetishistic overvaluation or misappropriation, on an irregular if not unreasonable reobjectification of the object that dislodges it from the circuits through which it is what it typically is. Thingness is precipitated as a kind of misuse value. By *misuse value,* I mean to name the aspects of an object—sensuous, aesthetic, semiotic—that become legible, audible, palpable when the object is experienced in whatever time it takes (in whatever time it is) for an object to become another.

This distinction brings a kind of instability into focus wherein the thing becomes manifest between multiple objectifications. Within the shimmering splinters of glass, glass can become something else. Or, to offer another narrative example (of what can be exemplified only syntactically, only in time): in the process of using a knife as a screwdriver, of dislocating it from one routinized objectification and deploying it otherwise, we have the chance (if just a chance) to sense its presence (its thinness . . . its sharpness and flatness . . . the peculiarity of its scalloped handle, slightly loose . . . its knifeness and what exceeds that knifeness) as though for the first time. For the first time, perhaps, we thus also sense the norms by which we customarily deploy both knife and screwdriver. My concern, then, is not to unveil the meaning of things in their proper thingness, or to describe the fate of pure objects abstracted from their use, and neither is it to privilege the thing *(das Ding)* over things *(die Sachen).*[4] For the life of things made manifest in the time of misuse is, should we look, a secret in plain sight—not a life behind or beneath the object but a life that is its fluctuating shape and substance and surface, a life that the subject must catalyze but cannot contain.

My title, "The Secret Life of Things," no doubt brings to mind a line from Wordsworth or Shelley, or one of Hoffmann's uncanny tales, or one of several surrealist images—if not Tristan Tzara's image of knives on their feet, then perhaps Aragon's image of keys humming to themselves.[5] Although such animation is not my concern in the following pages, I will in fact be preoccupied by the 1920s, the decade when things emerge as the object of profound theoretical engagement (Lukács, Heidegger, Benjamin), which is the decade after objects and things are newly engaged by (or *as*) the work of art (Pound, Duchamp, Williams, Gertrude Stein). The record of Virginia Woolf's engagement appears in a very short story she titled "Solid Objects." It is in fact a story not about solidity, but about the fluidity of objects—about how they decompose and recompose themselves as objects of new fascination. It is about the materials that make up the material object world, about the transvaluation of those materials into less and more than their familiar properties. It is about dislocating material—nothing but glass—from an instrumentalist teleology and into an aesthetic scene, although not one authorized by the dictates of Distinction or the System of Objects, but content instead with intensely private, inconspicuous display.

Woolf began to write the story in November 1918, at the close of World War I, and she published it in the *Athenaeum* in 1920. The story concerns a man named John who discovers a smooth lump of glass on the beach and brings it home and places it on his mantle, using it as a paperweight. The discovery incites him to seek out other objects that remind "him of the lump of glass," anything "so long it [is] an object of some kind, more or less round, . . . anything—china, glass, amber, rock, marble," the paradigmatic shape and size in fact bringing the specificity of the material into question.[6] At first studying the objects displayed in the windows of curiosity shops, he becomes increasingly obsessed and finally roams London with "a bag and a long stick," ransacking "all deposits of earth," searching "all alleys and spaces between walls," in his search for discarded objects that might become for him "specimens" (85). As he discovers other remnants—pieces of broken china, a bit of iron—his collecting impulse becomes, from his friends' perspective, pathological. Before long he abandons the life he has led as a politician on "the brink of a brilliant career," a man standing for Parliament (82). Indeed, in most respects he abandons his life, "devot[ing] himself more and more resolutely to the search," suffering "fatigue and derision," but still "consumed by [the] ambition" to add to his little collection (85).

The story has hardly fascinated Woolf's readers, who have been far more captivated by the life of the subject, the fate of individuality, and the vicissitudes of consciousness in her fiction. Yet a small critical consensus reads "Solid Objects" as a cautionary tale warning against aesthetic absorption at the expense of the practical, the ethical, the political.[7] Woolf, let us say, managed not to succumb to what Clive Bell disparaged as his contemporaries' "metaphysical-moral doctrines concerning the cowiness of cows and the thing in itself."[8] But her own boredom with politics as usual, what she called her "natural disposition to think Parliament ridiculous," would suggest that the moral of the story might not be read so unequivocally.[9] She herself stopped accompanying her husband Leonard on his political campaigns in 1919. At the end of the war, she wrote of the war that "the whole thing [was] too remote and meaningless to come home to one either in action or in ceasing to act" (*Diary*, 215). And she was eager to eschew conversation about the "bitter, impatient, powerful" lower classes (220). Such comments suggest that one might say of the story what Bell said of art more generally, that "no one could be much worse placed than the political moralist for seeing whatever there may be to be seen in what is, at once, strange and subtle."[10]

What is strange and subtle in Woolf's story, however, is the way it bears witness, however unconsciously, to the political economy of Great Britain during and immediately after the Great War. In other words, I want to point out how John's encounter with these material fragments—a piece of glass, of broken china, and of iron—is not just embedded within a trajectory of English aesthetics (Ruskin to Fry) or a genealogy of modernism (say, Hulme's "poetics of sensual immediacy and fragmentary vision"), but also embedded between the domestic crisis of wartime scarcity in London and the postwar industrial crisis provoked by the British commitment to free trade.[11] Although the fragments may thus be thought of as souvenirs of the unreal city, their very collection erases that context from the narrative as such.[12] But elsewhere, Woolf makes it clear how the war impinged on the material practice of art. She writes to Vanessa Bell about the problem of securing her paint: "The difficulty about paints is that they're made with oil, 'Now you may not know [a merchant has explained to Woolf] that every gun when it's first cast has to be dipped in a bath of oil.'"[13] She records in her diary the physical threat to art posed by the raids on London: "The Academy is storing its precious pictures, only 18 in number, in some Tube. They are told to expect immense bombs at the end of the month, which will dig 20 feet deep, & then explode" (*Diary,* 138). Yet "Solid Objects," without ever invoking the war, provides instead an account of the aesthetic—or an account of what we might call the relation between aesthetics and politics, between art and the economy—that is a history of the senses fundamentally altered by the facts of wartime scarcity and postwar depression. One might argue that the story's displacement of the psychological with the *materiological* is Woolf's uncharacteristic exploration of the antihumanist modernism advanced by T. E. Hulme. Her capacity to narrate a new subject/object dynamic, however, seems catalyzed instead by the transgression of economic habits, both domestic and international—in a word, by the Western world's misuse of material for martial ends, by the transposition of material into matériel.

As literary criticism wrestles itself out of the homogenizing habits of new historicism and the heterogenizing habits of cultural studies, one version of a new materialism asks how material culture impresses itself on the literary imagination. Another asks how literature itself works to imagine materiality; how it renders a life of things that is tangential to our narratives of modern production, distribution, and consumption; how it can contribute to a materialist phenomenology that does not bracket history, but asks both *how,* in history (how, in one cultural formation), human subjects and material objects constitute one another, and *what* remains outside the regularities of that constitution that can disrupt the cultural memory of modernity and modernism. If Simmel was right to argue, circa 1900, that the increased access to things that characterizes modernity results in the loss of the thingness of things, then we should recognize how various aesthetic practices work to compensate for that loss. Indeed, it would be perfectly reasonable to account for the recent academic attention to objects (not to say things) as a reaction against the declaration of—if not some compensatory response to the fact of—the further disappearance of the object within an increasingly mediated (digitally mediated) universe.

Woolf's story might thus be read as moralizing against such materialist fascinations, if it does not rather, as I will suggest, investigate a different kind of fascination, indeed a kind of fetishism that seems like an alternative mode of inhabiting modern culture. By consecrating the valueless material object, such fetishism confounds political economy's account of value, alienates itself from any enlightenment horror of waste, and settles happily into an unhuman (not antihumanist) history. "Solid Objects" manages to revise the question of the object and the question of things while clarifying the risk of that revision, which is always a risk to what Woolf's story narrates as the aesthetic subject. "One day," the narrator recounts, "starting from his rooms in the Temple to catch a train in order to address his constituents, his eyes rested upon a remarkable object lying half-hidden in one of those borders of grass which edge the bases of vast legal buildings. . . . [He] drew the piece of [broken] china within reach of his hands. As he seized hold of it he exclaimed in triumph," and he missed his train (82–83). Such exhilaration, staged in relation to the emblems of modernity (the train, the legal buildings, parliamentary democracy, the commuter temporality) is irreducible to consumer desire or the structure of cathexis described by psychoanalysis; it instead testifies to the enigmatic excess that characterizes the physical world, especially its bits and pieces, the discarded remains of modern objects. Insofar as the aestheticization of this refuse leaves John in a condition of social sclerosis, however, "aesthetic autonomy" manifests itself here not as the object's distance from consumer culture but as the utter isolation of the individual (the aesthetic subject). Some other reading of the story might indeed argue that John's obsession with inorganic objects is in fact inseparable from what Freud described, in his own postwar text, as the drive toward the inorganic that is the drive toward death.

Let me turn now to a clarifying disjuncture in William James's psychology—clarifying because it temporalizes, *narrating* the interaction between the somatic and the cognitive—to offer some handle on the object/thing distinction. Working within and against the associationist tradition, James points out, in his chapter on the perception of space, how the coalescence of our sensations in and as a thing depends on habit. This means that we grant to objects their full physicality (however partially glimpsed) because we are accustomed to doing so. Real form (what Husserl would come to call the inauthentic image as opposed to the authentic image we actually see) is *habitually* conjured up. In his somewhat prescient understanding of mind as matter (with which he works to refine the Humean position), James argues that habitual objects "plough deep grooves in the nervous system," so that there is a path of least resistance through which, for instance, our sensations of grayness and thinness and length become the apperception of a knife.[14]

In his chapter on the "perception of things," however, he tells the story of what happens when our habits are broken—when, for instance, we look at a landscape with our heads upside down or when we turn a painting bottom upward: "The colors grow richer and more varied, we don't understand the meaning of the painting, but, to compensate for the loss, we feel more freshly the value of the mere tints and shadings."[15] James understands perception and "naked sensation" as different cerebral conditions that cannot take place at the same time because sensations in themselves do not add up.[16] One might say, rather, that we need to understand two distinct, dynamic, intertwined materializations: one where we seem to begin with sensations, which precipitate perception, and one where the proximate sensuous engagement lies between one and another perceptual horizon. The viewer's perceptual "failure" (as in the case of nonfigurative painting) prompts a different kind of attention; but, in the routine of daily life, perception perpetually forecloses sensuous experience in order to render the material world phenomenal, which means rendering it inhabitable. What I want to underscore is how in James the difference between the apperceptive constitution of the thing, in what I would call its objecthood, and the experience of the thing, in what I would call its thinghood, emerges in the moment (and no doubt only as a moment) of reobjectification that is a kind of misuse: turning the picture bottom up, standing on one's head. The point may be less that "sensation is one thing and perception another," and more that the experience of sensation depends on disorientation, both habit and its disruption.[17]

In the case of Woolf's story, the point is not that the familiar object has been defamiliarized into unreconstituted fragments (which is to say discrete, fragmented sensations), but rather that literal fragments become objects, without any of the coherence or familiarity we associate with objects. Peripatetic though he is, John resembles less modernity's flaneur than the bricoleur, "speak[ing] not only *with* things . . . but also through the medium of things," reordering debris the way a kaleidoscope—to borrow Lévi-Strauss's figure—transforms bits of glass into a "new type of entity."[18] But if John perceives new structural patterns, he also manages to experience texture and shape in such a way that materials themselves—unchanneled through the habitual object—become the objects of his fantasy. Familiar materials—glass, china, iron—are debanalized, appearing all but magical: "It was impossible to say whether it had been bottle, tumbler, or window-pane; it was nothing but glass; it was almost a precious stone" (*House,* 80). Not objects, but materials—"nothing but glass"—have been released from any readiness-to-hand. Free from their incorporation into the familiar object world, they seem to assume lives of their own as John grants them a kind of agency. The piece of broken china

> looked like a creature from another world—freakish and fantastic as a harlequin. It seemed to be pirouetting through space, winking like a fitful star. The contrast between the china so vivid and alert, and the glass so mute and contemplative, fascinated him, and wondering and amazed he asked himself how the two came to exist in the same world, let alone to stand upon the same narrow strip of marble in the same room. The question remained unanswered. (83)

By not answering the question, both John and the narratorial voice grant the materials their sovereignty, but they do so not (as Baudrillard would have it) from a state of abjection, but in a state of wonder.

Woolf's story might thus be located within a continuum of modernist attention to materials, from, say, Otto Wagner's 1895 vision of a future architecture dominated by "the prominent use of materials in a pure state" to Marinetti's futurist cult of metals and Jünger's "poems of steel," to Donald Judd's 1965 description of the "aggressive" specificity of materials and the "objectivity" that inheres in the "obdurate identity of a material."[19] In closer proximity to Woolf, her friend Roger Fry, in the manner of Ruskin, repeatedly argued on behalf of the aesthetic importance of compositional substance, singling out the fate of china. He objected to Wedgwood (by now the preferred cornerstone in accounts of eighteenth-century consumer society) because it set "a standard of mechanical perfection which to this day prevents the trade from accepting any work in which the natural beauties of the material are not carefully obliterated by mechanical means."[20] Whereas Fry's answer to the problem was replacing mechanical production with craftsmanship, "Solid Objects" answers the problem of mechanical perfection by introducing the imperfection wrought by accident—by engaging the shard. At times, Woolf clearly shares Fry's fundamental aesthetic judgment. In *Orlando* (1928), the men of genius Orlando accompanies in the eighteenth century

(Addison, Pope, Swift) collect "little bits of coloured glass," demonstrating a kind of restrained appreciation for material that stands in contrast to the monumental accumulation of Victorian clutter—"crystal palaces, bassinettes, military helmets, memorial wreaths . . . telescopes, extinct monsters, globes, maps, elephants, and mathematical instruments"—a rubbish heap of Victorian history, a pile of "heterogeneous, ill-sorted objects" perceived by Orlando as a "garish erection."[21] But "Solid Objects" suggests that the residues of such clutter, the objects decomposed into little bits, as it were, can still compel us in their rudimentary substantiality, conveying both the natural and unnatural beauties of material.

Writing in the *Athenaeum* the year before Woolf's story appeared there, Fry laments the fate of materials within the Victorian object. Describing the inappropriate use of material to fashion all the Victorian *objets* that "gratify fatuous curiosity" and appeal to "social emotions" rather than "aesthetic feelings," he concludes that "the use of material at this period seems to be the least discriminating, and the sense of quality feebler, than at any previous period of world history."[22] The familiar Bloomsbury dismissal of Victoriana here achieves a materialist specificity inherited from the likes of William Morris. But Fry stops short of wondering what might in fact be learned about "social emotions" from the ill-suited use of materials. His role as artist and art critic no doubt prevented his taking an interest in the kind of disjuncture between material and form that captivated Benjamin as a legible sign of utopian longing. With a logic learned from *The Eighteenth Brumaire,* Benjamin imagines that the decorative use of iron, rather than its structural deployment, marks the way novelty first emerges in and depends on residual form, which is the way social dissatisfaction with the present expresses itself in a citational longing for the future: a longing that cites a past that is anterior to the recent past. "These tendencies deflect the imagination (which is given impetus by the new) back upon the primal past."[23] Whereas Ruskin believed that the "constant use of cast-iron ornaments" marked the "degradation of our national feeling," Benjamin read it retrospectively as marking an otherwise unexpressed desire to abandon a degraded present.[24]

If for Benjamin the point of considering such disjuncture is to imagine how a collective unconscious "thinks" forward by thinking back to a classless society, for Woolf the point is more the way attention to the substance of iron, for instance, can provide access to a "primeval history" that is no longer anthropocentric. The story begins to answer the question of how we could bring materials into history as something other than the history of their use, in industry or art. When John, perpetually scouring the crannies of London in his quest to add to his collection, finds a piece of iron under a furze bush in Barnes Common, his sense of time becomes cosmological.

> It was almost identical with the glass in shape, massy and globular, but so cold and heavy, so black and metallic, that it was evidently alien to the earth and had its origin in one of the dead stars or was itself the cinder of the moon. It weighed his pocket down; it weighed the mantelpiece down; it radiated cold. And yet the meteorite stood upon the same ledge with the lump of glass and the star-shaped china. (*House,* 84–85)

The passage is mobilized by a dialectic of proximity and distance, familiarity and alterity, that is at once spatial and temporal. The utterly ordinary, which is also otherworldly, can be pocketed and domestically displayed without ever being domesticated. Woolf records not only what it would feel like to desire material per se as a personal possession, but also how such a possession might change the scale of one's historical imagination, how the cosmological might insinuate itself into the daily. To name the scrap of modern iron a "meteorite" is to dislodge it from the homogeneous structure of time, and to say not that the distant past lingers within the present, but that this past is present as a kind of surface with which we can make intimate contact, as though touching one history in and as another.[25] If the story's temporality seems somewhat abstract or confused—"Day after day passed. He was no longer young" (*House,* 85)—this is because John's archaeology of the modern, his engagement with material as an end (not a means), has dislodged him from the temporal dictates of modern life. The *vie privée* of things becomes something other than the history of the object's production and exchange, and something other than its representation in, or transformation into, the work of art.

With James's help, we can redescribe the modernity that Simmel renders—where the ability to dominate things is coupled with the inability to establish contact with things—as the intensification of a basic perceptual process, or as a perceptual process that has become a social logic. In the twenties this sociopsychological, sociosensual problematic achieved its full theorization. On the one hand, Lukács asserts that reification "conceals above all the immediate—qualitative and material—character of things as things." On the other, Heidegger, without ever specifying Lukács, complains that such arguments always fail to describe for us what "we are to understand *positively* when we think of unreified *Being.*" And Benjamin, in a much-quoted passage from "One-Way Street" (providing a non-Heideggerian response to such a complaint), describes how children's engagement with the material world reveals the capacity to transform things, bits of cultural detritus, into new things—a kind of recycling that never replicates the world as it is, but rather reminds us, in the mode of spontaneous collage, that things might be other than they are.[26]

"Any object," Woolf writes in "Solid Objects," "mixes itself so profoundly with the stuff of thought that it loses its actual form and recomposes itself a little differently in an ideal shape which haunts the brain" (82). This activity of recomposition, which moves John's encounter from the sensuous and material to the phenomenal and the psychological, returns to the material by granting him a different mode of engagement with the city. That is, just as John mediates the transformation of the lump of glass into a "precious gem," so too the glass transforms his relation to urban space. It provokes him to walk through London with "his eyes upon the ground," especially attracted to the alleys where "such objects often occurred"—"thrown away, of no use to anybody, shapeless, discarded" (82). To say that objects *occur* is to suggest that objects have a temporality: they don't happen to be there so much as they happen. And the way that they happen distorts John's pedestrian quest to match the shape of the smooth lump of glass; instead, he seems propelled only by a new responsiveness to form as such. The broken piece of china "as nearly resembl[es] a starfish as anything—shaped, or broken accidentally, into five irregular but unmistakable points" (83). His new optical, tactile consciousness does not permit him to leave a curious object behind; he misses a meeting in order to secure the shard. John may exhibit the typical passions of the new collector, but one cannot quite say just what it is that he collects. And he makes no effort to express himself in his exhibition; rather, the lives of these things—the glass contemplative, the china vivid, fitful, surreal—overwhelm his life.

In his essay on surrealism, Benjamin confidently proclaims that the poet too perceives the immense force, the revolutionary energy, that resides within discarded artifacts, those "enslaved and enslaving objects."

But in the more telegraphic "Traumkitsch," where he imagines a history of dreams, the unconscious seems severely limited. The dreams of today, he writes, are a "short cut to banality"; in our dreams "there is a gray coating of dust on things"; and in dreams the hand touches objects "at their most thread-bare," where they are "worn through by habit." The dreamwork fails to recapacitate us as children, who never (according to habit) "clasp a glass" but "snatch it up."[27] It is a kind of misapprehension, an untoward reobjectification, a kind of misuse that clears the dust away.

It was with the "impulse of a child," Woolf writes, that John slipped the lump of glass inside his pocket "promising it a life of warmth and security" (81). When on the beach, and having left off a political argument with his friend Charles ("Politics be damned!"), John distracts himself by "burrow[ing] his fingers down, down into the sand," his eyes becoming "clear transparent surface[s] . . . expressing nothing but wonder, which the eyes of young children display" (80). Such rhetorical recourse to the child, figurative or literal, also helps Roger Fry to taxonomize the "economy" of the senses, as he called it, and above all to differentiate between looking and mere seeing. Although it is children who genuinely "look at things with some passion," the adult retains "something of this unbiological, disinterested vision," the testimony to which he finds in those collections of objects (like John's) that are otherwise unremarkable but "have some marked peculiarity of appearance that catches his eye." Fry's essay "The Artist's Vision," also published in the *Athenaeum* in 1919, provides the simplest theorization of what Woolf is up to in her story. It is as though Fry has translated James's psychological point (which originally stumbled onto the aesthetic, onto questions of landscape and painting) and transformed it into a point about the aesthetic and nonaesthetic subject. "We were given our eyes to see things, not to look at them," a fact that he takes to be a biological necessity given that the "very considerable ignorance of visual appearances" becomes a practical matter.[28] When Woolf herself writes about "the cinema" (which, according to the surrealists, disclosed in the photogenic object the fact that things have lives of their own), she describes its ability to provide audiences with a new field of sensation; she reiterates Fry's point but she also nationalizes it, describing "the English unaesthetic eye" as "a simple mechanism which takes care that the body does not fall down coal-holes."[29]

If the unhabituated child perpetually appears in contrast as the engaged aesthetic subject (although Benjamin calls attention not to a disinterested appreciation of the material world, but to an interested, spontaneous reconfiguration of that world), this is not a reinstallation of the Wordsworthian subject, for whom nature and not the detritus of culture exists as the fully engaging aesthetic object. Still, Woolf's story, because the child appears only as a vehicle for describing John's reactions, poses a complex of inescapable questions. Is John's response childlike in the profundity of its willingness to see and to feel the material world anew, or is his behavior a lamentable childish retreat? Is this an inspired act of transgression or simply a regression? Is this a regrettable withdrawal from politics or the recognition that politics needs to begin elsewhere—with some experience of the profound otherness of the everyday?

The story's ambiguity has everything to do with the proximity or specularity of, on the one hand, the life of things and, on the other, commodity culture as usual. For John is in what would be recognizable as the throes of consumer desire—"the determination to possess objects that even surpassed these tormented the young man" (*House,* 85)—were it to have appeared in Zola's *Au bonheur des dames* or Dreiser's *Sister Carrie.* His desire anticipates a later moment in the history of bourgeois consumerism where consumption and collection seem increasingly conflated. Any newly purchased object—not just the Hummel figurine but also the bottle cap and the Beanie Baby—can be declared by the manufacturer to be *collectible.* If, writing of the early-nineteenth-century interior, Benjamin could imagine that the collector's responsibility was "the Sisyphean task of divesting things of their commodity character," and of freeing things from "the drudgery of being useful," in the late twentieth century the preservation from this drudgery became the means of increasing consumer desire.[30]

So too, of course, the secret life of things—whether it is the fitfulness of a piece of broken china, or knives standing on their feet, or sponges swimming free at last on the river—might be declared a literalization of our alienation as Simmel describes it, where, "by their independent, impersonal mobility," objects "complete the final stage of their separation from people."[31] And yet it is precisely by giving in to—thinking or working through—reification and alienation, and by identifying a profounder separation (not of objects but of things), that Adorno came to reidentify ethical possibility: "If a man looks upon thingness as a radical evil . . . he tends to be hostile to otherness, to the alien thing that has lent its name to alienation, and not in vain."[32] For Simmel, the problem of modernity can be characterized by the fact that "objects and people have become separated from one another," that objects can no longer be "assimilated by the individual."[33] For Adorno, the problem has become the very will-to-assimilation. He designates the happiness of philosophy, over and against the "imperialism of annexing the alien," as residing "in the fact that the alien, in the proximity it is granted, remains what is distant and different."[34] Were we to grant "Solid Objects" a place between Simmel's sociology and Adorno's philosophy, we would read it as a narrative of things accumulated but not arranged, intimate but unassimilated ("extimate" in their simultaneous proximity and distance), accreted as vivacious fragments that belong to no whole. The ethics of the story thus reside in Woolf's depiction of an experience—of experience—that activates for the fragment a life of its own.

Although "Solid Objects" narratively engages topics conceptualized elsewhere, Woolf's diary during these years records no consistent concern for material objects. We read other diarists, after all, to hear about things. Woolf writes about reading and thinking and talking and writing. Just as, in *Orlando,* the young nobleman's "disease of reading" can temporarily turn all his riches—"carpets, sofas, trappings, china, plate, cruets, chafing dishes and other movables often of beaten gold" (74–75)—into mist, so too in Woolf's own daily record her reading and writing tends to obscure any encounter with the physical world. If she writes about objects, she tends to write about them as signs, in the effort to determine how possessions characterize those who possess them: "art lamps and iridescent plates," for instance, seem to demonstrate the gentility of one "farmer husband" (*Diary,* 248).

In her stories, however, material objects seem a condition of narratability. "Moments of Being" records the thoughts of a woman in search of a lost pin, the finding of which puts a stop to the story. "The New Dress" records the way social anxiety is most keenly mediated by material possessions. The point of "The Lady in the Looking Glass" is that possessions that apparently reveal a life in fact keep it concealed from view. An extraordinary dangling modifier in the story suddenly shifts the burden from the unnamed narrator to the possessions themselves, as though they spent their time contemplating the woman who possesses them:

"Under the stress of thinking about Isabella, her room became more shadowy and symbolic; the corners seemed darker, the legs of chairs and tables more spindly and hieroglyphic" (*House,* 89). It is as though the object world, by concerning itself with human subjects, becomes both more and less legible, clearly significant but indecipherable.

Although Woolf's novels never think through artifacts so exclusively, they continue to foreground the way objects mediate human relations, including the self's relation to itself. Orlando's past returns to her in the twentieth century through her former possessions, housed in a museum (*Orlando,* 318–19). In *Night and Day* (1919), when Mrs. Hilbery exclaims, "Dear things! Dear chairs and tables! How like old friends they are," the dearness resides in the family history that the objects express, in the objects' august legibility, a result of the fact that "we live in things," as Mrs. Swithin explains to the man who "fingers sensations" in *Between the Acts* (1941).[35] Those novels construct a universe where, as Benjamin would have it, interiors are legible in traces left by their occupants, and where collected objects contain for the collector elaborate narratives of their collection. In Woolf's version of the argument, within our houses, within our rooms, we are "surrounded by objects which perpetually express the oddity of our own temperaments and enforce the memories of our own experience." Thus a whole morning spent in Italy, the iron table and the breeze and the vines and the pillars, "rise[s] up in a cloud from the china bowl on the mantelpiece," a bowl purchased during an Italian holiday.[36]

But the fragments collected in "Solid Objects"—which, the more one reads Woolf, seems itself to be an unrepresentative fragment—have only a fantasized and fantastic provenance: perhaps the lump of glass is a gem "worn by a dark Princess," or perhaps it is from an Elizabethan treasure chest (80–81). The fragments express the oddity of someone else's temperament: John imagines that the shape of the china shard depends on the "conjunction [of] a very high house, and a woman of such reckless impulse and passionate prejudice that she flings her jar or pot straight from the window without thought of who is below" (84). As compellingly as this scene may describe a woman's frustration with the objects that materialize her domestic confinement, the scene results from John's mere conjecture. In other words, the difference that "Solid Objects" insists on is a difference that comes from dislodging objects from a history of their proximity to subjects, from liberating artifacts out of their status as determinate signs, from rendering a life of things that is irreducible to the history of human subjects.

Yet the pathos of *Jacob's Room* (1922), among other novels, depends precisely on that reduction—on the symbolic and metonymic power of objects. The novel displays the evanescence of the protagonist's life as a relation to the material object world. Woolf's poetics of space is in fact a poetics of the object. We first read about the boy climbing on rock—"one of those tremendously solid brown, or rather black, rocks which emerge from the sand like something primitive"—and then about him lost at the beach and "sobbing, but absent-mindedly" running "farther and farther" to discover just what it is that he's glimpsed "among the black sticks and straw."[37] Despite his family's insistence, he refuses to give up the sheep's skull, whitened by water and wind, there at the beach; he sleeps with it at the foot of the bed. The boy's attachment to the natural object that most readily suggests permanence, rock, becomes instead an attachment to bone, the quintessential memento mori that expresses the proximity between the animate and inanimate.

A child's fascination with the natural world—children collecting beetles and butterflies (in chapter 2)—devolves into more mundane arrangements, such as Jacob's room at Cambridge, with its "round table and two low chairs," with "yellow flags in a jar on the mantelpiece" (38). And the novel gradually taxonomizes the adult fascination with objects. Consumer desire keeps Fanny captivated by "Evelina's shop off Shaftsbury Avenue," where "the parts of a woman were shown separate," skirts and boas and hats and shoes displayed without the logic of the ensemble (121). Indian philosophy prompts Jinny Carslake to cherish "a little jeweler's box containing ordinary pebbles picked off the road. But if you look at them steadily, she says, multiplicity becomes unity" (131). And a recognizably romantic sensibility compels Jacob himself to cherish the Acropolis (148). In the midst of these competing modes of cathexis, the narrator offers a fully thematizing, ambiguating account of the relation between things of the world (actions) and things in the world (mere things) as Jacob begins to think seriously about his future, about going into Parliament, perhaps, about the question of the British Empire, the question of Home Rule in Ireland: "For he had grown to be a man, and was about to be immersed in things—as indeed the chambermaid, emptying his basin upstairs, fingering keys, studs, pencils, and bottles of tabloids strewn on the dressing-table, was aware" (139). Once immersed in mere things, Jacob is about to immerse himself in things, as his new possessions testify. He is cut off from aspiring to the political life and the sense of political economy that John willfully abandons in "Solid Objects." The concluding tableau of the novel, then, evolves less from the idea of absence (Jacob's death in the war) and more from a lingering presence, all the unburied remains, those possessions no longer possessed. A room lived in and permanently left is not haunted, but uncanny: "One fibre in the wicker arm-chair creaks, though no one sits there." And the overwhelming question for those left is what to do with the objects that linger: holding out a pair of Jacob's old shoes, his mother asks, "What am I to do with these?" (176). If, as Baudrillard would maintain, the subject's destiny passes into the object, what is the object's destiny beyond the life of the subject? What sort of obsolescence is this?

The affective power of the novel's close demonstrates the metonymic potency of material objects, which is inseparable from their potency to convey the realism of the novelistic universe, not just in the work of Dickens or Balzac, say, but also in experimental fiction. Woolf came to believe that the birth of the novel as we know it—*Robinson Crusoe*—must be thought through the figure of the "large earthenware pot," which she posits as an emblem of Defoe's authority (which is fiction's authority) to overwhelm the reader with the wholeness of an imagined world and to interrupt romantic fantasy with novelistic fact. "By believing fixedly in the solidity of the pot and its earthiness, he has subdued every other element to his design; he has roped the universe into a harmony."[38] In the power of the earthenware pot as Woolf imagines it, which is Defoe's capacity to novelize the universe, there is something of Stevens's jar on a hill in Tennessee, transforming the landscape around it, if not something of Heidegger's jug, the thing that things the world.[39] But when solid objects become the explicit object of Woolf's address, the coherence of the solid object that makes the world cohere gives way to the solidity of fragments; there is no earthenware pot, but simply "a piece of china of the most remarkable shape... shaped, or broken accidentally, into five irregular but unmistakable points" (*House*, 83). Although the emphasis on the accidental shape of the china fragment might be said to ally the story with the dadaist and surrealist faith in the irrational and the contingent, the point is more that reevaluating the material world seems to depend on its reuse and on some violence that violates the coherence of the object. Whereas John imagines this violence as the

Figure 17.1. The damaged printing works in Long Acre. Reprinted from *The Times History and Encyclopedia of the War* 19 (1919): 270.

act of an angry woman (hurling a "jar or a pot" out the window), the violence that the story nowhere imagines but everywhere intimates is the violence of war.

As John hunts in "the neighborhood of waste land where the household refuse is thrown away," and then comes to "haunt the places which are most prolific of broken china, such as pieces of waste land between railway lines, sites of demolished houses, and commons in the neighborhood of London" (*House,* 82, 83–84), it is hard not to envision him as a character roaming the city streets and rat's alley of *The Waste Land,* the poem the Woolfs would publish two years later (see Figure 17.1). But such a convergence, itself part of a more widespread representation of postwar London as the unreal city, foregrounds a crucial contrast.[40] In place of the dolorous voice of *The Waste Land,* shoring cultural fragments against the spiritual ruin of the cityscape, John serendipitously accretes material fragments within which he finds all the spirit he needs.

And if war-traumatized London makes sense as the (underspecified) setting for the story, that trauma would seem to be specifically material, not spiritual. Although Woolf could dismiss the war as "remote and meaningless," she also lamented that "one has come to notice the war everywhere," meaning that "everything is skimped," that butcher shops are closed, that cards are required for "most foods," that other shops display "tins, or cardboard boxes" that are empty (*Diary,* 100).[41] Given the facts of wartime scarcity, the point is less that her diaries seem so evacuated of material objects and more that the world they describe has been so evacuated: "If you see a plum, it is invariably a decoy plum" (*Diary,* 112). Although the accounts of the raids on London, the mattresses dragged to the cellar, are the more obvious reminder of the presence of the war in her diaries and letters, there is a subtler but ubiquitous sense of how the things of the world—such as paper and paint—have become the materials of war. In this context, then, the intermittent material fascinations of her 1918 summer diary attain more significance: "I think it was on Friday that I was given my green glass jar by the chemist—for nothing! It's a jar I've always coveted; since glass is the best of all decorations, holding the light & changing it" (*Diary,* 170).[42]

If Woolf's pleasure in this green glass jar resurfaces in John's pleasure in the green lump of glass found on the beach, it does so embedded in a culture of scarcity that precipitates a different quality of cathexis. Glass had become the focus of national concern, as glass manufacturers transformed major plants into munitions factories.[43] Moreover, the arrested import of Jena glass from Germany and Austria, and of chemical glass from Bohemia, had created a so-called glass-famine in Britain, especially severe in the production of microscopic and photographic lenses.[44] As the *Geographic Journal* explained in its review of the reports from the Ministry of Munitions, there was hope that "British glass sands" would support domestic production needs. But if to the ministry it seemed as though these sands had sufficient silica content and the right grain, in fact the postwar search for the best sand led British crystal manufacturers back to Fontainebleau and to Loch Aline, Scotland.[45] For the iron in the English sand gave indigenous glass a green hue; it was *verre de fougère.*[46] The image of John "burrowing his fingers down, down, into the sand" and discovering there "a large irregular lump" of green glass might thus be read as an image less of discovery than of productivity—a production of glass out of the domestic glass sands of Britain and a recognition of its particular beauty. Still, it is not material as such (neither the sand nor the glass), but the whole process of retrieving and reanimating the ambiguous remnant that catalyzes John's fascination.

Between 1912 and 1930, Francis Bakley published some six books and dozens of articles on English glass; in retrospect, this looks like an act of mourning, composed as it was in the midst of general doubts about the longevity of the English production. The problem was not simply that glass manufacturers had been making lightbulbs, rods, and tubes for wartime industry, but also that free trade made cheap imports a perpetual threat to the financial success of domestic stemware once the war was over. The Society for Glass Technology was organized in 1916, as was a Department of Glass Technology at Sheffield, in the specific effort to sustain the nation's importance in the history of glass manufacture.[47] But by 1924, 70 percent of the British market was supplied by imports, factories closed, and glassmakers were left unemployed in the face of Continental competition.[48]

If the wartime and postwar history of glass in Britain can help to reframe "Solid Objects" as a story about the modern fate of materials, then the history of iron intensifies the same point. And the history of iron *and* glass, as instantiated by the Crystal Palace, chronicled the serial and international prospects of modernity.[49] Still, the story of Great Britain's iron trade was perpetually felt as a national tragedy, a narrative of decline from the Industrial Revolution and the thriving imperial economy. In standard histories, the vast iron and coal resources of England were understood as the necessary condition of the eighteenth-century Industrial Revolution. As Leonard Woolf revised this history, the Industrial Revolution and empire converged as an "intense preoccupation with material things," a demand for raw materials, coupled with production technologies, that resulted in "the whole world [being] ransacked for mines and metals" and in international competition for the control of resources.[50] The globalization that culminates in war, and in the compression of time and space that has been said to constitute modernity, originates with what we might call a passion for materials. When Virginia Woolf begins to write a story about accumulating materials in the month of the war's close, she thus writes an allegory of that war's origin, but an allegory with a difference—the difference marked by the bricoleur's confusion of ends and means, by an alternative economy where value results from an uninstrumentalizing passion for things.

During the war, the need for scrap in the production of bombs led the military to search the English countryside and to return to major battlefields to recover metal.[51] The imperial passion for materials had become a warring Europe's obsession with iron and steel. In an article titled "Coal and Iron in War," the *Fortnightly Review* stressed the industrial, economic rationale of Germany's aggression by publishing excerpts of a confidential memorandum (submitted to the chancellor from leading industrial and agriculture societies in May 1915) that underscored the importance of the long-term weakening of enemy nations, using iron as a case in point. The *Review* itself proclaimed that the current British supply of pig iron and steel was utterly "inadequate to our needs."[52] The problem of this war of attrition, as we have come to call it, had boiled down to the "essential question," in Sir John French's words, of "munitions, more munitions, always more munitions," and after a Ministry of Munitions was organized (with Lloyd George appointed minister), the ministry took over such crucial production centers as the Cumberland and Lancashire iron mines.[53]

In the history of English iron, 1882 marks the record year for exports, dominated by the sale of railroad iron to colonial markets, but by the close of the century, exacerbated by the McKinley tariff of 1890 and the British policy of free trade, Great Britain lost those markets (the United States supplying Canada with 70 percent of its iron and steel requirements) and found its domestic market flooded with "iron dumping" from Belgium, Germany, and the United States.[54] Although the war secured the domestic market for British manufacturers, other nations increased their own producing capacity, making 1921–31 the "Black Decade" of the British iron industry.[55] The price of bar iron had been controlled during the war, but that control was removed in 1919; by 1921 the prices of such rudimentary objects as nuts and bolts had risen to five times what they were before the war.[56] When in his obsessive search John discovers "a very remarkable piece of iron" under a furze bush, he encounters the element that had become the focus of national and international obsession.

All this is to say that if John's "serious ambitions" are met with a "lack of understanding" that is repeated in the critical consensus about the story, we might nonetheless begin to understand his behavior as an alternative mode of experiencing scarcity (*House,* 85). In Europe, more so than in the United States, the war intensified a Taylorist horror of waste, not just of time but of substances. This was the war in which all citizens were summoned to participate as national subjects: "each one of us"—

Figure 17.2. German conservation poster, 1917. Hoover Institution Archives. The text reads, "There is enough aluminum, copper, brass, nickel, zinc in the country. Turn it in—the army needs it." Translation from Peter Paret, Beth Irwin Lewis, and Paul Paret, *Persuasive Images: Posters of War and Revolution from the Hoover Institution Archives* (Princeton, N.J.: Princeton University Press, 1992).

"you and each one of you."[57] In their effort to involve civilians in the military project, governments took out ads and relied on posters as the new medium for communicating with the masses, for bringing the war into the civilian everyday (Figure 17.2). Saving fat for use in explosives, collecting the metal needed for scrap in the making of bombs—these activities constituted a new kind of materialism, a requisite bricolage, a recognition that the materials of everyday objects could have another life (Figure 17.3). As Aragon came to put it, beneath the silver-plating, teaspoons too were made of lead.[58]

Indeed, if the engagement Woolf narrates in "Solid Objects" can be understood as registering and aestheticizing, however inversely or perversely, the newly stipulated attention to materials throughout Europe, then the story can grant us a different access to familiar accounts of modernism and the object. Whether one assumes that the readymade was meant to attack the world of art, to foreground the role of the artist,

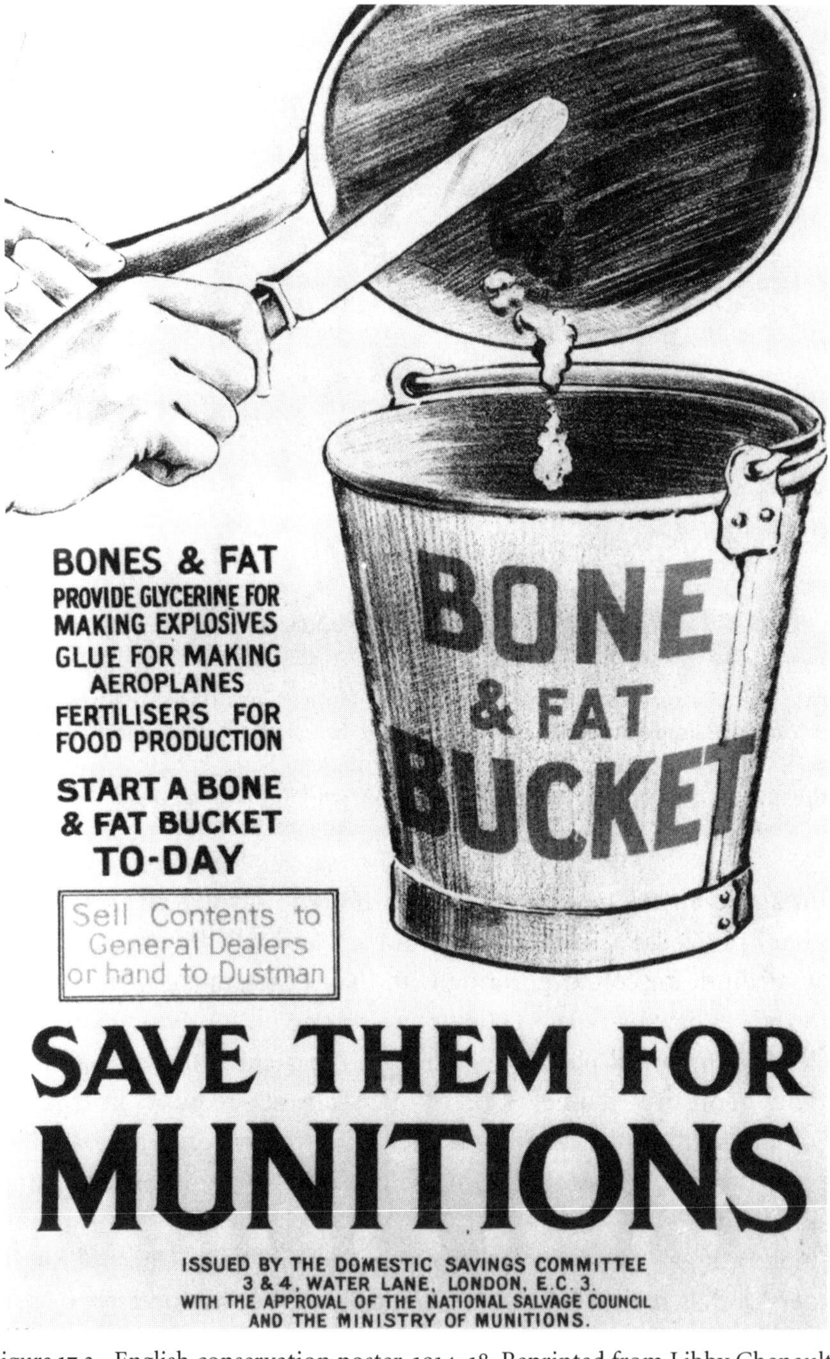

Figure 17.3. English conservation poster, 1914–18. Reprinted from Libby Chenault, *Battlelines: World War I Posters from the Bowman Gray Collection* (Chapel Hill: Rarebook Collection, Wilson Library, University of North Carolina, 1988).

or to dislodge common objects from the tyranny of use, Duchamp first promoted his readymades when the making of any common object—a urinal, a bottle rack, a snow shovel—was threatened all over Europe by the requirements of martial manufacturing. The various governmental demands to rethink the material world, and to revise the notion of waste toward a notion of recomposition, might lurk behind what Benjamin calls the "materialistic, anthropological inspiration" that provoked the surrealists to discover some revolutionary potential in discarded objects.[59] As for anthropological inspiration as such, we can describe the fetishism Woolf portrays as an alternative economy, an intensely private and privatizing reorientation of value, that offers a specular image of the alternative economies that anthropologists made visible in the 1920s. In *Argonauts of the Western Pacific* (1922), based on fieldwork done in New Guinea and North Melanesia during the war, Malinowski introduces "law and order into what seemed chaotic and freakish" by describing the function of apparently meaningless objects in the Kula.[60] When Mauss revises those conclusions to emphasize the irrationality of such practices, he deliberately juxtaposes "irrational expenditure" to the Western image of *Homo oeconomicus* as "a calculating machine" devoted to "frigid utilitarian calculation."[61] Although Bataille would go on to celebrate various modes of *dépense* as such, Mauss's own ethical conclusions, argued in explicit relation to the European war, emphasize how a stable sociality, a kind of solidarity that depends on competition, can emerge out of the respect and reciprocity of "the gift." The intense isolation of the individual in "Solid Objects" would be anathema to Mauss. Yet Woolf's image of reappropriating, valorizing, and aestheticizing waste, no less than Mauss's image of wasting valuable property, is underwritten by the sense that the economic reason of the West has been exhausted.[62] Which is to say that the history of objects as we know it (the history of objects as we know them) will never challenge the Enlightenment's history of itself. The challenge comes from the history of things, and from the histories in them.

"Solid Objects" begins with a narratorial consciousness that registers, as though through binoculars or through a zoom lens, a barely perceptible detail that slowly comes into focus as two human bodies. Woolf thus manages to record, in this gradually clarifying perception, something like the momentary development of sensation into perception:[63]

> The only thing that moved upon the vast semicircle of the beach was one small black dot. As it came nearer to the ribs and spine of the stranded pilchard boat, it became apparent from a certain tenuity in its blackness that this spot possessed four legs. . . . [The] mouths, noses, chins, and check stockings of the two speakers became clearer and clearer; the smoke of their pipes went up into the air; nothing was so solid, so living, so hard, red, hirsute and virile as these two bodies for miles and miles of sea and sandhill. (79)

These bodies—rendered as body parts, and as parts that help designate the form of the pilchard boat—achieve their solidity in the context of the seascape. But once they settle into their wholeness (once they assume, let us say, the phantasmatic image of the coherent human body) the "only thing" that can mark such solidity is some other thing. As John burrows his fingers into the sand, they finally curl "round something hard—a full drop of solid matter," which turns out to be a "green tint," a lump of glass, smoothed by the water into a veritable green gem (80). "It pleased him; it puzzled him; it was so hard, so concentrated, so definite an object compared with the vague sea and the hazy shore" (81). The definiteness of the solid object seems rather to expose the vagueness of politics ("Politics be damned!"), pushing politics into the background, as objects sometimes do in Woolf's diary: "I have bought another glass jar for 2/-. These things are in the foreground. It is partly due to them . . . that I don't write first & foremost of the German offer of peace" (*Diary,* 199). If we grant "Solid Objects" a (specifically) peripheral place in the British literature of World War I, and even grant Virginia Woolf's shortest fiction some relation to Leonard Woolf's tireless work on behalf of the League of Nations, then this story will assume a very different role: to demonstrate how utterly pedestrian passions can be understood as a longing for something other than the return of the same, for the fragments of the West to be reassembled differently.

Although the solidity of human bodies in the story gives way to the solidity of glass, solidity as such certainly gives way to a kind of fluidity—"the green thinned and thickened slightly as it was held against the sky or against the body" (81)—just as it gives way to elaborate fantasy: "Perhaps after all it was really a gem; something worn by a dark Princess trailing her finger in the water as she sat in the stern of the boat and listened to the slaves singing as they rowed her across the Bay" (80–81). What prevents solidity from becoming the point, what capacitates the imaginative encounter, is the incoherence of the fragment. John does not quite succumb to what Simmel describes as the "the present vividly felt charm of the fragment" that distances us "from things" because "reality is touched not with direct confidence but with fingertips that are immediately withdrawn."[64] Rather, John's tactile engagement gives him license to explore some other unhuman reality: "John turned it in his hands; he held it to the light; he held it so that its irregular mass blotted out the body and extended right arm of his friend" (81). The fragment appears in "Solid Objects" as the figure of the material metonym whose metonymic function has been arrested—the unconsummated metonym, as it were. The unconsummated metonym is the figure, or the conceptual image, that Woolf offers us to think the object/thing dialectic, to think the world anew. John collects broken parts that aren't really parts *of* anything determinable: "It was impossible to say whether it had been bottle, tumbler, or window-pane; it was nothing but glass." His materialism, where parts are related not to wholes but to other parts, enacts a kind of redemption that refuses the (Heideggerian) temporality of recuperation.

John's fetishism does not depend on substitution, but merely dynamizes the excess that characterizes any object, even the paper clip, the rubber band, the empty glass. If the recent work on *objects* (consumer objects, museal objects, ethnographic objects) "responds to the imperative to know about material needs, wants, and desires," then work on *things* should assume the task of discovering, in the history of objects, material desires, or the desire for material, that will forever be lost in the histories of consumer society or ethnographies of cultural exchange. At the very close of the story, John's friend Charles, depressed by the disarray of the room and utterly confused by his friend, asks, "What made you give it up?" meaning to ask just what prevented John from pursuing his political career. When John answers, "I've not given it up," he means that he has not abandoned his search (85). He could hardly give it up because his passion has become irrepressible. And he refuses to feel guilt about his new pleasure because, rather than discovering one solid object or another, he in fact discovers some other desire. The desire to historicize this desire cannot help but limit its potential to overcome affectively the specificities of time and of place, its potential to sense multiple histories materialized in (or by) the discarded remnant, the curious remainder. The war precipitated a national fixation on materials that enabled Woolf to imagine some more challenging, exhilarating material fixations. But we repeat the error she remonstrates against if, accumulating bits and pieces of this history, we believe that they form the whole story.

Notes

I would like to thank the "Aesthetic Subjects" conference participants—and especially David McWhirter, Martin Jay, and Robert Kaufman—for their responses to the original paper on which this chapter is based. Noel Jackson assisted me with the research that helped to transform the talk into an essay. As always, I owe an immeasurable debt to patient readers who are generous friends: Homi Bhabha, Jessica Burstein, James Chandler, Miriam Hansen, Elizabeth Helsinger, W. J. T. Mitchell, Janel Mueller, and Lesley Stern.

1. Jean Baudrillard, *Fatal Strategies,* trans. Phillip Beitchman and W. G. J. Niesluchowski (New York: Semiotext[e], 1990), 111–13.

2. Theodor W. Adorno, *Negative Dialectics,* trans. E. B. Ashton (New York: Continuum, 1997), 140, 193, 185. At the close of his career, Adorno writes an impassioned plea on behalf of the fullness of the "somatic moment" that grants us access to things (193).

3. See Arjun Appadurai, "Introduction: Commodities and the Politics of Value," in *The Social Life of Things: Commodities in Cultural Perspective,* ed. Arjun Appadurai (New York: Cambridge University Press, 1986), 57; Victoria de Grazia, introduction to *The Sex of Things: Gender and Consumption in Historical Perspective,* ed. Victoria de Grazia and Ellen Furlough (Berkeley: University of California Press, 1996), 10. See also Daniel Miller, ed., *Material Cultures: Why Some Things Matter* (Chicago: University of Chicago Press, 1998); Steven Lubar and W. David Kingery, eds., *History from Things: Essays on Material Culture* (Washington, D.C.: Smithsonian Institution Press, 1993); Mihaly Csikszentmihalyi and Eugene Rochberg-Halton, *The Meaning of Things: Domestic Symbols and the Self* (New York: Cambridge University Press, 1981); Susan M. Pearce, ed., *Experiencing Material Culture in the Western World* (London: Leicester University Press, 1997). More recent efforts to produce material objects (and the materiality of objects) as a new object of knowledge include Daniel Tiffany, *Toy Medium: Materialism and Modern Lyric* (Berkeley: University of California Press, 1999); Miguel Tammen, *Friends of Interpretable Objects* (Cambridge: Harvard University Press, 2001); Bill Brown, ed., "Things" (special issue), *Critical Inquiry* (fall 2001).

4. See Martin Heidegger, "The Thing," in *Poetry, Language, Thought,* trans. Albert Hofstadter (New York: Harper, 1971), 163–86; Jean Baudrillard, *The System of Objects,* trans. James Benedict (New York: Verso, 1996), 85–106; Jacques Lacan, *The Seminar of Jacques Lacan, Book VII, The Ethics of Psychoanalysis 1959–1960,* trans. Dennis Porter (New York: W. W. Norton, 1992), 19–86. I should say that in Lacan's "fable" of Jacques Prévert's collecting impulse, he anticipates much of my point. Prévert's empty matchboxes, which he threaded together by displacing the drawer of one box into the cavity of the contiguous box, ran in a line over the mantle and across a wall. As Lacan understands it, the exhibit enables the matchboxes to tran-

scend their status as objects, to show "the Thing that subsists in a match box." This "arrangement demonstrated that a match box isn't simply something that has a certain utility... that the match box all by itself is a thing with all its coherence of being" (114). This thingness, however, is precisely not the Thing that ultimately concerns Lacan—the Thing that names the unsymbolizable Real in its totality (as interiority and exteriority).

5. See Tristan Tzara, "Highway Single Sun," trans. Charles Simic and Michael Benedikt, in *The Poetry of Surrealism: An Anthology,* ed. Michael Benedikt (Boston: Little, Brown, 1974), 92; and see Louis Aragon, "Tercet," trans. Michael Benedikt, in the same volume, 155. In the literary history of surrealism, one could do worse than isolate the theory and poetry of Francis Ponge as the clearest celebratory encounter with material objects, culminating in *Le Parti Pris des Choses* (1942). In "Plus-que-raisons" (1930), he had argued that there is "no possible compromise between taking the side of ideas or things to be described, and taking the side of words. Given the singular power of words, the absolute power of the established order, only one attitude is possible: taking the side of things all the way" ("Plus-que-raisons," in *Nouveau Recueil* [Paris: Gallimard, 1967], 32). The history of such claims in their relation to the dicta of Pound (the "direct treatment of the *thing*") and Williams ("no ideas but in things") has yet to be written. The standard account of the postromantic, Anglo-American effort to disclose the sensuous proximity of the material world outside the subject/object opposition remains J. Hillis Miller, *Poets of Reality: Six Twentieth-Century Writers* (Cambridge: Harvard University Press, 1966).

6. Virginia Woolf, "Solid Objects," in *A Haunted House and Other Stories,* collected by Leonard Woolf (New York: Harcourt, Brace, 1944), 82. Page numbers for quotations from this and other stories will be provided in the text with the abbreviation *House.*

7. See, for instance, Robert A. Watson, "'Solid Objects' as Allegory," *Virginia Woolf Miscellany* 16 (1981): 3–4; Dean R. Baldwin, *Virginia Woolf: A Study of the Short Fiction* (Boston: Twayne, 1989), 19–20; Panthea Reid, *Art and Affection: A Life of Virginia Woolf* (New York: Oxford, 1996), 241; Hermione Lee, *Virginia Woolf* (New York: Alfred A. Knopf, 1997), 370. Douglas Mao interrupts this consensus with a reading of the story that introduces a wide-ranging account of Woolf's place in the genealogy of Victorian, aestheticist, and modernist attention to material objects. See Douglas Mao, *Solid Objects: Modernism and the Test of Production* (Princeton, N.J.: Princeton University Press, 1998), chap. 1.

8. Clive Bell, "Art and Politics," in *Since Cézanne* (New York: Harcourt Brace, 1922), 198. The topic of "things," when it comes to Woolf's fiction, has traditionally been rendered as the topic of "things in themselves," and has been pursued foremost through *The Waves.* See, for instance, Frank D. McConnell, "'Death among the Apple Trees': *The Waves* and the World of Things," *Bucknell Review* 16 (December 1968): 23–39; Igor Webb, "'Things in Themselves': Virginia Woolf's *The Waves,*" *Modern Fiction Studies* 17 (winter 1971–72): 570–73.

9. *The Diary of Virginia Woolf,* vol. 1, ed. Anne Olivier Bell (New York: Harcourt Brace Jovanovich, 1977), 173. Page numbers for further quotations from this volume of Woolf's diary will be provided in the text with the abbreviation *Diary.*

10. Bell, "Art and Politics," 198.

11. Miriam Hansen, "T. E. Hulme, Mercenary of Modernism, or, Fragments of Avantgarde Sensibility in Pre-World War I Britain," *ELH* 47 (summer 1980): 379. In

A Genealogy of Modernism: A Study of English Literary Doctrine 1908–1922 (New York: Cambridge University Press, 1984), Michael Levenson traces the schism between Bloomsbury and the movements with which Hulme's ideas are associated, futurism and vorticism (120–23). If in the following pages I seem to imply that within Woolf's story we can detect some transcendence of that schism, I hardly mean to suggest that this is anything but inadvertent, and my use of James, Simmel, Benjamin, and Adorno is meant to avoid domesticating Woolf's text too readily.

12. On the distinction between the souvenir and the collection, see Susan Stewart, *On Longing: Narratives of the Miniature, the Gigantic, the Souvenir, the Collection* (Baltimore: Johns Hopkins University Press, 1984), chap. 5.

13. Woolf to Vanessa Bell, 17 January 1918, *The Letters of Virginia Woolf,* vol. 2, ed. Nigel Nicolson (New York: Harcourt Brace Jovanovich, 1976), 210.

14. William James, *Principles of Psychology* (Cambridge: Harvard University Press, 1983), 891. One could homologize this claim to the idea that regulative discursive iteration effects materiality, but part of my point in this essay, of course, is to begin elsewhere—to suppose that there is an elsewhere that can regulate or interrupt discourse.

15. Ibid., 727.

16. Ibid.

17. Ibid.

18. Claude Lévi-Strauss, *The Savage Mind* (Chicago: University of Chicago Press, 1966), 21, 36. By quoting this use of the kaleidoscope image I mean, further, to intimate just how prevalent glass has been in the modern imaginary. In "Between Walls," William Carlos Williams shows how the particular quality of glass allows a broken object to assume greater luminosity than a whole one (*The Collected Earlier Poems* [New York: New Directions, 1966], 381).

19. Otto Wagner, *Moderne Architektur,* quoted in Sigfried Giedion, *Space, Time, and Architecture* (Cambridge: Harvard University Press, 1941), 318; Donald Judd, "Specific Objects" (1965), in *Complete Writings 1959–1975* (New York: New York University Press, 1975), 187. For a discussion of Marinetti, see Jeffrey T. Schnapp, "The Fabric of Modern Times," *Critical Inquiry* 24 (autumn 1997): 191–245. See also Jessica Burstein, "Prosthetic Fictions: Cold Modernism in Wyndham Lewis, Mina Loy, and Evelyn Waugh" (Ph.D. diss., University of Chicago, 1998); and, for an overview of the visual arts, see Ellen H. Johnson, *Modern Art and the Object* (New York: Harper & Row, 1976).

20. Roger Fry, "Wedgwood China" (1905), in *A Roger Fry Reader,* ed. Christopher Reed (Chicago: University of Chicago Press, 1996), 192.

21. Virginia Woolf, *Orlando: A Biography* (1928; New York: Harcourt Brace Jovanovich, 1956), 208, 232–33. Page numbers for further citations of this work appear in parentheses in the text.

22. Roger Fry, "The Ottoman and the Whatnot," *Athenaeum* 27 (June 1919): 529–30. To further specify the difference between "social emotions" and "aesthetic feelings," Fry developed the notion of the "opifact," an object meant to gratify certain social desires (in Thorstein Veblen's sense) that falls short of being an art object. See Roger Fry, *Art and Commerce* (London: Hogarth, 1926), 8.

23. Walter Benjamin, "Paris, Capital of the Nineteenth Century" (1935), in *The Arcades Project,* trans. Howard Eiland and Kevin McLaughlin (Cambridge: Harvard University Press, 1999), 4.

24. John Ruskin, *The Seven Lamps of Architecture* (1849; New York: Dover, 1989), 56.

25. On such temporal structures in historiography, see Siegfried Kracauer, *History: The Last Things before the Last* (Princeton, N.J.: Marcus Wiener, 1995), 139. The topic is of course central in the work of Benjamin. See, for instance, Beatrice Hanssen, *Walter Benjamin's Other History: Of Stones, Animals, Human Beings, and Angels* (Berkeley: University of California Press, 1998).

26. Georg Lukács, *History and Class Consciousness*, trans. Rodney Livingstone (Cambridge: MIT Press, 1971), 92; Martin Heidegger, *Being and Time*, trans. John Macquarrie and Edward Robinson (New York: Harper & Row, 1962), 72; Walter Benjamin, "One-Way Street," trans. Edmund Jephcott, in *Selected Writings*, vol. 1 (Cambridge: Harvard University Press, 1996), 449–50. For a sense of Heidegger's *Being and Time* as a response to Lukács, see Lucien Goldmann, *Lukács and Heidegger: Towards a New Philosophy*, trans. William Q. Boelhower (London: Routledge, 1977).

27. Walter Benjamin, "Surrealism," trans. Edmund Jephcott, in *Selected Writings*, vol. 2 (Cambridge: Harvard University Press, 1999), 210; Walter Benjamin, "Dream Kitsch," trans. Howard Eiland, in *Selected Writings*, 2:3. On Benjamin's sense of the possible mimetic appropriation of the material world, which he called "innervation," see Miriam Bratu Hansen, "Benjamin and Cinema: Not a One-Way Street," *Critical Inquiry* 25 (winter 1999): 306–43. Elsewhere I have focused on scenes of children engaging playthings: see Bill Brown, "How to Do Things with Things (a Toy Story)," *Critical Inquiry* 24 (summer 1998): 935–64; and *The Material Unconscious: American Amusement, Stephen Crane, and the Economies of Play* (Cambridge: Harvard University Press, 1996), 167–98.

28. Roger Fry, "The Artist's Vision," *Athenaeum* 11 (July 1919): 594–95.

29. Virginia Woolf, "The Cinema," in *Collected Essays*, vol. 2 (New York: Harcourt Brace, 1950), 268. Woolf's point about the cinema is that the temporality it offers might enable the English to engage a reality "more real, or real with a different reality from that which we perceive in daily life." But she goes on to imagine the surreal possibility that the cinema will offer "abstractions," "visual emotions," some way of visualizing "thought in its wildness" (271). In "Solid Objects," John's tactile engagement with material is coupled with a new sensitivity to abstract form: "He was often astonished, as he came to go into the question more deeply, by the immense variety of shapes to be found in London alone" (84).

30. Benjamin, "Paris, Capital of the Nineteenth Century," 9.

31. Georg Simmel, *The Philosophy of Money*, trans. Tom Bottomore and David Frisby (New York: Routledge, 1990), 460.

32. Adorno, *Negative Dialectics*, 191.

33. Simmel, *The Philosophy of Money*, 460.

34. Adorno, *Negative Dialectics*, 191.

35. Virginia Woolf, *Night and Day* (New York: Harcourt Brace, 1920), 22; Virginia Woolf, *Between the Acts* (1941; New York: Harcourt Brace, 1970), 70.

36. Virginia Woolf, "Street Haunting: A London Adventure," in *Collected Essays*, vol. 4 (New York: Harcourt Brace, 1967), 155–56.

37. Virginia Woolf, *"Jacob's Room" and "The Waves"* (New York: Harcourt Brace, 1980), 9, 10. Page numbers for further citations of this work appear in parentheses in the text.

38. Virginia Woolf, "*Robinson Crusoe*," in *Collected Essays*, vol. 1 (New York: Harcourt Brace, 1950), 75. For the best discussion of Woolf's essay, see Daniel Ferrer,

Virginia Woolf and the Madness of Language, trans. Geoffrey Bennington and Rachel Bowlby (London: Routledge, 1990), 141–48. For an account of Woolf's novels in the context of object relations theory, see Elizabeth Abel, *Virginia Woolf and the Fictions of Psychoanalysis* (Chicago: University of Chicago Press, 1989). For a discussion of objects in Woolf's novels that emphasizes how they "hang loose" without ever comprising a "whole world of which the objects are parts" (in other words, performing an antithetical function to the pot in *Robinson Crusoe*), see Rachel Bowlby, *Virginia Woolf: Feminist Destinations* (Oxford: Basil Blackwell, 1988), 117–27. For an account of how the subjective apperception of objects in Woolf's novels corresponds with G. E. Moore's psychology, see Harvena Richter, *Virginia Woolf: The Inward Voyage* (Princeton, N.J.: Princeton University Press, 1970), 67–69. For an account of Woolf's most explicit engagement with Hume's questions about the separation of subject and object, see Gillian Beer, "Hume, Stephen, and Elegy in *To the Lighthouse,*" in *Virginia Woolf: The Common Ground* (Ann Arbor: University of Michigan Press, 1996), 29–47. And for an account, prefaced with a reading of Woolf's essay, of Defoe in relation to the eighteenth-century china trade, see Lydia H. Liu, "Robinson Crusoe's Earthenware Pot," *Critical Inquiry* 25 (summer 1999): 728–57.

39. It would be possible to call attention to how Woolf's realist mode, with its verisimilar rendering of decor, transforms into a modernist mode where objects no longer have an identifiable relation to humans or to one another. And yet such schematic narratives, as Bowlby suggests, erase the very instability that characterizes Woolf's objectifications even as a fictional chronicler (*Virginia Woolf,* 120). In "Solid Objects," John's relation to the things he collects seems more like the sort of relation described in Leonard Woolf's novelistic account of Hambantota life in Ceylon, *The Village in the Jungle* (1926), where Silindu's profound intimacy with the jungle provokes his isolation both from his fellow villagers and from the British officials.

40. See Paul Fussell, *The Great War and Modern Memory* (New York: Oxford University Press, 1975), 325–26. For discussions of Woolf's novels in relation to war, see the essays collected in Mark Hussey, ed., *Virginia Woolf and War: Fiction, Reality, Myth* (Syracuse, N.Y.: Syracuse University Press, 1991).

41. Writing to Lytton Strachey before his visit to Asheham, Woolf explains that "you'll have to bring whatever cards for meat, sugar, butter you possess as we are strictly rationed here," or, alternatively, "get your cook at Belsize to get you a week's rations of butter, sugar and meat which you pack in your bag and bring with you" (24 March 1918, 27 March 1918, *Letters of Virginia Woolf,* 227, 228).

42. Woolf's interest in glass extends from the material to the rhetorical. In her diary, she explains of *Electra* that "traditional plots which have been made & improved & freed from superfluities by the polish of innumerable actors & authors & critics" become "like a lump of glass worn smooth in the sea" (*Diary,* 184). And when Orlando is frustrated by the way familiar metaphors encumber any thought or expression of love, Woolf uses the metaphor of the thing of glass: "Every single thing, once he tried to dislodge it from its place in his mind, he found thus cumbered with other matter like the lump of glass which, after a year at the bottom of the sea, is grown about with bones and dragon-flies, and coins and the tresses of drowned women" (*Orlando,* 101).

43. See T. C. Baker, *The Glassmakers: Pilkington, the Rise of an International Company 1826–1976* (London: Weidenfield & Nicolson, 1977), chap. 15; Pilkington Brothers, *Now Thus—Now Thus, 1826–1926* (London: Joseph Coaston, 1926), 59–63.

44. "Glass-Famine in Britain," *Literary Digest* 51 (16 October 1915): 836.

45. See "British Glass-Sands," *Geographic Journal* 51 (May 1918): 335–36; Great Britain Board of Trade, *Hand Blown Domestic Glassware* (London: HMSO, 1947), 24.

46. See C. E. N. Bromehead, "Natural Resources in Relation to the Arts," *Geographical Journal* 63 (June 1914): 488–89.

47. R. J. Chesterton, *English Glass and the Glass Used in England, circa 400–1940* (London: George Allen & Unwin, 1984), 230.

48. Great Britain Board of Trade, *Hand Blown Domestic Glassware,* 21, 24.

49. As the architect Charles Downes originally emphasized, the construction was modular, and the materials were "not of such a nature as to restrict the construction of similar buildings to any particular country." Charles Downes and Charles Cowper, *The Building Erected in Hyde Park for the Great Exhibition of the Works of Industry of All Nations, 1851* (London: John Weale, 1852), ii.

50. Leonard Woolf, *Imperialism and Civilization* (New York: Harcourt, Brace, 1928), 41, 42, 44. He goes on to specify that the manufacturers, who were "the harbingers of imperialism in the hills and plains of Asia and the forests of Africa," went there to obtain "tin or iron or rubber or tea or coffee" (49).

51. See D. L. Burn, *The Economic History of Steelmaking 1867–1939* (Cambridge: Cambridge University Press, 1940), 369.

52. Y., "Coal and Iron in War: The Importance of Alsace and Lorraine," *Fortnightly Review* 108 (November 1917): 709. The German memorandum reads, for instance: "For cast-iron shells alone, which are an inferior substitute for those in steel, an average production of 4000 tons of iron per day has been necessary. If the production of pig-iron and steel had not been doubled, the war could not have been continued" (700).

53. Sir John French, quoted in *The Times History and Encyclopedia of the War* 5 (12 October 1915): 309. To track the control of glass and iron production and distribution, see N. B. Dearle, *An Economic Chronicle of the Great War for Great Britain and Ireland* (London: Oxford University Press, 1929). For a general account of munitions manufacturing, see Sir Llewellyn Woodward, *Great Britain and the War of 1914–1918* (London: Methuen, 1967), chap. 30.

54. See W. Cunningham, *Western Civilization in Its Economic Aspects,* vol. 2 (Cambridge: Cambridge University Press, 1900), 227–28; J. Stephen Jeans, *The Iron Trade of Great Britain* (London: Methuen, [1940?]), 150, 139.

55. See T. H. Burnham and G. O. Hoskins, *Iron and Steel in Britain 1870–1930* (London: George Allen & Unwin, 1943), 46; Burn, *The Economic History of Steelmaking,* chap. 15. For a contemporaneous, international overview, see Edwin C. Eckel, *Coal, Iron, and War* (New York: Henry Holt, 1920). For details, see the *Iron and Coal Trades Review* (London), an illustrated weekly that began publication in 1866.

56. See Great Britain Board of Trade, *Report on Iron and Steel Products* (London: HMSO, 1920), 3–5.

57. From a poster quoting Sir Douglas Haig, quoted in *The Times History and Encylopedia of the War* 15 (14 May 1918): 461.

58. Louis Aragon, "Drinking Song," trans. Michael Benedikt, in *The Poetry of Surrealism: An Anthology,* ed. Michael Benedikt (Boston: Little, Brown, 1974), 154. One way to read Woolf's story, then, would be to understand John himself as a militaristic figure—increasingly strategic, goal focused, and obsessive—as someone

whose senses have been transformed by war's engulfing transformation, by its capacity to conscript even those who appear uninvolved.

59. Benjamin, "Surrealism," 209. This is hardly to argue that there is not a more explicit, more vibrant, and more politically fraught connection between Benjamin's investment in the surrealists and his depiction of the war as an "immense wooing of the cosmos." See Hansen, "Benjamin and Cinema," 326–28.

60. Bronislaw Malinowski, *Argonauts of the Western Pacific* (Prospect Heights, Ill.: Waveland, 1984), 9. The "simple action—this passing from hand to hand of two meaningless and quite useless objects (the arm-shells and necklaces)—has somehow succeeded in becoming the foundation of a big inter-tribal institution" (86).

61. Marcel Mauss, *The Gift: Forms and Functions of Exchange in Archaic Societies,* trans. Ian Cunnison (New York: W. W. Norton, 1967), 74.

62. Thus William Pietz, in his influential history of the concept of fetishism, explains that the "worship of haphazardly chosen material objects" became the "paradigmatic illustration of what was *not* enlightenment." William Pietz, "The Problem of Fetish, IIIa: Bosman's Guinea and the Enlightenment Theory of Fetishism," *Res* 16 (autumn 1988): 106. See also pts. 1 and 2, *Res* 9 (spring 1985): 5–17; and *Res* 13 (spring 1987): 23–45. And see William Pietz, "Fetishism and Materialism: The Limits of Theory in Marx," in *Fetishism as Cultural Discourse,* ed. Emily Apter and William Pietz (Ithaca, N.Y.: Cornell University Press, 1993), 119–51.

63. Woolf narrativizes such a development in "The Mark on the Wall," in *House,* 37–46. An ambiguous, abstract mark turns out to be a snail. Insofar as the story represents an attraction to "the impersonal world which is proof of some existence other than ours," an attraction satisfied by the "solidity" and "reality" of materials ("Wood is a pleasant thing to think about"), "The Mark on the Wall" can be reasonably paired with "Solid Objects." But the latter utterly differentiates itself by fixating on the fragment, the specifically cultural remainder that will never assume coherence as a familiar object, animate or inanimate.

64. Simmel, *The Philosophy of Money,* 474.

CHAPTER EIGHTEEN

Arresting Images

Kathleen Stewart

> Thinking involves not only the flow of thoughts, but their arrest as well. Where thinking suddenly stops in a configuration pregnant with tensions, it gives that configuration a shock.
>
> —Walter Benjamin, "Theses on the Philosophy of History"

Opening Things

Arresting images are a modern habit born out of the surge of signs, capital, and the sensoriums of public culture surge through circuits of image and matter. Lodged in the senses, and carrying the aesthetic charge of the senses, they are states of suspense filled with resonance.[1] Like a hunter tracking his way, or prey, they sniff out tracks in the networks of the new global order to mark moments of impact and reenchantment when circulating things suddenly enter the senses and literally make sense. Seducing and repelling us with the look and smell of an incipient vitality, they figure the immanent intensity or force of what Deleuze calls affect, or the two-sidedness of things where the virtual meets the actual and where what matters is the seeping edge of potentiality itself.[2] Felt as a sudden eruption or interruption, this shimmering transformation of matter and image into a common sensate affect can come as a shock. But it is also a constant in the continuous trembling that haunts the stable gaze and in the proliferation of images and sensibilities that constantly exceed the requirements of what we call reason, order, and "common sense."[3]

Affect is the promise, or threat, that something is happening—something new, emergent, and capable of impact. It may be half noted out of the corner of the eye or sensed as a figure shadowing the commonsense world. Or it can be put into words as that which escapes or exceeds enclosure and stasis to become a figure of vitality and even freedom.[4] But whether it haunts or is courted as a welcome reprieve from symbolic gridlock, affect gathers its force to make image touch matter by moving through the senses. It becomes the medium of the senses' contact and copy, and its power is the power of synaesthesia. It is precisely not the collection of named "feelings" or "emotions" invented in discourses of morals, ideals, and known subjectivities but something else that forms their raw material and exceeds them. It is more precisely and literally captured as the sudden and lingering intensity of things that give pause, if only for a minute—sights that hit with a tactile force and sounds that surge through the stomach.[5] Circulations in moments of vital impact.

Arresting Images

I remember childhood as a collection of arresting images that hinge on sensory details and open onto luminous scenes of affect: my kindergarten class walking back from Woolworth's carrying a box full of furry yellow chicks, the warming spring sun on our backs; the smell of shimmering red tulips in my mother's garden married to the taste of found raspberries and tart rhubarb ripped out of the ground while she wasn't looking and eaten with a spoonful of dirt. My mother dressing to go out in a beautiful black dress and red lipstick cuts to the brilliant red blood that exploded from the face of the boy next door as he fell from a cliff and landed face down on the cement in front of me, and then to the rhythm of shocks, days later, as my father and the other men tore the cliff apart boulder by boulder and each giant rock hit the ground, and shook the glasses in the kitchen cabinet of the quiet, shaded pantry with an impact that seemed transformative. I remember a spectral scene of my little brother hunched over in the pine trees that hugged the house and then, walking back from school a few hours later, the sight of the house engulfed in flames and the driveway full of fire trucks with flashing red lights and ear-piercing sirens. The phrase "playing with matches" seems to be written across the blue sky. Or there was the day when my grandparents—all four of them—came to visit from out of state and they were floating up the treacherous driveway in a big wide car as I stood on the side and watched. Then the right wheels were sliding off the icy edge and the big car hung suspended over the cliff. The white heads in the backseat sat very still while I ran, yelling for my father. Or there was that tense moment when my sister crushed her fingers in the milk delivery door at the top of the cellar stairs and she was screaming, drawing my mother to the spurting blood, while the wild rabbits we had captured that morning ran around the cellar in a secret chaos. Sunday drives were ice cream cones dripping down our fingers as we sat crowded into the backseat, a complex order of silent conspiracies, betrayals, and realignments as the youngest were wordlessly defrauded of their ice cream without setting off the alarm that would alert the front seat. I remember this latter as a scene of sticky fingers and huge, silent tears running down fat baby cheeks. There were strange, jarring performances like the one at the VFW hall where my sister was the "can-can" girl covered in clanking cans and I was the "balloon girl" dancing in floating plastic spheres to the song about "the itsy-bitsy, teeny-weeny, yellow polka-dot bikini" while everyone laughed.

Arresting images interrupt the run-on story of everyday life with an aesthetic sensibility that literally articulates, or "makes matter," the Event itself—the moment of recognition that changes the nature of recognition, or the encounter that erupts out of the order of representations we use to lay claim to a self, or an era, or a cultural politics. The moment of shock—the Event made sensate—erupts as a shadow suddenly revealed skirting the order of ideal representations of things like family, church, and law. So, for instance, my early Catholic school years are literally articulated in screen memories of sensate excess and shock: my little brother scared to the point of vomiting every day on our walk to school, the big leather strap in the back of the room, the ruler coming down on knuckles, the voice of the priest behind the dark confessional curtain asking if I had ever been impure (and was it alone or with others?), the bishop's giant ruby ring as he slapped my face at the altar of my confirmation. I know Family as a viscerality through screen images of walking through neighborhoods with my mother as night fell, peering together into picture windows to catch a glimpse of a lamp by a reading chair or a shelf of knickknacks on the wall as still lifes of modernity at rest. Or Saturday mornings spent sitting around my grandmother's table while she and my mother and all of my aunts told graphic stories under the guise of keeping track of a massive kinship network when the simple effort to recall married names systematically would key the sudden, repetitive eruption of images of alcoholism, accidents, violence, cancers, and other disastrous ends. Or there is the scene of my father trying to hand-feed me all through my life as if he were a bird dropping food into the open mouth of his young. Or the shocking moments of his helpless panic, like the dark, bitter-cold morning he crawled on his old hands and knees up the steep icy driveway in a desperate effort to get me to the airport on time.

The technologies of family, church, law, and nation lay confident claim to affect as a capturable content of known and expected "feelings,"[6] but affect itself—–that which surges into view along the jumpy border of the actual and the virtual—is their raw material and their only renewable resource. Alphonso Lingis describes an encounter with the jumpy move of affect one day when he was visiting a mine on the Arctic Circle:

> The young miner who showed me the mine put out every cigarette he smoked on his hand, which was covered with scar tissue. Then I saw the other young miners all had the backs of their hands covered with scar tissue.... when my eye fell on them it flinched, seeing the burning cigarette being crushed and sensing the pain.... The eye does not read the meaning in a sign; it *jumps* from the mark to the pain and the burning cigarette, and then jumps to the fraternity signaled by the burning cigarettes.[7]

Circulation and Impact

The arresting images of everyday life are innumerable, and they are at once vastly familiar and entirely uncharted, roosting here and there in strange and ordinary moments of impact and emergent affect. At odd moments of spacing out, a strange malaise may come over you. Something tempts a shift in perspective—a sidestep that brings an uncanny, alien presence into the field of vision.[8] An object insists on being seen. Whether through the tricks of trauma or the seductions of compulsive beauty,[9] something captivates you in a field of reciprocal gazes that can not be reduced to the subject's superior one-point perspective. It provokes what Lyotard calls "the extinction of... the subject's mirror... of its most elementary capacity for synthesis" and opens instead to the circuitry of circulation and impact, matter shifting into image shifting into matter.[10] This is not necessarily a bad thing. It's not a good thing either. But it is, necessarily, an aesthetic event of the senses.

These days, spectacular graphics of disaster, monstrosity, and strangeness literally "bring to light" the mass subject and the very notion of a "public."[11] The airwaves are filled with images of the man who bursts into his ex-girlfriend's trailer, shooting her and her new lover in their bed, or the "educated couple" who calmly go away on vacation, leaving behind a hundred cats—some dead, some alive, wild ones living in the walls. On the nightly news we see the arrested image of the trailer wrapped in crime scene tape and the cat cages and cans of unopened cat food all over the house.

Reality TV gives us still lifes of the poor and outcast or the rich and famous. And then car ads break in. The big shiny object whisks you along a beautiful wilderness road and then sweeps to a quick stop; the camera pans back to ponder the big shiny car in a quiet moment of fantasy realized. In the end, you picture yourself both "in" the car and just where you are, watching, inhabiting the power of the tuned-in spectator.

America's Most Wanted shows photos of bank robbers with and without beards so you can scan the faces at the 7-Eleven for a match. This, of course, is a technology of self-discipline in which the citizenry feeds on its moments of visibility—its moments of failure, of excess "action," of surges into the limelight, and of abjection. But it is also, first, a game in which the viewer mimics the moves of the TV and becomes an active participant in its logic of image production and recognition. The seduction, it seems to me, is not in a catharsis of mean-spirited, festering alienation but in the vitality of the game itself. In the game you can make the connection between the image on the screen and the walking simulacrum of social life that is the trip to the 7-Eleven.

Some people make the trip to the 7-Eleven several times a day, expending energy in excess of the weekly shop to the supermarket grid. They go for cigarettes and beer and bad food and lottery tickets and all those things poor people shouldn't spend their money on. It's irrational. But it keeps them in the loop of the citizen as consumer and performs an action on the loop itself, taking it further into the logic of excess and expenditure, taking that logic itself to the point of excess and visibility and to a point of satisfaction in which a tension is finally spent.

Those people at the 7-Eleven who are on the lookout for the face out of place may be adding a dimension of excitement to their four-trips-a-day habit. Others may be surveiling Otherness from the righteous pose of those just stopping in for the efficiency of a quart of milk midweek. Layers of alienation and the vitality of action/reaction twist in rich and tense confusion and rub shoulders in sudden impulses of seduction or repulsion.

Mimesis in a State of Shock

When affect makes its jump between the visible thing, the idea, and the social sensibility, it can leave in its wake uncanny connections between otherwise disparate states of arrest, like shock and recluse. Take, for instance, the uncanny resemblance some of us feel between the dazed state of trauma and the enforced cluelessness, or cocooning, we now call "home." In both, a space of heightened affect engulfs the subject in an aesthetic/sensory scene. Affect jumps into view as the shock of an unassimilated trauma, or it drifts dreamily onto center stage in the profoundly secluded space of the bourgeois interior. Either way, sensually charged objects resonate with an absence/presence whether they are hypervisible and charged with excess or held at bay and haunting.

From the perspective of affect, the link between shock and a cushioned recluse is direct, seductive, and mimetic. That is, shock and cocooning are not "opposite emotions"—as we might picture them, for instance, in the image of the traumatized subject who runs home to hide and finds relief—but practices with a deep affinity. Both track the immanence of affect lodged in a scene of arrest. Both are haunted by immanence and both dream of a satisfaction of the senses, or the completion or expenditure of an overwhelming affect. Both states of a jumpy arrest, they stage both the search for an ending and the intensity of immanence itself. The same momentary "satisfaction" of the haunted senses can come at the sight of an accident or at the sight of the perfect cocoon room when you come home at night and close the door behind you. But even as dread comes to a head in a moment of shock it threatens to erupt again; even as the cushioned fantasyland of recluse snaps into place it takes on the jumpy logic of the fetish moving through circuits of repression and return, spectrality and concrete substance.[12] The very act of holing up in your living room produces dread of what is "out there," even to the point where going out itself becomes traumatic. Then the search for the arresting presence is renewed and redoubled.

Think of standing in line in a supermarket. You're already impatient but then you get desperate when something goes wrong with the register and you're stuck there, unable either to go forward or to move to another register. You are caught in a system of circulation but unable to move. So you pick up a magazine to zone out. You open to the picture-perfect centerfold of a scene at rest in *Country Living* or *Home and Garden* and relax into the invented aura. Or, alternatively, you skim the tabloid headlines for the thrill of shock. This is another way of doing the same thing, of literally "relaxing" the jumpy move of affect. You come back to life, engaged by an object/scene. The tactile image literally satisfies the move of affect to actualize something that is tempting or haunting.

Glamour magazines do this too. They give you not so much a model, or a blueprint, of how to look and what to wear as the magic of affect itself. Models frozen in time and space stare back at you in a scene that stages the jump from fantasy to actual body/image and back. Affect is captured in an affecting presence at rest.[13] The world of sports spectatorship is stuffed to overflowing with this jump of affect.

The arrested image seduces the spectator with the copy that is also contact.[14] In its popular art form—the film—it whispers to us, in an inaudible murmuring, "Love me."[15] And it promises, in return, both the bubble of the living fantasy and the little but profound shocks of recognition and encounter that seem to awaken something. As Taussig has argued, it is the capacity of modernity's mimetic machines to pump out contact-sensuousity that makes Benjamin's "profane illumination" possible.[16] "Not what the moving red neon sign says—but the fiery pool reflecting it in the asphalt."[17] An "optical unconscious" born in a commodified world grows sensuously vibrant in the circulating impacts of surround-sound movies, ads, malls, car phones, and daydreams.

Quiet Time in the Middle Ground

The "middle class," then, is not just a "norm" or ideal that signals safety and stasis but a womblike space of affect where forms of sentimentality and a longing for interiority have become tactile.[18] Here, affect is a vitality and hope launched against the nightmare image of social entropy and the vicious blank-screen affect of Other people "out there" who just don't care. Dread is dredged up as the other to the dream of an unhaunted home. What is called the "middle class"—what people thinking as "Americans" now want to identify with—is the affective space where the hegemonic claim to channel trauma into beauty is actualized: the self-help movement; privatization; the banality of franchise culture; exhilarated consumerism; "sensible," solid accumulation; family values; the utopia of colorful decor; instant and easy communication; ever-new techno-gadgets; repetitive risk routines like the stock market and the daily lottery; and the constant stimulation of the senses and the passions through synaesthetic images, sounds, touches, and smells. The "middle class" is the state of being "inside" the central, hooked-up jumps of affect and privy to the enabling technologies and circuitry of circulation itself. The objects of mass desire have become the very affects of circulation and accumulation themselves—travel; the stock market; information networks; movie fantasies; the accumulation of money, things, and life stages; and the sensible conspicuous consumption of the big, beautiful, basic, intensely sensate commodity-to-live-in like the perfect bathroom done in the textures of old stone or the country farmhouse getaway.

"Outside" is the nothingness, the refused access, that produces a "wilding" scene of crime, chaos, drug-addled monsters, danger, disease, and decay. "Inside," the American Dream settles down into a little vignette stuffed to overflowing with scenes of aesthetic connection. Vitality and potentiality unfold as if automatically or effortlessly, but anxiety is the ground over which they march. Houses painstakingly kept up, yards kept trim and tended, the little family stands beside the sports utility vehicle in the driveway looking up, stock portfolios in hand, everything insured, payments up-to-date, fat-free diet under their belts, Community Watch systems in place. Martha Stewart offers advice on the finishing touches. A dreamy nostalgia conflates with a resurgent modernist image-affect of the new and clean and up-to-date.

Both ideals and materiality grow to excess in the womb of the middle ground, where their transmogrification is both automatic, it seems, and a desperate goal—all that matters. Here, affect literally senses itself through the repetitions of the jump from ideal to matter to ideal. There are big projects, like remodeling, and daily projects, like shopping, making lists, keeping a diary, or taking pictures. Little pleasures are hooked up to the big picture.

Some people watch the stock market channel like others watch the weather channel, hour to hour, minute to minute—like it's background, like it's company, like it knows what's going to happen. The visceral image on the screen is both comforting and exciting: the maps and charts and talking heads, the bright colors and simulated thunderstorms, the big, cheery schoolroom suns, the feeling of being in the middle of something big and inevitable, watching it unfold, deciding what action to take, riding the ups and downs of vitality itself. The weather and the stock market become the subjects of conversation-lite: What's the weather gonna do? What's the stock market gonna do? Who knows? That's life, we're all in it together.

The middle ground implodes under the weight of its own literal embodiment as it plays itself out to the point of exhaustion.[19] Remember the suburban ideal, for instance, now transmogrified into the new and improved planned community (which is, in turn, sinking fast even as it is dead set on the path of hegemonic realization). Some critiques of middle-ground excesses claim a decontaminated distance capable of judging them to death. Others, like this one, or like contemporary films that parody suburbia and the nuclear family, take the tack of tracking the affect and drawing it down its own road to banal actualization. But either way, the flat specters of suburbia and the middle class do not die. Far from it—their very ordinariness make them heroes and objects of fascination for the restless gaze of a spectator seeking out scenes of arousal and tactility and for the snoop sniffing out tracks of circulation and impact.

The circulation (exchange value) of late capitalism now depends on the labor of looking. The sensorium is retooled by the hours on the couch watching images cut between ads and stories and news, surfing between channels, and cutting back and forth from the screen to the scene in your house.[20] Affect swells and flexes its muscles as the habit of watching images touch matter grows.

Action movies of masculinity play out a fast-switching dialectic of impending disaster and last-minute reprieve in which agency (or the action/reaction of affect) awakens and takes on a muscled mass. Movies made for women imagine a picture-perfect scene of an Inside—a Home filled with tangible objects that Mean or a Self filled with the intricate dramas of dreams launched, wounded, and finally satisfied or left behind. Affect itself is laid out on the carpet like a beautiful fetish that it is okay to love.

Out There

Meanwhile, "the streets" are littered with cryptic, half-written signs of personal/public disaster like the daily sightings of homeless men and women holding up signs of abjection and will while puppies play at their feet. Here, the arresting image strikes the senses with a negating, yet mesmerizing, force. The graphic lettering that pleads for the attention of the passing cars glances off the eye as something to avoid like the plague; abjection itself is felt as a contagion.[21] But it is also the fascination of catastrophe, or the sense that something is happening—the surge of affect toward the scene of abjection, or profound homelessness.

The sign of homelessness pleads to be touched, if only in passing, by the dry wind left in the wake of the passing cars. The act of looking at it is other to the power (and anxiety) look that looks in order to mime the desire of others[22]—my desire is your desire and we are all together in the mass desire. The sign on the side of the road makes a gesture toward an ideological center that claims the value of willpower and must leave open the possibility of redemption. But the image of the sign itself offers no affect to mime, no line of vitality to follow, no intimate secret to plumb, no tips to imbibe for safety or good health or the search for things new and vibrant with collective envy. Instead, something sticks out of the side of things like the shock of the Real—Žižek's blot on the camera, Lyotard's "inhuman," Lacan's unassimilated something not quite exhausted by the symbolic.[23]

Even to glance out of the corner of the eye at the sign on the side of the road is a mesmerizing and repellant sidestep. And what it finds in the scene it glances through, half-panicked, is not an affective lead but the abject surge to be included in the very wind of circulation itself. Its message is too starkly one of begging and too perfect to the letter; it points to a painful vulnerability that will try anything, or to parody or fraud.

A dollar bill stuck out of a car window gets a quick surge forward from the one with the sign and the heightened, but unassimilated, affect of a raw contact. "God bless you."

Now we're trudging the rough terrain of bodies, sensuous accumulation, impact.

An Image Gets Stuck in the Middle of Your Brain

Laurie Anderson had a performance exhibit at the Soho Guggenheim called *Your Fortune, $1*. A spooky white plastic owl perched on a stool in a darkened corner of the museum spewed out a stream of two-bit advice, trenchant commentary, and stray advertising lingo plucked out of a realm of sheer circulation. The owl's mechanical yet sensuously grainy voice droned on and on, transfixing me in a flood of Hallmark greeting-card shlock and moments of shocking recognition. One of these moments of shock came when it said something, I swear, that I had already been anxiously chanting to myself: "Sometimes when you hear someone scream it goes in one ear and out the other. Sometimes it passes right into the middle of your brain and gets stuck there." The flow of circulating signs stopped dead in its tracks. I went home and wrote down a story that had been lodged somewhere in the middle of my brain ever since I'd heard it.

The story starts with a question lodged in a tactile, sensate anxiety and then opens onto an aesthetic scene of the senses. The question: Do you ever wake up in the morning, or in the middle of the night, with a sense of sudden dread and start scanning your dreamy brain for the memory of what you've done or a premonition of what's coming? Some do this all the time; for *us*, this is just what morning has become—a grievous mourning, a "morning" of a different order. The Aesthetic scene of the senses: my big iron bed brushes up against windows onto the back deck. Tropical breezes waft over me in the night, carrying the sweet and fetid smells of kumquat trees and mimosa blossoms. In the dawn there are wild bird cries—mourning doves and grackles. And before that, at certain hours in the still of the night, the train cries in the near distance. When I have guests I give them my bed and they wake up talking about the iron bed and the whistling train as if they feel pleased to be set down in some kind of American Heartland pulsing with the high lonesome sound of nostalgic machine dreams roaming the landscape. But I know why the train sings, so I am only too happy to lay myself down a pallet on the living room floor and fall into a deep sleep with only the smell of old ashes from the fireplace.

The train sings for Bobby—a homeless drunk who laid himself down on the tracks one night and passed out as if he, too, could lay down a pallet and escape. Bobby and his old lady had been down at the free concert at the river and they got into a fight. So Bobby stomped off and ended up at the tracks alone, licking his wounds in the abjection of his own night airs. The train had the pull of the high, lonesome sound in the distance for a drunk taking stock and wallowing in a booze-soaked moment of reprieve. The romance of the whistling train draws close, as if it were the only thing left. As if its promise of tactility and power could chase away his ghosts, Bobby laid himself down on the icy cold tracks and closed his eyes in a bodily movement surging, simultaneously, toward an abject ending and the dream of contact with the iron substance of a public world that might include him. Then, in the middle of the long train passing over him, he raised his head, awakening. They say that otherwise it would have passed right over him. But who can sleep at a train passing over? Now the train screams out a warning when it approaches that place on the tracks not far from my iron bed. It often wakes me. Or it lodges in my sleep and comes as an unknown shock of anxiety in the morning.

Sometimes the screech of the night train breaks into the light of day, like when I'm stopped at the railroad crossing on the way to the office. The scene of cars and trucks waiting fills with the wild force coming down the tracks. Scenes take shape, like the day a boxcar full of Mexican illegals drifted slowly by and the men at the door were waving and smiling at us like this was their fifteen minutes of fame and we were the welcoming audience. In West Virginia when we waited for the coal trains that would block the only road out of the holler, sometimes for hours, we would get out and lean on the trucks, gazing into the scene as we talked. Sometimes a confident claim would begin to circulate that someday, someone was gonna get a pile of dynamite, blow the train in half, and clear the road for good.

Something in this confidence—the exuberant waving of the new immigrants, the explosive claims in the coal camps, Bobby's lying down to sleep on the tracks—lends itself to Benjamin's dialectics of intoxication.[24] It is the kind of intoxicated confidence that surges between life and dream and cheers on the reckless daydream that a "something else" will suddenly appear on the ravenous horizons of the order of things.

It's as if the subject is literally "touched," or punctured, by a scene and makes herself its convulsive possession.[25] There is abjection in this, but there is also at the same time a vital move to take on a force with sufficient intensity to capture it in the senses. On the one hand, the confident-abject surge is what Hal Foster calls traumatic realism, or a figuring that, like traumatic memory, fails to represent the inflicting force as an object in a symbolic order and therefore feels compelled to literally re-present it over and over, miming the original haunting impact.[26] But it is also the confidence of a subject constituted in the vital move itself—the subject surging to bear an affect, or surging toward an actualization.[27] In this sense it has to be seen not as a lack but as a fullness.[28] Its extreme vulnerability (all of those unwarranted hopes) comes not from a disconnection with reality, or a false consciousness, but from the passionate connection of the subject who goes with the flow in an intoxicated moment. It's not as if sober distance promises a true alternative. Rather, it clings to the other extreme—the self-discipline of affect beaten down to reason.

Signs of the Senses

Walking along the river in Austin in the early morning, I always stop on a high bridge that overlooks scenes of fishermen floating in the still water, giant blue herons and swans poised on drowning tree trunks, and mansions perched on distant cliffs. One morning there was a crude sign taped to the bridge. Below it there was a shrine: yellow ribbons, a votive candle with the image of the Sacred Heart of Jesus on it, and a half dozen burned sticks of incense stuck into the half-burned wax. The sign was both cryptic and stark. At the top was the inscription of the names of star-crossed lovers you can picture repeated over and over on school notebooks and graffitied train trestles. The names were crossed out.

> **Angela and Jerry**

Then the sign-shrine opened onto a cryptic reference to a crime against life, love, and the nation committed by federal agents and the local Austin police department.

> Relationship destroyed, *WITH MALICE* by Federal Agents & A.P.D.
>
> for beliefs guaranteed under U.S. Constitutional Bill of Rights.
> I miss you Angela, Jessica & Furry Dog Reef –
> Always,
> Jerry

Below this there were several graphics. One was a heart pierced by an arrow and inside it the words "Yankee Girl." Another was a box that had inside it the words "Please come back." Then the message repeated, with an added stress both on the loss and on the artist's signature:

> Angela, Jessica and Furry Dog Reef . . . *I MISS YOU.*
> May God have mercy on the souls of the *HATEFUL, EVIL, VINDICTIVE* people who conspired to take you from me, and did so with success.
> Angela, I will love you always and forever.
> I miss you, babe,
> Jerry

At the bottom was another pierced heart encircling the words "Yankee Girl."

You can feel the satisfaction in the making of this sign-shrine. Satisfaction as a force, and end, in itself spoken through the bright, blunt, sensate aesthetics of the sign. You can see the demand for satisfaction quivering like flesh in the wavering letters and violent slashes. Bitter fury is its vitality. The grief, fury, and longing it builds, condenses, and heaves at you is not an "expression" of a state of mind, an affect shimmering over an inner content,[29] but a state of the senses making contact with pen and paper and matches. It's theatrical. It's both cryptic and as crystal clear as a scream. In the surge to gather itself to the point of intensity and arrest, it both slashes at itself and spits at the world. It has a strange fullness. Something in its violent surface resists closure and points to a residue; something refuses to disappear.[30]

It's the kind of thing you see every day, in the elaborate poetics of graffiti, for instance: the signatures left so artfully, the politics of slashing through them, crossing them out, erasing them, replicating them all over town. Or in the young girls who "cut" themselves so they can feel alive or, literally "come to their senses." These are inscriptions on surfaces that have no hidden message even though the story line is far from clear. They draw attention, hold a visual fascination. Their surfaces insure against surplus value, or the translation of desire into the abstract and transcendent terms of the symbolic order.[31] They do not ask for interpretation or construct the subject who would assign them a meaning. Yet every day such signs of the senses—these dramas of surge and arrest—are given meaning, or normalized, by reference to "underlying systems" of signification that make them readable as texts. Now we're back in the land of sheer circulations, exchange value, economies, and equilibriums. We enter the unnatural calm of another form of arrest. Then the question becomes, Will the gesture of the shrine-sign shimmer as a curiosity passed on an everyday walking path, and will you feel a little jolt as you pass? Or will the scene resist synaesthesia—in one eye and out the other?

The Optical Eye Also Lunges for Affect

Noticing the shimmer can be dangerous for the thing shimmering. West Virginia. Tommy Creek Holler.[32] Bobby's worried about the Whittakers down by the church. They're grown now and wild looking and there's been trouble with some rich kids from town who think they're freaks worth capturing on camera.

I remember a powerful still life of the Whittakers from years ago. I went inside their place for the first and only time on a home visit with the doctor from the clinic. The mother was in congestive heart failure and sat, with her swollen ankles propped up, in a beat-up recliner. A half dozen teenage boys grunted and gestured and ran in and out of the house, showing us things. A group of as many younger children sat around on the old mattresses on the floor where they slept. They smiled at us.

Then the mother died. The father put on an old cowboy hat and a beautiful, cheap red and yellow satin cowboy shirt with sequins and drifted off. Mary Jo, the oldest, was able to take care of the others, cashing their disability checks and walking every day to the little store at the end of the holler to get weenies, Ding Dongs, coffee, and little cans of sweet evaporated milk.

The others from Tommy Creek helped keep them together, carrying them to the hospital and fighting to keep their disability. Someone gave them an old trailer, now decayed and collapsing on the spot. In recent years, broken down cars have piled up there too, and some of the Whittakers have built their own shacks. Two of the women go to the Tommy Creek Free Will Good Hope Baptist Church next door, and they testify in a language no one can understand but everyone feels is special; they hug them and tell them they love them. When I drive past their place on the narrow holler there are always several Whittakers standing frozen in the yard, watching me pass. The sight is a graphic moment of arrest. Usually someone will smile and wave back at me as I drift slowly past.

The trouble started when a visiting preacher in from Beckley spotted them on his way to the Tommy Creek church and went back and told his congregation. A church committee came visiting with food and clothes. Then, Bobby says, they realized what they had here and they came back at Christmas with a video camera. A group of teenagers who saw the video in their church were seized by it and surged toward the Whittakers one dark night in the thrill of anticipated encounter. Somehow they found the place down the dark holler and they threw rocks at the Whittakers's shacks to draw them out. A few weeks later they returned, and this time the Whittaker men came out showing guns. Bobby was afraid that the next time the rich kids would be back shooting.

An escalating exchange was sparked by a visceral encounter of images. In a video that blankly recorded an arresting image, young embodiments of a modern middle-ground-in-the-making came face-to-face with an otherness that compelled a closer look. The order of representation gave way to a more violently affective contact. Speeding toward the Whittakers and then calling them out in the night, the kids from Beckley locked spaces and lines of movement together in a provisional hierarchy of relations. They surged toward the scene of their confident excitement, and the Whittakers learned their part in the face of threat: the headlights shining in their sleepy eyes and the crack of hostile shouts.

The Body Throws Itself through Space and Encounters Sheer Impact

Impact makes the social, whether good or bad or both. I was in a small town in southwest Texas and had stopped to eat in the only café in town, which turned out to be one of those places with great steaks and pies and checkered table cloths, where the local ranchers hang out at the end of the day talking crops and fertilizer and machine equipment and everyone notices those passing through. The sun had gone down and I was halfway through my steak and fully into my nostalgia and the excitation of otherness brought to the senses when a biker couple came in limping. I watched them closely as they talked intently and exchanged startled looks. When I got up to leave they called me over to their table and asked if I was heading out on the west road that night and if I would look for bike parts on the road. No, I wasn't, why? They had a story to tell. They had hit a deer coming into town and had lost some bike parts in the dark. The deer, they said, had fared much worse. They were shaken up by the sudden, violent, physical encounter and compelled to repeat the event as the sentience of it still reverberated in their senses. I was only too happy to play the part of audience, caught by the promise and threat of affect's surge.

Notes

1. On the aesthetic charge of the senses, see Paul Trembath, "Aesthetics without Art or Culture: Toward an Alternative Sense of Materialist Agency," *Strategies* 9/10 (1996): 122–51. See also Brian Massumi, "The Autonomy of Affect," in *Deleuze: A Critical Reader,* ed. Paul Patton (Cambridge, Mass.: Blackwell, 1996), 217–39.

2. Gilles Deleuze, *The Logic of Sense,* trans. Mark Lester (New York: Columbia University Press, 1990). See also Massumi, "The Autonomy of Affect," 235–36.

3. See Jacques Derrida, *Specters of Marx: The State of Debt, the Work of Mourning, and the New International,* trans. Peggy Kamuf (New York: Routledge, 1994); Avery Gordon, *Ghostly Matters: Haunting and the Sociological Imagination* (Minneapolis: University of Minnesota Press, 1997).

4. Massumi, "The Autonomy of Affect," 229.

5. See Michael Taussig, "Tactility and Distraction," *Cultural Anthropology* 6 (1991): 147–53.

6. Massumi, "The Autonomy of Affect," 234.

7. Alphonso Lingis, "The Society of Dismembered Body Parts," in *Deleuze and the Theatre of Philosophy,* ed. Constantin Boundas and Dorothea Olkowski (New York: Routledge, 1993), 296.

8. Slavoj Žižek, *Looking Awry: An Introduction to Jacques Lacan through Popular Culture* (Cambridge: MIT Press, 1995).

9. Hal Foster, *Compulsive Beauty* (Cambridge: MIT Press, 1997).

10. Jean-François Lyotard, *The Inhuman,* trans. Geoffrey Bennington and Rachel Bowlby (Stanford, Calif.: Stanford University Press, 1991), 157.

11. See Lauren Berlant, *The Queen of America Goes to Washington City* (Durham, N.C.: Duke University Press, 1997); Hal Foster, "Death in America," *October* 75 (1996): 37–59; Mark Seltzer, *Serial Killers: Death and Life in America's Wound Culture* (New York: Routledge, 1998); Michael Warner, "The Mass Public and the Mass Subject," in *The Phantom Public Sphere,* ed. Bruce Robbins (Minneapolis: University of Minnesota Press, 1993), 234–56.

12. Foster, *Compulsive Beauty,* 197.

13. Robert Armstrong, *The Affecting Presence* (Urbana: University of Illinois Press, 1971).

14. See Michael Taussig, *Mimesis and Alterity* (New York: Routledge, 1993); Michael Taussig, "Physiognomic Aspects of Visual Worlds," *Visual Anthropology* 8 (1992): 15–28.

15. Christian Metz, *The Imaginary Signifier: Psychoanalysis and the Cinema,* trans. Celia Britton, Annwyl Williams, Ben Brewster, and Alfred Guzzetti (Bloomington: Indiana University Press, 1982), 14.

16. Taussig, *Mimesis and Alterity*; Walter Benjamin, "Surrealism: The Last Snapshot of the European Intelligentsia," in *Reflections,* ed. P. Demetz (New York: Schocken, 1978), 177–92.

17. Walter Benjamin, "One-Way Street," in *Reflections,* ed. P. Demetz (New York: Schocken, 1978), 61–94.

18. See Wendy Brown, *States of Injury: Power and Freedom in Late Modernity* (Princeton, N.J.: Princeton University Press, 1995); Matthew Archer, "Gated Governmentality" (master's report, University of Texas, 1997); Joan DeJean, "Did the Seventeenth Century Invent Our Fin de Siècle? Or, the Creation of the Enlightenment That We May at Last Be Leaving Behind," *Critical Inquiry* 22 (1996): 790–816.

19. See Steven Shaviro, *The Cinematic Body* (Minneapolis: University of Minnesota Press, 1993), 263.

20. See Jonathan Beller, "Cinema, Capital of the Twentieth Century," *Postmodern Culture* 4, no. 3 (1994).

21. See Mike Davis, *Ecology of Fear: Los Angeles and the Imagination of Disaster* (New York: Henry Holt, 1998).

22. See Trembath, "Aesthetics without Art or Culture."

23. Žižek, *Looking Awry*; Lyotard, *The Inhuman*; Jacques Lacan, *Écrits: A Selection*, trans. Alan Sheridan (London: Tavistock, 1977).

24. Benjamin, "Surrealism."

25. Foster, *Compulsive Beauty*, 199. See also Taussig, "Physiognomic Aspects of Visual Worlds," 27.

26. Foster, *The Return of the Real* (Cambridge: MIT Press, 1996). See also Cathy Caruth, *Unclaimed Experience: Trauma, Narrative, History* (Baltimore: Johns Hopkins University Press, 1996); Lacan, *Écrits*; Lyotard, *The Inhuman.*

27. See Daniel Smith, "Deleuze's Theory of Sensation," in *Delueze: A Critical Reader*, ed. Paul Patton (Cambridge, Mass.: Blackwell, 1996), 29–56.

28. See Elizabeth Grosz, *Volatile Bodies: Toward a Corporeal Feminism* (Bloomington: Indiana University Press, 1994).

29. See Lingis, "The Society of Dismembered Body Parts."

30. See Shaviro, *The Cinematic Body.*

31. Ibid.

32. See Kathleen Stewart, *A Space on the Side of the Road: Cultural Poetics in an "Other" America* (Princeton, N.J.: Princeton University Press, 1996).

CHAPTER NINETEEN

The Adult's Imagination of the Child's Imagination

Michael Taussig

I

To talk of the adult's imagination of the child's imagination is inevitably to enter the aesthetic no less than the political nature of secrecy. That this is ultimately an ethical issue carrying quick and slow-release charges of pleasure, on account of pain and destruction, I plan to demonstrate, beginning with Walter Benjamin sizing up Plato's famous argument in the *Symposium,* the argument being, according to Benjamin, that for eros, truth lies not in a process of exposure that destroys the secret, but in a revelation that does *justice* to it.[1] He says secret and he means hidden truth, and when you equate truth and secret like this it seems to me there is more than a hint of mystery and fate working in cahoots, awaiting the magic of the diviner extracting the rabbit from the hat. As does Plato—for instance, with the magic of the vision of the Form of the Beautiful, which gives complete knowledge of the truth concerning the universe. The result of a sacred pilgrimage. And if the equation of truth with secrecy seems corny and melodramatic, so be it. It's certainly the equation most of us make most of the time and have done so, in the West, for millennia.

Doing justice here is where aesthetics and ethics converge, because so much hinges on the tight relation between truth and beauty, it being the outer form of the beautiful, in Benjamin's interpretation, that at first attracts yet conceals to eros, the impassioned observer, the truth within the beloved object of desire, and second because if we ponder the notion of a "revelation that does justice," we realize the necessity for some theatrical unmasking, some performative finesse, beautiful in its perfection, as if beauty and truth not only converge in that unmasking, but truth lies as much in this act as in the eventual product of an ideal form drawn out from the obscurity within. Recall Benjamin's anxiety about the need to handle with exquisite care the unfolding of truth hidden in beauty. Not an exposure, he says, that would destroy the secret, but a revelation that does it justice. Indeed, when Benjamin tries to denote what he means by a just revelation, he figures the process as the burning up of the husk of the beautiful outer appearance of the secret as it enters into the realm of ideas—"that is to say," he adds, "a destruction of the work in which the external form achieves its most brilliant degree of illumination."[2]

So we pass from outer substance to inner idea, from the shimmering world of appearance, beautiful as it may be, to the secret within, and justice, our third term, our ethical term, additional to and vitally necessary for truth and beauty, insists that beauty has its splendid funeral pyre so as to reveal properly and do justice to what lies within. Justice is conflagration, a beautiful conflagration.

But this is more than death and transformation by means of death, as if that were not mysterious enough. It is as if beauty has all along been waiting for this incendiary moment, which shall further magnify its beautiful self to the uttermost, so as then to die; and in dying its very beauty reaches not only perfection but an ability, heretofore absent, to reveal its inner self, when, as Benjamin puts it, "the external form achieves its most brilliant degree of illumination." Death, we might say, is enlightenment, where another form of beauty, that of ideas, is regnant.

I want to point attention here to the destructive element required for justice to occur, justice as in a revelation that does justice to the secret, a destructive element akin to sacrifice, even self-sacrifice by means of an inspired defacement, like unmasking only more violent, more negating—more fiery—it being the fires of destruction that bring enlightenment and without which truth would languish.

II

Beauty thus exists so as to be destroyed as by fire, and it is the power of the light issuing forth from destruction that shall do justice to truth. Perhaps this is a just fate for beauty to exist so as profitably to die, beauty being so close to art and art being held in such suspicion by Plato because of what he understood to be art's disorienting confusing copying of copying, piling appearance onto appearance, and so forth. He allows beauty its moment, so to speak, but only a moment, so long as it can be fired up and through the flames of sacrifice allow its content to enter the sacred realm of pure ideas.

Yet the whole operation sounds so artistic, so sacred, so priestly even, so artfully contrived. Is this an unjust smuggling of art in the back door, so to speak, a defacing and destructive beautiful art that would banish art thus and forever? And if this is possible or even the case, how can we speak of justice as in a revelation that does justice to the secret, as opposed to an exposure that destroys it, when that justice is achieved through use of unjust means such as art?

This is what Nietzsche had in mind, I think, as the target of his broadest critiques of philosophy and Christianity, this unjust use of art to destroy art. It is very much at the core of his critique of the will to truth and will to power, passions that strive to appropriate and harness mimicry and Dionysian powers of representation, to put them in service of the struggle for power—something we can see around us in the workplace, for instance, on a daily basis. Plato's puppet, Socrates, frequently the object of Nietzsche's scorn, is thus derided for his naive illusion, for his "unshakable faith that thought, using the thread of logic, can penetrate the deepest abyss of being, and that thought is capable not only of knowing being but even of *correcting* it. This sublime metaphysical illusion accompanies science as an instinct," Nietzsche adds, "and leads science again and again to its limits at which it must turn into art—which is really the aim of this mechanism."[3] (And note that for Nietzsche, Socrates "was also a great erotic"!)[4]

To my mind, to equate truth with the secret within is already to predestine the conversation toward the inescapable function of theater and art in Plato's terms as a negative force, an excessive force, we could add, excessive in that it escapes the logic of his dialogical method, which strives to pin down the one and just meaning of the truth within. Having set up a theater of truth composed of a front and a hidden behind, like certain puppet shows, it is disingeneous—but understandable—to then deny art any function and even to revile it. Art then would be the hidden factor, the secret within the secret that allows justice to be done.

This was certainly Nietzsche's and later Freud's view of what Nietzsche stated repeatedly, that all human life is sunk deep in untruth, that truth is based on error and deception. This was art and art was the lie necessary for all of this to function over the millennia of human history. A terrible legacy mocks us academic intellectuals hell-bent on discovering truth's secrets hidden behind facades of our own making such that every time we expose, we conceal, and without concealing we could not expose. Where's the ethic or even intelligence in that? Where the grounds for optimism? There is none of course, hence the effort to get "beyond good and evil."

If Plato's notion of truth is thereby turned on its head as untruth's victory, what happens to Benjamin's advice, that truth lies not in exposure but in a revelation that does justice to it? What sort of revelation are we talking about? Would truth then require a dissimulation of dissimulation, a gay science epistemology for a Nervous System ontology? And what does it mean to say, as Nietzsche does, "We destroy only as creators"? Is this the same as the revelatory incandescence of the secret's husk, or does it point to the need for philosophy to change tracks, as it were, and become an art so as to outsmart the art that is the deception, the brooding patience, and the mimicry, that is the struggle for power and will to knowledge that is social existence? In that case, criticism would need to redefine itself in a more realistic manner, coming to grips with the melodrama, even childishness, of the tension of the secret within and thus its astonishing capacity to coalesce illusion with *jouissance.*

III

If Plato sets the scene of truth with men in love, it is Nietzsche who repeatedly asks, What if truth is a woman? The difference between the figuration of truth as man or as woman here is the measure of the enormous difference in attitude toward sensuous appearance and truth as secrecy disguised by such appearance. Plato sees truth guided by eros very much in terms of penetration of depth, whereas for Nietzsche this is a sad and even silly commentary on man taken in by his self-created illusions. Not that Nietzsche is against illusions per se—far from it. Is not his whole being invested in the notion that truth is sunk in untruth? Thus Plato's man must seem childish to Nietzsche, childish philosophically, that is—not because of his carnal love, not because of eros, but because of the seriousness of his love of truth to the detriment of fantasy. In which case he is not childish enough.

This brings to mind not merely two poles and the ambivalence of the child as either stupid or wise, devil or innocent, but also the metamorphoses of spirit Nietzsche tries on for his newly secured philosophical confidence in 1883, first becoming the uncomplaining, reverential, weight-bearing camel, then the lion, king of the hunt, and finally the child. Because the central task is to create new values for Western civilization, he discards the long-suffering Platonic-Christian composite that is the camel, ship of the desert, and takes spirit-possession of the lion, it being necessary to *seize the right* to new values. How does the lion achieve this? Well, "once it loved this 'Thou Shalt' as its holiest thing; now it has to find illusion and caprice even in the holiest, that it may steal freedom from its love."[5] That is why the lion is needed for this theft. It itself is a transformed spirit, even, we might say, the spirit of transformation, and it is this and thus by living in a becoming that is a discarding of the burden of religious duty and of obedience to sacred prohibitions. But note that this discarding is a twisting from within, indeed a sacredly inspired rearrangement of elements that "finds illusion and caprice even in the holiest." And it is this that provides "freedom from its love," as if deliberately rejecting Plato's equations of love with beauty, beauty with truth, and truth with the mystical secret.

But then why invoke the child? What can the child do that the lion cannot and leaves unfinished, according to Nietzsche? Because the "child is innocence and forgetfullness, a new beginning, a sport, a self-propelling wheel, a first motion, a sacred Yes." In other words, whereas the lion steals the right to create by sacredly negating the sacred negation, finding illusion and caprice in holiness, it is the child who then goes on actually to create something as "a self-propelling wheel."[6] This must be what Nietzsche has in mind when he says in *The Gay Science* that we destroy only as creators.

Thus we move from man as truth to woman as truth and thence to child, from camel to lion to child, paralleling a movement of truth from secret depths to appearance and thence to a third and most amazing state, dazzling and daring, that I take to be *neither* appearance *nor* depth, now figured in the child, a state Nietzsche elsewhere envisaged as "midday, time of the shortest shadow, end of the longest error." Why time of the shortest shadow? Because with the dissolution of depth in the Platonic theater of truth, so appearance disappears as well.[7] What is left?

Where shall we turn? "Is there still any up or down? Are we not straying as through an infinite nothing?" We hear the madman with the lantern ranting in the bright morning hours. At least there is the golden sunlight, giving without receiving as it goes under the ecstatic turbulence of the sea. "Truly, even now nothing remains of the world but green twilight and green lightning."[8]

This state, this stateless state, we might say, is what is to be figured in the child following camel and lion, and I venture myself now to figure this figure in a highly specific mise-en-scène: namely, *the adult's imagination of the child's imagination.* Here truth as a just revelation of secrecy takes unexpected turns, and the death and destruction involved in unmasking the outer appearance is subject to a new formulation.

IV

Is it concept, or thing, or sheer movement of becoming, this stateless state of the adult's imagination of the child's? Or all of the above? I take it to be a vast cultural resource appropriated by modernity, and by the state in particular. Kafka serves as a signpost here, yet it is Benjamin's gloss on Plato's metaphysics as involving an almost self-willed death of beauty as appearance, with its subsequent revelation of truth as secrecy, that I wish to keep firmly in mind—but now in an ironic, almost mocking mode, as something a little too melodramatic to swallow whole, as something absurd yet at the same time the stuff of nightmares and muteness. For we cannot swallow it whole, and the tongue at times that may be crucial in the history of nations no less than of individuals lies choked. This mix of the mute-absurd is where the child enters into the historically contrived space of death, basic to the pressure of the pretensions of sovereignty, whose sacred icons are endowed with more than life. The dead are thus not metaphoric but literal, thanks to the invocation by adult of the child.

Such a child exists in some time outside of time, half in and half outside adult reckoning, as when adults talk about serious things, including children, in the child's hearing, as though the child cannot hear, or when they switch back and forth between addressing the child sitting there in front of them one minute as object and next minute as subject. The comic aspect of this, as when adults confidentially lower their voices to stage whispers, testifies to what we might call "absurd epistemology," the child put into the position of being and not being there, part eavesdropper, part idiot, part fairy, and the considerable powers for fantasy, disavowal, and contradiction in this epistemology are further magnified, it seems to me, by the adult imagining of this imagining, using this child, so to speak, as a way of making metaphor literal and almost viscerally effective.

I first started thinking of this in Venezuela, where the relation between stately presence and the spirits of the dead has achieved hyperbolic intensity. But this relation is by no means restricted to the apparent exotica of postcolonial societies. I see the same play and the same almighty power of the adult's imagination of the child's in the mythic realism of phenomena like George W. Bush, or Alan Greenspan, not to mention the dollar-wise mysteries of "confidence" Greenspan's leadership of the Federal Reserve Bank so far inspires. I see it in the famous "gray area" of the police as spectral beings in modern democracies that Benjamin points to in his "Critique of Violence," violence as in *Gewalt,* also meaning authority.[9] The gray area where the specter emerges is where law, in being administered by the police, ceases in fact to exist, yet it is this swamp that sustains stately forms. Before me I see a young man in upstate New York in handcuffs pressed up against his car. It is a cold night. The troopers have set up a roadblock for what they call a sobriety check. My friend is told to get out of our car because when he answered the policeman his mouth was too closed. He gets out, lifts his hands, and the policemen freezes. "I didn't tell you you could raise your arms," he shouts. "Everything you do, step by step, you have to ask my permission." The stupidity is palpable. And monstrously evil. There can be no response. One is struck dumb. Over his shoulder I see the young man in handcuffs completely humiliated and helpless as the troopers don't even pretend, now, to be searching his car. Long black flashlights, ominously long like billy clubs, wave still more cars down as they exit off the ineptly titled freeway. I look in the mute-absurd neither for reason nor for justice. Yet neither will it suffice to categorize this as irrational. Where I do find resonance is in the continuous becoming of the adult's imagination of the child's.

For a long time, months, maybe a year or so, in Venezuela, I'd been aware of pictures on walls in cities and small towns, on the walls of schools, in central plazas, by the sides of busy streets and occasionally highways. Childish pictures of the Wars of Independence from 1811 to 1822, cosmic origin of the modern, independent, nation-state. Bright red-coated soldiers and horses and machetes scattered across verdant plains, plus crude portraits in ornate frames, plus slabs of pulsing national colors like jet streams skipping over bus stops and around corners, the nation itself let loose and flowing along the contours of the manmade environment. Without thinking, I assumed these childish murals engirdling the nation-state were in fact painted by children. Only later did it occur to me that this was a dissimulation, that the paintings were painted by adults to look as if they were painted by children—that this was a style, a technique, such as "naive painting." But such labels detract from the point that the confusion or the possibility of confusion was there in the heart of the work as to whether they were genuinely childish or adult executions thereof.[10]

What struck me as most salient here is not only that the modern child's imagination serves as some sort of imagined reservoir for the adult fantasy writ into the daily functioning of society, but that what is most at stake is the working of the rules by which social intercourse courses, rules that are spectacularly interesting for their being more honored in the breach than in the observance. If there are social laws, this is their being, binding formality with informality, the said with the unsaid, the rule with its actual practice, and what Émile Durkheim drew attention to as the noncontractual elements of contract, what some of us call "culture."

Asked by the College of Sociology to define the sacred in everyday life in 1938, Michel Leiris responded by invoking childhood—his own—claiming that the sacred existed in the humblest things, outside of the official forms of religion, the state, or morality. What he demonstrated by his method invoking the child was that such a perspective on the sacred in modernity was the outcome of the adult's imagination of the child's.[11] And let us not forget the severity of the intellectual and political issues facing the College of Sociology under whose auspices this address was delivered, attempting to rework a Marxist version of Hegel's dialectic locked in incessant labor of the negative so as to get a better grip, among other things, on the modern state in general, and on fascism in particular. Let us also note that Leiris's literary activities at that time were much bound to his ethnographic interests, notably concerning secret societies.

V

The modern state is the great container of secrecy, and this accounts for the mysterious hence mystical excess that is its authority and legitimacy—in a word, its *power*—which is when we recall Elias Canetti, with his adage in *Crowds and Power* that secrecy lies at the very core of power.[12] They are coterminous terms. Not *crowds* and *power*, but *secrecy* and *power*. Yet what is more important, real and pure secrecy, which must be very scarce, a horizon, really, at the outer limit of the possible, or what I call "public secrecy," which is I think extremely widespread and consists in knowing what not to know, a sort of active unknowing? Such knowing unknowing is truly an art form, and there is no doubt about its being at the crossroads where aesthetics and ethics meet. Such knowledge is also what makes the world go round, far more mischievous and complicated and real than "ideology" or "discourse," terms that have leadenly occupied the discussion of ideas and mental life in politics and history over the past few decades.

The management of public secrecy is a delicate affair, testimony to the cunning of socialized humanity, and something that can devour its would-be managers. Its delicacy no less than its power lies in the adroitness with which one can use revelation so as to conceal further, a trick writ firmly into the formula, "knowing what not to know." So much for the calculated naïveté of Enlightenment, which is an attempt to use unmasking so as to appropriate the power of mystery without the mystery itself.

All secret societies, with their flamboyant masking and unmasking, are built on the principle whereby unmasking churns and thickens mystery instead of dissipating it. As described in ethnography from Tierra del Fuego, Central Amazonia, Melanesia, Australia, New Guinea, and Central and West Africa, secret societies invariably divide truth into two parts, men and men about to be initiated on one side and women and chidren on the other. This division into knowers and those who know what not to know is crucial. It provides the life energy of the society, the key to its fabulous fantasies and ability to fantasize fabulously. Make no mistake: the secret is a public secret, and the women, if not the children, are pretty savvy about knowing what not to know. The kids? That's another story.[13]

VI

The emperor: Well, he has no clothes. Right? And who says so? The only one to say so? Why, the child, the "little child," to be precise. There are several points here to consider carefully.

The child reveals the concealed truth. The concealed truth is that the emperor is concealed by nothing.

These clothes are said by one and all throughout the kingdom to have a "magical quality."[14]

This magic consists of the assertion by the swindlers who pretend to weave the cloth that a stupid person or one unfit for his official position in state service cannot see the cloth. The secret, however, is that these weavers weave nothing. But nobody will say that. Everyone can see it, but nobody will say it. In fact, when the emperor begins his procession under his crimson canopy through the streets so as to show off his new clothes, all the people of the town declare how beautiful his clothes are.

> "But he doesn't have anything on," cried a little child.
>
> "Listen to the innocent one," said the proud father. And the people whispered among each other and repeated what the child had said.
>
> "He has nothing on," shouted all the people at last.
>
> The emperor shivered, for he was certain that they were right; but he thought, "I must bear it until the procession is over." And he walked even more proudly.

Note it is the adults—or, more precisely, adult society—who are taken in by the magic of the cloth. Not the child. Also note that following the revelation, the emperor says to himself, "I must bear it," and walks on more proudly than before.

The child's act can be seen in two different ways. One is that the child, in its immaturity, in its ethical immaturity, that is, sees and talks straight. The eye no less than the tongue is innocent. It is a piercing eye yoked to a blurting tongue. It is truth itself. And truth here means unsocialized being. The child is a "little child" and has not yet mastered the art of knowing what not to know. "Listen to the innocent one," said the proud father.

A quite different way of seeing this child's act is to regard the child as anything but innocent. This child is a sophisticated player, taking advantage of adult positioning of the child as innocent and ethically (not to mention sexually) immature so as to untwist, or give a further twist to, the public secret—that which we all know but cannot articulate, namely, that the emperor has no clothes. This child knows only too well what not to know, but for some reason or other—and this is really what is so strange and wonderful—cannot but blurt it out. Refusing the obligation inherent in the gift, this child instead commits it to sacrifice, but not the sort envisaged by Benjamin for Plato's dream of a mystical revelation that would do justice to the secret as revealed truth. Instead this is sacrifice based on profitless loss as formulated by Bataille, where he writes that sacrifice consecrates that which it destroys,[15] or where the anthropologist Evans-Pritchard, in his 1936 study of Nuer religion in central Africa, emphasizes sacrifice of cattle as not so much a gift of flesh as it is the taking of the gift of life.[16] It is this gift of negation, with its ensuing turbulence, that would seem to be the truth this child will implicate.

VII

This child performs the basic split in belief that allows contradiction and conflict to persist, no less than multiple realities and interpretations. And as such, this child bears an intimate relation to a spirit—like the spirits of the dead and like Eros too, the spirit of love, given definition by Plato, in the voice of the woman mystic, Diotima, as one "who conveys the messages to the gods from men and to men from the gods, prayers and sacrifices to the one, commands and rewards to the other. Being of an intermediate nature," she goes on, "a spirit bridges the gap between them and prevents the universe from falling into two separate halves. Through this class of being come all divination and the supernatural skill of priests in sacrifices and rites and spells and every kind of magic and wizardry."[17]

Everything that is spirit, in other words, is half god and half man, and Socrates' very first question indicates here that a spirit is inherently childish, if not a child. "Who are his parents?" he asks Diotima with respect to Eros. And how childlike Eros turns out to be! From his mother he inherits want, or dependence; from his father, cunning and tricks, and he is always on the hunt for knowledge. A strange character—for when he wins he always loses, and he is neither wise nor ignorant.

But then is this not the model of Plato's dialogues, storybooks for children, with the principal actors more often than not acting stupid or precociously smart, being grudgingly led by the nose down the stepwise path of logic? Is not the very structure of the dialogue, as pilgrimmage to truth, thus one immense public secret?

VIII

"My gift to the world," says the epigraph to my 1,096-page volume of Andersen's fairy tales. And thus I cannot but think of the adult's imagination of the child's imagination as being a series of exchanges like gift exchange in which the adult relates to the world via the gift of his imagination of the child's, except that when it comes to the secret of the gift, the child in question cannot resist the temptation to spend it.

Children love gifts. Christmastime for many children, such as the ones for whom Hans Christian Andersen wrote, brings the secret and the gift together with secret preparations by adults of their gifts, and with the adult determination to keep the spirit of Christmas alive in the figure of the mythical gift giver, Santa Claus.

Yet cynics love to point out that the gift is notoriously unstable and contradictory. It appears as altruistic and spontaneous, while at the same time it is calculated and instrumental. Because many analysts see the gift relationship as basic to the social bond anywhere, this contradiction assumes enormous importance in social theory. It is the function of the public secret, as we see with the emperor's state, to harness the power of this contradiction. Indeed, social contradictions are powerless until they find their home in such secrecy and the immense creativity of which it is capable.

Children love gifts. They also love secrets. Above all they love to reveal them—that is, to spend them in almost ceremonious displays of what Bataille famously termed *dépense* or expenditure, and which, for him, entailed not the release of some dammed-up instinctual flood, but the labor of the negative as with negation of the negation, the breaking of the rule. Thus Bataille's "general economy," that new science by which he hoped to show how a human sacrifice, the construction of a church, or the gift of a jewel is no less interesting than the sale of wheat, does not apply to the child who has not assimilated the rule, that innocent child of whom the father standing in the crowd is so proud.[18] Only the child who in some way, no matter how dim, realizes the presence of the taboo in breaking it can be said to love secrets so as to spend them.

IX

This gift brings to mind Benjamin's note in his arcades project, that "every childhood achieves something great, irreplaceable for mankind." What he had in mind was a prehistoric impulse located in the modern commodity, it being the child's eye that draws out the archaic symbolism in the new technology, while for the adult the relevant and contrasting terms are not the archaic but the new, history, and fashion itself, fashion as the death rite of the commodity. "Through its interest in technical phenomena, its curiosity about all sorts of discoveries and machinery," he writes, "every childhood ties technological achievement to the old, symbolic worlds."[19] Yet what is understated here is that the commodity is thus the outcome of a dual viewpoint, brought to a fine yet unstable focus in the adult's imagination of the child's, the instability underwriting the single most important critical weapon in Benjamin's arsenal, what he calls the "dialectical image." Here death and the child, therefore, are no strangers, as with Adorno's notion, cited by Benjamin, comparing the dialectial image to an antediluvian fossil wherein history passes through death into a petrified, primordial landscape.[20] This face of death, the gift of the child, irradiates the new, child and adult's eye.

X

This child, as figured in the adult's imagination of the child's imagination, is not the child destined to be "father of the man." Nor is this child the bearer of culture, learning the language and codes so as to provide continuity. As against these developmental notions of the child, as against this faith in a continuum, the child in the adult's imagination of the child's imagination is more like a soap bubble radiating colors while floating in the air, spinning off who knows where into a referentless world where a magical prehistory of humankind intersects with Enlightenment realism, the child being not only a fairy-tale fabulist, but notorious for telling it like it really is. Quite a feat.

In this modern spin on things, one thing stands out, and that is the importance of prehistory, a special time before time when magic held sway, things could easily transform into other things, and women, children, and sometimes animals, but not men, had the magic. Enter with a vengeance the fairy story and the rise of children's literature, in large part, in Europe, due to the efforts of seventeenth- and eighteenth-century women. William Blake belongs to this world, as does Nietzsche in his effort to create new values. And it is this notion of prehistory in modernity that permeates Benjamin's study of time and figuration in Kafka's writing. "In Kafka," writes Benjamin, "the written law is contained in books, but these are secret; by basing itself on them the prehistoric world exerts its rule all the more ruthlessly."[21]

In modern society this haunting of the present by such a prehistory finds a specially powerful place in our children's culture. This prehistory is, you could say, "mythic," but not in at least one of the meanings given to myth by the academic discipline of anthropology as a social charter. To the contrary, such a mythic reality of prehistory recruits childhood in the same way adults watching a movie sink into the screen as imaginary signifiers take over their bodies.

"Don't worry, my dear, it's only a movie!" Attempting to explain this takeover by the movies, Christian Metz draws attention to the function of the fetish in Freud's formulation as a keener way of approaching Coleridge's famous "suspension of disbelief." Metz argues that the split in belief as expressed in the fetish, of believing and not believing at the same time, of dis/avowing, provides a basis for understanding the power of movies as real and not as artful copying of reality—in Metz's words, how "spectators can sustain their credulousness in all incredulousness."[22]

Here Metz reminds us of a legendary history that he says is frequently invoked by the second and subsequent generations of moviegoers, like ourselves, cinema's "children," you might say. The legendary history such "children" like to relate, he says, concerns cinema's very first spectators. They were supposedly a credulous lot. They were, we could say, "prehistoric" in their ability to take things literally and in their studied inability to peel representations off from reality. Take the spectators of the Lumière brothers' famous film at the Grand Café in Paris in 1895, who were said to have fled their seats in terror when the train hurtled toward them on the screen.

And Metz immediately compares this story—his point being that it does not at all matter whether it is true or false—with the ethnology of secret societies, where informants regularly declare, he says, that "'long ago we used to believe in the masks' (these masks that are used to deceive children, like our Father Christmas, and adolescents learn at initiation that the 'masks' were in fact adults in disguise)." The belief, in other words, is relegated to a long ago, says Metz, but this "long ago" is more like a continuous past that extends into the present such that it is coextensive, he asserts, with "childhood, when one really was duped by masks." As such it nurtures the unbelief of today, nurturing it, however, through denegation by "attributing credulity to the child and to former times."[23]

Could the adult's imagination of the child's be plainer? Here it is the attribution by adults, as to the literal-mindedness of the child, which allows the metaphoric power of the adult imagination to spread its wings—to believe, that is, in a langauge before the Fall when names and things were unified.

All this, then, is owed Andersen's little child, Andersen's "gift to the world," the child who saw the emperor had no clothes and thus saw through the public secret that allowed magic its purchase on reality in the magic of the state. This child still loves secrets, as gifts to be unwrapped, as secrets to be spent, and thus the entire complex apparatus of language and representation in human society is subject to a meritorious division of signifying labor, between adults who know that signs, like conventions, are arbitrary, yet nevertheless cannot make sense without also believing the very opposite—namely, that there is a magical and mimetic link as strong as steel between words and things.

This is why one of the more endearing events of academic life in recent years has been the professor who, instead of doing justice to the secret, exposes it so as to destroy it. Perhaps eros flees at this point. I do not know. But pleasure there must be in such exposure, in the will to power in shocking students with the news that the linguistic sign is arbitrary, the ensuing silence bearing testimony to the fact that nobody can really believe it. Nor should they. Really. But they have their part to act in this drama of revelation. As children verging on academic adulthood, it is for them to decide, as so many children before them, whether they will be initiated into the secrets of knowledge so as to become real men or slide either side of the public secret in the luxury of their immaturity, gracelessly, getting it wrong, so that others, and language itself, can get it right in this eternal return of the world history of signification. This, their "gift to the world."

XI

Yet does not this very striking capacity for mimesis and literalization on the part of what we might call the "prehistorical child," as in the adult's imagination of the child's, itself depend upon and give rise to magic and delightful, dadalike, nonsense? This suggests that in the very process of realizing language, such mimesis undoes it as well, precisely because language itself operates with the illusion of a one-to-oneness with things, and yet this secret as to its illusory ability to portray and faithfully represent cannot be questioned too long or with any degree of seriousness. A public secret if ever there was one—and hence the very place for a shuddering encounter between child and emperor! Thus the adult's imagination of the child's has it both ways. The child who is recruited to sustain the mimetic illusion of language is also the child who can plunder the secret of language for the buried treasure therein—spending it, we might say, as Bataille describes the poet dedicated to the profitless loss of language, spending it as we saw earlier with the child's love of gifts, which now includes its own gift to language as well.

This spending that involves exposure of the dadalike nonsense of the linguistic sign is in fact a principal component of the sacred in everyday life, at least in the opinion of Michel Leiris, who, invoking the adult's imagination of the child's, makes quite a point about linguistic expressions serendipitously discovered by children. In fact, he devotes two pages of his seven-page essay on the sacred to just this point, perhaps because he sees in such childhood discoveries a key to language. What he has in mind is the phenomenon of *mis*hearing and *mis*reading by the child, because from his point of view such mis-takes partake of, and hence create, not just the sacred but the *left* sacred, combining magic with the turbulent powers of transgression, the illegitimate and the unethical. He has no hesitation in placing the freshly minted words that come from mishearing and misreading in the same category as certain objects and places that evoke the left sacred in the adult's imagination of the child's, places like the secret society he and his brother formed in the bathroom.

As examples, he provides his use of *réusement* instead of *heureusement* and his learning how to pronounce the name Moses, which he had until then only read, a correction with all sorts of implications for other words connected by spelling, sound, and biblical association.

Réusement and *heureusement* formed a conjunction paralleled by the way his family distinguished between the sand pit and the sand quarry *(sablonnière, sablière),* as well as between two types of paper airplanes they baptized as "rectilinear" and "curvilinear." These "sacred" games with language exemplify the critical power of difference, but so as to exemplify *différance.* That is the point. They establish the systematicity of the system and the power of presence thus generated, only to spend it.

Apart from these sorts of mis-takes, Leiris includes the act of naming as also crucial to this left-sacred experience, as one would gather from theoretical approaches to language as bound to a prehistory of God's naming things before the Fall. Here then, the child replaces God, as Leiris recounts his naming, as with the name "The Empty Hall," by which name he and his brothers referred to a group of rocks in the area where his family went for summer vacations. Then there is the breaking up of names, as happened after the Fall and the expulsion from paradise and the ensuing confusion of Babel with the arbitrariness of the signifier. This is what it seems to me Leiris is evoking when he mentions from his childhood biblical studies the name Rebecca, for instance, conjuring images and associations of certain clothes and soft gestures, raisins, and a prolonged breaking up of the name into syllables and letters, especially, in good rebuslike and surrealist fashion, the *R,* all of which was testimony, in the adult's imagination of the child's, to the word's exoticness, "to the strangeness it harbored," a strangeness that included, he thought, the fact that such words "speak to you by themselves."

Such strangeness, which perhaps too abstractly can be labeled as "left sacred" and the effect of transgression, involved for him a sense of vertigo (reminding us of the Fall), by means of which such words often acted in his childhood as keys, "either because surprising perspectives were opened through their very resonance or because, discovering one had always mutilated them, suddenly grasping them in their integrity somehow seemed like a revelation, like a veil suddenly torn open or some outburst of truth."[24]

This is the unmasking and defacement we began with in Benjamin's gloss on Plato's image of truth as a secret idea form to be revealed by the destruction of the physical husk containing it. And it would be hard to say which account is the more mystical. Leiris makes no bones of the fact that this play with words as names and as things is—for the child he was—a shift from a profane to a sacred state, which we might gloss as the child's reinsertion of God's language into the semiotic play of difference that characterizes language as we know it today. This eternal return of God's language in the activity of the child, however, is what creates the transition from the profane to the sacred, whereas with Plato, it requires an already established mystical force to drive the flames that consume the husk. While in Plato's system that mystical force lies outside the system dependent upon it, in the adult's imagination of the child's, the left sacred exists as the power of the secret exchanged as a gift between adult and child. Eros is here not derived from Freud's allegory of Oedipus. Instead, the oedipal itself is derived from an eros defined first and foremost as the passionate love of secrecy and the riddle containing it, a love bound to its spending as in the figure of the adult's imagination of the child's.

Notes

1. Walter Benjamin, *The Origins of German Tragic Drama,* trans. John Osborne (London: New Left, 1977), 31.
2. Ibid.
3. Friedrich Nietzsche, *The Birth of Tragedy,* in *Basic Writings of Nietzsche,* ed. and trans. Walter Kaufmann (New York: Vintage, 1968), 95–96.
4. Friedrich Nietzsche, *Twilight of the Idols,* trans. R. J. Hollingdale (London: Penguin, 1990), 42.
5. Friedrich Nietzsche, *Thus Spoke Zarathustra,* trans. R. J. Hollingdale (London: Penguin, 1969), 55.
6. Ibid.
7. Nietzsche, *Twilight of the Idols,* 51.
8. Friedrich Nietzsche, "The Madman," in *The Gay Science,* trans. Walter Kaufmann (New York: Vintage, 1974), 181, 247.
9. Walter Benjamin, "Critique of Violence," in *Reflections,* trans. Edmund Jephcott (New York: Harcourt Brace Jovanovich, 1978).
10. For background, see Michael Taussig, *The Magic of the State* (New York: Routledge, 1997).
11. Michel Leiris, "The Sacred in Everyday Life," in *The College of Sociology (1937–39),* ed. Denis Hollier (Minneapolis: University of Minnesota Press, 1988), 24.
12. Elias Canetti, *Crowds and Power,* trans. Carol Stewart (New York: Farrar, Straus & Giroux, 1984), 290.
13. Michael Taussig, *Defacement* (Stanford, Calif.: Stanford University Press, 1999), 99–220.
14. Hans Christian Andersen, "The Emperor's New Clothes," in *The Complete Fairy Tales and Stories* (Garden City, N.J.: Doubleday, 1974), 78.
15. See Georges Bataille on sacrifice, "Hegel, Death, and Sacrifice," trans. Jonathan Strauss, *Yale French Studies* 78 (1990): 9–28; and Georges Bataille, *The Accursed*

Share: An Essay on General Economy, 3 vols., trans. Robert Hurley (New York: Zone, 1988). See also E. E. Evans-Pritchard, *Nuer Religion* (Oxford: Oxford University Press, 1956), 272–86.

16. Evans-Pritchard, *Nuer Religion,* 276.

17. Plato, *The Symposium,* trans. Walter Hamilton (London: Penguin, 1951), 81.

18. See Bataille, *The Accursed Share.*

19. Walter Benjamin, "N [Theoretics of Knowledge, Theory of Progress]," *Philosophical Forum,* 15, nos. 1–2 (1983–84): 6.

20. Ibid., 6.

21. Walter Benjamin, "Franz Kafka: On the Tenth Anniversary of His Death," in *Illuminations,* ed. Hannah Arendt, trans. Harry Zohn (New York: Schocken, 1968), 115.

22. Christian Metz, *The Imaginary Signifier: Psychoanalysis and the Cinema* (Bloomington: Indiana University Press, 1985), 73.

23. Ibid.

24. Leiris, "The Sacred in Everyday Life," 29.

Contributors

Leo Bersani was until recently the Class of 1950 Professor of French at the University of California, Berkeley. His many books on psychoanalysis, literature, and the visual arts include *Baudelaire and Freud, The Freudian Body: Psychoanalysis and Art, The Culture of Redemption,* and *Homos.* He is coauthor (with Ulysse Dutoit) of *The Forms of Violence* and *Arts of Impoverishment: Beckett, Rothko, Resnais.*

Susan Bordo is professor of English and women's studies and holds the Otis A. Singletary Chair in the Humanities at the University of Kentucky. Her books include *Unbearable Weight: Feminism, Western Culture, and the Body,* which was a *New York Times* Notable Book of 1993 and nominated for a Pulitzer Prize; *Twilight Zones: The Hidden Life of Cultural Images from Plato to O.J.;* and *The Male Body: A New Look at Men in Public and Private.* She lectures widely on contemporary culture and the body.

Bill Brown is George H. Pullman Professor of English at the University of Chicago, where he is also a member of the Committee on the History of Culture and a coeditor of *Critical Inquiry.* He is the author of *The Material Unconscious: American Amusement, Stephen Crane, and the Economies of Play* and *A Sense of Things: The Object Matter of American Literature.* He is the editor of *Reading the West: An Anthology of Dime Novels* and of "Things," a special issue of *Critical Inquiry.*

Beatriz Colomina is professor of architecture at Princeton University and founding director of the Program for Media and Modernity. She is the author of *Privacy and Publicity: Modern Architecture as Mass Media* and the editor of *Sexuality and Space* and *Architectureproduction.* She is currently working on a book on the relationships between war and modern architecture.

Ulysse Dutoit teaches French at the University of California, Berkeley. His work is concerned primarily with the visual arts, especially film and painting. He is coauthor (with Leo Bersani) of *The Forms of Violence* and *Arts of Impoverishment: Beckett, Rothko, Resnais.*

Lee Edelman is professor of English at Tufts University. He is the author of *Transmemberment of Song: Hart Crane's Anatomies of Rhetoric and Desire* and *Homographesis: Essays in Gay Literary and Cultural Theory.* He is currently working on two manuscripts, "No Future: Queer Theory and the Death Drive" and "Hollywood's Anal Compulsion: Cinema, Psychoanalysis, Sexuality."

Maureen Harkin teaches English and humanities at Reed College. She has published articles on Adam Smith, Henry Mackenzie, and Matthew Lewis, and is completing a study of the work of Smith and its links to theories of fiction, history, and aesthetics.

Howard Horwitz teaches in the English department at the University of Utah. He is the author of *By the Law of Nature* and is completing "Administrative Aesthetics," a manuscript on the interrelations between literature and the social sciences in the United States at the beginning of the twentieth century.

Audrey Jaffe is research associate at the Center for Cultural Studies, University of California, Santa Cruz. She is the author of *Vanishing Points: Dickens, Narrative, and the Subject of Omniscience* and *Scenes of Sympathy: Identity and Representation in Victorian Fiction.* She is currently working on a book about the image of the graph in Victorian and contemporary culture.

Martin Jay is Sidney Hellman Ehrman Professor of History at the University of California, Berkeley. Among his books are *The Dialectical Imagination, Adorno, Marxism and Totality, Permanent Exiles, Fin-de-Siècle*

Socialism, Force Fields, Downcast Eyes, and *Cultural Semantics.* He is now working on a book about the discourse of experience in modern European and American thought.

Kay Bea Jones is associate professor at The Ohio State University's Knowlton School of Architecture. She has published in *The Discipline of Architecture* (Minnesota, 2001), *Journal for Architectural Education, Anfione Zeto, Metamorphosi,* and *Competitions.* She received a Collaborative Practice Award from the Association of Collegiate Schools of Architecture for her role in producing cohousing for single-parent university students, which she is designing for occupancy in 2003.

Robert Kaufman is assistant professor of English at Stanford University. He is currently completing two related studies, "Negative Romanticism, Almost Modernity: Keats, Shelley, and Adornian Critical Aesthetics" and "Experiments in Construction: Frankfurt School Aesthetics and Contemporary Poetry." His essays have been published or are forthcoming in *Critical Inquiry, October, American Poetry Review, Modern Language Quarterly, The Cambridge Companion to Adorno, English Literary History,* and *Studies in Romanticism.*

Alphonso Lingis is professor emeritus of philosophy at Pennsylvania State University. He is the author of *Excesses: Eros and Culture; Libido: The French Existential Theories; Phenomenological Explanations; Deathbound Subjectivity; The Community of Those Who Have Nothing in Common; Abuses; Foreign Bodies; Sensation: Intelligibility in Sensibility; The Imperative;* and *Dangerous Emotions.*

Joseph Litvak is professor of English at Tufts University, where he teaches Victorian literature and culture. He is the author of *Caught in the Act: Theatricality in the Nineteenth-Century English Novel* and *Strange Gourmets: Sophistication, Theory, and the Novel.* He is currently writing a book on Jews in mass culture.

Douglas Mao is associate professor of English at Cornell University. He is the author of *Solid Objects: Modernism and the Test of Production* and is working on a study of modernism, aesthetic environments, and human development.

Pamela R. Matthews is associate professor of English at Texas A&M University, College Station. She is the author of *Ellen Glasgow and a Woman's Traditions* and the editor of the forthcoming *Perfect Companionship: Ellen Glasgow's Selected Correspondence with Women.* She is working on a book about Joan of Arc in America.

David McWhirter is associate professor of English at Texas A&M University, College Station. He is the author of *Desire and Love in Henry James* and the editor of *Henry James's New York Edition: The Construction of Authorship.* He is completing a study of James's late-1890s fiction.

Barbara Maria Stafford is William B. Ogden Distinguished Service Professor of Art History at the University of Chicago, where her teaching focuses primarily on eighteenth- and nineteenth-century art and theory. She is the author of *Visual Analogy: Consciousness as the Art of Connecting; Body Criticism: Imaging the Unseen in Enlightenment Art and Medicine; Artful Science: Enlightenment, Entertainment, and the Eclipse of Visual Education;* and *Good Looking: Essays on the Virtue of Images.*

Kathleen Stewart teaches anthropology and cultural studies at the University of Texas at Austin. She is the author of *A Space on the Side of the Road: Cultural Poetics in an "Other" America,* as well as a variety of articles on aspects of the U.S. political imaginary, including the American Dream, the materiality of desire, conspiracy theory, banality, apocalypticism, the sensory impact of the new economy, and the aesthetics and politics of everyday life. She is completing a manuscript, "The Private Life of Public Culture," based on fieldwork in Las Vegas; Orange County, California; and Austin, Texas.

Kathryn Bond Stockton is associate professor of English at the University of Utah. She is the author of *God between Their Lips: Desire between Women in Irigaray, Brontë, and Eliot,* and her articles have been published in *boundary 2, Novel,* and *Cultural Critique.* She is writing a book on debasement, engaging switchpoints between black and other queer connections to anal economics, miscegenation, stone butch wounds, and the brain's prophylactic relations with the dead.

Judith Stoddart is associate professor of English at Michigan State University, where she teaches Victorian literature and cultural theory. Her publications include *Ruskin's Culture Wars: Fors Clavigera and the Crisis of Late Victorian Liberalism* and essays on nineteenth-century nationalism and historicism and Victorian aesthetic theory. Her current projects include a book on theories of perception and Victorian sentimentality, and a study of early-Victorian theories of the public sphere.

Michael Taussig is professor of anthropology at Columbia University. His fieldwork and writing—on topics ranging from commodity fetishism and colonialism to terror, magic, and secrecy—have resulted in several books, including *The Nervous System, Mimesis and Alterity: A Particular History of the Senses, The Magic of the State,* and *Defacement.*

Index

Aalto, Alvar, 51, 66n.8
Abrams, M. H., 16
absolute music, 11
abstraction: Janus face of, 253
adoration: as violent, 35
Adorno, Theodor W., xiv, xxiii–xxiv, 160–61, 162, 165, 367, 398, 424n.2; articulation of construction, 373, 374–75, 377–88; constructivism as alternative to productionism, 380–82, 384–85; on expression and mimesis, 378–80; geometry as signifying merely calculative rather than constructivist phenomena to, 392n.16; imagining a modernism that might come after modernism, 387; Kantian base of critical procedures of, 374; Kracauer study sessions on Kant, 391n.12; on modern art, 381, 394n.28; on natural beauty, 194–95, 224n.7; reidentification of ethical possibility, 410–11; resurgence of interest in, xvii; reworkings of Kant, 369–70. *See also Aesthetic Theory* (Adorno)
adult's imagination of child's imagination. *See* child's imagination, adult's imagination of
advertising: assault on beauty myth to sell beauty-enhancing products, 217–18; campaigns stressing attractiveness, 191; Calvin Klein, 147–48; Murad ad, authentic self and cultural projection indistinguishable in, 306–8; Toothpaste International ad as archetype of modern vulgarity, 162
aesthetic(s): as anti-aestheticist, 368, 377; art and, 4–27, 194–95; as artistics, expanding traditional understanding of, xvi; current theoretical instability of, xiv; economics and, xiv; ethics and, xxi–xxii; in everyday life, 432–46; history of, xvii–xviii, 5–8, 16–18, 24n.13, 194–203, 206–8, 372–73 (*see also* eighteenth-century aesthetics, theorizing popular practice in; Victorian sentimental narrative painting); identity and, 297; identity between aestheticization and, 367, 368; immanent, xxvi; inarticulateness of, xv; as Kant's third form of pleasure, 9; Marxist, 372–73; origination as "an idiom of the body," xvii; politics and, xv, xvi, xvii, 18–19, 366–70, 372, 373; productive tensions in, xiii–xiv; quasi-conceptuality of Kantian, 374–75, 379–80, 394n.26; return from exile, xiii–xiv; as sign of onset of modernity, xviii; situational, 77; of vulgarity, xxi, 167–68. *See also* debasement, queer aesthetics of; Jewishness, aesthetics of

aesthetic autonomy, 403
aesthetic discourse: emergence of, xvii
aesthetic evaluation: detachment of pure gaze of, 192
aesthetic experience: artwork as integral dimension of, 20–21; cognitive powers mobilized by, 9; empirical nature of, 83–89; Kames on link between social order and, 180–85; medieval anticipations of, 24n.13; natural supernaturalism vs. Kantian notion of, 17–19; perpetuation of, by poetry, 322–23, 326; purposeless, phenomenon of, 382, 385, 388; separation from work of art, 3–27
aesthetic experiment: intellectual and emotional apparatus for accessing "the new" constructed by, 375
aestheticization: identity between the aesthetic and, 367, 368; of politics, 18–19
aesthetic judgments, 9–10; shared enjoyment evoked by, 10
aesthetic knowledge: organicist ideal of, 83
aesthetic message: Kames's concept of, 184
aesthetic response: class difference in, 181; psychobiology of, 251–67
Aesthetic Theory (Adorno), xix, 162, 194–95, 369, 374, 378–87; on Hegel's complete conceptualism, 380, 394n.27; Hullot-Kentor's translation of, 370–71; mutual constitution and deconstruction of modern aesthetic stasis and dynamism in, 386–87; quasi-conceptuality and aporetic reflective judgment in, 394n.26
aesthetic value, xv; nineteenth-century notions of universal, 78–79
affect, 431–32, 434; captured in affecting presence at rest, 437; jump of, 434, 436–37, 438; link between shock and cushioned recluse for, 436–37; middle class as womblike space of, 437–39; toward scene of abjection, surge of, 440
Agamben, Giorgio, xxiv–xxv
"agreeable," the, 8
Agrippa of Nettesheim, 264
Ahmad, Aijaz, 390n.5
Ahrentzen, Sherry, 69n.40
AIDS, 39, 40–42
aiesthesis, Greek, 6
Ain, Gregory, 354
aisthesis, xvi
algorithms: limitations of as model for cognition, 262, 263
Alison, Archibald, 17, 76–77
allegory: Benjaminian, 389n.5; Jameson's mobilization of, 389–90n.5
"allographic" works, 4
Allston, Washington, 93
Althusser, Louis, 189n.32, 189n.34, 303, 304–5, 343n.51
ambiguity, 343n.59
ambiguity of language: Basic English's imprecision exemplifying, 329–30; Richards on, 315–20
ambivalence: Bhabha's definition of, 331–35
American Beauty (film), 128, 146, 148, 152n.35
American Dream, 438
American identity: "melting pot" model of, 335–36
America's Most Wanted, 435
Amor Victorious (Caravaggio), 102
analogy, 318; as cross-cortical model for mental combination, 251–52, 259, 262–65; indescribable intimacies turned into publicly shareable, 255; joining impulses of, 262, 263; as nonalgorithmic technique for binding known to unknown, 263
Andersen, Hans Christian, 460, 463
Anderson, Benedict, 300, 327
Anderson, Laurie, 440–41
Angel Standing in the Sun, The (Turner), 76, 89–95, 97n.32; cabinet size of, 93; resistance to explanation, 94
Anker, Suzanne, 252
anorexia among young women, 133, 151n.20
Anthropology from a Pragmatic Point of View (Kant), 196, 197

anti-essentialist constructivism, 372
anti-Semitism, 161
antisublime aesthetics: of Gerard, 176–79; of Kames, 180–85
anxiety about preference for beauty, 190–91, 202, 215
aporetic reflective judgment, 380, 382, 394n.26
Appadurai, Arjun, 399
appetencies: competition among, 320, 321; poetry and cultivation of capacity to coordinate, 322–23
Aragon, Louis, 400, 419
Architectural Design, 355; "Eames, a Celebration" special issue, 356
architecture, xix; American postwar embrace of modern, 352, 353; avant-garde, 56–58; centrality of feminist critical theory to contemporary, 64–65, 69n.38, 69n.40; civic-social, 64; Eames House, xxiii, 347–65; as exhibition, 361; Hadid and, xix, 44–69; modernisms in, 50–54; beyond modern models, 54–58; neomodern, 49–50; photocollage method used in, 357–58; postwar way of living, Case Study House Program and, 352–54
Architecture d'aujourd'hui, L' (film), 360
Argonauts of the Western Pacific (Malinowski), 421, 430n.60
aristocracy: beauty and, 209; neo-aristocracy of celebrities, 210–12; Yeats's defense of privileges of, 209–10
Armstrong, Isobel, xxviin.5
arresting images, 431–48; affect and, 431–32, 434; childhood as collection of, 432–34; circulation and impact, 434–36; event made sensate, 433–34; mimesis in state of shock, 436–37
art(s): aesthetics and, xix, xxiv–xxvi, 4–27, 194–95; analogizing visually concordance between matter and thought through, 265; artwork as integral dimension of aesthetic experience, 20–21; constructionist-expressionist history of, 383; destruction of aesthetics to liberate, xxv; ethics and, 12; formed material objects as artwork, 22; Kant's celebrated definition of, 10; modern, Adorno on, 381, 394n.28; plasticity of response (good taste) cultivated by, 322; Plato's suspicion of, 450–51; separation of aesthetic experience from work of, 3–27
"Art and Objecthood" (Fried), 14–15
Art as Experience (Dewey), 19–21
art centers/galleries: architecture of, 48, 56–65
art dealer: spectator positioned with perspective of, 73–74
artisan and fine artist: distinction between skilled, 5
artist: spectator positioned as, 73
artistics: expanding traditional understanding of aesthetics as, xvi
"Artist's Vision, The" (Fry), 409
Arts & Architecture (magazine), 358, 361; Case Study House Program sponsored by, 352–54; competitions organized by, 353
Arts of Impoverishment (Bersani and Dutoit), 112
Arts on the Level (Krieger), 14
ascription: norm of, 212–13, 214, 219
Asher, Michael, 15
Asplund, 66n.8
assimilation of Jews, 155, 156
attentive listening, 11
Aulenti, Gae, 68n.36
"autographic" works, 4
automutilation, 274, 292n.21
autonomous subject, 331
avant-garde, 26n.35; architecture of historical, 359, 362; Russian, 65n.2
avant-garde architecture, 56–58; feminist conception of, 56–57
Aymonino, Aldo, 58

Bacchino Malato (Caravaggio), 99, 100, 101–3, 114
Bacchus, Uffizi (Caravaggio), 100
bad taste as root evil, 314–15. *See also* Richards, I. A.
Baillie, John, 187n.10

Bakley, Francis, 417
Balcony, The (film), 153–56
Balcony, The (Genet), 153
Ball, Alan, 146, 152n.35
Ballerina Sand Box, 261
Banham, Reyner, 352
Barcelona Pavilion (Mies van der Rohe), 61
baroque cabinet of curiosities, 264
baroque poetics, 263
Barthes, Roland, 166
Basic English, 339n.11, 342n.41; as best mechanism for achieving maximization of response, 327; formalism and, 313–16, 337n.1; goal of, 326; supranational ideal and, 329–30
Basic English and Its Uses (Richards), 328–30
Bataille, Georges, 106, 273–74, 285, 288, 292n.16, 421, 459, 460–61, 464
Battersby, Christine, 202, 226n.27
Baudelaire, Charles Pierre, 386
Baudrillard, Jean, 300, 397, 398, 405, 414
Bauer, Gary, 232, 233
Baumgarten, Alexander, 6, 7
Beach, Christopher, xxviin.7
beauty, 190–229; anxiety about preference for, 190–91, 202, 215; aristocracy and, 209; capacity to provoke us to rethink and change our lives, xxvi; difference between ugliness and, 296, 297; disinterested pleasure in, 9; effortlessness of, 207, 208–10; effort visible in, 220–24; ethnicity and, 227n.45; existence to be destroyed as by fire, 450–51; expressive theory of, 197–98; gendering of, 199–201; genius and, 208–9; Heidegger on, 121n.10; Hume on, 6; justice and, tension between, 190–98, 206, 228n.51; Kant on morality and, 12, 201–2; labor theory of, xxi, 206–24; morality and, 12, 195–98, 201–6; natural, Adorno on, 194–95, 224n.7; opportunities for undertaking effort at, 218–20; privileging of, as grotesque anachronism, 206; rewards of corporeal, 202–3; Scarry on, 191, 215–16, 228n.51; shame as kind of blush in face of, 288; shift from object of, to experience of, in aesthetic discourse, 5–8; subjectivity and, 194–206; supermodels and, 211–13; tendency of aesthetic criticism to universalize, xiv; theodicy of, xxv, xxvi; unfolding of truth hidden in, 450; as wound, 273
beauty culture, America's, 156–57
beauty myth: advertising assault on, to sell beauty-enhancing products, 217–18; feminist critique of, 216–18
Beauty Myth, The (Wolf), 216
Beckett, Samuel, 105, 112, 386, 387
Bell, Clive, 401
Bell, Vanessa, 401
Benjamin, Walter, xvii, xxv, 6, 18, 61, 68n.34, 367, 370, 374, 389n.5, 410, 427n.27, 431, 437, 454, 459, 465; anxiety about unfolding of truth hidden in beauty, 450; arcades project, 461; on architecture, 55; on decorative use of iron, 406; on "dialectical image," 461; dialectics of intoxication, 442; on dreams, 409; on Plato's argument in *Symposium,* 449; on surrealism, 408–9, 421
Bennett, Joan, 340n.22
Bennett, Tony, xvi
Bentham, Jeremy, 341n.26
Benthamite economy of mind, 320, 341n.26
Berman, Russell A., 370
Bernstein, J. N., 370
Bersani, Leo, xx, xxvi, 112, 269
Between the Acts (Woolf), 412
"Between Walls" (Williams), 426n.18
Bhabha, Homi, xxiii, 316, 331–35, 336, 389n.5
"binding problem," 253, 259
Blackface, White Noise: Jewish Immigrants in the Hollywood Melting Pot (Rogin), 156
Blair, Hugh, 340n.20
Blake, William, 462
Bloody Mama (film), 157
Blunden, Anna, 88
Body Criticism (Stafford), 253

Boots of Leather, Slippers of Gold (Kennedy and Davis), 275, 293n.29, 294n.30
Bordo, Susan, xx–xxi
Boswell, James, 180
Boule, André-Charles, 260
Bourdieu, Pierre, xiv, xx, 12, 97n.28, 158, 171, 185, 192, 193, 224n.3
bourgeois aesthetic: sublime as, 175
bourgeois formalism, 372
bourgeois social order: shift from feudalism and absolutism to, 172. *See also* eighteenth-century aesthetics, theorizing popular practice in
Bourne, Randolph, 335–36
box art, 253–55
Boy with a Basket of Fruit (Caravaggio), 100, 101, 104–5
brain as computer/information processor, 255–56, 262, 263, 264
Brando, Marlon, 166
Braque, Georges, 252
Brecht and Method (Jameson), 396n.42
Breuer, Marcel, 62
Brewer, John, 171
Bridge House, 358
Brillat-Savarin, Anthelme, 255
British Art Gallery (Kahn), 63
Brontë, Charlotte, 204–6, 226n.30
Brown, Bill, xxiv
Brown, Wendy, 214
Brownmiller, Susan, 143
Bruce, Lennie, 136
Buck-Morss, Susan, 370
Burbank, Luther, 327
Bürger, Peter, 26n.35
Burke, Edmund, 174–75, 179, 195, 198–202, 203, 207, 226n.27
Burney, Fanny, 204
Bush, George W., 455
Butler, Judith, 189n.32, 302, 303, 311n.14

Cabinet on Stand (Varin and Boulle), 260
Cage, John, 383
Calling of St. Matthew, The (Caravaggio), 107, 110–11
Camilla (Burney), 204
Campbell, Hugh, 340n.20
Campbell, Naomi, 221
Canetti, Elias, 457
capitalism: circulation (exchange value) of late, 439
Caravaggio, xx, 99–122; act of looking in paintings of, 100–101; *Amor Victorious,* 102; *Bacchino Malato,* 99, 100, 101–3, 114; *Bacchus,* Uffizi, 100; *Boy with a Basket of Fruit,* 100, 101, 104–5; *Calling of St. Matthew,* 107, 110–11; *David with the Head of Goliath,* 117–20; decapitation, images of, 99, 100, 117–20; *Decapitation of St. John the Baptist,* 99; emphasis on apparently unfathomable nature of the erotic, 103–6; enigmatic body in paintings of, 106–7; *Entombment,* 103; experiments with relationality, 107, 112–13; *Gypsy Fortune Teller,* 107–10, 111, 113, 114, 120, 120n.3; kinds of concealment painted by, 111–12; light emanating from figures of, 113; mode of connectedness posited by, 103, 114; *St. John the Baptist with a Ram,* 114–17, 120, 121n.11, 122n.11; *Salome Receiving the Head of St. John the Baptist,* 99; self-portraits in paintings by, 99, 101, 102, 117–20; *Victorious Cupid,* 100, 105, 114, 116, 122n.11
Carlyle, Thomas, 16
Carmichael, Stokely, 136
Cascardi, Anthony, 370
Case Study House Program, 352–54
castration: decapitation and, 100, 118–19, 120
castration complex, 291n.9
Castro, Fidel, 221
celebrity culture, 227n.42; neo-aristocracy of, 210–12; relegitimation of social hierarchy in, 193–94; super-models as test of public tolerance for, 211–13
Center for Contemporary Art (Centro per le Arti Contemporane [CAC]) in Rome, 58–62
certainty, discursive, 256
Chagall, Marc, 170n.16

chance: love and, 40
Chenal, Pierre, 360
child, the, xxiv, 449–67; as concept, 233, 237–39, 242–45; continuous becoming of, 455; Eames architecture and, 356–57; as engaged aesthetic subject, 409, 410; engagement with material world, transformation in, 408; left sacred in, 464–65, 466; Nietzsche and, 453–54; revelation of concealed truth by, 458–59; stateless state of adult's imagination of imagination of, 454–56. *See also Lolita* (Nabokov), moral content of
childhood: as collection of arresting images, 432–34
Child Pornography Prevention Act of 1996, 138, 142
child's imagination, adult's imagination of: as gift exchange, 460–61; stateless state of, 454–56
Christmas Carol, A (Dickens), xxi, 234–39, 240; Scrooge as embodiment of *sinthom*-osexuality, 235–39, 240, 242; Tiny Tim, 234, 237, 239, 240; truth about nature of neighborly love in, 237–38
Chronicle of Higher Education, xiii
Churchill, Winston, 313
Churchland, Patricia, 255
Churchland, Paul, 255
Cincinnati Contemporary Art Center (Hadid), 48, 59, 60
cinema. *See* film
cinematic looking: inequality between men and women in, 192–93
circus: Eames on, 347–49
citizenship: citizen as consumer, 435; rights as citizen, 205–6; supranational, 328–31, 334
civic-social architecture, 64
class difference in aesthetic response, 181. *See also* eighteenth-century aesthetics, theorizing popular practice in
class status: Kames on taste as inseparable from, 181–83
Clifford, James, 86
closure: theoretical disappearance of, 27n.53
clothes: cultural stereotypes of, 289n.1; Eames costume, 349; Freud on, 270–71; modesty/protection/decoration trinity of motives for, 290n.5, 291n.9
clothes, martyrdom to, xxii–xxiii, 268–94; cloth of communal adherence, 279–81; cloth of curve, 281–87; cloth of loneliness, 275–78, 289; cloth of woundedness, 270–74; curve of cloth, 287–89; sacrifice and, 273–74, 288–89; social holdings of self-debasements, 269; types of cloth wounds, 270
"Coal and Iron in War" *(Fortnightly Review),* 418, 429n.52
Cocteau, Jean, 38
cognition: brain as computer/information processor, 255–56, 262, 263, 264; brain's "binding" capacity, 253; cognitive compression, modernist vs. postmodernist view of, 253. *See also* neurobiology, combinatorial aesthetics of
Cohen, Ed, 304
collage, 252; box art as intensification of, 253–55
collection: collecting impulse in Woolf's "Solid Objects," 400–401, 403; consumption and, conflation of, 410; objects containing elaborate narratives of their, 412
College of Sociology (France), 456
Colomina, Beatriz, xxiii
color correspondences, 255
combinatorial aesthetics of neurobiology. *See* neurobiology, combinatorial aesthetics of
commodification of anticommodification, 228n.56
commodity: prehistoric impulse located in modern, 461
commonplace: art of the, 16–17; transformed into work of art by educated eye, 88
Common Sense (Paine), 342n.47
communal adherence, cloth of, 279–81
Company (Beckett), 112

compulsory emulation of taste, 180–85
computational philosophy of consciousness, 255–56, 262, 263, 264
Comte, Auguste, 83, 96n.19
consciousness: computational philosophy of, 255–56, 262, 263, 264; critical, need for, 149; as inherently visual, 257–58
conservation posters: English (1914–18), 420; German (1917), 419. *See also* wartime scarcity in England
Constable, John, 17
constructedness of sentimental response, 73
construction/constructivism, 370; as Adorno's alternative to productionism, 380–82, 384–85; Adorno's articulation of, 373, 374–75, 377–88; anti-essentialist, 372; Benjaminian, 389n.5; ongoing interrelationship of expression and, 378–80, 382, 383, 393n.22; rational constructionism, noninstrumentalized, noncoercive, 376–77; reassembly of materials to achieve self-expression of the material, 378–80; stasis and, 385–86; "Vers une musique informelle," discussions of necessity and radicality of, 383–84
consumer: citizen as, 435
consumer desire, 410, 413
consumption: clothing in context of, 290n.5; collection and, conflation of, 410
contextual feminism, 69n.40
contingency, 343n.59
conversion narrative of identity politics, 301
Cordaro, Michele, 121n.3
Cornell, Joseph, 253–55, 259
Corpus Hermeticum, 258
cosmetics, 160–61
cosmetic surgery: history of, 229n.57
Cours de philosophie positive (Comte), 96n.19
Cousin, Victor, 13
Cover Girl (film), 166
Crary, Jonathan, 92, 98n.35
Crick, Francis, 251, 253
Crisp, Quentin, 289n.1
critical consciousness: need for, 149
critique-of-aesthetic-ideology critics, 368
Critique of Judgment (Kant), 7, 372; Adorno on, 195, 369, 374, 384; on beauty and genius, 208; ethics and aesthetics in, 197, 198; object as "as-if" concept in, 11; paradox of simultaneous "demand for agreement" and actual impossibility of achieving consensus about the beautiful, 375–77; sublime in, 12–13; three forms of pleasure in, 8–9
Critique of Practical Reason (Kant), 372
Critique of Pure Reason (Kant), 8, 369, 372
"Critique of Violence" (Benjamin), 455
Crowds and Power (Canetti), 457
Crowther, Paul, 13
Cruise, Tom, 148
Crystal Palace, 417
cubism, 252
cultural artifacts: extension of aesthetic appreciation to, 18
cultural embodiment, 295–312; Dorian Gray as, 305; imaginary body of culture, 299; of modern male homosexual identity, 298–300, 302, 309; Murad advertisement offering both authentic self and, 306–8
cultural feminism, 69n.40
cultural narrative: formation of, 297, 311n.4; identity visible only when marked as, 306
cultural stereotypes of clothing, 289n.1
culture: demystification of, 192; difference between practice and, 309; identity and, 298–300, 302, 309; imaginary body of, 299, 310; as interpretation of set of practices, 305
Culture of Redemption, The (Bersani), xxvi
Cunanan, Andrew, 232
Cuzin, J.-P., 120n.3

Danby, Francis, 93
Danto, Arthur, xxv, 68n.28
Darnton, Robert, 171
Darwin, Charles, 262
Davenport, Charles B., 341n.32
David with the Head of Goliath (Caravaggio), 117–20
Davy, Humphry, 98n.35
death as enlightenment, 450
death drive, 231, 403; of Scrooge in *Christmas Carol,* 238
debasement, queer aesthetics of, xxii, 268–94; cloth of communal adherence, 279–81; cloth of curve, 281–87; cloth of loneliness, 275–78, 289; cloth of woundedness, 270–74; curve of cloth, 287–89; sacrifice in, reasons for, 288–89; social holdings of self-debasements, 269; types of cloth wounds, 270
decapitation: Caravaggio's images of, 99, 100, 117–20; castration equated with, 100, 118–19, 120
Decapitation of St. John the Baptist, The (Caravaggio), 99
deconstruction: pantextualist breaching of boundary between ergon and parergon of, 14
decoration: as motive for clothes, 290n.5, 291n.9
"De divisione naturae" (Erigena), 8
de Grazia, Victoria, 399
Deleuze, Gilles, 431
delight in the good, 8–9; aesthetic experience distinguished from, 9–10
de Man, Paul, 389n.5
democracy(ies): democratic impulse in novels, 204–5; democratization of content, 16; police as spectral beings in modern, 455; spatially motivated democratizing, 121n.6; supermodels as affront to effort-reward relation in, 212
demystification of culture, 192
Dennett, Daniel, 255
Department of Glass Technology (England), 417
desert: problem of, 215; "public honor and individual desert," 220–23
"Design for Postwar Living" competition (1943), 353
design practice: Vattimo's definition of, 58
destruction of aesthetics to liberate art, xxv
Dewey, John, 7, 19–21, 26n.43, 26n.48
Dialectic of Enlightenment (Horkheimer and Adorno), 160–61, 378
Diary of Anne Frank, The (stage and screen versions), 163–64
diaspora identity, 336
Dickens, Charles, xxi, 234–42
Dickie, George, 10, 12
Diderot, Denis, 255
differentiation of value spheres, 3–4
Diotima, 459
Discourse on Inequality (Rousseau), 206–7
discursive certainty, 256
disinterestedness, aesthetic, 14–19; aestheticization of politics and, 18–19; concept of, 8, 9, 10; implications for art object, 11; moral imperative and, tension between, 13; privileging of, 14–15
disseminated spatial concealment, 120
Distinction (Bourdieu), 192, 224n.3
distributive justice, 215–16, 227n.43
distributive principles, 212–13
division of labor, 3
Dowd, Maureen, 153
Dowling, Linda, 296, 300, 301, 311n.4, 312n.28
Downes, Charles, 429n.49
dreams: Benjamin on, 409
Dreiser, Theodore, 410
Drei Studien zu Hegel (Adorno), 392n.12
Drescher, Fran, 158
Drozdik, Orshi, 252–53
Dubos, Jean Baptiste, 7
Duchamp, Marcel, 15, 16, 253, 261, 421
Dupee, F. W., 136
Durkheim, Émile, 456
Dutch style and coloring of painting, 85–86

Dutoit, Ulysse, xx, 112
dynamism, 381, 386–87

Eagleton, Terry, xiv, xvii, xviii, xxii, 78–79, 172, 173, 185, 224n.3, 314, 341n.27
Eames, Charles, xxiii, 348; on circus, 347–49; on gifts, 355–56; plywood war products of, 353–54; on "quality" of good architect, 350–51
Eames, Ray, xxiii, 348, 350, 353–54
Eames cards, 356
Eames chair, 351, 356
Eames House, xxiii, 347–65; under construction, 347, 348; craftsmen working on, 349–50, 364n.8; design as rearrangement of limited kit of parts, 350, 364n.11; distinction between design and occupant blurred in, 350–51; as exhibition or showroom, 361–62; film on (1955), 359–60; as gift, 356–57; house as shock absorber, 351; as multiscreen performance, 360; process of decision making in, 357; published and scrutinized, 352, 364n.16; shift between first and second versions of, 358–60; as site of fashion photographs, 362; standardization of components of, 354
Eaton, Marcia, 70
Eco, Umberto, 264
economic benefits of physical attractiveness, 211–13
economic forces: aesthetic judgments and, xiv
economic modern (low) architecture, 51
Edelman, Gerald, 255
Edelman, Lee, xxi–xxii, 304
education: Richards's view of, 325–26
effort: effortlessness of beauty, 207, 208–10; labor theory of beauty and, 218–20; reward and, correspondence between, 212; subjectivity governed by, 223–24; sublime and, 207, 208
ego-ideal, 242
Eighteenth Brumaire, The, 406
eighteenth-century aesthetics, theorizing popular practice in, 171–89; aristocracy of culture, 185–86; Gerard and, xxi, 173–74, 175, 176–79, 186; Kames and, xxi, 173–74, 175, 180–85, 186; nonelite audiences and, 171–76
Eimert, Herbert, 383
Eisenman, Peter, 51, 69n.41
Elements of Criticism (Kames), 180–85, 186
Eliot, George, xxi–xxii, 242–46, 248n.19
Ellis, Havelock, 327
embodied spectator, 86–87
emotion and physiological sensation: interconnection of, 86
empirical nature of aesthetic experience, 83–89
empiricism, scientific, 77
Empson, William, 313
Encyclopedie (Diderot and D'Alembert), 258
English glass, 417
enigmatic signifier, 112, 113–14
enigmatic subject, 111–12
Enlightenment models of social function of aesthetics, 171–89; emergence as separate discourse, 172; of Gerard, 176–79, 186; of Kames, 180–85, 186
Entenza, John, 353–54, 356, 362
Entenza House, 350
Entombment, The (Caravaggio), 103
equality: promotion of justice affiliated with promotion of greater, 191
equipoise of ordered experience: Bhabha's something-else-besides as later avatar of, 331–35, 336; perpetuation of, by poetry, 324, 326
Erfahrung, 5
ergon and parergon (work and frame): deconstruction's pantextualist breaching of boundary between, 14
Erigena, Johannes Scotus, 8
Erlebnis, 5
eros and eroticism, 459, 466; Caravaggio's emphasis on, 101–20; erotic address, 106, 111–12, 114; femme-butch relations, 279–81; love and chance, 40; lust, 35, 38; truth guided by, 449, 452; voluptuous pleasure, 32–33, 38–39. *See also Lolita* (Nabokov), moral content of

Erythrocytes (Drozdik), 252–53
Esprit Nouveau, L' (Le Corbusier), 354
"Essay on Beauty" (Jeffrey), 77
Essay on Taste (Gerard), 176–79, 186
Essays on the Nature and Principles of Taste (Alison), 17, 77
"Eternal [or Perpetual] Peace" (Kant), 384, 385
ethics: Adorno's reidentification of ethical possibility, 410–11; aesthetics and, xxi–xxii; art and, 12; of images' production, 148; of representation, xx
ethnicity: beauty and, 227n.45
eugenics, 326–27, 341n.32
Evans-Pritchard, 459
exercise technologies: beauty effort and, 218
experimentalism, 57, 58
expression, 378–80, 393n.22; construction and, relation between, 382, 383
expressive theory of beauty, 197–98
Eyes Wide Shut (film), 128, 148–49

Face of Love: Feminism and the Beauty Question, The (Lambert), 216
Face Value: The Politics of Beauty (Lakoff and Scherr), 216
Fallacies of Hope (Turner), 92
fantasy, 230–32; clothing as act of, 274; of feminist butch relations, 279–81; in Genet's *Querelle,* 282–87; sacrifice and, 274, 292n.21; of self-hailing, 303–5; about ugliness, *Picture of Dorian Gray* as, 296; undergirding reality itself, Scrooge's refusal to participate in, 236–37
Farnsworth House, 359, 362, 363
fashion as system, 290n.5. *See also* clothes, martyrdom to
fashion models, 211–13
Fechner, Gustav, 5, 98n.35
Feinberg, Leslie, 276, 279–82, 288, 289, 293n.26, 293n.28
Fekete, John, 338n.4
Feminine Mystique (Friedan), 136
"Femininity" (Freud), 270–71
feminism, 136; centrality of feminist critical theory to contemporary architecture, 64–65, 69n.38, 69n.40; critique of beauty myth, 216–18; feminist butch relations, 279–81; feminist conception of avant-garde architecture, 56–57; Hadid and, 48–49, 56–57; liberal feminist stance, 69n.40; power, 143–44; second-wave, 143; third-wave, 143–44; Wollstonecraft and, 201, 203
femme-butch relations, 279–81
Ferry, Luc, xviii
fetishism, 402–3, 423–24, 430n.62; as alternative economy, 421; split in belief as expressed in fetish, 462–63
Ficino, Marsilio, 258
Fiddler on the Roof, 170n.16
film: arrested image in, 437, 439; inequality between men and women enforced by pleasure of cinematic looking, 192–93; power of, 462; Woolf on cinema, 409, 427n.29
Film (Beckett), 105
fine artist and skilled artisan: distinction between, 5
fine arts as virtual arm of government, 184
Fish, Stanley, 335
Fisher, Amy, 126
Fisher, Philip, xxv
Flugel, J. C., 271–72, 290n.5, 291n.9
formalism, 317; Basic English and, 313–16, 337n.1; bourgeois, 372; breaking total meaning into contributory meanings, 318–19; limitations of, 321–22; true, of Richards's aesthetic theory, 324–25
formed material objects: as artworks, 22
Foster, Hal, 367, 442
Foucault, Michel, 302, 309, 311n.4, 311n.14
Frankfurt school, 21; "critical theory," 367; Kantian legacy maintained by, 372; studies of Adorno, 370–71; tensions between mass culture and, 390n.7

freedom: of Richards's supranational aesthetic subject, 330–31; of satisfied person, 321
French, John, 418
French realist art, 97n.28
Freud, Sigmund, 179, 236, 237, 242, 246, 305, 451, 466; death drive, 403; on ego-instincts vs. sexual instincts, 247n.12; on origins of male homosexuality, 241, 247n.13; theory of narcissism, 240, 241; on vanity of women, 271; on women's genital deficiency, 270–71
Friday, Nancy, 216
Fried, Michael, 14–15
Friedan, Betty, 136
Friedlander, Walter, 122n.11
Frith, William Powell, 87
Fry, Roger, 405, 406, 409, 426n.22
functionalism: Vattimo's criticism of, 54–55
Furniss, Tom, 226n.27
Fuss, Diana, 309
futurism, reproductive, 242, 245, 246
Futurists, 18
futurity: fantasmatics of, 230–32. *See also sinthom*-osexuality

Gage, John, 97n.33
Gallagher, Catherine, 11
Galton, Francis, 341n.32
Garches (Le Corbusier), 360
Gay Science, The (Nietzsche), 453
gaze of aesthetic evaluation: detachment of pure, 192
Gehry, Frank, 62
gendering of beauty, 199–201
Genet, Jean, 153, 268, 273, 282–87, 288, 292n.16, 294n.31
Genette, Gérard, 4
genital deficiency: Freud on women's, 270–71
genius: beauty and, 208–9; Kant on, 208
geometry, 392n.16
George, Lloyd, 418
Gerard, Alexander, xxi, 173–74, 175, 176–79, 186
Gere, Richard, 229n.61
German Ideology, The (Marx and Engels), 367, 368, 372
Geulen, Eva, 391n.8
gift: adult's imagination of child's imagination as gift exchange, 460–61; Eames' concept of, 355–56; Eames House as, 356–57; of negation, 459; sociality emerging out of respect and reciprocity of the, 421; as unstable and contradictory, 460
Gilbert, Creighton, 121n.11
Giovannini, Joseph, 65n.2
Girard, René, 312n.29
"girl-children": cultural shifts in attitudes toward bodies of, xxi. *See also Lolita* (Nabokov), moral content of
Gladwell, Malcolm, 289n.1
glass: architectural use of, 60, 68n.28; prevalence in modern imaginary, 426n.18; wartime scarcity in England and, 416–17; Woolf's interest in, 416, 428n.42
Glimpses of the U.S.A. (film), 356, 360
Godard, Jean-Luc, 371, 390n.7
Gold Standard and the Logic of Naturalism, The (Michaels), 372
Goodman, Nelson, 4
gossip, 36
Graff, Gerald, 314, 319, 338n.6
graffiti, 444–45
Grant, Lee, 153–56, 157, 167; blacklisting of, 155–56; family name, 155
Great Britain's political economy: during and just after Great War, 401–2, 403, 416–21
Greco-Egyptian temple priests: talismanic thaumaturgy used by, 258
Greenspan, Alan, 455
Gregori, Mina, 108, 121n.11
Griffith, Melanie, 139–40
Gris, Juan, 252
Guggenheim Museum, 56
Guillory, John, xiv, xv
gym culture: rise of, 219
Gypsy Fortune Teller, The (Caravaggio), 107–10, 111, 113, 114, 120; in Capitoline Museum, 108–10, 120n.3; in Louvre, 107, 108

Habermas, Jürgen, 3, 12
habit(s): disruption of, effect of, 404; objects granted full physicality out of, 403–4; Richards on, 319, 323–24, 326, 341n.31
Hackman, Gene, 159
Hadid, Zaha, xix, 44–69; art centers by Office of Zaha Hadid, 48, 56–65; distinction from other neomodern architects, 49–50; as experimentalist, 58; expressive form privileged over legibility of deterministic orders, 55; liberated domestic space of, 53–54; perceptions of, 48; preference for interiority porous to exterior, 63; reconsideration of role and form of wall, 61–62; use of glass, 60; works in progress, 48
Haiken, Elizabeth, 229n.57
Hall, Radclyffe, 271, 272–73, 275–78, 288, 289, 292n.23, 293n.25
Hall, Stuart, 336
Hall, Thomas, 71–74, 75
Hamilton, James, 98n.35
Hand-Book of Taste, or How to Observe Works of Art, 82–83, 84, 91, 98n.34
Hansen, Miriam, 161, 163, 370
Hanslick, Eduard, 11
Hanssen, Beatrice, 370
Harkin, Maureen, xxi
Harpham, Geoffrey Galt, xiv, xviii, 391n.8
hate, 42
Hefner, Hugh, 134
Hegel, G. W. F., 373, 392n.12; condescension to the aesthetic as source of knowledge, 388; importance to Adorno, 379, 380, 393n.25; relentless dedication to the conceptual, 380, 394n.27
Heidegger, Martin, 121n.10, 408
Helsinger, Elizabeth, 97n.31
Hermes, Alice, 166
Herzog & de Meuron, 49
Hesser, Amanda, 247n.17
Hipple, Walter, 173, 182
Hirsch, Foster, 167
history-as-sacrifice-of-subjectivity, 378
History from Things (Lubar and Kingery), 398
Hoch, Hannah, 252
Hochschild, Jennifer, 212
Hoff-Sommers, Christina, 143
Hofmann, Hans, 359, 362
Hogarth, William, 87
Homages to the Romantic Ballet (Cornell), 254–55
Home, Henry, 175
homeless men and women, 439–40
homosexuality: embodiment of modern male homosexual culture, 298–300, 302; Freud on origins of male, 241, 247n.13; homoeroticism in Caravaggio, 106–7; narcissism associated with homosexual desire, 241–42; originary moments in instantiation of modern male homosexual identity, 298–300, 302; among prison inmates, 36; queer theory, xxi–xxii, 235; *sinthom*-osexuality embodied by, 232–33. *See also* debasement, queer aesthetics of; lesbianism; *Picture of Dorian Gray, The* (Wilde); *sinthom*-osexuality; transsexuals
honesty, 37, 41
Hong Kong: the Peak men's club in, 44, 45, 48
honor: problem of individual desert and public, 220–23
Hood, Thomas, 85, 87
Hoohendahl, Peter Uwe, 370
Hope in a Jar (Peiss), 156
Horkheimer, Max, 160, 165
Horn, Rebecca, 261
Horwitz, Howard, xxiii
House: After Five Years of Living (film), 359–60
House Un-American Activities Committee, 155–56
How to Read a Page (Richards), 322, 325
Huhn, Tom, 370
Hullot-Kentor, Robert, 370, 377, 378
Hulme, T. E., 401, 402, 425n.11
Hume, David, 6, 7, 23n.7; "standard of taste" argument, 172, 175, 177

Husserl, Edmund, 403
Hutcheson, Francis, 7

Iamblichus, 258
IBA housing project (Berlin) (Hadid), 49–50
idealism, 76; ontological, xxiii, 316, 324–30, 337
identity: cultural embodiment of modern male homosexual, 298–300, 302, 309; desire for, as desire to belong, 303–5; diaspora, 336; implication of aesthetics for understanding, xxii–xxiii; "melting pot" model of American, 335–36; as system of interests, 317; visible only when marked as cultural narrative, 306
identity politics, xxiii, 297–98; conversion narrative of, 301; Fuss's definition of, 309; reconceived as creation of desirable identity, 309–10; visibility and, 299–300
ideological state apparatuses, 189n.34
illusion, verisimilar, 263
Illustrated London News: visitors to 1843 Royal Academy exhibition from, 80, 81–82; Westminster exhibition (1843) illustrated in, 80–81
imaginary body of culture, 299, 310
"imagined communities" (Anderson), 300, 327
imitation: Burke on, 174–75
immanent aesthetics, xxvi
immanent works, 4
immaterialization of reality, 14
Industrial Revolution, 417
inequality: Rousseau on, 206–7
informal music, 383–86, 387
inscription of homoerotic desire, 304
instituting relationalities, 113
interface, 259
interlanguage, 342n.41
international relations: Richards's view of, 328
Interpretation in Teaching (Richards), 317, 339n.19
intersubjective community, 10
intersubjectivity: construction of, 377
Into the Light of Things (Leonard), 16–17
investments: norm of, 212, 213, 219
Ion (Plato), 178
iron: Benjamin on decorative use of, 406; history of English, 417–18; in "Solid Objects," access to primeval history through, 406–7
Irons, Jeremy, 139, 151n.28
irony: understanding, 318–19

Jacobi, F. H., 17
Jacob's Room (Woolf), 413–14
Jaffe, Audrey, xxiii
James, Henry, 253
James, William, 321, 323, 403–4, 407
Jameson, Fredric, 366, 368–72, 374, 377, 383, 388, 396n.42; on Adorno's "guerrilla raids" on *Critique of Judgment,* 369, 371; distancing of Adorno from Kant, 369–72
Jane Eyre (Brontë), 204–6, 226n.30
Janeway, Elizabeth, 139
Jaucourt, Louis de, 258–59
Jauss, Hans Robert, 16, 18, 26n.48
Jay, Martin, xix, xxv, 161, 370, 377, 388
Jay, Peter A., 232
Jazz Singer, The (film), 156
Jeffrey, Francis, 77
Jenkins, Dorothy, 349
Jespersen, Otto, 342n.41
Jewishness, aesthetics of, 153–70; aesthetics of vulgarity, xxi, 167–68; assimilation and, 155, 156; black-Jewish cultural politics and, 156, 160; culinary/cultural tradition and, 157–58; Jewish speech and, 166–68; mimesis and, 160–62, 165; popular image of, 158–59
Jewish performance: counteraesthetic of, xxi
Johnson, E. D. H., 70
Johnson, James, 11
Johnson, Samuel, 180
Jolson, Al, 156
Jones, Kay Bea, xix
Jones, Nancy, 145–46

jouissance, 231–32
Judd, Donald, 405
Jünger, Ernst, 18, 405
justice: beauty and, tension between, xx, 190–98, 206, 228n.51; destructive element required for, 450; distributive, 215–16, 227n.43; promotion of greater equality affiliated with promotion of, 191; self as subject of, defined by its effortfulness, 223–24; social, 212; truth in revelation that does justice to it, 449–50, 452

Kael, Pauline, 128, 132, 158, 160, 165
Kafka, Franz, 454, 462
Kahn, Louis, 51, 66n.8, 68n.36; New Haven galleries by, 63
Kames, Lord, xxi, 7, 173–74, 175, 180–85, 186
Kant, Immanuel, xvii, 3, 7, 13, 14, 195–98, 203; Adornian construction and, 379–80; Adorno's reworkings of, 369–70; beautiful defined by, 380; on beauty and justice, 195–98; on beauty and morality, 12, 201–2; on beauty and nobility, opposition between, 226n.28; contradiction of art in aesthetics of, 394n.26; on genius, 208; Hegel and, 373, 379, 380, 388, 392n.12, 393n.25, 394n.27; notion of aesthetic experience, natural supernaturalism vs., 17–19; productive imagination, 24n.10; proposal for eternal or perpetual peace, 384, 385; quasi-conceptuality of aesthetic of, 374–75, 379–80, 394n.26; on sublimity, 225n.22; turn toward geometry as basis for implied construction within pure intuition, 392n.16. *See also Critique of Judgment; Critique of Practical Reason; Critique of Pure Reason*
Katz, Ephraim, 155
Kaufman, Robert, xxiii–xxiv
Keaton, Buster, 105
Kesey, Ken, 136
"kiddy porn," 147–48
Kidman, Nicole, 149
Kierkegaard: Construction of the Aesthetic (Adorno), 377–78
King of the Hill (TV sitcom), 212
Kipnis, Jeffrey, 66n.3
Kircher, Athanasius, 264
Kirwan, James, xxviin.9
Kittredge, George Lyman, 340n.20
Klein, Calvin, 147–48
Kneller, Jane, 226n.27
knowledge: knowing what not to know (active unknowing), 457, 458; organicist ideal of aesthetic, 83
Koolhaas, Rem, 49, 52
Korsmeyer, Carolyn, 225n.24
Kossuth, Joseph, 15
Kournikova, Anna, 126
Kozlowsi, Karen, 157
Kracauer, Siegfried, 391n.12
Kramer, Larry, 232–33, 238
Krieger, Murray, 14, 27n.53
Kristeva, Julia, 298
Kubrick, Stanley, xx, 126, 127–28, 142, 148, 149, 163, 164

labor theory of beauty, xxi, 206–24; effort visible in, 220–24; exercise technologies and, 218; opportunities for undertaking beauty effort, 218–20; supermodels and, 211–13
labor-theory-of-value productionism, 372
Lacan, Jacques, 105, 230, 237, 239, 424n.4, 440; mirror scene, 312n.26; on *sinthome*, xxi, 231, 236
Laclau, Ernesto, 336, 343n.58
"Lady in the Looking Glass, The" (Woolf), 411
Lakoff, Robin, 216, 217
Lambert, Ellen Zetzel, 216
Landesgartenschau (Hadid), 44, 47
Lane, David, 248n.21
Langella, Frank, 151n.27
language: act of naming things, 465–66; ambiguity of, 315–20, 329–30; *mis*hearing and *mis*reading by child creating, 464–66. *See also* Basic English
Languages of Art (Goodman), 4
Laplanche, Jean, 111–12, 114, 240

Last Judgment (Michelangelo), 93
Late Marxism: Adorno, or, The Persistence of the Dialectic (Jameson), 369, 371, 372, 391n.8
Late Show with David Letterman, The, 221
laughter at life and death, 42
Lauren, Ralph, 165
Lavater, Johann Caspar, 196, 197, 198, 225n.16
League of Nations mental economy, 328
Le Corbusier, 49, 61, 66n.8, 353, 354, 360
Lectures on Aesthetics (Hegel), 5
Lectures on Rhetoric and Belles Lettres (Blair), 340n.20
left-sacred experience, 464–65, 466
Leiris, Michel, 456, 464–65
Leonard, George, 16–17
lesbianism: in Feinberg's *Stone Butch Blues,* 279–82, 293n.26, 293n.28; in Hall's *Well of Loneliness,* 275–78, 292n.23, 293n.25; Mannish Lesbian's refusal of women's clothes and stigma of, 272–73. *See also* homosexuality
Lessing, G. E., 17
Letters on Aesthetic Education (Schiller), 13
Levenson, Michael, 426n.11
Lever House, 50
Levine, George, xxviiin.7
Lévi-Strauss, Claude, 404
LF one (Hadid), 55
liberal feminist stance, 69n.40
liberalism: imperative to impartiality of modern, 335
Lichtenberg, Georg Christoph, 197–98, 225n.16
Light Construction (MoMA exhibition), 49, 66n.5
Lileks, James, 214
Limbaugh, Rush, 143
Lingis, Alphonso, xix, 434
lipstick, 154, 155, 156–57, 160–61
listening: attentive, 11; passive, 11
literature: beauty and morality in nineteenth-century novels, 204–6; formation of communities circumscribed by their members' shared knowledge and, 300. *See also specific titles*
Litvak, Joseph, xxi
Lolita: textual and visual representations of, xx–xxi
Lolita (Kubrick film), 126, 127, 128–37, 151n.29; cast of, 129–30; censorship of, 129; compared to Lyne version, 138, 139, 140; Winters as Charlotte Haze in, 129, 163–66
Lolita (Lyne film), 126, 127–28, 137–47; Annabel episode, 138–39; cast of, 139–40; orgasmic Lolita in, 141, 142–43, 152n.30
Lolita (Nabokov), moral content of, 125–52; *American Beauty* as moral descendant, 146–47; cultural career of *Lolita,* 126; in empire of images, 147–49; Kubrick film version, 126, 127, 128–37, 151n.29; Lolita's body size and shape, 132–33; Lyne film version, 126, 127–28, 137–47
Lolita Story, The (documentary), 139, 151n.28
loneliness, cloth of, 275–78, 289
Long Bay Gaol (Australia), 33, 35
Longinian rhetorical sublime, 174
"lookism": campaigns against, 191, 213–16
Lo's Diary (Pera), 126, 143–44
Louvre, the, 5
love, 42; chance and, 40; neighborly, 237–38; Plato on beauty-inspired, 203
Lukács, Georg, 407
Lumière brothers film (1895), 462
lust, 38; as violent, 35
Lyne, Adrian, xxi, 126, 127–28, 137–47, 148
Lyon, Sue, 128, 130, 132, 134, 136
Lyotard, Jean-François, 434, 440

Macherey, Pierre, 179
magic: alliance between medicine and, 258–59. *See also* child's imagination, adult's imagination of; fantasy
Mahon, Denis, 120n.3
Mailer, Norman, 136
Malinowski, Bronislaw, 421, 430n.60

Malone, Annie Turnbo, 156
Mancini, Giulio, 108
Mandel, Ernest, 372
"Mannish Lesbian" of 1920s, 272–73
Mao, Douglas, xxi, 425n.7
Marcuse, Herbert, 22
Marinetti, Emilio, 18, 405
"Mark on the Wall, The" (Woolf), 430n.63
Martin, John, 93
Martin, Judith, 227n.42
martyrdom to clothes. *See* clothes, martyrdom to
Marxian critical theory traditions, 367–68
Marxism and Form (Jameson), 371, 372
Marxist aesthetics: long-historical view of Kantian crux in, 372–73
Mason, James, 130, 134, 140, 164
mass culture, 160–62; as mask culture, 162; tensions between Frankfurt school theory and, 390n.7
mass subject, 434–35
Master Card: commercials for, 228n.56
Material Cultures: Why Some Things Matter (Miller), 398
materialism: horror of waste during World War I and, 419–21. *See also* "Solid Objects" (Woolf)
materialist theories of the aesthetic: *Angel Standing in the Sun* associated with, 94
Matter, Herbert, 362
Mauss, Marcel, 421
Mazursky, Paul, 168
McCallum, Pamela, 338n.4
McCoy, Esther, 351
McKlosky, Mary, 10
McLuhan, Marshall, 259
Meaning of Meaning, The (Richards), 322
medicine: alliance between magic and, 258–59
medieval anticipations of aesthetic experience, 24n.13
Mellor, Anne, xxviin.7
"melting pot" model of American identity, 335–36
Mencius on the Mind (Richards), 318
Mendes, Sam, 146, 152n.35
mental economies, 328
Merleau-Ponty, Maurice, 110
Messiaen, Olivier, 383
metaphor, 332; Richards on, 317–18, 340n.21
Method acting, 166–67
Metz, Christian, 462–63
Michaels, Walter Benn, 302, 305, 310, 311n.4, 372
Michelangelo, 93, 122n.11
middle class: ideals and materiality in, 438–39; social utopian dream of expanding, 52; as womblike space of affect, 437–39
Mies van der Rohe, Ludwig, 49, 51, 61, 66n.8, 362, 363; exhibition at MoMA, 358, 359, 360–61
Millett, Kate, 143
mimesis: Adorno on, 378–80; aesthetics of Jewishness and, 160–62, 165; capacity of "prehistorical child" for, 464; in state of shock, 436–37
Mind Zone for London's Millennium Dome (OZH), 44
Minima Moralia (Adorno), 381–82; reflection on alternatives to productionism, 384–85
Minnie's Boys, 165
misuse value: thingness precipitated as kind of, 399, 404
mob discontent and violence: Gerard's fear of lower-class rhapsodic response and, 178–79, 186
modernism: modernist view of cognitive compression, 253; of Richards, 337; wall's role in architectural, 61; Woolf's exploration of antihumanist, 402–3, 405, 419
modernisms in architecture, 50–54; economic, 51; oppositional, 50–51; pure, 51, 66n.8; social, 51–53, 66n.9
modernity: the aesthetic as sign of onset of, xviii; end of, 54; notion of prehistory in, 462
modernization: typified by increasing differentiation of value spheres, 3

modesty: as motive for clothes, 290n.5, 291n.9
Moir, Alfred, 108, 114
Molly (Jones), 145–46
"Moments of Being" (Woolf), 411
Monk, Samuel, 173
monumental artifact versus vessel: dilemma of, 56
moral imperative: tension between aesthetic disinterestedness and, 13
morality, beauty and, 12, 195–98, 201–6; Kant on, 201–2
Moretti, Franco, 204–6, 226n.30, 300
Morgan, Robin, 143
Moritz, Karl Philipp, 7
Mork & Mindy (TV), 397
Morricone, Ennio, 138
Morris, William, 406
Moses und Aron (Schönberg), 383
Moss, Kate, 221
Mouffe, Chantal, 335, 336, 343n.58, 343n.59
movies. *See* film
Mulready, William, 87
Multiple Definition: words as instances of, 316, 317
Mulvey, Laura, 192–93, 194
Murad advertisement: authentic self and cultural projection indistinguishable in, 306–8
Murdoch, Rupert, 161
music: absolute, 11; informal, 383–86, 387

Nabokov, Dmitri, 150n.8
Nabokov, Vera, 125, 127, 128, 135
Nabokov, Vladimir, xx, xxi, 125–52; screenplay for Kubrick's *Lolita,* 128–29. *See also Lolita* (Nabokov), moral content of
naming, act of, 465–66
narcissism, 240–42; associated with homosexual desire, 241–42; of the Other, 241, 245, 246; paradoxes of, 241; pedocentrism's triumph over, 245–46; primary, 240; secondary, 240; of Silas Marner, 243
nation(s): ambivalent idea of, 332; identification through, 327–28; supranational citizenship beyond, 328–31, 334; transnational identity and, 332–36
nationalism: as general model of identity, 298
Nations and Peace (Richards), 327–28, 329
natural beauty: Adorno on, 194–95, 224n.7
natural selection, 262
natural supernaturalism, 16, 17; Kantian notion of aesthetic experience vs., 17–19
negation: gift of, 459
Negative Dialectics, 369
neo-avant-garde, 48, 65n.2
neomodern architecture, 49–50
Nervi, Pier Luigi, 58
Nestle, Joan, 293n.26
Neuhart, John, 364n.11
Neuhart, Marilyn, 364n.11
neurobiology, combinatorial aesthetics of, xxii, 251–67; analogy and, 251–52, 259, 262–65; box art, 253–55; brain's "binding" capacity, 253; collage, 252; role played by qualia, 254–55; sense perception as avenue to embodied self-awareness, 256–57
New Criticism, 314, 337, 338n.4
"New Dress, The" (Woolf), 411
new mind, 257–63
New Music, 383, 387
Newton, Esther, 292n.23
Newton, Isaac, 255
New Woman, 275, 292n.23; refusal of women's clothes, 272–73
Next Stop, Greenwich Village (film), 168–69
Nicholsen, Shierry Weber, 370
Nietzsche, Friedrich, 22, 451, 452–54, 462
Night and Day (Woolf), 412
Night of the Iguana (film), 349
noble sex: men as, 200, 201
noesis, 6
nonelite audiences, eighteenth-century aesthetics and, 171–76; Gerard on, xxi, 173–74, 175, 176–79, 186; Kames on, xxi, 173–74, 175, 180–85, 186

norm: of ascription, 212, 213, 214, 219; of investments, 212, 213, 219
Noten zur Literatur (Adorno): Nicholsen's translations of, 370
novels: beauty and morality in nineteenth-century, 204–6; democratic impulse in, 204–5
Nozick, Robert, 227n.43
Nunokawa, Jeff, 301

objecthood, 404
objectifications: thing manifested between multiple, 399
objective self-sufficiency: condition of, 6, 23n.5
objectivity: as "as-if" concept in Kant, 11; rhetoric of, 11
objects: containing elaborate narratives of their collection, 412; destiny beyond life of subject, 414; granted full physicality out of habit, 403–4; recomposition of, 408; symbolic and metonymic power of, 413–14. *See also* "Solid Objects" (Woolf)
Observations on the Feeling of the Beautiful and Sublime (Kant), 195–97, 198, 200–201, 208, 226n.28
Odets, Clifford, 167
Oedipus, 466
Office of Zaha Hadid, 44
"Of the Standard of Taste" (Hume), 6, 175, 177
Ogden, C. K., 313, 318, 339n.11, 342n.41
O'Hara, Frank, 216
Ohmann, Richard, 314, 341n.27
Oklahoma!, 165
On Beauty and Being Just (Scarry), xxviin.4, 191, 215–16, 228n.51
One Touch of Nature makes the whole World Kin (Hall), 71–74, 75, 88; positions of spectator in, 73–74
"One-Way Street" (Benjamin), 408
ontological idealism, xxiii, 316; ontological formalism of Bhabha, 333–35; of Richards's aesthetic theory, 324–30, 337
opifact: notion of, 426n.22
oppositional modern (high) architecture, 50–51
optimal aesthetic subject: paradoxes attending Richards's characterization of his, 321
organicist ideal of aesthetic knowledge, 83
Orlando (Woolf), 405–6, 411, 412
Other, the: narcissism of, 241, 245, 246
Our America (Michaels), 302, 311n.4
Ow, David, 252
Oxford Hellenistic tradition: homosocial codings of, 300

Paglia, Camille, 143
Paine, Thomas, 342n.47
painting: of Caravaggio, 99–122; circular format for, 93; Dutch style and coloring of, 85–86; Victorian sentimental narrative, 70–98
pantheism controversy, 17
Parti Pris des Chose, Le (Ponge), 425n.5
passive listening, 11
Pater, Walter, 299
Paulson, Ronald, 97n.31
Peak, the (men's club in Hong Kong), 44, 45, 48
Pearson, Karl, 341n.32
Peirce, C. S., 340n.20
Peiss, Kathy, 156
Penrose, Roger, 262
pensière débole (weak thought), 54, 67n.15
Pera, Pia, 126, 127, 143–44, 145, 150n.8
performance art: Turner's paintings as, 92
perpetuation: of aesthetic experience, by poetry, 322–23, 326; aesthetic representation as, 323; of equipoise of ordered experience, by poetry, 324, 326
Persistent Desire: A Femme-Butch Reader, The (Nestle), 293n.26
Philosophical Enquiry into the Origin of Our Ideas of the Sublime and Beautiful (Burke), 174–75, 198–202, 207
Philosophy of New Music, The (Adorno), 393n.22

Philosophy of Rhetoric (Campbell), 340n.20
Philosophy of the Inductive Sciences, The (Whewell), 76
photocollage method, 357–58
Physiognomical Fragments (Lavater), 196, 198, 225n.16
physiognomy: Kant on, 196–97
physiological sensation and emotion: interconnection of, 86
Piano, Renzo, 58, 68n.36
Picabia, Francis, 261
Picasso, Pablo, 252
Picture of Dorian Gray, The (Wilde), xxiii, 208–9, 295–312; Dorian's beauty, 296; Dorian's relation to his picture, 296–97; as fantasy about ugliness, 296; identity as image of social life in, 303–5; picture as accumulation of experience, 305–6; picture-painting scene, 302–3, 304, 305; specific historical and sexual context of, 300–301; value of ugliness in, 305–6, 308
pietà: in Feinberg's *Stone Butch Blues,* 289; in Genet's *Querelle,* 285, 286–87; martyrdom to clothes as, 268–69
Pietz, William, 430n.62
plainstyle, 287, 289n.1
Plato, 178, 245, 317, 449, 454, 459; Athenian Stranger of, 241–42; on beauty-inspired love, 203; notion of truth, 449, 451, 452, 465; suspicion of art, 450–51
Playboy magazine, 134
pleasant, the, 8
pleasure, 8–9, 32–33, 38–39, 91
Plotinus, 258
"Plus-que-raisons" (Ponge), 425n.5
poetry: cultivation of capacity to coordinate appetencies and, 322–23; as mode of discrimination that does not discriminate, 324–25; perpetuation of experience by, 322–23, 326; Richards on, 315
poiesis, 6
police: as spectral beings in modern democracies, 455
political economy of Great Britain: during and just after Great War, 401–2, 403, 416–21
Political Unconscious, The (Jameson), 366, 368, 371, 372
politics: aestheticization of, xxv, 18
Ponge, Francis, 425n.5
Pontalis, J.-B., 240
Poseidon Adventure, The (film), 158, 159–60
positivist myths, 52
postcolonial theory, 331, 336
postidentitarian subject, 336
postmodernist view of cognitive compression, 253
postnationalist model of Bhabha, xxiii, 331–35, 336
"postulate" of "universal voice," 376
postwar way of living: Case Study House Program and, 352–54. *See also* Eames House
power: secrecy and, 457; taste and, xiv–xv
power feminism, 143–44
Power of Beauty, The (Friday), 216
Practical Criticism (Richards), 315–19, 325, 340n.22
Pragmatist Aesthetics (Shusterman), 20
pragmatist tradition, 21
prehistory: importance of, 461–63
primary narcissism, 240
Principles of Literary Criticism (Richards), 314, 316
Proclus, 258
production and productionism: Adorno's constructivism as alternative to, 380–82, 384–85; labor-theory-of-value, 372
Proper Meaning Superstition, 330
protection: as motive for clothes, 290n.5
Proust, Marcel, 254
psychoanalytically constituted subject, 111
Psychology of Clothes, The (Flugel), 271–72
"public honor and individual desert": problem of, 220–23

public secret, 457, 464
pure modern (high) architecture, 51, 66n.8
purposeless aesthetic experience: phenomenon of, 382, 385, 388

qualia: role played in process of cognitive binding by, 254–55
quantitative rationalism, 256
quasi-conceptuality of Kantian aesthetic, 374–75, 379–80, 394n.26
queer aesthetics of debasement. *See* debasement, queer aesthetics of
queer theory, xxi–xxii, 235. *See also* homosexuality; *Picture of Dorian Gray, The* (Wilde)
Querelle (Genet), 273, 282–87, 294n.31

Ragas, Meg Cohen, 157
rationalism, quantitative, 256
Rawls, John, 227n.43
Read My Lips: A Cultural History of Lipstick (Ragas and Kozlowsi), 157
realism, traumatic, 442
reality TV, 435
"Really Useless 'Knowledge': A Political Critique of Aesthetics" (Bennett), xvi
recomposition: of objects, 408; revision of notion of waste toward notion of, 421
redemptive aesthetic, xxvi
Redgrave, Richard, 75, 76, 83–89, 93, 94–95
Reflecting Pool (Viola), 257
reflective judgment, aporetic, 380, 382, 394n.26
relationalities, instituting, 113
religion as search for lost intimacy: Bataille on, 274
Rembrandt, 93
reobjectification, 404
repetition, rhapsodic, 176–79, 186
representation: ethics of, xx
Republic (Plato), 317
"revelation that does justice": notion of, 449–50, 452
Revell House, 356
Reverdy, Pierre, 252
reward and effort: correspondence between, 212
Reynolds, Joshua, 17
rhapsodic repetition, 176–79, 186
"Rhetoric of Temporality, The" (de Man), 389n.5
Richards, I. A., xxiii, 313–44; on ambiguity of language, 315–20; Bhabha's ambivalent subject and, 331–35; on emancipation from words, 323–26; formalism and Basic English, 313–16, 337n.1; on metaphor, 317–18, 340n.21; modernism of, 337; onto-logical idealism of, 324–30, 337; on satisfaction and being, 320–23; on transcending the nation, 326–30
Riddle, Nelson, 138
Rietveld, Gerrit, 66n.8
rights: beauty and, 204–6
Riley, Terry, 49
Rimbaud, Arthur, 395n.40
Robinson Crusoe, 414
Rogers, Samuel, 92
Rogin, Michael, 156
Roiphe, Katie, 126, 143
Rome, Center for Contemporary Art (Centro per le Arti Contemporane [CAC]) in, 58–62
Roosevelt, Franklin Delano, 313
Rorty, Richard, 229n.61
Rosenthal, Lyova. *See* Grant, Lee
Rousseau, Jean-Jacques, 206–7
Rowe, Colin, 60
Royal Academy exhibitions of 1840s: viewers of, 79–82, 91
Rubens, Peter Paul, 93
Rubinstein, Helena, 156
Rudd, Mark, 136
Ruskin, John, 90, 93, 97n.32, 406
Ruskin and the Art of the Beholder (Helsinger), 97n.31
Russian avant-garde, 65n.2
Russo, John Paul, 338n.1, 339n.11, 340n.21

Saarinen, Eero, 350, 351, 358
sacred in everyday life: Leiris's definition of, 456; principal component of, 464

sacrifice: fantasy and, 274, 292n.21; in feminist butch relations, 281; in Genet's *Querelle,* 285–87; gift of negation, 459; martyrdom to clothes and, 273–74, 288–89; in queer aesthetics, reasons for, 288–89
"Sacrificial Mutilation and the Severed Ear of Vincent Van Gogh" (Bataille), 274, 292n.21
Sade, Marquis de, 255
St. John the Baptist with a Ram (Caravaggio), 114–17, 120, 121n.11, 122n.11; multiple fanlike structures in, 116
Salome Receiving the Head of St. John the Baptist (Caravaggio), 99
Samara, Lucas, 253
Santa Cruz (California) City Council: antidiscrimination ordinance of, 213–14
Sartor Resartus (Carlyle), 16
satisfaction: narcissistic, association with *sinthom*-osexuality, 240–42; Richards on, 320–23; supranational model's similarity to mental economy of, 329
Saussure, Ferdinand de, 340n.20
Scarpa, Carlo, 66n.8
Scarry, Elaine, xv, xxiv, xxv, xxviin.4, 191, 215, 228n.51
Schaper, Eva, 11
Scherr, Raquel, 216, 217
Schiff, Stephen, 126, 138–39, 141, 142
Schiller, J. C. F. von, 13
Schlegel, Friedrich, xix
schmaltz, 158
Schönberg, Arnold, 383
Schopenhauer, Arthur, 13
Schrift, Shirley. *See* Winters, Shelley
Science and Poetry (Richards), 315, 328
scientific empiricism, 77
Scottish turnpike roads: Kames on effect of network of, 183–84
Scrooge *(Christmas Carol):* as central literary embodiment of *sinthom*-osexuality, 235–39, 240, 242
Seagram Building, 50, 66n.6
Searle, John, 262
secondary narcissism, 240
second reflection: subject in, 382–83
second-wave feminism, 143
secrecy, 466; equation of truth with, 449, 451–52; power and, 457
secret(s): equating truth with secret within, 449, 451–52; erotic, in Caravaggio, 107, 108–11, 112, 114–17; of gift, 460–61, 463; real and pure versus public, 457, 459, 460, 463, 464
secret life of things, 397–430. *See also* "Solid Objects" (Woolf)
secret societies, 457, 462–63
Sedgwick, Eve Kosofsky, 296, 300–301, 311n.6
Seeds of Time, The (Jameson), 391n.8
Seinfeld, Jerry, 157
self: implication of aesthetics for understanding, xxii–xxiii; as subject of justice, defined by its effortfulness, 223–24
self-awareness: coherence associated with, 257–58; importance of networked spatial relations in construction of, 251–52; sense perception as avenue to embodied, 256–57
Sellers, Peter, 128
Sempstress, The (Redgrave), 75, 76, 84–89, 94–95; Thackeray's critique of, 86, 87, 89
sensationalism, 76, 77
senses: signs of the, 443–44
sentimental narrative painting, Victorian. *See* Victorian sentimental narrative painting
sentimental response: constructedness of, 73
Sex of Things, The (de Grazia and Furlough), 398
sexual agency and potency of women, 143–45. *See also Lolita* (Nabokov), moral content of
Seymour, Jane, 217
Shaftesbury, Anthony Ashley Cooper, 7, 8, 10
shame: clothes and, 271, 282, 291n.9; as kind of blush in face of beauty, 288

Shelley, Also Known as Shirley (Winters), 154
Sherrington, Charles, 321
shock, 433–34; mimesis in state of, 436–37
Shusterman, Richard, 20, 21, 26n.43
signifier and signified: nonidentity between, 333
signs: communication operating through, 318, 340n.20; of the senses, 443–44
Silas Marner: The Weaver of Raveloe (Eliot), xxi–xxii, 242–46, 248n.19
Silverman, Kaja, 300
Simmel, Georg, 402, 407, 423; on separation of objects and people, 410, 411
sinthome: Lacanian, xxi, 231, 236; loom in Silas Marner as figure for machinelike insistence of, 244
sinthom-osexuality, 230–48; association with narcissistic satisfaction, 240–42; embodied by homosexuality, 232–33; Scrooge as central literary embodiment of, 235–39, 240, 242; of Silas Marner, 242–46
situational aesthetics, 77
Slabs (Hong Kong from "the Peak") (Hadid), 44
Slutzky, Robert, 60
Smith, Tony, 15
Smithson, Alison, 355, 356
Smithson, Peter, 355, 356, 357–58
Snowstorm, The (Turner), 93
Sobieski, Leelee, 148–49
social and the aesthetic: relation of, 174–75
social justice, 212
Social Life of Things, The (Appadurai), 398
social modern (low) architecture, 51–53, 66n.9
social order: aesthetic experience as privileged means to reconciling, 183; Kames on link between aesthetic experience and, 180–85; poetry and, 315
Society for Glass Technology (England), 417
Socrates, 188n.16, 451, 459
Soderholm, James, xxviiin.7
"Solid Objects" (Woolf), xxiv; as allegory of war's origin, 417–21; alternative economy portrayed in, 417, 421; collecting impulse in, 400–401, 403; ethics of, 411; fetishism in, 402–3, 421, 423–24; fragments in, 404–5, 423; liberation of artifacts from their history in, 412–13; recomposition of objects in, 408; rhetorical recourse to child in, 409, 410
Sollors, Werner, 300
"Song of the Shirt, The" (Hood), 85
Sound of Music (film), 349
South Pacific (film), 349
Spacey, Kevin, 146
Speak Memory (Nabokov), 136
spectator: growing anxiety in art world about effect of embodied, 86–87
Spheres of Justice: A Defense of Pluralism and Equality (Walzer), 220–23
Spinoza, Baruch, 16
Spivak, Gayatri, 336
Stafford, Barbara Maria, xxii
standardization, 354
standard of taste argument, 172, 175, 177; Kames's transformation of problem of, 181–83
stasis, 385–87; construction and, 385–86; mutual constitution and deconstruction of modern aesthetic, 386–87
Stations (Viola), 256–57
Stein, Clarence, 66n.9
Steiner, George, 22
Stella, Frank, 120
Stendhal, 22
Stevens, Stella, 160
Stewart, Kathleen, xxiv
Stewart, Martha, 438
Stieglitz, Alfred, 261
stigma of lesbianism, 272–73
Stockton, Kathryn Bond, xxii
Stoddart, Judith, xx
Stoller, Ezra, 66n.6
Stolnitz, Jerome, 10

Stone Butch Blues (Feinberg), 273, 276, 279–82, 288, 289, 293n.26, 293n.28
Strachey, Lytton, 428n.41
Strasberg, Lee, 167
Subjectivity, xviii, 6, 116; beauty and, 194–206; governed by effort, 223–24; in interaction with world characterized by spatial flux, 252; as mode of experience, 333; "splitting" or "ambivalence" involved in, 331–32
sublime: antisublime aesthetics of Gerard, 176–79; antisublime aesthetics of Kames, 180–85; in Burke, 226n.27; effort and, 207, 208; Kant on, 225n.22; Longinian rhetorical, 174; as manifestly bourgeois aesthetic, 175; privileging of discourse on, 174
suburbs, 52, 439
supermodels, 211–13; affiliation with ascriptive differentiation, 212–13
supernaturalism, natural, 16, 17–19
supranational citizenship, 328–31, 334
"Sur l'eau" *(Minima Moralia)*, 381–82, 385–86, 387
surrealism, 408–9, 421, 425n.5
Suvari, Mena, 146, 152n.41
Swain, Dominique, 140, 148
Symonds, John Addington, 299
sympathetic emulation of aesthetic models: Kames on, 180–85
sympathies and antipathies: theory of, 259
sympathy: Burke on, 174–75
Symposium (Plato), 203, 449
Synesius, 258

Tafuri, Manfredo, 57
Taglioni's Jewel Casket (Cornell), 254–55
Tailhade, Laurent, 18
Tale of Two Cities, A (Dickens), 239–40
talismanic thaumaturgy used by Greco-Egyptian temple priests, 258
taste: activism retained in ancillary notion of, 6; bad, as root evil, 314–15; Basic English to develop, 316; complicity with domination, 191–92; compulsory emulation of, 180–85; Gerard's "simple principles" of, 176–77; *Hand-Book of Taste* (1843), 82–83, 84, 91, 98n.34; as inseparable from class status, Kames on, 181–83; Jeffrey's theory of, 77; nineteenth-century notions of universal, 78–79; power and, xiv–xv; Redgrave's notion of, 83–84; "standard of taste" argument, 172, 175, 177; unsupported, 319–20
Taussig, Michael, xviii–xix, xxiv, 437
Taylor, F. W., 320
Ten Commandments (film), 349
Terragni, Giuseppe, 66n.8
textual response: importance of precision in, 177–78
Thackeray, W. M., 86, 87, 89
"theatrical" style of beholding, 14–15
theodicy of beauty, xxv, xxvi
Theory of Fictions (Bentham), 341n.26
Theory of Religion (Bataille), 274
Theses on Feuerbach (Marx), 368, 372
thinghood, 404
thingness: precipitated as kind of misuse value, 399, 404
things: secret life of (*see* "Solid Objects" [Woolf]); outside subject/object trajectory, 398
third-wave feminism, 143–44
"Third World Literature in the Era of Multinational Capitalism" (Jameson), 389n.5
Thompson, E. P., 173–74
Tiny Tim *(Christmas Carol)*, 234, 237, 239, 240
transcendent works, 4
"transhistorical" imperative, 366, 368
transnational identity, 332–36; Bhabha on, 332–35; Bourne's effort to imagine, 335–36
"Transparency: Literal and Phenomenal" (Rowe and Slutzky), 60
transsexuals, 28–43
Trauerspiel (Benjamin), 389n.5
trauma: resemblance between cocooning of "home" and dazed state of, 436
traumatic realism, 442
"Traumkitsch" (Benjamin), 409

truth, 113; concealed, child's revelation of, 458–59; equated with secrecy, 449, 451–52; figuration as man or as women, difference between, 452; guided by eros, 449, 452; Plato's notion of, 449, 451, 452, 465
Tschumi, Bernard, 52
Turner, J. M. W., 76, 89–95, 98n.34. *See also Angel Standing in the Sun, The* (Turner)
Turner, Lana, 227n.42
Turner, Ted, 161
24 Cathcart Road: international-style London residence at, 53–54
Tzara, Tristan, 400

ugliness: difference between beauty and, 296, 297; fantasy about, 296; value of, in *Picture of Dorian Gray,* 305–6, 308
Undine Giving the Ring to Masaniello (Turner), 92
Undoing Aesthetics (Welsch), xviii
U.S. Plywood Association: competition (1944) sponsored by, 353
universality, xvii; of the beautiful, Kant on, 380; universalizing tendencies of prevailing standards of aesthetic judgment, xiv; universal victimization, 229n.61; "universal voice," "postulate" of, 376
Un-Private House, The (MoMA exhibition), 49, 66n.5
unsupported taste, 319–20
"urban 'graft'": Roman CAC as, 59
utopianism, aesthetic, 382, 383

value spheres: differentiation of, 3–4
Van Gogh, Vincent, 274, 292n.21
vanity of women: Freud on, 271. *See also* beauty
Varin, Jean, 260
Vattimo, Gianni, 54–55, 56, 58, 62, 64, 65
Veblen, Thorstein, 320
Venus Envy (Haiken), 229n.57
verisimilar illusion, 263
Versailles mental economy, 328
"Vers une musique informelle" (Adorno), 383–86, 387
victimization, universal, 229n.61
Victoriana: Bloomsbury dismissal of, 406
Victorians, British Painting 1837–1901, The (1997 National Gallery exhibit), 71
Victorian sentimental narrative painting, 70–98; changing intellectual climate and, 77–79; Hall's *One Touch of Nature makes the whole World Kin,* 71–74, 75, 88; *Hand-Book of Taste* and, 82–83, 84, 91, 98n.34; Redgrave's *The Sempstress,* 75, 76, 84–89, 94–95; Royal Academy exhibitions of 1840s, 79–82, 91; and Turner's *The Angel Standing in the Sun,* 76, 89–95, 97n.32
Victorious Cupid (Caravaggio), 100, 105, 114, 116, 122n.11
Vidler, Anthony, 60, 63, 67n.11
Villa d'Avray (Le Corbusier), 360
Village in the Jungle, The (Leonard Woolf), 428n.39
Villa Savoye (Le Corbusier), 360
Vindication of the Rights of Woman (Wollstonecraft), 201
Viola, Bill, 256–57
violence: mob discontent and, Gerard's fear of lower-class rhapsodic response and, 178–79, 186; police as spectral beings in modern democracies, Benjamin on, 455; violation of inner space, 35; of war, Woolf and, 415–16
visibility: identity politics and, 299–300
"Visual Pleasure and Narrative Cinema" (Mulvey), 192–93
Vitra fire station (Weil-am-Rhein, Germany), 44; Hadid's painting of, 46
Voisin, Gabriel, 353, 354
voluptuous pleasure, 38–39
vulgarity: aesthetics of, xxi, 167–68. *See also* Jewishness, aesthetics of

Wagner, Otto, 66n.8, 405
Walker, C. J., 156
wall: role and form of, 61
Walzer, Michael, 220–23, 227n.43

war: postwar way of living after World War II, 352–54; as spectacle, celebration of, 18–19; violence of, Woolf and, 415–16. *See also* World War I
Warren, Austin, 314, 338n.5
wartime scarcity in England, 416–21; material practice of art and, 401–2
waste: World War I and horror of, 418–21
Waste Land, The, 415
Watson, John, 340n.25
Way of the World, The (Moretti), 204–6
Weber, Max, 3
Wedgwood china, 405
Wellek, René, 314, 338n.5
Well of Loneliness, The (Hall), 271, 272–73, 275–78, 288, 289, 292n.23, 293n.25
Welsch, Wolfgang, xvi, xviii, xxv, xxviiin.20
Wendell, Barrett, 340n.20
Westminster Hall: exhibition in (1843), 80–81
Wexner Center for the Arts at Ohio State University in Columbus, 51
What's Fair? (Hochschild), 212
Whewell, William, 76
Wilde, Oscar, xxiii, 208–9, 211; defense against charges of homosexuality, 298–99
Wilder, Billy, 355–56, 362
Williams, Rachel, 227n.42
Williams, Robin, 397
Williams, William Carlos, 426n.18
Winters, Shelley, xxi, 153–70; aesthetics of vulgarity of, xxi, 167–68; as Charlotte Haze in *Lolita,* 129, 163–66; family name, 154–55; Lee Grant incident, 153–56, 157, 167; as Method actress, 166–67; in *Next Stop, Greenwich Village,* 168–69; in *Poseidon Adventure,* 158, 159–60
Wolf, Naomi, 143, 216
Wolin, Richard, 370
Wollstonecraft, Mary, 201, 203
woman/women: as archetype of beauty, 195; burden of beauty placed on, 216–17; fictions on beauty and morality of, 203–6; Freud on vanity of, 271; gendering of beauty and, 199–201; moral capacity of, Kant on, 201–2; New Women's refusal of women's clothes, 272–73; postwar rebellion against conventional wives and mothers, 133–34; sexual agency and potency of, 143–45
Wood, Michael, 152n.30
Woodmansee, Martha, 76
Woolf, Leonard, 417, 422, 428n.39
Woolf, Virginia, xxiv, 400–424; *Between the Acts,* 42; on cinema, 409, 427n.29; diaries of, 411, 416, 422; *Jacob's Room,* 413–14; "Lady in the Looking Glass," 411; "Mark on the Wall," 430n.63; material objects as condition of narratability in, 411–12; "Moments of Being," 411; "New Dress," 411; *Night and Day,* 412; *Orlando,* 405–6, 411, 412; violence of war and, 415–16. *See also* "Solid Objects" (Woolf)
Wordsworth, William, 17
"Work of Art in the Age of Mechanical Reproduction, The" (Benjamin), 367
World as Will and Representation (Schopenhauer), 13
World War I, 416–17; need for scrap in, 417–21; political economy of Great Britain during and just after, 401–2, 403, 416–21; scarcity of glass in, 416–17; Taylorist horror of waste intensified by, 418–21
World War II: postwar way of living after, 352–54
woundedness, cloth of, 270–74
Wright, Frank Lloyd, 56, 66n.8
Wright, Howard, 66n.9

Yeats, William Butler, 209–10
Young Hegelianism, 367, 368, 389n.5
Your Fortune, $1 (Anderson), 440–41

Zaha Hadid: The Complete Buildings and Projects, 44
Zammito, John, 11
Žižek, Slavoj, 229n.61, 230, 440
Zola, Émile, 410
Zoosemiotics (Anker), 252
Zuidervaart, Lambert, 370